3D Graphics Programming in Windows™

Philip H. Taylor, Jr.

Addison-Wesley Publishing Company
Reading, Massachusetts • Menlo Park, California
New York • Don Mills, Ontario • Wokingham, England
Amsterdam • Bonn • Sydney • Singapore • Tokyo
Madrid • San Juan • Paris • Seoul • Milan
Mexico City • Taipei

Many of the designations used by manufacturers and sellers to distinguish their products are claimed as trademarks.Where those designations appear in this book, and Addison-Wesley was aware of a trademark claim, the designations have been printed in initial capital letters or all capital letters.

The author and publishers have taken care in preparation of this book, but make no expressed or implied warranty of any kind and assume no responsibility for errors or omissions. No liability is assumed for incidental or consequential damages in connection with or arising out of the use of the information or programs contained herein.

Library of Congress Cataloging-in-Publication Data

Taylor, Philip, H., Jr.
    3D graphics programming in Windows / Philip Taylor.
        p. cm.
    Includes index.
    ISBN 0-201-60882-0
    1. Computer Graphics. 2. Windows (Computer programs) 3. Three
-dimensional display systems.   I. Title
T385.T375 1994
006.6'765—dc20   94-8469
                CIP

Sponsoring Editor: Philip Sutherland
Project Manager: Eleanor McCarthy
Production Coordinator: Lora Ryan
Cover design: Chad Kubo
Back cover imaging courtesy of Thurston Productions, Inc.
Set in 10 point Palatino by Total Concept Associates

1 2 3 4 5 6 7 8 9-BAH-9897969594
First printing, August 1994

Addison-Wesley books are available for bulk purchases by corporations, institutions, and other organizations. For more information please contact the Corporate, Government and Special Sales Department at (800) 238-9682.

This book is dedicated to the memory of

Kathy Marie Ornelas
1962-1992

All who knew her loved her.

Contents

Chapter 11   Implementing the 3D Modeler **683**

Acknowledgments

I owe distinct thanks to several blocks of source code and several books. The SDK examples DIBView and MakeApp, the public domain ray tracers MTV and DKB (along with Craig Lindley's book about DKB), and the Stevens/Watkins books have all contributed code ideas. Both of the Watt books were instrumental in my personal quest for graphics fulfillment. Jim Blinn's Corner, in *IEEE Computer Graphics & Applications* over the years, has contributed to my graphics understanding. And all graphics programmers bow in homage to Foley and van Dam, because they are always there when you need them.

A production like this is only possible because of the efforts of a great many people. In this case, there are three distinct sets: hardware, publishing, and technical. Hardware people who were nice to me (and who have good products) include Celia Booher at TrueVision (24-bit cards), Brian Burke at STB (S3-based products), and, last but not least, Scott Weatherall at ATI (Ultra and Wonder cards). I can highly recommend their products and their companies. The Addison-Wesley people who hung with me and helped make this book happen include Julie Stillman, Elizabeth Rogalin, Karen Goeller, Eleanor McCarthy, Claire Horne, Phil Sutherland, Keith Wollman, and many others. Technical thanks to Tanj Bennet, Troy Chevalier, Peter Eden, Lars Frid-Nielson, Matt Pietrek, Ron Praver, Jeff Richter, Andrew Schulman, and Victor Stone. Thanks to Joel Diamond and Jon Howell. Special thanks to Dan Richardson for being my main reader and reviewer and Tim Dolbeare for additional reading. The production of the back cover could not have happened without Thurston Productions, Inc. and Russell Smith.

A special thanks to Cameron Myrvold and all at Microsoft Developer Relations. Personal thanks to my family (all of them), the knights of the basement (Rick and John), and, last but not least, for being there when I needed someone, Mark Mullin. If I forgot anyone I apologize.

Introduction

This book will help you build a geometric modeler that runs under Windows. With this modeler, you can create pictures of three-dimensional objects like cubes, pyramids, and spheres. Along the way, you'll gain an understanding of the separate but related issues of graphics system design, a windowing system's impact on graphics systems, and the requirements of geometric modeling. Throughout, I'll also discuss design issues, so you can make informed judgments of your needs versus the environment of the book.

Some of the design issues I'll cover include a definition of the feature set, consistency, clarity, good graphics practice, and good Windows "citizenship." These issues are also representative of the design criteria used to form such near-standard graphics systems as the Programmers Hierarchical Interactive Graphics System (PHIGS) and the Graphical Kernel System (GKS). I'm not trying to create a PHIGS for Windows in this book, but I am attempting to instill an appreciation for graphics system design and the knowledge of how to build a modeler.

This means that this book is also about developing the code. The best way to understand how to program something is to see its implementation. I'll use several standard implementation techniques in the course of developing the libraries and applications; most importantly, in developing an API (application programmer interface) for 3D graphics application development. Application development using the routines in the library is thus fundamental to this book. We'll develop several demo programs using portions of the library before developing the complete application. This helps you see how various pieces of the library are used, and how to use them in concert within an application.

The approach I use concentrates first on the fundamental routines and then on their use. This is a project-oriented approach with clear goals and immediate results. Hopefully, you won't see this as just a collection of code; I've tried to provide explanations to help you not only understand what's included here, but also where you can go later for individual explorations.

This individual exploration is the key to it all. If you can't take this material and create further magic of your own, this book has not met my goal: to give you, as a programmer, insight into the design of a graphics system and into applications that use this graphics system to further illuminate the 3D graphics issues. It's also my goal, of course, to give you a working modeler to make pretty pictures with.

Approach

To build a geometric modeler, you need (from a 3D graphics standpoint) the support of basic routines in the Windows environment. You also need higher-level support, in the form of drawing surfaces and 3D mathematics. Once you have this substrate, you also need support for the modeling process. A set of modeling services completes an API to do 3D modeling under Windows.

Developing the support libraries and the modeler involves a blend of theory and practice. Theory provides the foundation for understanding the material. That's why I've included the design-related material: to explain the why of what's being done. Practice, on the other hand, makes it real. And that's why the code is here: to provide the how. An ordered solution requires design (and an understanding of design issues) and implementation techniques.

The first step on our road is developing the basic support services under Windows. On the library side, this translates into the construction of DLLs and support services: the WLib DLL, the G3DLib DLL, and the M3D modeler support services, which together make up the tools for building the modeler application. We'll use mainly pre-packaged services or APIs for this. Additionally, Chapters 4 through 7 (all of Part II) contain sample applications that illustrate the APIs of the WLib and the G3DLib.

The application side of this process translates into the construction of the modeler application. We'll start with a codebase provided by Microsoft in the Windows Software Development Kit (SDK). The modeler will show the use of the M3D API and a solution to 3D modeling.

Table I-1 gives a top-level view of the source code provided in this book. See Appendix B for exact details on source contents, installation instructions, and compiling.

Table I-1.   Source Code in 3D Graphics Programming in Windows

Libraries and Apps	Description
Libraries	
WLib	Helper functions for Windows at the primitive level
G3DLib	Higher level services, provide new "types"
M3D	Modeler support services
Applications	
Samples	Each chapter in Part II (4, 5, 6, & 7) has sample apps
WinMod3d	The geometric modeler application

Organization

With those goals, this book is made up of three parts. **Part I: Foundations** lays the groundwork for the rest of the book. It describes the parts of a geometric modeler and the components that the support libraries need to provide. **Part II: Constructing a 3D Graphics System** is where the implementation of the support libraries begins. It includes a detailed and procedural description of the design and development process. **Part III: Using a 3D Graphics System** takes a step-by-step approach to exposing the internals of a 3D modeling application that allows both wireframe and ray-traced images.

There are three chapters in Part I. Chapter 1, "3D Graphics, Modeling, and Windows," develops the key issues and conceptual framework for the entire book. Chapter 2, "3D Modeler Application Architecture," frames the modeling application that is the principal product of Part III, and introduces the support required from the libraries developed in

Part II. The last chapter in Part I, Chapter 3, "3D Library Design," explores four key areas: the raster graphics services needed within the Microsoft Windows world, the linkage between the raster GDI and the vector-based 3D graphics system, the vector-based 3D graphics system itself, and the modeler services.

Part II has 4 chapters. Chapter 4, "WLib Library Construction," implements the policy-free primitive layer of Microsoft Windows services. Chapter 5, "G3DLib Construction Part I: Drawing Surface and General Support Services," develops a strategy for display-surface management, linking the raster GDI and the vector-based 3D graphics systems. Chapter 5 also explores the support and utility services for coordinates and the window-viewport mapping, as well as providing additional math support. Chapter 6, "Graphics Primitives and Attributes," presents the output primitives of the graphics system; these primitives are responsible for displaying points, lines, and more. The last chapter of this section, Chapter 7, "Vector Math, Transforms, and Viewing Primitives," helps you design and implement the features of a graphics system that provides the three-dimensional mathematics of the system.

Part III has the last 4 chapters of this book, and completes the development of the modeler. Chapter 8, "Modeling, the Modeling Support Services, and Description Languages," describes the internals of a modeling application, including the development of description languages for models and scenes, and a generic tokenizer for parsing these languages. Scenes contain objects. Chapter 9, "3D Objects and Scenes," develops the objects used by the modeler and the details of their representation. Chapter 10, "Polygon Drawing and Object Tracing," presents the 3D graphics upon which the modeler is based: visibility tests and sorting, illumination models, shading geometry, and ray tracing. Chapter 11, "Implementing the 3D Modeler," wraps up the material from the preceding chapters and completes the geometric modeler.

Audience

Experienced Windows programmers will get the most out of this book, although any programmer who wants to learn more about graphics will benefit as well. I assume you know C, have read the source examples and documentation in the SDK, and that you've read the classic Windows programming book *Programming in Windows* by Charles Petzold (Microsoft Press). This book has been updated from the 1988 Windows 2.0 version and is an indispensable resource for any beginning Windows programmer. Since I assume you've read it, I don't duplicate any of its excellent coverage of basic Windows topics.

This means you must already understand event-driven programming message-loops, window and dialog procedure callbacks, GDI (Graphics Device Interface), client areas, and so on. If you do not, get Petzold before tackling this book. I'm not going to try to do a better job of explaining how to program Windows. We're just going to do it. In particular, the basics of bitmaps, palettes, GDI primitives, and printing are assumed.

To those of you who are worried about the math required to "do graphics," don't worry too much. I've assumed you have some exposure to geometry and trigonometry — no more. You need slightly more advanced math to really understand projection geometry, transformations, and intersections, but I'll give you some explanation with those topics. For truly detailed explanations that are beyond the scope of this text, I recommend that every serious graphics programmer have at least Foley and Van Dam's *Computer Graphics: Principles and Practice* (Addison-Wesley, 1990) and Alan Watt's *Fundamentals of Three-Dimensional Computer Graphics* (Addison-Wesley, 1989), or the equivalent. Foley and Van Dam is an exhaustive treatise on the breadth of computer graphics; Watt is a comprehensive coverage of three-dimensional graphics.

While I'll give you all the material necessary to understand and write these graphics programs, I won't go into the exhaustive detail that these other books contain on every topic. With the content and source provided in this book, and those additional references as your guideposts, you can expand the capability of the system as far as your time permits.

Conventions

I've included several visual cues for you in the layout of this book. Module layout charts for the current design entity (library or application), as shown below in Figure I-1, appear with section titles (within chapters) to indicate which topic is being covered. The current section is highlighted, and the other sections are shaded. This technique gives you a "roadmap" of where you are. For example, the graphic in Figure I-1 would accompany a section called "Shells: The Continuous Demo."

Figure I-1.   Example of the Guideposts Used To Mark the Way

Shells: The Continuous Demo

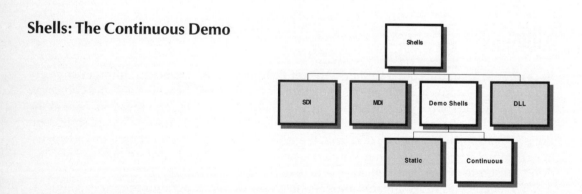

Throughout this book, I use DOS to refer to both MS-DOS® and PC-DOS®. Windows refers to Microsoft Windows™.

I've also established some typographical conventions to help with the information density. Table I-2 explains these conventions.

Table I-2.   Typographical Conventions

Convention	Description of Convention
CreateWindow	Bold letters indicate native Windows types, structs, or API functions.
InitEveryMdiApp	Bold Italic indicates types, structs, or API functions developed in this book.
`lpCmdLIne++`	Monospaced type indicates code chunks or messages.
...	Ellipses used to indicate skipped code.
Defined term	Italics indicates a term that is defined in the glossary.

Part I
Foundations

1 3D Graphics, Modeling, and Windows

In This Chapter

- General introduction.
- Definition of general 3D graphics concepts, general geometric modeling concepts, and classical graphics influences.
- A discussion of strategy and tactics used for this design and this implementation of these 3D libraries and this geometric modeler.

Introduction

One tool you can use to make "pretty pictures" in 3D graphics is a **geometric modeler.** A geometric modeler uses 3D graphics systems and data structures to construct an internal representation of a 3D geometric world then display or render it. In this book, I'll take you through the step-by-step design and construction of a basic geometric modeler and its 3D graphics and Windows support libraries. Some of the larger issues that must be resolved to pull this task off include underlying graphics and memory issues, 3D graphics library design, 3D viewing system issues, the design and representation of 3D geometrical objects, and more. The process of designing and building the support libraries and the geometric modeler will acquaint you with these issues and one solution for them as you carry them from design to implementation.

Constructing a geometric modeler takes more than understanding what a rotation matrix is. Handling 3D data in any amount gets bulky and you'll quickly find that modeler-level 3D graphics requires even more from a graphics library than the basic 3D demo program. The ability to perform real-world actions like reading and writing images, printing them, and exchanging data with other applications is as important as the ability to handle three-dimensional data. One without the other fails to provide a sufficient basis for application-building without a lot of effort from the application programmer. Combine this with a GUI environment like MS-Windows that provides both a rich graphics environment and relatively sophisticated memory management (as well as a well-developed set of user expectations), and it becomes clear that applications and application programmers need something more than random chunks of code manipulating numbers.

In this book, we will develop two separate, yet related, systems to accomplish the goal of building a modeler: a set of support libraries, and a skeleton application structure that provides a template to construct the modeler around. With these components, you will have a logical framework for developing 3D-graphics-aware Windows applications.

So how should we design this inter-related set of systems? Before we can decide, it will help to review a little history with an eye to understanding previous, similar efforts. Programmers as well as philosophers need to take to heart the truism "those who cannot remember the past are condemned to repeat it."

A Little History

Attempts to define "standard" graphics APIs have been undertaken throughout the history of computer graphics. The ACM/SIGGRAPH Graphics Standards Planning Committee (GSPC) Core System definition was first published in 1977 and revised in 1979. Core, as it is referred to, is no longer a factor in the graphics programming community, but its influence is felt in all subsequent work pertaining to graphics standards. The current standards can be broken down into two functional groupings: API-related standards and graphics metafile standards. API-related standards include GKS and PHIGS. Metafile standards include CGM and CG-VDI.

In 1985 GKS, or Graphical Kernel System, was declared the ISO API standard. Its primary weakness was its failure to address 3D. Its descendant GKS-3D went into review in late 1986. PHIGS, or Programmer's Hierarchical Interactive Graphics System, came about to address the modeling community's needs and was approved in 1988. PHIGS+ extends PHIGS in the area of rendering and complex models. PEX is a version of PHIGS for use in the X-Windows environment (Release 11) and provides some important lessons for implementing 3D graphics in a GUI environment.

Metafile standard CGM, or Computer Graphics Metafile, is a standard for capturing, transferring, and archiving graphic image data. CGM deals with file storage and retrieval as well as issues relating to machine-independent image transfer. CG-VDI, or Computer Graphics–Virtual Device Interface, is a low-level device interface standard for system implementers. This defines a standard control interface for graphics devices, which allows another form of device-independence.

In exploring these "lessons learned," two major themes emerge:

- Device independence, and
- API development.

Ideally, the device-independent model frees the programmer from the details of the screen and printers' separate imaging models. This is important, because, in many cases, the lifetime of hardware is shorter than the lifetime of an application program. The underlying graphics hardware might also undergo radical changes. So programmers spend a significant amount of time "porting" programs from one hardware platform to another. A common imaging model, like the one provided in Windows, is a good base from which to start. A device-independent interface frees the application programmer from the burden of caring what the hardware platform is. This may seem obvious, but it is worth keeping in mind that device independence is one of the basic lessons of application programming.

Similarly, applications and application programmers use an API to provide higher-level tools and avoid the lower-level details. Some of the benefits from and reasons for developing an API are:

- Code reuse: An API is designed for use in many projects, so it is not tied to a particular application.
- Application program portability: Code that uses an API to hide details on one platform can be ported to another mainly by porting the API.
- Application programmer portability: Once an application programmer has learned how to use the API to perform a specific task, the time required to do that task again on the next project is greatly reduced.

Typically, an API lets you concentrate on solving the real problems, even if it does add some overhead in terms of learning and run-time cost. As a general resource, an API provides many benefits that reduce the application programmer's burden. The moral is: an application programmer's time is limited, so any tool or technique that maximizes it is worthwhile. A graphics system API is such a tool.

An API usually consists of a combination of definitions, data structures, and functions. The "rules of the road," or policy, define how the programmer interacts with the library. The data structures and the functions work together to define a system you can use to build applications. This API, along with the policy for using it, is the medium through which you, the application programmer, express your solution to problems.

Some Basic Concepts

There is a crucial coupling between the application and its library (or libraries). Applications require services and libraries provide them. The domain of problems that an application can solve by using a particular library is limited by the content and richness of the library. If the library's contents are too specific, only a certain class of problems can be solved. If the contents are too general, it may require too much investment of time and effort by the application programmer to learn and use the library. This tension and the design decisions that resolve it are the key issues in implementing a library. In any system, understanding the components available and the relationships between them is not only a prerequisite for grasping the strengths and weaknesses of the system, but also for successfully using it.

While designing and building the libraries and the geometric modeler in this book, we will explore these issues. We'll work through several sample programs before constructing the modeler, but the modeler itself serves as the best illustration of this process—design, construction, exploration, and re-design.

General 3D Graphics Concepts

Keeping in mind the goal of building a geometric modeler and its underlying 3D support, it's time to explore some topics:

- 3D graphics concepts,
- 3D modeling concepts, and
- classical API issues.

Once you understand the basics of 3D graphics and geometric modeling, we'll take a quick look at classical API influences in the last section of this chapter. Then, you'll be ready to tackle the rest of the work in this book.

Basic 3D Graphics

You need to understand the basic concepts of a 3D graphics system before you can build a geometric modeler. Before you can run, you must first learn to walk. Without a solid foundation in these areas, any attempt to do more advanced tricks is liable to fail.

Underlying any 3D graphic system are:

- coordinates and coordinate spaces,
- 3D objects, and
- viewing systems, including the viewing pipeline and projections.

Coordinates and coordinate spaces are a fundamental concept in 3D graphics. Modelers and viewing systems generate views of 3D objects; these views are defined using coordinates. Coordinates, or points, exist within a coordinate space: a system consisting of a number of dimensions, an origin, and a range of values the system is defined for. 3D graphics systems are based on multiple coordinate spaces, which is one of the main causes of confusion.

Objects are defined by two main characteristics: their geometry and their surface properties. Geometry defines position and shape; surface properties determine color and texture. Again, geometry implies coordinates. Three-dimensional objects have at least three values; typically x, y, and z.

Viewing systems manage the set of transformations that allow object definitions and their mathematical coordinates to become visible pixels. This transformation process is usually called the *viewing pipeline*; it consists of the standard linear transformation matrices for translation, scaling, and rotation. Instead of stooping to raw matrix math, the viewing system provides tools that let you move points through the pipeline without the pain of linear algebra.

Figures 1-1 through 1-3 depict the sequence of coordinate spaces you'll become familiar with by the time you're done with this book. They include:

- Object Coordinates or "oc,"
- World Coordinates or "wc,"
- Eye Coordinates or "ec," and
- Screen Coordinates or "sc."

Objects are defined in their own local, or "object," coordinate system (object-x [ox], object-y [oy], and object-z [oz]). Objects are then instantiated into "world" coordinates (wx, wy, and wz), which may include a local transformation defining the size, orientation, position or scale, rotation, and translation of that object in world space. Figure 1-1 shows a simple example of this, an object that has been moved to a particular spot. Note that without understanding the object's default size, orientation, and position it is difficult to say whether any scaling or rotation is involved.

Figure 1-1.   Object and World Coordinate Systems

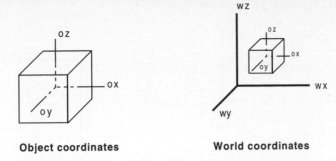

Object coordinates   World coordinates

Since objects exist collectively for the first time in world coordinates, world coordinates are the beginning of the viewing pipeline. The viewing parameters and transformation operate on objects to convert their world coordinates into "eye" coordinates. The viewing system lets you define the transformation used to move from world to eye coordinates. This is illustrated in Figure 1-2.

Figure 1-2.   World and Eye Coordinate Systems

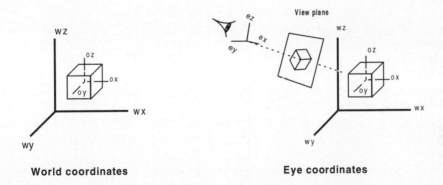

World coordinates   Eye coordinates

Once the objects have been transformed to eye coordinates, the eye coordinates must be projected into two dimensions and mapped into "screen" coordinates. When the object has been transformed to screen coordinates you are finally dealing with the pixels on the screen. Figure 1-3 shows the higher-level view of this last step.

This final step across the 3D-2D interface is actually a two-step process. The first step, shown in Figure 1-4, is the projection of 3D coordinates into 2D coordinate space. This typically results in real-number results called *window* or *logical* coordinates. These window coordinates must be mapped in the second step (shown in Figure 1-5) to *viewport*, or *physical*, coordinates.

Figure 1-3.   Eye and Screen Coordinate Systems

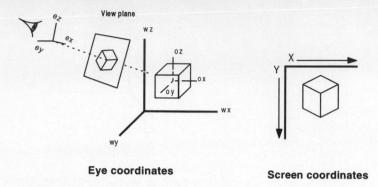

Figure 1-4.   Projecting 3D Objects into 2D Space

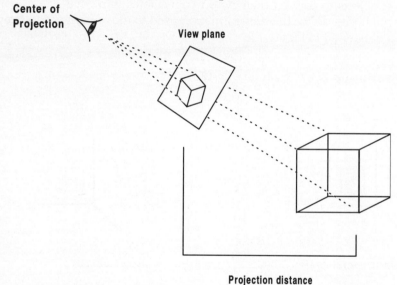

It is important to remember that, in a Windows environment you cannot use the entire physical display. This means that "screen" anything has to be rethought in terms of the windowing system and its coordinates. Be that as it may, the end result of 3D operations is typically 2D window coordinates that must be "mapped" to 2D viewport coordinates before any drawing operations can take place.

These coordinates are shown in Table 1-1.

The projection operation defines how eye coordinates are transformed into 2D coordinate space resulting in window coordinates. Two common projection transformations are supported: parallel and perspective.

Parallel projections simply use the x and y values of the coordinates, resulting in scenes that do not distinguish between near and far objects. The perspective projection compensates for depth by dividing the x and y coordinate value by the value of the z coordinate. You see this in Figure 1-4.

Figure 1-5. Mapping 2D Window Coordinates to 2D Viewport Coordinates

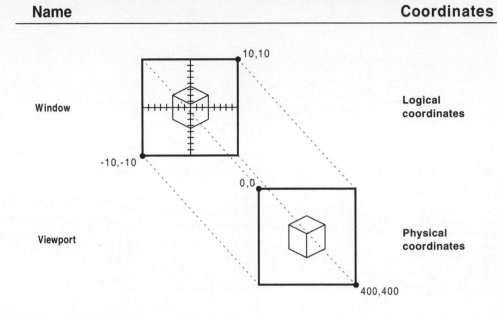

Table 1-1. Classical coordinates

System	Coordinate Type	Operation
System 2 (3D)	Object	Instantiate
	World	Transform
	Eye	Project
	Screen	See System 1
System 1 (2D)	Screen "window"	Map
	Screen "viewport"	Draw

The last step of the process maps projected 2D coordinates into screen or device space. Projected 2D coordinates are still real-value numbers: 2D window coordinates ("sw" in short-form notation, "s" for screen) that must be mapped to 2D viewport coordinates (or "sv"), as illustrated in Figure 1-5.

It's very important to keep these distinct coordinate spaces and operations separate in your head, while understanding where in the pipeline actions occur. At the end of the pipeline you generate output and draw the image. If your only goal is to perform wireframe drawing, you're done at this point. But more realistic image generation requires more advanced techniques, bringing us to the realm of modeling and rendering.

3D Modeling

A model is an artificial construct we make to simulate and help us understand a concept. Geometric models contain information that mathematically describes objects. Three-dimensional objects grouped into "scenes" let you create anything from completely artificial worlds

Figure 1-6. A 3D Cartesian World

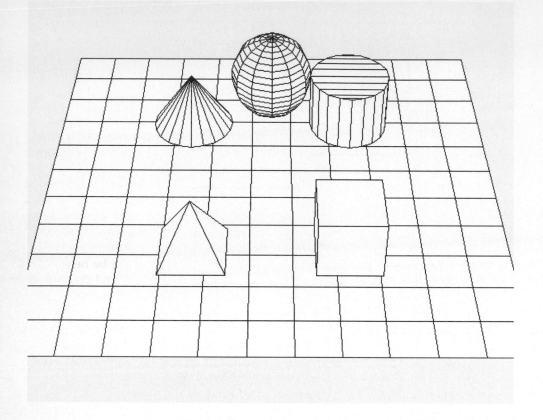

to simulations of the real world, as illustrated in Figure 1-6. Thus, a 3D model, sometimes referred to as a Cartesian model, is a computer simulation of a real or imagined world, constructed in the computer out of a set of primitive objects. The objects in the scene are transformed through the various coordinate spaces, then rendered to create an image. A geometric, or 3D, modeling program lets you create and render these 3D worlds. The parts of a geometric modeler are:

- shape representations,
- the user interface, and
- tools.

The *representation* defines what a shape is, the *user interface* determines how shapes are specified, and the *tools* manipulate the shapes.

For example, 3D objects can be represented as surface boundaries or volumetric solids. If you choose a surface boundary representation, surfaces are represented by faces and vertices, or points. If you choose volumetric representation, surfaces are represented using Constructive Solid Geometry (CSG).

A specification language lets you describe scenes containing objects; usually in scene data files that are parsed by the modeling program in the world-generation phase.

To actually see this world, the model must be drawn or rendered. It is important to distinguish between models and their rendering. Models describe objects and their properties. Rendering transforms the model into a picture on the screen.

Finally, interactive tools let you manipulate the model and color post-processing tools let you manipulate the generated image. In a commercial application, these tools usually include an editing facility. For simplicity's sake, however, the modeler we'll build in this book does not provide any run-time editing capability. Within that limitation, the user interface lets you modify the camera position and generate another view of the model by binding the arrow keys on the keyboard to the camera's x, y, and z positions. Environment options like background color, a 3D axis for orientation, and print control, as well as capabilities like saving to a file and sharing on the clipboard, provide further output control.

Color post-processing manipulates the color intensity values resulting from shading and ray-tracing rendering techniques. This builds on a solid-color specification and generation system, usually by implementing color mixing models and "color palette" services. From this basis, histograms and their graphs provide a visual approach to the color analysis technique for the final image's color generation.

Now that you understand the physical implementation process, it will be helpful for you to understand the logic behind it. By understanding both the practical and philosophical issues, you'll be able to figure out strategies for dealing with them, and, more crucially, the limitations of any scheme you develop to implement a particular strategy.

A useful logical structure for discussing modeling is Abstraction-Representation-Implementation (ARI) decomposition, which was set forth by Barzal in *Physically Based Modeling for Computer Graphics* (Academic Press, 1992), diagrammed in Figure 1-7. In this book, "structured modeling" is our goal and ARI is the method we'll use to achieve it.

Figure 1-7.   Structured Analysis of Modeling

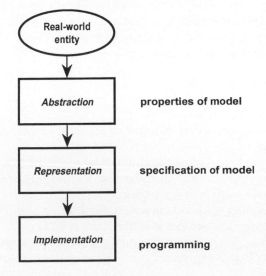

A model is the implementation, using a representation, of an abstract thing or entity. The thing being modeled is distinct from the model itself, but the relationship between the thing and its model is conceptually maintained. This system of modeling can also help you understand someone else's models if you simply invert it and ask yourself these three questions:

- What is being attempted (the *abstraction*)?
- What is the approach (the *representation*)?
- What are the details (the *implementation*)?

A simple example will clarify this concept. Let's pick the ubiquitous teapot as the thing to be modeled and a wireframe image as our desired result. The relevant aspects of the teapot, the set of features and characteristics you need to capture, are the *abstraction*. To do wireframe rendering all you need is the collection of points that describe its outline. This being the case, the *representation* can be as simple as a list of faces containing vertex indices and a list of vertexes. The *implementation* then needs to provide face, vertex, and list subsystems to support the representation of the model and its underlying 3D graphics.

A more important example is the geometric modeler that we'll be building here. Its *abstraction* must be sufficient to support the needs of a polygon modeler and raytracer. Its *representation* will be a dual one that combines the needs of both polygon shading and object tracing. The *implementation* will derive from these.

You can see from these examples that this questioning process can be a useful aid in understanding someone else's modeling scheme. If you can't decompose a scheme into these three parts, problems may exist either in the model or in your understanding of it—both bad situations. However, as Barzal himself says, this is not to say that this is the method you should use to decompose every modeling system you run into, nor must you shoehorn all knowledge into these three boxes. ARI is just one system for decomposition; it is a useful guide to understanding models and is good at pointing out areas of fuzziness.

You now have a way to create a mental framework to measure the logical quality and consistency of a given system. But how do you measure the internal *quality* of the system? Some common metrics used include:

- computational cost,
- effectiveness,
- complexity, and
- data acquisition.

Computational cost is measured in terms of storage, construction time, rendering time, and general usage time.

How well the model represents the thing to be modeled is an indicator of the model's *effectiveness*; but you need to keep in mind that a representation that is adequate for one application may not be sufficient for another.

Complexity represents a trade off between effectiveness and cost. A good general rule is: "The more effective the representation is, the more it will cost."

The ease with which the necessary geometric data can be acquired is what we refer to as *data acquisition*. Data that is captured or created in one form may need to be converted to another before it can be used. Geometry creation quickly becomes the most important practical issue for modelers.

Acquiring the geometry data to feed the rendering engine is a continual quest, and a specification language for scene description is an important tool in this quest. Using a language lets us uncouple the model from the application to build a general-purpose geometrical modeler, the grail at the end of our quest. Language is a powerful tool to express problems in the "real" world, and this is the case in the graphics world as well. When we use a scene description language, we describe objects to the modeler based on the properties allowed by the description language. This textual representation is parsed and translated into an internal representation stored by the modeler.

Three components help determine the image quality of the system:

- shape and shape representation,
- viewing geometry, and
- rendering.

Shapes and their representation define what can be modeled and heavily influence the scene designer's choices and capabilities. Viewing geometry determines how the image is presented to the rendering phase of the program. For example, simple viewing geometry may save rendering time at the cost of image appearance. Rendering can be as simple as wireframe drawing or as complex as ray tracing. Wireframe drawing is the equivalent of "stick-figure" rendering; shading and ray tracing attempt to take into account how light behaves. This use of an "illumination" model produces very nice images. The term *photorealistic* is used to refer to ray-traced images because of their optical accuracy; although the threshold of the term "photorealistic" seems to move upwards every year.

Now that the conceptual details of modeling are clearer to you, it's time to examine the components of a geometrical modeler. This will help us to understand both the modeling application and its support services.

In the abstract, modeling consists of shape representations, a user interface, and tools. In practical terms, a modeler consists of the following phases:

- world generation, or "front end,"
- world manipulation, or "gut functions,"
- world rendering, or "back end," and
- color post-processing, or "tools."

The front end is the user interface; it also performs the translation of input into the internal representation used by the modeler—3D objects. To understand the internals of 3D objects, you must understand both data structures and math. The guts of the modeler let you manipulate this world using the viewing system. In our geometric modeler we won't be building in the real-world editing facilities that you would need in a commercial application; for simplicity's sake, we'll allow a "view-only" approach involving only camera motion.

The back end performs additional transformations of the representation using the desired rendering type and various rendering functions. Because of the simplicity of the modeler we're building here, this limits our required implementation to viewing-system and rendering functions.

The end result of the back-end transformation varies. *Wire-frame rendering* produces points that are joined by lines. *Hidden-line rendering* (also known as **H**idden-**L**ine, **H**idden-**S**urface **R**emoval or HLHSR) produces points that define a polygon that is filled with some constant color. *Polygon shading* also produces points that form polygons, but the fill color is calculated using an illumination model. *Ray tracing* produces pixels the colors of which are calculated using an illumination model. An *illumination model* describes the interaction of light sources with the surface properties of the objects being rendered.

When an illumination model is used, color and its representation become important. Typically, color internal to the modeler uses RGB (red-green-blue), indicating that it is composed of three color components. RGB values are defined in the range [0,1] and are floating-point values. The native color systems of computing hardware are usually defined as an integer range. For example, for 24-bit color this range is [0,255] for each component. Depending on the hardware and the implementation, intensities may require post-processing using color analysis to achieve your desired result.

The glue binding these modeling phases together is the internal representation of objects. Wireframe drawing and solid shading both operate upon an explicit representation containing vertices and facets that define surfaces. In contrast, ray tracing uses analytic or equation-based forms to describe objects. Bridging this "representation gap" within the modeler is one of the challenges that we must solve to get the whole thing to work.

Now that you have an understanding of 3D graphics and modeling concepts it is time to examine some API issues.

API Design Issues

In the previous several sections, we identified the "pieces" that needed to be developed. It is now time to look at how we can develop those pieces—identifying the functions and data structures the API should provide for the application programmer's use comes first. We already know we need an API, but what should it contain? Once again, we turn to some history to provide a foundation for developing our answers.

The history of computer graphics tells us how to break down the components of a basic 2D graphics software package:

1. graphics setup,
2. data plotting routines,
3. graphics output primitives,
4. graphics attribute manipulation,
5. graphics input primitives,
6. segment manipulation, and
7. debugging.

Most 3D systems depend on underlying 2D components. A typical breakdown for a 3D package, derived once again from classical graphics, is:

1. graphics setup,
2. three-dimensional world-view routines,
3. graphics output routines,
4. graphics input routines, and
5. graphics object routines.

You can clearly see the overlap with the 2D breakdown but the dependencies may not be as readily apparent. Even less obvious are the connections that allow coexistence with a raster-oriented windowing system. It may be helpful to look at the following intersection of our 2D and 3D breakdowns:

1. graphics setup,
2. graphics output primitives,
3. graphics attribute manipulation,
4. graphics input primitives,
5. three-dimensional world-view routines, and
6. graphics object routines.

This intersection depends on basic window-to-viewport mapping and the underlying concept of coordinates. We can begin to see the basic components that are required, as well as which of the 2D functionality we'll need to build on.

This breakdown still does not take into account the influence of the windowing system or GUI with which these classical graphics services must coexist. The experience of PEX development shows us that the windowing system affects:

1. the window environment itself (as compared to no windowing environment),
2. coordinate systems,
3. input events,
4. color, and
5. errors (plus a catchall miscellaneous).

The windowing environment affects the ways the user and programmer view devices, since windows allow the display to be shared. This affects all output primitives, as well as coordinate systems and the underlying window-to-viewport transformation. Event handling cannot escape being characterized by the window system. Color and its support are important components of a graphics system; the degree to which a device-independent color model can be provided greatly eases a library-implementer's job. Errors and many other odds-and-ends are also affected by the environment. By now you are starting to get an idea of the scope involved.

You can now see, from a pure graphics and modeling viewpoint, the main pieces involved in geometric modeling. History has provided insight into some relevant design issues. Now that you have the high-level understanding of a geometric modeler's components and needs, it's time to consider our implementation of it.

Implementation Strategy

Strategy is the grand plan; tactics is a local battle. In this case our main strategic issue is identifying the pieces; our tactical challenges lie in defining how to implement and deliver them.

Design is kind of like skinning a cat—there's more than one way to get to the finish line. But, no matter which path you take, general rules like avoiding coupling, implementing policy-free primitives, and presenting a consistent programming model and interface are a good idea.

Two elements define the path we take here:

- Build service libraries to encapsulate as much as possible and provide abstraction where appropriate.
- Construct a template application to build the modeler around.

This design has two levels—the macro and the micro. The macro, or strategic, perspective deals with the high-level view, or the "How are we going to accomplish this?" question. The micro, or tactical, perspective deals with the low-level details, or the "What are we going to build?" question.

The Macro Perspective

From the macro perspective the libraries and the modeler share common techniques. In the library, a two-layered approach of policy-free primitives and policy-implementing components is combined with two implementation techniques: extensible APIs, and wrapper layers.

For the modeler, the application architecture is guided by two other implementation techniques:

- simple Model-View-Controller (MVC) structure, and
- function pointers for state machine control and list mapping.

Extensible APIs allow for controlled growth. Using only a few standard techniques results in systems that allow both the designer and the user the chance to grow. Wrapper layers are used here to provide programmers with components defining usage rules or "policy" and to free them from many of the underlying implementation details.

MVC is a simple but powerful way to structure internals. A controller provides views of data (here called the "model"). Function pointers structure the internals of both the state-machine control logic and the 3D objects. Control functions clarify main driver logic within the application and structure the execution cycle of the state machine. Mapping functions operate on repetitive data structures (like lists) and provide a method of applying a function to each object in the list. When you need to process a data object repeatedly in the same manner, this mapping function technique can be valuable.

All of these techniques give you a sound, structured design perspective firmly grounded in the real world.

The following areas influence the actual design of the libraries:

- feature set and general implementation issues, and
- performance and algorithms.

Feature set design is a tricky thing, and it is difficult to satisfy all classes of uses, as shown by the previous attempts at standard APIs (like PHIGS). Still, the API model has been proven in classical computer graphics, and its influence will become obvious in the definition of the system I use here.

Feature set is a minimum set of functionality that must be present in the finished system. This, in turn, defines the implementation issues. Let's defer for a moment the actual contents of the feature set, and examine the implementation issues in greater detail. They include:

- operating-system-related issues,
- general graphics issues, and
- 3D graphics issues.

Operating system concerns boil down to the usual worries, such as error-handling and recovery, inquiry functions, and memory management. The general graphics issues consist of all the things other than the 3D environment, like support for color, coordinates, display surface management, graphics attributes, graphics input, and graphics output. 3D issues include number representation (fixed-point, float, or double), 3D or 4D mathematics, the type of viewing system, object representation, illumination, shading, and surface property features.

As I explained a little earlier (in the classical API feature set discussion), window systems add to our mess concerning color, coordinates, environment, input, and graphics primitives, not to mention the expectations of users for certain base levels of functionality. The intersection of these topics—a 3D graphics system that is windowing-system aware—presents us with many different opportunities for solutions.

Another important issue under the topic of both graphics and Windows is performance. These can be broken down into two areas: algorithmic, and system-related (Windows).

The O ("big-oh") notation is used to classify algorithms by the "order of running time," as follows:

- $O(1)$—constant,
- $O(\log N)$—logarithmic,
- $O(N)$—linear,
- $O(N\log N)$, usually called "NlogN,"
- $O(N^2)$—quadratic.

From this, you should readily see that quadratic algorithms should be avoided; it's every programmer's wish that every program they write will run in constant time, no matter how much you ask it to do! In general, though, the topic of algorithmic performance in the graphics realm is outside the scope of this book. In the interest of clarity and readability I've chosen to work with a simpler algorithm rather than a fast one, but I'll discuss the design decisions where I've chosen simplicity, and I'll give you references to the literature on faster methods. This does not mean the choices I make here are "bad"; I've kept the implications of "big-oh" in mind to avoid quadratic behavior (for example, in the sorting algorithm for visible surface determination). This decision does have a cost, though, and you'll see that, too.

In the area of Windows performance, your alternatives are more limited. There are two performance areas you'll need to examine with Windows in mind:

- floating-point, and
- graphics output.

Most of the time, programmers don't stop to consider floating-point—it's just something that happens when you use float or double types. Unfortunately, in the Windows environment you can't afford to be that blithe. In DOS, the currently executing application "owns" the machine, but this is not true in Windows. Figure 1-8 shows the picture for enhanced-mode Windows (we'll ignore 286 or protected-mode in this discussion). Enhanced mode performs its magic through a combination of the Virtual Machine Manager (VMM) and Virtual Device Drivers (VxDs) to virtualize hardware. The floating-point coprocessor is hardware, and has a corresponding VxD, the VMCPD (Virtual Math CoProcessor Device). This allows the VMM to manage coprocessor "contexts."

As the picture shows, this introduces one level of overhead; the mediation between the virtual machines. For Windows applications, the picture is even worse, as you can see in Figure 1-8. All Windows applications "live" in the same virtual machine—the system virtual machine. Within that virtual machine, if multiple Windows applications try to access the math coprocessor, some form of mediation must again take place. WIN87EM.DLL handles this mediation for the System Virtual Machine and Windows applications. This means that, on average, Windows applications can expect floating-point performance that is between 2 and 3 times slower than a plain DOS application (2 mediation layers plus overhead).

One of the most important and time consuming of the other tasks that WIN87EM.DLL performs is run-time floating-point exception handling. Exception polling occurs in WIN87EM.DLL, and it is costly. But this feature, coupled with support for per-task instancing of application-installed exception handlers, at least means that you get a payback for the performance cost. Very good exception handling can be installed, as you'll see in a little while.

And there is one other good piece of news in all this overhead: The VMCPD only performs "coprocessor context" switches on demand, instead of on task-switch time. This has important implications for background processing—as long as only one application at a time is performing floating-point, a task switch will not force it to give up the coprocessor. Nice!

Graphics output is another major performance concern. Without rewriting driver primitives, there are some things you're stuck with in Windows. One of these is slower graphics performance than that of programs that directly address the hardware (although Windows' line-drawing speed isn't that bad, really). Never fear however, there are some programming tricks that you can perform to improve performance, be efficient, and not add additional penalties, including:

Figure 1-8. Floating-Point Hardware and Performance

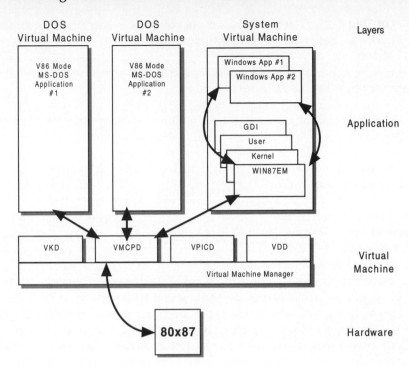

- drawing surface strategies,
- primitive usage strategies, and
- GDI drawing tool/attribute strategies.

Bitmaps and the client area of a window are the simplest examples of drawing surfaces. A common technique for eliminating flicker and allowing frame-by-frame composition is known as the *off-screen bitmap*. In this technique, the Bitblt operator transfers an off-screen image to the screen. Bitblt is a single operation and by transferring one bitmap at a time, the underlying pixel, line, and polygon operations are hidden from the user.

Primitives need to provide both one-shot and repetitive-usage functions. They also need to be attribute-aware by providing an attribute-override capability. Graphics Device Interface (GDI) pen and brush strategies attempt to localize and minimize creation/selection/deletion costs. You also need to maintain an awareness of the resource load the application is placing on the system. Later in this book, I'll discuss these techniques and issues and any advantage you can take from them.

In another sense, though, you can't solely be concerned with performance, since you're trying to build a well-behaved Windows application. Actions like using background processing to avoid locking the machine, judicious feedback to the user, and setting up for the post-processing phase all exact some cost. The *PeekMessage* background processing technique does not add much overhead if the user does nothing. Feedback, by its nature, costs.

Micro Perspective

We've handled the basics of "why"; now let's get back to "what." From the micro perspective two components define our implementation:

- the modeling application and its development, and
- the service libraries and their development.

The modeling applications' foundation is a simple shell application. The shell begins with the SDK sample MakeApp, which is found in the \SAMPLES\MAKEAPP subdirectory of a full-blown SDK installation. MakeApp may seem innocuous, but it provides a lot of bang for the buck, and every SDK owner has it. On top of the MakeApp foundation, there are three phases of development:

- value-added development,
- multiple-view extensions, and
- Model-View-Controller layer.

Whether you call them shells, application templates, or something else, they are useful. MakeApp in particular provides regular naming and construction, 16-bit/32-bit independence, and more, along with a canned generation process that provides simple but effective automation of the process of "cutting" an application.

Some simple enhancements add to this basic framework. You need several flavors of shells to satisfy a wide variety of requirements. For example, both SDI (Single Document Interface) and MDI (Multiple Document Interface) styles have their use. These are constructed on top of MakeApp. Some other enhancements, like drag-drop, command-line parameter handling, and private profile files, again add value to the basic shell. Finally, both Toolhelp and floating-point exception handling (for robustness) round out the additions to the basic shell layer.

Once you've created the basic shell layer, it is time to begin developing the modeling application. First, you'll extend the basic shell to use a multiple-view representation. This differs from MDI in that the multiple-view representation defines what happens inside a document or document window. MakeApp does not subdivide the client area, but instead treats it as one surface. The multiple-view extensions change this and present the user with a subdivided client area made up of specialized child-window classes. These children are:

- the main, or image, view pane,
- the scene info pane,
- the histogram display pane (for color analysis), and
- the session log pane.

At this point these children are just "stubs" waiting for further construction.

WinMod3D Geometric Modeler

The modeling application, known as *WinMod3D*, gives you a way to implement the child-view stubs. The modeler uses these multiple view panes to give the user a variety of feedback. For example, the image view contains the 3D image. While creating 3D images is the purpose of the modeler, these images by themselves can be difficult to interpret. In this case, "info" and "hist" panes give additional feedback to the user.

The info pane only changes one time for each pipeline run since it displays static information about the scene (like viewpoint, number of objects, number of lights, and more). This helps the user place the image in its appropriate context.

The hist pane, or histogram, display is a slightly different story. It displays a rough plot mapping the color intensities of the image to a 236-bin histogram. Even though this aliases values, the result is a realistic mapping into the 236 available "slots" in the Windows palette for 256 color adapters. The data structure that manages this sits behind the rough plot. The frequency with which you choose to update this data structure determines your performance overhead. In the polygon model, shader overhead exists at the polygon level; in the ray tracer scenario, the overhead is at the pixel level. You might say "ouch," but the plot of intensity values does give useful feedback about the color density in your image.

The running transcript (or at least the last 32K of it) is available for you to scroll back through, and the entire transcript is saved to file transcript.log in your current working directory. Every transcript call costs, too.

On top of all that, the title bar is used at various critical junctures to "flash" messages to the user about what is going on. This is the easiest way to communicate visually with the user without implementing a status bar, but it does flicker quite a bit and cost cycles. When you're rendering a really large model, you'll probably like this a lot more than when you're working with a small one. If the coupling and feedback really bother you and you want to wring the last ounce of performance out of your system, it's easy to change this code.

All of the sub-views I've just described act together to provide good feedback about the internal state of the modeler. Application management tasks get trickier when multiple views come into play. The Model-View-Controller, or MVC, paradigm I mentioned earlier (which was first popularized in Smalltalk systems) can help you handle this. Using a simple state machine as the basis of the controller, the multiple-view representation will provide views to the user and the underlying 3D data structures will serve as the model. In this case, the internals of the application shell will be upgraded to serve as our geometric modeling application.

You use all this I've just described to support the phases of the modeler I described earlier:

- world generation (front-end),
- world manipulation (core-functions),
- world rendering (back-end), and
- color post-processing (tools).

Object representation is the glue that binds all these phases together. Object representation lets the modeler describe objects in terms of both polygons (for polygon mode) and equations (for raytrace mode). If the object internals need to reflect this dualism, the external specification language will have to as well. We'll begin by working with the Neutral File Format (NFF) developed by Eric Haines for the Standard Procedural Database (See "A Proposal for Standard Graphics Environments," *IEEE Computer Graphics & Applications*, Vol. 7, No. 11, Nov. 1987, pp. 3-5) and add extensions as we need to. NFF is designed to test various rendering algorithms and efficiency schemes, and lets you describe the geometry and surface characteristics of objects, the placement of lights, and the setting of viewing parameters. Even though it was originally intended for use with ray tracing, we can add support to it for wire-frame and shaded drawing, as well as additional ray-tracing features. We'll take the first step in this direction by extending the scene-description language to add a control file containing vertex and facet information. Next, by choosing carefully the range of objects to be defined, we can match our ability to define arbitrary sets of vertex and facet data with our ability to mathematically describe an object, allowing us to render an object in multiple ways. Finally, by doing a minimum of texture-mapping the checkerboards and other textures that signify ray tracing will be supported.

The specification language feeds the front end that translates this external representation into the internal representation the modeler uses in its data structures (shown in Figure 1-9). This results in the creation of the object list with its dual representation.

Figure 1-9.   Modeler Data Flow

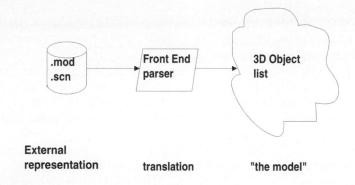

Explicit face and vertex representations are ideal for wireframe and shaded drawing. One reason this is important, even if you're not doing wireframe rendering, is that the wireframe viewer is a very useful tool in picture development. You can create scenes that are arbitrarily complex, so a simple mechanism for verifying your image geometry is essential. A wireframe renderer is an ideal way to do this.

While wireframe drawings are adequate to get the sense of a scene, they don't make a very great impression, as shown in Figure 1-10.

Hidden-line and shaded images are an intermediate step. Using the same object representation as you just did with the wire frame viewer, you can, with a little more work, generate better images. Your move beyond wireframe drawing involves two steps: visible polygon surface determination, and polygon surface shading.

It's here that we first face the problem of hidden surfaces. If we use visible-surface determination, we can generate a hidden-line rendering. By accepting some limitations in our scene (most notably that objects cannot intersect), performing depth-sorting, and drawing in z-order, we can come to a pretty satisfactory solution to the visibility and hidden-surface problem. An example of an HLHSR image that could result from this process is shown in Figure 1-11.

Figure 1-10.   Wireframe Image

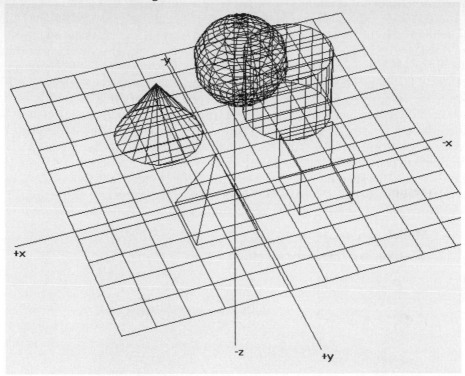

Figure 1-11.   Hidden-Line Image

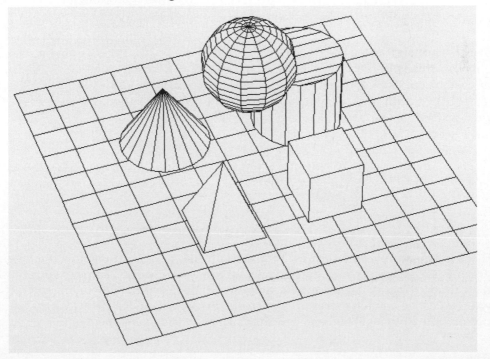

By using a subset of our illumination model we can determine the color to shade a polygon. Shading typically occurs in two flavors: *flat* (or *diffuse*), and *specular* (or *Phong*) shading.

Flat shading is a subset of Phong shading. It's good enough for you to get an impression of where the lights and objects are in a scene, but it ignores highlights on shiny surfaces.

Phong shading is an empirical model for highlighting, and works best when implemented as a pixel-level technique. If you use a scan-line polygon shader instead of polygon filling (which uses the underlying Windows GDI output primitive), the Phong technique starts looking even more attractive. But for true Phong shading, your process needs to do averaging across adjacent faces prior to the interpolation step. In our modeler, the explicit face/vertex representation maintains no adjacency information. This means the incremental shading technique will show unacceptable artifacts from the lack of averaging. Taking this into account means only flat shading is really feasible with this system. Still, this is good enough to show relationships between objects and lights. And Phong shading still does not take into account interactions between objects. An example gray scale flat-shaded image is shown in Figure 1-12.

Figure 1-12. Flat-Shaded Image in Grayscale

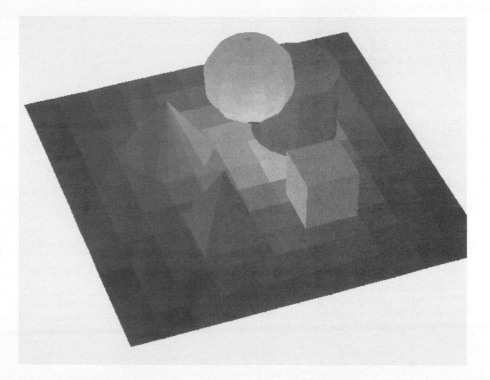

These images, while better than wireframe, still lack realism. The whole point behind ray tracing is to generate realistic images. So, when you've created a scene to your satisfaction, it's time to trace it. Ray tracing elegantly solves the problem of modeling interactions between reflective and refractive surfaces; in other words, it models the way light bounces off objects. The illumination model and shading are a major component of the ray-tracing process. I don't want to go into too much detail on shading yet, so suffice it to say that the illumination model describes how the surface properties of objects, light sources, and viewing geometry interact, and that it allows a mathematical calculation of color.

What results from either the polygon-shading calculations (for each polygon) or the ray-trace shading calculations (for each pixel) is an x,y,z triplet of floating-point RGB color values in the range of [0,1]. These values are typically mapped to a [0,255] integer range, which takes up a byte of storage. One byte each for red, green, and blue results in 24-bit color, or 16.7 million colors.

This is where hardware comes into the picture. Eight-bit color cards display only 256 colors, so something has to give. We use a process called *color reduction* to analyze the image and pick the colors to use. If you're working with 15-bit cards displaying 32,768 colors (32K) or more, it is worth your while to use the 24-bit bitmaps and let the hardware figure it out. There are perfectly adequate Windows and other 24-bit drivers that define the rules for displaying a 24-bit image in 15 bits, so you don't need to reinvent the wheel. But all this does complicate the process of generating an image.

I use a simple solution to solve the problem of displaying 24-bit color in an 8-bit machine. I create a grayscale of the image, using one of several available methods, to display its 8-bit intensities. Figure 1-13 shows an example of a ray-traced grayscale image. The grayscale methods available include simple averaging and displaying one channel (all 8-bits) of the red, green, and blue color channels. The original 24-bit intensities are stored, and a post-processing phase revisits them once the image is complete.

Figure 1-13. Basic Ray-Traced Image in Grayscale

With your image's original 24-bit values stored and the grayscale values in hand, there are three color resolutions you need to deal with:

- 4-bit "plain" VGA (16 colors),
- 8-bit (256 colors), and
- 15-bit (32,768 colors) and higher.

If you have a 15-bit (or higher) color card, colors could be directly assigned from the intensity buffer, making this post-processing step unnecessary. The rules for handling 15-bit cards and 24-bit bitmaps make it possible to treat any resolution above 15-bit as 24-bit, easing the burden a bit.

However, the polygon shader draws GDI polygons that are filled by brushes. Creating and destroying thousands of brushes "on-the-fly" would increase your rendering time immensely. So rather than do that, the system grayscales in 32K color mode (and above), and performs color reduction as a post-processing step.

Handling 8-bit and plain VGA (4-bit) uses a subset of the original colors. Generating this subset uses color reduction or *color quantization*, resulting in a palette of colors used to map the intensity values in the image buffer. This requires a color-model system and the ability to manipulate color palettes.

Windows provides the Palette Manager to help you do just that. If you use the Palette Manager in conjunction with the program's generation of the palette colors you will produce a subset of the colors represented in the intensity buffer.

There are two methods of palette generation: fixed and adaptive. Arbitrarily fixed palettes usually result in unsatisfactory images. But several algorithms exist to generate palettes that "adapt" to the content of images. The best-known of these are:

- Uniform
- Popularity,
- Median-cut, and
- Octree.

Which method works best? That depends on the image itself. Histograms provide a tool to examine the intensities and determine which method to use. Images with few colors can use the first two of these methods and save time. Images with many colors require a more sophisticated approach to color selection to make a satisfactory image.

Once the modeler is built, scene development and data acquisition become the issue. You should use test pictures to validate the renderer and re-validate whenever you add features. Even though test pictures are usually not very interesting, you'll notice how the question of data and geometry very quickly becomes the central issue.

How do you generate scenes and scene data? Three methods of scene generation are common: manual, algorithmic, and external. *Manual* implies just that. This is a labor-intensive method, whether you use a text editor or an interactive interface. *Algorithmic* scene generation is used to compute a scene from a program. The Standard Procedural Database, which I've already mentioned, provides a base set of algorithmically generated standard images to test a renderer. You can also acquire geometry data from *external* sources like a CAD program, but that usually requires conversion between the representation from the CAD program and the representation of the renderer.

Service Libraries

What about the libraries, you ask? The service-library implementation presented here consists of three layers:

- A Windows and operating-system layer—the WLib,
- A 3D-support layer—the G3DLib, and
- A 3D-modeler support layer—the M3D modeler-support services.

The WLib is the lowest layer, consisting of policy-free primitive routines that provide useful Windows services, but that do not enforce much mechanical structure for using them. The goal of this library is simply to provide primitive building blocks, so the only usage policy it dictates is the create/use/destroy sequence familiar to Windows programmers who've dealt with memory or GDI. Since this library provides Windows services, it is natural to mimic Windows' organization. Therefore, WLib contains three subsystems like Windows: kernel, GDI, and user functions. The kernel subsystem contains memory and error-handling routines. The GDI subsystem follows with color, palette, bitmap, and DIB (Device Independent Bitmaps) routines. Finally, the user subsystem provides useful clipboard and mouse routines. Table 1-2 shows this organization.

Table 1-2.   WLib Subsystems

WLib Subsystems	Description
WLib Housekeeping	Standard DLL routines for initialization and termination
Kernel	Memory and error handling
GDI	Color, palettes, bitmaps, and DIBs
User	Clipboard and mouse

The next library, G3DLib, is a layer built on the WLib primitives. The G3D routines provide usable 3D foundation components and define the policy for using these components. The G3DLib also contains three subsystems. The first subsystem, *Drawing Surfaces*, is the basis for the interface between abstract 3D coordinates and the 2D screen. Its *canvas* is a standard Windows off-screen bitmap coupled with an off-screen memory Device Context (DC), encapsulated in a wrapper. A canvas supports solving the "coordinates in a window system" problem I discussed earlier, and provides smooth screen updates. The next subsystem, *General Support*, adds a standard inquiry capability, histogram support, math, and graphics primitive output to the canvas. On this foundation, the final subsystem, *3D Support*, adds the vector, matrix, and viewing system routines. Table 1-3 shows these subsystems.

Table 1-3.   G3DLib Subsystems

G3DLib Subsystems	Description
G3DLib Housekeeping	Standard DLL routines for initialization and termination
Drawing Surface	Canvas and genv drawing-surface management
General Support	Useful services, like inquiry and math
3D Support	3D mathematics support

The last layer defines the 3D-modeler support services (or M3D). The five parts of M3D follow the phases of the modeler. The "Front End Part I" and "Front End Part II" routines provide script language and 3D object instantiation support. The "Core Functions Part I" and "Core Functions Part II" routines allow simple manipulation and rendering. The final set of routines, "Post Processing," address the color problem and provide support for producing 8-bit images from 24-bit data. Table 1-4 delineates the subsystems of the M3D Modeler support services.

Table 1-4. M3D Subsystems

M3D Subsystems	Description
Front End Part I	Provides script language support
Front End Part II	Provides 3D-object instantiation support
Core Functions Part I	Provides world manipulation
Core Functions Part II	Provides world rendering
Post Processing	Provides color post-processing support

Figure 1-14. Chapter Road Map of Coverage: Libraries and Applications

	Libs			App		
	WLib	G3DLib	M3D SS	MakeApp	Multiple Views	MVC State Mechanism
Chapter 1	●	●	●	●	●	●
Chapter 2				●	●	●
Chapter 3	●	●	●			●
Chapter 4	●					
Chapter 5		●				
Chapter 6		●				
Chapter 7		●				
Chapter 8			●			●
Chapter 9			●			
Chapter 10			●			●
Chapter 11			●	●	●	?

This dual strategy of applications and libraries combines to provide building blocks enabling the development of the modeler. Figure 1-14 shows you, chapter-by-chapter, where each component, library, and application is covered in this book. The programmer interface, covered in Chapter 3, is the most visible part of a library. Chapter 2 provides more detail about the internals of a geometric modeler, and introduces the MVC concept and the multiple-view extensions to the basic shell. Part II steps you through implementing the WLib and the G3DLib, delivered as DLLs. And finally, Part III helps you implement the M3D modeler-support services and the MVC-like geometric modeler.

Before you leap into the details, though, you need some guiding principles, or tactics, to help you control the implementation and allow easier reading of the code. The MakeApp shell gives us our initial kick-start.

Implementation Tactics

Now that we've got the strategy mapped out, we need a tactical model for organizing the project. The obvious tactical decisions about external details like stub files, stub makes, the build environment, and directory structures, as well as internal details like programming style and naming conventions are important. A global application architecture is nice too, but is not sufficient by itself. We need a common culture to level the playing field and serve as a prototypical programming model. Throughout this book, I use one such project culture.

We're going to begin with a code base provided by Microsoft in the SDK. The MakeApp application provides solutions to many basic development problems. It uses the Hungarian style for variable naming. It uses the new features of the 3.1 SDK to isolate porting issues. It provides a well-thought-out modularization. It also lacks some of the finishing touches that would make it truly useful, so there's a definite opportunity to add value.

First, let's discuss the original MakeApp. The components of the base MakeApp application template are shown in Table 1-5; the C source files are shown in Figure 1-15. The source files in this sample application are App, Frame, Client, and Dlg. The app.c module contains the main-level routines, including the master initialization and termination routines, and the main loop. The frame.c module contains routines to manage the desktop-level functionality expected of a frame window. The client.c module insulates client-area management or display. These window-class modules and the makewc.c template module (not shown in the diagram) provide working examples of how to use the message-cracker macros. Finally, the dlg.c module contains working examples of the MakeApp solution for dialogs.

A default module-definitions file, a resource file containing resources, an icon file, a version resource, a dialog template file, a makefile, and a linker response file round out the build process. Default resources include a menu with a defined help menu, a string table, and dialog templates. The string table contains entries for application name, titlebar title, window class, and startup menu entries.

The dialog templates are for the sample dialogs.

Table 1-5.   MakeApp Source Components

Files	Description
Main	
app.c, app.h	Application layer with global initialization, winmain, and global termination.
makeapp.h	Main include file
Window classes	
frame.c, frame.h	Top-level window class, the desktop window
client.c, client.h	Client area window class, pass-through layer
Command layer	
dlg.c, dlg.h	Dialog handlers
Support	
makewc.c, makewc.h	Stub window class
menu.h, dlgdefs.h, resource.h	Helper header files
makeapp.rc, makeapp.ico	Resource files
makeapp.def, makeapp.ver	Definition and version file
makeapp.bat, makeapp2.bat	Generator batch files
rep.exe	Search and replace program for generation process

Figure 1-15.   MakeApp Source Components

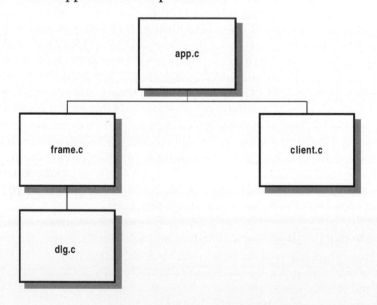

While these are simple beginnings, MakeApp provides nicely thought out layering for you to use—and use it you will. The first major change you'll make adds view panes within the client area. This client module absorbs most of the changes, leaving the frame layer unaware of any second-generation descendants. Besides the view pane additions, you'll expand the desktop-level functionality in the frame layer with application-specific menu and dialog handling, drag-drop, and help. Little niceties like a splash screen dialog provide the finishing touches.

Besides providing a platform for this growth, this template application dictates that files share a common naming convention and structure, making it much easier to manage many window classes. This convention also provides some of the replication features of this framework. The following file naming convention is used:

- The filename is the name of the window-class source and include file (excluding the .c or .h).
- ClassName is the class name used for function name prefixes (for example, ClassName_OnCommand, etc.).
- TYPENAME is the name of the instance data-structure type (for example, size of TYPENAME);
- Ptrtype is the name to use for pointers to instance data (for example, TYPENAME* ptrtype.)
- AppPrefix_ is the class-name prefix to use for the registered classname. The underscore must be included (for example, **CreateWindow**(...," AppPrefix_ClassName", . . .)).
- Appname is the name of the main application header file (for example, #include "appname.h").

Understanding the naming conventions in the code is critical to being able to read it.

MakeApp applications use a standard header-file strategy in addition to this naming convention. The C run-time library headers, a good example of header-file strategy, have two important properties: *idempotence* and *independence*. This means they can be both included multiple times and that they can be included in any order. To avoid having to worry about idempotence the MakeApp-derived header files use a #define constant to determine whether they have been included already.

Listing 1-1 shows how to guard against multiple inclusion. Bracket the header with a test for the absence of a constant. Within the brackets, define the constant. If the test succeeds, you enter the #define block for the first time, define the constant so that you can't get here again, then fall through to the body of the header. If the test fails, you've already been here, so you don't need to include this code again.

Listing 1-1.   Guarding Headers Against Multiple Inclusion

```
#ifndef _INC_VWWND
#define _INC_VWWND
...

#endif // !_INC_VWWND
```

Using this technique, we define two classes of headers: main and mini. Each mini-header defines items for a specific source file or subsystem. The main header for each library includes all of the mini-headers. Each application also has a main header that includes the library main headers and application mini-headers that it needs. In the case of order dependencies, the main headers shield each library or application source file from them.

Now comes the beauty of MakeApp. With the components of a minimum shell and some global renaming, we can manually modify the shell into base code for a new project.

Let's look at exactly what we need to do to accomplish this. Our goal is to make an application that is completely distinct from MakeApp. To change one application into another requires the following:

- Change the module name and exports in the def file.
- Change the class name for **RegisterClass** and **CreateWindow**.
- Change any resources and resource identifiers.
- Change the .exe name in the make and linker response files.
- Change the main source filename (optional).

This is a lot of work for little gain. These components do not isolate us (the programmers) from the uniqueness issue, and the process gives us a huge opportunity to make errors.

Now, here's the new, quick-and-easy way. A nifty little application called rep.exe lives in the MakeApp directory of the 3.1 SDK samples. It automates the transformation I've just described, which frees us from needing to do it all manually. MakeApp gives us both a batch file and the rep.exe global search-and-replace engine that automates this error-prone task. The MakeApp utility "cuts" a template application for us.

Besides copying the template files, rep.exe renames the files, functions, and constants in the makefiles, source files, header files, and resource files. It acts as a crude code generator. As files are added to the base code, the batch-file-turned-code-generator must be modified so the new "cut" will work accordingly.

The common naming convention makes this work in the makefile, source files, headers, and resources. Rep.exe then does its magic. The makefile is structured for easy growth; the source files are organized into a layered app-frame-client hierarchy for clear lines of responsibility; and the resource file implements some cool things like a version resource that helps with installation.

There's the high-level view of the project environment. It contains well-designed modularization, a naming convention for many of the elements of an application (source files, data structures, classnames, etc.), a header-file strategy, and a crude code generation capability that uses DOS copy and rep.exe.

From a low-level view, the source uses Microsoft's message-cracker macros to structure the code. The message-cracker macros provide a portable and type-safe method to deal with window messages, their parameters, and their return values. Instead of separating message parameters with casts and HIWORD/LOWORD macro invocations, you declare and implement a function with parameters and return value that match a cracker signature. The message crackers pick apart the parameters, call your function, and return the appropriate value from the message. Message forwarders use **DefWindowProc**, **SendMessage**, or **PostMessage** to forward messages to a function. In our implementation, we'll use the HANDLE_MSG macro to improve readability wherever possible. All message handling in the window procedure will be uniform in appearance, thereby reducing "noise" in the code.

By using these macros you do not have to worry about what parameters go where and what kind of casting you need to do. The message crackers, control APIs, and macros will all help your application's portability to 32-bit Windows. This template application is also fully STRICT compatible. Windows.h in the 3.1 SDK introduced many new features for ease of use and robustness; including the STRICT option.

For the details on how these macros perform the voodoo that they do so well, you should read the .txt files in the SDK and windowsx.h. Reading Windows.h, windowsx.h, and the other header files will improve your overall knowledge of Windows. I am continually amazed at how much I continue to glean from careful rereading of Windows.h.

The technique I've just shown you (in the MakeApp SDK example) may be the most useful to you in the long run, or you may already use some code generation tool to speed your application generation. Whichever is the case, the key here is to use tools; for my purposes in this book, the MakeApp template provides them for us.

MakeApp is the basis for our tool, but it is not complete enough by itself to be useful for our needs. We'll derive four application architectures from MakeApp: an SDI shell, an MDI shell, a static graphics demo architecture, and a dynamic graphics demo architecture. SDI and MDI are the two most common interface styles around. Static graphics demos that draw once and dynamic graphics demos that draw forever are both useful, too.

Additionally, a DLL shell will ease the startup strain on libraries, and round out our basic building blocks. Figure 1-16 shows the building blocks we'll derive from MakeApp.

Simple drag-drop functionality, command-line parameter handling, a private profile file, and some other niceties are also built into the shell architectures to add value. These features make the MakeApp code a nicer breed of Windows application.

Figure 1-16.   MakeApp-Derived Shells

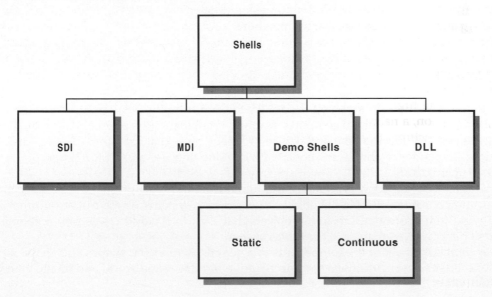

While the features I've just described are niceties, features more concerned with robustness—like exception handling—are also provided. Two major classes of error are of concern to a modeling application: resource errors (like memory and GDI resources) and floating point calculation errors.

Toolhelp.DLL lets you install an interrupt handler by using **InterruptRegister** at your application's startup. It also lets you deinstall the handler at application termination using **InterruptUnregister**. This traps exceptions like GP fault, integer division by zero, stack fault, and invalid op-code. The first class of errors can be managed using this functionality.

This still does nothing for floating-point exceptions. The Microsoft Developer Network CD contains a wonderful article, "Floating-Point in Microsoft Windows" (with sample example code), that discusses exception handling and performance issues. The sample shows how to install and deinstall exception handlers for both DLLs and applications, using **signal** out of the Run-Time Library.

Combine these two techniques with **Throw** and **Catch** and you can handle a wide range of errors without "crashing." The WLib will provide macros to make this even easier for you, and I'll introduce you to a programming style for using the macros.

The G3DLib also uses the macros. The Toolhelp functions are not used in our DLL, since they're primarily intended for use in an application.

The modeling application, on the other hand, uses all three techniques: Toolhelp exceptions, floating-point exceptions, and Throw/Catch macros.

That finishes our discussion of tactics. You've seen how we'll enhance and extend the basic MakeApp code. We now have five building blocks to work with: two types of demo shells, two types of application shells, and a DLL shell. These ready-made components used in simple variations and a basic application-generator process dramatically reduce the amount of new and different material you'll need to deal with.

Granted, these building-block shells may be too simplistic to base your next "killer" application on, but to help you learn, I've built the demos, and example programs of the book are built on them. In Chapter 2, we'll significantly strengthen this scaffolding by adding a multiple view capability. We'll continue building on our MakeApp foundation throughout the book, but you have to start somewhere.

Summary

No matter what you attempt, you should try to learn from the past.

I introduced the history of computer graphics implementation efforts, which has shown the value of API development and device independence. Windows provides the basics of device independence and in this book we'll develop and use an API for 3D graphics and geometric modelers.

We reviewed the concepts that are the foundation of all 3D graphics systems: coordinates and coordinate spaces, 3D objects, and viewing systems. These can be summarized by saying that coordinates make up objects that exist in a world created by a geometric modeler and viewed using a 3D graphics system.

We then talked about the components of a geometric modeler: shapes and shape representations, shape specifications and specification interfaces and world and image manipulation tools.

The method I use to decompose (examine) geometric modeling systems is to ask three questions:

- What is being attempted (abstraction)?
- What is the approach (representation)?
- What are the details (implementation)?

This ARI decomposition is a form of structured modeling and provides a valuable logical framework for analysis and design.

We then discussed a set of nonprogramming issues involving system and image quality, and I suggested some ways to approach measuring quality in this context.

Getting into the "meat" of the modeler, I broke modeler processing into phases:

- world generation (front end),
- world manipulation (core functions),
- world rendering (back end), and
- color post processing (tools).

The front end translates for the core functions and participates in world generation. World manipulation uses the viewing engine and core functions to change the image. The back end uses the rendering engine and core functions to generate the images. Image post-processing puts the finishing touches on the model.

Our overall implementation strategy boils down to two sets of components: a geometric modeling application and service libraries.

To do this, I combined a macro design based on a two-layer policy-free/policy-implementing approach and using common implementation techniques with basic decisions on the library feature set, performance and algorithms, and other general issues.

I used the MakeApp SDK sample as a starting point, and used all of this "macro-perspective" to provide a micro view of the modeling application and its three phases of development (plus the three service library implementations):

- expand MakeApp into various shells,
- expand basic shell into multiple-view representation, and
- clean up the internals by using a Model-View-Controller-like approach.

The library implementation also has three layers:

- Windows and operating system,
- 3D support, and
- 3D object geometry.

Tactically, the MakeApp-derived shells and project culture are the common bond between the libraries, demo programs, and applications developed in this book. They provide building blocks and are constructed according to a style and structure that forms a common language for the code.

I outlined three sets of enhancements that we'll make to MakeApp:

- new features and exception handling,
- multiple-view extensions, which we'll see in Chapter 2, and
- Model-View-Controller, which is discussed in Chapter 2 and later.

What's Next?

We'll fill in more of the details of modeling (including the beginning of MVC) with a quick look at the multiple-subview framework in Chapter 2. When we've accomplished that goal, Chapter 3 presents more detail on the support libraries.

2 3D Modeler Application Architecture

In This Chapter

- Discussion of modeler architecture, some common threads, and the multiple-view extensions to MakeApp.
- A general view of the WinMod3D modeler.
- Exploration of common themes between the simple demo and WinMod3D modeler applications with regard to regular API usage, canvas- and graphics-environment-based drawing, world manipulation and rendering based on 4D vectors and matrices, and the results of living in the Windows environment.
- Implementation of the multiple-view extensions to MakeApp, using child windows to present multiple renditions of data.
- Preparation for the further MVC extensions we'll do in Part III.

Introduction

In the last chapter, we took a high-level view of modeling. Now it's time for more details. Much of our implementation won't actually happen until we get to Part III, but here we get started with the internals that support WinMod3D, the modeler we're developing.

There are three parts to this chapter: the first describes the modeling architecture; the second describes common threads for API programmers, and in the third part we'll start expanding the MakeApp shell into the multiple-view shell.

The description of the modeling architecture starts with an overview of MVC implementation and the M3D modeler-support services. This gives us the foundation for starting to describe the implementation we're using here. We'll then move to the next level of detail on world generation, world manipulation, world rendering, and image post-processing, which further define the set of services we'll need for our implementation.

When we approach the section on "common threads," it will be quickly apparent that graphics applications have a certain exploitable regularity. These common threads, evidenced by the basics of simple 3D applications and 3D modelers, allow maximum gain from a minimum of code and effort. Not only is API-usage itself a "meta-thread," the canvas- and graphics-environment-based drawing, vector and matrix-3D mathematical underpinnings, and the Windows environment are all basic components of the code we'll be dealing with here, from simple demo applications to the modeler itself.

Finally, implementing the multiple-child window interface in the last section of this chapter expands on the MakeApp shell code. In the process, it provides the application skeleton that we'll depend on for WinMod3D and its development in Part III.

Modeler Architecture I: WinMod3D Strategy Overview

In Chapter 1, I introduced the concepts of 3D objects, the modeler's "world," and various ways to view objects and scenes within the modeler's world. Now that you're familiar with those concepts, we'll move on to a description of 3D objects and the object list, and 3D manipulations on the object list.

To maintain object compatibility in all modes, we start with a limited set of objects that are describable in both explicit face/vertex terms as well as in mathematical or analytic representation. Polygon mode, as I discussed previously, needs only face and vertex data. Ray-trace mode requires that we be able to mathematically describe objects and the inter-section of a line with the object. Objects that are supported in both modes include:

- Perfect sphere,
- Infinite plane,
- Cylinder and cone, and
- Box and pyramid.

We use an external database-generator process to build data files containing face and vertex information for each object. Our scene description language directly references this object data file. (Data files for the types I just mentioned and the generation process itself are two of the main subjects of Chapter 9.) Both internal representations of the modeler are created from the data in this external process.

In polygon mode, faces are defined by vertices. *Faces* are defined as rectangles and tri-angles, and a *vertex* is defined as a 3D-point that represents specific x, y, and z coordinates. The face list contains the points that define the object; the point list stores the defining coordinates. This simplicity makes it easier to create new objects in polygon mode.

In ray-trace mode, both the sphere and the plane can be described by single equations. The cylinder, cone, box, and pyramid are not as simple. Cylinders and cones are defined by simplified quadratic equations for their bodies, but their endcaps are defined by a circle. Boxes and pyramids are similarly defined from the starting point of a set of rectangles, then rely on triangles or rectangles to complete them.

The circle, rectangle, and triangle are really just plane figures and can be handled with a variation of the infinite-plane code. Thus, they're not treated as separate objects in the scene description language. Rather, they are lower-level components used to make the cylinder, cone, box, and pyramid in the ray-trace representation.

As long as you add both representation methods in parallel, you'll have no problem extending the system. This quickly leads you to higher-order mathematics, though, since even a basic shape like a torus is a quartic surface (or an equation in powers of 4) and must be described as such in ray-trace representation. The basic assumption here is that both forms of 3D must be present for the modeler to function correctly. This is your key point to remember for expansion.

OK, you know how objects are defined. Now, let's go over combining objects to create scenes. The visibility method you choose has a strong influence on the limitations you'll experience in creating a scene. Your biggest problems happen when two objects try to oc-cupy the same space. Polygon representation can't handle this, even through ray-tracing can. There's actually another representation problem here as well, but you'll find out about that one in Chapter 10.

When you're creating a scene, you're the director. You place the objects and position the camera. You need to be aware of object size, the extents of all objects in a scene (the range of possible polygon vertex/ray-object location values), camera position, light location, and distance relative to the objects. Sound a little like photography and picture composition? You are right. It is. The ray tracer can be thought of as a pseudo-camera capable of producing reasonably nice images—when you're creating ray-traced images, you're composing a picture.

3D-viewing systems and their mathematical underpinnings let you operate on the objects in a scene and produce graphic output. We use two representations of the 3D-viewing system, similar to the way we handled the object list. The first representation is a matrix, defined in 4x4 or 4D notation, that stores the transformation from world space to eye space for polygon mode. We discussed this in Chapter 1, remember? The second representation is a group of vectors, defined in 4D notation, that are used to generate the rays for ray-trace mode. In either of these cases, we bind the arrow keys on the keyboard to camera position, allowing you control while viewing the scene.

But you do not have infinite power as director of these mathematical actors. This viewing system has some limitations. First, no clipping is performed. Clipping is a process of testing points for relevance in a view of a scene. Second, there are no special checks for crossing the origin, having the distance between the from- and at-point equal zero (very bad), etc. Everything is fine as long as you keep the camera in a region sufficiently far away from objects to avoid the "fish-eye" effects from lack of clipping, outside of objects (driving inside an object can be useful at times but is not supported here), and away from the origin (because of the lack of tests). Comparatively speaking, this is a very big valid region with plenty of opportunity for nice images. You can get reasonably close to either the origin or the edges of an object, but checking in the arrow key handling thwarts your attempts to enter a "bad" region. Figure 2-1 and Figure 2-2 show an example of what happens if you don't have clipping and special checking. Figure 2-1 is right before the problem occurs, and Figure 2-2 shows the problem.

Once you have your objects and a camera, it's time to render. The polygon visibility process uses quicksort to gain the "NlogN" advantage, implying a contiguous block of memory treated as a list structures. (See your run-time library reference to verify that this is true in your configuration.) The implications of this decision should be obvious—with thousands of polygons in the scene, thousands of visible polygons result. You need to be able to manipulate huge pointers and deal with blocks of memory larger than 64K. This, by the way, implies a huge memory model in 16-bit Windows 3.1. Objects in either polygon or ray-trace mode share surface-property definitions, including color, surface coefficients, and texture definition. If a property is not needed, it is ignored, but the presence of these properties is a big help with expansion. Another extensible feature is the use of user-definable color and materials lookup tables. The default set of colors is derived from the X-11 implementation, but it is not the only possible set. In the same manner, the default set of materials can easily be replaced or expanded.

Since the polygon representation doesn't maintain face-adjacency information, it is limited to flat shading. This is not a limitation because a ray-traced mode exists. The ray tracer uses the same algorithm for the specular calculation as a Phong shader, so the adventurous among you should have no problem extending the polygon shader if you want to.

Figure 2-1. Wireframe Drawing Without Clipping — Still Valid

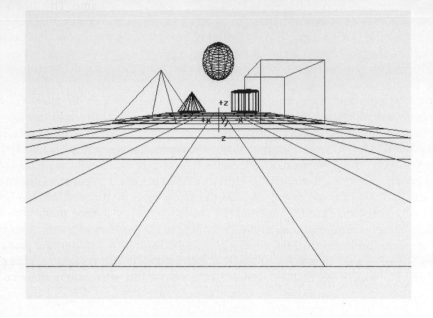

Figure 2-2. Wireframe Image Without Clipping — Showing Errors

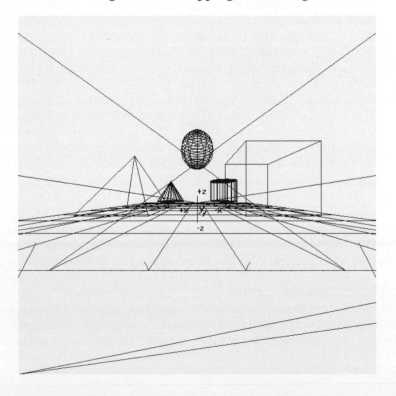

The existence of ray-trace mode means that you can regard polygon shading as a "preview" mode. First, you position the objects and view them in wireframe. Then, add lights and view them flat-shaded. Finally, when everything is "just right," you ray-trace the image. This doesn't mean the other types of shading aren't valuable; Phong shading is much faster than ray-tracing and can actually be fairly realistic, with a little tweaking (shadows and textures). So if you're serious about 3D graphics you probably should investigate polygon-shading further.

The ray tracer implements reflection and specular highlights. This tracer, however, doesn't support refraction, so it cannot trace glass. There are provisions in the intersection code that will let you add this if you want, but the definitions are only there to show you what needs to be done. It's not implemented in the scope of this book.

Figure 1-9 showed the flow of data in the modeler, from the external to the internal data representation. Then, Figures 1-10 through 1-14 showed four different results of converting that internal representation to an image (wireframe, hidden line, flat-shaded, and ray-traced). The figure you're about to see is separated into polygon and ray-trace mode processes. Each of these processes consists of manipulating and rendering the 3D object list (or *model*) to produce the image on the canvas or view. For your clearer understanding, I've simplified the process shown in Figure 2-3 somewhat. Here, I've used the canvas, or drawing surface, I used in Chapter 1. The internal data flow is from the data structures (3D object list) to the canvas.

Figure 2-3.   More Modeler Data Flow

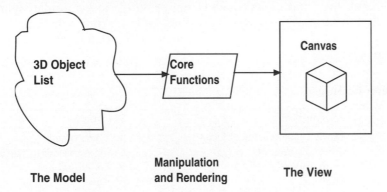

WinMod3D uses the canvas for all its output. This is an important and fundamental concept. Since our graphics system lives in the Windows environment, it cannot simply map to absolute screen coordinates (I discussed this in the classical coordinate section of Chapter 1). A well-behaved Windows application draws only within its client area, not on the entire screen. This presents a problem for the window-viewport mapping operation. PEX and its design, however, shows a guiding light here, by providing the programmers who use it with a drawable surface area as the basic currency of their drawing.

There's a parallel concept here, in the canvas. It is an offscreen drawing surface (in Windows parlance, a *memory DC* and a *memory bitmap*). The canvas "double-buffers" output; and it is owned by a graphics environment whose job is to manage the final coordinate mappings for the canvas. This means that this graphics environment/canvas pair supports the classical notion of a window and a viewport.

The bitmap drawing surface is sufficient for wireframe and simple hidden-line renderings. However, the rendering modes for flat-shading and ray-tracing add illumination models, requiring additional handling. In polygon mode, each face stores its color value, a technique that's only valid when one color is used for the entire face (like flat-shading). For ray-trace mode, this isn't sufficient.

You need a way to store each calculated value, instead of immediately using it for output to the bitmap drawing surface of the canvas. But it's the canvas that once again comes to our rescue. A *HEAVY* variety of canvas provides a parallel memory array tailor-made to be a memory buffer or intensity buffer. You can use the face or the memory buffer to store the calculated intensity values for each mode, supporting the post-processing. The post-processing phase uses the stored the image data to generate the final image without needing to further manipulate the 3D object list.

The post-processing operations manage the final part of color image production. Post-processing also targets the canvas for its output. To do this, it uses either the value stored with each face in the visible face list or the value at the current pixel location in the memory buffer associated with each canvas. This intensity buffer and color analysis are used with library routines for color and palettes to generate the final image.

From external to internal representation, through manipulation and rendering to grayscale, and finally to color image generation, the process is now complete. Our system's capabilities with regard to the content of scenes, the possible views of them, and the final resulting colored image are defined by these features. While the canvas is our target, its the 3D viewing system and the illumination models that provide the manipulation and rendering operations that make image generation possible. Table 2-1 shows the feature set and similarities for polygon and ray modes. Table 2-2 shows the limitations defined by the approaches we'll take here.

Table 2-1. Modeler Features

Feature	Polygon Mode	Ray Mode
Representation	Explicit face/vertex object	Analytic object
Surface properties	Color, coefficients	Color, coefficients, textures
Viewing	From, lookat	From, lookat,up
Lights	Multiple	Multiple
Output	8 or 24 bit	8 or 24 bit

Table 2-2. Modeler Limitations

Feature	Polygon Mode	Ray Mode
Representation	No adjacency info	No general solver
Surface properties	No texture, specular	No refraction
Viewing	No clipping	N/A
	From manipulation only	From manipulation only
Scene sizes	Limited by selectors/memory	Limited by selectors/memory

At this point, you should have a good general concept of our system. Now, our problem boils down to getting to a working application from this point. The answer is: an abundance of building materials, use of commonality, and a sound framework.

The framework gives us a canned architecture that our modeler can leverage. As such, it uses multiple views and an MVC paradigm to manage those multiple views. The libraries contain service routines for your support. The support libraries provide a wide range of basic Windows-helper, drawing-surface, 3D mathematics, and modeler-specific graphics functions.

The three support components—WLib DLL, G3DLib DLL, and M3D Support Services— each contribute their part. The most visible components are the canvas and graphics environment, 4D vectors, matrices, transformations, and the 3D objects. All graphics output revolves around the drawing-surface subsystem of the G3DLib, which is built on the lower-level WLib code. Likewise, mathematical operations are based on the vectors and matrices provided by the 3D-support subsystem of the G3DLib. The M3D support services give you helper functions for all phases of the modeler, including 3D object support.

There are several common threads between the sample applications and the WinMod3D modeler when it comes to building materials. The canvas and graphics environment constitute your drawing surface and manage window-viewport mapping. 4D vectors and matrices do world manipulation and rendering. And you must remember that Windows environment issues are larger than our modeler-specific issues. The modeler information is specific; the off-screen drawing, fundamental mathematical operations, and Windows citizenship concerns are general.

We use the MakeApp SDK sample to jump-start our development process. A family of shells were manufactured for use in further construction: WinMod3D requires enhancements to these base shells. The principle change we'll make is creating the multiple-view subsystem, which will produce a multiple-rendition representation of the world. We are going to use a four-pane system in WinMod3D, which the enhanced application shells are designed to provide in a stub implementation. The details of this are in the last section of this chapter.

Our modeler also uses the MVC (model view controller) abstract design technique as a paradigm to guide future changes. Using a model or data structure, a program can control multiple views. This is very much like the Smalltalk MVC, and is a very powerful organizing principle for the internals of an application.

Modeler Architecture II: WinMod3D and the MVC Paradigm

As I just stated, we're going to use the MVC paradigm as our organizing principle. It provides a method for managing internal data structures, output, and input. Internal data structures are the models, managed by a controller, who presents views to (and receives input from) users. WinMod3D uses this technique to provide multiple renditions of the scene to provide feedback to the user. This technique is both useful and common. For applications that require special windows for display and user interaction, the Model-View-Controller paradigm proves especially valuable. For a broader discussion of MVC, consult *Inside Smalltalk, Volume II*, by Pugh and Lalonde (Prentice-Hall 1991).

Briefly stated, the three components are:

- Model: core application data,
- View: responsible for providing a visual representation of the model, and
- Controller: sits between the user and the model/view, arbitrating the interface.

[In this context, I use the term model to refer to data structures, structured programming, and abstraction—not 3D models and modeling.]

Some of the advantages of MVC are:

- It supports multiple views.
- It lets you interchange controllers, allowing you to tailor user modes (for example, expert versus novice).
- It separates input (controller interactions) from output (display of views).

Figure 2-4 shows the coupling in an MVC system. Our limited implementation hardwires the required views, allowing us to dispense with the arbitrary superview-view-subview hierarchy and its extensibility, and dependency tracking of Smalltalk's MVC.

Figure 2-4.   MVC Diagram

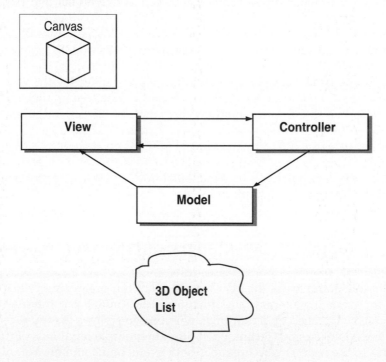

A state machine is a natural choice as the basis of the controller. The multiple-view side of the equation fits right in to the existing MakeApp framework. If we subdivide the client area into several different panes, then implement several child-view window classes within the client area, we'll achieve our desired result: the model is the scene, the 3D objects it contains, and any additional support it requires.

How does this map to the actual modeling application? In the last chapter, you saw that a modeler consists of the following phases:

- world generation (front-end),
- world manipulation (guts),
- world rendering (back-end), and
- color post-processing (tools).

Table 2-3 maps these modeler phases to the actions taken by the MVC system. As you can see, the controller has direct responsibility for arbitrating the interface, creating and destroying model data, manipulating and rendering the model data, and modifying the image data for the color post-processing phase.

Table 2-3.   Modeler Phases and MVC

Modeler Phases	MVC Action
World generation	Controller arbitrates interface, creates model, pipelines model.
World manipulation	Controller arbitrates interface, pipelines model.
World rendering	Controller arbitrates interface, pipelines model.
Color post-processing	Controller arbitrates interface, modifies view data directly, updates view.

To recap, then, MVC boils down to:

- **model** = internal data structures
- **view** = display panes
- **controller** = internal control structures and variables, managing the pipeline of model data

The controller manages the user interface (menu and keyboard), internal data structures, and view-display regions. What the user is allowed to do, the contents of the data structures, management and manipulation of data, and what occurs within those regions are the details of the capabilities of the modeling application.

Modeler Architecture III: WinMod3D and M3D Support Services

Once again we need to refer to phases of implementation for capabilities (by now, this should be pretty familiar):

- World generation,
- World manipulation,
- World rendering, and
- Postprocessing.

The very existence of the system presupposes WLib and its Windows services, as well as G3DLib and its general graphics services, but each of these phases in turn determines the contents of the M3D services. The arrangement of the functional areas in the library and this discussion are shown in Table 2-4.

Table 2-4.   M3D Support Services by Modeler Phase

Modeler Phases	M3D Subsystem	M3D Contents
World generation	Front End Part I	Model and scene description language support
	Front End Part II	3D object instantiation,
		lights, surface properties, lookup tables
World manipulation	Core Functions Part I	World and object manipulation/transformation
World rendering	Core Functions Part II	More surface properties, lights,
		illumination models, texturing
Color post-processing	Post-Processing	Color analysis and quantization

Front-End, Part I: World Generation

Scene-description languages are central to world generation. There are two issues, completely aside from scene specifics, that we need to consider in passing input specifications to a 3D rendering engine: projection type and rendering type.

The modeling parameters specify a modeling *pass*. For any single scene file, there are many different possible passes. Listing 2-1 shows an example of some parts of the modeling specification we'll use.

Listing 2-1.   Modeling Specification Example

```
RES
  XRES    = 400
  YRES    = 400

PROJ
  PARA    = 1

RENDER
  WIRE    = 1

SCENE
  GEOMETRY = plane.scn
```

When a scene has been defined in a modeling context, its specification controls the details of the scene's contents. Typical scene-description languages contain at least:

- viewing system definitions,
- global illumination definitions,
- light sources, and
- objects.

A more syntactically accurate example of a scene description language is shown in Listing 2-2. First and foremost, the scene must define the eye or viewpoint location. The scene-description language uses the pinhole camera system and specifies a from,lookat,up system. Light sources produce shaded images. 3D objects are the actors on the stage of our images. An object's color is determined and controlled by its surface-property definitions and the illumination model. These elements are enough to script a scene. They also imply data structures and service routines. Chapter 8 completes this picture when we implement the tokenizer and the parsers for both the modeling script and the scene script languages.

Listing 2-2.   Syntactic Elements of Sample Scene-Description Language

```
"v"  - viewing vectors and angles
"l"  - positional light location
"b"  - background color
"a"  - ambient background light
"o"  - object definition
```

Front-End Part II: 3D Objects

3D objects are the most important entities in our scenes. Bridging the requirements of a polygon shader with those of a ray tracer means supporting a dual representation scheme for object internals. The wireframe and shader rendering engine uses a polygonal representation for surfaces. Each object is decomposed into faces that are defined by vertices. Faces are the rectangles and triangles that make up the object; vertices are the 3D coordinates used to describe them. A vertex is a three-dimensional point in space, used here to represent the defining points of a rectangle.The polygon-based subsystem uses this representation scheme (as shown in Figure 2-5). The topology is described by the list of faces; the geometry, by the faces and vertices. The vertices in the list are assumed to be in counterclockwise order, as viewed from the outside of the object. Sample circuit directions are also shown.

Figure 2-5. Polygon-Based Face and Vertex Representation

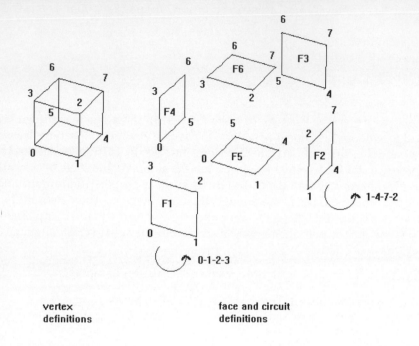

vertex
definitions

face and circuit
definitions

An analytic internal form based on the generalized quadric formula shown in Equation 2-1 is more suitable for the ray-tracing technique. This is the most general form of the equation, and it suffers from too much generality. This formula defines the family of infinite quadric surfaces. Without a way to bound them, cylinder and cone surface definitions would be a pain. So instead, we use a subset of this equation to define the sheet associated with the cylinder and cone, then use the special-case circle implementation to cap it, as shown in Equation 2-2. Similarly, we define the box and pyramid in terms of rectangles and triangles.

Equation 2-1. Generalized Quadric Formula

$$AX^2 + BY^2 + CZ^2 + DXY + EXZ + FYZ + GX + HY + IZ + J = 0$$

Equation 2-2. Simpler Subset of Quadric Formula

$$AX^2 + BY^2 + CZ^2 + Ey = D$$

All three of these plane figures can be implemented on top of the infinite plane definition, as shown in Equation 2-3. Finally, we define the sphere by Equation 2-4. With these basics, and a little trickiness for the plane, our ray-object definitions are complete.

Equation 2-3. Plane Formula

$$AX + BY + CZ + D = 0$$

Equation 2-4. Sphere Formula

$$X^2 + Y^2 + Z^2 - r^2 = 0$$

We store both representations internally. Depending on the rendering you want, you'll use either the explicit polygon surface representation or the analytic quadratic formula representation to generate the image. A reasonable subset of objects that can be represented using this dual system is shown in Figure 2-6. These objects define the content of simple scenes, and can be used to define other objects in turn.

Figure 2-6. 3D Objects

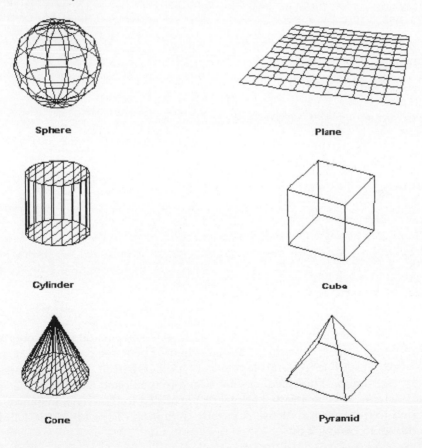

Sphere

Plane

Cylinder

Cube

Cone

Pyramid

A data structure pseudo-definition that represents surface properties is shown in Listing 2-3. The surface-property definitions are used in conjunction with the illumination model to calculate color values. An initial color, combined with the surface-property coefficients and a texture definition, is sufficient to define the surface's appearance. You do this through a two-part specification of color and material.

For convenience, we define an ASCII name for the color in the structure. A color lookup table containing an ASCII name/RGB value pair and a binary search algorithm help with this. Similarly, a material structure that contains a shape-name coupled to a set of coefficients and a texture, along with a lookup table and binary search, can be a great convenience. Both of these tables are loaded "on-the-fly" and are user-definable. Listing 2-4 shows some sample colors and materials by name. Common colors like red, as well as more unique colors like salmon, are defined. Materials like a checkered (or chessboard) pattern, a smooth surface, and a mirrored surface are shown as examples.

Listing 2-3.   Surface Property Data Structure

```
typedef struct t_surfaceprops
{
  Color
  Coefficients
  Texture
} SURFACEPROPS ;

typedef SURFACEPROPS FAR *LPSURFACEPROPS;
```

Listing 2-4.   Example Color and Material Names

```
//color
Plum
Red
Salmon
//materials
chessboard
countertop
mirror
```

Now that we have all these wonderful new 3D objects and the data structures and API routines to implement them, how do we manage them? The scene data structure, pseudo-defined in Listing 2-5, defines several elements of type **LPOBJECT.** This data structure is a linked-list representation. When elements are added to the linked list at runtime, it grows in a dynamic fashion. This means that as objects are added to the scene, instances are created and added to the appropriate list. A pseudo-definition of the **LPOBJECT** linked list structure is shown in Listing 2-6.

Listing 2-5.   SCENE Data Structure

```
typedef struct tagSCENE
{
  viewpoint
  background and ambient light
  list of objects ( type LPOBJECT )
  list of lights ( type LPOBJECT )
  counters
} SCENE;

typedef SCENE FAR * LPSCENE;
```

Listing 2-6.   LPOBJECT Linked-List Data Structure

```
typedef struct t_object
{
  struct t_object FAR *next;
  unsigned short        o_type ;
.
.
.

  LPVOID                o_data ;
} OBJECT ;

typedef OBJECT FAR *LPOBJECT;
```

These script elements and data structures allow objects to be defined in a text file. Then, the parsing part of the front-end translates the definition from script language to instantiated object in memory. As scene elements are parsed, scene elements are instantiated then linked to the correct list. The scene is now ready to be manipulated. Chapter 9 describes the instantiation details for each object type up to the point where it is added to the object list.

The object list is central to all of this. It is created from the description language, and the object-mapping functions, which are under control of the state machine, are activated to manipulate the elements of the list.

Core Functions Part I: World Manipulation

The task of generating an image is split between manipulation and rendering, although there's a fine line between the two.To clarify the difference in this application, we'll limit world manipulation to simple camera movement and image generation; no support for run-time editing. This limited manipulation capability involves three distinct classes of actions:

- generating the viewing system,
- pipelining the points, and
- handling camera movement.

How do you use the viewing system to make images? We'll use a two-part strategy; one deals with Windows and 2D coordinates, and the other deals with 3D graphics and coordinates. The viewing system and pipeline handle the 3D graphics; the canvas/graphics environment pair manages the 2D coordinates.

We need to assign some names to help us keep everything straight. Since the 2D canvas target is at the bottom of the food chain, let's call the window-viewport coordinates "System One." All "screen" coordinates (in classical terms) or canvas coordinates in our terms fall under this category. Window-viewport mapping for each canvas is managed by its own graphics environment. The 3D coordinate system built on top of the 2D system is called "System Two." Object, world, and eye coordinate systems are the responsibility of the 3D support functions in System Two.

This bounty of coordinates is compounded by the dual representation modes, which require separate paths in the image creation process. For polygon and ray-trace modes there are separate viewing-system generation and pipelining processes.

Figure 2-7 shows this dual path from the 3D objects to final image. You'll find this dual path discussed not only in this section on manipulation, but also in the next, on rendering. The polygon and ray-trace mode processes perform the manipulation and rendering operations that result in an image. The canvas is the target of all their output.

Figure 2-7.   Dual-Processing Path

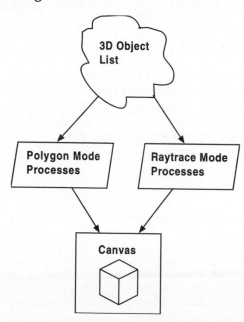

The key to remember is that two separate representation systems are coming together. This is usually the cause of the confusion and misery in 3D graphics. The 2D output system that is the foundation of System One is where the pixels hit the pavement. It encompasses the window and viewport coordinate systems of the canvas. The projection operation binds System One to System Two.

System Two is the 3D internal world of the modeler. It encompasses object, world, and eye coordinates. The instantiation process and the camera move System-Two points down the pipeline to eye coordinates. This is where System Two ends and System One begins. The linkage between the two systems is the eye-to-screen operation: projection in polygon mode, and pixel ray generation/object intersection in ray-trace mode. The operation on eye coordinates yields 2D window coordinates that are user-defined real values. These real values are then mapped into viewport coordinates that are integer values.

It may be helpful to think of these different systems as "coordinate spaces" through which points must pass before they become "screen coordinates" or pixel-based values. Table 2-5 maps the notation of system to operation by mode. Starting with System One, we define the window, or logical, coordinate system to be the real valued range [-10.0,-10.0] to [10.0,10.0]. This is SW coordinate space. Next, we define the viewport on the integers in the interval [0,0] to [400,400], a range that we intend to be mapped to pixels. This viewport defines or, more properly, *is* the canvas, and is SV coordinate space. You can do this at canvas-creation time to initialize the graphics environment to the proper values, as shown in Listing 2-7. You could also use the *G3D_WV_SetWindow* and *G3D_WV_SetViewport* functions to redefine the window-viewport mapping, when needed, as shown in Listing 2-8. Figure 2-8 illustrates the window-viewport mapping process, and shows the relationship between a viewport and a canvas.

Table 2-5.   Coordinate Pipeline and Notation

System	Coordinate Type	Operation by Mode		Notation
		Polygon	*Ray-Trace*	
System 2 (3D)	Object	Instantiate	Instantiate	xo
	World	Transform	Eye-ray generation	xw
	Eye	Shade	Pixel-ray generation	xe
		Optional hide/shade projection	Object intersection	
	Screen	See System 1	Shade	xs
System 1 (2D)	Screen "window"	Map	N/A	xsw=xs
	Screen "viewport"	Draw	Draw	xsv
	Client area	Blit	Blit	N/A

Listing 2-7.   Defining the Window-Viewport Mapping at Canvas-Creation Tim

```
rW.left    = -10.0;
rW.bottom  = -10.0;
rW.top     = 10.0;
rW.right   = 10.0;
rV.left    = 0;
rV.top     = 0;
rV.right   = 400;
rV.bottom  = 400;


psv->genv = G3D_GEnv_Create(psv->hwnd,LIGHT,NULL,
               WHITE_CANV,rW, rV);
```

Listing 2-8.   Redefining the Window-Viewport Mapping

```
rW.left    = -10.0;
rW.bottom  = -10.0;
rW.top     = 10.0;
rW.right   = 10.0;
rV.left    = 0;
rV.top     = 0;
rV.right   = 400;
rV.bottom  = 400;
G3D_WV_SetWindow(pvwwnd->genv,
     rW.left,   rW.bottom,
     rW.right,  rW.top);
G3D_WV_SetViewport(pvwwnd->genv,
     rV.left, rV.top,
     rV.right, rV.bottom);
```

Notice that the depiction of window-viewport coordinates is Cartesian, with the origin in the left bottom; GDI places the origin at the left top. The window-viewport mapping we've discussed so far is completely out of the realm of GDI. We use the GDI window-viewport mapping functions in this system simply to remedy the coordinate-origin switch. They allow us to do that quite easily and transparently to all math code by handling it at the display surface level, not the math level. This greatly simplifies the basic window-viewport transformation—it just doesn't care about GDI, never did, and never will.

System Two, the 3D artificial world, is a little bit trickier. Again, earlier in this chapter and back in Chapter 1, I showed you the coordinate systems we need to deal with. The final system shown in Chapter 1 was screen coordinates, which map to our canvas coordinates, making them a System-One concern. System Two is concerned with everything *before* screen coordinates.

Figure 2-8.   Visualizing Window-Viewport Mapping Underneath the Canvas

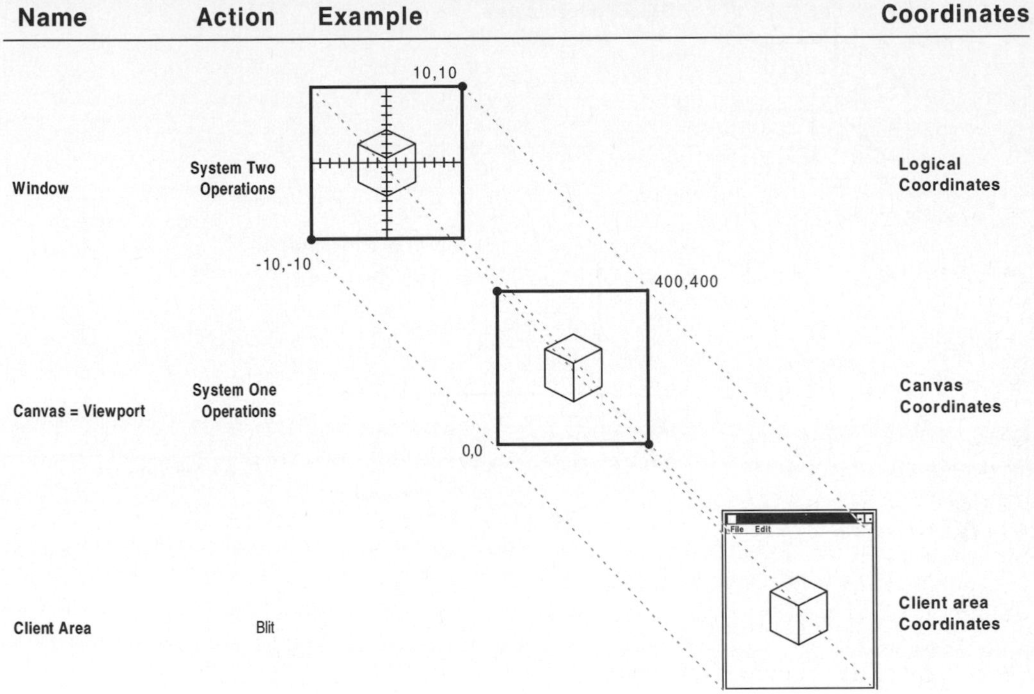

Name	Action	Example	Coordinates

Window	System Two Operations	10,10 -10,-10	Logical Coordinates
Canvas = Viewport	System One Operations	400,400 0,0	Canvas Coordinates
Client Area	Blit	File Edit	Client area Coordinates

Figure 2-9 shows the System Two coordinate systems from object to eye coordinates. We can now concentrate on these. 3D objects exist in object coordinates. They are then instantiated into a scene from their object coordinates during the world-generation phase, resulting in a set of world coordinates as shown in the first two parts of Figure 2-9. Our job is to get from object coordinates to eye coordinates in both modes. As discussed earlier, once objects are instantiated, this consists of generating the viewing system and pipelining the points.

Generating the viewing system for each mode is not really that difficult. The polygon mode builds a 4D matrix using the camera routines that build a matrix representing the camera location. The ray-trace mode builds a set of 4D vectors that define the *eye or root ray;* these are used in constructing the *pixel rays,* which are shot through each pixel in the canvas.

In polygon mode, the viewing system is a single viewing transform. What is called a "camera" in this system is represented as a composite transform matrix. The matrix is defined as a 4x4 matrix: what is known as 4D homogeneous coordinates.

In ray-trace mode, the viewing system is really a set of vectors that represent the viewer's eye, sometimes called the *eye-ray.* It is used in conjunction with a pixel location to generate a pixel ray that is shot into the scene. These vectors are also defined using 4D homogeneous coordinates.

Figure 2-9.   The 3D-Viewing Coordinate Systems

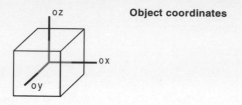

Object coordinates

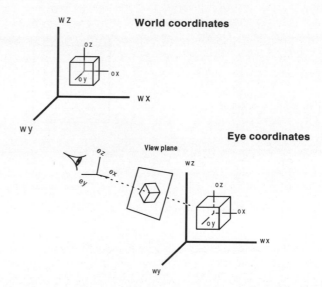

World coordinates

Eye coordinates

Pipelining the points involves the entire coordinate hit parade. Once instantiation is behind us, the polygon mode operations include transform, optional calculate visibility (hide), optional calculate color using illumination model (shade), project, map, and draw. From there the canvas is blitted using GDI's **BitBlt** function to the client area. In ray-trace mode, operations include generating the eye ray, iterating across the drawing surface and generating pixel rays, intersecting objects using pixel rays, calculating each pixel's color using illumination-model and intersection information (shade), and drawing. Again, from this point the canvas is blitted to the client area.

In polygon mode, world coordinates are transformed to eye coordinates and then projected to screen coordinates. This world-to-eye transformation is the basis of the viewing system. Behind the scenes, we create a transformation matrix that describes the world and is used in the pipeline.

The setup routines shown in Listing 2-9 give you an easy way to initialize a viewing system. All polygon modes, from wireframe to simple hidden-line to flat-shaded, use the camera matrix returned from these routines. Moving from world coordinates to eye coordinates is as easy as iterating and applying the matrix to each point by matrix multiplication. That just leaves moving from eye coordinates to screen coordinates. In point of fact, the process of moving from eye coordinates to screen coordinates is a little more complicated.

Listing 2-9.   Polygon-Mode Viewing System Generation

```
G3D_View_InitEye(pvwwnd->genv,
                 Theta, Phi);
 G3D_View_InitCamera(pvwwnd->genv,
          vecFrom,veclookAt,vecUp,dViewAng);
```

First, there is a projection step. The projected screen coordinates then leave the 3D system to be mapped into the 2D system; they will be mapped from the window coordinate system to the viewport coordinate system, as shown previously in Figure 2-8. The whole process of moving through the pipeline boils down to a transformation, a projection, and a mapping. This process transforms a particular world with its scene by its camera location.

An example is in order. Listing 2-9 showed you how to initialize the viewing system for polygon mode; now Listing 2-10 shows you an example of moving a point in world coordinates (**Pw**) through the viewing transformation pipeline.

Listing 2-10.   Moving a Point Through the Pipeline

```
G3D_Xfrm_TransformPoint(&ep,wp,lpT);
G3D_Xfrm_ProjectPoint(&sp,ep,vtype);
G3D_Coords_UsertoDev(pv->genv,sp.x,sp.y,&xv1,&yv1);
```

First, the transformation moves the point to eye coordinates, point **Pe,** by calling *G3D_Xfrm_TransformPoint* with the viewing transformation matrix. Once a point has been transformed, it may need to be projected. *G3D_Xfrm_ProjectPoint* takes an eye point, **Pe,** and generates a screen coordinate point, **Ps.** The resultant point is a screen window coordinate, **Psw.** This is also known as a *user coordinate point,* since the user also defines the window. User coordinate point is the name we'll adopt for these functions to avoid confusion with the term window. We still need to map to the screen viewport, which we'll denote **Psv.** *G3D_Coords_UsertoDev* does just that, and is the last transform of the object vertex points before we use them in a 2D drawing primitive. This is also known as a *device coordinate point,* since it maps to the screen device in a classical system.

This function manages the mapping from screen window coordinates to screen viewport or canvas coordinates, and is purposely named without using the terms "window" or "viewport." It maps from a "user-defined" floating-point space to a "device-defined" integer space. The device coordinate cannot refer to the screen directly because Windows owns the screen, so here it maps to a canvas and the graphics environment that manages it. It just so happens in this case that viewport is equivalent to canvas.

The polygon modeler uses this matrix, but the ray tracer initializes the viewing system in a slightly different way. The ray tracer uses world coordinates for shading purposes; polygon mode uses eye coordinates. Still they both use the same set of three vectors to define the eye in the world.

Ray-trace mode uses an eye ray and a pixel ray. Referring to the third part of Figure 2-9, pixel rays are shot from the eye through the viewplane and into the scene, where they (hopefully) intersect objects. The eye ray is constructed from the same inputs as the camera functions. The pixel ray is made from a combination of the eye-ray components and the current pixel. Listing 2-11 contains these two ray-trace mode viewing system generation functions.

Listing 2-11.   Ray-Trace Mode Viewing System Generation Functions

```
void WINAPI MakeEyeRay(VWWND * pv,
      VECTOR4D from,VECTOR4D at,  VECTOR4D up,
      LPVECTOR4D rS,LPVECTOR4D rU,LPVECTOR4D rV,
      LPRAY Ray);
void  WINAPI MakePixRay (VWWND *  pv,
      VECTOR4D rS,  VECTOR4D rU,  VECTOR4D rV,
      int rx, int ry,
      LPRAY     Ray);
```

Using pixel rays, the modeler performs object intersections, and feeds the results into the shader. The shader then calculates the color at a pixel: this is where rendering starts (it will be covered in the next section). The mapping into 2D coordinates has also been done for us here. Drawing operations occur at the pixel location without another mapping needing to take place.

Now we need to handle camera movement. The user can modify the current camera position by using the arrow keys on the keyboard—in other words, the camera-positioning controls are bound to the keyboard arrow keys. This has to be dealt with in both modes.

What happens if the world changes in polygon mode? No problem. Modifying the current world transformation has the effect of moving the eye location and the viewing plane and changing the scene. Update routines, shown in Listing 2-12, make it easy to generate an adjusted viewing matrix.

What if the world changes in ray-trace mode? Again, no problem. Modifying the current eye location is easily accomplished by invoking the ray generators from Listing 2-11. Each object may have some dependencies on the current viewing location for optimization, but a mapping function just for this purpose allows a simple loop to accomplish the "reorientation" of the world. Listing 2-13 contains the interface to the "cover" function that hides this loop.

Listing 2-12.   Polygon-Mode Viewing System Update

```
G3D_View_MoveEye(pvwwnd->genv,
            OX,OY,OZ, OD,);

G3D_View_MoveCamera(pvwwnd->genv,vecFrom);
```

Listing 2-13.   Ray-Trace-Mode Viewing System Update

```
void RayCalcVisibility(VWWND *pv);
```

Between these two sets of processes and support functions, it is easy to generate and manipulate viewing systems. This makes it simple to include the camera movement capability you need for basic interactivity in the modeler.

This is quite a bit of processing, and we have, so far, skipped the rendering phase. Table 2-6 shows these functions in relation to the steps they are meant to perform.

Table 2-6.   System One and System Two Pipeline/Function Mapping

System	Coordinate Type	Operation by Mode	
		Polygon	*Ray-Trace*
System 2 (3D)	Object	Instantiate,G3D_View_Initxxx,	Instantiate
	World	G3D_Xfrm_TransformPoint	MakeEyeRay
	Eye	optional hide/shade	MakePixRay
		G3D_Xfrm_ProjectPoint	(Intersect(...))
	Screen	See System 1	Shade
System 1 (2D)	Screen "window"	G3D_WV_Setxxx	G3D_WV_Setxxx
		G3D_Coords_UsertoDev	N/A
	Screen "viewport"	draw line,polygon	Draw pixel
	Client area	G3D_Genv_Paint blit	G3D_Genv_Paint
		to client area	blit to client area

Note the reversed order in the table; coordinates end in System One so this table follows the nature of the coordinate-system flow. At this point you have seen a quick tour of the guts of a modeler. Now, let's look at rendering.

Core Functions Part II: World Rendering

Now that you've seen the manipulation actions, the next step is the rendering process. We'll support three basic renderings in our modeler:

- wireframe,
- hidden-polygon, and
- ray-traced.

Let's return briefly to the System One initialization shown in Listing 2-7 and Listing 2-8 to recap the process of using the viewing systems to make images. The user coordinate space corresponding to the logical window was defined using a real-number range from −10.0 to 10. Then we used an integer-value range to define the physical viewport-coordinate space. This, in turn, defined a canvas used as the output destination of all drawing operations. The application contains a world model that is a linked list of objects. The viewing system defines a world transformation. Each object in the scene may have a local transformation. The rendering phase transforms the model into an image. We use two forms of representation in the modeler: an explicit representation of a collection of points that can be run through the viewing pipeline, and an analytic representation for the ray tracer that yields the accumulated pixel intensities from ray-object intersections.

In the cases of wireframe and shaded rendering, the transformation information is used to operate on the vertex information stored for each object. The generalized wireframe drawing process is shown in pseudo-code in Listing 2-14. Each object is constructed of faces that in turn are made of vertices. Each vertex (or point) is run through the viewing transformation pipeline. The resultant transformed points are then used to generate the image. Listing 2-15 shows an example of output-primitive *G3D_GEnv_Line,* which draws a line on a canvas.

Listing 2-14.   Generalized Wireframe Vertex Drawing Process

```
for each object {
        for all faces in object {
                for all points in a face  {
                                local transform object
                                perform world to eye transform
                                perform projection transform if necessary
                                map to device coordinates
                                draw
                }
    }
}
```

Listing 2-15.   Drawing a Line at the End of the Pipeline

```
G3D_GEnv_Line(pvwwnd->genv,
            xv1,yv1);
            xv2,yv2);,
            (DWORD)hPen);
```

How do you use the viewing system to make better images than the wireframe image? You can use either shading or ray-tracing. These techniques each use a different approach to solving the hidden-surface problem.

The shading technique uses what is known as *Z-sort* and *painters algorithm* rendering. This is an object-space method that makes decisions about visibility in three-dimensional or object coordinates (x-y-z is the Z in Z-sort). The renderer constructs objects from a polygon-based representational scheme that consists of faces and vertexes (just like wireframe). If a scene is restricted to solid objects that are wholly in front of or wholly behind any other object, we can sort the surfaces in order of distance from the viewpoint (by z axis) and draw the objects from back to front using the painters algorithm.

Using the dot product for each polygonal surface visibility test lets us remove or *cull* the back faces of objects. The dot product operation calculates the angle between two vectors and is used to determine whether the surface faces toward or away from the viewpoint. This, of course, assumes that all our polygons are closed. This test also eliminates polygons that contribute nothing to the scene, like those that are totally hidden by another object. Drawing in back-to-front order ensures that the obscured polygons are drawn over, and the color value for each pixel in the polygon is calculated using the illumination model. Listing 2-16 shows a pseudo-code implementation of this process. The result is a polygon drawn as shown in Listing 2-17.

Listing 2-16.   Generalized Hidden Polygon Drawing

```
for each object {
        for all faces in object {
                    for all points in a face  {
                                    local transform object
                                    perform world to eye transform
                                    calculate a surface normal for the face
                                    if the dot product is positive
                                        place surface(object)in visible
                                        list
                    }
            }
}
z-sort the visible surface ( object )list
for z = max to z = min {
        for each visible object
                calculate pixel intensities
}
```

Listing 2-17.   Drawing a Polygon at the End of the Pipeline

```
G3D_GEnv_Polygon(pv->genv,
        (LPPOINT)&pgdi,(long)fi->ni+1,
        NULL(DWORD)rgbGray[max(run,0)]);
```

The ray-tracing algorithm uses the same coordinate spaces and the same viewing transformation; the only differences are the representation and the method of generating the image. But the entire approach is different. It is what is known as a point-sampling algorithm. Instead of looping across objects, you shoot rays through each pixel, basically making an iteration across the pixels. Objects are constructed from an analytic representation of the generalized quadratic surfaces. Using some algebra, some calculus, and many brain cells, the derivation of a generalized quadric intersection and quadric normals can be converted to code. Intersections determine which objects affect the color of the image. As a ray strikes an object, the pixel through which the ray passes takes on the color of the closest intersected object. The ray-object intersection calculations use the viewing system as well as many vector-math functions to calculate normals, intersections, and intermediate results (See Listing 2-18 for the pseudo-code to the ray tracing algorithm.) The shading processes in both modes perform an immediate draw in grayscale and require post-processing to put color on the screen. The grayscale output of the ray tracer is shown in Listing 2-19, where function **DrawGrayPixel** is shown.

Listing 2-18.   Generalized Object Tracing

```
for each row{
  for each column{
    shoot a ray through pixel
    for each object {
      calculate ray-object intersection
      if intersection is closest ( t smallest )
        save intersection
    }
    if intersection
    {
    calculate point of intersection
    calculate normal
    for each light source {
        shoot a ray from intersection to light
        for every object but current intersection
          calculate light ray-object intersection
          if no intersection point not in shadow
            calculate intensity using this light
        }
      }
    else
        set intensity to background
    use intensities to set screen and save buffer
  }
}
```

Listing 2-19.   Drawing a Pixel at the End of the Pipeline

```
void WINAPI DrawGrayPixel(HDC hdc,int xc, int yc, int graycol);
```

Calculating color involves using the surface that is normal for either the visible polygon or the intersected object, together with the illumination model. Here, both the polygon drawing and object tracing use related illumination models and shading geometry. The flat-shader uses a subset of the illumination model that is used by the ray tracer. Figure 2-10 illustrates the geometry involved in shading, and Chapter 10 explores this in detail.

The surface in question, the eye or viewpoint (V in Figure 2-10), and the light source (L in Figure 2-10) combine with the surface normal (N in Figure 2-10) and the reflected vector (R in Figure 2-10) in the illumination model. The surface property definitions are used with the illumination model to calculate color values.

Two illumination models are used in WinMod3D. Polygon mode uses a flat-shaded illumination model and ray-trace mode uses a specular and reflection model. The illumination models assume that each light source is located at a point infinitely distant from the objects in the scene. In the case of flat-shading, the model uses ambient and diffuse lighting components to mimic basic lighting. In ray-traced shading, the model not only uses ambient and diffuse lighting components to mimic basic lighting, it also uses specular and reflected components to add to the realism. Both modes use ambient lighting for the background

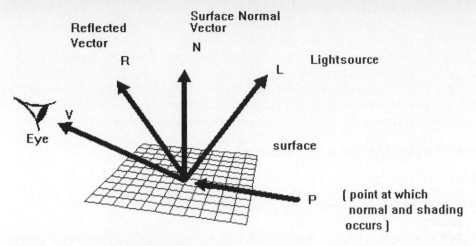

Figure 2-10.   Shading Geometry

illumination that is everywhere in a scene. This is indicated by use of the *ka* ambient coefficient and the ambient term in the equations. Both modes also use diffuse lighting to mimic scattered light. This is indicated by the use of the *kd* diffuse coefficient and the diffuse term in the equation. The ray tracer uses specular light to model highlights or shiny spots. This is indicated by the *ks* specular coefficient and the specular term. Finally, the ray tracer bounces or reflects rays, which is indicated by a recursive invocation of the shading equation.

Equation 2-5 shows the flat-shading model, which does not take into account either highlights or interactions between objects that are due to reflection or refraction but does, however, mimic basic lighting.

Equation 2-5.   Flat-Shading Illumination Model

$$I = Iaka + kd \sum_{j=l}^{j=ls} I_{Lj}(\overline{N} * \overline{L}_j)$$

Taking highlights into account means adding a specular term to the equation. This is an empirical term named after its inventor, Bui Phong. The equation governing Phong shading is shown in Equation 2-6. Adding the specular lighting component increases the quality of the image, but this model still does not account for reflected light.

Equation 2-6.   Phong-Shading Illumination Model

$$I = Iaka + kd \sum_{j=l}^{j=ls} I_{Lj}(\overline{N} * \overline{L}_j) + ks \sum_{j=l}^{j=ls} I_{Lj}(R * V)^n$$

A better model would account for reflection and would allow mirrored images. Basically, this improvement amounts to recursively evaluating Equation 2-6 if the surface is reflective, thereby causing a "bounce." By simply adding recursion to the ray tracer the realism of the rendered scenes increases greatly. This represents half of what is usually called the *transmissive* term because it models transmitted light. The other half of the transmitted term is refraction, which is not handled here.

Equation 2-7 shows how to model the transmission term, based on Turner Whitted's classic paper *An Improved Illumination Model for Shaded Display* (CACM, Vol. 23 No. 6). It requires both a *kt* transmission coefficient and an IOR index of refraction parameter. Support for this is embedded in the data structures for surface properties and intersections, but I've only included it here as a provision for expansion—you'll have to do the rest yourself.

Equation 2-7.   Improved Illumination Model

$$I = I_a + k_d \sum_{j=l}^{j=ls} (\overline{N} * \overline{L}_j) + k_s S + k_t T \text{ where } I_{Lj} = 1$$

While the *kt* and IOR coefficients are defined, they are left unused because we're not supporting refraction. The typical refractive shader uses the *ks* coefficient to guide the reflection recursion and the *kt* coefficient to guide the refraction recursion. Our tracer instead uses the IOR value to define reflectivity, meaning that highlights and reflection are controlled separately. This does require a small amount of redefinition when you add refraction, but refraction will require you to make other changes as well.

To summarize, our job was to create a canvas and a viewing system, and either move points through the pipeline or iterate across each pixel, calculating intersections and color intensity values then drawing to the canvas. This repetitive process of either moving points down the graphics pipeline and performing shading—either drawing polygons or drawing pixels—defines 3D graphics modeling. While this sequence is central to our goal, this is by no means all that can be done with this API. These are just actions that are necessary to perform the task of generating an image from a model. Again, remember that this process has generated both stored intensity values for post-processing and a grayscale immediate view. The last step in the process of image-generation is color reduction or *colorization*.

Color Post-Processing

You've finally reached the promised land! While you can generate a grayscale showing image intensity at run-time, this is like watching a color movie in black and white. It's okay, but it's not great. I know, I know, you want color! Using the values in the intensity buffer you can color-process an image.

First, though, you need color. RGB describes colors in terms of red, green, and blue components. Windows GDI uses an internal integer form of RGB called CRT. Most graphics systems specify color using floating-point [0,1] RGB representation. Several other popular color systems exist as well. Implementations of RGB-to-CRT and back conversions, and conversions for other color systems, provide the basis for describing and handling color.

Now that you have basic color representation and conversion routines, how do you show that color on the screen? This process is very dependent on hardware display drivers. If your target machine has a 24-bit color card, the values saved in the intensity buffer can drive the output with no additional processing. Even if you use 15-bit color (with 32,768 color values available) the process of color quantization can largely be ignored.

For 256-color drivers, which are currently the most popular, we can't ignore this process. The 256-color cards dominate today's market, so we need to be able to work with 8-bit images to be effective and backward-compatible. The speed at which hardware decreases in cost and increases in capability means that the limitation of current display systems will eventually disappear. However, we're stuck with it today. This means working with the Windows Palette Manager. Only by building a Windows GDI palette object that corresponds to your color specification, then using it to create brushes and the like, can you hope to get accurate colors.

The Palette Manager forces two things on us:

- palette object creation and management, and
- palette handling application policy.

Once you have color specification and realization, you need numbers to specify with. These result from the contents of the intensity buffer, through a process called *color quantization*. We'll use two of the generally accepted methods: popularity and median cut.

The *popularity* algorithm is the easiest method to implement and gives acceptable results. It simply picks the n most popular colors. This could be up to 256, but under Windows we should limit ourselves to 236 colors so that we don't spoil the color-mapping of other applications' non-client areas.

The *median cut* algorithm solves the same problem, but with better results. It attempts a sort around regions of similar colors to better preserve the original color content of the image.

The processing for either method uses histograms. Histograms provide statistics (in this case, on color content) and are perfect tools for determining which colors to use. Once you create the palette, it is simple to remap a 256-color image. Apply the colors, and you get a pretty picture. You can save this image, load it into any program that reads bitmaps, share it on the clipboard, print it—in other words, you can do any of the normal operations a user would expect. This is possible, once again, because of the API and the canvas model. Table 2-7 shows the steps involved for both 8-bit and 24-bit color.

Table 2-7. Color Post-Processing Steps

Modes	
8-bit	*24-bit*
Generate intensities	Generate intensities
Update histogram	Update histogram
Use gray palette	Directly assign colors
Post-process using color analysis	N/A

Common Threads

Several common threads weave the libraries and applications together. In total, there are four major themes:

- API usage,
- Canvas-based drawing,
- 4D vector and matrix mathematics, and
- Windows environment techniques.

All Windows applications make library API calls, draw using canvases, use 4D vectors and matrices, and live in the Windows environment. While the API is important, canvas-based drawing is the cornerstone of our system. It is a unifying theme, because all things must come together at the screen or drawing surface.

API Usage

Because of the way it dominates the landscape, API usage is, in a way, more fundamental than even the concept of a drawing surface and its manifestation as GENVs and CANVASes, which is the most single visible common drawing thread. Windows services, the graphics environment and canvas, output primitives, and 3D support all come from the API. If you haven't guessed it yet, you are going to see a lot of API calls—API usage is a central topic of this book. Canvas and graphic environment usage, which I've already presented, are examples of how ubiquitous the API is.

For an API to be successful there must be some rhythm or regularity to its use. That is certainly true here. The graphics environment is "home base," and a great deal of the canvas part of the library deals with the graphics environment data structures, and operations on them. The G3D Library provides an illustration of the interaction of a GENV with the system. Coordinates, graphics output primitives, and attributes all have an intimate relationship with a GENV.

The Graphics Environment and Canvases

The graphics environment and the canvas it provides are major features of the application environment. They provide display-surface management, a crucial element of a graphics package designed for a GUI environment. This is an off-screen display surface that provides a double-buffered approach to output. In addition, it directly supports the ray-trace post-processing with the memory buffer used as the intensity buffer.

All output is to the canvas, and the paint operation blits the canvas to the client area. In that sense, the canvas is the atomic unit of drawing. It's also the first example of API usage that dominates application internals—a natural and expected outcome of API development. Indeed, if this were not the case, the libraries would have failed in their purpose.

The services are designed around a structure, shown in Listing 2-20. The standard set of creation, destruction, and access routines are provided, all operating on instances of the data structure—*far pointers,* if you will.

Listing 2-20.   GENV Structure

```
typedef struct _glgenv {
    HWND     hw;
    double   uxmin,uymin;
    double   uxmax,uymax;
    LONG        dxmin,dymin;
    LONG        dxmax,dymax;
    double   a,b,c,d;
    LPCANVAS lpcanv;
} GLGENV;
```

Providing an opaque structure as a token to operate on, an *instance,* is a standard technique used by Windows as well.

The creation function for GENVs, shown in Listing 2-21, has two flavors, LIGHT and HEAVY. LIGHT graphics environments contain a canvas that consists of a bitmap. HEAVY graphics environments contain, in addition to a bitmap, a memory array representing the display surface. This memory array, sometimes known as an intensity buffer, stores the results of calculations. These two flavors provide the flexibility that make the canvas such a valuable tool. Right now, you don't need more detail on the internals of this: We will probe it further in Chapters 3 and 5. What is important is GENV and CANVAS usage and what they provide.

Listing 2-21.   Two Flavors of GENVs

```
//
pvwwnd->genv = G3D_GEnv_Create(pvwwnd->hwnd, LIGHT, NULL,
            BLACK_CANV,rW,rV);
//
pvwwnd->genv  = G3D_GEnv_Create(pvwwnd->hwnd, HEAVY, INT32,
            WHITE_CANV,rW,rV);
```

4D Vectors and Matrices

Inevitably, the mathematics behind these coordinates surface as a major theme of graphics. The term *coordinates* is, unfortunately, heavily overloaded. In addition to the multiple abstract coordinate spaces created to perform 3D graphics, there are more mundane 2D coordinate systems at the canvas level. In this discussion, we are more concerned with the abstract 3D representation.

We use the *vector* as the mathematical unit to represent a point. Operations that act on two points—add, subtract, and the like—have a direct graphical representation. Matrices store transformations that operate on points. Because the matrix needs to operate on the vector or point, they must share dimensions. It is convenient to use a 4D representation for both vectors and matrices. The formal name for 4D coordinates is *homogeneous coordinates.*

Homogeneous coordinates originated as a geometry tool for solving projection problems. They are also one of those cute tricks mathematics is known for. This one is goes like this:

A problem in n space has a corresponding problem in $(n+1)$ space. Sometimes the results are easier to either understand or figure out in $(n+1)$ space. What is true for $(n+1)$ is true for n by induction.

In our case, it's valuable to restate the problem in a different space. For example, when we deal with the concept of a point at infinity in 3D space it causes difficulties. A restatement of the problem in 4D space, however, permits a representation that makes it possible to deal with the concept with ordinary analytical tools, not mind-bender stuff like infinities.

Listing 2-22 shows the definition of a 4D vector. It includes the expected x, y, z of a 3D Cartesian coordinate system, as well as a fourth parameter, w, often called the *scale factor*. Briefly, [x y z] is represented as [wx wy wz w] where w is set to 1 in this version of homogeneous coordinates. Listing 2-23 shows the definition of a 4D matrix. It follows this by using a 4x4 definition. If this isn't too clear to you at this point, don't worry about it too much—we'll go over it again in Chapter 7. And besides, the libraries take care of most of this for you.

Listing 2-22.   Definition of a 4D Vector

```
typedef struct V4D
{
DOUBLE x,y,z,w;
} VECTOR4D, *PVECTOR4D, far *LPVECTOR4D;
```

Listing 2-23.   Definition of a 4D Matrix

```
typedef struct M4D
{
   DOUBLE T[4][4];
} MATRIX4D,*PMATRIX4D, far *LPMATRIX4D;
```

Windows Environment Techniques

The influence of the Windows environment is pervasive. This is not necessarily a bad thing, as Windows applications have certain advantages in memory and graphics. In particular pseudo-multitasking, access to a large amount of memory, (mostly) device-independent graphics, and an event-driven input model are important features of the Windows environment that we can use here. Once again, we see that these features are derived from the underlying Windows components (although sometimes the separation between Kernel and User is blurred): User, GDI, and Kernel.

User: Windows and Events
The MVC framework we use here relies on a multiple-view scheme. That scheme is realized in this environment by a set of cooperating child windows hidden from the upper,

desktop-level window by the layering inherited from MakeApp. The framework also depends on the event and messaging system of Windows. Startup, menu, mouse, and keyboard events signal user input, while the internal operation of the modeler signals program changes of state.

The multiple views are implemented by defining a set of child window classes and managing their creation/manipulation/destruction in a layer separate from all graphics processing. In addition, we'll need to the manage the data content. The state machine that we'll implement in Part III will help with this chore. It provides a link between the child views, the modeler data, and the Windows event system. Input and update events also occur and we'll need to handle them as well. The normal processing of a window procedure is enough for some of these events, but others are more important and need to be dealt with by the state machine.

GDI

The Graphics Device Interface, or GDI, gives you a wide range of support. In particular, you'll use the color specification, color management, bitmaps, and graphics output facilities from the support libraries. In addition, the GDI RGB color routines, the Palette Manager and palettes, bitmaps, and graphics output primitives for drawing points, lines, and filled polygons provide you with a rich array of 2D raster services.

The canvas architecture depends on bitmaps and graphics output primitives. These GDI elements contribute to all drawing that is done in the modeler. Additionally, the post-processing phase relies on support with the:

- color system,
- Windows color palette,
- histogram bin data structure, and
- intensity buffer.

There's also an array of GDI brushes pre-allocated to speed up the grayscale drawing process. This saves repetitive brush creation/deletion time during shading. These services, coupled with the rough plot of the histogram and the color analysis services, make good use of the graphics capabilities of the Windows environment. And, as I said before, if you have a display adapter capable of at least 32K colors, life and post-processing is easier.

Kernel: Memory and Background Processing

Modelers use prodigious amounts of memory, and WinMod3D is no exception. The 3D object list of modeler data structures places the most burden on the memory manager: it uses many blocks of memory. In addition, the visibility process in polygon mode also uses huge blocks of memory to store the visible-face list.

I'll discuss background processing, the final dominant characteristic of this environment, in more detail here because the other topics are all covered later.

Background processing in Windows involves various schemes for using **PeekMessage** and allowing both processing and dispatching to happen at some predetermined granularity. This requires a significant amount of thought into the unit of background processing you choose to allow coordination between the user interface and calculations.

New information, available in Windows 3.1, has slightly changed the rules for performing peeks. Listing 2-24 shows the way we used to do it; this is no longer the best approach. If there is no background processing to do, this loop continues to run without waiting for messages, preventing the system from going into idle mode. This failure to allow Windows to go into an idle state as soon as background processing is complete adversely affects system performance, "idle-time" system processes such as paging optimization, and power management on battery-powered systems.

Listing 2-24.   Inefficient Background Processing

```
// This PeekMessage loop will NOT let the system go idle
  for (;;)
    {
    while (PeekMessage(&msg,NULL,0,0,PM_REMOVE))
     {
       if (msg.message == WM_QUIT)
           return TRUE;

       TranslateMessage(&msg);
       DispatchMessage(&msg);
      }

    BackgroundProcessing();
}
```

This loop needs to be rewritten with the following two properties:

1. Process all input messages before performing background processing, which provides good response to user input.
2. "Idle" (wait for an input message) when no background processing needs to be done.

Listing 2-25 shows function **App_ProcessNextMessage,** which has these two desirable properties. It peeks, dispatches any input messages, and uses **WaitMessage** to indicate that no background processing needs to occur. It uses **App_Idle** as a scheduler routine. This is much better code, but it still leaves most of the burden on the application and application designer to provide an architecture that can take advantage of background processing.

Creating an architecture that uses background processing effectively involves decoupling drawing calculations and display updates. The decoupling itself is primarily an application issue, although libraries cannot make any assumptions or perform any actions that would hinder background processing. From an application-design standpoint, and in keeping with the principle of TANSTAAFL (there ain't no such thing as a free lunch), if calculations and display aren't driving each other, some external force must assume control. In other words, you have to write the code to control the process and allow message processing if you want a responsive application rather than one that disappears into a long calculation and drawing loop.

Listing 2-25. App_ProcessNextMessage

```c
BOOL App_ProcessNextMessage(APP* papp)
{
    // If we've already processed a WM_QUIT message, just return TRUE.
    //
    if (papp->fQuit)
        return FALSE;

    // If a message exists in the queue, translate and dispatch it.
    //
    if (PeekMessage(&papp->msg, NULL, 0, 0, PM_REMOVE))
    {
        // See if it's time to quit...
        //
        if (papp->msg.message == WM_QUIT)
        {
            papp->codeExit = (int)papp->msg.wParam;
            papp->fQuit = TRUE;
            return FALSE;
        }
        // Call the message filter hook to handle
        // accelerators, modal dialog messages, and the like
        //
        if (!CallMsgFilter(&papp->msg, MSGF_MAINLOOP))
        {
            TranslateMessage(&papp->msg);
            DispatchMessage(&papp->msg);
        }
    }
    else
    {
        // No messages: do idle processing.
        // If the idle proc need not be called any longer,
        // call WaitMessage() to suspend the application.
        //
        if (!App_Idle(papp))
            WaitMessage();
    }
    return TRUE;
}
```

This is where your application architecture comes in. As we start to zero in on final details of the modeler, you'll see this issue again. For now, simply remember that some controlling process has to handle the user interface and arbitrate the calculations and drawing, and it must do this at a specific granularity. We'll need to use some coupling in what might seem like unnatural places to accomplish this and accommodate the controller.

In **App_Idle,** Listing 2-26, I've invoked the **View_Draw** method. This couples the app/frame layers that handle UI with the subview View layer that handles calculations. The App and Frame layers handle message processing and the UI, and are now explicitly coupled to the display layers, allowing a certain granularity of background processing to occur. It also lets the layers closer to the desktop arbitrate processing.

Listing 2-26.   App_Idle

```
BOOL App_Idle(APP* papp)
{
// Return TRUE to get called again
// (i.e., there is more work to do),
// FALSE if there is no more idle processing to do.
//
    if ( papp->ds.bDraw )
    {
        View_Draw();
        return TRUE;
    }
    else
        return FALSE;
}
```

View_Draw drives the background processing, and as units of the image are generated, it forces updates to each of the other subviews. It operates as a minion of the simple controller in this respect. Internal to the subview View layer, it still needs to perform some peeking internal to the calculation and draw loop to allow the machine to be responsive. Thus, the responsibility of the display layer is to:

- determine the granularity of the coupling between subviews,
- perform the calculations and drawing, and
- enable background processing by peeking.

In these examples, coupling granularity varies, but the key idea is that as a unit of the job is done, **PeekMessage** is called to process messages. This is explicitly provided for in the examples by the coupling between the control layer and the subviews. Note that this scheme is *only* meant for these examples. Specific applications usually have requirements that defeat any general plan. However, this approach is a pretty good place to start: you can always alter how the calculations are split and the coupling granularity to conform to your circumstances. When we get to Part III, our modeler will do exactly that. Just remember to perform well-behaved background processing when you use or modify this feature of the environment.

Multiple-View Framework

Now that you understand the needs of a modeler and the common threads, it is time to investigate our prototype architecture a bit further. The MakeApp architecture is a cascaded series of handlers. Each layer handles some details and, in turn, delegates some of them down the ladder. MakeApp made the first principled division of labor, partitioning the application into "window dressing" (app, frame, and client) and "display" (view) handling. App delegates to frame. Frame delegates to client. Client then delegates to view. Display specialization in the basic shell ends at the child class view.

This is too limited for our purposes, so it's our first target for modification. Instead of one view class taking up the entire client area, we'll subdivide the client area into subviews, allowing the modeler to present multiple renditions of the data.This multiple-view framework is very useful to show internal program state and to help user interaction with the program. You can see how this interface looks based on the screen capture from a single document interface (SDI) application in Figure 2-11.

Figure 2-11.   Multiple-Subview SDI Application

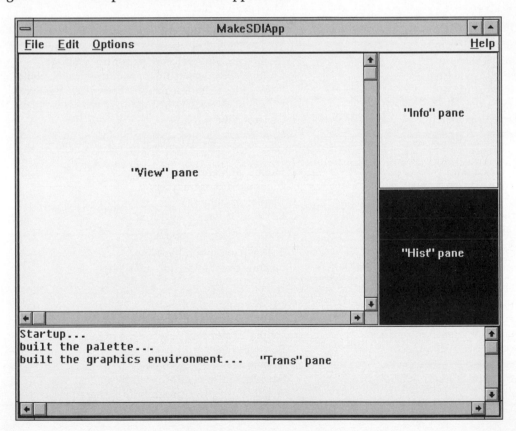

Figure 2-11 shows the components of the SDI multiple-view framework in terms of child window classes. For implementation purposes, we'll divide our discussion into *window dressing* and *display*. In the "window dressing" section, the additions to the client layer we make to handle multiple sub-views are the most global and visible change from the base MakeApp template. The window-dressing layer also adds an error-handling module, in addition to the internal changes we make to the existing modules. The "display" layer consists of four child window classes that manage various display areas, or panes. These four classes perform the image drawing, provide general image information, show an image histogram, and display a transcript of the running session. The display layer has three additional modules, the hist, info, and transcript, as well as another set of internal changes. This is shown textually in Table 2-8 and graphically in Figure 2-12.

Table 2-8.   Multiple-View Extensions and MakeApp

Files	Description
Main	
app.c,app.h	Application layer with global initialization,winmain, and Global termination
msdiapp.h	Main include file
Window classes	
frame.c,frame.h	Top-level window class, the desktop window
client.c,client.h	Client area window class, pass-through layer
pview.c,pview.h	Child of client, has main view output responsibility
pinfo.c,pinfo.h	"",provides text information about pview contents
phist.c,phist.h	"",provides intensity histogram of pview contents
pscroll.c,pscroll.h	General pane scrolling
ptrans.c,ptrans.h	"",provides running transcript of program session
Command layer	
cmd.c,cmd.h	Menu-command handlers
cdlg.c,cdlg.h	Common dialog handlers
odisdlg.c,odisdlg.h	Display options
err.c,err.h	Error reporting
Exception Handling	
err.h,handler.asm.fault.h	Toolhelp exception handling
fpsig.c,fpstuff.c,floatapp.h,floatdll.h	Floating point exception handling
Support	
util.c,util.h	Utility support routines
helpids.h,strtab.h	Further refinements of resource headers
menu.h,dlgdefs.h,resource.h	Helper header files
msdiapp.rc,msdiapp.ico	Resource files
msdiapp.def,msdiapp.ver	Definition and version file
msdiapp.bat,msdiapp2.bat	Sdi template generator batch files
rep.exe	Search and replace program for generation process

Figure 2-12.   Multiple-View SDI Framework Source Components

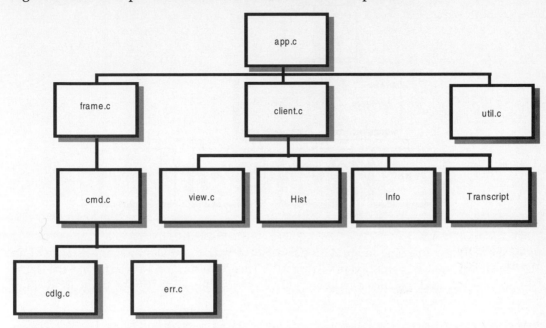

Before we dive into the details, let's examine the data structure hierarchy this tree of window classes presents.Table 2-9 shows the window class to instance data structure mapping and Figure 2-13 shows the tree with the app module inserted at the top. This should clearly indicate to you which modules are associated with window classes and the instance data structure ownership.

Table 2-9.   Window Class Mapped to Instance Data Structure

WindowClass	Instance Data Name	Description
Frame	FRAME	Top-level window class, the desktop window
Client	CLIENT	Client area window class, pass-through layer
View	VWWND	Child of client, has main view output responsibility
Info	INFOWND	"", provides text information about pview contents
Hist	HISTWND	"", provides intensity histogram of pview contents
Trans	TRANSWND	"", provides running transcript of program session

Figure 2-13. SDI Data Structure Hierarchy

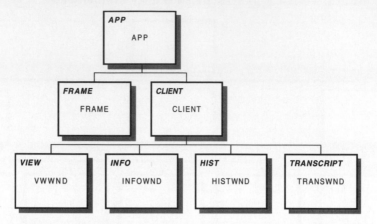

In the window dressing layer, **APP** has a global variable that stores an instance of an *APP* structure, which is stubbed in Listing 2-27. This stores important values like the frame window handle and instance handle for global access, thus allowing the main application layer to control the frame window and frame layer.

Listing 2-27.   App Master Structure

```
typedef struct tagAPP
{
...
HWND      hwndMain
HINSTANCE hinst;

} APP;
APP g_app;
```

The frame window stores, in instance data, a *FRAME* structure that has a handle to the client window. It also controls a client window with it to manage the UI of the window dressing layer. Client has an element for each of the display layer classes in its structure and also stores this in instance data. At this layer, the tree grows branches. It is Client's place to be a buffer layer to shield any code above it from knowledge of what's below. The four display layer classes each have a structure to help in performing their own duties; they each store this in instance data as well. Listing 2-28 shows the stubs of these structures and the ownership-establishing elements. This complements Figure 2-13, which shows the data structure hierarchy. Between the data structures, ownership relations, and the module layout from Figure 2-11, the face of the shell with its window dressing and display components should be coming into clearer focus for you.

Listing 2-28.   Window-Dressing Layer and Display-Layer Data Structure Stubs

```
//
// window dressing layer
//
typedef struct tagFRAME
{
...
HWND hwndClient
} FRAME

typedef struct tagCLIENT
{
...
HWND hwView, hwInfo, hwHist, hwTrans;
} CLIENT
//
// display layer
//
typedef struct tagVWWND
{
...
} VWWND
typedef struct tagHISTWND
{
...
} HISTWND
typedef struct tagINFOWND
{
...
} INFOWND
typedef struct tagTRANSWND
{
...
} TRANSWND
```

Window Dressing-Frame Handling

The frame layer performs many of the normal duties of a WinApp. It handles the menu and desktop interactions in this scheme. In addition to the normal desktop features it provides, graphics applications must also take into account palette-handling details, since the sub-views depend on palettes and correct palette handling. This involves writing handlers for the WM_QUERYNEWPALETTE and WM_PALETTECHANGED messages, and the top-most window must handle these messages. In this architecture, each layer gets a chance to handle an event, then forwards the message on down the chain.

The frame menu handling funnels interesting events to the client layer, which in turn hands them off to the appropriate subviews. This allows the subviews to participate in the complicated dance we are doing with a minimum of coupling. The client layer is inter-posed to both concentrate and encapsulate the details of subview handling. Frame doesn't care, and isn't affected by, which internals are actually hooked up. Instead Client, which knows the details anyway, is the affected layer.

In keeping with this philosophy, *Frame_OnCommand* contains additional blocks that provide the funnel. Let's go "down the spout" and examine one of the handlers contained in *Frame_OnCommand. File_Open* which is shown in Listing 2-29, invokes the client layer **LoadFile** handler and lets the handling dribble further down the funnel.

The frame palette handling, like the command handling, acts as a traffic cop and directs the messages on their merry way. The individual display panes must implement the actual palette handling policy because they are the ones responsible for rendering the data, not Frame. The palette handling functions, contained in Listing 2-30, forward the message using the forwarder macro.

Listing 2-29. Frame File_OnOpen Handler

```
void File_OnOpen(FRAME* pfrm, int id, HWND hwndCtl, UINT code)
{
...
    LoadFile(pfrm->hwndClient,pfrm->szFileName);
...
}
```

This is the extent of the change to the Frame layer. The change is relatively localized because of the effort we spent in creating the shells. This is where we get the payoff from that effort, and application building becomes a process of assembling prefabricated components into the desired final product, adding only the minimal changes needed for that particular purpose. Next, we'll look at the client layer changes.

Listing 2-30. Frame_OnQueryNewPalette and Frame_OnPaletteChanged

```
BOOL Frame_OnQueryNewPalette(FRAME* pfrm)
{
    FORWARD_WM_QUERYNEWPALETTE(pfrm->hwndClient,SendMessage);
    return TRUE;
}


void Frame_OnPaletteChanged(FRAME* pfrm,HWND hwndPaletteChange)
{
    FORWARD_WM_PALETTECHANGED(pfrm->hwndClient,
            hwndPaletteChange,
            SendMessage);
}
```

Window Dressing-Client Handling

The Client layer is primarily just a funnel to channel events from the frame layer to the individual display panes. In the basic shell, most actions are simply pass-throughs. But even this minimalist approach will be perturbed slightly by the code expansion we're undertaking. The order of the creation and destruction of the subviews is now important. The resource utilization by the child windows requires that we handle them in a certain order. For instance, the transcript pane must be created before the first transcriptable action and destroyed after the last one. If this is not true, a bad memory write is bound to occur.

This structural internal dependency is a direct result of the application architecture. In the code, facts like this are critical to an overall understanding of what is going on. See Listings 2-31 and 2-32 for details.

Listing 2-31. Client Create Block

```
//
// critical to init transcript before view
//
    pcli->hwTrans    = Trans_CreateWindow(pcli->hwnd,
                             0,
                             HEIGHT + 2,
                             rc.right + 1,
                             (rc.bottom - HEIGHT),
                             TRUE);
    if (!pcli->hwTrans)
        return -1;
//
// starts transcripting right away
//
    pcli->hwView     = View_CreateWindow(pcli->hwnd,
                             0,0,
                             WIDTH + 1,
                             HEIGHT + 1,
                             TRUE);
    if (!pcli->hwView){
       return -1;
    }
    pcli->hwInfo     = Info_CreateWindow(pcli->hwnd,
                             WIDTH + 2,
                             0,
                             (rc.right - WIDTH),
                             HEIGHT/2 - 1,
                             TRUE);
    if (!pcli->hwInfo) {
       return -1;
    }
    pcli->hwHist     = Hist_CreateWindow(pcli->hwnd,
                             WIDTH + 2,
                             HEIGHT/2,
                             (rc.right - WIDTH),
                             HEIGHT/2,
                             TRUE);
    if (!pcli->hwHist) {
       return -1;
    }
```

Listing 2-32.   Client Destroy Block

```
void Client_OnDestroy(CLIENT* pcli)
{
// force the order
//
   if ( pcli->hwHist )
      DestroyWindow(pcli->hwHist);
   if ( pcli->hwInfo )
      DestroyWindow(pcli->hwInfo);
   if ( pcli->hwView )
      DestroyWindow(pcli->hwView);
   if ( pcli->hwTrans )
      DestroyWindow(pcli->hwTrans);
}
```

The menu command layer also participates in this funneling, as we've already seen. For example, the **LoadFile** routine, shown in Listing 2-33, redirects the CMD_FILEOPEN event onto the view, info, and hist layers.

Listing 2-33.   Client LoadFile Function

```
void LoadFile(HWND hwc, LPSTR szFileName)
{
   CLIENT* pcli = Client_GetPtr(hwc);

   FORWARD_WM_COMMAND(pcli->hwView, CMD_FILEOPEN, NULL, NULL,
      SendMessage);
   FORWARD_WM_COMMAND(pcli->hwInfo, CMD_FILEOPEN, NULL, NULL,
      SendMessage);
   FORWARD_WM_COMMAND(pcli->hwHist, CMD_FILEOPEN, NULL, NULL,
      SendMessage);
   return ;
}
```

The WM_QUERYNEWPALETTE and WM_PALETTECHANGED message handlers in the client layer further redirect these messages to the subviews that are concerned. Within the client layer, the architecture lets you hide decisions about which specific sub-views need to be palette-aware. In this manner, the client layer takes over the function of the bottom of the funnel and directs the flow. In this example, the palette messages are redirected only to the view and hist panes. The info pane provides a text representation of the current image, so it does not need to be palette-aware to perform this duty. This is a simplifying design decision—usually a sign that it is a good decision. Listing 2-34 shows the client palette handlers using another set of forwarder macros. This concludes our exploration of the window dressing. Now we'll move on to the display panes.

Listing 2-34.   Client Palette Message Handlers

```
BOOL Client_OnQueryNewPalette(CLIENT* pcli)
{
    FORWARD_WM_QUERYNEWPALETTE(pcli->hwHist, SendMessage);
    FORWARD_WM_QUERYNEWPALETTE(pcli->hwView, SendMessage);
    return TRUE;
}

void Client_OnPaletteChanged(CLIENT* pcli,HWND hwndPaletteChange)
{
    FORWARD_WM_PALETTECHANGED(pcli->hwHist,
            hwndPaletteChange,
            SendMessage);
    FORWARD_WM_PALETTECHANGED(pcli->hwView,
            hwndPaletteChange,
            SendMessage);
}
```

Display Panes–Text Mode Transcript Handling

The transcript window is different from the view, info, and hist panes. It exists as a TTY-style output window, so it's natural to consider it first. Here, you encounter its API for the first time. Transcription depends on the services provided by the libraries. The transcript-class creation and destruction use the API functions *G3D_Trans_Create* and *G3D_Trans_Destroy* to instantiate a transcript. (See Listing 2-35 for a usage example.) This enables transcripts, but adding text to a transcript is handled by function *G3D_Trans_Add*. This function in turn is wrapped in variable-argument list function **Trans_Printf.** So how does the transcript get generated?

Listing 2-35.   Trans_OnCreate and Trans_OnDestroy

```
BOOL Trans_OnCreate(TRANSWND* ptranswnd, CREATESTRUCT FAR*lpCreateStruct)
{
...
    winio_hwnd = G3D_Trans_Create(g_app.hinst,
                    ptranswnd->hwnd,
                    (LPSTR) NULL,rcT);
...
}

void Trans_OnDestroy(TRANSWND* ptranswnd)
{
...
    G3D_Trans_Destroy(winio_hwnd);
...
}
```

Trans_Printf lets us code the transcript lines as shown in Listing 2-36—it's not exactly stdio, but isn't that far from it.   Using the "%" token technique for providing the transcript entries makes creating them essentially a no-brainer for the programmer: you simply use the same string-formatting sequences that are known and loved everywhere. Now all that you need to do is use the token returned by *G3D_Trans_Create* and decorate the code by sprinkling it with calls like Listing 2-36 at various key sequences to let the user know what's going on.

Listing 2-36.   Transcript Entry Generating Call Sequence

```
Trans_Printf(winio_hwnd,"from=(%.14e,%.14e)\n",
    (float)cptLL.real, (float)cptLL.imag);
```

Display Panes–Graphics Mode: Info, Hist, and View Handling

Tried-and-true text-based representation has its purpose, but graphics mode is where all the action is. In general, the child windows, view, info, and hist all have a parallel construction. They have an instance structure that contains a graphics environment pointer. The SOMEVIEW structure, shown in Listing 2-37, contains a graphics environment and a font. The graphics environment is a standard component of the window instance structure from now on. Any window that uses GENV services stores the instance returned by the library with the window instance data. This makes the graphics environment easily available to all normal processing of the window procedure. Common operations like creation, destruction, scrolling, painting, printing, and more are all provided by the graphics environment.

Listing 2-37.   SOMEVIEW Structure

```
typedef struct tagSOMEVIEW
{
    HWND   hwnd;
    LPGENV genv;
...
} SOMEVIEW;
```

Creation and Destruction

Creation and destruction are quite simple. A sample instantiation of a graphics environment is shown in Listing 2-38. This operation requires two rectangles: one defines a logical or window coordinate system, the other, a physical or viewport coordinate system. *G3D_GEnv_Create* uses these rectangles to create a canvas and set up the coordinate mappings. Internally, this process consists of creating a bitmap and setting up a DC with the appropriate values. In a similar manner *G3D_GEnv_Destroy* reverses the process. Both of these functions are shown in example blocks in Listing 2-38.

Listing 2-38. SOMEVIEW_OnCreate and SOMEVIEW_OnDestroy

```
BOOL SOMEVIEW_OnCreate(SOMEVIEW* psv,
                       CREATESTRUCT FAR* lpCreateStruct)
{
... app specific ...
//
// create the genv and its lightcanvas
//

    psv->genv  = G3D_GEnv_Create(psv->hwnd,LIGHT,NULL, WHITE_CANV,rW,rV);
    if ( !(psv>genv) )
        return FALSE;

... app specific ..

}
void SOMEVIEW_OnDestroy(SOMEVIEW* psv)
{
... app specific
//
// de-select the canvas, destroy the genv and its lightcanvas
//

    G3D_GEnv_Reset(psv->genv,ID_BITMAP);
    G3D_GEnv_Destroy(psv->genv);
}
```

General Display Strategy

Besides using canvas-based drawing, two other critical components of the display strategy are as follows:

- Generalized scrolling is shared.
- Calculations and display are decoupled.

We'll develop a generalized pane scroller, used by multiple panes, to simplify providing scrollable views. Second, the architecture I present here clearly distinguishes between generating an image and rendering it to the display. This disconnects the calculating code and the display code.

The GENV contains the two rectangles for the logical window and the physical viewport. Sometimes image size is greater than the available display area, in which case we implement a scrolling technique to allow the user to move around the image. It is up to the application to determine when and if scrollable views are needed.

Note that the calling sequence for the horizontal and vertical scrolling functions is slightly different. Previously, I've shown examples of passing an instance data structure to these functions, which ties the function to the single window class that owns the instance data structure. This implementation causes the function to expect a window handle and makes it able to be used by any window class. *Pane_HScroll* is shown in Listing 2-39. *Pane_VScroll* is identical, except for the assignment to nVertorHorz. They both exist to set up a call to **Pane_Scroll. Pane_Scroll** is a generic scrolling function, shown in Listing 2-40, that sets up a call to the Windows function ScrollWindow.

Listing 2-39. Pane_HScroll

```
void WINAPI Pane_OnHScroll(HWND hwnd,HWND hwndCtl,UINT code, int pos)
{
    int  xBar;                          // Where scrollbar is now.
    int  nMin;                          // Minumum scroll bar value.
    int  nMax;                          // Maximum scroll bar value.
    int  dx;                          // How much to move.
    int  nOneUnit;                      // #pixels f LINEUP/LINEDOWN
    int  cxClient;                     // Width of client area.
    int  nHorzOrVert;                   // horizontal or vertical?
    RECT rect;                         // Client area.

    GetClientRect (hwnd, &rect);
    nHorzOrVert = SB_HORZ;
    cxClient    = rect.right - rect.left;
    cxClient    = width;
    PaneScroll(hwnd,code,pos,nHorzOrVert,cxClient);
}
```

Listing 2-40. Pane_Scroll Generic Function

```
void WINAPI PaneScroll(HWND hwnd,UINT code, int pos,
            int nHorzOrVert, int cClient)
{
    int  xBar,nMin,nMax,dx,nOneUnit;;
    RECT rect;                         // Client area.
    GetClientRect (hwnd, &rect);
    nOneUnit = cClient / SCROLL_RATIO;
    if (!nOneUnit)
       nOneUnit = 1;
    xBar = GetScrollPos (hwnd, nHorzOrVert);
    GetScrollRange (hwnd, nHorzOrVert, &nMin, &nMax);
    switch (code) {
        case SB_LINEDOWN:               // One line right.
           dx = nOneUnit;
           break;
        case SB_LINEUP:                // One line left.
           dx = -nOneUnit;
           break;
        case SB_PAGEDOWN:               // One page right.
           dx = cClient;
           break;
        case SB_PAGEUP:                // One page left.
           dx = -cClient;
           break;
```

```
      case SB_THUMBPOSITION:           // Absolute position.
         dx = pos - xBar;
         break;
      default:                         // No change.
         dx = 0;
         break;
   }
   if (dx) {
      xBar += dx;
      if (xBar < nMin)  {
         dx  -= xBar - nMin;
         xBar = nMin;
      }
      if (xBar > nMax) {
         dx  -= xBar - nMax;
         xBar = nMax;
      }
      if (dx)  {
         SetScrollPos (hwnd, nHorzOrVert, xBar, TRUE);
         if (nHorzOrVert == SB_HORZ)
            ScrollWindow (hwnd, -dx, 0, NULL, NULL);
         else
            ScrollWindow (hwnd, 0, -dx, NULL, NULL);
         UpdateWindow (hwnd);
      }
   }
}
```

SOMEVIEW_OnSize manages the scroll bars and the WM_SIZE message, and helps implement a scrolling display. Using the canvas size as a maximum, *SOMEVIEW_OnSize,* shown in Listing 2-41, sets up scrollbars and sets the critical global values cxScroll and cyScroll. The cooperation between the scrolling and the sizing code is a typical example of coupling in Windows applications.

Listing 2-41. SOMEVIEW_OnSize

```
void SOMEVIEW_OnSize(SOMEVIEW* psv, UINT state, int cx, int cy)
{
   int        cxScroll, cyScroll, cxCANVAS = 0, cyCANVAS = 0;
   RECT       rect;

      // Find out the dimensions of the window, and the current
      //  thumb positions.

   GetClientRect (psv->hwnd, &rect);
   cxScroll = GetScrollPos (psv->hwnd, SB_HORZ);
   cyScroll = GetScrollPos (psv->hwnd, SB_VERT);
```

Listing 2-41.   (*cont.*)

```
    // If we are in "stretch to window" more, or the current
    //  thumb positions would cause "white space" at the right
    //  or bottom of the window, repaint.

  if ( cxScroll + rect.right  > 200 ||
       cyScroll + rect.bottom > 200 )
     InvalidateRect (psv->hwnd, NULL, FALSE);

  if (!IsIconic (psv->hwnd) )
     SetupScrollBars (psv->hwnd, 200, 200);
}
```

Painting

The *cx* and *cy* values that determine the scroll position (returned from **GetScrollPos**) are used by the call to **G3D_GEnv_Paint** in **SOMEVIEW_OnPaint,** as shown in Listing 2-42. The key detail here is that the WM_PAINT handler simply renders the generated image contained in the canvas to the screen. The necessary drawing calculations and the actual drawing must occur at some other location if background processing is going to be possible. This transforms the entire nature of the WM_PAINT message. It is now simply a time for repairing the damage to the client area display by blitting the canvas to the screen. The WM_PAINT handler has no conception of calculations, drawing, background processing, or whatever. It performs a one-step, simple process without much ado.

Listing 2-42.   SOMEVIEW_OnPaint

```
void SOMEVIEW_OnPaint(SOMEVIEW* psv)
{
    PAINTSTRUCT ps;
    RECT        rDst,rSrc;
    HDC         hdc;
    int         xScroll,yScroll;
    GetClientRect(psv->hwnd, (LPRECT)&rDst);
    GetClientRect(psv->hwnd, (LPRECT)&rSrc);
    xScroll = GetScrollPos  (psv->hwnd, SB_HORZ);
    yScroll = GetScrollPos  (psv->hwnd, SB_VERT);
    rSrc.left   = xScroll;
    rSrc.right  -= xScroll;
    rSrc.top    = yScroll;
    rSrc.bottom -= yScroll;
    hdc    = BeginPaint(psv->hwnd, &ps);
    G3D_GEnv_Paint(psv->genv,hdc, rDst,rSrc,FALSE);
    EndPaint(psv->hwnd, &ps);
}
```

With these operations in hand, we've finished the basics of converting the graphics environment API and its canvas display surface for our use.

We could spend time going over printing, loading, and saving files, the clipboard, and more, but these topics would only serve to reinforce the key lessons of this chapter:

- The layered architecture is easy to extend and maintain.
- Graphics environments and API calls provide valuable services.

Summary

I defined architecture in three steps: overall, MVC, and M3D support (in terms of the modeler phases). The overall architecture of WinMod3D consists of both a polygon and raytrace mode for each of six objects (sphere, plane, cylinder, cone, box, and pyramid) including illumination models. The MVC architecture handles (or controls) user input and manages presentation (or viewing) of the 3D object list (or model). The M3D support libraries provide helper functions for every phase in WinMod3D. We revisited the phases of a modeler:

- world generation (front-end),
- world manipulation (guts),
- world rendering (back-end), and
- color post-processing (tools).

In developing 3D graphics applications in general, and our geometric modeler in specific, four major themes stand out:

- API usage,
- canvas-based drawing using an off-screen bitmap,
- 4D vectors and matrices using homogeneous coordinates, and
- Windows environment issues, including background processing.

The multiple-view framework is built on top of MakeApp, and I described it in terms of a division of labor into window dressing, and a display layer.

The window dressing layer is the familiar Frame and Client layer from MakeApp. The multiple-view extensions add four display classes to provide management for:

- View—displays the primary view,
- Info—displays viewpoint and scene information,
- Hist—displays a histogram of the color information in the view pane, and
- Trans—maintains a running transcript.

This contributes to an application environment by giving the user good feedback. From a practical standpoint, the multiple-view framework provides good value and leverages the time invested in it. Likewise, the common needs of these applications make the development of a useful API possible. The API then provides a body of work in a standard form, further leveraging your investment.

So far this has been nothing more than a standard application of good design and programming practice in a windowed 3D environment.

What's Next?

Chapter 3 continues the tale of the API and wraps up Part I.

Part II deals with the implementation of both the WLib and the G3DLib APIs at length. Chapter 4, on the Windows side, provides some enlightenment about low-level Windows issues. Chapter 5 presents the Drawing Surface services, including the canvas, as well as General Support services and routines. Chapter 6 develops the output primitives and attributes. Chapter 7 rounds out the G3DLib with the core 3D services.

Part III then develops the 3D object geometry library and the modeling application.

3 3D Library Design

In This Chapter

- Introduction to the three implementation techniques that the support libraries use.
- Discussion of the components and interdependencies within the libraries.
- Initial sketch of the contents for all three libraries.

Introduction

Our modeler implementation revolves around two areas:

- modeler architecture, architectural techniques, and components, and
- the support libraries, implementation techniques, and other components we need to build the modeler.

In Chapter 1 we looked at the high-level view of modeling, then got into more detail in Chapter 2, with a discussion of architecture and required features. This chapter is concerned with the support libraries that provide many of the components used to construct the modeling application. Before I describe the details of the implementation, we'll need to take a diversion into implementation techniques so that you understand the essence of three common practices:

- extensible APIs,
- wrapper layers, and
- function pointers for control and mapping.

Once that's out of the way, we move to an overview of the components provided by the support libraries, and look at the interdependencies in the libraries. Finally we'll get into the details of the API.

Macro View Part I: Implementation Techniques

The programmer interface is the most visible component of any API. In this component, there are general design problems that must be solved separately from the graphics design issues. When we look at the graphics design issues, we're able to develop a list of the components we'll need; by considering the "practical" and "packaging" issues, we'll be able to implement the API.

We know from past experience that extensibility and scalability are two features we need to design into the implementation and packaging. Providing for extensibility is a balancing act between current requirements and future expectations — a tightrope that the designer must walk. We use three common implementation techniques to accomplish this:

- general extensible API rules,
- wrapper layers, and
- function pointers for control and mapping.

You probably already use the generally accepted extensible API techniques; and Windows itself definitely does. These techniques include using structures and structure parameters, version and size fields, dynamic or variable-sized structures, variable arguments, and callback functions.

Wrapper layers further enhance extensibility goals by placing a layer, or *encapsulation*, between you and the underlying system. A typical encapsulation provides a component built from a data type and functions that operate on that type. Components are even more useful when a unifying conceptual model supports their use.

There are two basic methods for providing components. Method One "exposes" a component or object. This type of wrapper layer does construction, destruction, and operations upon this object and forces the programmer to follow its rules, or *policy*. Method Two hides the object and exposes some pre-packaged functionality. Wrappers like this hide the allocation and destruction functions, forcing the programmer to follow a simpler policy, and suffer some loss of absolute control over program actions. Method Two is more of a simple "black-box," as compared to Method One, which is more involved and general.

Other benefits we'll gain from implementing a wrapper layer are portability, version protection, and parameter validation above and beyond what the base platform gives. There are also benefits in simplification and standardization. The most important benefit, however, is a component that encapsulates functionality and, hopefully, makes your life easier.

Function pointers provide a valuable role in structuring and defining this system. The internals of both the state machine controller and the 3D objects use this implementation technique to delegate responsibility. In the case of the state machine, it's the states and not the machine that own the code. For 3D objects, the objects, not the rendering loop, own the code.

In either case, the technique is to store the function with the data object itself, in an object-oriented programming style. The application code to apply these functions across a table or list, for instance, becomes very generic, permitting some open-endedness. A new state or object implements versions of these functions and then can be added to the table or list (or pipeline, or whatever) and operate in the desired manner. For 3D objects, specifically, this approach has another advantage. You can treat the "derived" objects as though they are instances of the "base" class. To the loop body code that operates on these lists, it is the base object that provides the interface: these more-specialized objects are treated as plug-compatible. The grungy details are kept with each of the different primitives and thus do not affect the application code. While this falls short of true OOP, this provides a crude polymorphism and is a nice technique.

As the system grows, it still needs to be able to deliver and perform: this is most often what is meant by *scalability*. The notion of scalability extends beyond extensibility. If the ability exists to something once, can it be done *n* times? What is the effective size of *n*? At what value of *n* does the performance of the system saturate? If a set of services are to be scalable, the value of *n* needs to be significantly greater than 1. This set of issues addresses performance.

Memory management plays a key role in the scalability of both the underlying 3D support and the more-advanced 3D object geometry services. Much of the value of the system comes from the abstractions it provides, not just the math it handles. Data structures provide points, vectors, transforms, and the like, constituting the conceptual model you can use to solve problems. Object geometry is built on these basic abstractions to provide a higher-level interface. But the system itself must provide and manage instances of these entities.

Instance creation implies memory allocation. Some operations result in the creation of instances, while others act on existing instances and expect far pointers as a target. Instances also need to be freed when you're done with them. Listing 3-1 shows a sample data structure and one of each of these tasks. The **VECTOR4D** data structure is the basis for 4D homogeneous coordinates. *VNew4D* returns a far pointer to a 4D vector initialized with the values **a**, **b**, and **c**. *NVCross4D* returns, as a result, a far pointer to a vector created from the cross-product operation. *VSet4D* accesses the elements of the vector (first parameter **lpV**) and assigns them the values in the next 4 parameters: **x**, **y**, **z**, and **w**. *VDel4D* deallocates the memory associated with the instance represented by the far-pointer parameter.

Listing 3-1.   Instance Management

```
typedef struct V4D
{
      DOUBLE x,y,z,w;
} VECTOR4D;

typedef VECTOR4D far *LPVECTOR4D;

LPVECTOR4D    WINAPI VNew4D(DOUBLE a,DOUBLE b,DOUBLE c);
LPVECTOR4D    WINAPI NVCross4D(VECTOR4D v1,VECTOR4D v2);
void          WINAPI VSet4D(LPVECTOR4D lpV,
                    DOUBLE x,DOUBLE y,DOUBLE z,DOUBLE w);
int           WINAPI VDel4D(LPVECTOR4D lpV);
```

Thus, we have a family of functions that allocate new instances of a data type, operate on existing instances, and deallocate instances. It is, by definition extensible, provides a wrapper, and is the basis of a standard construction — the mark of a regular API. We'll add to this higher-level objects based on a common definition that expose standard functions by using function pointers; we'll also use a crude polymorphism to simplify the main body of core loops. This regularity helps the client programmer and is an indication that maybe, just maybe, our design is satisfactory. That is, after all, our goal. And these three techniques will help us achieve it.

Extensible APIs

"Extensibility" is more than a buzzword. It lets you gain a crucial edge over future change. Practical design methods for accommodating future growth are not "black art." If you've written Windows applications before, you're already familiar with several of these methods, since Windows is designed to be extensible and uses many of these same techniques. An API is the set of function calls, structures, and constants contained in a master header file. Common extensible programming methods for an API include:

- structure parameters,
- size fields,
- variable-sized structures,
- variable-argument functions, and
- callback functions.

Using structures for parameters gives you a measure of protection against change. Changes to the content of the structure do not automatically change the functions that use the structure. Listing 3-2 shows a sample structure and function prototype. The function prototype can accommodate changes in the structure without disturbing the public API.

Listing 3-2.   Structure Parameters

```
typedef struct tagSS {
        int  member1;
        BOOL member2;
} SOMESTRUCT

void SomeFunction(int param, SOMESTRUCT *pss);
```

Size fields allow a measure of robustness and version resilience. Functions that use public structures check the size "fail-safe" fields to make sure invalid reads and writes do not occur. Future versions of the library can use this field to help "old" versions of client code avoid access elements that are defined in newer versions. The Toolhelp API uses this technique in the structure walking subsystem; Listing 3-3 contains the Toolhelp **MODULEENTRY** structure definition that illustrates this concept.

Listing 3-3.   Size Fields

```
typedef struct tagMODULEENTRY
{
    DWORD dwSize;
    char szModule[MAX_MODULE_NAME + 1];
    HMODULE hModule;
    WORD wcUsage;
    char szExePath[MAX_PATH + 1];
    WORD wNext;
} MODULEENTRY;
```

Listing 3-4. Variable-Sized Structures

```
typedef struct tagLOGPALETTE
{
    WORD     palVersion;
    WORD     palNumEntries;
    PALETTEENTRY palPalEntry[1];
} LOGPALETTE;

typedef struct vertex
{
    WORD                vpNum;
    VECTOR4D            vp[1];
}VERTEX;
```

Listing 3-4 shows the Windows **LOGPALETTE** data structure and the M3D support services *VERTEX* data structure. Both are examples of variable-sized data structures that have a fixed header and a variable data portion. The header contains components that define the size of the variable part that is dynamically allocated. Referencing the dynamic portion as an array of structures makes code that accesses elements of the structure easier to read as well as to write. (See Listing 3-5 for an example.) A loop allows indexed access to the elements of the structure that are allocated at run-time. The equivalence of pointers and arrays in C makes this easy for us.

Listing 3-5. Variable-Sized Structure Access

```
for ( i = palpad; i <= NUMGRAYCOL + palpad; i++ )
{
    /* assign into palette */
  pPal->palPalEntry[i].peRed   = min(255,i);
  pPal->palPalEntry[i].peGreen = min(255,i);
  pPal->palPalEntry[i].peBlue  = min(255,i);
  pPal->palPalEntry[i].peFlags = PC_RESERVED;
}
```

Variable argument list functions are a specialty of C. The keyword **_cdecl** lets the compiler know that the function that follows uses the normal C calling convention, with arguments pushed from right to left. The calling function manages the stack. This technique depends on the **strFmt** parameter acting as a template to define the rest of the arguments. Usually this is implemented as a standard **printf** string. At runtime, the function scans the **strFmt** string for clues about the passed parameters and does the right thing. This lets you write functions that accept any number of arguments in any order. Listing 3-6 shows an example of this.

Listing 3-6.   Variable-Argument Functions

```
int FAR _cdecl Trans_Printf(HWND hw, LPSTR strFmt, ...);
```

Callbacks are an elemental part of Windows. Window classes are defined by the callback window procedure. The same is true for dialog boxes. Printing and abort procedures also use callbacks. They should be familiar enough to you that you don't need an example here.

These are some practical methods for building an extensible API, but these methods alone are not sufficient to guarantee your result. Inherent in these methods is programmer knowledge and cooperation. The API amounts to a contract between the system's providers and its consumers. If you follow the rules, you will be mostly protected.

Wrapper Layers

Wrapper layers are a mechanism both to encapsulate and hide details and to provide an abstraction. For example, the drawing surface is an abstraction. It is a wrapper around the elements of the WLib and GDI that are necessary to construct the abstraction, but that need to be hidden to effectively use the abstraction. Some of the benefits of a wrapper layer include:

- portability,
- version protection,
- parameter validation,
- simplification and standardization, and
- a unifying conceptual model.

A wrapper layer, like structures and structure parameters, is a mechanism for managing change (which is what a port is, after all). By isolating all references to functions, structures, and their like within the wrapper layer we achieve a degree of independence from the underlying substrate.

A few simple rules guide the construction of a wrapper layer. First, you need to define an interface or API. In the course of the definition, both functions and data structures need to be wrapped, since one of the prime rules of wrapping is to never expose a type provided by the third-party library being encapsulated. Next, you need to use the concepts of an extensible API, which requires isolation from change and encapsulation from underlying details. Finally, you must provide useful abstractions or components.

There are two basic methods for providing components. As previously discussed, the first method exposes a component or object and provides construction, destruction, and operations upon this object. In this case, the application creates, destroys, and invokes operations upon objects. The second method hides the object and exposes only some pre-packaged functionality. Here, the application knows nothing about any underlying object — the wrapper provides only the desired operation, while hiding the underlying component. Method one clearly defines a create-use-destroy policy, but is more general than the second method. You can use method one to build method two. Keep in mind, though, that while method two might appear simpler, in the long run it does not give you as much flexibility.

These simple rules guide the way to code that is more maintainable and that may be more reusable (depending on the abstractions it supports) than raw seat-of-the-pants coding. The WLib did exactly this for Windows primitives, with the exception of the explicit use of platform types. In our application, we're not trying to hide Windows, but except for that, we'll use the concept of a wrapper layer around GDI, bitmaps, palettes and the like. The G3DLib does the same with the graphics environment and its canvas, histogram, transcript, vector, matrix, composite transform matrix, and camera.

In addition to insulation or independence from change and portability issues, there are a couple of other nice features that result from creating wrapping layers and extensible APIs: version protection and resilience. These are issues that are becoming increasingly important in the industry. You already see a modicum of this with Microsoft's data formats in OLE 1.0 and 2.0. Parameter validation, return value checking, and error-handling in general can be significantly cleaned up in the wrapper layer, and it also lets you provide this additional support in increments behind the scenes, without affecting your application code. Developing and using a layer of your own devising also allows for simplification and standardization of the interface, providing a useful tool in that respect.

One final, major detail goes largely unsung, but may be the most important for the success of the wrapper as a conceptual model. This is the notion of *syntax* and *semantics*. *Syntax* deals with the grammatically correct invocation (I know you thought you left grammar behind, but it's everywhere) of the API. The API has its own syntax, obviously, and the compiler is usually pretty good about telling us what is grammatically correct. You, the designer, define the syntax of the API, so syntax usually is neither seen nor heard from except in the definition and building phase.

Semantics, on the other hand, deal with the meaning associated with a particular action. This includes both what happens when action x occurs and the conditions under which action *x* is allowed. In general, then, semantics are the relationship between an action and what happens (what it means to the system).

Semantics do not disappear into the compile process. In a wrapper layer the semantics enforce the usage policy. Here, you're allowed to do this, here you can't. Here, you must do this only in a particular order, passing the required set of magic words back and forth. Here, you need to understand the binding between the functions and their actions, because if you don't invoke them correctly what you expect won't happen. As if that's not bad enough, the semantics of the wrapper layer may also be influenced by the underlying substrate. Abstractions like a drawing surface are well and good, but there is a point at which you have to select the proper objects into the Windows device context, and you must be able to specify these attributes. Just managing this balance between control and access is not enough — you must also maintain efficiency and a reasonable cost, or the abstraction won't be worth using. Achieving this balance is a tough goal but it can be achieved.

Another often-forgotten aspect of this type of setup is programmer head-space, or "some abstraction is good but too much is bad." This means that, while the drawing surface is a nice concept, if the drawing objects are radically different from GDI objects, the system may contain too many new and unfamiliar creations for the programmer to learn effectively. We'll revisit this issue as I develop the later discussions about drawing tools, output primitives, and output attributes. This is more of a practical concern than a true wrapper issue, but is a point worth noting: Do what is appropriate and no more.

Function Pointers: State Machines and Mapping Functions

Function pointers are used in two key places in the modeler: within the state machine to control execution, and within the 3D objects to control behavior.

Taken one step at a time, the first detail we need to know about is function pointers. Listing 3-7 contains a C function-pointer definition. The use of function pointers within the state machine lets our application transition from one state to the next to invoke the correct control logic. This frees us to create an extremely clean main driver loop. In a similar manner, using function pointers in the 3D object data structure lets us write nice, tight little loops that simply call the element itself to accomplish the task. This action of applying the function is referred to as *mapping*.

Listing 3-7.   Function-Pointer Definition

```
int    (*somefunc) () ;
```

The state machine uses a table-driven approach that associates an array of function pointers with the table entries, as shown in Listing 3-8. This allows some partitioning and reuse among the control functions, and the transition simply chains up to five (0-4) of these control functions together. This could also be done with just one function and the use of a wrapper around the smaller functions, but this is really an insignificant detail. The important detail is the function pointer itself.

Listing 3-8.   State Table Function-Pointer Usage

```
typedef struct tagS_TABLE
{
...
   int   (*flist[5])(STATE * cur);

} S_TABLE;
```

The structure of function pointers embedded in the **LPOBJECT** list-element data structure defined in Chapter 2 provides a mechanism to associate functions with the 3D objects themselves. A sample of this type of structure definition is contained in Listing 3-9. This is a crude form of object-orientedness, and is useful for both structuring internal control loops and maintaining extensibility.

Listing 3-9.   3D Object Function-Pointer Structure Definition

```
struct t_objectprocs
   {
//debugging
...
//polygon-(explicit)
...
//quadric-(analytic)
..
//cleanup
..

   } * o_procs ;
```

The clarity of the loop contained in Listing 3-10, from a code readability standpoint, is much greater than if the face/vertex access and transformation process were exposed in-line. This is the greatest structural benefit of this technique. Another side benefit is the ease with which you can add a new object, because most of the behavior of the 3D objects is captured in this group of function pointers.

Listing 3-10.   Function-Pointer Invocation and Control Loop Structure

```
//
//   transform vertex list to eye coords
//
for ( i = 0; i < pv->mWorld->Scene->nObjs && pfrm->bDraw;i++)
{
      LPOBJECT    ot;

         ot    = GetElement(pv->mWorld->Scene->ObjectList,i+1);
               (ot->o_procs->transform(ot,vtype==CMD_PERSP?tPerspProj:tParaProj));
}
//
```

This clearly shows why you'll want to use this technique; there should also be enough technical details for you to follow along. We've not only concluded the function pointers for both state machines and mapping functions, we've also completed the discussion of implementation techniques. Now we need to consider what components we're providing using these techniques.

Macro View Part II: Components

Considering the Windows types as one layer, there are four layers of components. Some of these are interdependent on each other, as well as being dependent on Windows. When you understand the data types, their uses, and their dependencies you'll know quite a bit about any library.

Provided Abstractions

First and foremost, our system works in the Windows environment. It is natural, therefore, for the WLib to follow the Kernel, GDI, and User breakdown. The Kernel routines provide memory and error handling, but define no types. It is a simple wrapper, and adds no abstraction overhead. In the GDI area, the underlying Windows abstractions — color, bitmaps, brushes, fonts, pens, and palettes — are used directly. While you don't usually need to be concerned with the GDI data structures, when you're working with color, bitmaps, and palettes you need to be.

We'll use a wide range of services for color and color generation, from basic color and palettes to histograms, intensity buffers, and color analysis. But it all starts with color. We'll enhance the basic Windows color capability by adding four new color types and wrapping around Windows own color system.

Classical graphics uses a [0,1] floating-point valued color system. Windows' own system, RGB, ranges from [0,255]. The Windows system is really a hardware system, and thus is wrapped and called "CRT." Conversions between CRT and RGB support movement between the convenient RGB and the necessary CRT. RGB is convenient because normal intensity values range between [0,1] (exactly the RGB range). Shading and tracing compute color in RGB space. Drawing to the screen, on the other hand, requires CRT space and a necessary conversion. Classical graphics also define alternate color systems. Three of these are supported here. CMY (Cyan, Magenta, Yellow) is a system used in color printing processes (also known as CMYK, where K is black). HSV and HLS are two more color systems that may have some use.* While the modeler itself uses the RGB and CRT systems, the color and material lookup tables are user-definable. You could then make a new color table in one of the other systems and change the code using the services for that system. Shell definitions for the color systems are shown in Listing 3-11.

Listing 3-11.   Shell Definitions for Color Systems

```
typedef struct
{
...
} CRT;
typedef struct
```

---

*HSV (Hue-Saturation-Value) and HLS (Hue-Lighting-Saturation) describe color in a manner best suited to artists as opposed to the screen and printer color systems.

```
{
...
} RGB;

typedef struct
{
...
} CMY;
typedef struct
{
...
} HSV;
typedef struct
{
...
} HLS;
```

Windows bitmaps are the principle display surface in this system. If you need to review this topic, see the SDK documentation and the DIBView sample application, or Petzold (as cited in the bibliography of this book) for the basics on bitmaps and DIBs, output to the screen and printer, and file I/O. All output from drawing routines goes to a display surface. The paint logic for a window class that uses a display surface reduces to blitting the bitmap to the client area. This display-surface philosophy places little burden on the framework of the program, instead dropping a plug-in system with a minimum of plugs into the existing application framework. When the plugs become one basic function call (like the paint logic), growing the application is greatly simplified. This work still has to happen somewhere, though, since there's no such thing as magic or instantaneous matter-energy conversion. Luckily, the state machine and mapping functions have made it easier to bury the details. Still, somewhere a function is drawing to a bitmap, then Windows' paint logic is repairing the damage to the client area.

Bitmaps are also used for reading and writing files, as well as for printing. For reading and writing bitmap files, it is necessary to become familiar with the Windows bitmap and DIB data structures. While bitmaps are the display surface currency, the currency to and from disk is a DIB. This is a simple conversion, since there is always a palette associated with a bitmap in 256 color mode, and a DIB is basically a bitmap plus a palette in the same mode. In 32K color mode and higher, we can dispense with the palette, but we still grayscale the image and post-process it for two reasons: the brush creation/destruction cost, and the pre-view nature of polygon mode. This is not the reasoning behind making "automatic" colorization the default mode, but you could easily change this behavior of the program. Printing the bitmap is a special case, because the print logic uses the gray bitmap. If you avoid having the printer driver re-grayscale, you'll gain both speed and a bit more quality in the gray resolution of the printout, a side benefit of mucking about with palettes and grayscale. Printing adds a type of its own to manage various print options, including scaling, the pseudo-definition of which is shown in Listing 3-12.

Listing 3-12.　Shell Definition for Print Options

```
typedef struct
{
...
} FAR *LPPRINTOPTIONS, PRINTOPTIONS
```

All of this means that palettes are with us and cannot be ignored. Again, palettes have been around since Windows 3.0 and are covered in the SDK documentation as well as on the Microsoft Developer Network (MSDN) CD, which every serious Windows programmer should have a copy of. The basics of the palette data structures, the GDI palette functions, and the message applications must handle should be familiar. Bitmaps and palettes are tied together, but the palette data structure is usually used for palette creation and discarded immediately.

Here, we'll take a slightly different approach. We'll retain the palette structure and use it as input into the brush array creation process. Since native color in the modeler is RGB, any run-time color requests must be translated from RGB to CRT. The palette creation process already did this and stored the result in the palette array. It is really convenient to defer destruction of this structure, then, and use this, along with some palette indexing, to get CRT color values for GDI brush creation. Why? Even though the brush arrays allow us to avoid *most* brush creation "on-the-fly," it's hard to avoid brush creation altogether. The data structures used and provided are shown in Figure 3-1.

Figure 3-1.　WLib Data Structures

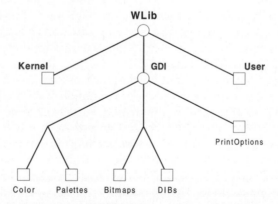

As you see, WLib provides very low-level primitives and not much in the way of new abstraction, just a packaging of the necessary Windows elements.

The G3DLib, on the other hand, provides both the bridge between raster and vector worlds (with the Drawing Surface Services), a wide range of routines in General Services, and the basic vector and matrix functions in 3D Support Services.

The Drawing Surface Services provide off-screen display surfaces, which we've referred to here as a "canvas." This is the principle abstraction that lets us bridge between the raster and vector worlds. A canvas wraps the off-screen bitmaps, DCs, brushes, and other GDI objects required for basic drawing.

This is the first use of the WLib and its bitmap and palette routines. Note that this is not the only use of the WLib routines, just one specific use; you can use the WLib routines to construct other libraries. The canvas abstraction is only one way to use those functions, but a valuable one.

Besides the display surface of a canvas and its drawing tools and color (managed by the palette), traditional notions of window and viewport are needed. Here a "graphics environment" or *GENV* provides coordinate-management services for a canvas. It "owns" the canvas and defines a (usually) floating-point range for the window, along with an integer domain for the viewport. The user-to-device coordinate-mapping functions operate on *GENVs*. This allows you to do all modeler calculations in floating-point without considering the output details. After projection, the floating-point screen coordinates represent traditional window coordinates, so they must be mapped to viewport coordinates before output. Not only are the window-viewport definition and mapping provided, but the traditional output primitives are recast in graphics environment form. The graphics environment and canvas definitions are shown in Listing 3-13.

Listing 3-13. Graphics Environment and Canvas Definition

```
typedef struct
{
   ...

} CANVAS;

typedef struct tagGENV
{
    ...
    LPCANVAS lpcanv;
} GENV;
```

What is not shown is that the canvas itself is a combination of lower-level primitives. The canvas lets you associate an intensity buffer of values with a bitmap buffer of pixels. Each of the buffer components of the canvas is important, but remains invisible to the higher level except for semantic actions forced by the dual nature of the canvas. Value-access functions are a prime example of this. Two flavors must be provided at the exportable level if you are to have a documented way of getting at the bits. Programmers always want to get at the bits; it's hard to avoid this, and it probably should not be avoided, so I've explicitly coded for it here. This is one place where the dual nature of the underlying canvas "seeps through."

The graphics environment supports the window and viewport mapping information, as well as the output primitives. It does this by internal variables and a dependency on the canvas. The graphics environment manages the window-viewport mapping and allows the canvas to manage bitmaps, DCs, and drawing tools like pens and brushes.

The General Support Services add the histogram, inquiry, transcript helper, and math functions. The histogram data structure is an array representing a simple group of bins that can store a count to build a mechanism for collecting and displaying statistics. The system often needs to do inquiries on various key parameters about the graphics capability and system capabilities. Inquiry capability is provided, but adds no types. The transcript services provide a child window class intended to simplify the creation of running transcripts (a good thing for debugging). This is based on code from David Maxey and Andrew Schulmans' article ("Call Standard C I/O Functions from Your Windows Code Using the WINIO Library," *MSJ* Vol 6, Iss. 4), although probably not in a way intended by the original authors. Any ugliness is, of course, my fault (sorry David and Andrew). Here, only two parts of the entire structure of WINIO are used: memory and text management, and the **printf**-style variable argument interface. This is enough to bootstrap a simple but effective transcription service. Listing 3-14 contains the shell definitions for both histogram and transcript types. General Support Services also provide some math helper routines, but these are simply trig functions (like sine and cosine) or conversions and the like. They add no new types.

Listing 3-14.   Histogram and Transcript Definitions

```
typedef struct
{
...
} HIST;

typedef struct tagWINIOWND
{
...
} WINIOWND
```

The 3D Support Services add vectors and matrices. As previously discussed, this implementation of vectors and matrices uses 4D notation, even though it might seem like more is required, especially for the viewing system with all this talk about cameras. The camera is represented by a matrix that is the result of a sequence of operations, a composite or concatenated matrix. The camera can also be represented by the three vectors that guide the construction of the matrix — the from, lookat, and up vectors. In either case, another type is not strictly required. If you feel like further encapsulating this implementation, you can certainly do that, but what's here is enough to get the job done. Listing 3-15 defines the *VECTOR4D* and *MATRIX4D* types, finishing up G3DLib. It might seem at this point that we haven't accomplished much. But the truth of the matter is that these few types are the basis for all graphics output and for all mathematics. That is quite a bit, and it's good that we can accomplish this with a minimum set of types; there's less to learn and remember. Figure 3-2 illustrates the service areas and data structures for the G3DLib.

Listing 3-15.   VECTOR4D and MATRIX4D Definitions

```
typedef struct
{
...
} VECTOR4D;

typedef struct
{
...
} MATRIX4D
```

We need to consider the modeler and object geometry library, or M3D, together, because

Figure 3-2.   G3DLib Data Structures

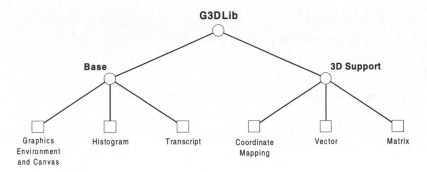

the whole is more than the sum of the parts, and the picture will be clearer from this. There are types in five areas:

- control structures,
- model/scene management,
- front end,
- objects, and
- properties and post-processing.

As you might expect, the first two categories are more closely identified with the application, while the last three categories are provided by the library. An example might be illustrative — the scene structure (category 2) owns a list (category 1) of objects (category 3).

The control structures, as already mentioned, include the two groups of function pointers for control logic and object behavior, along with their management in the state table and object list. The function-pointer groups and the owning data structures are shown in Listing 3-16. These two constructs make up much of the infrastructure of the modeler. They help manage what might be properly known as the "Model" in the MVC scheme, or the model and scene data structures.

Listing 3-16.   State Table and 3D Object List Definitions

```
//state table
typedef struct tagS_TABLE
{
...
   int  (*flist[5])(STATE * cur);

} S_TABLE;

// object list
struct t_objectprocs
{
...
} * o_procs ;

typedef struct t_object
{
   struct t_object FAR *next;
   unsigned short        o_type ;
   unsigned short        o_id ;
//
   struct t_objectprocs
   {
   ...
   } * o_procs ;

} OBJECT
```

In the model/scene management category there are types for both the model and the scene, to be consistent with the existence of two description languages: one for modeling information and one for scene information. These two types are defined in Listing 3-17. You can see the interrelationships between the model, its scene, and a canvas. At the same time, the modeler uses several other structures that operate at a higher level than the 3D object. These include the viewpoint and the extent related to a scene, as seen in Listing 3-18. In addition the ray and intersection data structures are key structures in the ray tracer, and light sources are used in both the polygon drawer and the object tracer. Listing 3-19 contains these types. Figure 3-3 shows the data structures for the control and global levels.

Listing 3-17.   SCENE and MODEL Definitions

```
typedef struct tagSCENE
{
// scan res
   int           scanX;
   int           scanY;
// eye and transforms
   VIEWPOINT     Eye ;
```

```
   LPMATRIX4D      Tx;
   MATRIX4D        t;
// background
...
//objects
   LPOBJECT        ObjectList;
...
// HLHSR
   LPFACELIST      VisFaces;
//shading
   LPOBJECT        LightList;
   int             nLights;
   VECTOR4D        Ig;

} SCENE;

typedef SCENE FAR * LPSCENE;

// model data structure for single-frame modeler

typedef struct tagMODEL
{
...
//canvas res
   int             nxVRes;
   int             nyVRes;
// scene properties
...
//scene scriptfile
...
   LPSCENE         Scene;
// object extents to "autoframe" the scene
   EXTENTS         Extents;
} MODEL;
```

Listing 3-18.   VIEWPOINT and EXTENTS Definitions

```
//viewpoint vector cache
typedef struct t_viewpoint
{
...
} VIEWPOINT;

// scene extents

typedef struct tagEXTENTS
{
...
} EXTENTS;
```

Figure 3-3. Control and Global-Level Data Structures

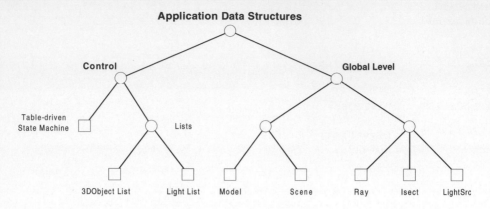

Listing 3-19. RAY, ISECT, and LIGHTSRC Definitions

```
//ray
typedef struct t_ray
{
...
} RAY;

// ray intersection
typedef struct t_isect
...
} ISECT ;

//light source
typedef struct t_light
{
...
} LIGHTSRC;
```

The front end adds only a simple token structure, in keeping with its basic nature. This is defined in Listing 3-20. This same tokenizer is used for both description languages by virtue of neglecting keywords. The tokenizer recognizes that some construct other than white space or a comment is in the input stream, but the parser for each description language takes over from there. This is not really in keeping with current language theory, but it makes for convenient reuse here.

Now we must consider the meat of the system — 3D objects. We've already defined the overall object structure (the list-element structure). It is, in many ways, simply a shell to place in the list and wrap the dual representation. Each representation has a set of types. The explicit representation has an "owning" data structure, the *EX3DOBJECT*, wrapping the underlying polygon surface representation. The *POLYSURFACE* data structure in turn owns *FACE* and *VERTEX* elements. This hierarchy is shown in Listing 3-21.

Listing 3-20. TOKEN Definition

```
typedef enum
{
...
}TOKEN;
```

Listing 3-21. EXPLICIT Types

```
//A VERTEX is a 4d homogeneous coordinate
typedef struct t_vertex
{
...
}VERTEX;
//A FACE is a plane figure consisting of a list of vertices.
//represented here as an array.  The corners in the list are
//assumed to be in counterclockwise order as viewed from the
//outside of an object.
typedef struct t_face
{
...
}FACE;
typedef struct t_facelist
{
...
}FACELIST;
// POLYSURFACEs are solid,polygonal objects
// The topology is completely described by the list of faces;
// the geometry is described by the faces and vertices.
typedef struct t_polysurface
{
...
} POLYSURFACE ;
//explicit [face/vertex]
typedef struct t_explicit_3Dobject
{
...
   int                 nV,nF,nVinF;
   POLYSURFACE         o_psurf ;
...
} EXPLICIT3DOBJECT ;
```

Unfortunately, the ray objects are not quite so simple or uniform. The sphere and plane objects have their own definition, *SPHERE* and *PLANE*, which are quite simple. The cylinder, cone, box, and pyramid are a different story. While *CYLINDER, CONE, BOX*, and *PYRAMID* types are defined in Listing 3-22, their actual implementation is not quite so simple. First, the endcaps on the cylinder and the cone are represented by circles. Next, the box and pyramid are represented using rectangles and triangles. So why is this different from the explicit representation? These are *projections* of a circle, a rectangle, and a triangle on a plane, and, as such, require an additional test once the plane surface is intersected to determine whether the intersection coincides with the plane figure. (You will see more of this in Chapters 9 and 10.) The upshot is that a simple polygon and circle data structure are used as helpers by the **NGON** and **QUADRIC** data structures (not shown here). There is additional work taking place, but it is not as critical to understanding the overall picture as these pieces. These four data structures present enough of the details to see what is going on.

Listing 3-22.   Ray Object Types

```
typedef struct t_sphere
{
...
} SPHERE;
typedef struct t_plane
{
...
} PLANE;

typedef struct t_box
{
...
} BOX;
typedef struct t_pyramid
{
...
} PYRAMID;

typedef struct t_cone
{
...
} CONE;

typedef struct t_cylinder
{
...
} CYLINDER;
```

Figure 3-4 shows the object data structures, both explicit and analytic. That leaves surface properties and color post-processing. The surface-property structures take two parts: the three properties used in the object definition itself, and the two used to create that definition. The object surface properties are made up of three parts:

- color,
- coefficients, and
- texture.

Figure 3-4.   3D Object Data Structures

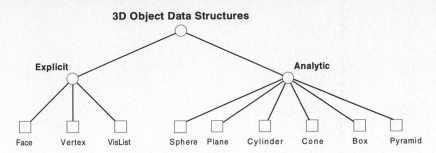

This definition is created from a color and a material specification. A material is a convenient way to name a pair of surface coefficients and a texture. Using a color name and a material name, the color and material lookup tables, and binary searches, we accomplish the conversion of the specification into a definition. Listing 3-23 contains the shell definitions for these types.

Listing 3-23.   Surface-Property Structures

```
//color
typedef struct t_color_entry
{
        char        ce_name[64] ;
...
} COLORENTRY;
// surface coefficients
typedef struct t_surfacecoeffs
{
 //coefficients
...
} SURFCOEFFS ;
//materials
typedef struct t_material
{
...
} MATERIALENTRY;
//
//lookups
typedef struct t_color_array
{
...
  COLORENTRY ceColors[1];
} COLORARRAY;
typedef struct t_material_array
{
...
    MATERIALENTRY meMaterials[1];
}MATERIALARRAY;
```

Listing 3-23.   (cont.)

```
//properties
typedef struct t_surfprops
{
 //name
...
 //color
...
 //coefficients
...
 //texture
...

} SURFPROPS
```

   In addition, the color post-processing phase defines some additional types. The histogram structure is useful for the rough plot, but we also need a structure to manage the thousands of entries that can result from shading. Both popularity and median cut add types as well. The popularity algorithm requires two types: an entry and an array of entries to store the color information during the quantization process. The median cut algorithm also uses a new type: a three-dimensional histogram or "box." Conceptually, smaller boxes represent the regions in this three-dimensional space that are selected as the final values, but we don't create a type to handle this. The definitions of post-processing structures are shown in Listing 3-24. Figure 3-5 depicts the property structures. The post-processing structures, like the *TOKEN* structure from the front end, are self-evident.

Listing 3-24.   Post-Processing Structures

```
typedef struct tagPPCOLORENTRY
{
...
} PPCOLORENTRY;
typedef struct tagGENNEDCOLORS
{
...
    HPPPCOLORENTRY   hpCEntry;
} GENNEDCOLORS;
typedef struct tagMEDIANBOX
{
...
} MEDIANBOXES
```

Figure 3-5.   Property Structures

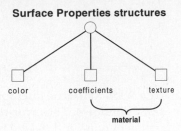

Library Interdependencies

You already know that this implementation consists of the three layers shown in Figure 3-6:

- A Windows and operating system layer
- A graphics and 3D support layer, and
- A modeler support layer.

Figure 3-6.   Libraries and Applications

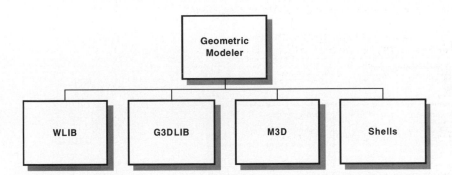

Now, you've seen an overview of the data structures for the WLib, the G3DLib, the M3D services, and certain key application structures.

It is natural for you to ask how these pieces fit together. Fully appreciating the functionality of the three libraries is not sufficient in itself to follow the design, you must also understand their interdependencies. There is always a limit on the possible, so understanding the environment, the provided abstractions, and the dependencies puts you in the drivers seat in being able to really use the libraries. Without this hard-won knowledge, you will still be able to use the modeler and the libraries, but extending the code will be proportionately more difficult.

There are four dependency threads:

1. Windows,
2. the WLib,
3. the G3DLib, and
4. the M3D routines.

Windows underlies everything. The WLib makes no attempt to define new abstractions, it simply wraps the existing ones from Windows. The error-reporting and memory functions in the Kernel services and the color, bitmap, and palette functions in the GDI services are the result of this wrapping process and serve the other libraries. The WLib layer is the foundation for all to come.

The G3DLib bridges two distinct worlds — the raster nature of Windows and the vector nature of 3D graphics. For this reason we need two distinct strategies: one raster and one vector. The graphics environment and canvas-drawing strategy provides the necessary elements to manage the interaction with Windows. The bitmap and palette routines from the WLib help produce the canvas and graphics environment abstraction. These elements comprise the raster end of the solution. For the 3D subsystem and the vector world, the 4D homogeneous coordinate system is the anchor point for the 3D viewing system. Vector services, matrix transforms, and the viewing system primitives are all constructed on the 4D definitions.

The M3D modeler-support routines are also based on the 4D homogeneous coordinate routines. The explicit and analytic representations both heavily depend on the vector library. The camera and the transformation process use the matrix routines. Figure 3-7 illustrates the dependencies between the three libraries.

Figure 3-7.   Library Interdependencies

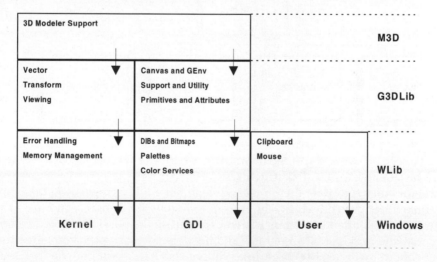

These interdependencies are another instance of coupling, and understanding the issues at this deeper level are critical to good design-thinking. In the next sections of this chapter you will be exposed to more detail about the exported functions, the most visible part of the API. Once the scope of the libraries has been exposed, you will be ready for implementation, which we'll start in Part II.

Micro View

You've already been introduced to the implementation techniques and the data structures component. The interconnections and dependencies I've described should increase your understanding of the libraries. That leaves the API definition itself. The API is the most visible part of any library. The API — WLib, G3DLib, and M3D — is presented here in overview form.

Windows Services Library

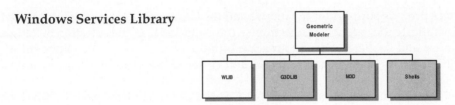

Targeting a windowed environment like MS-Windows exacts a cost. Applications must perform certain actions to "live" in the environment. The WLib provides a set of standard services that encapsulates the common actions. This consolidates the interface to standard Windows services for graphics applications into a single library.

The three main components of Windows are Kernel, GDI, and User. WLib contains three parts that parallel those components. WLib Kernel services include error-handling and memory management. WLib GDI services provide color, palettes, bitmaps and DIBS, and printing routines. WLib User services enable the mouse and the clipboard. See Figure 3-8.

The Kernel services component consists of standard error-handler and memory management routines. Error-handling needs to be designed in; otherwise it's never done, or never done right. That process has already begun and will be continued. Memory management is always a trade-off between accepting the default allocator and all of its faults, or implementing a separate allocation scheme under local control. This is a thorny issue and can be a time drain. The key is to avoid wasting time implementing a grand scheme, while still preparing for a future of change.

The GDI services must provide simple manipulation of bitmaps and palettes. Bitmap creation and destruction, reading and writing bitmap files, printing bitmap images, copying bitmaps; these are fundamental operations. Palette operations are much simpler: creation, destruction, animation, and copying are supported by the API. Bitmaps and palettes are not enough, though. Palettes are a method for specifying color. To allow maximum control over color specification for palettes, you need good color-mixing services.

Figure 3-8.   WLib Windows Services

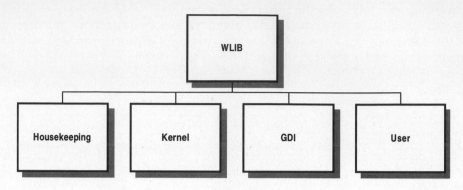

User services provide support for the mouse and the clipboard. *Rubber-banding* is a technique used to indicate the extent of a selection — the boundaries of the selection rectangle. Using the mouse and rubber-banding to mark a bitmap for copying to the clipboard is a very common action. By using bitmap, mouse, and clipboard services, we can accomplish this easily.

Table 3-1 shows the files contained in this project. The next sections expand on this table and discuss the exported API.

Table 3-1.   Source Files for WLib

Files	Description
WLib Housekeeping	
wl_init.c,wl_init.h	library global initialization
wl_term.c,wl_term.h	library global termination
wl_err.c,wl_err.h	library error reporting
wl_inc.h	main include file that applications reference
Kernel	
mem.c,mem.h	memory service layer
err_hndler.h	TRY/CATCH macros
GDI	
color.c,color.h	Color systems
palette.c,palette.h	Palette services
bitmap.c,bitmap.h	Bitmap services
dib.c,dib.h	DIB services
file.c,file.h	File I/O for DIBs and bitmaps
print.c,print.h	Printing for bitmaps
User	
clipbrd.c,clipbrd.h	Clipboard copy
mouse.c,mouse.h	Mouse selection rectangle

WLib Kernel Services

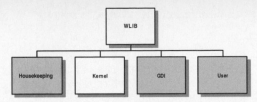

Error handling is crucial to any robust system. Programs usually contain about 80% error handling and 20% core code. To this end, we'll build a choke-point error-handling scheme into our application. By simply providing one call and an ordering scheme, different types of errors can all be handled through a common interface. We increase robustness by adding the floating-point exception handling discussed in Chapter 1. Resource-allocation failures are one of the most significant kinds of failures we need to handle; so developing a method for treating resource allocation is a key piece of our strategy. I'll also provide you with a TRY and CATCH methodology for writing the code to guard allocations and do reporting, as shown in Listing 3-25.

Listing 3-25.   Error Handling in Wl_err.c and Err_handler.h

```
// errors and memory

// error reporting
BOOL WINAPI WL_Error_Init(void);
BOOL WINAPI WL_Error_Process(DWORD dwErrorCode);
void        WL_Error_Report(WORD wErrorType,LPSTR lpszMsg);
BOOL WINAPI WL_Error_Term(void);
// error handling
TRY
CATCH
ENDCATCH
EXCEPT
```

It's not sufficient to manage memory simply by calling the Windows Global routines, but we don't want to get into a complete exploration of the intricacies of memory management. All we need is basic memory management with the capability to add two important additional features: memory tracking and subsegment allocation.

A simple wrapper layer will give us the ability to transparently add these features. Performance optimization cannot happen without performance data. When we need performance data, a memory tracking layer is a valuable tool. At some point the sheer number of allocation requests becomes a problem in terms of the selector limit; our subsegment allocation scheme alleviates this problem. This wrapper layer uses the global allocation macros in windowsx.h to provide the basic memory management calls, as shown in Listing 3-26.

Listing 3-26.   Memory Management Routines in mem.c

```
//memory management
BOOL        WINAPI WL_Mem_Init(void);
LPVOID      WINAPI WL_Mem_Alloc(UINT flags, DWORD size);
LPVOID      WINAPI WL_Mem_Realloc(LPVOID lpv,DWORD size,UINT flags);
HGLOBAL     WINAPI WL_Mem_Handle(LPVOID lpv);
HGLOBAL     WINAPI WL_Mem_Free(LPVOID lpv);
BOOL        WINAPI WL_Mem_Term(void);
```

WLib GDI Services

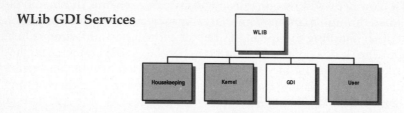

I've provided a wide range of color-mixing routines here so that you'll have an easy leg up into GDI's RGB-based color mixing scheme, no matter what scheme you're familiar with. This approach allows data defined in a foreign color system to be migrated easily into the Windows environment. Once you understand color, palettes are your next step in achieving fuller mastery over the environment. Within the Windows environment, it is necessary to use palettes to access more than the "system palette" colors in 8-bit systems; I've provided a set of helper routines for this. See Listing 3-27 for function prototypes.

Listing 3-27.   Color and Palette Functions in color.c and palette.c

```
// color and palettes
// color
BOOL        WINAPI WL_Color_Init(void);
BOOL        WINAPI WL_Color_RGBtoCRT( RGB FAR * rgbV, CRT FAR * crtV );
BOOL        WINAPI WL_Color_CRTtoRGB( CRT FAR * crtV, RGB FAR * rgbV );
BOOL        WINAPI WL_Color_RGBtoCMY( RGB FAR * rgbV, CMY FAR * cmyV );
BOOL        WINAPI WL_Color_CMYtoRGB( CMY FAR * cmyV, RGB FAR * rgbV );
BOOL        WINAPI WL_Color_RGBtoHSV( RGB FAR * rgbV, HSV FAR * hsvV );
BOOL        WINAPI WL_Color_HSVtoRGB( HSV FAR * hsvV, RGB FAR * rgbV );
BOOL        WINAPI WL_Color_RGBtoHLS( RGB FAR * rgbV, HLS FAR * hlsV );
BOOL        WINAPI WL_Color_HLStoRGB( HLS FAR * hlsV, RGB FAR * rgbV );
BOOL        WINAPI WL_Color_Term(void);
//palettes
BOOL        WINAPI WL_Pal_Init(void);
BOOL        WINAPI WL_Pal_Create(LPLOGPALETTE lpPal)(void);
BOOL        WINAPI WL_Pal_Destroy(HPALETTE hp);
int         WINAPI WL_Pal_MakeIdentityPal(LPLOGPALETTE pPal)
int         WINAPI WL_Pal_ColorsInPalette(HPALETTE hPal);
HPALETTE WINAPI WL_Pal_CreateDIBPalette (HANDLE hDIB);
HPALETTE WINAPI WL_Pal_CopyPaletteChangingFlags(HPALETTE hPal,BYTE bNewFlag);
void        WINAPI WL_Pal_AnimatePalette (HWND hWnd, HPALETTE hPal);
BOOL        WINAPI WL_Pal_Term(void);;
```

Bitmaps are the basic unit of drawing in this system. Device Independent Bitmaps (DIBs) provide a measure of protection against device-driver dependency. Essentially, a DIB is a bitmap and a palette that, taken together, specify image bits and a color mapping. Using DIBs as the unit of file I/O is natural. DIBs can be written to a file and read on a machine with a different display driver. This is not always the case with regular bitmaps, also known as DDBs (Device-Dependent Bitmaps). There is also a set of functions to support using of DDBs for display along with using DIBs for storage. See Listing 3-28.

Listing 3-28. Bitmaps and DIBs in bitmap.c, dib.c, and file.c

```
// bitmaps and DIBS
//bitmaps
BOOL        WINAPI WL_Bitmap_Init(void);
HBITMAP     WINAPI WL_Bitmap_Create(HDC hdcMem,
                   int ox, int oy, int ex, int ey);
HBITMAP     WINAPI WL_Bitmap_Copy(HDC hdcMem,HBITMAP hb,
                   HPALETTE hp, int ox,int oy, int ex, int ey);
BOOL        WINAPI WL_Bitmap_Delete(HBITMAP hb);
BOOL        WINAPI WL_Bitmap_Term(void);
// DIBS
BOOL        WINAPI WL_DIB_Init(void);
DWORD       WINAPI WL_DIB_DIBWidth(LPSTR lpDIB);
DWORD       WINAPI WL_DIB_DIBHeight(LPSTR lpDIB);
WORD        WINAPI WL_DIB_DIBNumColors(LPSTR lpbi);
WORD        WINAPI WL_DIB_PaletteSize(LPSTR lpbi);
LPSTR       WINAPI WL_DIB_FindBits(LPSTR lpbi);
HBITMAP     WINAPI WL_DIB_DIBToBitmap(HWND hw,HANDLE hDIB,
                   HPALETTE hPal);
HANDLE      WINAPI WL_DIB_WinDIBFromBitmap(HWND hw,
                   HBITMAP hBitmap,DWORD dwStyle,WORD wBits,
                   HPALETTE hPal);
BOOL        WINAPI WL_DIB_Term(void);
// file io
BOOL        WINAPI WL_File_Init(void);
BOOL        WINAPI WL_File_DIBFiletoDDB(HWND hw,LPSTR szFile,
                   HPALETTE FAR * lphp);
BOOL        WINAPI WL_File_DDBtoDIBFile(HWND hw,HBITMAP hb,
                   HPALETTE hp, LPSTR szFile);
BOOL        WINAPI WL_File_Term(void);
```

Printing is fundamental. Period. We'll be able to render color images on black-and-white printers. True, it's not color, but it's still usable. Using abort procedures and other tricks of the trade will allow us to do a credible job of it, too. Printing is the second use we will make of background processing. The print API, shown in Listing 3-29, has only one visible routine, **WL_Print_PrintDIB**. The rest of this subsystem consists of helper functions largely devoted to supporting the visible interface. Those of you who are only interested in using the API need consider nothing more. But for those of you who are interested, the implementation of the guts of printing proves quite fascinating. Later, in Chapter 5 you will see how to use this substrate to construct the canvas print facility using **G3D_GEnv_Print**.

Listing 3-29.   Printing Bitmaps in print.c

```
//printing
BOOL    WINAPI WL_Print_Init(void);
DWORD   WINAPI WL_Print_DIBPrint (HDC      hPrnDC,
                                  HWND     hDlgAbort,
                                  LPSTR    lpDIBHdr,
                                  LPSTR    lpBits,
                                  LPRECT lpPrintRect,
                                  WORD wUnits,
                                  DWORD dwROP,
                                  BOOL fBanding,
                                  BOOL fUseEscapes,
                                  LPSTR lpszDocName);
DWORD   WINAPI WL_Print_BandDIBToPrinter (HDC hPrnDC,
                      HWND    hDlgAbort,
                      LPSTR lpDIBHdr,
                      LPSTR lpBits,
                      LPRECT lpPrintRect);
DWORD   WINAPI WL_Print_PrintABand (HDC hDC,
                HWND    hDlgAbort,
                LPRECT lpRectOut,
                LPRECT lpRectClip,
                  BOOL fDoText,
                  BOOL fDoGraphics,
                 LPSTR lpDIBHdr,
                 LPSTR lpDIBBits);
BOOL    WINAPI WL_Print_DeviceSupportsEscape (HDC hDC, int nEscapeCode);
void    WINAPI WL_Print_TranslatePrintRect (HDC hDC,
                    LPRECT lpPrintRect,
                    WORD    wUnits,
                    WORD    cxDIB,
                    WORD    cyDIB);
HDC     WINAPI WL_Print_GetPrinterDC (void);
DWORD   WINAPI WL_Print_DoStartDoc (BOOL bUseEscapes, HDC hPrnDC,
                              LPSTR lpszDocName);
DWORD   WINAPI WL_Print_DoSetAbortProc (BOOL bUseEscapes,HDC hPrnDC,
                              FARPROC lpfnAbortProc);
DWORD   WINAPI WL_Print_DoStartPage (BOOL bUseEscapes,HDC hPrnDC);
DWORD   WINAPI WL_Print_DoEndPage (BOOL bUseEscapes,HDC hPrnDC);
DWORD   WINAPI WL_Print_DoEndDoc (BOOL bUseEscapes,HDC hPrnDC);
FARPROC WINAPI WL_Print_FindGDIFunction (LPSTR lpszFnName);
BOOL    WINAPI WL_Print_Term(void);
```

WLib User Services

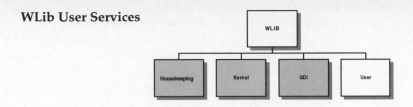

Mouse and clipboard support go hand in hand. The mouse marks the region of interest with a "rubber-band rectangle" technique. This region is then used in clipboard operations or other graphics processing. We'll develop both mouse and clipboard routines to provide these techniques. Listing 3-30 shows the function prototypes for the mouse and clipboard routines.

Listing 3-30. Clipboard and Mouse Functions in clipbrd.c and mouse.c

```
// clipboard
BOOL          WINAPI WL_Clipbrd_Init(void);
HANDLE        WINAPI WL_Clipbrd_RenderImmed(HWND hw,int cf,
                     HDC hdcS, HANDLE h1, HANDLE h2);
BOOL          WINAPI WL_Clipbrd_RenderDelay(HWND hw,int cf);
BOOL          WINAPI WL_Clipbrd_Term(void);
//mouse
BOOL          WINAPI WL_Mouse_Init(void);
void          WINAPI WL_Mouse_DrawRect( HWND, LPRECT, BOOL, HDC);
BOOL          WINAPI WL_Mouse_Term(void);
```

A tree layout of the API, Figure 3-9, gives a good bird's-eye view of the subsystems, and is useful to compare to the data structure tree diagram for the WLib, as shown in Figure 3-1.

Figure 3-9. WLib API

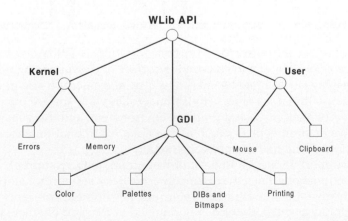

That concludes coverage of WLib. At this point, you've seen the API, the data structures, and the dependencies. Chapter 4 provides the implementation that complements this overview, and these routines are critical to every demo and application provided here. Since memory and GDI are effectively dealt with, we're now free to consider the next level. There is always another level, and here there are actually several. The next one on the list is G3DLib. It makes heavy use of the WLib services in providing the graphics environment and canvas.

G3D 3D Support Library

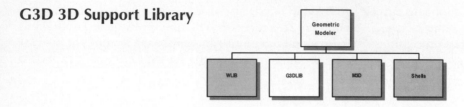

The 3D support library, or "G3D," can be broken down into three broad areas of functionality. The Drawing Surface Services provide a necessary layer around the raster GDI and prepare a gateway to the vector future. General Services provide a range of functions like transcription and basic mathematics functions. 3D Support Services provide the 4D homogeneous coordinate mathematics that underlie this 3D graphics system. This functional decomposition is illustrated in Figure 3-10.

Figure 3-10.   G3D Library

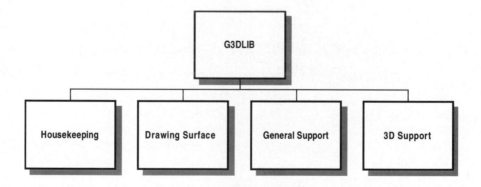

Drawing Surface Services provide a drawing surface or canvas analogous to the "drawable" of PEX. Display-surface management is a crucial element to any graphics package that needs to exist within a graphical environment. Drawing-surface management functions are provided by the canvas and graphics environment, and this subsystem serves to hide the Windows environment as much as possible. Additional functions add the window-to-viewport mapping to the canvas abstraction.

The General Support Services add a set of histogram, inquiry support, math, and session-transcription functions. Histogram functions are basic support for storing count data. Inquiry capability gives you the ability to determine key numeric constants in the environment. Transcription is useful both for debugging and as a record of where you have been.

Besides the math functions provided by the Run-Time Library (RTL), we'll also implement additional conversions and transcendental support.

While the canvas abstraction is very important, it still does not address 3D graphics. To "do 3D," you need some form of a vector library, a matrix transform library, and viewing system setup routines. The 3D support subsystems give you that capability. Primitives and Attributes formalize graphics output and attributes, with the canvas as the target. The target of output functions is the canvas, but since the source is the output of the 3D calculations, this treatment is not unwarranted (even if it might seem more natural to consider primitives as part of the Drawing Surface Services). Next are vectors, transforms, and viewing primitives. Together, they add the final essential ingredient — the three-dimensional world-view system. Along the way to building the viewing system, we'll develop the vector and matrix routines. These underlying routines are available at the API level.

Table 3-2 shows the source files in the G3DLib build. Once again, the files are separated into three different functional areas, although there is some overlap between math functions in the general area and *GENV* output functions in the 3D area.

Table 3-2.   G3DLib Source Contents

Files	*Description*
G3DLib Housekeeping	
gl_init.c,gl_init.h	Library global initialization
gl_term.c,gl_term.h	Library global termination
gl_err.c,gl_err.h	Library error reporting
g3d_inc.h	Main include file that applications reference
Drawing Surface	
glgenv.c,glgenv.h	Graphics environment, manages coords for canvas
canvas.c,canvas.h	Canvas provides offscreen drawing surface for genv
bmpbuff.c,bmpbuff.h	Light part of canvas, hidden
membuff.c,membuff.h	Heavy part of the canvas, hidden
coords.c,coords.h	Coordinate mapping
winview.c,winview.h	Window/viewport using coord layer
General Support	
inquiry.c,inquiry.h	System inquiry, hides GetDeviceCaps/GetSystemMetrics
hist.h,hist.h	Histogram support
math.c,math.h	General math functions
trans.c,trans.h	Session transcript global window class based on WINIO
3D Support	
prims.c,prims.h	Output to genv
vec4d.c,vec4d.h	Vector functions
matrix.c,matrix.h	Basic matrix functions
xform.c,xform.h	Matrix transforms
viewing.c,viewing.h	Viewing systems

G3D Drawing Surface Services

Keep in mind, you're working within Windows. You don't have the luxury of simply "assuming control" over the horizontal and the vertical. Some "drawing area" must be provided and maintained or the system fails to provide a useful set of building blocks. The canvas abstraction hides the inclusion of drawing tools like pixel color, line pen, and fill brush. It also hides details like whether a canvas is constructed of a bitmap only or of a bitmap and an intensity buffer. The canvas and all this graphics information are encapsulated within the concept of a graphics environment. Using the graphics environment API makes one nice neat package for performing Windows graphics tasks. The graphics environment API is shown in Listing 3-31. Notice that the underlying canvas routines are not visible; a perfect example of encapsulation and information hiding (well mostly). As in real life, nothing is perfect, and occasionally you need to go down to the basement. The canvas level is actually accessible, but we won't get into those details until Chapter 5.

Listing 3-31.   Graphics Environment Functions in glgenv.c

```
// util
void        WINAPI G3D_GEnv_Clear(LPGENV genv,HBRUSH hbrClear);
void        WINAPI G3D_GEnv_Update(LPGENV genv);
void        WINAPI G3D_GEnv_Size(LPGENV genv,
                        RECT   rcDst);
// screen and printer io
void        WINAPI G3D_GEnv_Paint(LPGENV genv,
                        HDC    hdc,
                        RECT   rcDst,
                        RECT   rcSrc,
                        BOOL   fRectDefined);
void        WINAPI G3D_GEnv_Scale(LPGENV genv,
                        HDC    hdc,
                        RECT   rcPaint,
                        BOOL   fRectDefined);

BOOL        WINAPI G3D_GEnv_Print(HINSTANCE      hInst,
                        HWND          hw, LPGENV genv,
                        FARPROC       lpAbortProc,
                        FARPROC       lpAbortDlg,
                        HWND          hDlgAbort,
                        BOOL      FAR *bAbort,
                        LPPRINTOPTIONS lpPOpt, LPSTR szJobName);
// file io
BOOL        WINAPI G3D_GEnv_Load(HWND hw, LPGENV genv,LPSTR szFileName);
BOOL        WINAPI G3D_GEnv_Save(HWND hw,LPGENV genv,LPSTR szFileName);
// tool access
```

```
BOOL        WINAPI G3D_GEnv_SetVal(LPGENV genv,int Element, DWORD Value);
DWORD       WINAPI G3D_GEnv_GetVal(LPGENV genv,int Element);
BOOL        WINAPI G3D_GEnv_Reset(LPGENV genv, int Offset);
void        WINAPI G3D_GEnv_Use(LPGENV genv, int Offset);
// pixel access
BOOL        WINAPI G3D_GEnv_SetPix(LPGENV genv,
                                   int OffsetX,int OffsetY, HPVOID Value);
HPVOID      WINAPI G3D_GEnv_GetPix(LPGENV genv,int OffsetX,int OffsetY);
BOOL        WINAPI G3D_GEnv_SetMem(LPGENV genv,
                                   int OffsetX,int OffsetY, HPVOID Value);
HPVOID      WINAPI G3D_GEnv_GetMem(LPGENV genv,int OffsetX,int OffsetY);
```

The graphics environment, our unifying theme, is the basis for our application's coexistence with Windows. Providing and manipulating the graphics environment is the primary purpose of the display-surface management routines. In order to bind that subsystem to the three-dimensional viewing system, the graphics environment contains the window-to-viewport mapping layer that manages transformations between device coordinates and user coordinates. Remember, using a canvas transforms the traditional coordinate systems, changing viewport or device coordinates into canvas coordinates. Window or logical coordinates remain a "user" coordinate system, so named because the user determines the range of values for the system. Listing 3-32 shows the coordinate mapping and window-viewport functions.

Listing 3-32.   Graphics Environment Coordinate Functions in winview.c and coord.c

```
// support and utility
void        WINAPI G3D_GEnv_SetWindow(LPGENV genv,
                                      int wxo, int xyo,
                                      int wxe, int wye);
void        WINAPI G3D_GEnv_SetViewport(LPGENV genv,
                                        int vxo, int vyo,
                                        int vxe, int vye);




void        WINAPI G3D_GEnv_UsertoDevice(LPGENV genv,
                                         int   uxo, int   uyo,
                                         LPINT dxe, LPINT dye);

void        WINAPI G3D_GEnv_DevicetoUser(LPGENV genv,
                                         int   dxo, int   dyo,
                                         LPINT uxe, LPINT uye);
```

G3D General Support Services

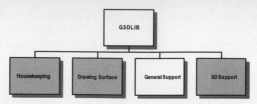

General Support provides histogram, inquiry, math, and transcript functions. These services are a grab-bag of extras that can be very useful. For example, we use a plot of the number of occurrences of a particular color in an image — a histogram — in the modeler. Histogram support is the underlying mechanism that supports the statistics; plotting is handled by the modeler. Most graphics systems allow inquiry into system capabilities and the value of system parameters like screen size and pixel depth. The **GetDeviceCaps** and **GetSystemMetrics** are used in one function to provide a "one-stop shopping" approach to inquiry. Math functions extend the RTL with conversions, different coordinate systems, and additional transcendental functions. Finally, the transcription routines provide a window class for outputting debugging information.

Histograms give us valuable feedback about image data content. They are an analysis tool that help form the foundation of color manipulation and enhancement techniques. The histogram services here encapsulate a "bin" data structure in which our application can store the histogram frequencies. Manipulating this information is left to the application: for example, the rough plot provided by the hist view pane and the sweeping of the bins done by the color quantization routines.

This library provides basic tools like histograms without attempting to cross the boundary (blurry as it is) between 3D graphics and image processing. See Listing 3-33 for the exported histogram functions.

Listing 3-33.   Histogram Functions in hist.c

```
BOOL    WINAPI G3D_Hist_Init(void);
LPHIST  WINAPI G3D_Hist_Create(int bins);
BOOL    WINAPI G3D_Hist_Clear(LPHIST lph);
BOOL    WINAPI G3D_Hist_Set(LPHIST lph,int bin);
long    WINAPI G3D_Hist_FindMostPopular(LPHIST lph);
BOOL    WINAPI G3D_Hist_Destroy(LPHIST lph);
void    WINAPI G3D_Hist_Term(void);
```

Inquiry functions provide a wrapper or interface not only to system values but also to the methods of obtaining these values. This functionality frees you from having to worry about how to get display resolution or pixel depth information under Windows and whether it is in **GetDeviceCaps** or **GetSystemMetrics** or what. This system independence proves to be a powerful thing. Listing 3-34 shows this single-routine service, ignoring the initialization and termination routines.

Listing 3-34.   Inquiry Functions in inquiry.c

```
BOOL        WINAPI G3D_Inq_Init(void);
DWORD       WINAPI G3D_Inq_Inquire(HWND hw, WORD wSysValue);
BOOL        WINAPI G3D_Inq_Term(void);
```

It's also helpful to provide additional support with general math routines. The functions provided by C and its run-time library are adequate, but it is always nice to have the extra support. In addition, the vector, matrix, and viewing systems use some of these functions. Finally, in polygon drawing and object tracing we'll make even more use of these functions. Listing 3-35 shows the exported API for general math routines.

Listing 3-35.   General Math Exported Functions in math.c

```
// general math
long        WINAPI G3D_Math_Round(double x);
long        WINAPI G3D_Math_Trunc(double x);
double      WINAPI G3D_Math_Sqr(double x);

double      WINAPI G3D_Math_CosD(double Angle);
double      WINAPI G3D_Math_CosR(double Angle);
double      WINAPI G3D_Math_ACosD(double Angle);
double      WINAPI G3D_Math_SinD(double Angle);
double      WINAPI G3D_Math_SinR(double Angle);
double      WINAPI G3D_Math_ASinD(double Angle);
double      WINAPI G3D_Math_TanD(double Angle);
double      WINAPI G3D_Math_TanR(double Angle);
double      WINAPI G3D_Math_ATanD(double Angle);
double      WINAPI G3D_Math_Power(double Base, int Exponent);
double      WINAPI G3D_Math_Log(double x);
double      WINAPI G3D_Math_Exp10(double x);
int         WINAPI G3D_Math_Sign(double x);
// conversions
double      WINAPI G3D_Math_Radians(double Angle);
double      WINAPI G3D_Math_Degrees(double Angle);
void        WINAPI G3D_Math_Cylr2Cart(double R,
                        double Theta, double Z,
                        LPDOUBLE x,
                        LPDOUBLE y,
                        LPDOUBLE z );
void        WINAPI G3D_Math_Cart2Cylr (DOUBLE   x,
                        DOUBLE    y,
                        DOUBLE    z,
                        LPDOUBLE R,
                        LPDOUBLE Theta,
                        LPDOUBLE Z );
```

Listing 3-35.   (cont.)

```
void         WINAPI G3D_Math_Sphr2Cart(double R,
                          double Theta, double Phi,
                          LPDOUBLE x,
                          LPDOUBLE y,
                          LPDOUBLE z );
void         WINAPI G3D_Math_Cart2Sphr(DOUBLE   x,
                          DOUBLE   y,
                          DOUBLE   z,
                          LPDOUBLE R,
                          LPDOUBLE Theta,
                          LPDOUBLE Phi);
```

Another debugging aid (besides error-reporting) is the session transcript. Within the shell applications there are provisions for session transcription, and we tie up that loose thread with these services. From both the debugging and reporting points of view, session transcription gives both you and the application user valuable feedback. Listing 3-36 shows the contents of the transcription services.

Listing 3-36.   Transcription Functions

```
BOOL         WINAPI G3D_Trans_Init(void);
HWND         WINAPI G3D_Trans_Create(HINSTANCE hInst, HWND hwP,
                          LPSTR strTitle,RECT rcP);
void         WINAPI G3D_Trans_Add(WINIOWND*  pwiniownd, BYTE FAR *pch,
                          unsigned  cch);
void         WINAPI G3D_Trans_Destroy(HWND hwnd);
BOOL         WINAPI G3D_Trans_Term(void);
```

G3D 3D Support Services

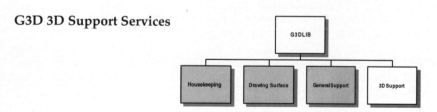

We need two more pieces to fully address 3D graphics: output and more math. As I mentioned before, you need not only some form of graphics output, but also a vector library, a matrix-transform library, and viewing system setup routines. Output primitives and attributes add the functions you'll need to draw points, lines, and other geometrical shapes. In addition, attributes control the appearance of these graphical objects, so you'll need some minimal attribute policy. Vectors, transforms, and viewing system routines are what create the multi-dimensional nature of the system.

Primitives and attributes add the functions you need to draw points, lines, and other geometrical shapes. Primitives operate in 2D coordinate space, which means that the application must draw line segments in viewport coordinates after the viewing transform occurs. The primitive functions extend the access routines provided by the canvas. Canvas access routines allow array-like access to a (row,column) location in the canvas. Output primitives let us draw in a more natural manner on the display surface. Listing 3-37 shows the exported output primitive functions.

Listing 3-37.   Primitive Exported Functions in prims.c

```
// prims
BOOL      WINAPI GL_GEnv_Point(LPGLGENV glgenv, int x, int y,
                          DWORD hbr);
BOOL      WINAPI GL_GEnv_Text(LPGLGENV glgenv,
                          int     x1, int y1,
                          LPSTR   lpText,
                          LONG    tLen);
BOOL      WINAPI GL_GEnv_Line(LPGLGENV glgenv,
                          int x1, int y1,
                          int x2, int y2, DWORD dwColor);
BOOL      WINAPI GL_GEnv_Rect(LPGLGENV glgenv,
                          int     x1, int y1,
                          int     x2, int y2,
                          DWORD   hpen,
                          DWORD   hbr);
BOOL      WINAPI GL_GEnv_Ellipse(LPGLGENV glgenv,
                          int     x1, int y1,
                          int     x2, int y2,
                          DWORD   hpen,
                          DWORD   hbr);
BOOL      WINAPI GL_GEnv_Tri(LPGLGENV glgenv,
                          int     x1, int y1,
                          int     x2, int y2,
                          int     x3, int y3,
                          DWORD   hpen,
                          DWORD   hbr);
BOOL      WINAPI GL_GEnv_Polyline(LPGLGENV glgenv,
                          LPPOINT pPoly,
                          DWORD   dwColor,
                          DWORD   hpen);
BOOL      WINAPI GL_GEnv_Polygon(LPGLGENV glgenv,
                          LPPOINT pPoly,
                          DWORD   dwColor,
                          DWORD   hpen,
                          DWORD   hbr);
```

Attributes, as I've said, control the appearance of these graphical objects. GDI provides basic attributes like brushes, fonts, palettes, and pens. These are the only attributes this system really needs, so rather than introduce another abstraction and more API functions, we simply piggyback on the existing GDI functions. Yes, this is a violation of wrapping, and makes any possible future porting to a non-Windows platform more problematic. However, this approach is extremely simple and forces no new learning on the user. By depending directly on the GDI objects, we force certain policy and semantic decisions in line with the way GDI does things.

How is this used, in a more practical sense? It helps us keep with our desire to provide both repetitive and one-shot attribute control. The internals of the canvas contain named "slots" for attributes. These are the default for every output primitive. The primitive routines, in their interface, contain parameters for pens, brushes, or whatever. This is the one-shot override capability.

The typical usage pattern is thus twofold. At graphics-environment creation time you select the default attributes using *G3D_GEnv_SetVal* and the #define manifest constants for the attribute slots. At the point of any output primitive, an attribute override may take place for the duration of that call only. This places the burden for attribute management (pen, brush, etc.) squarely on the application and provides only a mechanism for usage. Beyond that, most of the work involved in using attributes is involved in synchronization. For instance, as long as the memory DC that the canvas uses and the output-target client-area DC contain the same attributes and are in sync, output will behave as expected. If the device contexts get out of sync, you get garbage. Any changes made to attributes in the graphics environment must be reflected in the client DC in the end to prevent this. The palette attribute is the most obvious, but don't forget about DC origins and extents. The DC origin and extent values are changed by the mucking about with window-viewport mappings. Bitmap copy operations and output to the client DC (both typically use **BitBlt** or **StretchBlt**) must take this into account. Never fear, I'll give you a wide range of examples to show exactly how to handle this in the most common situations.

Just like the general math routines operate independent of the graphics environment, the vector, transform, and viewing system routines operate in a purely mathematical way. We'll look at two common, independent viewing systems. First, there's a simple 4-parameter viewing system suitable for simple demo programs, illustrated in Figure 3-11. Then, once we've looked at the basics of 3D world definition and how to use the vector and transform libraries, we'll go on to a more complicated and useful viewing system, shown in Figure 3-12. The from/lookat/up pinhole camera system is the basis of a powerful viewing environment, and is the viewing system upon which our modeler is built. Vector functions, matrix functions, and the viewing primitives are similar to math functions, since they operate independently in an abstract mathematical space. At some later point we will provide some glue between the viewing system and the canvas as well.

Figure 3-11. Four-Parameter Viewing System

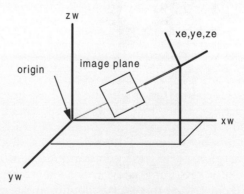

Figure 3-12.   From/Lookat/Up Viewing System

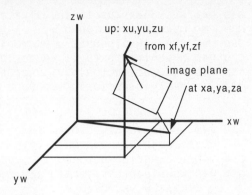

Points in space, or coordinates, can be represented by a vector. In this system, coordinates and vectors are fundamentally interchangeable. The vector routines provide a set of vector operations in 4D homogeneous coordinates. The basic tools you'll need for this are dot products, cross products, and normals, and, of course, basic operations like addition and subtraction. This classical breakdown does not, however, consider the memory management aspect of service systems. In order for a vector package to scale, we must build in memory management; for example, a modeler creating a scene of 1,000 four-sided polygonal objects has 4,000 vectors to manage, in addition to the 1,000 faces. Instance-management is, therefore, key.

Operations that return new instances as well as in-place operations are very important to this strategy. This means that most functions have two flavors. The vector normal function is a good example of this. The first flavor takes two vectors as parameters and returns a new vector as the normal. The second flavor takes three parameters, the first of which is a far-pointer, to a vector that will contain the result. This meets most programming requirements. Listing 3-38 displays the vector API.

Listing 3-38.   Vector Exported Functions in vec4d.c

```
#define VECTOR4DX(v) ((v).x)
#define VECTOR4DY(v) ((v).y)
#define VECTOR4DZ(v) ((v).z)
#define ONE4D        1
#define ZERO4D       0
#define DOUBLEINF4D  0x7FFFFFFF


// vector instance management
LPVECTOR4D  WINAPI G3D_V4D_VNew4D(DOUBLE a,DOUBLE b,DOUBLE c);
void        WINAPI G3D_V4D_VSet4D(LPVECTOR4D lpV,
                      DOUBLE x,DOUBLE y,DOUBLE z,DOUBLE W);
int         WINAPI G3D_V4D_VDel4D(LPVECTOR4D lpV);
//
DOUBLE      WINAPI G3D_V4D_VDot4D(VECTOR4D v1,VECTOR4D v2);
DOUBLE      WINAPI G3D_V4D_VMag4D(VECTOR4D v);
```

Listing 3-38.   (cont.)

```
LPVECTOR4D    WINAPI G3D_V4D_NVCross4D(VECTOR4D v1,VECTOR4D v2);
LPVECTOR4D    WINAPI G3D_V4D_NVNorm4D(VECTOR4D v);
LPVECTOR4D    WINAPI G3D_V4D_NVScale4D(DOUBLE s,VECTOR4D V);
LPVECTOR4D    WINAPI G3D_V4D_NVAdd(VECTOR4D V1,VECTOR4D V2);
LPVECTOR4D    WINAPI G3D_V4D_NVSub4D(VECTOR4D V1,VECTOR4D V2);
LPVECTOR4D    WINAPI G3D_V4D_NVDiv4D(VECTOR4D V,DOUBLE s);

//in place ops
void          WINAPI G3D_V4D_VCross4D(LPVECTOR4D lpV,
                            VECTOR4D v1, VECTOR4D v2);
void          WINAPI G3D_V4D_VNorm4D(LPVECTOR4D lpV, VECTOR4D v);
void          WINAPI G3D_V4D_VScale4D(LPVECTOR4D lpV,
                            DOUBLE s,VECTOR4D V);
void          WINAPI G3D_V4D_VAdd4D(LPVECTOR4D lpV,
                            VECTOR4D V1, VECTOR4D V2);
void          WINAPI G3D_V4D_VSub4D(LPVECTOR4D lpV,
                            VECTOR4D V1, VECTOR4D V2);
void          WINAPI G3D_V4D_VDiv4D(LPVECTOR4D lpV,
                            VECTOR4D V,DOUBLE s);
```

Matrix services provide both basic and transform services. Basic matrix operations include the basic translate, rotate, and scale, but this is not enough. The zero operation, matrix identity, transpose operator, and value-setting operator complete the matrix services. As always, instance management, instance-generating operators, and in-place operators are provided. See Listing 3-39 for details.

Listing 3-39.   Matrix Manipulation Functions in matrix.c

```
// instance management
LPMATRIX4D    WINAPI G3D_M4D_MNew4D(void);
int           WINAPI G3D_M4D_MDel4D(LPMATRIX4D lpM);

// new instance ops
LPMATRIX4D    WINAPI G3D_M4D_NZero4D(void);
LPMATRIX4D    WINAPI G3D_M4D_NIdentity4D(void);
LPMATRIX4D    WINAPI G3D_M4D_NTranspose4D(LPMATRIX4D T);
LPMATRIX4D    WINAPI G3D_M4D_NTranslate4D(VECTOR4D V);
LPMATRIX4D    WINAPI G3D_M4D_NUniformScale4D(DOUBLE s);
LPMATRIX4D    WINAPI G3D_M4D_NScale4D(VECTOR4D);
LPMATRIX4D    WINAPI G3D_M4D_NRotateX(DOUBLE);
LPMATRIX4D    WINAPI G3D_M4D_NRotateY(DOUBLE);
LPMATRIX4D    WINAPI G3D_M4D_NRotateZ(DOUBLE);
LPMATRIX4D    WINAPI G3D_M4D_NMatrix4D(
                      DOUBLE m11,DOUBLE m12,DOUBLE m13,DOUBLE m14,
                      DOUBLE m21,DOUBLE m22,DOUBLE m23,DOUBLE m24,
                      DOUBLE m31,DOUBLE m32,DOUBLE m33,DOUBLE m34,
                      DOUBLE m41,DOUBLE m42,DOUBLE m43,DOUBLE m44);
```

```
// in place ops
void          WINAPI G3D_M4D_Zero4D(LPMATRIX4D lpZ);
void          WINAPI G3D_M4D_Identity4D(LPMATRIX4D lpI);
void          WINAPI G3D_M4D_Transpose4D(LPMATRIX4D lpTt,
                     LPMATRIX4D T);
void          WINAPI G3D_M4D_Translate4D(LPMATRIX4D lpT,VECTOR4D V);
void          WINAPI G3D_M4D_UniformScale4D(LPMATRIX4D lpS,
                     DOUBLE s);
void          WINAPI G3D_M4D_Scale4D(LPMATRIX4D lpT,VECTOR4D P);
void          WINAPI G3D_M4D_RotateX(LPMATRIX4D lpM,DOUBLE deg);
void          WINAPI G3D_M4D_RotateY(LPMATRIX4D lpM,DOUBLE deg);
void          WINAPI G3D_M4D_RotateZ(LPMATRIX4D lpM,DOUBLE deg);
void          WINAPI G3D_M4D_Matrix4D(LPMATRIX4D lpM,
                 DOUBLE m11,DOUBLE m12,DOUBLE m13,DOUBLE m14,
                 DOUBLE m21,DOUBLE m22,DOUBLE m23,DOUBLE m24,
                 DOUBLE m31,DOUBLE m32,DOUBLE m33,DOUBLE m34,
                 DOUBLE m41,DOUBLE m42,DOUBLE m43,DOUBLE m44);
```

Matrices are used for transformation operations. Vectors and matrices can be transformed, and the transform routines provide that capability. In addition, matrices can be concatenated together to form what is known as a *composite transform matrix* or *CTM*. The transform layer provides a simplified version of the standard instance-management and operator routines. Listing 3-40 shows the interface to this transform layer.

Listing 3-40.   Transform Functions in xform.c

```
//   Transform constants
#define DEND        0
#define SCALE       1
#define TRANSLATE   2
#define ROTATEX     3
#define ROTATEY     4
#define ROTATEZ     5
#define PROJECT     10

//   Projection types
#define PARALLEL    20
#define PERSPECTIVE 21

// vector by matrix transforms
void          WINAPI G3D_Xfrm_TransformPoint(LPVECTOR4D Pout,
                                             VECTOR4D Pin,
                                             LPMATRIX4D Tx);
void          WINAPI G3D_Xfrm_TransformNPoints(LPVECTOR4D  lpP,
                                               LPVECTOR4D  lpD,
                                               int         cnt,
                                               MATRIX4D    T);
```

Listing 3-40.   (cont.)

```
// matrix by matrix transforms
void            WINAPI G3D_Xfrm_TxT4D(LPMATRIX4D C,
                                      LPMATRIX4D A,LPMATRIX4D B);
// projection
void            WINAPI G3D_Xfrm_ProjectPoint(LPVECTOR4D Pout,
                                             VECTOR4D   Pin,
                                             int        nType);
void            WINAPI G3D_Xfrm_ProjectNPoints(LPVECTOR4D lpP,
                                               LPVECTOR4D lpD,
                                               int        cnt,
                                               int        nType);


//generate arbitrary transform

int             FAR cdecl G3D_Xfrm_MakeTM(LPMATRIX4D lpT,int a,...);
```

The viewing-system services are the last component of the G3DLib. The interface is extremely simple, consisting of initialization and update routines for each of the viewing systems shown in Figure 3-11 and Figure 3-12. These routines exist at the top of the pyramid. The vector, matrix, and composite transform routines provide the foundation on which the viewing systems are built. This allows a narrow interface to provide a lot of power. And, in case something unanticipated comes up, the basic vector and matrix routines can be made to do just about anything if you need them to. Listing 3-41 shows the viewing system interface routines.

Listing 3-41.   Viewing System Exported Functions in viewing.c

```
LPMATRIX4D      WINAPI G3D_View_InitEye(LPGENV    genv,
                                        VECTOR4D  vp,
                                        double    vs);
void            WINAPI G3D_View_MoveEye(LPGENV     genv,
                                        LPMATRIX4D Tx,
                                        VECTOR4D   vp,
                                        double     vs);

LPMATRIX4D      WINAPI G3D_View_InitCamera(LPGENV    genv,
                                           VECTOR4D vFrom,
                                           VECTOR4D vLookAt,
                                           VECTOR4D vUp,
                                           double   ang,
                                           double   vd,
                                           double   vs);
void            WINAPI G3D_View_MoveCamera(LPGENV     genv,
                                           LPMATRIX4D Tx,
                                           VECTOR4D   vFrom,
                                           VECTOR4D   vLookAt,
                                           VECTOR4D   vUp,
                                           double     ang,
                                           double vd,  double     vs);
```

That concludes the G3DLib. You now understand how the graphics environment and its canvas bridge the raster-vector gap, and provide both window-viewport mapping and output primitives and attributes. With a drawing surface in hand, the 3D support enables the drawing of 3D output on this surface. Figure 3-13 depicts, in tree form, the layout of the API. It's finally time to put another layer together—the final layer—that of scenes, objects, and surface properties.

Figure 3-13. G3DLib API

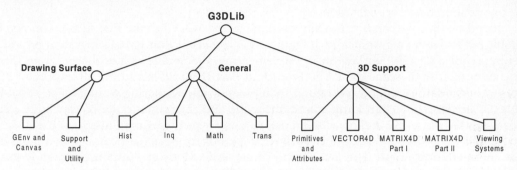

M3D Modeler Support Services

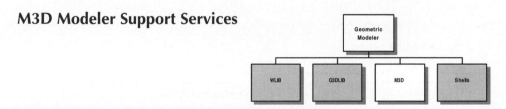

Now you have a canvas, output primitives, and attributes with which to draw; and vectors, transforms, and viewing systems to calculate the values to draw. But what do you calculate and what do you draw? Three-dimensional objects, that's what. You need scenes and objects, and support for them, to build a geometric modeler. The modeler and the M3D Modeler Support Services are tightly coupled around the five data-structure areas:

- control,
- model/scene,
- front end,
- 3D objects and surface properties, and
- post-processing.

The control area contains the state machine and object list functional areas. The state machine is clearly in the application domain. The linked-list services are on the borderline. They are more general, so we should consider them as part of the M3D Support Services, but the discussion on them fits better as an application topic. Model and scene management are also more property considered as application details.

That leaves the front end, core functions that manipulate objects and properties, and the post-processing functions. The front-end supports both language translation and object instantiation. It encompasses the script language element to 3D objects instantiated in memory.

Once objects are created and installed in the list, they can be manipulated and rendered —these are the core functions. Manipulation here consists of the transformation and ray-generation processes, along with camera movement. All of the rendering methods share surface properties and the illumination model. The rendering phase is bound to the color post-processing by surface property support for color, coefficients, and texture, realized as a color and material specification.

Based on this, we can functionally decompose the M3D into the five sections shown in Table 3-3 and shown graphically in Figure 3-14. The **Front End Part I** subsystem provides support for a description language. Implementing a language makes the program independent of specific scene data. The **Front End Part II** routines add the all-important 3D-object instantiation support. Without it, manipulation and rendering would not be possible. Next, **Core Functions Part I** implements the world and object manipulation capability. Rendering takes the world and objects and makes a pretty picture; **Core Functions Part II** supports object rendering and defines surface properties for object appearance that are used by the rendering phase. The last section of the M3D Modeler Support Services is **Post-Processing.** Here color analysis and image-colorization support are implemented.

Table 3-3.   M3D by Subsystem

M3D Subsystems	Description
Front End Part I	Provides script language support
Front End Part II	Provides 3D object instantiation support
Core Functions Part I	Provides world manipulation
Core Functions Part II	Provides world rendering
Post-Processing	Provides color post-processing support

Figure 3-14.   M3D Object Geometry Services

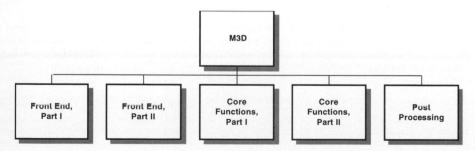

Front End Part I

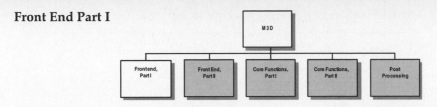

First we need to tackle some language issues. A simple modeler can get by with one description language to describe the contents of a scene. To provide easy extensibility, we'll separate out the modeling control parameters from the scene geometry. To that end, we'll use both a simple modeling script language and a simple scene script language here. To help with this, I'll provide an extremely simple, but sharable, tokenizer. On top of that, we'll also implement conversions and other helper functions.

Table 3-4 shows the source components in the Front End Part I subsystem. I've generalized support for languages a bit, with a separation into both tokenizing and parsing modules. The language is the important item here, though, so the description languages are next.

Table 3-4.   Front-End Part I Source Components

M3D Subsystems	Description
Front End Part I	Provides script language support
token.c,token.h	Description tokenizing
parse.c,parse.h	Model and scene description parsing

The modeling script gives us direct control over:

- canvas size,
- initial rendering type,
- color lookup table specification,
- material lookup table specification,
- shading and tracing environment variables, and
- scene geometry description file.

A scene description referenced in the modeling script controls the world definition. However, this begs a language definition. With regard to tokens in the scene description, we'll refer back to the NFF format described in Chapter 1, with some extensions and changes. The NFF tokens are compared to the new WinMod3D tokens in Table 3-5.

Table 3-5. NFF Versus WinMod3D: Scene Description Tokens

Token	NFF	WinMod3D
v - viewing vectors and angles	yes	yes
l - positional light location	yes	yes
b - background color	yes	yes
a -global ambient background light	n	yes
f - object material properties	yes	n, available in "o"
c - cone or cylinder primitive	yes	n, available in "o"
s - sphere primitive	yes	n, available in "o"
p - polygon primitive	yes	n
pp - polygonal patch primitive	yes	n
o - common object definition	n	yes

The "v" token, the "l" token, and the "b" token are used without change. We'll add an "a" token for ambient light. The "f" token defining surface properties, and the "c," "s," "p," and "pp" tokens defining objects are replaced with a single "o" token, which represents a common object definition. This common object definition provides for

- primitive specification (type name and associated face-vertex file name),
- surlace color and material properties specification,
- local scale, rotate, and translation specification.

As Table 3-6 shows, WinMod3D supports the sphere, infinite plane, cylinder, cone, box, and pyramid primitive types. Instead of a separate surface-property specification and an "object gets last defined surface" policy, the policy places a color and material element in the common object definition. Listing 3-42 shows a sample object definition.

Listing 3-42.   Example Object Definition

```
o
box
box.dat
COLOR     Tan
MATERIAL  oak
SCALE     20.0  10.0    10.0
ROTATE     0.0   0.0     0.0
TRANSLATE  0.0   0.0     0.0
end
```

The color and material specifications combine to define the appearance of the object. Table 3-7 again compares NFF versus WinMod3D properties. The exact meaning and use of these parameters will be described in detail in Chapter 10. The local transformation elements in the common object definition provide a parallel to the NFF definitions. With this local transformation, we control the positioning of objects within the world (although in ray-trace mode some objects currently ignore the local rotation).

Table 3-6. **NFF Versus WinMod3D: Objects in Description Language**

Object	NFF	WinMod3D
Sphere	yes ,s	yes, o sphere
Plane	no	yes, o plane
Cylinder	yes, c	yes, o cylinder
Cone	yes, c	yes, o cone
Box	no	yes, o box
Pyramid	no	yes, o pyramid
Polygon	yes, p	no
Polygonal patch	yes, pp	no

Table 3-7. **NFF Versus WinMod3D: Supported Surface Properties**

Description	NFF	WinMod3D
Object Material Properties	f red green blue K_d K_s shine K_t ior	COLOR Name (in lookup table)
		Name red green blue
		MATERIAL name (in lookup table)
		Name TextureName k_a k_d k_s shine k_t ior
scanf formats	f %g % g % g % g %g % g %g % g	Name %g %g %g
		Name %s %g %g %g %g %g %g
Individual Surface Properties, Compared		
color	yes	yes
k_a	no	yes
k_d	yes	yes
k_s	yes	yes
shine	yes	yes
k_t	yes	yes, unused
ior	yes	yes, overloaded for reflection
texture	no	yes

Description languages imply script files, parsing, and all kinds of messy details. Parsing implies some data formats and data conversion. Low-level data format conversions, the tokenizer, and both a model and scene parser complete Part l of the front end. The color and material specifications, along with the common object definition, are covered in Part II. This low and midlevel support let you customize the existing parser or write a better front-end.

I'll give you a simple set of routines to convert from a text-based representation in the script files to numeric representation internal to the program (as shown in Listing 3-43) along with routines *gettoken*, *parse_scene*, and *parse_model*, shown in Listing 3-44.

Listing 3-43.   Example Conversion Routines in parse.c

```
void WINAPI LoadVector(FILE *InFile, LPVECTOR4Da lpV);
void WINAPI LoadWord(FILE * InFile,WORD *a);
void WINAPI LoadText(FILE * InFile,LPSTR a);
```

Listing 3-44.   Tokenizing and Parsing in token.c and parse.c

```
//token.c
TOKEN WINAPI gettoken (char FAR *, FILE FAR *);
//parse.c
void  WINAPI parse_scene (FRAME * pfrm,VWWND * pv,
     LPMODEL theModel, LPSCENE theScene,
     char FAR  * filename, FILE FAR * infile);
void  WINAPI parse_model (FRAME * pfrm,VWWND * pv,
     LPMODEL theModel,char FAR  * filename, FILE FAR * infile);
```

Front End Part II

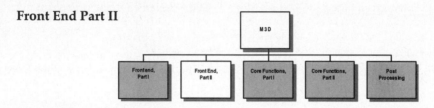

The model description language defines a color table with a color specification, and a material table with a material specification. The scene description adds a common object definition. The parsing phase performs an action for each recognized token. Typically, that results in making memory copy of one of these three specifications. Dealing with these three specs characterizes the Part II routines. Table 3-8 shows the source code components of this subsystem.

Color depends on the way light and objects interact in both the real world and our simulation of it in the modeler. Light sources can have a wealth of functionality, including details like spotlights. This has its cost in implementation and execution. Our implementation associates only a color value with a light source, so the object's surface properties have a dominant impact on scene colorization.

Surface-property descriptions consist of three parts: a color, a set of coefficients, and a texture. Color is easy to specify, but coefficients and texture need an organizing principle to be manageable. This takes form here as the named material specification. This explains why there are two lookups and not three—looking up a material gives both a set of coefficients and a texture.

The color needs of the modeler are well served by the underlying routines of the WLib, but a more convenient representation is a text color name. A table of common color names (derived from the X-Windows source code and used by many public-domain ray tracers) is supported with a binary lookup function, shown in Listing 3-45. *MakeColorLookupTable* takes a color table specification and builds a color table. *FreeColorLookupTable* destroys one. Key-value pairs of names and RGB color values are stored in a *COLORARRAY* table and *LookupColorByName* provides mapping from name to value.

Table 3-8   Front End Part II Source Components

M3D Subsystems	Description
Front End Part II	Provides 3D object instantiation support
Surface Properties	
ccolor.c,ccolor.h	Color lookup
material.c,material.h	Material lookup
Object Support	
Polygon Objects	
explicit.c,explicit.h	Face-vertex polygon helpers
ray-trace objects	
sphere.c,sphere.h	Perfect sphere
plane.c,plane.h	Infinite plane
simples.c,simples.h	Circle,rectangle, and triangle helpers
simquad.c,simquad.h	Simplified quadratic helpers
cylinder.c,cylinder.h	Uses simplified quadratic and circle
cone.c,cone.h	Uses simplified quadratic and circle
box.c, box.h	Uses rectangles
pyramid.c, pyramid.h	Uses a rectangle and triangles

Listing 3-45.   Color Name Support in ccolor.c

```
LPCOLORARRAY WINAPI MakeColorLookupTable(LPSTR SrcFile);
int         WINAPI FreeColorLookupTable(LPCOLORARRAY Colors);
int         WINAPI LookupColorByName(LPCOLORARRAY Colors,
                   char * name, Color color);
```

The material API works much the same way. *MakeMaterialLookupTable* takes a material table specification and builds a material table. *FreeMaterialLookupTable* handles its destruction. Key-value pairs of names and coefficient/texture definitions are stored in a *MATERIALARRAY* table: mappings from name to value are provided by *LookupMaterialByName*, as shown in Listing 3-46.

Listing 3-46.   Material Support in material.c

```
LPMATERIALARRAY WINAPI MakeMaterialLookupTable(LPSTR SrcFile);
int    WINAPI FreeMaterialLookupTable(LPMATERIALARRAY Materials);
int    WINAPI LookupMaterialByName(LPMATERIALARRAY Materials,
              char * name, LPSURFPROPS match);
```

That leaves the common object definition. This takes two forms — the *visible*, which is seen by the scene parser, and the *internal*, which takes care of the differing needs of the dual representation. At the topmost, visible level, a series of instantiation functions, referred to generically as *Makexxx*, perform the visible service. These functions are shown in Listing 3-47.

Listing 3-47. Object Instantiation Functions in Ray-Trace Source Modules

```
//plane.c
LPOBJECT WINAPI MakePlane (LPSCENE theScene,
PLANE plane,LPSTR szObjFileName,
EX3DOBJECT ex3DObj);

//sphere.c
LPOBJECT WINAPI MakeSphere(LPSCENE theScene,
SPHERE sphere, LPSTR szObjFileName,
EX3DOBJECT ex3DObj);

//box.c
LPOBJECT WINAPI MakeBox(LPSCENE theScene,
BOX box, LPSTR szObjFileName,
EX3DOBJECT ex3DObj);

//pyramid.c
LPOBJECT WINAPI MakePyramid(LPSCENE theScene,
PYRAMID pyramid, LPSTR szObjFileName,
EX3DOBJECT ex3DObj);

//cylinder.c
LPOBJECT WINAPI MakeCylinder(LPSCENE theScene,
CYLINDER cylinder, LPSTR szObjFileName,
EX3DOBJECT ex3DObj);

//cone.c
LPOBJECT WINAPI MakeCone(LPSCENE theScene,
CONE     cone, LPSTR szObjFileName,
EX3DOBJECT ex3DObj);
```

Underneath, each representation has a set of routines. Listing 3-48 contains the explicit representation support. *MakeExObject* uses *LoadData* and *Load3DObjectFile.*

Listing 3-48.   Face-Vertex Representation Support in explicit.c

```
void WINAPI SetFace( LPFACE fi, int Index, int Value);

void WINAPI LoadData(FILE          *objfile,
                     LPOBJECT      theMaster,
                     LPEX3DOBJECT this,
                     int           LastVertex, int LastFace,
                     int VertexNumInFace);

void WINAPI Load3DObjectFile(LPSCENE theScene,LPOBJECT theMaster,
                LPSTR ObjFileName, LPEX3DOBJECT theObject);


LPEX3DOBJECT WINAPI MakeExObject(LPSCENE theScene,
LPOBJECT theMaster, LPSTR szObjFileName, EX3DOBJECT ex3DObj );
```

Listing 3-49 contains the analytic representation support, consisting of the *MakeAnxxx* functions, that takes the explicit data and mathematically derives the setup for the analytic representation.

Listing 3-49.   Analytic Representation Support in the Ray-Trace Source Modules

```
LPSPHERE        MakeAnSphere(SPHERE sphere);
LPPLANE         MakeAnPlane(PLANE plane);
LPSIMPLENGON    MakeAnBox(BOX box);
LPQUADRIC       MakeAnCylinder(CYLINDER cylinder);
LPSIMPLENGON    MakeAnPyramid(PYRAMID pyramid);
LPQUADRIC       MakeAnCone(CONE cone);
```

Front-end support has now taken us from ASCII-text script language to objects in memory and in a list (ignoring further details of the linked-list routines for now). The manipulation and rendering processes are next.

Core Functions Part I— World Manipulation

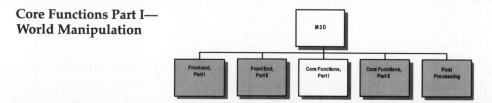

Manipulation involves camera positioning. It also represents the start of the image-generation process, by its operations on the objects in the object list. The support services give us the ability to manipulate objects; they also depend on the linked-list functions specific to WinMod3D. Table 3-9 lists the source files involved. Again, you'll see the 3D object source. From instantiation through rendering, the 3D objects are part of the process and the source reflects this.

Table 3-9.   Core Functions Part I Source Components

M3D Subsystems	Description
Core Functions Part I	Provides world manipulation
Generic Object Support	
object.h	Generic +3D object definition
linklist.c,linklist.h	Linklist routines for type "object"
3D Object Support	
polysurf.h,raysurf.h	Polygon and ray-trace definitions
Polygon Objects	
face.c,face.h	Face-vertex polygon helpers
Ray-trace Objects	
sphere.c,sphere.h	Perfect sphere
plane.c,plane.h	Infinite plane
simples.c,simples.h	Circle,rectangle, and triangle helpers
simquad.c,simquad.h	Simplified quadratic helpers
cylinder.c,cylinder.h	Uses simplified quadratic and circle
cone.c,cone.h	Uses simplified quadratic and circle
box.c,box.h	Uses rectangles
pyramid.c,pyramid.h	Uses a rectangle and triangles

One of the central themes of this book is the use of dynamic data structures like lists and the structuring of the application around the use of mapping functions on the list elements. Linked lists require *self-referential data structures* — ones that reference themselves. The **OBJECT** data structure shown in Listing 3-50 is a good example.

Listing 3-50.   Self-Referencing Declaration in object.h

```
 typedef struct t_object
{
   struct t_object FAR *next;
...
} OBJECT ;
```

This declaration makes it possible to walk a chain or list of these data structures. I'll give you simple list routines that do just that. See Listing 3-51 for the interface. The key to this is the function-pointer structure, shown in Listing 3-52, that groups the basic behavior of the 3D objects into one package.

Listing 3-51. List Functions in linklist.c

```
void      AddToList(LPOBJECT FAR *ListPtr, LPOBJECT Item);
unsigned FreeList (LPOBJECT FAR *ListPtr);
LPOBJECT GetElement(LPOBJECT ListPtr,unsigned short Object_id) ;
unsigned PrintList(LPOBJECT ListPtr,HWND hw);
```

Listing 3-52. 3D Object Function Pointers in object.h

```
struct t_objectprocs
   {
//debugging
     int    (*print) () ;
//polygon-(explicit)
     int    (*transform) () ;
     int    (*drawedges) () ;
     int    (*drawface) () ;
//quadric-(analytic)
     int    (*intersect) () ;
     int    (*normal) () ;
//cleanup
     int    (*free) () ;
   } * o_procs ;
```

Print and *free* are related to housekeeping, while ***transform*** and ***intersect*** are for manipulation. That leaves the rendering capability.

**Core Functions Part II—
World Rendering**

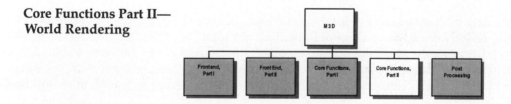

The object function-pointer structure contains methods to support both rendering and manipulation. This means that the 3D object source is involved in this subsystem, too, making it the third one in a row. The rendering phase depends on light sources, and also adds the rendering methods themselves. The rendering methods provide the control code that invokes the object function pointers where appropriate. See Table 3-10 for the source components to Core Functions Part II.

Table 3-10   Core Functions Part II Source Components

M3D Subsystems	Description
Core Functions Part II	Provides world rendering
Polygon Objects	
polydraw.c,polydraw.h	Polygon drawing modes
face.c,face.h	Face-vertex polygon helpers
Ray-trace Objects	
trace.c,trace.h	Ray-trace drawing mode
sphere.c,sphere.h	Perfect sphere
plane.c,plane.h	Infinite plane
simples.c,simples.h	Circle,rectangle, and triangle helpers
simquad.c,simquad.h	Simplified quadratic helpers
cylinder.c,cylinder.h	Uses simplified quadratic and circle
cone.c,cone.h	Uses simplified quadratic and circle
box.c,box.h	Uses rectangles
pyramid.c,pyramid.h	Uses a rectangle and triangles
Lights	
light.c,light.h	Light sources
Shading and Surface Properties	
illume.c,illume.h	Illumination model
surfprop.c,surfprop.h	Surface property definition
Texturing	
textures.c,textures.h	procedural texturing

Whereas the *transform* and *intersect* methods in Listing 3-52 belong to manipulation, the *drawedges, drawface,* and *normal* methods are used for rendering. The modeler uses the surface property data, along with the object geometry data, to generate a color. Once the color is calculated, it checks the texture definition. If a texture other than smooth is defined, it "perturbs" the color value to create a textural overlay on top of, or in addition to, the base color.

The surface-property data structure is shown in full in Listing 3-53. These properties are used in conjunction with the mapping functions and the polygon drawing and object tracing service functions shown in Listing 3-54. The mapping and service functions are used internally, under control of the state machine, to perform the rendering. The state machine controls function *RenderObjectList,* which in turn uses *PolyRenderObjectList* or *RayRenderObjectList,* shown in Listing 3-55.

Listing 3-53.   Surface Property Data Structure in surfprop.h

```
typedef struct t_surfprops
{
 //name
   char         szName[64];
 //color
   char         szColor[64];
   Color        surf_color ;
 //coefficients
   VECTOR4D     surf_ka ;     //ambient
   VECTOR4D     surf_kd ;     //diffuse
   VECTOR4D     surf_ks ;     //specular
   double       surf_shine ; //phong shine factor
   VECTOR4D     surf_kt ;//(reflection and refraction )
   double       surf_ior ;    //index of reflectionn/refraction
 //texture
   char         szTexture[64];
   int          surf_tid;
   LPVOID       surf_texdata;
} SURFPROPS ;
```

Listing 3-54.   Rendering Support Functions in illume.c and textures.c

```
//gray helpers in illume.c
void WINAPI Put_Gray_Pixel(HDC hdc,int xc, int yc, int run);
void WINAPI PerformGray(LPVECTOR4D vI,long far * col, int type);
//poly shade in illume.c
void WINAPI ShadePoly(VWWND    * pv,
                   LPVECTOR4D TotW,
                   LPOBJECT   Object,
                   VECTOR4D   Normal, VECTOR4D   Point,
                   LPVECTOR4D Color);
//ray shade in illume.c
void WINAPI ShadePoint( VWWND     * pv,
                   LPVECTOR4D TotW,int Depth,
                   LPOBJECT   Object, LPRAY       Ray,
                   VECTOR4D   Normal,VECTOR4D   Point,
                   LPISECT    hit,
                   LPVECTOR4D Color);
//texture in textures.c
void WINAPI Texture(VWWND *pv,
                   LPOBJECT Object, LPRAY IRay,
                   VECTOR4D N, VECTOR4D IPt,
                   LPVECTOR4D TexCol);
```

Listing 3-55.   Application Rendering Control

```
void WINAPI RenderObjectList( VWWND *pv,
                              HDC    hDC,
                              int    vtype,
                              int    rtype);

void WINAPI RayRenderObjectList(pv,hDC,vtype,rtype);

void WINAPI PolyRenderObjectList(pv,hDC,vtype,rtype);
```

Now the rendering process has generated a grayscale image. During this process, values are saved to support the post-processing of the image.

Post-Processing

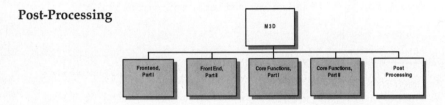

The rendering process leaves a legacy of intensity values on either a face (for polygon mode) or a pixel (for ray-trace mode) basis. Those values must be converted to color values from the gray values used in "on-the-fly" rendering. The polygon faces, the canvas intensity buffer, the histogram, and the color analysis functions combine to generate color when working with 256-color drivers. In 32K-color mode or higher, direct color assignment is used in the post-processing step. Table 3-11 shows the source included in post-processing. Besides the popularity and median cut routines, there is the overall quantization process for both the visible face list and the intensity buffer.

Table 3-11   Post-Processing Source Components

M3D Subsystems	Description
Post-Processing	Provides color post-processing support
quantize.c,quantize.h	Quantization control
mcut.c,mcut.h	Median cut
popular.c,popular.h	Popularity

You've already seen the data structures for the popularity and median cut algorithms; the functions are in Listing 3-56.

Listing 3-56.   Post-Processing Functions in mcut.c and popular.c

```
void WINAPI Popularity(void);
void WINAPI MedianCut(void);
```

At this point, we can save the image either in color or in grayscale. This completes our look at the M3D API. A tree-layout of the M3D is shown in Figure 3-15, concluding the consideration of the three support libraries in general. The modeler itself, with the state machine controlling the object list, finalizes the picture.

Figure 3-15.   M3D API

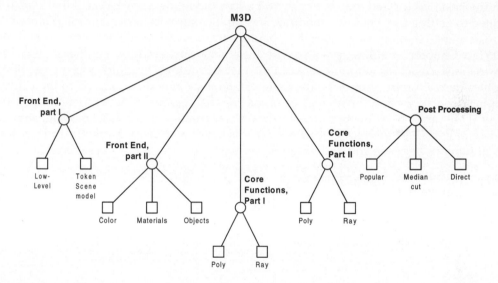

Summary

The implementation techniques used here include:

- extensible APIs,
- wrapper layers, and
- heavy usage of function pointers in the state machine and object list.

Using these practical concepts with the design issues from Chapters 1 and 2, we developed the system, its architecture, and the API.

The basic architecture of the system consists of three layers:

- A Windows, and operating system layer,
- A 3D support layer, and
- A modeler support services layer.

We looked at the data structures and the interconnectedness of the libraries, as well as the API for all three layers. The components of the individual libraries have each, in turn, been discussed as well. I explained the key design decisions, and you know all about the exported API.

Now it's time to really get our hands dirty with implementation details. Part II will take care of that, so get ready.

What's Next?

It might seem like we're handling quite a bit of material, and we are. We need a lot more than the basic vector and matrix library to build a modeling application. All of Part II is devoted to getting the Windows and basic 3D graphics support under control. (Figure 3-16 is a road map to the contents of Part II.) Chapter 4 focuses on the Windows support library, the WLib. Chapter 5 follows up with a critical element: canvas support in the G3DLib. The drawing surface acts as a bridge between the raster Windows graphics and the vector 3D graphics here. Output primitives, the topic of Chapter 6, are also coupled to the canvas. Chapter 7 concludes Part II with the vector matrix, and viewing system functions essential to any 3D library. These functions must exist for construction of the M3D modeler support services in Part III to succeed. Once you have this material under your belt, Part III will be all that remains between you and the ability to generate nice 3D graphics images.

Figure 3-16.   Part II Topical Road Map

DLLs

	WLib	G3DLib Drawingn Surface	G3DLib General Support	G3DLib Primitives and Attributes	G3DLib Vectors	G3DLib Matrices	G3DLib Viewing
Chapter 4	●						
Chapter 5		●	●				
Chapter 6				●			
Chapter 7					●	●	●

Figure 3-17 is the topical road map for Part III. There are two sets of elements — functional in the support library and structural within the modeler — shown in relation to each other. Where detailed coverage of these topics fits in is also shown. Chapter 8, "Modeling Architecture, the Modeling Support Services, and Description Languages," and Chapter 9, "3D Objects," are both devoted to front-end topics on all fronts. Chapter 10, "Polygons and Rays," is concerned with the balance of the core functions. Finally, Chapter 11, "Implementing the 3D Modeler," completes the architectural and functional elements that make up the modeler.

Figure 3-17.   Topical Road Map for Part III

	M3D			Modeler			
	Front End	**Core Functions**	**Post Processing**	**Front End**	**Lookups, Objects**	**Mapping Functions**	**MVC State Mechanism**
Chapter 8	●			●	●		●
Chapter 9	●	●		●	●	●	
Chapter 10		●			●	●	●
Chapter 11		●	●		●	●	●

4 WLib Library Construction

In This Chapter

- Key library issues and WLib contents, including Kernel, GDI, and User issues.
- Beginning of the demo program sequence that continues until Part III.

Introduction

We have an easy-to-understand global strategy for the Windows services library (WLib) — provide policy-free primitives. We will partition this library into Kernel, GDI, and User services, as illustrated in the decomposition diagram in Figure 4-1, which parallels Windows' own main components. The source contained here is shown in Table 4-1, repeated from Chapter 3.

The name *Kernel* implies the core, or the heart; error handling and memory management can certainly be described with this term. With our watchword being "policy-free," these are lightweight services, since the cost of using them and the mental model they force on you are minimal.

Figure 4-1.   WLib First-Order Decomposition

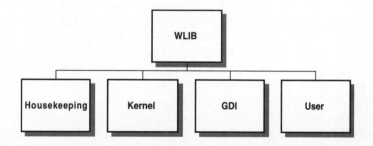

Table 4-1. WLib Source Modules

Files	Description
WLib Housekeeping	
wl_init.c,wl_init.h	library global initialization
wl_term.c,wl_term.h	library global termination
wl_err.c,wl_err.h	library error reporting
wl_inc.h	main include file, applications reference this
Kernel	
mem.c,mem.h	memory service layer
err_hndler.h	TRY/CATCH macros
GDI	
color.c,color.h	color systems
palette.c,palette.h	palette services
bitmap.c,bitmap.h	bitmap services
dib.c,dib.h	DIB services
file.c,file.h	file I/O for DIBs and bitmaps
print.c,print.h	printing for bitmaps
User	
clipbrd.c,clipbrd.h	clipboard copy
mouse.c,mouse.h	mouse selection rectangle

Similarly, our GDI services attempt to incur a minimum of overhead while providing their features. The color services include several color-mixing models and conversion routines, and let you program color independent of the Windows implementation. In the 8-bit color world, you must use the palette services that GDI provides to gain access to colors beyond the reserved or "system" colors. If you don't use palettes and a palette-based specification system, all you'll get are dithered colors. For this reason, it's desirable to have a generic manipulation of Windows' palette capability in GDI services.

While palettes assure correct coloration, bitmaps are used as the fundamental drawing surface. Bitmaps and palettes working together are a powerful combination. These two service categories are where we start to really use our strategy of instance management and instance operations as a standard interface. Creation, copying, reading, writing, and destroying are all important support routines. In this case, they are simply wrappers around GDI bitmap objects. In future service categories, we'll extend this approach to structures of our own devising.

Printing a bitmap and making it look good are also very important. We'll get into an approach to printing that is slightly more involved than the basic print cycle you get in all beginning Windows programming books. This will give you better results, and will be the foundation of the print routines in WLib.

Mouse and clipboard support, components of user services, go hand in hand, as I discussed in Chapter 3. Selection is one of the primary uses that can be made of the mouse. The classic selection method is to use a "rubber-band" rectangle to indicate the selected region. This rubber-banding allows good visual runtime feedback. Rubber-banding is the only component we're concerned with of mouse services.

The clipboard is used for data sharing. As you make images, you'll have two important pieces of data to share — the bitmap and the palette that together represent an image. Copying images to the clipboard is a basic data-interchange facility.

Packaging is as important as implementation. Windows gives you the option of using dynamic link libraries (DLLs) in addition to the standard object library packaging. DLLs provide shareable services, which are available to multiple applications or instances with all clients sharing one copy of DLL code in memory. The WLib is implemented as a DLL to share with both the G3DLib and the modeler application.

Using the DLL vehicle, the library also provides services to end-user programmers. You, of course, will be the first end-user programmer of these library services, when we construct G3DLib, starting in Chapter 5. DLL delivery means worrying about DLL startup and termination, a housekeeping duty.

These are the services provided in WLib. Take a look at the detailed decomposition diagram shown in Figure 4-2.

Figure 4-2.   Second-Order WLib Decomposition

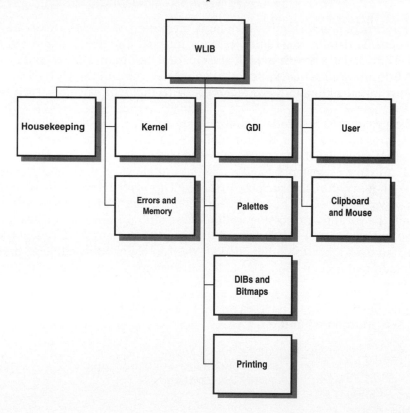

WLib Library Housekeeping

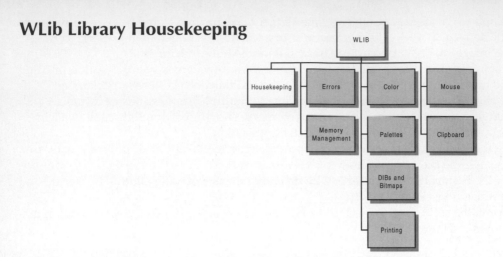

Before we leap into actual service subsystem implementation, we need to take care of some small, library-specific details. Most libraries have internal initialization and termination requirements. They usually have a default startup, and all libraries must contain and export a stub **WEP** routine. This is explicitly taken into account in the DLL shell, and you simply add your initialization and termination code to that template code each time you need a new DLL.

One nice feature of the shell code is a library-specific name in the assembler startup. When the generator process is run, this function is renamed with the library prefix. When you have to debug multiple DLLs, a feature like this can come in very handy. In the case of the WLib DLL, the library instance handle is set at initialization time, and global strings that are very similar in nature and purpose to the shell app global strings are set up as well. After that, all service subsystems have a shot at initialization. While in this case these subsystems actually perform no processing, calling these stub routines minimizes the turbulence of changes. For now, all subsystems contain a stub initialization function and the library startup invokes this "do-nothing code." You can change this either to disable the stub calls or to add real initialization code to the subsystems when you need it. See Listing 4-1 for *WL_Main*.

Listing 4-1.   WL_Main in wl_init.c

```
int CALLBACK          WL_Main(HANDLE hModule,
                          WORD wDataSeg, WORD cbHeapSize,
                          LPSTR lpszCmdLine) {
   hLibInst = hModule;
   if ( cbHeapSize )
      UnlockData(hLibInst);
   LoadString(hModule, IDS_DLLNAME,      gszDLLName,
   sizeof(gszDLLName));
```

```
    LoadString(hModule, IDS_LOADSTRFAIL,  gszLoadStrFail,
sizeof(gszLoadStrFail));
    LoadString(hModule, IDS_ALLOCFAILURE, gszLockErrorMsg,
sizeof(gszLockErrorMsg));
    LoadString(hModule, IDS_LOCKFAILURE,  gszAllocErrorMsg,
sizeof(gszAllocErrorMsg));
    WL_Error_Init();
    WL_Mem_Init
    WL_Color_Init();
    WL_Pal_Init();
    WL_Bitmap_Init();
    WL_DIB_Init();
    WL_File_Init();
    WL_Print_Init();
    WL_Mouse_Init();
    WL_Clipbrd_Init();
    return (bInit);
}
```

Termination code is even simpler. In Windows 3.1 or Win31, the SDK documentation clarified the details on **WEP** functions and exit codes, and here we've explicitly coded for both releasing the DLL and system exit. For these exit-code cases, all service sub-system termination handlers are invoked. Notice the symmetry with the initialization handler. Once again the termination handlers are stubs. See Listing 4-2 for the **WEP** code.

Listing 4-2.   WEP in wl_exit.c for wl.dll

```
int WINAPI WEP (int fSystemExit){
    switch(fSystemExit)
    {
        case WEP_FREE_DLL:
        case WEP_SYSTEM_EXIT:
          if ( bInit )
          {
              WL_Mouse_Term();
              WL_Clipbrd_Term();
              WL_Print_Term();
              WL_File_Term();
              WL_DIB_Term();
              WL_Bitmap_Term();
              WL_Pal_Term();
              WL_Color_Term();
              WL_Mem_Term();
              WL_Error_Term();
          }
          return 1;
          break;
    }
}
```

WLib Kernel Services: Error

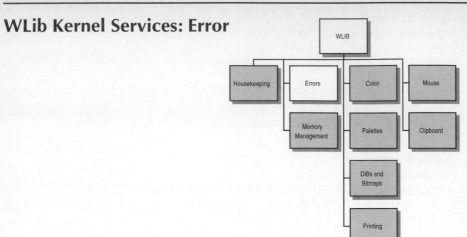

A standard error scheme is an important component of a well-designed system. The scheme implemented here includes both a reporting mechanism and a policy for a structural style that code should conform to. Creating the error-reporting/handling layer early and incorporating it wherever applicable is critical to robust, production-quality code development. Another side effect of designing the error layer early is that it forces some decisions that significantly affect the structural shape of the system. This programming style combined with the reporting mechanism ensures that the error is reported with some detail, and, wherever it can, makes recovery possible.

Installing exception and signal handlers in this DLL and the G3DLib is too much policy for the DLLs, so I've deferred it to the application. The modeler employs Toolhelp exception handlers and floating-point signal handlers to define policy. The issue of balance between the DLL and the application is discussed in more detail on the Microsoft Developer Network Services CD in the article "Floating Point in Windows," which has been available since Disk Four. If you really want to have DLL-level handlers, read this article.

Deciding what constitutes an error is our first order of business. WLib gives us the basic building blocks of the Windows environment. In this layer, we can directly use underlying Windows API calls and resources. Our primary concern, then, is unguarded resource allocation. There are two kinds of resources used here: heap-based memory objects, and GDI objects (especially bitmaps, brushes, and palettes). Failures with these resource types are defined as error classes, so all we need to do is fix on an error handling strategy to guard these resource allocations.

Guarding resource allocation is easiest when you use a standard structural style. This provides a basis for implementing the code: conform to the style and all will be well. Once an error occurs, it has to "hit" the interface and be presented to the user or reported in some way. By using this structural style, we explicitly code for error handling at the point of resource allocation, and report any that occur. These two pieces, the error handling and reporting, together are what is generally known as "error handling." See Listing 4-3 for the error API that provides this functionality.

Listing 4-3.   Error API in wl_err.c and errhandler.h

```
// error reporting
BOOL WINAPI WL_Error_Init(void);
BOOL WINAPI WL_Error_Process(DWORD dwErrorCode);
void        WL_Error_Report(WORD wErrorType,LPSTR lpszMsg);
BOOL WINAPI WL_Error_Term(void);
// error handling
TRY
CATCH
ENDCATCH
EXCEPT
```

Providing a structuring style and a reporting mechanism does force your hand, with the benefit of simplification and standardization. This is what is known as a *mental model*. When we give a programmer tools that make it easy to implement a scheme, the scheme is more likely to get used.

Error Reporting

Guaranteeing operation of the error-reporting mechanism in low-resource situations is a developer-friendly feature. The error-reporting mechanism responds with at least some minimal error message instead of just failing and making matters worse. To achieve this goal, certain key error string values are cached in global variables. The cached strings use IDC_, while normal error strings use IDS_. Then the final reporting routine, here *WL_Error_Report*, always reports something. But it's important to note that you must cache error conditions for allocating and locking memory to avoid a catch-22 in the error handler.

The failure of **LoadString** itself is another candidate for caching. This function is shown in Listing 4-4.

Listing 4-4.   WL_Error_Report in wl_err.c

```
void        WL_Error_Report(WORD wErrorType,LPSTR lpszMsg)
{
   LPSTR lpszErrorMsg;

   switch( wErrorType ){
        case IDC_ALLOCFAIL:

            lpszErrorMsg=gszAllocErrorMsg;
            break;
        case IDC_LOCKFAIL:

            lpszErrorMsg=gszLockErrorMsg;
            break;
        case IDC_LOADSTRINGFAIL:

            lpszErrorMsg=gszLoadStrFail;
            break;
```

Listing 4-4.   (cont.)

```
        default:    //if wErrorType = NULL, already loaded
            lpszErrorMsg=lpszMsg;
            break;
    }
  MessageBeep(MB_ICONEXCLAMATION);
  MessageBox(NULL, (LPSTR)lpszErrorMsg, gszDLLName,
            MB_ICONEXCLAMATION | MB_OK);

    return;
}
```

Routine *WL_Error_Report* actually hits the user interface with an error message. *WL_Error_Process* has responsibility for processing error codes and retrieving resource strings from the string table. It attempts to use the error-code value, map it to a string ID, and load a string from the string table in the resource fork using **LoadString**. If it succeeds, the error is reported using **MessageBeep** and then **MessageBox**. If the load fails, the failure is reported using one of the cached string values (see Listing 4-5). This basic concept is used in both DLLs and applications.

Listing 4-5.   WL_Error_Process in wl_err.c with General Errors Shown

```
void FAR PASCAL WL_Error_Process(DWORD dwErrorCode)
{
   WORD   wStringID;

   switch(dwErrorCode)
   {
//
// general
//
        case GENERR_ALLOCFAILURE:
            wStringID=IDS_ALLOCFAILURE;
            break;
        case GENERR_LOCKFAILURE:
            wStringID=IDS_LOCKFAILURE;
            break;
        case GENERR_LOADSTRFAIL:
            wStringID=IDS_LOADSTRFAIL;
            break;
        case GENERR_FINDFILEFAIL:
            wStringID=IDS_FINDFILEFAIL;
            break;
        case GENERR_LOADFILEFAIL:
            wStringID=IDS_LOADFILEFAIL;
            break;
```

```
//
        case 0:    //User may have hit CANCEL or we got a *very* random
error
        default:
           return;
    }
    if (!LoadString(hLibInst, wStringID,
       gszBuffer, sizeof(gszBuffer)))
    {
        WL_Error_Report(IDC_LOADSTRINGFAIL,NULL);
        return;
    }

    WL_Error_Report(NULL,gszBuffer);

    return;
}
```

Error Handling

An error-handling strategy coded in adherence to policy benefits from a uniform feel to the code, but may suffer from some heavy-handedness. If you develop this style first, you'll eliminate the need for retrofitting. At this point, it's less important to worry about the exact nature of a coding style that uses an error-handling flavor than it is to make the decision to use one.

My first decision was to use the little-known functions **Catch** and **Throw** to implement a recovery mechanism. Lately, **Catch** and **Throw** have gotten some attention in technical articles. These functions work much like **setjmp** and **longjmp,** and can be the basis of reasonably useful error-handling code.

Wrapping them in macros makes it easier to use them. Both C++ and NT give us a model for these macros. The second edition of Bjarne Stroustrup's book *The C++ Programming Language* (Addison-Wesley, 1991) described an exception-handling mechanism using the keywords TRY and CATCH. Microsoft's Windows NT implements TRY and EXCEPT.

Implementing TRY, CATCH, and ENDCATCH macros allows us to mimic the structured exception handling of C++ and Windows NT. Because these macros are very similar to the C++ and NT models, we'll be able to port this code to either of these underlying mechanisms without much effort.

The **TRY** macro, seen in Listing 4-6, hides the details of calling **Catch**. An automatic is used for the **CATCHBUF** and the error return value. It calls **Catch**, then prepares the code body for the if block. The **CATCH** macro, seen in Listing 4-7, hides the end of the code body block and the beginning of the error-catching block with the else that matches the if after the **Catch**. The **END_CATCH** macro, seen in Listing 4-8, ends the error-handling block. All blocks that perform resource allocations are then structured to look like the example in Listing 4-9.

Listing 4-6.   TRY Macro in errhndler.h

```
      CATCHINFO ci;

#define TRY          \
{                                                          \
   int        err;         \
   err = Catch((LPCATCHBUF)&ci.state); \
   if ( err == 0 ) \
{
```

Listing 4-7.   CATCH Macro in errhndler.h

```
#define CATCH             \
   } \
   else      \
   {
```

Listing 4-8.   ENDCATCH Macro in errhndler.h

```
#define END_CATCH   \
   }  \
}
```

Listing 4-9.   Example TRY/CATCH Block

```
TRY
{
  if ( some error )
  {
    Throw((LPCATCHBUF)ci.state,errorcode);
  }
  return TRUE;
}
CATCH
{
   switch(errorcode)
   {
      case someerror:
            handle_error();
            break;
      default
            return NULL;
            break;
   }
}
END_CATCH
```

The **TRY** block can only be exited by successful completion. The result of any failure within the if block is a call to **Throw**, which causes the **CATCH** block to gain control. The application programmer calls the Windows function **Throw** with the ci.state variable. This "invisible" definition is a pain, but we can live with it since it's always the same.

This work could be further hidden by asking the DLL to manage instances and use a stack of **CATCHBUF**s along with a function to hide the **Throw** call and the variable. This is an area for significant research and expansion by any of you who feel adventurous, but this functionality suffices for our immediate purposes. Every module that includes this header can use these macros.

WLib Kernel Services: Memory Management

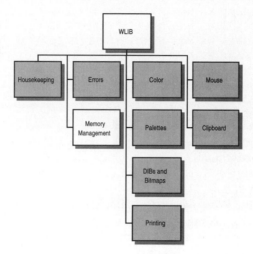

The goal of our memory-management layer is to provide lightweight services that will isolate the body of the code from any underlying implementation. This enables us to transparently add memory tracing or subsegment allocation. Windows has a hard limit of 8192 selectors available for memory allocation, because all Windows applications share one Local Descriptor Table (LDT) in enhanced mode. Any really serious application has to deal with this issue. The subsegment allocation I just mentioned is one solution, but for now we'll ignore this issue. We'll deal with the selector-limit problem when it hits us down the road, instead of immediately, but it is a reasonable simplification to begin with. In general, an application cannot assume that it will be able to get more than half of the available selectors, or 4192. For our purposes, even when we consider the overhead in the application and the libraries, that still leaves a few selectors for the scene and its objects. The details of object representation and implementation are what will more closely determine our absolute limit here, and we'll revisit this issue in Chapter 9. However, this is an important limitation for you to know about, in general, so that you fully understand the design decision that affects the library, and the limitations this imposes.

Windowsx.h, which is used heavily in the production of the shells, again provides a set of macros that manage pointers. Basing our routines on these macros will gain us the portability of **STRICT**, at the cost of assuming protected mode only and using pointers instead of handles (Windows 3.1).

Once again, we defer our ability to write subsystem initialization and termination routines. If and when tracking, reporting, or subsegment allocation are added, we would have to revisit this decision. Allocating, resizing or reallocating, retrieving the handle, and freeing are the basic services that a memory layer should provide. The API contains functions that provide these services as shown in Listing 4-10.

Listing 4-10. Memory API in mem.c

```
//memory management
BOOL        WINAPI WL_Mem_Init(void);
LPVOID      WINAPI WL_Mem_Alloc(UINT flags, DWORD size);
LPVOID      WINAPI WL_Mem_Realloc(LPVOID lpv,DWORD size,UINT flags);
HGLOBAL     WINAPI WL_Mem_Handle(LPVOID lpv);
HGLOBAL     WINAPI WL_Mem_Free(LPVOID lpv);
BOOL        WINAPI WL_Mem_Term(void);
```

The allocation and reallocation functions do perform resource allocation, but they're not coded using the TRY/CATCH style. Libraries have a hard time anticipating exactly what to do in a low-level case like this. They leave it up to the application to do the allocation within the scope of the TRY/CATCH block. Here, *GlobalAllocPtr* is simply called directly, as shown in Listing 4-11. The usage of these functions is more important than all the gory implementation details. Listing 4-12 shows how to use *WL_Mem_Alloc*. It looks remarkably like using the Windows global allocator, doesn't it? This means the learning curve is nil. Paralleling this, Listing 4-13 shows how to deallocate memory using *WL_Mem_Free*, a simple process of passing in the pointer that is no longer needed.

Listing 4-11. WL_Mem_Alloc Implementation

```
HPVOID WINAPI WL_Mem_Alloc(UINT flags, DWORD size)
{

    return (HPVOID)GlobalAllocPtr(flags,size);
}
```

Listing 4-12. Sample Memory Allocation Block

```
//
lpbb        = WL_Mem_Alloc(GHND,sizeof(BMPBUFF));
```

Listing 4-13. Memory De-Allocation Call

```
//
WL_Mem_Free(lpbb);
```

The other members of this API mimic the usage of the Windows global allocators very closely, and because of this I don't need to show them all individually. As you encounter them in the body of the code, just remember they are thin wrappers that perform exactly like the Windows routines. The difference is that when the selector limit begins to plague your imaging, you can rewrite the allocation layer to perform what is known as "sub-allocation." Inserting this layer lets you make this significant change without affecting client code — always a good thing.

WLib GDI Services: Color

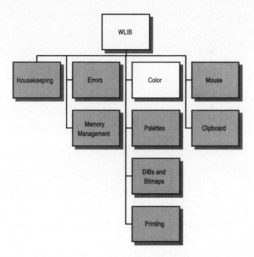

The foundation of all of our color support consists of the basics of color specification systems or mixing models, and services that provide conversion between these models and the GDI color model. The palette services and specifications in the modeler, the color lookup table, the quantization code — all these are clients of the underlying color code. The color API is shown in Listing 4-14. To understand color, you need to understand color mixing models.

Listing 4-14. Color API in color.c

```
// color
BOOL    WINAPI WL_Color_Init(void);
BOOL    WINAPI WL_Color_RGBtoCRT( RGB FAR * rgbV, CRT FAR * crtV );
BOOL    WINAPI WL_Color_CRTtoRGB( CRT FAR * crtV, RGB FAR * rgbV );
BOOL    WINAPI WL_Color_RGBtoCMY( RGB FAR * rgbV, CMY FAR * cmyV );
BOOL    WINAPI WL_Color_CMYtoRGB( CMY FAR * cmyV, RGB FAR * rgbV );
BOOL    WINAPI WL_Color_RGBtoHSV( RGB FAR * rgbV, HSV FAR * hsvV );
BOOL    WINAPI WL_Color_HSVtoRGB( HSV FAR * hsvV, RGB FAR * rgbV );
BOOL    WINAPI WL_Color_RGBtoHLS( RGB FAR * rgbV, HLS FAR * hlsV );
BOOL    WINAPI WL_Color_HLStoRGB( HLS FAR * hlsV, RGB FAR * rgbV );
BOOL    WINAPI WL_Color_Term(void);
```

Color Specification Systems

Color mixing models are a way to characterize color samples in an orderly manner, so that the relations between colors are obvious, and to provide a framework for the specification of colors. Color specification systems are an implementation of specific mixing models.

There are two types of color mixing models: hardware-oriented and user-oriented. Hardware-oriented systems depend, in some form, on mixing red, green, and blue components in a Cartesian system. Two hardware-oriented models are in common use: RGB (Red-Green-Blue) and CMY (Cyan-Magenta-Yellow). We'll provide services for both of these models.

User-oriented color systems are based on the artists' concepts of tint, shade, and tone. User-oriented color systems attempt to present a color specification system that is both more perceptually uniform and easier to use. HSV (Hue-Saturation-Value) and HLS (Hue-Lightness-Saturation) are common examples of user-oriented systems, and we'll also develop their library routines in this section.

When using any color specification system, you must differentiate from the truly hardware-dependent specification mechanism (in this case GDI and its idealization of the Cartesian-based model). This GDI color space, called CRT (Cathode-Ray-Tube) here in reference to its hardware dependency, is limited to integral values from 0 to 255 for any individual component and a DWORD in total. This makes the transformation from a floating-point specification system into CRT space potentially an information-losing proposition. Delaying the transformation of color specifications into CRT color space until the last possible moment maintains the information's integrity until the screen pixels are actually set to a value. This means you must carry around values in data types other than the native Windows RGB; you must also invoke a conversion routine at brush creation time. For now, I'll defer the detailed consideration of the RGB-to-CRT (and back) conversions until I've discussed all the abstract systems. This will let you consider color specification in the abstract without thinking about device-dependencies, which helps your implementation "hide" physical details from most of the code base. First we will develop all the other color specification systems and their respective conversions in terms of RGB; only then will we define RGB and the CRT translations.

Hardware-Oriented Systems

Hardware-oriented mixing models are directly related to the hardware (obviously), whether screen or printer. RGB is a screen mixing model and CMY is a printer mixing model. They are based on additive and subtractive models, respectively. You can meet most graphics applications' needs by providing both a screen and a printer mixing model.

RGB
The red-green-blue (RGB) color mixing model (see Figure 4-3) is a simple and direct specification mechanism that is directly related to the physical properties of monitors. In this model, red, green, and blue phosphors are combined according to a Cartesian coordinate system structure usually referred to as the "RGB Cube." This system uses floating-point representations for the red, green, and blue components (see Listing 4-15). The data type

that handles these values simply uses floats for the individual components. RGB is defined in the interval [0,1] in the abstract; conversion routines to and from GDI's representation are simple, based on the mapping between the two spaces as shown in Listing 4-16. At this point, I'll delay consideration of the details of the RGB-to-CRT conversions.

Figure 4-3. RGB's Floating-Point Color Cube

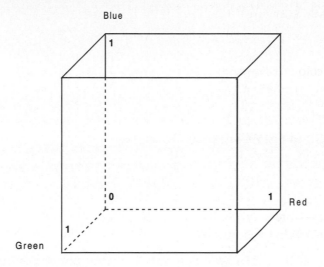

Listing 4-15. RGB Structure

```
typedef struct {
        float        fRed;
        float        fGreen;
        float        fBlue;
} RGB;
```

Listing 4-16.   RGB-to-CRT Conversion Formulas

```
RGBvalue = CRTvalue / 255;
CRTvalue = RGBvalue * 255;
```

CMY

The alternate hardware-based color description system CMY is printer-oriented. CMY(see Figure 4-4) is a variant that uses subtractive, rather than additive, colors. The CMY model is used in many hard-copy devices that depend on the concept of using pigments on paper to represent color. This system is sometimes modified slightly and called CMYK, where K is a black ink, rather than depending on a combination of the other three inks to produce black. Floating-point values once again represent the constituent components. We follow good practice and exactly parallel what we did for RGB, so we define a data structure encapsulating the information and conversion routines that convert CMY to and from RGB, as seen in Listings 4-17 and 4-18. Now that we've defined a data structure and a mathematical relation, we need to develop the service routines that provide the actual conversion services. Using the naming scheme for service routines, the new routines are named *WL_Color_CMYtoRGB* and *WL_Color_RGBtoCMY*. As you see in Listing 4-19, these routines are a straightforward implementation of the formulas from Listing 4-18 and their implied inverses.

Listing 4-17.   CMY Structure

```
typedef struct {
        float          fCyan;
        float          fMagenta;
        float          fYellow;
} CMY;
```

Listing 4-18.   RGB-to-CMY Conversion Formulas

```
Cyan    = 1 - Red;
Magenta = 1 - green;
Yellow  = 1 - Blue;
```

Listing 4-19.   CMY Service Routines

```
BOOL WINAPI WL_Color_RGBtoCMY( RGB FAR * rgbV, CMY FAR * cmyV )
{

        // convert RGB to CMY
         cmyV->fCyan    = (float)1.00 - rgbV->fRed;
         cmyV->fMagenta = (float)1.00 - rgbV->fGreen;
         cmyV->fYellow  = (float)1.00 - rgbV->fBlue;

         return( TRUE );

}

BOOL WINAPI WL_Color_CMYtoRGB( CMY FAR * cmyV, RGB FAR * rgbV )
{

        // convert CMY to RGB
        rgbV->fRed   = (float)1.00 - cmyV->fCyan;
        rgbV->fGreen = (float)1.00 - cmyV->fMagenta;
        rgbV->fBlue  = (float)1.00 - cmyV->fYellow;

        return( TRUE );

}
```

Figure 4-4. CMY Color Cube

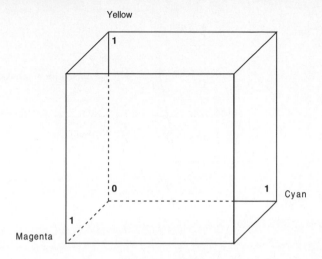

User-Oriented Systems

User-oriented color systems are based upon artists' conceptual models and psychological perception models, rather than a hardware dependency. HSV (sometimes called HSB) and HLS are two widely used user-oriented models. HSV and HLS are related in that both attempt to address deficiencies in RGB related to visual uniformity and ease-of-use. Unfortunately, they are not completely successful in that respect. These systems are not perceptually uniform, so the measured and perceived distance between two colors is not always equal. For instance, it is possible to define colors that appear the same, but that have different values for the respective parameters. However, both of these systems are easier to use for color specification than RGB or CMY.

HSV

HSV uses an adaptation of the perceptual color model to give you a way to specify colors based upon the parameters' hue, saturation, and value. From a topological standpoint, HSV can be best described as a six-sided cone, or *hexcone*. The value parameter is represented by a vertical line through the central axis of the cone, with the top representing white (V = 1) and the bottom representing black (V = 0). Value (V) thus represents the lightness or *luminance* component. Each vertex of the hexcone corresponds to one of the primary or secondary colors and is referenced by hue in degrees (red is at 0 degrees, green at 120, etc.). The remaining parameter, saturation, is represented as a vector that extends horizontally from the value axis and corresponds to the purity or *vividness* of the color, and its variation from neutral gray (0) to the most vibrant (1). See Figure 4-5 for the visual representation of this concept.

Figure 4-5. HSV Hex Cone

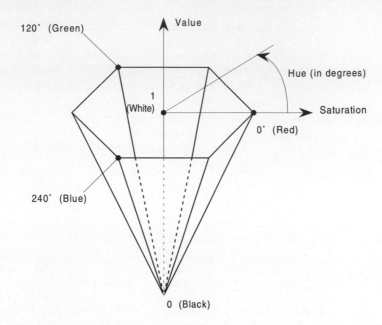

Again, we'll follow good practice and parallel our setup with RGB and CMY. First, we define a data structure as shown in Listing 4-20. Once again, this data structure provides a floating-point representation for the components.

Before you read further about implementing HSV, you need to understand the meaning of *achromatic* and *chromatic* light: your implementation must handle the details of both cases. *Achromatic* light is black, white, and shades of gray. Intensity counts! *Chromatic* light has color. We'll implement conversion routines for the relationships implied by the hexcone in functions **WL_Color_HSVtoRGB** and **WL_Color_RGBtoHSV**, respectively, but I'm not going to show these conversions here. The bulk of the algorithm you need to implement for this is shown in *Computer Graphics: Principles and Practice* by James D. Foley and Andries Van Dam (Addison-Wesley, 1990). The code is also contained in the libraries on your disk.

Listing 4-20.   HSV Structure

```
typedef struct {
        float           fHue;
        float           fSaturation;
        float           fValue;
} HSV;
```

HLS

HLS is another artists' conceptual system developed by Tektronix circa 1978. This time, color is defined in terms of hue, lightness, and saturation. From a topological standpoint, HLS can be best described as a double-ended cone, or a hexcone stacked on top of another hexcone. Hue is the angle around the vertical of the double hexcone, with red at 0 degrees. Some HLS systems use blue at 0 degrees, but we'll use red to maintain consistency with the HSV definition. The colors around the perimeter appear counterclockwise: red, yellow, green, cyan, blue, and magenta. This is the same order as in the HSV single hexcone. In fact, you can think of HLS as a stretching of HSV, in which white is deformed upwards to create the upper hexcone. Value becomes lightness and ranges from 0 at the base to 1 at the apex. As in HSV saturation is measured radially from the vertical axis. See Figure 4-6.

Figure 4-6. HLS Double Hexcone

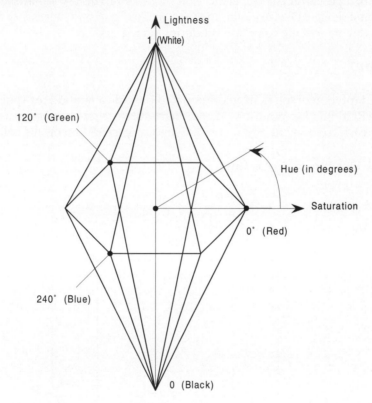

Just as we did for RGB, CMY, and HSV, we'll define a data structure and conversion routines. The data structure, shown in Listing 4-21, again provides a floating-point representation for its components. We then implement the conversion formulas through the functions *WL_Color_HLStoRGB* and *WL_Color_RGBtoHLS*, which are again not shown.

Listing 4-21. HLS Structure

```
typedef struct {
      float         fHue;
      float         fLightness;
      float         fSaturation;
} HLS;
```

This completes our overview of the abstract color-specification systems, and we've constructed most of a powerful color-specification subsystem. The key remaining piece is rendering color on a device. Device Color, the next section, gives the necessary final touches: conversion to device-specific color and rendering on the display.

Device Color

GDI uses an adaptation of the RGB color model to provide a method for specifying colors. GDI maps the RGB floating-point-based system into an integer-based system with a range of 0 to 255 for each component. See Figure 4-7 for a representation of this color cube.

Figure 4-7. GDI's Integer Color Cube

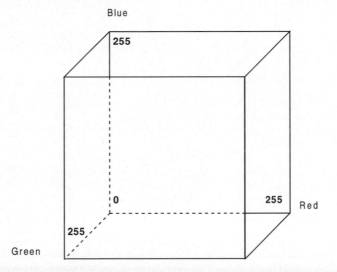

It's natural to call this the CRT color-specification system, since that is essentially what it is. We'll again follow good practice and parallel what we did for all the other specification systems, beginning with defining a data structure as shown in Listing 4-22. This is the first non-floating-point representation, and it uses a DWORD for the components of the color. This is consistent with the internal GDI representation, which is shown in Figure 4-8. Note that this is the internal form based on the **RGB** macro and a **COLORREF**. The two other macros used to generate RGB values, **PALETTERGB** and **PALETTEINDEX**, are a variation that we'll consider during our discussion of Windows' palettes.

Listing 4-22. CRT Structure

```
typedef struct
{
        BYTE            cRed;
        BYTE            cGreen;
        BYTE            cBlue;
        BYTE            cUnused;
} CRT;
```

Figure 4-8.   Internal Form of RGB in GDI

You have the data representation for CRT colors and an understanding of the relationship between these two specification systems, so what do the conversion routines look like? As shown in Listing 4-23, they implement the simple relation that was shown in Listing 4-16. Now you can define a color in terms of RGB, CMY, HSV, or HLS *and display it*. To render the color from any system other than RGB, first convert the color to RGB, then to CRT.

Listing 4-23.   WL_Color_CRTtoRGB and WL_Color_RGBtoCRT

```
BOOL WINAPI WL_Color_CRTtoRGB( CRT FAR * crtV, RGB FAR * rgbV )
{

        // convert CRT to RGB
        rgbV->fRed   = (float)crtV->cRed    / 255.00;
        rgbV->fGreen = (float)crtV->cGreen  / 255.00;
        rgbV->fBlue  = (float)crtV->cBlue   / 255.00;

        return( TRUE );
}
BOOL WINAPI WL_Color_RGBtoCRT( RGB FAR * rgbV, CRT FAR * crtV )
{

        // convert RGB to CRT
         crtV->cUnused = 0;
         crtV->cRed    = (BYTE)rgbV->fRed    * 255.00;
         crtV->cGreen  = (BYTE)rgbV->fGreen  * 255.00;
         crtV->cBlue   = (BYTE)rgbV->fBlue   * 255.00;

        return( TRUE );

}
```

We've completed developing four color-specification systems: two hardware-oriented and two user-oriented. We have mapped these systems into device-dependent GDI colors through the CRT color abstraction. Table 4-2 summarizes some values for each color system.

Table 4-2.   Sample Color Values

Color	RGB	CMY	HSV	HLS	CRT
Black	0,0,0	1,1,1	0,0.0,0.0	0,0.0,0.0	0, 0, 0
White	1,1,1	0,0,0	0,0.0,1.0	0,1.0,0.0	255, 255,255
Green	0,1,0	1,0,1	120,1.0.1.0	120,0.5,1.0	0, 255, 0

There are, however, a couple of problems you should be aware of. As Charles Petzold has so aptly noted in his "Environments" column in *PC* magazine, if you don't use the Palette Manager, you only get 16 colors on VGA and 20 colors on 8514 displays when using 256-color drivers. Even more interesting, as Petzold pointed out in his column "Color Complexities and Craziness" in *PC* magazine (April 30, 1991, Vol. 11, Issue 7), color selection is not as straightforward as it seems. In brief, selecting colors with the Palette Manager is not consistent with normal color selection, so don't mix palette-based and RGB-based color selection. This is also discussed on the MSDN CD in "Tech Articles: GDI." The strategy here is to use palette-based color specification to get at colors other than the system colors and to get consistent color selection.

WLib GDI Services: Palettes

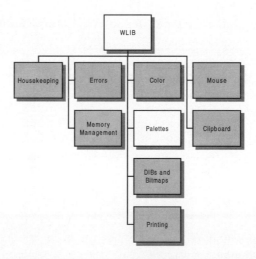

Our next goal is to get at the rest of those colors, because exacting as this discussion was, you can still only see 16 colors on the screen for VGA and 20 for 8514/A in 8-bitmode without palettes. While this is initially quite frustrating, the requirement that you use the Palette Manager to manipulate colors almost makes sense in a windowed environment. Palettes were new to Windows in version 3.0 and were a welcome addition. Now, with 256-

color video cards so common, you can get appealing images in this environment with just a little bit of work. With card/driver combinations that provide higher colors, this work will not be sacrificed.

To illustrate the power of palettes, we'll use a demo program to display the base RGB-color cube and then recast it using palettes. This shows the very visible improvement in color-manipulation abilities you get by using palettes. Here, the split between application and library becomes apparent. The application needs to create a palette. So how can the library understand this ahead of time? The answer is that it can't. At this level of services, all we can provide is a shell for creating and destroying structures without knowledge of the contents of those structures.   Palette contents and more application-specific palette management are policy issues that must be left to specific applications and their programmers to determine what is needed. The palette API is shown in Listing 4-24.

Listing 4-24. Palette API in palette.c

```
//palettes
BOOL     WINAPI WL_Pal_Init(void);
BOOL     WINAPI WL_Pal_Create(LPLOGPALETTE lpPal)(void);
BOOL     WINAPI WL_Pal_Destroy(HPALETTE hp);
int      WINAPI WL_Pal_MakeIdentityPal(LPLOGPALETTE pPal)
int      WINAPI WL_Pal_ColorsInPalette(HPALETTE hPal);
HPALETTE WINAPI WL_Pal_CreateDIBPalette (HANDLE hDIB);
HPALETTE WINAPI WL_Pal_CopyPaletteChangingFlags(HPALETTE hPal,
BYTE bNewFlag);
void     WINAPI WL_Pal_AnimatePalette (HWND hWnd, HPALETTE hPal);
BOOL     WINAPI WL_Pal_Term(void);;
```

Windows Palette Fundamentals

Remember that there are two aspects to the Palette Manager and using palettes:

- palette object creation and management, and
- application palette-handling policy.

Application policy has no place in a library, so I've deferred the discussion of palette messages and how an application handles them until we're ready to examine an application using palettes. The palette object, its creation, and its management are our concern at this point.

The **LOGPALETTE** structure is the hub around which the palette routines operate. The **LOGPALETTE** struct contains a header with a version flag and the numentries count for numentries **PALETTEENTRY** elements, as shown in Listing 4-25. The **PALETTEENTRY** elements are variable-sized structures, whose sizes are determined at run-time (as discussed in Chapter 3 under Extensible APIs).

Listing 4-25.   LOGPALETTE and PALETTEENTRY Data Structures

```
typedef struct tagLOGPALETTE {   /* lgpl */
    WORD          palVersion;
    WORD          palNumEntries;
    PALETTEENTRY palPalEntry[1];
} LOGPALETTE;

typedef struct {      /* pe */
    BYTE   peRed;
    BYTE   peGreen;
    BYTE   peBlue;
    BYTE   peFlags;
} PALETTEENTRY;
```

We'll populate this and call **CreatePalette** for a handle, as you might expect. **SelectPalette** enables the palette for a particular DC. The palette is independent of any DC and can be shared across DCs, but beware — a change to a palette shared like this affects all the DCs that use that palette. There's also an important hidden implication: all the DCs used to share a palette *must* be of the same physical device type. To use the palette, the application must follow **SelectPalette** with **RealizePalettte**. The palette GDI object is deleted using **DeleteObject** as with any other GDI object.

To actually get at those colors in a DC, we use macros **PALETTEINDEX** and **PALETTERGB** to help create brushes. The **PALETTEINDEX** macro lets you select color values by index (directly, in other words), and is convenient in 256-color mode. This is especially convenient for palette animation. The **PALETTERGB** macro method is necessary for 24-bit color devices. This method selects by value, and matches to a palette, if appropriate. For this reason, the **PALETTERGB** method is our preferred solution.

Standard Palette Services

The standard interface includes allocation, deallocation, copying, and animating routines. *WL_Pal_Create* and *WL_Pal_Destroy* are wrappers around the GDI routines **CreatePalette** and **DestroyObject**, as shown in Listing 4-26. The intended usage of these routines is shown in Listings 4-27 and 4-28.

Listing 4-26.   WL_Pal_Create and WL_Pal_Destroy

```
HPALETTE WINAPI WL_Pal_Create(LPLOGPALETTE pPal)
{
    HPALETTE hp = NULL;

    hp = CreatePalette(pPal);

    return hp;
}
```

```
BOOL     WINAPI WL_Pal_Destroy(HPALETTE hp)
{

    DeleteObject(hp);
    return TRUE;
}
```

Listing 4-27.   Palette Creation Block

```
LOGPALETTE FAR * lpPal
//
... palette setup
//
 hp = WL_Pal_Create(lpPal);
//
 ...
```

Listing 4-28.   Palette Destruction Block

```
...
//
  WL_Pal_Destroy(hprgb);
//
...
```

The application initializes the entries in the variable-sized palette data structure and creates a handle to a palette object using *WL_Pal_Create*. This is a normal palette handle in all respects, and, in addition to being manipulable by this API, the normal GDI object and palette functions can still operate on it. An application de-allocates the palette using *WL_Pal_Destroy*, hiding the GDI usage.

The next function creates an identity palette. This palette has its first and last 10 entries set to the system colors. Creating an identity palette reduces the load on GDI in performing color mapping. Windows reserves a group of palette entries for a fixed number of colors. These *system colors* are used for drawing screen elements like scroll bars. Windows also uses these system colors as replacements when inactive windows request more color entries than are available in the system palette. Windows puts the system colors at the top and bottom of the system palette to ensure that logical operations (such as XOR) work correctly. Figure 4-9 shows this arrangement.

By arranging logical palettes the same way that Windows arranges the system palette, you can avoid unexpected color changes and improve the speed at which your application draws (this is even more true if you use DIBS instead of bitmaps — a modification that you could make without much difficulty at this point).

Figure 4-9.   IdentityPalette Organization

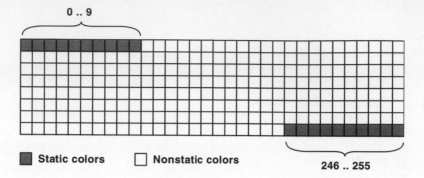

Listing 4-29 shows *WL_Pal_MakeIdentityPal*. It uses *GetSystemPaletteEntries* to force the first and last 10 entries to be "system colors."

Listing 4-29.   WL_Pal_MakeIdentityPal

```
int        WINAPI WL_Pal_MakeIdentityPal(LPLOGPALETTE pPal)
{
    HDC hdc = CreateDC("DISPLAY",NULL,NULL,NULL);
    int nNumPC, nNumSC, nNumSP,spot;

    nNumSP = GetDeviceCaps(hdc,SIZEPALETTE);
    nNumSC = GetDeviceCaps(hdc,NUMRESERVED);
    if ( nNumSC != 0 )
        num = nNumSC/2;
    else
        num = 10;
    spot = (pPal->palNumEntries-num);
    GetSystemPaletteEntries(hdc,
                        0,
                        num,
                        &(pPal->palPalEntry[0]));
    GetSystemPaletteEntries(hdc,
                        (nNumSP-num),
                        num,
                        &(pPal->palPalEntry[spot]));
    DeleteDC(hdc);
    return 0;
}
```

Animating a palette is performed by invoking *WL_Pal_Animate* as shown in Listing 4-30. Internally, this function uses a for loop (see Listing 4-31) to move entries in the data structure over a slot. Performing this action repetitively over time results in the appearance of animation.

Listing 4-30. Palette-Animating Block

```
...
//
        WL_Pal_AnimatePalette(pvwwnd->hwnd,hprgb);
//
...
```

Listing 4-31. Palette-Animation Internals Block

```
...
//
    for (i = 0;  i < wEntries - 1;  i++)
lpPalEntries[i] = lpPalEntries[i+1];
//
...
```

Copying palettes, shown in Listing 4-32, is performed using the API function *WL_Pal_CopyPaletteChangingFlags*. This function allows either simple copying or a copy that toggles the flag bits for each palette entry. To refresh your memory, I've repeated the PALETTEFLAG #defines in Listing 4-33.

Listing 4-32. Palette Duplication Block

```
...
//
  case CF_PALETTE:
      h = WL_Pal_CopyPaletteChangingFlags(hprgb, 0);
      break;
//
...
```

Listing 4-33.   Palette Entry Flag Defines

```
    /* Palette entry flags */
    #define PC_RESERVED   0x01 /*palette index used for animation*/
    #define PC_EXPLICIT   0x02 /*palette index is explicit to device*/
    #define PC_NOCOLLAPSE 0x04 /*do not match color to system palette*/
```

Each palette-using application has to decide which flags are appropriate and use them at palette setup time to initialize the flags entry.

WL_Pal_ColorsInPalette is a general-purpose routine that is used both internally and externally to the palette services. An example of a calling sequence is shown in Listing 4-34.

Listing 4-34.   WL_Pal_ColorsInPalette Usage

```
...
//
 wEntries = WL_Pal_ColorsInPalette (hPal);
//
...
```

WL_Pal_CreateDIBPalette supports the DIB-to-DDB conversion required by file I/O. Listing 4-35 shows this function taking a handle to a DIB as a parameter.

Listing 4-35.   WL_Pal_CreateDIBPalette Usage

```
...
//

*lphp = WL_Pal_CreateDIBPalette(hDIB);
//
...
```

Bitmap and DIB services are next on our agenda, so finishing up palette services with the DIB-dependent routine *WL_Pal_CreateDIBPalette* is timely. On that note, we're finished with palette services.

WLib GDI Services: Bitmaps and DIBs

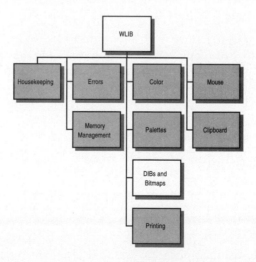

Bitmaps and DIBs are critical to our fundamental control of Windows graphics. Bitmaps are, in the end, what finally get put on the screen and printer. We'll use a bitmap and a palette as our fundamental drawing surface. This gives us the ability to generate a DIB at any moment — an added measure of device-independence. DIBs are a way of shielding bitmaps from most device dependencies, and are the unit of file I/O. You should notice that most of the bitmap and DIB code I use here is derived from the DIBView sample application. This sample is pretty much the final word on DIB, palette, and bitmap handling because it is based on the code used in the Driver Compatibility Test (DCT) test suite that is delivered in the Device Driver Kit (DDK).

First, we'll examine bitmaps. Then, under the topic of file I/O, we'll get into DIBs. The bitmap services are based around our familiar friend, the standard interface. The DIB routines are intended to support the bitmap functions; they are "internal" services, so they're not written with either the same intent or interface.

Bitmap Data Structures

The DDB bitmap structures, while they may be familiar, are worth a quick look. This structure is shown in Listing 4-36. It contains elements describing width and height, as well as color depth. The raw bits are available from the last element, a far pointer.

Listing 4-36.   BITMAP Structure in Windows.h

```
typedef struct tagBITMAP
{
    int       bmType;
    int       bmWidth;
    int       bmHeight;
    int       bmWidthBytes;
    BYTE      bmPlanes;
    BYTE      bmBitsPixel;
    void FAR* bmBits;
} BITMAP;
```

To accommodate differences between early OS/2 and Windows, the bitmap color entry structures, shown in Listing 4-37, come in two flavors. Studying both flavors helps you write DIB-neutral code; even though the save operation defaults to creating a Win3x DIB, it's nice that the load operation doesn't need to care when it encounters the alternate format.

Listing 4-37.   BITMAP Color Entry Flavors in Windows.h

```
/* Bitmap Header structures */
typedef struct tagRGBTRIPLE
{
    BYTE      rgbtBlue;
    BYTE      rgbtGreen;
    BYTE      rgbtRed;
} RGBTRIPLE;
typedef RGBTRIPLE FAR* LPRGBTRIPLE;


typedef struct tagRGBQUAD
{
    BYTE      rgbBlue;
    BYTE      rgbGreen;
    BYTE      rgbRed;
    BYTE      rgbReserved;
} RGBQUAD;
typedef RGBQUAD FAR* LPRGBQUAD;
```

Just so you are aware of the memory requirements of large bitmaps, Table 4-3 contains some sample numbers at common widths, heights, and pixel depths.

Table 4-3. Bitmap Memory Requirements

Amounts of Video Memory for Various Display Resolutions				
Width (pixels)	Height (pixels)	Depth (bits per pixel)	Colors	Memory (bytes)
320	200	1	2	8000
320	400	1	2	16000
320	400	4	16	64000
640	480	1	2	38400
640	480	4	16	153600
640	480	8	256	307200
1024	768	8	256	786432
2048	1536	8	256	3145728
640	480	16	32,768*	614400
1024	768	16	32,768*	1572864
2048	1536	16	32,768*	6291456

* This assumes 5 bits each for red, green, and blue.

Bitmap Service Routines

Again, our strategy influences the course of development, and, in turn, the content of the API. The usual creation, destruction, and copying functions are provided, but the needed file I/O services are found in the DIB layer. This means that the canvas abstraction needs to be aware of this separation, but since we're handling it all, that's okay.

Listing 4-38 shows the bitmap API, and Listings 4-39 and 4-40 show the creation destruction functions and key parts of the copy function. Bitmaps, like palettes, are simple wrappers around the GDI objects of the same names, so the creation and destruction functions *WL_Bitmap_Create* and *WL_Bitmap_Destroy* contain calls to **CreateCompatibleBitmap** and **DeleteObject**. *WL_Bitmap_Copy* is noteworthy for its DC hacking. The origins, extents, and mode of the source DC must be emulated by the target DC to guarantee correct operation of the copy function.

Listing 4-38. The Bitmap API in bitmap.c

```
BOOL        WINAPI WL_Bitmap_Init(void);
HBITMAP     WINAPI WL_Bitmap_Create(HDC hdcMem,     int ox, int oy,
                                        int ex, int ey);
HBITMAP     WINAPI WL_Bitmap_Copy( HDC hdcMem,
                                    HBITMAP hb,HPALETTE hp,          int ox,
    int oy,
                                    int ex, int ey);
BOOL        WINAPI WL_Bitmap_Destroy(HBITMAP hb);
BOOL        WINAPI WL_Bitmap_Term(void);
```

Listing 4-39. Bitmap Creation/Destruction Functions

```
HBITMAP WINAPI WL_Bitmap_Create(HDC hdcMem,
                                int ox, int oy,
                                int ex, int ey)

{
     HBITMAP  hb;
     hb  = CreateCompatibleBitmap( hdcMem,
                                   ex-ox,
                                   ey-oy);

     return hb;
}
//
BOOL   WINAPI WL_Bitmap_Destroy(HBITMAP hb)
{
     DeleteObject(hb);
     return TRUE;
}
```

Listing 4-40. Bitmap Copy DC Hacking Block

```
SetMapMode(hdcMemD,GetMapMode(hdcMem));
dwo     = GetWindowOrg(hdcMem);
dwe     = GetWindowExt(hdcMem);
SetWindowOrg(hdcMemD,LOWORD(dwo),HIWORD(dwo));
SetWindowExt(hdcMemD,LOWORD(dwe),HIWORD(dwe));
dvo     = GetViewportOrg(hdcMem);
dve     = GetViewportExt(hdcMem);
SetViewportOrg(hdcMemD,LOWORD(dvo),HIWORD(dvo));
SetViewportExt(hdcMemD,LOWORD(dve),HIWORD(dve));
```

Using these functions is extremely simple, as you can see by the interface. Listing 4-41 contains a call to *WL_Bitmap_Create*; this is the same call *WL_Bitmap_Copy* uses.

Listing 4-41. Bitmap Create Invocation

```
hclone  = WL_Bitmap_Create(hdcMem,ox,oy,ex,ey);
```

This leaves the saving of DIBs that support loading and saving bitmaps. These DIB discussions give you service routines that are of immediate value; they do not investigate every nook-and-cranny of GDI's implementation of DIBs. Here, we are pragmatic rather than pioneering with respect to our requirements from GDI.

DIB Data Structures

Flavors of DIB data structures include the BITMAPCOREHEADER structure shown in Listing 4-42, and the BITMAPCOREINFO structure shown in Listing 4-43, which are used by OS/2 DIB format. The COREINFO has a COREHEADER and RGBTRIPLE color table peculiar to OS/2 1.x.

Listing 4-42. BITMAPCOREHEADER Structure

```
typedef struct tagBITMAPCOREHEADER {     /* bmch */
    DWORD     bcSize;
    WORD      bcWidth;
    WORD      bcHeight;
    WORD      bcPlanes;
    WORD      bcBitCount;
} BITMAPCOREHEADER;
```

Listing 4-43. BITMAPCOREINFO Structure

```
typedef struct tagBITMAPCOREINFO {  /* bmci */
    BITMAPCOREHEADER bmciHeader;
    RGBTRIPLE        bmciColors[1];
} BITMAPCOREINFO;TMAPCOREHEADER;
```

Windows 3.x bitmaps use a slightly different format. The BITMAPINFOHEADER shown in Listing 4-44 contains, among other things, a compression field that this API ignores. A BITMAPINFO contains an INFOHEADER and a color table composed of RGBQUADS. This structure is shown in Listing 4-45.

Listing 4-44.   BITMAPINFOHEADER Structure

```
typedef struct tagBITMAPINFOHEADER {     /* bmih */
    DWORD   biSize;
    DWORD   biWidth;
    DWORD   biHeight;
    WORD    biPlanes;
    WORD    biBitCount;
    DWORD   biCompression;
    DWORD   biSizeImage;
    DWORD   biXPelsPerMeter;
    DWORD   biYPelsPerMeter;
    DWORD   biClrUsed;
    DWORD   biClrImportant;
} BITMAPINFOHEADER;
```

Listing 4-45.   BITMAPINFO Structure

```
typedef struct tagBITMAPINFO {  /* bmi */
    BITMAPINFOHEADER    bmiHeader;
    RGBQUAD             bmiColors[1];
} BITMAPINFO;
```

The file-based representation of a DIB is contained in the BITMAPFILEHEADER data structure, which is followed immediately by either an INFO or COREINFO structure. The FILEHEADER structure is shown in Listing 4-46. Figure 4-10 compares the Windows and OS/2 file organizations, which completes our breeze through the DIB data structures.

Listing 4-46.   BITMAPFILEHEADER Structure

```
typedef struct tagBITMAPFILEHEADER {     /* bmfh */
    WORD    bfType;
    DWORD   bfSize;
    WORD    bfReserved1;
    WORD    bfReserved2;
    DWORD   bfOffBits;
} BITMAPFILEHEADER; .
```

Figure 4-10. Windows and OS/2 DIB File Organizations Compared

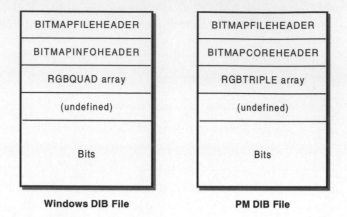

DIB Service Routines

These routines provide support for bitmap and palette file I/O. Listings 4-47 and 4-48 show the internal DIB and DIB-file I/O API that provides this support. There is no reason why you cannot use these underlying routines; indeed, they are exported and used by G3DLib in Chapter 5. Mainly, though, they are meant to be hidden away in the internal implementation of the canvas abstraction.

Listing 4-47.   Internal DIB API in dib.c

```
BOOL        WINAPI WL_DIB_Init(void);
DWORD       WINAPI WL_DIB_DIBWidth (LPSTR lpDIB);
DWORD       WINAPI WL_DIB_DIBHeight (LPSTR lpDIB);
WORD        WINAPI WL_DIB_DIBNumColors (LPSTR lpbi);
WORD        WINAPI WL_DIB_PaletteSize (LPSTR lpbi);
LPSTR       WINAPI WL_DIB_FindBits (LPSTR lpbi);
HBITMAP     WINAPI WL_DIB_DIBToBitmap (HWND hw, HANDLE hDIB,
                    HPALETTE hPal);
HANDLE      WINAPI WL_DIB_WinDIBFromBitmap(HWND hw,HBITMAP Bitmap,
                    DWORD dwStyle,WORD wBits,HPALETTE hPal);
BOOL        WINAPI WL_DIB_Term(void);
```

Listing 4-48.   Internal DIB-File I/O API in file.c

```
BOOL        WINAPI WL_File_Init(void);
BOOL        WINAPI WL_File_DIBFiletoDDB(HWND hw,LPSTR szFile,
                    HBITMAP FAR * lphb, HPALETTE FAR * lphp);
BOOL        WINAPI WL_File_DDBtoDIBFile(HWND hw,HBITMAP hb,
                    HPALETTE hp, LPSTR szFile);
BOOL        WINAPI WL_File_Term(void);
```

The *WL_DIB_DIBtoBitmap* and *WL_DIB_BitmapToDIB* functions are the guts of the file I/O and conversion process. You saw the file-function prototypes in Listing 4-48. To perform this valuable service, they use the file I/O services, especially routines *WL_File_DIBFiletoDDB* and *WL_File_DDBtoDIBFile*, which are in prototype form in Listing 4-49. Listings 4-50 and 4-51 show usage examples for the two file-subsystem helpers. For a deeper look at the entire DIB, DDB, and file I/O code, check out the source disk and/or DIBView.

Listing 4-49.   DIBToBITMAP, BITMAPToDIB Conversion Prototypes in dib.c

```
HBITMAP WINAPI WL_DIB_DIBToBitmap(HWND hw,HANDLE hDIB,
                  HPALETTE hPal);
HANDLE  WINAPI WL_DIB_BitmapToDIB (HBITMAP hBitmap, HPALETTE hPal);
```

Listing 4-50.   WL_DIB_DIBFiletoDDB File I/O Block

```
...
//
WL_File_DIBFiletoDDB(hw,szFileName, &hb, &hp);
if ( !hb && !hp )
{
      Throw((LPCATCHBUF)&_ci.state,BBERR_LOADFAILURE);
}
//
...
```

Listing 4-51.   WL_DIB_ DDBtoDIBFile File I/O Block

```
...
//
if ( !WL_File_DDBtoDIBFile(hw,lpbb->hbmMem,lpbb->hpS,szFileName))
{
      Throw((LPCATCHBUF)&_ci.state,BBERR_SAVEFAILURE);
}
//
...
```

WLib GDI Services: Printing

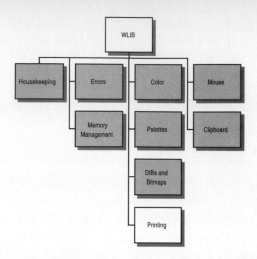

Starting with Petzold's printing shell as our initial model means that we've included abort handling and banding, but this is not enough. A full-featured printing subsystem usually provides more functionality, and WLib is no different. Key components of the printing strategy are:

- Print options data structure and dialog,
- Job and page control API, and
- custom grayscaling.

It's worth the extra effort to provide a data structure and some standard print options. The data structure shown in Listing 4-52 implements variable scaling. Variable scaling is not difficult to implement and turns out to be quite useful. Formalizing the job- and page-control API helps clean up the main print body (in terms of code readability and maintenance). Listing 4-53 shows a rough form of printing internals. The sequence amounts to: retrieving a printer DC, performing mode and rectangle setup, then using the job- and page-control to bracket a call to *WL_Print_DIBPrint*. Finally, the printer DC must be released.

Listing 4-52.   PRINTOPTIONS Data Structure in print.h

```
typedef struct
{
    BOOL bStretch;
    BOOL bPrinterBand;
    BOOL bUse31PrintAPIs;
    WORD wPrintOption;
    WORD wXScale;
    WORD wYScale;
    WORD biStyle;
    WORD biBits;
} FAR *LPPRINTOPTIONS, PRINTOPTIONS;
```

```
      // Values used for wPrintOption in PRINTOPTIONS

#define PRINT_BESTFIT          IDRB_BESTFIT
#define PRINT_STRETCH          IDRB_STRETCH
#define PRINT_SCALE            IDRB_SCALE
```

Listing 4-53.   Example Print Code

```
if ( WL_Print_GetPrinterDC () )
{
   SetStretchBltMode (hPrnDC, COLORONCOLOR);
   WL_Print_TranslatePrintRect(hPrnDC,...);
   WL_Print_DoStartDoc (bUseEscapes,hPrnDC, lpszDoc);
   WL_Print_DIBPrint(hPrnDC,..);
   WL_Print_DoEndDoc (bUseEscapes,hPrnDC);
   DeleteDC (hPrnDC);

}
```

As you'll see in Chapter 5, this will all be hidden by the canvas abstraction.

The final component of print strategy is a print palette. This is, again, not strictly an issue for WLib, since it's a component of the graphics environment (again, covered in Chapter 5).

Briefly, the graphics environment uses this parameter, if present, to improve print quality. In most cases, a gray-level output can be generated during the rendering phase. Using the information from this output at print time, in the form of a grayscale print palette, improves the printout quality by helping the driver decide what shade of gray a particular color dithers to.

Let me make a small diversion to discuss an important bug and an interesting feature. Fran Finnegan's "Questions and Answers" column in *Microsoft Systems Journal* (Volume 7, No. 7) discusses a bug in the HP II printer driver. **BitBlt** can fail when moving between SVGA-resolution screens and printing using the HPPCL driver. While converting different formats requires work, usually the driver-writer solves this problem (after all, that's why they get the "big bucks"). In this case, though, the HP driver punts the problem back to the printer user. If you have one of these printers, you'll need to read Fran's column and fix the code. I haven't spent copious amounts of time trying to guarantee this won't happen and add special cases to the code in the library; I, too, am punting this one back to you. Sorry!

The feature applies to one of the internal routines of the print subsystem that uses an interesting technique. This may appear to have nothing to do with the topic at hand, and in a certain sense you're right. But I still think you'll find this information useful. *WL_Print_FindGDIFunction* is similar to the **GET_PROC** used in *Undocumented Windows*, by Schulman, Maxey, and Pietrek (Addison-Wesley, 1992). This function is an example of run-time dynamic linking, except that in this case we are only interested in GDI functions. *WL_Print_FindGDIFunction* returns the function address of one of the new Win31 print functions. If the function doesn't exist, it returns null. In this manner, you can determine the presence or absence of Win31 at run-time and, therefore, use 3.1-specific functions, while still allowing your program to load under 3.0. This technique also exposes some important facts about compile/link-time dynamic linking versus run-time dynamic linking and the underlying system. See Listing 4-54.

Listing 4-54.   WL_Print_FindGDIFunction

```
FARPROC WL_Print_FindGDIFunction (LPSTR lpszFnName)
{
   HANDLE hGDI;

   hGDI = GetModuleHandle (szGDIModule);

   if (!hGDI)
      return NULL;

   return GetProcAddress (hGDI, lpszFnName);
}
```

With that, we've finished our discussion of both printing and the GDI services.

WLib User Services: Mouse

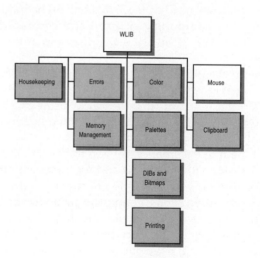

I've mentioned previously that mouse and clipboard support go hand in hand. Once we have a bitmap in a window, what do we want to do with it? Copy it to the clipboard is the most obvious answer. Another is to select an area using the mouse and operate on that selection. The mouse marks the region of interest with a rubber-band rectangle technique. Then the region is used in clipboard operations or other graphics processing.

Listing 4-55 shows the Mouse API. It provides one service and one service only: marking the selection rectangle. Rubber-banding is pretty easy; you simply handle the WM_xBUTTONDOWN, WM_MOUSEMOVE, WM_xBUTTONUP for both buttons (in case the user swaps the meaning of the buttons in the control panel) with code similar to that in Listings 4-56, 4-57, and 4-58.

Listing 4-55.   Mouse API in mouse.c

```
//mouse
BOOL          WINAPI WL_Mouse_Init(void);
void          WINAPI WL_Mouse_DrawRect( HWND, LPRECT, BOOL, HDC);
BOOL          WINAPI WL_Mouse_Term(void);
```

Step one, the button-down case, causes the first point, known as the *anchor point*, to be drawn. Note the use of **DPtoLP**, which is necessary because of the DC attribute hacking we'll be doing. **SetCapture** captures mouse events for this process, even when the mouse is outside the boundary of this window.

Listing 4-56.   Button-Down Mouse Handling

```
case WM_LBUTTONDOWN:
...
//
      pSelected.x = x;
      pSelected.y = y;
      DPtoLP(hdc,&pSelected,1);
      // draw the new rectangle
      WL_Mouse_DrawRect(pvwwnd->hwnd,
                  &pvwwnd->rcZoom,
                  TRUE,
                  hdc);
                  (HDC)G3D_GEnv_GetVal(pvwwnd->genv,ID_DC));
      SetCapture(pvwwnd->hwnd);
...
//
```

Once the anchor is dropped, step two extends the selection rectangle. This operation uses ROP code magic to enable a "redraw" directly on top of a first draw to restore the pixels. This is followed by drawing the rectangle again to the new specification, after the requisite **DPtoLP** translation.

Listing 4-57.   Mouse Move Code Block

```
case WM_MOUSEMOVE:
...
//
WL_Mouse_DrawRect(pvwwnd->hwnd, &pvwwnd->rcZoom,
                  FALSE,hdc);
                  (HDC)G3D_GEnv_GetVal(pvwwnd->genv,ID_DC));
pMove.x = x;
pMove.y = y;
DPtoLP(hdc,&pMove,1);
```

Listing 4-57.   (cont.)

```
// update the selection rectangle
if (pMove.x <= pSelected.x)
    pvwwnd->rcZoom.left   = pMove.x;
if (pMove.x >= pSelected.x)
    pvwwnd->rcZoom.right  = pMove.x;
if (pMove.y >= pSelected.y)
    pvwwnd->rcZoom.top    = pMove.y;
if (pMove.y <= pSelected.y)
    pvwwnd->rcZoom.bottom = pMove.y;

WL_Mouse_DrawRect(pvwwnd->hwnd,&pvwwnd->rcZoom,
                  TRUE,hdc);
                  (HDC)G3D_GEnv_GetVal(pvwwnd->genv,ID_DC));
...
//
```

Step three simply turns off capture, using **ReleaseCapture** in this example. This leaves the selection rectangle visible. If you wanted to erase the selection rectangle, you'll just have to add one more call to *WL_Mouse_DrawRect* to add to this block.

Listing 4-58.   Mouse Up Code Block

```
...
//
case WM_LBUTTONUP:

  ReleaseCapture();
//
...
```

The key to this is the ROP code. **PatBlt** is the low-level GDI function used to implement the rubber-banding. It uses the DSTINVERT code to allow the draw/undraw sequence to work as we need it to. See Listing 4-59 for an example **PatBlt** invocation.

Listing 4-59.   Example PatBlt Call

```
PatBlt (hdcBM,
        lprc->left,
        lprc->bottom,
        1,
        -(lprc->bottom - lprc->top),
        DSTINVERT);
```

WLib User Services: Clipboard

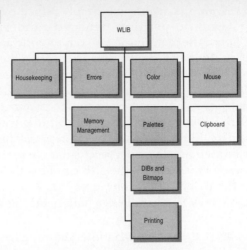

Standard clipboard support enables the shareability of data and interoperability of applications within the Windows environment. It is user-friendly and, at minimum, serves as a good copy service. It allows the modeler to naturally share bitmaps with other tools in the environment. Clipboard supports three formats:

- DIB,
- palette, and
- bitmap.

There are two modes to rendering data in the Windows clipboard. *Immediate mode*, the simplest, requires you to immediately supply the clipboard with data. A more sophisticated method, called *deferred mode*, lets you defer supplying the data until a later time. The messages WM_RENDERFORMAT, WM_RENDERALLFORMATS, and WM_DESTROYCLIPBOARD must be handled to perform the "at a later time" work as part of the application policy. I've provided support for immediate mode, and deferred rendering is supported as well, with a little help from you.

Immediate rendering, as its name implies, immediately places data on the clipboard. Deferred rendering places a token identifying the application that "owes" the clipboard a handle. When another application requests clipboard data, the owing application receives a notification and must pay its "IOU." Listing 4-60 contains the function prototypes for the clipboard API.

Listing 4-60.   Clipboard API in clipbrd.c

```
// clipboard
BOOL        WINAPI WL_Clipbrd_Init(void);
HANDLE      WINAPI WL_Clipbrd_RenderImmed(HWND hw,int cf,HDC hdcS,
                                    HANDLE h1, HANDLE h2);
HANDLE      WINAPI WL_Clipbrd_RenderDelay(HWND hw,int cf);
BOOL        WINAPI WL_Clipbrd_Term(void);
```

WL_Clipbrd_RenderDelay simply puts the NULL token on the clipboard, which signifies its wish to perform deferred rendering. With a clever use of the routine *WL_Clipbrd_RenderImmed*, you can provide an interface for both immediate and deferred rendering. Both of these routines expect that the clipboard is opened before they are called, and both expect you to close the clipboard afterward as well.

WL_Clipbrd_RenderImmed provides the three-format support, but does it in a slightly unusual fashion. It has two "handle" parameters that are used as follows. First, it uses *WL_DIB_BitmapToDIB* and both a bitmap handle and a palette handle as parameters to generate a DIB representing the bitmap/palette pair. Next, it uses *WL_Bitmap_Copy* and both a bitmap handle and a palette handle to duplicate the bitmap with its color information intact. Finally, since the DIB contains the palette that should be placed on the clipboard, the palette processing uses *WL_Pal_CreateDIBPalette*. So in this invocation the function uses a DIB handle as a parameter. Table 4-4 contains a recap of this mapping.

Table 4-4.   CF_FORMAT-Handle Mapping for WL_Clipbrd_RenderImmed

Format	Parameters (handles)
DIB	h1 = bitmap
	h2 = palette
BITMAP	h1 = bitmap
	h2 = palette
PALETTE	h1 = DIB

Listing 4-61 shows the implementation of the immediate function. The deferred rendering support is simpler.

Listing 4-61.   WL_Clipbrd_RenderImmed

```
HANDLE        WINAPI WL_Clipbrd_RenderImmed(HWND hw,int cf,HDC hdcS,HANDLE
h1, HANDLE h2)
{
    HANDLE h;
    BITMAP bm;

    switch (cf)
    {

        case CF_DIB:
            h = WL_DIB_BitmapToDIB (h1, h2);
            break;
        case CF_BITMAP:
            GetObject (h1, sizeof (bm), (LPSTR)&bm);
            h = WL_Bitmap_Copy(hdcS,
                               h1,
                               h2,
                               0,       0,
                               bm.bmWidth, bm.bmHeight);
            break;
```

```
            case CF_PALETTE:
                h = WL_Pal_CreateDIBPalette(h1);
                break;
        }
        if (h)
            SetClipboardData (cf,h);
        return h;
    }
```

Listing 4-62 shows function *WL_Clipbrd_RenderDelay*. It is a cover function for invoking **SetClipboardData** with a NULL data handle for the clipboard format passed in as a parameter. The application policy for the messages remains to complete deferred rendering.

Listing 4-62.   WL_Clipbrd_RenderDelay

```
BOOL        WINAPI WL_Clipbrd_RenderDelay(HWND hw,int cf)
{
    SetClipboardData (cf,NULL);
    return TRUE;
}
```

Table 4-5 summarizes the messages, the reasons they are generated, and the action a program should take in response.

Table 4-5.   Deferred Rendering and Windows Messages

Message	Reason for generating	Action
WM_RENDERFORMAT	GetClipboardData called on your deferred format	Render data without emptying clipboard
WM_RENDERALLFORMATS	Your program terminates while owing a deferred format	Render data with emptying clipboard
WM_DESTROYCLIPBOARD	Some other program calls EmptyClipboard	Cancel deferred format

Now comes an example of deferred rendering. In the application you then respond to the two Windows messages for deferred rendering: WM_RENDERALLFORMATS and WM_RENDERFORMAT. The RENDERALLFORMATS handler generates WM_RENDERFORMAT messages for each format the app supports. The WM_RENDERFORMAT handler invokes various library functions for each format. The example in Listing 4-64 shows both WM_RENDERALLFORMATS and WM_RENDERFORMAT handlers. Simple.

Listing 4-63. Example of Initializing Deferred Rendering

```
...
    if (!OpenClipboard (pfrm->hwnd))
       return;
    EmptyClipboard ();
    WL_Clipbrd_RenderDelay(pv->hwnd,CF_BITMAP);
    WL_Clipbrd_RenderDelay(pv->hwnd,CF_DIB);
    WL_Clipbrd_RenderDelay(pv->hwnd,CF_PALETTE);
    CloseClipboard ();
...
```

Listing 4-64. Handling Deferred Rendering

```
void    View_OnRenderAllFormats(VWWND* pv)
{
    if (!OpenClipboard (pv->hwnd))
       return;
    EmptyClipboard ();
    SendMessage(pv->hwnd, WM_RENDERFORMAT, CF_BITMAP,  0L);
    SendMessage(pv->hwnd, WM_RENDERFORMAT, CF_DIB, 0L);
    SendMessage(pv->hwnd, WM_RENDERFORMAT, CF_PALETTE, 0L);
    CloseClipboard ();
    return;
}
HANDLE View_OnRenderFormat(VWWND* pv,UINT fmt)
{
    HANDLE  h;
    HPALETTE hpT;
    if (Model == CMD_RGB) hpT = hprgb;
    else hpT = hpcmy;
    switch(fmt){
       HDC hdc = (HDC)G3D_GEnv_GetVal(pv->genv,ID_DC);
       case CF_BITMAP:
           h = WL_Bitmap_Copy((HDC)G3D_GEnv_GetVal(pv->genv,ID_DC),
                       (HBITMAP)G3D_GEnv_GetVal(pv->genv,ID_BITMAP),
                               hpT,0,0,g_app.Width, g_app.Height);
           break;
       case CF_DIB:
           h = WL_DIB_BitmapToDIB((HBITMAP)G3D_GEnv_GetVal(pv->genv,
                               ID_BITMAP),hpT);
           break;
       case CF_PALETTE:
           h = WL_Pal_CopyPaletteChangingFlags(hpT, 0);
           break;
    }
    if ( h )
       SetClipboardData(fmt,h);
    return h;
}
```

That concludes our discussion of the User services and finishes our treatment of WLib. Next I'll show you an example of how to use some of these services before we tackle the canvas abstraction in Chapter 5.

Usage: Color Cube Demo

The easiest introduction to using the API is the color cube demo. This demo illustrates the theoretical RGB color cube, and there are a wide variety of methods for rendering this fundamental figure. To be effective, it requires you to use logical and physical representations for both coordinates and color values. But be wary, 256-color mode takes more effort than just using more colors.

After all is said and done, it is not that much extra work to use the Palette Manager, as you'll see in the suite of demo code. Palette creation, use, and destruction is only part of the story, though. Using palettes in a windowing environment entails sharing a resource and forces you to some policy actions.

The color cube is an archetypal demo, a hoop that every graphics programmer must jump through and get out of their system. With the color cube, you can show your control over the available spectrum of color gracefully within one simple demo program. This elegance and simplicity is one of the constantly repeated facets of good graphics demos and a visible display of mastery.

Now, let's talk about exactly what the RGB color cube is and how we go about constructing one.

The details of logical/physical drawing will have to wait. For now, suffice it to say that we describe the logical picture we wish to display, then draw it into the graphics window, using Windows' own functions to map that into a graphics viewport. Logically, we want to draw a cube consisting of rectangular "patches" of color. This cube represents "slices" from the abstract RGB color cube. The slices march through the red, green, and blue segments of the cube showing various colors.

First, we need to take care of some housekeeping details. We want to draw a 5x5x5 cube. (Trust me — this is what we want.) We chose an odd number of patches so that we can see the gray line through the exact center of the cube. Five is an auspicious number since it's the number of patches that you can see distinctly at any size. We need to separate the patches by a constant margin. We also want to frame this in the center of our logical window.

The example first draws a row of red patches xSpot and ySpot in size. The patches are separated by xSpace and ySpace between the rows, and X and Y are staggered by xDiff and yDiff in each row to give the illusion of depth and 3D. We also need to get the y origin correct, since GDI places it in the upper left, and the representation we'll use places it in the lower left. This results in an image as diagrammed in Figure 4-11.

On to the implementation. If we take the standard application shell, we need only change the *View_OnPaint* routine to provide graphics output. The *View_OnPaint* routine invokes the *View_Draw* routine, which then calls *CubePaint*. View modifications are shown in Listing 4-65. This *CubePaint* function is the key to the implementation, as shown in Listing 4-66. First *CubePaint* clears the background with a black brush. It then uses a switch statement to arbitrate color mixing models.

Figure 4-11.   Color Cube Conceptual Diagram

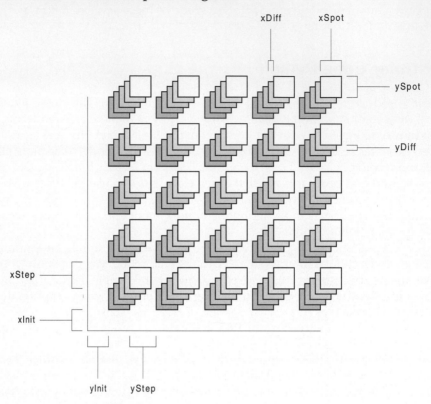

Listing 4-65.   View Module Modifications

```
void View_Draw(HDC hdc,RECT rect)
{
   CubePaint(hdc,rect);
}
void View_OnPaint(VWWND* pvwwnd)
{
    PAINTSTRUCT ps;
    RECT        Rect;
    HDC         hdc;

    hdc = BeginPaint(pvwwnd->hwnd, &ps);
    GetClientRect(pvwwnd->hwnd, (LPRECT)&Rect);
    View_Draw(hdc,Rect);
    EndPaint(pvwwnd->hwnd, &ps);
}
```

Listing 4-66.   CubePaint

```
void CubePaint(VWWND* pvwwnd,HDC hdc,int Model, RECT Rect)
{
    HBRUSH        hBrush,hbrO;
    char          szModel[80];

    hBrush = CreateSolidBrush((long)0x00000000);
    hbrO   = SelectObject(hdc, hBrush);
    PatBlt(hdc, 0, 0, pvwwnd->rV.right, pvwwnd->rV.bottom, PATCOPY);
    SelectObject(hdc, hbrO);
    DeleteObject(hBrush);

    if ( !hprgb || !hpcmy )
       return ;

    LoadString(g_app.hinst,IDS_TITLE,szTitle,32);
    switch(Model)
    {

      case CMD_RGB:
         DrawRGBColorCube(hdc,Rect);
         LoadString(g_app.hinst,IDS_RGB,szModel,32);
         break;
      case CMD_CMY:
         DrawCMYColorCube(hdc,Rect);
         LoadString(g_app.hinst,IDS_CMY,szModel,32);
         break;
      case CMD_CRT:
         DrawGDIColorCube(hdc,Rect);
         LoadString(g_app.hinst,IDS_CRT,szModel,32);
         break;
    }
    lstrcpy((LPSTR)(LPSTR)szNewTitle,(LPSTR)szTitle);
    lstrcat(szNewTitle," - ");
    lstrcat((LPSTR)szNewTitle,(LPSTR)szModel);
    if ( g_app.hwndMain)
       SetWindowText(g_app.hwndMain,(LPSTR)szNewTitle);
}
```

The cube routines are very similar. We are going to see quite a bit of this code, so you need a general understanding of its form. This code shows definitions, size calculation, and iteration parts that loop across the color components and draw color patches according to our specifications. See Listing 4-67.

Listing 4-67.   Generalized Cube Drawing

```
DrawGDICube(hDC)
HDC     hDC;
{
    int             x, y, xSize, ySize;
    int             xSpot, ySpot, xSpace, ySpace, xInit, yInit;
    int             xDiff, yDiff;
    HBRUSH          hBrush;
    long            r, g, b, n;
//
//  define logical sizes
//
//  iterate across the three color components, red,green,blue
//      and draw the cube
//
}
```

The logical sizing code, as shown in Listing 4-68, provides a 1200x1200-unit drawing area with the sign of the y extent flipped to account for the difference between GDI and Cartesian coordinates. Patches of color 125 units square begin at an initial offset of 20. Rows are offset by 100 units, and patches within a row are staggered by 30 units.

Listing 4-68.   Logical Cube Sizing

```
xSize = 1200;
ySize = -1200;

xSpot = 125;
ySpot = 125;

xSpace = 100;
ySpace = 100;

xDiff = 30;
yDiff = 30;

xInit = 20;
yInit = 20;
```

The code shown in Listings 4-68 and 4-70 intimately depend on a DC that is set up as shown in Listing 4-69. Setup code like 4-69 is common, and code very much like it is contained in the canvas abstraction. In the course of providing a window-viewport abstraction in the graphics library, you also need to deal with the underlying Windows implementation.

Listing 4-69. DC Specifications

```
//
// dc/drawing ... to be moved to canvas support
//
    SetMapMode(hdc, MM_ANISOTROPIC);
    SetWindowOrg(hdc, 0, 0);
    SetWindowExt(hdc, 1200, -1200);
    SetViewportOrg(hdc, 0, 0);
    SetViewportExt(hdc, Rect.right-Rect.left, Rect.bottom-Rect.top);
```

Listing 4-70.   Drawing Loop

```
long Pal[] = {0x00000000,0x00000040,0x00000080,0x000000C0,0x000000FF};

    for (g=0; g<5; g++)
    {
        y = ySize + yInit + (g * yDiff);
        for (b=0; b<5; b++) {
            x = xInit + (g * xDiff);
            for (r=0; r<5; r++) {
                n = Pal[r] + (Pal[g] << 8) + (Pal[b] << 16);
                hBrush = CreateSolidBrush(n);
                hBrush = SelectObject(hDC, hBrush);
                PatBlt(hDC, x, y, xSpot, ySpot, PATCOPY);
                hBrush = SelectObject(hDC, hBrush);
                DeleteObject(hBrush);
                x += xSpot + xSpace;
            }
            y += ySpot + ySpace;
        }
    }
```

I've included the drawing loop shown in Listing 4-70 for illustration purposes only; it is a naive straight-GDI implementation of the color cube. It is simple, uses no palettes, and draws the patches. This routine iterates across the three color components in the interval of [0,255].   Pal is an array containing hard-coded values for the 5 uniform slices through the RGB color space. A brush to draw the patch is created using **CreateSolidBrush**. The brush object is selected using **SelectObject**. The iteration then selects a slice layer and draws the rectangles for it using **PatBlt**. The brush is then deselected and deleted.

The problem with this function is that it's completely tied to GDI color, brushes, and such. This usage and type of color specification provides no level of abstraction above CRT. Here's where color services ride to the rescue. To use our color service routines, simply rewrite the loop as shown in Listing 4-71, where the iteration now assigns RGB values between 0 and 1 rather than using the Pal array that was tied to GDI color. When the color is needed to do on-screen rendering, the RGB values are converted to CRT and used in **CreateSolidBrush**, along with the usual GDI housekeeping. It's easy to use these color services and they let us specify color in the logical [0,1] space rather than in the [0,255] representation of the platform. We could do the same for the CMY specification system, yielding a *DrawCMYCube*. These could even be combined in our demo program using a mixing model menu, with one global variable for current menu choice and a paint handler that uses a switch and the global to determine the drawing method. I've given you the idea of using this logical form and creating instances of it that use a particular color scheme to draw the cube. This is enough that you should be able to implement it as an easy exercise, if the idea strikes your fancy.

Listing 4-71.   RGBCube Using Color Services

```
for (g=0; g<5; g++)
{
    rgbColor.fGreen = (float)g * 1./4.;
    y = ySize + yInit + (g * yDiff);
    for (b=0; b<5; b++) {
        x = xInit + (g * xDiff);
        rgbColor.fBlue  = (float)b * 1./4.;
        for (r=0; r<5; r++) {
            rgbColor.fRed   = (float)r * 1./4.;
             WL_Color_RGBtoCRT( &rgbColor, &crtValue );
            hOldBrush = SelectObject(hDC,
                CreateSolidBrush(*((DWORD*)&crtValue)));
            PatBlt(hDC, x, y, xSpot, ySpot, PATCOPY);
            DeleteObject( SelectObject(hDC,hOldBrush) );
            x += xSpot + xSpace;
        }
        y += ySpot + ySpace;
    }
}
```

By repeating the drawing loop with the addition of a palette routine, we show another face to this simple code and permit a quick compare and contrast with the other two (simpler) examples. Remember, too, that without palettes in 256-color mode you don't get what you ask for. Implementing one program in multiple ways can be very instructive.

Listing 4-72 shows the RGB palette-creation routine. Once you have a palette, it's pretty trivial to modify the drawing loop. Assuming the palette is selected into a DC, use the palette value to generate a brush. This change in brush specification, which is now using the **PALETTERGB** macro, is not a great deal of code change, but if you execute it on a 256-color device it results in a significant difference. When you use the brush in a DC that has our palette selected, voilá, a brush of the correct color is created. This brush is used, as shown in Listing 4-73, to draw the color patch. But don't forget, every brush that gets created must also be destroyed. To say there is a cost associated with this is an understatement. Before we develop the application we'll rectify this cost. For now, though, tuck this issue in the back of your mind.

Listing 4-72.   Arbitrary RGB Palette Creation

```
HPALETTE InitRGBPalette(void)
{
    long        r, g, b, n;
    CRT         crtValue;
    RGB         rgbColor;
    LOGPALETTE  *pPal;
    HPALETTE    hp;
//
// setup palette for 125 colors
//
    pPal = (LOGPALETTE *)LocalAlloc(LPTR,sizeof(LOGPALETTE) +
            125 * sizeof(PALETTEENTRY));
    if ( !pPal )
       return 0;
    pPal->palNumEntries = 125;
    pPal->palVersion    = 0x300;
    n                   = 0;
    for (g=0; g<5; g++) {
        rgbColor.fGreen = (float)g * (float)1./(float)4.;
        for (b=0; b<5; b++) {
            rgbColor.fBlue  = (float)b * 1./4.;
            for (r=0; r<5; r++) {
                rgbColor.fRed   = (float)r * 1./4.;
// convert RGB and display crt equivalent numerical values
                WL_Color_RGBtoCRT((LPRGB)&rgbColor,(LPCRT)&crtValue );
// assign into palette
                pPal->palPalEntry[n].peRed   = crtValue.cRed;
                pPal->palPalEntry[n].peGreen = crtValue.cGreen;
                pPal->palPalEntry[n].peBlue  = crtValue.cBlue;
                pPal->palPalEntry[n].peFlags = PC_RESERVED;
// bump pointer
                n++;
            }
        }
    }
    hp = WL_Pal_Create(pPal);
    LocalFree((HANDLE)pPal);

    return hp;
}
```

Listing 4-73.   Palette-Based Drawing

```
for (g=0; g<5; g++)
  {
        y = ySize + yInit + (g * yDiff);
        rgbColor.fGreen = (float)g * 1./4.;
        for (b=0; b<5; b++){
```

Listing 4-73.   (cont.)

```
        x = xInit + (g * xDiff);
        rgbColor.fBlue  = (float)b * 1./4.;
        for (r=0; r<5; r++){
            rgbColor.fRed   = (float)r * 1./4.;
// display palette colors
            WL_Color_RGBtoCRT( &rgbColor, &crtValue );
            lsClr = PALETTERGB(crtValue.cRed,
        crtValue.cGreen,crtValue.cBlue);
            hBr        = CreateSolidBrush( *((DWORD*)&lsClr) );
            hOldBrush = SelectObject(hDC,hBr);
            PatBlt(hDC, po.x, po.y, ps.x, ps.y, PATCOPY);
        DeleteObject( SelectObject(hDC,hOldBrush) );
            x += xSpot + xSpace;
        }
        y += ySpot + ySpace;
    }
}   .
```

Figure 4-12 shows what happens without a palette; Figure 4-13 shows the result of all this careful work with palettes. Compare it carefully with Figure 4-12 and you will see the

Figure 4-12. RGBCube without Palettes

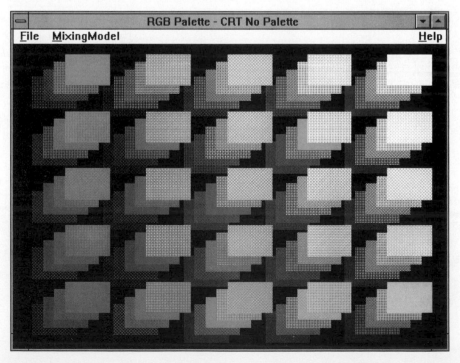

Figure 4-13. RGBCube with Palettes

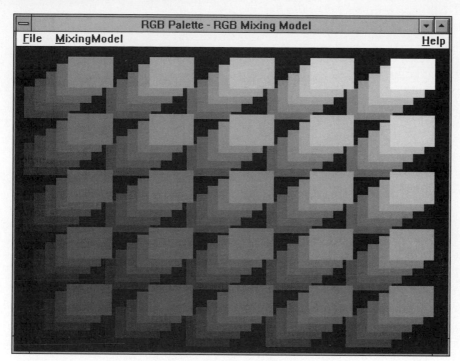

benefits of using palettes. The dithering that's apparent in Figure 4-12 disappears and the color patches are clearly solid colors in Figure 4-13.

If you've been paying close attention, you'll notice that displaying two instances of this demo uses more than 236 colors (250 to be exact); this implies that using multiple instances and trying to show both RGB and CMY palettes simultaneously will exceed the hardware limits. Windows responds to this by giving a black brush for those palette entries — not exactly a graceful degradation. If we wanted to be really clever, we would be careful not to create extra brushes for the default colors that are present in these two palettes. Then we could display both application palettes simultaneously. This is a lot of work for a demo program, though. For now, just be aware of the issue, because it's the tip of the application-policy iceberg.

Summary

The WLib, paralleling Windows, is divided into:

- Kernel,
- GDI, and
- User.

Kernel contains services for error handling, and memory management. GDI contains routines to handle:

- color,
- palettes,
- DIBs and bitmaps, and
- printing.

Finally User services provide functions for mouse handling and clipboard data sharing. That concludes the discussion of low-level Windows services. You made it!

What's Next?

While it's inevitable that Windows will creep into our code, the services we've just covered provide ready-made tools for many occasions. The Kernel, GDI, and User services will be under a heavy load starting in Chapter 5: Base, Support, Utility, and Math. In Chapter 5, we use the bitmap and palette routines to build the graphics environment and the canvas services, which are the fundamental drawing routines of the system.

5 G3DLib Construction Part I: Drawing Surface and General Support Services

In This Chapter

- Clarify the split of the G3DLib into Drawing Surface, General Support, and 3D Support services. This chapter covers the first two of these categories.
- Present Drawing Surface components: drawing-surface management, support, and utility.
- Present General Support components:
  —histograms,
  —inquiry,
  —math, and
  —transcripting.

Introduction

We now have a foundation layer in WLib. These primitives provide the basics, but aren't enough to let us ignore the windowing system's underlying details to see our way to 3D graphics. We can't spend our time worrying about bitmaps and DCs. What we need is a shift in level that leaves all that behind. How do you do this?

A common technique is to give a programmer both a conceptual model and tools to implement that model; a *layer*, if you will. In this layer, we need to package the raster notions of the underlying windowing system in anticipation of the 3D support services and their requirement for coherently implemented coordinates.

What we'll do here is package a drawable surface in an API, providing a higher-level concept than a bitmap. This acts as a bridging layer that provides a necessary encapsulation around the WLib services, while adding features that address the coordinate needs of the 3D support services. The graphics environment provides this bridging layer. Internally, it builds a canvas and provides you with double-buffering services that enable screen refresh, file I/O, printing, and data sharing. This also serves as a unifying concept in the mental model we'll use in this system. The graphics environment uses the canvas abstraction to provide display surfaces and coordinates. Drawing-surface and coordinate management are constructed around the graphics environment and the canvas it owns.

The coordinates of the display surface meet the coordinates of the 3D graphics pipeline at the point of the user-to-device transformation; what is traditionally known as *window-viewport mapping*. Think of it as a line in the code. Above the line, you're clearly in the realm of 3D computer graphics, where 3D mathematics support comes into play. Below the line, the windowing system's impact is felt, where raster strategy is involved. In between these two, there are some generally useful functions packaged into a general set of routines. The major division of the library—Drawing Surface, General Support, and 3D Support services— is reflected in the decomposition diagram of Figure 5-1. As it shows, we can't forget the usual housekeeping chores, either.

Figure 5-1.   G3DLib First-Order Decomposition

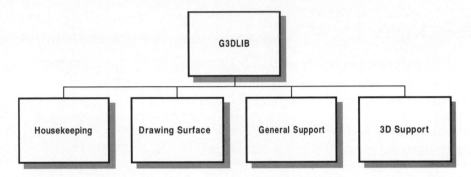

Drawing Surface services are the conceptual model followed for all drawing operations. The drawing surface or canvas is the target of all output primitives and is usually blitted as a unit to the client area of some window to present output to the user. The Drawing Surface services themselves are comprised of two sets of routines:

- Drawing Surface canvas and graphics environment management
- Drawing Surface support and utility.

This is shown in Figure 5-2.
Drawing surface management is a two-part process.

1. The canvas provides the drawing surface.
2. The graphics environment provides the coordinate mappings.

The canvas routines allocate an off-screen raster drawing surface where the vector operations are performed. Using an offscreen raster surface allows a double-buffering of the image to be displayed. The drawing surface is then moved to the screen, usually through a bitblit (not to be confused with the Windows implementation called, of course, **BitBlit**). An extension to this approach adds a memory buffer to cache the intermediate calculated values, allowing a color mapping to sweep into the off-screen area. Both methods have their uses; it is up to you to decide which to use and when.

Externally, you have access to the *GENV* data structure and API, and internally you have the canvas abstraction to handle most of the details. Within the graphics environment, key values and components are maintained for your convenience. Windows has a similar concept with its notion of a device context (DC) and the values maintained in it. The DC is a core GDI concept, but I don't want to discuss the many important details asso-

Figure 5-2. G3DLib Drawing Surface Services

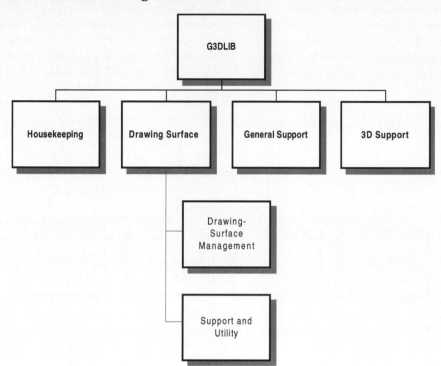

ciated with DCs and Windows programming. For our purposes, it's more important to expand upon the DC and maintain more information about what objects are being used and what actions are currently being performed.

Graphics environment routines are centered around the graphics environment structure; they provide set and get functions that form a query and manipulation structure for our interface to GDI. The G3DLib provides for creation and destruction of instances of *GENV*s, as well as functions that let you manipulate *GENV*s for your benefit.

The drawing surface support and utilities contain coordinate-definition and mapping functions as well as the window and viewport functions. The support and utility functions calculate both user and device coordinates for the window-viewport paradigm. Window and viewport definition, a simple wipe, and conversion between the user coordinates of the window and the device coordinates of the viewport are the heart of this API.

Within General Support services, there are routines that handle:

- histogram,
- inquiry,
- math, and
- session transcripting.

Histograms are a valuable tool when we're processing the images we create.

Inquiry functions determining various hardware and software capabilities are a standard component of graphics systems. Since we use Windows as the substrate, inquiry must be able to bridge between Windows and the graphics system's requirements. General math functions enhance those provided in the standard run-time library.

Session transcripts enable reporting on events, which is useful for maintaining an action log as well as debugging the system. Figure 5-3 contains a detailed decomposition diagram showing this.

Figure 5-3.   G3DLib General Support Services

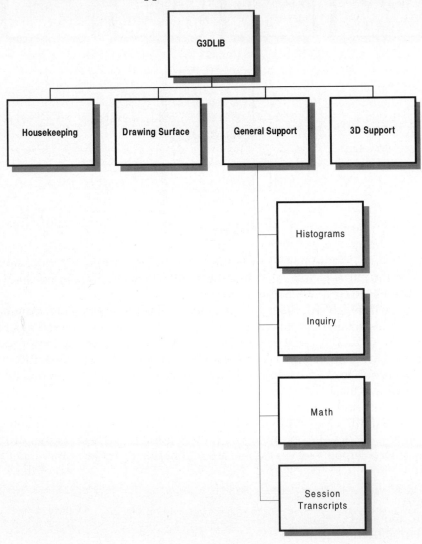

Histograms are extremely useful for examining the color content of an image. They also provide a bridge into image processing, by allowing an examination of the frequency of occurrence of data: in this case, color values. When combined with the color services you've seen, the memory buffer that's used as an intensity buffer, and the application support (rough plot of histogram bin data, color analysis), I think you'll agree that quite a bit of code goes into color and color support.

In the more advanced techniques, the colors in an image are a combination of original color, surface properties, and lighting conditions: the result isn't known until the image is generated. When you're working with less than 16 million colors, you need some technique other than directly specifying the color. We'll use the technique of gray scale intensity rendering during image generation and post-processing for color generation. This lets us see an inexact rendering during image generation to make sure that our final product is worth waiting for and spending the processing cycles to colorize. Histograms are an important part of this process and I supply general routines to support histograms, as well as the additional grayscaling and colorizing routines that we'll develop later.

Inquiry functions put a standard wrapper around Windows' mechanism for determining various system values. This frees you from worrying about the underlying mechanism that determines important system values.

The math routines extend the support from the C run-time library in the area of transcendental and conversion routines. The need to handle radians and degrees, trig functions that use radians or degrees, and a few other "extras" just seem to crop up all the time. Experience will show you the value of these routines.

Session transcripts are a mechanism for tracing the execution path. This is useful for debugging and for reporting on the results of a particular session. You'll need a full-fledged transcripting layer to solve buffering and display problems that are beyond the scope of this book. Chief among them is the 64K boundary. Another is the behavior of **TextOut** across the boundary. Still, a simple transcripting layer provides some value, so we'll develop one.

This completes General Support services.

The critical 3D mathematics routines are our final set of routines. Within the 3D Support services you have:

- graphics output primitives and attributes, and
- vector, transform, and viewing system services.

Primitives and attributes add the functions you need to draw points, lines, and figures, along with control over the appearance of graphical objects that gives you a layer of output independence. And, last but not least, they support the component usually associated with 3D graphics: the expected vector, transform, and viewing system routines that provide the mathematical basis of the system. Figure 5-4 shows the decomposition of the 3D Support services.

Figure 5-4. G3DLib 3D Support Services

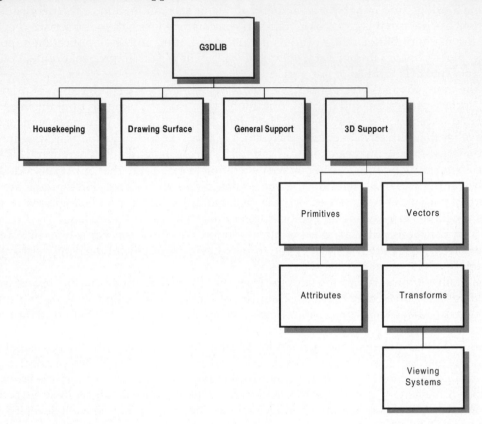

The primitives and attributes let us work above the GDI routines. If you decide to expand this system to include concepts like structures and bundles in PHIGS, this layer will prove very valuable. Likewise, if you want to port the basic API to any other system, it is critical that all graphics output is GDI-independent. Here we still use GDI objects directly, but the library graphics ouput primitives lay the foundaton for future independence.

Vector, transform, and viewing system primitives round out the G3DLib and prepare you for 3D objects and the modeler. Vector math in three dimensions is a fundamental component of the world of 3D graphics. Thankfully, you don't need much more than algebra and trigonometry to cope with vector math. Matrix transforms are the first "serious" math component. (Don't worry—I give you the code.) Building on the transforms, the viewing system primitives encapsulate the operations necessary to initialize and control 3D transformations.

That completes the initial description of the G3DLib (see Table 5-1). In Chapter 7 I'll get into the vector, transform, and viewing system routines. The primitives and attributes are the subject of Chapter 6. Only the Drawing Surface and General Support services are covered here in Chapter 5.

Table 5-1. G3DLib Source Modules

Files	Description
G3DLib Housekeeping	
gl_init.c,gl_init.h	Library global initialization
gl_term.c,gl_term.h	Library global termination
gl_err.c,gl_err.h	Library error reporting
g3d_inc.h	Main include file, applications reference this
Drawing Surface	
glgenv.c,glgenv.h	Graphics evironment,manages coords for canvas
canvas.c,canvas.h	Canvas provides offscreen drawing surface for genv
bmpbuff.c,bmpbuff.h	Light part of canvas, hidden
membuff.c,membuff.h	Heavy part of the canvas,hidden
coords.c,coords.h	Coordinate mapping
winview.c,winview.h	Window/viewport using coord layer
General Support	
inquiry.c,inquiry.h	System inquiry, hides GetDeviceCaps/GetSystemMetrics
hist.h,hist.h	Histogram support
math.c,math.h	General math functions
trans.c,trans.h	Session transcript global window class based on WINIO
3D Support	
prims.c,prims.h	Output to genv
vec4d.c,vec4d.h	Vector functions
matrix.c,matrix.h	Basic matrix functions
xform.c,xform.h	Matrix transforms
viewing.c,viewing.h	Viewing systems

G3DLib Library Housekeeping

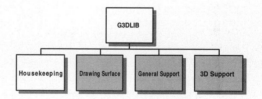

The G3DLib is built, like the WLib you met in Chapter 4, around the MakeDLL generator. It starts us off by creating shell modules for the initialization and termination routines (with the startup customized for this particular library). Then we create the various subsystems. Creating subsystems usually means changing both the initialization routine (in this case *G3D_Main*) and the termination **WEP** routine. In our case, we'll create each subsystem with the shell initialization and termination routines that are meant to be placed in *G3D_Main* and **WEP**.

In addition to considering the library-specific details we need to take care of at load and unload time, this library deals with error-handling and reporting. We use the **TRY/CATCH** routines internally, as well as the *WL_Error_Process* function; both are exports from WLib, but that's not enough. The G3DLib will also publish its own error-reporting function.

G3D_Main sets the library instance handle and global strings, which are very similar in nature and purpose to the shell app global strings, and loads them from the string table. After that, service subsystems have a shot at initialization (as shown in Listing 5-1). Notice that all subsystems are initialized; if any particular subsystem doesn't need to be, it can be removed from this sequence.

Listing 5-1.   G3D_Main in gl_init.c

```
int CALLBACK G3D_Main(HANDLE hModule,
                  WORD wDataSeg,  WORD cbHeapSize,
                  LPSTR lpszCmdLine){
    hLibInst = hModule;
    if (!LoadString(hModule, IDS_DLLNAME,
        gszDLLName, sizeof(gszDLLName)))
        return (FALSE);
    if (!LoadString(hModule, IDS_LOADSTRFAIL,
        gszLoadStrFail,  sizeof(gszLoadStrFail)))
        return (FALSE);
    if (!LoadString(hModule, IDS_ALLOCFAILURE,
        gszLockErrorMsg,  sizeof(gszLockErrorMsg)))
        return (FALSE);
    if (!LoadString(hModule, IDS_LOCKFAILURE,
        gszAllocErrorMsg, sizeof(gszAllocErrorMsg)))
        return (FALSE);
    G3D_BmpBuff_Init(); // base
    G3D_MemBuff_Init();
    G3D_Canv_Init();
    G3D_GEnv_Init();
    G3D_Hist_Init();
    G3D_Inq_Init();
    G3D_Trans_Init();
    G3D_Coords_Init(); // 3d
    G3D_WV_Init();
    G3D_Error_Init();
    G3D_Prims_Init();
    G3D_Attr_Init();
    G3D_GM_Init();
    G3D_Vec4D_Init();
    G3D_M4D_Init();
    G3D_XF_Init();
    G3D_VS_Init();
    return (bInit);
}
```

Termination code is just like the other DLL code. For both exit-code cases, we invoke all service subsystem termination handlers. Note the symmetry here with the initialization handler. See Listing 5-2 for the **WEP** code.

Listing 5-2.   WEP in gl_exit.c for G3D.DLL

```
int WINAPI WEP (int fSystemExit) {
    switch(fSystemExit)   {
        case WEP_FREE_DLL:
        case WEP_SYSTEM_EXIT:
            if ( bInit ) {
                G3D_VS_Term();    // 3d
                G3D_XF_Term();
                G3D_M4D_Term();
                G3D_Vec4D_Term();
                G3D_GM_Term();
                G3D_Attr_Term();
                G3D_Prims_Term();
                G3D_Error_Term();
                G3D_WV_Term();
                G3D_Coords_Term();
                G3D_Hist_Term();    // base
                G3D_Inq_Term();
                G3D_Trans_Term();
                G3D_GEnv_Term();
                G3D_Canv_Term();
                G3D_MemBuff_Term();
                G3D_BmpBuff_Term();
            }
            return 1;
            break;
    }
}
```

The error-reporting mechanism is a parallel construction similar to the code shown in Chapter 4. See Listing 5-3 for the function prototypes. *G3D_Error_Report* is responsible for the user interface; *G3D_Error_Process* handles the string resource access. Again, this block is initialized with the generic codes from the template-building process.

Listing 5-3.   Error Functions in gl_err.c

```
void WINAPI G3D_Error_Report(WORD wErrorType,LPSTR lpszErrorMsg);
void WINAPI G3D_Error_Process(DWORD dwErrorCode);
```

The categorization and definition of specific "interesting" error codes is our next order of business. The classes of errors that lie ahead have a lot to say about where the system is going, which makes them worth a moment's thought. Since they encompass the system, they naturally enforce global thinking—thinking about the definition of the library as a whole. Past practice and graphics standards attempts have categorized errors as:

- Invalid parameter,
- Request for or use of an unsupported feature,
- Math error (divide overflow etc.),
- bad operation for current state,
- general error (buffer overflow, etc.).

This is pretty straightforward. We've already covered the general case. Bad operations include actions like attempting to draw before viewing-system initialization occurs. A math error like divide overflow can happen in the perspective-projection division step if, for instance, an object definition is wrong. A request for an unsupported feature and an invalid parameter are related, but slightly different, cases of bad usage. A request for an unsupported feature is a type of invalid parameter that usually indicates unimplemented features or limitations of the system. A "normal" invalid parameter is usually a programmer error such as an inquiry using a #define that is not in the range of the defined inquiry values.

G3DLib Drawing Surface Services: Drawing Surface Management

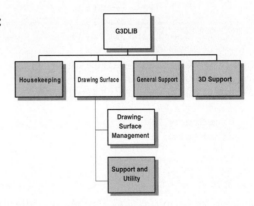

Once more, the goal of the display surface management routines is to provide a conceptual model and tools to orchestrate 3D graphics output within the windowing system. The canvas and graphics environment is the publicly visible solution. It allows a marriage of windowing system drawing requirements with the output needs of a 3D graphics system into a single package. This solution consists, as you would expect, of a data structure and an API. That's the external view. Internally, things are not quite so clean.

Wrapping layers are another element of the implementation strategies and complement the extensible API rules. The drawing surface is a wrapper around the elements of the WLib and GDI. It is both the display surface of the canvas and the coordinate management of the graphics environment, using the bitmap and palette elements of the WLib and GDI to do this. The drawing surface thus acts as both a tool and a conceptual model. But since the suite of routines that provide and operate on graphics environments is present, by definition it is a tool. By way of providing a single mechanism for graphics output, the graphics environment and its associated canvas provide a unifying structure or conceptual model for interaction with the display surface.

How it does this is another story. You already know it uses bitmaps, palettes, and more GDI. The *GENV* graphics environment data structure owns a *CANVAS*. All output modes need a bitmap for drawing output, so the *CANVAS* data structure owns a *BMPBUFF* to provide its bitmap component. A *CANVAS* with only a *BMPBUFF* can be constructed by using the LIGHT modifier at canvas-creation time. In our modeler, the histogram pane uses the LIGHT variant of the *CANVAS*.

Sometimes, it is convenient to store calculated values in addition to the drawing output. A *CANVAS* that provides this support is called HEAVY and uses the *MEMBUFF* to implement this feature. Raytrace mode in the modeler uses the *MEMBUFF* of the HEAVY variant as its intensity buffer. Figure 5-5 shows the hierarchy of this data structure, and the next section deals with the routines built around these four data structures. At the API level only the *GENV* and the *CANVAS* are visible.

Figure 5-5.   Drawing Surface Data Structure Hierarchy

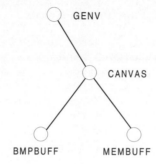

The GENV

The *GENV* structure is shown in Listing 5-4. Its content is split into two parts. The first consists of an *LPCANVAS,* a far-pointer to a canvas, which provides (at a minimum) the underlying bitmap for output. The second part provides elements that implement the window-viewport support. Notice the definition of two new structures, *FRECT* and *LRECT.* Internally, the classical window-viewport mapping is maintained in double for window coordinates and long for viewport coordinates.

Listing 5-4.   GENV Structure

```
typedef struct _glgenv {
    HWND        hw;
    FRECT       user;
    double      uxmin,uymin;
    double      uxmax,uymax;
    LRECT       device;
    LONG        dxmin,dymin;
    LONG        dxmax,dymax;
    double      a,b,c,d;
    int         Mode;
    LPCANVAS lpcanv;
} GENV;
typedef GENV NEAR *PGENV;
typedef GENV FAR  *LPGENV;
```

The Drawing Surface Management routines, shown in Listing 5-5, provide:

- new instance operations,
- screen and printer I/O,
- file I/O, and
- tool and value access.

These routines are the basis of drawing-surface management. In one package, the graphics environment provides read and write from the disk, display to the screen, output to the printer, and copy to clipboard services. Many of these operations boil down to one function call instead of a long sequence of Windows and DOS calls.

Listing 5-5.   Graphics Environment Functions in glenv.c

```
//new instance ops
LPGENV     WINAPI G3D_GEnv_Create(HWND hwnd,
                                   int ctype,    // canvas
                                   int vtype,    // values
                                   int stype,    // coloring scheme
                                   FRECT rW,
                                      lRECT rV);
void       WINAPI G3D_GEnv_Destroy(LPGENV glgenv);
// screen and printer io
void       WINAPI G3D_GEnv_Paint(LPGLGENV glgenv,
                        HDC     hdc,
                        RECT    rcDst,RECT   rcSrc,
                        BOOL    fRectDefined);
void       WINAPI G3D_GEnv_Scale(LPGLGENV glgenv,
                        HDC     hdc,
                        RECT    rcPaint,
                        BOOL    fRectDefined);
BOOL       WINAPI G3D_GEnv_Print(HINSTANCE      hInst,
                        HWND             hw,
                           LPGENV glgenv,
                        FARPROC          lpAbortProc,
                        FARPROC          lpAbortDlg,
                        HWND             hDlgAbort,
                        BOOL       FAR *bAbort,
                        LPPRINTOPTIONS lpPOpt,
                           LPSTR szJobName);
// file io
BOOL       WINAPI G3D_GEnv_Load(HWND hw, LPGLGENV glgenv,
LPSTR szFileName);
BOOL       WINAPI G3D_GEnv_Save(HWND hw,LPGLGENV glgenv,
LPSTR szFileName);
```

In addition to these operations we have tool and value access routines to manage drawing tools like pens, brushes, and palettes that are needed to draw and allow an array-like mechanism to manipulate individual pixel locations on the display surface. We'll expand on the ubiquity of the DC and the objects you incessantly select and deselect, providing a set of routines that mimic these actions, as shown in Listing 5-6. This gives you fine-grain control at the cost of semantically tying the policy structure of the subsystem to the Windows model. *G3D_GEnv_SetVal*, *G3D_GEnv_GetVal*, and *G3D_GEnv_Use* provide this mimicry. This implies that the canvas is tightly tied to the drawing objects for which these functions act. By picking a very generic set of drawing tools you can avoid too much dependency since almost every underlying graphics system (like GDI, GPI, or QuickDraw) uses pens, brushes, and palettes.

Listing 5-6.   GENV Tool Access and Value Access Routines in glgenv.c

```
// tool access
BOOL        WINAPI G3D_GEnv_SetVal(LPGLGENV glgenv,int Element, DWORD
Value);
DWORD       WINAPI G3D_GEnv_GetVal(LPGLGENV glgenv,int Element);
BOOL        WINAPI G3D_GEnv_Reset(LPGLGENV glgenv, int Offset);
void        WINAPI G3D_GEnv_Use(LPGLGENV glgenv, int Offset);
// pixel access
BOOL        WINAPI G3D_GEnv_SetPix(LPGLGENV glgenv,
                                int OffsetX,int OffsetY, HPVOID Value);
HPVOID      WINAPI G3D_GEnv_GetPix(LPGLGENV glgenv,int OffsetX,int
OffsetY);
BOOL        WINAPI G3D_GEnv_SetMem(LPGLGENV glgenv,
                                int OffsetX,int OffsetY, HPVOID Value);
HPVOID      WINAPI G3D_GEnv_GetMem(LPGLGENV glgenv,int OffsetX,int
OffsetY);
```

Accessing the buffer values is another useful operation. This mechanism is different from the point-output primitive (Chapter 6) in concept, even if the end result of both can be to set a pixel. We can use the access mechanism like an output primitive to set a value, but it can also be used to query the current value, and it allows access to both levels of the canvas. This final detail is the kicker—the true output primitive has no idea that the canvas is composed of multiple layers, which makes access different from output.

Semantically, unless we have a mechanism to distinguish the layers of the canvas, access to sub-components is not allowed. As an API designer, you make the call as to the "where"s and "how"s of this access mechanism, or whether to even allow it at all. In this case, the histogramming/grayscaling/colorizing process hinges on being able to access and modify underlying canvas values and force an update to appear. The *SetPix/GetPix* routines provide bitmap access, while the *SetMem/GetMem* routines provide memory-array access. All of this depends on the canvas layer lurking in the shadows. Before you're exposed to canvases, let's tackle the drawing-surface management routines, the *GENV* and internals.

An instance of a *GENV* is constructed using *G3D_GEnv_Create*. We must request one of the two flavors, LIGHT or HEAVY, to designate the use of either just a bitmap or a bitmap in conjunction with a memory array. If we request a HEAVY canvas, we have to specify the value type. I'll cover this in gory detail later, but for now Listing 5-7 shows the syntax for both invocation flavors.

Listing 5-7.   GENV and Canvas Creation

```
//
pvwwnd->genv  = G3D_GEnv_Create(pvwwnd->hwnd,
      LIGHT,NULL,BLACK_CANV,rectW,rectV);
//
pvwwnd->genv  = G3D_GEnv_Create(pvwwnd->hwnd,
      HEAVY,INT32,WHITE_CANV,rectW,rectV);
```

In addition to the canvas weight, memory value, and style parameters, *GENV* also contains the window handle and the window and viewport rectangles connecting the device coordinates of the bitmap to the user coordinates of the application-defined viewing system. Destroying an instance of a *GENV* operates on the token returned by the creation function, and is handled by the corresponding *G3D_GEnv_Destroy* function shown in Listing 5-8. The *GENV* token can then be used in load, paint, print, and save operations; see the sequence in Listings 5-9 to 5-12 for details on syntax. These functions provide the bulk of the functionality of the display surface.

Listing 5-8.   GENV and Canvas Destruction

```
G3D_GEnv_Destroy(pvwwnd->genv);
```

Listing 5-9.   GENV Load from File

```
G3D_GEnv_Load(pvwwnd->hwnd,pvwwnd->genv,szFileName);
```

Listing 5-10.   GENV Output to Screen

```
G3D_GEnv_Paint(pvwwnd->genv,
               hdcDst,rectDst,rectSrc,fSelectRectDefined);
```

Listing 5-11.   GENV Output to Printer

```
G3D_GEnv_Print(g_app.hinst,pvwwnd->hwnd, pvwwnd->genv,
               lpfnAbortProc,lpfnAbortDlg,hDlgAbort,
               (BOOL FAR *)&bAbortFlag,
               (LPPRINTOPTIONS) &poInfo, szFileName);
```

Listing 5-12.   GENV Save to File

```
G3D_GEnv_Save(pvwwnd->hwnd,pvwwnd->genv,szFileName);
```

Using these functions is just as simple as it looks. The tool and value access routines are not so obvious. The interface to these functions is shown in Listing 5-13, and Listing 5-14 shows how you can use the tool functions in one sequence to select and realize a palette, and in another sequence to retrieve the current pen.

Listing 5-13.   GENV Tool-Access Functions

```
// tool access
BOOL  WINAPI G3D_GEnv_SetVal(LPGENV genv,int Element,DWORD Value);
DWORD WINAPI G3D_GEnv_GetVal(LPGENV genv,int Element);
BOOL  WINAPI G3D_GEnv_Reset(LPGENV genv, int Offset);
void  WINAPI G3D_GEnv_Use(LPGENV genv, int Offset);
```

Listing 5-14.   GENV Tool Operation Examples

```
//specify palette and make active
G3D_GEnv_SetVal(pvwwnd->genv,ID_SCREENPALETTE,(DWORD)hprgb);
G3D_GEnv_Use(pvwwnd->genv,   ID_SCREENPALETTE);
// retrieve palette for use in another operation
WL_Pal_AnimatePalette(pvwwnd->hwnd,
(HPALETTE)G3D_GEnv_GetVal(pvwwnd->genv,ID_SCREENPALETTE);
```

The semantics of these functions consist of two simple rules; *SetVal/Use* to modify and *GetVal* to retrieve. Certain rules of GDI, especially those relating to palettes, require a two-step process of selecting and realizing, or activating, tools. The *SetVal/Use* pair mimics that model. **G3D_GEnv_SetVal** sets an element of the structure but does not perform the select into the memory DC. **G3D_GEnv_Use** selects a tool and, if necessary, also performs the realization operation. Where all this happens is not as important to you as the features it provides. In this way, the graphics environment, like a DC, allows a great deal of customization to fit the situation. This means the wrapping layer, while valuable as a tool and conceptual model, isn't a straight jacket at the same time.

The set of tools built in to the graphics environment helps define how complete and useful the wrapping is. This, of course, begs the question of what all the different items are that can be set, used, and got. Think of these as "slots" in the graphics environment that you can control. The slots that can be operated on are described in Table 5-2. The graphics environment gives you direct control over the contents of these slots. The value passed in must be 32-bit to maintain NT compatibility, and this code is very careful to make no assumptions about drawing tool sizes.

Still, strictly speaking, this is a violation of the first rule of wrapping (the one about exposing underlying Windows entities), but the value here lies in using the familiar without reinventing the wheel. This conceptual model is close enough to the GDI and DC model that it only requires minimal mental effort on your part to grasp this.

Table 5-2.   Graphics Environment/Canvas Attribute Slots

Slot	Purpose
ID_DC	Memory DC
ID_BITMAP	Primary drawing surface
ID_SCREENPALETTE	Matches client DC
ID_PRINTPALETTE	For grayscale "print" palette
ID_BCKCOLOR	Scene controls this
ID_TXTCOLOR	Automatically set based on above (B/W)
WHITE_CANV	Completely updates DC for this bckcolor
BLACK_CANV	Completely updates DC for this bckcolor
ID_PEN	Attribute for lines
ID_BRUSH	Attribute for fills
ID FONT	Attribute for text output

Another reason for doing it this way is performance and efficiency. When too many layers and abstractions get in the way, performance suffers. Another side effect of too much design is that you get divorced from the underlying substrate to the extent that a lack of understanding of the underlying details can lead you to make bad decisions. An understanding of some of the internal operations of a system can be an effective design tool, because it lets you make an informed decision about the costs/benefits of different technical approaches. This is not to say that you need to understand all the guts of the system, but a little basic knowledge helps make sense of things and helps you make better design decisions.

Since the underlying tools are the simple GDI tools, and are basically the same tools used in other GUI environments, this code is not as bad as it looks. For example, the DC is directly mimicked by the grafport of the Mac and the graph context, or GC, of X11. It both gives the familiar to us Windows programmers, and frees us from another cycle-eating layer; in general, it just seems like a valuable simplification. In this case, breaking the rules seems to be worth the cost and is a reminder that rules are meant to be used intelligently and not followed blindly.

The value-access functions are a mechanism to retrieve, modify, and update an x, y location on the canvas. An x, y pair indexes to the proper location. While our x and y offsets in the pixel and memory array are coordinates, they do not necessarily need to be 32-bit values to maintain NT compatibility. NT coordinates are 32 bits to increase the range for logical values in various mapping modes in a DC. The x and y we are concerned with here are physical values; realistically, a 2K x 2K bitmap is stretching the system. This means 16-bit x and 16-bit y is fine. Both the LIGHT and the HEAVY canvas will need a pair of functions; and *G3D_GEnv_SetPix/GetPix* and *G3D_GEnv_SetMem/GetMem* provide access to the bitmap and memory array, respectively. Listing 5-15 shows the API interface to the value access functions. Using these functions is as simple as providing an x, y offset to the desired location and providing a pointer of the proper type to receive the value. At graphics-environment construction time, if you specified a HEAVY canvas, you also specified a value type, so you're only keeping your contract with yourself here, as we all do when we program.

Listing 5-15. GENV Value-Access Functions

```
// value access
BOOL   WINAPI G3D_GEnv_SetPix(LPGENV genv,int OffsetX,int OffsetY, HPVOID
Value);
HPVOID WINAPI G3D_GEnv_GetPix(LPGENV genv,int OffsetX,int OffsetY);
BOOL   WINAPI G3D_GEnv_SetMem(LPGENV genv,int OffsetX,int OffsetY, HPVOID
Value);
HPVOID WINAPI G3D_GEnv_GetMem(LPGENV genv,int OffsetX,int OffsetY);
```

Listing 5-16 shows an example of using these functions to perform useful work. This code chunk is from the internal draw loop of a graphics demo program. The calculation loop has updated a memory location before this code is executed, so here it retrieves the pre-existing memory value using *G3D_GEnv_GetMem*, performs histogram and color calculations, and finally uses the derived value to update the pixel value using *G3D_GEnv_SetPix*.

Listing 5-16. GENV Value-Access Example

```
...
HPWORD hpw;
// get a pointer to the mem draw buffer and use calculated mem val hpw =
G3D_GEnv_GetMem(pvwwnd->genv,x,y);
...
//calculate value to set pixel to, based on x,y in hpw
...
// draw a pixel using bitmap buffer val
G3D_GEnv_SetPix(pvwwnd->genv,x,y,
                PixVal);
...
```

This clearly shows how the graphics environment provides a tool to make your life easier. This brief sequence of function calls performs some very powerful operations on your behalf and shows some of the power of the graphics environment. It also exposes two important features of the graphics environment:

- its provision of a conceptual model, which forces a policy of usage, and
- its dependency on the canvas with its bitmap and memory array.

Previously, we've only provided primitive services. You could use them in almost any fashion and the only rules they imposed were of the simplest kind, like "operate only on allocated instances." The graphics environment forces a policy of usage that goes well beyond this simple dictate. For output to screen and printer, reading and writing from disk, modifying attributes, and modifying values, it provides a suite of routines that semantically define the actions you can take. It also tries to enforce a consistent mental model of how to treat the display surface. This heavily flavors code that uses the graphics environment and influences how you code.

While providing this tool and model (as well as wrapping GDI), the graphics environment is itself a wrapper for more primitive basic services. These services are higher up the food chain than the low-level Windows bitmap services, but not by much. What this means is that the graphics layer is highly dependent on the canvas layer.

If we look at the implementation of the graphics environment rather than just the interface and usage we can clearly see this dependency. Listing 5-17 shows *G3D_GEnv_SetViewport*. Here we consider the classical viewport. This routine, which I'll cover in detail later in this chapter, gives you the ability in a single function call to set the viewport, resize the canvas to match the viewport, and clear the canvas.

Listing 5-17. GENV Internals for G3D_Genv_SetViewport

```
BOOL WINAPI G3D_GEnv_SetViewport(LPGENV glgenv,
                                       long vxo, long vyo,
                                        long vxe, long vye)
{
    RECT rcDst;
    G3D_WV_SetViewport(glgenv,vxo,vyo,vxe-vxo,vye-vyo);
//
// viewport size = canvas size
//
    rcDst.left   = rcDst.top = 0;
    rcDst.right  = vxe-vxo;
    rcDst.bottom = vye-vyo;
    G3D_GEnv_Size(glgenv->lpcanv,rcDst);
    return TRUE;
}
```

It uses the underlying window-viewport routine *G3D_WV_SetViewport* to set the viewport, then uses the utility routine *G3D_GEnv_Size* to resize and clear the canvas. It may not be obvious, but this function also defines a great deal of policy. It couples setting the viewport with resizing and clearing the canvas. Semantically, this binding could cause a problem unless we provide an alternate method to manipulate the viewport without affecting the canvas. When we consider the implementation of *G3D_GEnv_SetViewport* in the Support section (the *G3D_GEnv_SetWindow* companion function is deferred until then also), we'll look at this issue again. Here, I just want to illustrate the layer dependencies and the policy semantics bound into this function. It's inevitable that some of this occurs in a library, and understanding a library at this level is a key factor in effectively using it. Understanding the implementation of the graphics environment then exposes these dependencies and semantics; further understanding the canvas adds to your grasp of its features and limitations.

The CANVAS, BMPBUFF, and MEMBUFF

There are many ways to render an image. The naive approach renders directly into the client area. A much better technique uses an off screen bitmap that is then displayed in the client area. For the really demanding, a convenient technique is to maintain a shadow array in memory containing a representation of what is being drawn. This array usually contains pixel color values. This shadow array can then be post-processed as needed. Sometimes the post-processing is as simple as rendering it into the off-screen bitmap I just mentioned, then displaying it into the client area of the target window. Sometimes the pixel array values require much more processing to provide useful values, as is the case with color quantization and palette generation.

The principle components of the canvas are the bitmap and the memory array. The bitmap is an offscreen or memory bitmap. More important, a memory Display Context, or *memDC*, is created at the same time, and its lifetime is tied to the bitmaps. This combination allows directly blitting to the client area without the annoying process of creating a memory DC and destroying it in the usual Windows sandwich. The memory buffer is simply an allocated array.

This may seem simple and innocuous, but data representation rears its ugly head when we consider the set of value types to provide. For simplification, let's call the bitmap and DC combo a *bitmap buffer* or **BMPBUFF** and the memory array a *memory buffer* or **MEMBUFF**.

Now we can define the two canvas flavors. A LIGHT, or lightweight, canvas consists of a **BMPBUFF** or an offscreen bitmap and DC combo. Figure 5-6 depicts this "double-buffering" arrangement. A HEAVY, or heavyweight, canvas consists of *both* a **BMPBUFF** or offscreen bitmap and DC combo and an **MEMBUFF** or memory array; this is shown in Figure 5-7. This arrangement provides "triple-buffering," and is the principle mechanism for decoupling image calculation and display. By using these #defines, you specify the type of canvas you want created. Having both types of canvases gives you the building blocks to handle varying application needs.

Figure 5-6.   High-Level Diagram of Light Canvas

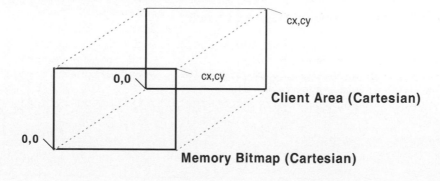

Figure 5-7.   High-Level Diagram of Heavy Canvas

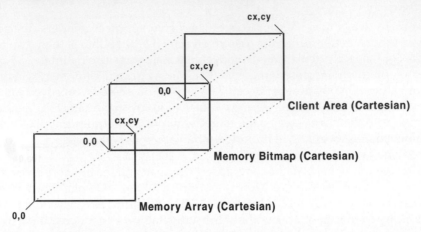

The first interesting thing you should notice about these figures is that the canvas is addressed using standard Cartesian coordinates, not the text-mode addressing that is the GDI default. The bitmap buffer and client area are, indeed, GDI-coordinate oriented in the beginning. To manage the coordinate origin change, we employ code like Listing 5-18 to change the mapping mode, and to modify the window-viewport coordinate mapping GDI uses to address bitmaps and the client area. First, it sets the window's y origin to a positive value, indicating that the y zero value should be translated by that amount. This effectively moves the origin from left-top to left-bottom. Next, it sets the window y extent to a negative value, indicating that values increase when moving upward; this is the opposite of default mode and gives us the effect we want. We use viewport values in the normal GDI fashion. This provides a swapping of the origin in GDI's mind, which allows the graphics system to address pixel values in a normal Cartesian fashion and have that transferred through GDI without interference. Figure 5-8 shows, side by side, the two pixel-addressing schemes; you can see that the Cartesian scheme is much more convenient for us.

Listing 5-18.   DC Coordinate Mapping Change

```
SetMapMode(lpbb->hdcMem, MM_ANISOTROPIC);
SetWindowOrg(lpbb->hdcMem,0,                      (rv.bottom-rv.top));
SetWindowExt(lpbb->hdcMem,rv.right-rv.left, -(rv.bottom-rv.top));
SetViewportOrg(lpbb->hdcMem,0, 0);
SetViewportExt(lpbb->hdcMem,rv.right-rv.left, rv.bottom-rv.top);
```

Figure 5-8.   GDI Versus Cartesian Coordinate Mapping

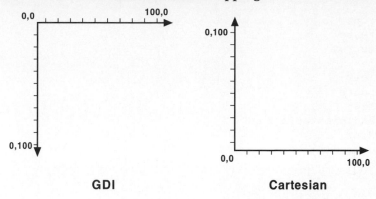

The Canvas

Most conveniently, the canvas and graphics environment hide all of this from us. Now that we've outlined our general strategy, we need to, once again, focus on the implementation tactics. Our two general rules are as follows.

1. Define a structure.
2. Define a standard set of routines that operate on that structure, providing a consistent set of basic operations (instance operations, utility, screen and printer output, file I/O, etc.).

The *CANVAS* structure, shown in Listing 5-19, is itself only a wrapper for the *BMPBUFF* and the *MEMBUFF*. The canvas API parallels the *GENV* API using the *CANVAS* structure. An important detail here is the usage of *LRECT*, or longs, for the coordinate values. The name space in Listing 5-20 illustrates this parallelism. I've omitted the parameter lists and return values for these functions in this listing because they are simple pass-throughs for the *GENV* parameters and returns.

Listing 5-19.   CANVAS Structure

```
typedef struct _canv {
    HWND          hw;
    int           ctype;
//
// w/v/mapping
//
    LRECT      rW;
    LRECT      rV;
//
// offscreen storage
//
    LPBMPBUFF     bb;
    int           vtype;
    LPMEMBUFF     mb;
} CANVAS;
```

Listing 5-20.   CANVAS Functions in canvas.c

```
//instance ops
G3D_Canv_Create
G3D_Canv_Destroy
//utility
G3D_Canv_Clear
G3D_Canv_Update
G3D_Canv_Size;
// screen and printer outout
G3D_Canv_Paint
G3D_Canv_Scale
G3D_Canv_Print
// file io
G3D_Canv_Load
G3D_Canv_Save
//  tool access
G3D_Canv_SetVal
G3D_Canv_GetVal
G3D_Canv_Reset
G3D_Canv_Use
//  value access
G3D_Canv_SetPix
G3D_Canv_GetPix
G3D_Canv_SetMem
G3D_Canv_GetMem
```

When we use the canvas layer as a pass-through, the mechanism by which the double and triple-buffering is provided is completely transparent to the graphics environment. You can change the internal behavior of the canvas and, as long as you don't disturb the API, the graphics environment and the user will be unaware of the change. That is, they'll be unaware of it as long as your changes provide equal or greater functionality and aren't buggy.

Internally, the graphics environment makes *CANVAS* calls. Listing 5-17 showed *G3_GEnv_SetViewport* invoking the canvas API. Listing 5-21 shows another sequence, this time part of the creation of the graphics environment. *G3D_Canv_Create* is called with a parameter list that is almost identical. The difference, though subtle, is extremely important and revolves around coordinates. It uses the *LRECT* rV parameter instead of the *FRECT* rW parameter. There's some sleight-of-hand involved here.

Listing 5-21.   GENV Creation Sequence Using G3D_Canv_Create

```
glgenv->lpcanv = G3D_Canv_Create(hwnd,ctype,vtype,stype,rV,rV);
G3D_WV_SetWindow(glgenv,rW.left,rW.bottom,rW.right,rW.top);
G3D_WV_SetViewport(glgenv,rV.left,rV.top,rV.right,rV.bottom);
```

The graphics environment manages the classical window-viewport mapping and is the only layer that knows about both floating-point window coordinates (*FRECT*) and long-integer viewport coordinates (*LRECT*). The canvas takes care of flipping the GDI window-viewport internally, and for it all to hang together GDI must believe that the bitmap has the same GDI extents with the origins flipped (resulting in Cartesian coordinates on the canvas). Using the rV parameter for both GDI window and GDI viewport accomplishes this for the extents, then code like Listing 5-18 takes over. The function prototypes for the two creation functions are contained in Listing 5-22 to highlight this difference.

Listing 5-22.   GENV and CANVAS Create Function Prototypes

```
// genv
LPGENV      WINAPI G3D_GEnv_Create(HWND hwnd,
                                   int ctype,    // canvas
                                   int vtype,    // values
                                   int stype,    // coloring scheme
                                   FRECT rW, LRECT rV); //CLASSICAL
// canvas
LPCANVAS    WINAPI G3D_Canv_Create(HWND hwnd,
                                   int ctype,    // canvas
                                   int vtype,    // values
                                   int stype,    // coloring scheme
                                   LRECT rW, LRECT rV);  //GDI
```

Let me repeat: two window-viewport systems are involved here:

- *GENV* and classical, and
- canvas and GDI.

The *G3D_WV_SetWindow/SetViewport* pair belong to the Support section and provide window-viewport mapping (in Cartesian coordinates) of a floating-point-valued range to a long-integer-valued domain in the classical sense. This is very different from the underlying Windows window and viewport routines, as we've already discussed. They are both integer-based systems and, therefore, useless in providing true range-domain mapping from floating-point to integer without assistance. In this system, we only use the Windows window and viewport routines to flip the origin of the coordinate system in GDI to match our Cartesian-based scheme. For this to work, the window and viewport extents passed to the GDI routines **SetWindowxxx** and **SetViewportxxx** must be equal.

Enough with the window viewport; let's get on to canvas details. If you examine the details of *G3D_Canv_Create* in Listing 5-23, you'll see that it clearly depends on the *BMPBUFF* and *MEMBUFF* layers. In another example, file I/O in Listing 5-24, the dependency is even clearer. From this code block it should be clear to you that the *BMPBUFF* and the *MEMBUFF* reside in separate files, a fact the layers above the canvas have no need to know.

Listing 5-23.   CANVAS Creation Sequence Using BMPBUFF and MEMBUFF

```
lpcanv->rW = rW;
 lpcanv->rV = rV;
 lpcanv->bb = G3D_BmpBuff_Create(hwnd,lpcanv->rW,lpcanv->rV,stype);
 if ( !lpcanv->bb )
 {
    Throw((LPCATCHBUF)&_ci.state,CANVERR_BMPBUFF_CRFAIL);
 }
 switch(ctype)
 {
    case HEAVY:
       lpcanv->vtype = vtype;
       lpcanv->mb    = G3D_MemBuff_Create(hwnd,
                                          vtype,
                                          (rV.right -rV.left),
                                          (rV.bottom-rV.top));
       if ( !lpcanv->mb )
       {
           Throw((LPCATCHBUF)&_ci.state,CANVERR_MEMBUFF_CRFAIL);
       }
       break;
 }
 return lpcanv;
```

Listing 5-24.   CANVAS File I/O

```
BOOL WINAPI G3D_Canv_Load(HWND hw,LPCANVAS lpcanv,
LPSTR szFileName){
    BOOL     r;
    r =  G3D_BmpBuff_Load(hw, lpcanv->bb,szFileName);
    switch(lpcanv->ctype) {
       case HEAVY:
       return G3D_MemBuff_Load(lpcanv->mb,szFileName);
    }
    return r;
}
BOOL   WINAPI G3D_Canv_Save(HWND hw,LPCANVAS lpcanv,
LPSTR szFileName){
    BOOL     r;
    r =  G3D_BmpBuff_Save(hw,lpcanv->bb,szFileName);
    switch(lpcanv->ctype){
       case HEAVY:
       return G3D_MemBuff_Save(lpcanv->mb,szFileName);
    }
    return r;
}
```

The decision to use two separate files is a trade-off in terms of file-system usage and complexity, but it allows the bitmap portion to be saved as a DIB on disk that is then usable by any tool that reads DIB files. The *MEMBUFF* values, on the other hand, have limited use by any other tool except the post-processing tools used in the modeler. This means that it's acceptable to use a non-standard format and dump the *MEMBUFF* values to a separate file. Once again, this clearly illustrates the dependency on the underlying *BMPBUFF* and *MEMBUFF.*

The Bitmap Buffer

The *BMPBUFF* and *MEMBUFF* are the underlying primitive layers in the graphics environment/canvas system. *BMPBUFF*s are built on the bitmap layer provided by WLib. The *BMPBUFF* structure, shown in Listing 5-25, contains elements to support the slots for the drawing tools, as well as the offscreen bitmap, DC, and window-viewport information. Remember that there are two window viewports here—the Windows-GDI one hidden by the canvas and the classical one provided by the canvas. The *BMPBUFF* API again parallels the *GENV* and *CANVAS* API, so I'll spare you the gory details. The key features of the *BMPBUFF* are as follows, all of which are accomplished while conforming to the standard interface.

- It provides the offscreen bitmap and memory DC (see Figure 5-9).
- It handles the flipping of the GDI window-viewport mapping.
- It manages one of the two separate files required by canvas I/O.

Figure 5-9.   Detailed Diagram of Light Canvas

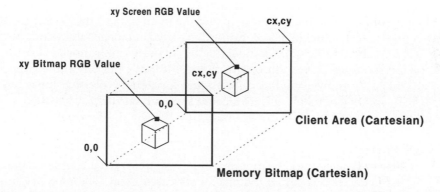

Listing 5-25.   BMPBUFF Structure

```
// bmpbuff structure declaration
typedef struct tagBmpBuff
{
    HWND        hwnd;
// mem dc support
    HDC         hdcMem;
    HBITMAP     hbmMem,hbmOld;
    int         width;
    int         height;
    RECT        rcBmp;
// palette support
    HPALETTE    hpS,hpP,hpOld;
// style
    int         stype;
// background and text color
    DWORD       bClr;
    DWORD       tClr,otc;
// attr
    HPEN        hp,hpo;
    HBRUSH      hbr,hbro;
    HFONT       hf,hfo;
} BMPBUFF;
typedef BMPBUFF NEAR *PBMPBUFF;
typedef BMPBUFF FAR  *LPBMPBUFF;
```

The *BMPBUFF* is the light canvas in many respects, even though it exists below the canvas. Since it contains the memory bitmap and the memory DC, the *SetPix/GetPix* functions at this level affect actual pixels. Because this canvas manages the window-viewport mapping, use of it and its accessing element (dx, dy) operates in the normal Cartesian fashion, as depicted in Figure 5-9. Additionally, the result that's placed on the clipboard and saved to a file is a Windows-standard bitmap and a palette. Note that these two objects make up a DIB, and one of them is easily created from a *BMPBUFF*. This, then, is the light canvas and the features, including double-buffering, it provides for you.

The Memory Buffer
Double-buffering combined with the memory buffer provides what could be called "triple-buffering." This is basically a big, dynamically allocated array. The memory buffer provides an "intensity buffer" to store the results of calculations. It's only really used for the ray-tracer and pixel-level drawing processes, because they map nicely into the array access provided by the memory buffer. As each pixel in the trace is calculated, the *_SetMem* function (which I'll show you in a little bit) can be used to cache the original calculated value before grayscaling. For filled polygons, this does not map easily; remember, we're using GDI, not a polygon scan-line converter that would map.

There is a twist, however. Data representation becomes a major issue (actually, a couple of major issues wrapped together). The actual data type and its accuracy and the linkage to the bitmap are both representation-related issues. The data type we pick for this memory buffer represents a trade-off between storage cost and value maintenance.

Integer-based buffers are repositories for integral values in the range $0 . . 2^{n-1}$, where n is the number of bits. A short integer has 16 bits, which means it can manage a range of 32K values. A long integer has 32 bits and is typically used to cache 24-bit color values, after RGB-to-CRT conversion but before grayscale.

Most needs are satisfied by providing only these two types; however, in the interest of providing policy-free primitives, we can also allocate a buffer of floating-point types. We'll do this mostly in the interest of completeness. It quickly illustrates issues you'll need to know about in dealing with the memory buffer, and points out the value-representation issues involved. Allowing for different data types within the internals of the *MEMBUFF* lets the application programmer make the trade-off between storage cost and value range. This is exactly what we want—the application programmer is the only one who knows what's most important for their application, and the only one who can make the trade-off and code it up.

The key to this approach is the concept of *void pointer*. It's all well and good to allow the client programmer to specify data type. The "gotcha" is in implementing a structure to accommodate this. We don't want a union because each field in a union must have a unique name. What we want is to be able to use only one name internally, regardless of type, to ease readability. A type tag and a pointer to void allows, using judicious casts, a general approach to this problem.

Before we deal with implementation of the *MEMBUFF*, a quick review of basic data types will fix in your mind the important aspects that influence the *MEMBUFF*. Table 5-3 shows common data types, along with their size in bits, their range of representable values, and their precision. The types.h file, *MBHEADER* structure, and *MEMBUFF* structure are shown in Listing 5-26. The manifest constants define the initial set of value types. We can extend this easily by simply defining an entirely new, parallel construct for each additional value type.

Table 5-3.   Data Types, Sizes, Ranges, and Precision

Type	Size	Range	Precision
WORD	16	-2^{15} to $2^{15}-1$	N/A
DWORD	32	-2^{31} to $2^{31}-1$	N/A
FLOAT	32	3.4×10^{-38} to 3.4×10^{38}	7 digit
DOUBLE	64	1.7×10^{-308} to 1.7×10^{308}	15 digit
LONG DOUBLE	80	3.4×10^{-4932} to 1.1×10^{4932}	19 digit

Huge pointer typedefs are a convenience, but the use of huge void pointers is essential to the correct operation of the *MEMBUFF* routines. The *MBHEADER* is used in file I/O. In the *MEMBUFF* structure, the width and height of this memory array, along with the vtype-type tag element, provide enough information both for initial memory allocation and for correct access to the values. The utype field contains the number of bytes for the vtype contained in the structure. Rather than using a switch everywhere and hardcoding this value, we'll initialize it once as a convenience. If for some reason these utype byte count values have to change, they're localized in one spot. Note, the v for void could just as easily be considered v for value. A couple of typedefs round out the header file of *MEMBUFF*-specific structures.

Listing 5-26.   Types.h and MEMBUFF Structure

```
#define INT16   1
#define INT32   2
#define REAL32 3
#define REAL64 4
#define REAL80 5
typedef WORD            _huge* HPWORD;
typedef DWORD           _huge* HPDWORD;
typedef float           _huge* HPFLOAT;
typedef double          _huge* HPDOUBLE;
typedef long double _huge* HPLDOUBLE;
typedef VOID            _huge* HPVOID;
typedef struct tagMBHeader {
  int     width;
  int     height;
  int     vtype;
  int     utype;
} MBHEADER;
typedef MBHEADER NEAR   *PMBHEADER;
typedef MBHEADER FAR    *LPMBHEADER;
typedef struct _mem_buff {
  int     width;
  int     height;
  int     vtype;
  HPVOID  hpv;
} MEMBUFF;
typedef MEMBUFF NEAR   *PMEMBUFF;
typedef MEMBUFF FAR    *LPMEMBUFF;
```

The API provided by the *MEMBUFF* layer is different from the parallel *GENV-CANVAS-BMPBUFF* axis. Listing 5-27 shows the minimal API needed by the *MEMBUFF*. Of the standard categories (instance, utility, output, file I/O, tool access, and value access), we only need instance operations, utility operations, file I/O, and value access operations.

Listing 5-27.   MEMBUFF API in membuff.c

```
// instance ops
LPMEMBUFF WINAPI G3D_MemBuff_Create(HWND hwnd,UINT utype,
                                    WORD x,WORD y)
void     WINAPI G3D_MemBuff_Destroy( LPMEMBUFF lpmb );
//utility
BOOL     WINAPI G3D_MemBuff_Clear( LPMEMBUFF lpmb);
BOOL     WINAPI G3D_MemBuff_Size( LPMEMBUFF lpmb,
                                  WORD x,WORD y);
//file io
BOOL     WINAPI G3D_MemBuff_Load(LPMEMBUFF lpmb,LPSTR szFileName );
BOOL     WINAPI G3D_MemBuff_Save(LPMEMBUFF lpmb,LPSTR szFileName );
// value access
```

```
HPVOID  WINAPI G3D_MemBuff_GetMem(LPMEMBUFF lpmb,
                                  WORD x,WORD y );
BOOL    WINAPI G3D_MemBuff_SetMem( LPMEMBUFF lpmb,
                                   WORD x,WORD y, HPVOID Value );
```

During allocation, the *MEMBUFF* layer performs the all-important sizing calculation:

$$size =(LONG)sizeof(vtype)*(LONG((LONG)x+1)*(LONG(Y+1));$$

where *vtype* is the parameter containing the base value type. This defines the size of a location in the array, *x* contains the array width, and *y* contains the array height. You must calculate the size of each type of value correctly or risk bad things like a general-protection violation exception 13 when you access memory that does not belong to you. Listing 5-28 shows the key switch block in *G3D_Membuff_Create* that arbitrates array size to avoid this "bad" event.

Listing 5-28. Core Memory Buffer Sizing Code

```
switch(lpmb->vtype){
 case INT16:
   size        =(LONG)sizeof(WORD)*(LONG((LONG)x+1)*(LONG(Y+1));
   lpmb->hpv   = WL_Mem_Alloc(GHND,size);
   lpmb->utype = 2;
   break;
 case INT32:
   size        =(LONG)sizeof(LONG)*(LONG((LONG)x+1)*(LONG(Y+1));
   lpmb->hpv   = WL_Mem_Alloc(GHND,size);
   lpmb->utype = 4;
   break;
 case REAL32:
   size        =(LONG)sizeof(FLOAT)*(LONG((LONG)x+1)*(LONG(Y+1));
   lpmb->hpv   = WL_Mem_Alloc(GHND,size);
   lpmb->utype = 4;
   break;
 case REAL64:
   size        =(LONG)sizeof(DOUBLE)*(LONG((LONG)x+1)*(LONG(Y+1));
   lpmb->hpv   = WL_Mem_Alloc(GHND,size);
   lpmb->utype = 8;
   break;
 case REAL80:
   size        =(LONG)sizeof(LDOUBLE)*(LONG((LONG)x+1)*(LONG(Y+1));
   lpmb->hpv   = WL_Mem_Alloc(GHND,size);
   lpmb->utype = 10;
   break;
}
```

File I/O is yet another chunk of code that is very dependent on the type of value contained in the *MEMBUFF*. The *MBHEADER* structure contains elements for the x and y size, as well as the type. This information is used as a file header for the *MEMBUFF* output with code like the examples shown in Listings 5-29 and 5-30.

Listing 5-29.   File Input Using MBHEADER

```
//
// x, y, val type
//
_lread(in,(LPSTR) &mbh,sizeof (MBHEADER));
x     = mbh.width;
y     = mbh.height;
vtype = mbh.vtype;
//
// read in a line
//
for( x = 0;
     x < lpmb->width;
     x++)
{
    offset = (LONG)lpmb->utype*LONG((LONG)x*LONG)lpmb->height);
    size   = (LONG)lpmb->utype   * (LONG)lpmb->height;
    _lread(in, (LPSTR) lpmb->hpv+offset, size);
}
```

Listing 5-30.   File Output Using MBHEADER

```
//
// write the header
//
 mbh.width  =  lpmb->width;
 mbh.height =  lpmb->height;
 mbh.vtype  =  lpmb->vtype;
_lwrite(out, (LPSTR)&mbh,
         sizeof (MBHEADER));
//
// write the lines
//
for (x = 0;
     x < lpmb->width;
     x++)
{
    offset = (LONG)lpmb->utype*(LONG)((LONG)x*(LONG)lpmb->height
    size   = (LONG)lpmb->utype   * (LONG)lpmb->height;
    _lwrite(out, (LPSTR) lpmb->hpv+offset, size);
}
```

The access functions also depend on the type tag to allow value-size arbitration and to operate correctly. *G3L_MemBuff_SetMem* uses the type tag and the requested value offsets x and y to calculate the appropriate offset, then uses the result to modify the value at that location. *G3D_MemBuff_GetMem* performs the same calculation to retrieve a pointer to the location containing the desired value. The memory-buffer coordinate system accessed with the x and y offset values is essentially a linear mapping of vertical lines or columns of the memory array onto the bitmap representing the screen. FORTRAN described this as column major order. Figure 5-10 illustrates this mapping internal to the *MEMBUFF* and Figure 5-11 places this in the context of the heavy canvas.

Using the x and y offsets to calculate the location of the requested value is a little more involved than calculating the size. Referring to Figure 5-10 again, an x offset requests a column, and a y offset specifies the location in that column. Then this offset is used with the appropriate cast to enable the compiler to do our work for us. Refer to Listing 5-31 for the code.

Figure 5-10.   Memory Buffer Coordinate Mapping

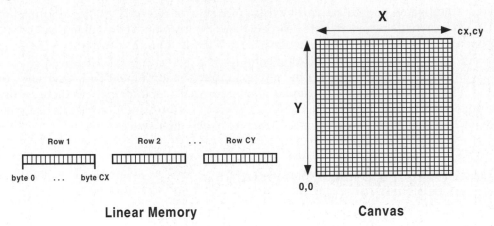

Figure 5-11.   Detailed Diagram of Heavy Canvas

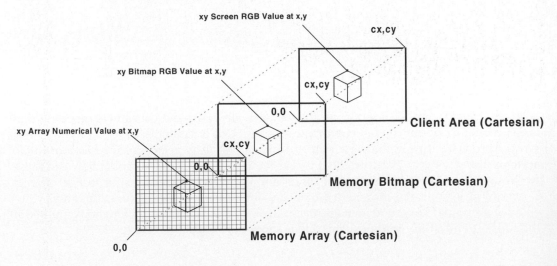

Listing 5-31. Memory Buffer Access Calculations

```
...
//calculate offset
col     = ((LONG)x * (LONG)lpmb->height);
offset = col + ((LONG)y;
...
// let compiler figure out which one it is
hpw       = (HPWORD)lpmb->hpv;
hpw      +=  offset;
...
```

I've omitted some particulars, but by this point you've received the grand tour of the display-surface management system; learned about the graphics environment and its subcomponents with their features, dependencies and limitations; and have seen the usage policy enforced by the graphics environment.

The canvas abstraction shadows the public graphics environment API. Internally, the graphics environment invokes its canvas analog for many operations that then devolve into a single function call. Next, the window-viewport support and graphics environment utility functions finish off the drawing-surface management services.

G3DLib Drawing Surface Services: Support and Utility

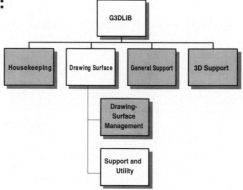

Support services provide support for the window-viewport and coordinate mapping that is a cornerstone of our overall coordinate strategy. Utility contains the clear, update, and size functions for the graphics environment and canvas. Any vector system has coordinate systems underlying it; Windows does too, as we've already seen. Mapping between these two coordinate systems (the graphics library and Windows) is the main purpose of support services. The graphics environment provided a slot for these mapping functions and a valuable "chokepoint" for you to manage this process. Three simple utility functions round out the support and utility routines. This API is shown in Listings 5-32 and 5-33.

Listing 5-32.   G3DLib Support Functions in glgenv.c

```
// window-viewport and coordinate mapping support in glgenv.c
BOOL      WINAPI G3D_GEnv_SetViewport(LPGENV glgenv,
int vxo, int vyo, int vxe, int vye);
BOOL      WINAPI G3D_GEnv_SetWindow(LPGENV glgenv,
double wxo, double wyo, double wxe, double wye);
//coordinate mapping in coords.c
BOOL      WINAPI G3D_GEnv_UsertoDev(LPGENV glgenv,
double x, double y, LPINT dcx, LPINT dcx);
BOOL      WINAPI G3D_GEnv_DevtoUser(LPGENV glgenv,
int x, int y, LPDOUBLE dcx,LPDOUBLE dcy);
```

Listing 5-33.   G3DLib Utility Functions in glgenv.c

```
// utility
void      WINAPI G3D_GEnv_Clear(LPGENV glgenv,HBRUSH hbrClear);
void      WINAPI G3D_GEnv_Update(LPGENV glgenv);
void      WINAPI G3D_GEnv_Size(LPGENV glgenv,
                        RECT   rcDst);
```

The window-viewport support lets you define a real-valued window coordinate space and a long integer-valued viewport coordinate space. Functions *G3D_GEnv_SetWindow* and *G3D_GEnv_SetViewport* perform these actions. I've already shown the code to *G3D_GEnv_SetViewport* in Listing 5-17. This function also enforces a major policy decision—the graphics environment forces the canvas size to equal the viewport size. This provides an equivalence in canvas and viewport coordinates that enables coordinate mapping. Canvas coordinates are viewport coordinates. However, canvas is not necessarily the same as client area. The issue of coordinate-space size is separate from the issue of drawing-surface size.

The issue of drawing-surface size in relation to client-area size is one of user interface policy more than anything else. If the drawing-surface size is the same as the client-area size, a *fixed-size policy* is in effect, which requires a resize of the drawing surface to match window resizes. If the drawing-surface size is not related to the client-area size, a *variable-size* policy is in effect and we must manage scrollbars for the user.

An unfortunate side effect of this is to penalize simple window-viewport remapping. This is easily rectified; simply export the *G3D_WV_* functions, then, if you need to, you can force a remapping without resizing the bitmap of the canvas as easily as doing two function calls.

Utility functions provide three basic operations—clear, update, and size—that enhance the graphics environment. The clear function provides a "wipe," using either a brush passed in as a parameter or the current background setting for the canvas. Next, the update function provides a method to force the screen output. Finally, the size function controls the resizing of the underlying bitmap and memory array. The *G3D_GEnv_SetViewport* function is already signed up as the first client of the size function.

Window-Viewport Support

Providing the public window-viewport support is handled by the two layers shown in Figure 5-12:

- window-viewport or *G3D_WV*, and
- coordinates or *G3D_Coords*.

Figure 5-12.   Window-Viewport Support Components

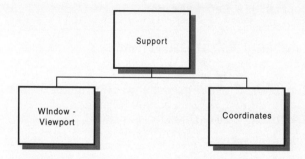

The *wv* layer, defined in Listing 5-34, provides functions *G3D_WV_SetWindow* and *G3D_WV_SetViewport*. As I discussed in Chapter 2, these functions let you define the window-viewport mapping in a manner similar to the classical form. This usage is shown again in Listing 5-35. We define a real-valued window of [10.0,-10.0] to [10.0,10.0] and map that to [0,0] to [400,400], as shown in Figure 5-13, by the code block in Listing 5-35.

Figure 5-13.   The Classical Window-Viewport Mapping

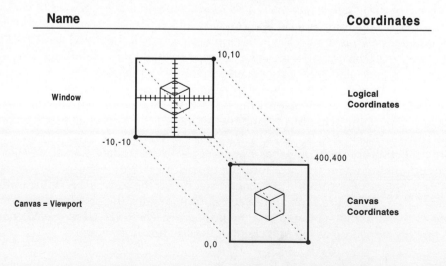

Listing 5-34.   WV Layer Functions in winview.c

```
BOOL  WINAPI G3D_WV_SetViewport(LPGENV glgenv,
int vxo, int vyo, int vxe, int vye);
BOOL  WINAPI G3D_WV_SetWindow(LPGENV glgenv,
double wxo, double wyo, double wxe, double wye);
```

Listing 5-35.   Using the WV Layer

```
rW.left   = -10.0;
rW.bottom = -10.0;
rW.top    = 10.0;
rW.right  = 10.0;
rV.left   = 0;
rV.top    = 0;
rV.right  = 400;
rV.bottom = 400;

G3D_WV_SetWindow(pvwwnd->genv,
      rW.left,  rW.bottom,
      rW.right, rW.top);
G3D_WV_SetViewport(pvwwnd->genv,
      rV.left, rV.top,
      rV.right, rV.bottom);
```

The implementation of these functions, shown in Listing 5-36, simply calls down to the *coord* layer to perform the appropriate action. The *coord* layer is defined in Listing 5-37.

Listing 5-36.   WV Implementation

```
BOOL WINAPI G3D_WV_SetViewport(LPGENV glgenv,
int vxo,int vyo,int vxe,int vye)
{

    G3D_Coords_SetDevice(glgenv,vxo, vyo, vxe, vye);
    return TRUE;
}

BOOL WINAPI G3D_WV_SetWindow(LPGENV glgenv,
double wxo, double wyo, double wxe,double wye)
{

    G3D_Coords_SetUser(glgenv,wxo, wyo, wxe, wye);
    return TRUE;
}
```

Listing 5-37.   Coord Layer in coords.c

```
BOOL        WINAPI G3D_Coords_SetDevice(LPGENV glgenv,
int dxo, int dyo, int dxe, int dye);
BOOL        WINAPI G3D_Coords_SetUser(LPGENV glgenv,
double uxo, double uyo, double uxe, double uye);
BOOL        WINAPI G3D_Coords_UsertoDev(LPGENV glgenv,
double x, double y, LPINT dcx, LPINT dcy)
BOOL        WINAPI G3D_Coords_DevtoUser(LPGENV glgenv,
int x, int y, LPDOUBLE ucx, LPDOUBLE ucy);
```

This layer provides the user and device coordinate metaphor. *G3D_Coords_SetDevice* is the trigger function. *G3D_Coords_SetUser* simply modifies dimension values in the graphics environment. *G3D_Coords_SetDevice*, on the other hand, not only modifies dimension values, but also recalculates the mapping variables necessary for the correct operation of *G3D_Coords_UsertoDevice* and *G3D_Coords_DevicetoUser*. The set functions are shown in Listing 5-38.

Listing 5-38.   G3D_Coords Setup Functions

```
BOOL WINAPI G3D_Coords_SetDevice(LPGENV glgenv,
int dxmin, int dymin, int dxmax, int dymax)
{
    glgenv->dxmin = dxmin;
    glgenv->dymin = dymin;
    glgenv->dxmax = dxmax;
    glgenv->dymax = dymax;

    glgenv->a = (glgenv->dxmax - glgenv->dxmin) /
( glgenv->uxmax - glgenv->uxmin );
    glgenv->b = glgenv->dxmin - glgenv->a * glgenv->uxmin;
    glgenv->c = (glgenv->dymax - glgenv->dymin) /
( glgenv->uymax - glgenv->uymin );
    glgenv->d = glgenv->dymin - glgenv->c * glgenv->uymin;
    return TRUE;
}
BOOL WINAPI G3D_Coords_SetUser(LPGENV glgenv
,double uxmin, double uymin, double uxmax, double uymax)
{
    glgenv->uxmin = uxmin;
    glgenv->uymin = uymin;
    glgenv->uxmax = uxmax;
    glgenv->uymax = uymax;
    return TRUE;
}
```

Listing 5-39 shows the corresponding mapping functions *G3D_Coords_UsertoDevice* and *G3D_Coords_DevicetoUser*. These exported functions provide direct access to the user-device mapping process and are the last functions called before using a graphics output primitive. I discussed the usage of these functions in Chapter 2. Now you've seen their implementation. We'll visit these functions one more time in the modeler application in Part III.

Listing 5-39.   G3D_Coords Mapping Functions

```
//
BOOL WINAPI G3D_Coords_UsertoDev(LPGENV glgenv,
double x, double y, LPINT dcx, LPINT dcy)
{
    *dcx = (int)(glgenv->a * x + glgenv->b);
    *dcy = (int)(glgenv->c * y + glgenv->d);
    return TRUE;
}

//
BOOL WINAPI G3D_Coords_DevtoUser(LPGENV glgenv,
int x, int y, LPDOUBLE ucx, LPDOUBLE ucy)
{
    *ucx = (double)((double)x - (double)glgenv->b ) / (double)glgenv->a;
    *ucy = (double)((double)y - (double)glgenv->d ) / (double)glgenv->c;
    return TRUE;
}
```

GENV Utility

The utility functions clear, update, and size, shown in Listing 5-40, are extremely trivial and delegate the actual work to the canvas layer. In the clear function, the clear itself is eventually performed by a **FillRect** GDI call. In the update function, an **InvalidateRect** forces a *G3D_GEnv_Paint*. And the size code simply deletes the old bitmap and creates a new one using the WLib bitmap creation routine *WL_Bitmap_Create*.

Listing 5-40.   Utility Functions

```
void   WINAPI G3D_GEnv_Clear(LPGENV glgenv,HBRUSH hbrClear)
{
    G3D_Canv_Clear(glgenv->lpcanv,hbrClear);
    return ;
}
void   WINAPI G3D_GEnv_Update(LPGENV glgenv)
{
    InvalidateRect(glgenv->hw,NULL,NULL);
    return ;
}
void   WINAPI G3D_GEnv_Size(LPGENV glgenv,
                           RECT    rcDst)
{
    G3D_Canv_Size(glgenv->lpcanv,rcDst);
    G3D_Canv_Clear(glgenv->lpcanv,NULL);
    return ;
}
```

This is all we need for now, but this architecture supports easy extension as you need new functions. We still need to cover histograms, inquiry, and session transcripts, before moving on to the 3D support component in the second half of this chapter and Chapters 6 and 7.

G3DLib General Support: Histograms

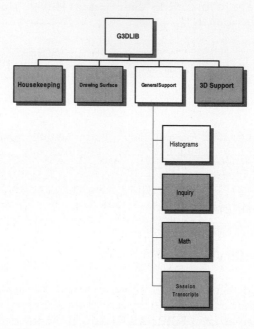

A histogram is a representation of a distribution, usually associated with the color content of an image. Histograms are often used in image processing, and there comes a point in color processing for illumination models where the line between 3D graphics and image processing blurs. Basing our colorization process on histograms makes applications based on this API easier to extend into the image-processing realm, since some of the data needed by image-processing functions is already available.

The histogram services are, again, very general and provide little policy. They include an opaque structure that represents a histogram and routines that create, manipulate, and destroy instances of that opaque structure. Listing 5-41 describes the histogram API.

Listing 5-41.   Histogram Functions in hist.c

```
BOOL    WINAPI G3D_Hist_Init(void);
LPHIST  WINAPI G3D_Hist_Create(int bins);
BOOL    WINAPI G3D_Hist_Clear(LPHIST lph);
BOOL    WINAPI G3D_Hist_Set(LPHIST lph,int bin);
long    WINAPI G3D_Hist_FindMostPopular(LPHIST lph);
BOOL    WINAPI G3D_Hist_Destroy(LPHIST lph);
void    WINAPI G3D_Hist_Term(void);
```

Our histograms are going to be very simple. The *HIST* structure they require simply maintains a count and a pointer to a block of memory. The count element specifies both the number of logical "bins" in the histogram and the size of the block of memory (multiplied by the data-type size). An additional typedef for your convenience is all we need in the way of data structures for histograms. This is shown in Listing 5-42.

Listing 5-42.   Histogram Structure

```
typedef struct tagHist
{
    int   bins;
    LPINT Hist;     // array of ints, each bin can represent 32k colors
} HIST;
typedef HIST FAR *LPHIST;
```

Routines that create and destroy instances of the *HIST* structure are correspondingly simple. *G3D_Hist_Create* takes a count as a parameter, initializes the bin element, then uses the count value to allocate memory. This routine uses the **TRY** and **CATCH** macros around the resource allocation calls. Notice that we use our *WL_Mem* routines from WLib to handle memory allocation, and also note the added bin with the +1. This is a behind-the-scenes cheat to provide an extra bin for the color black. *G3D_Hist_Destroy* takes apart this structure by freeing the memory allocated using our *WL_Mem* routines to perform this action. For details see Listing 5-43.

Listing 5-43.   G3D_Hist_New and G3D_Hist_Del

```
LPHIST WINAPI G3D_Hist_Create(int bins){
  LPHIST lph;
  TRY{
      lph          = WL_Mem_Alloc(GHND,sizeof(HIST));
      if ( !lph ){
         Throw((LPCATCHBUF)&_ci.state,GENERR_ALLOCFAILURE);
      }
      else{
         lph->bins    = bins;
         TRY{
            lph->Hist = WL_Mem_Alloc(GHND,sizeof(int) * bins + 1);
            if ( !lph->Hist ){
               Throw((LPCATCHBUF)&_ci.state,BBERR_MEMDC_CRFAIL);
            }
         }
      }
      CATCH {
         switch(_exk){
            case HISTERR_HARRAY_CRFAIL:
               G3D_Error_Process(_exk);
               break;
         }
```

Listing 5-43.   (cont.)

```
                WL_Mem_Free(lph);
                return NULL;
            }
            END_CATCH
        }
        return lph;
    }
    CATCH{
        switch(_exk){
          case HISTERR_ALLOCFAILURE:
          default:
            G3D_Error_Process(_exk);
            break;
        }
        return NULL;
    }
    END_CATCH
}
BOOL WINAPI G3D_Hist_Destroy(LPHIST lph)
{
  WL_Mem_Free(lph->Hist);
  WL_Mem_Free(lph);
  return TRUE;
}
```

We often need a routine to clear a histogram. It's also useful to be able to find the bin with the maximum value, or the "most popular" bin. Listing 5-44 shows both *G3D_Hist_Clear* and *G3D_Hist_FindMostPopular*.

Listing 5-44.   G3D_Hist_Clear and G3D_Hist_FindMostPopular

```
BOOL WINAPI G3D_Hist_Clear(LPHIST lph)
{
  int i;
  for (i = 0; i < lph->bins; i++)
     lph->Hist[i] = 0;
// account for scaling divide by making black = 1
  lph->Hist[lph->bins] = 1;
  return TRUE;
}
long  WINAPI G3D_Hist_FindMostPopular(LPHIST lph)
{
  int      i;
  long     mp;
  mp     = 0;
  for (i = 0; i <= lph->bins; i++)
     mp = (long)max(mp,lph->Hist[i]);
  return mp;
}
```

G3D_Hist_Clear zeroes all the bins except the "black" bin. This trick makes reliable scaling code that uses the maximum histogram value for a divisor. Little details like this in an API are very important. Both providing them and knowing about them can make the difference between an API that can really be used and one that you "go around" to get the job done. *G3D_Hist_FindMostPopular* walks the bins and returns the largest value. This function returns a long integer. Thus, if you decide that you want to accept the storage cost of promoting the histogram bins to long, your API already accounts for this. It's another small detail that you can take advantage of later.

The final routines to consider are *G3D_Hist_Set* and *G3D_Hist_Get*. *G3D_Hist_Set* increments the value for the specified bin. *G3D_Hist_Get* returns the value for the specified bin. Once again, these routines look simple, and they are. See Listing 5-45 for the details.

Listing 5-45. G3D_Hist_Set and G3D_Hist_Get

```
BOOL WINAPI G3D_Hist_Set(LPHIST lph,int bin)
{
  lph->Hist[bin]++;
  return TRUE;
}
int  WINAPI G3D_Hist_Get(LPHIST lph,int bin)
{
  return lph->Hist[bin];
}
```

As you may have surmised, we'll need more histogram routines as well. I haven't included them at this point for two reasons. The first is that we haven't yet created certain services these additional routines depend on. The second is that it's not clear that these additional routines are really library routines, rather than application routines that implement too specific a policy. For instance, without providing a general-purpose 2D plotting package, any attempt at visual displaying a histogram must be application-oriented. So we'll leave histograms as they are and proceed onward for now; when we get to the implementation of the modeler in Part III, we'll revisit the histogram output issue.

G3DLib General Support: Inquiry

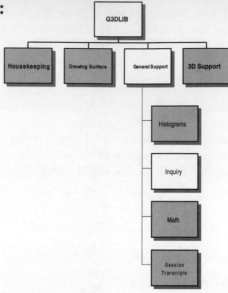

All graphics systems use certain key values to build and maintain their own internal states. Most use these values for various formatting and sizing operations, like obtaining maximum resolution in horizontal, vertical, and pixel depth directions. **GetSystemMetrics** and **GetDeviceCaps** are the familiar Windows functions used to retrieve these values, but directly invoking them is not as "nice" a programming practice as is interposing a layer between the application program and Windows.

The API provides one function, *G3D_Inq_Inquiry*, as Listing 5-46 shows. This function takes a constant parameter indicating which value is being queried.

Listing 5-46.   Inquiry Functions in inquiry.c

```
BOOL        WINAPI G3D_Inq_Init(void);
DWORD       WINAPI G3D_Inq_Inquire(HWND hw, WORD wSysValue);
BOOL        WINAPI G3D_Inq_Term(void);
```

The set of values that can be queried break down into two broad categories: color and screen values.

Color inquiry capability provides five queries:

- PALETTEDEV,
- SIZEPALETTE,
- NUMRESERVED,
- BITSPIXEL, and
- NUMCOLORS.

Color inquiry capability starts by determining whether the graphics device supports palettes. This is a simple call to **GetDeviceCaps** with an AND operation on the mask RC_PALETTE. Once we know whether we're working with a palette device, we need to know how many colors are in the palette and how many are reserved by the system. The bits-per-pixel value is a useful double-check on the value of the number of colors. We need this cross-checking because **GetDeviceCaps(hdc, NUMCOLORS)** may not work in all cases. The return code of **GetDeviceCaps** is an INT that implies 32767 as the maximum return value; hicolor cards break it. Actually, by casting to unsigned you can get past this particular limitation, but Truecolor cards still fracture **GetDeviceCaps**. You'll also notice the recursive call to unravel the NUMCOLORS problem. Listing 5-47 shows the sequence of code for the color-inquiry capability.

Listing 5-47.   Color-Inquiry Code Block

```
...
   switch ( wSysValue )
   {
      case PALETTEDEV:
         dwRet = GetDeviceCaps (hdc, RASTERCAPS) & RC_PALETTE;
         break;
      case SIZEPALETTE:
         dwRet = GetDeviceCaps(hdc,SIZEPALETTE);
         break;
      case NUMRESERVED:
         dwRet = GetDeviceCaps(hdc,NUMRESERVED);
         break;
      case BITSPIXEL:
         dwRet = GetDeviceCaps(hdc,BITSPIXEL);
         break;
      case NUMCOLORS:
         dwRet = G3D_Inq_Inquire(PALETTEDEV);
         if ( dwRet ) {
            dwRet = G3D_Inq_Inquire(SIZEPALETTE);
         }
         else {
            if ( G3D_Inq_Inquire(BITSPIXEL) >= 15 )
               dwRet = 2<<(G3D_Inq_Inquire(BITSPIXEL))-1;
            else
               dwRet = (unsigned)GetDeviceCaps(hdc,NUMCOLORS);
         }
         break;
...
   }
...
}
```

Screen-inquiry capability provides six queries:

- HORZRES,
- VERTRES,
- LOGPIXELSX,

- LOGPIXELSY,
- CLIENTXRES, and
- CLIENTYRES.

The first four of these queries use **GetDeviceCaps**. They provide general information about the absolute screen resolution. The last two use **GetClientRect** with the owning window to provide window-relative screen information. The split between absolute and relative information will continue, and is critical to smooth coexistence with the Windows environment. We don't want to be bad citizens by assuming control over the entire screen, so we must be constrained to the interior of a window. But some calculations are based on screen resolution, not client-area size. This trade-off results in the query-implementation choices for the screen inquiry code as shown in Listing 5-48.

Listing 5-48.   Screen-Inquiry Code Block

```
...
  switch ( wSysValue ){
...

    case HORZRES:
       dwRet = GetDeviceCaps(hdc,HORZRES);
       break;
    case VERTRES:
       dwRet = GetDeviceCaps(hdc,VERTRES);
       break;
    case LOGPIXELSX:
       dwRet = GetDeviceCaps(hdc,LOGPIXELSX);
       break;
    case LOGPIXELSY:
       dwRet = GetDeviceCaps(hdc,LOGPIXELSY);
       break;
    case CLIENTXRES:
       GetClientRect(hw,&rect);
       dwRet = rect.right - rect.left;
       break;
    case CLIENTYRES:
       GetClientRect(hw,&rect);
       dwRet = rect.bottom - rect.top;
       break;
    default:
       G3D_Error_Process(INQERR_INVALIDVAL);
       break;
   }
...


}
```

That is all that's needed in the inquiry subsystem. Next on our list is the Math component.

G3DLib General Support: Math

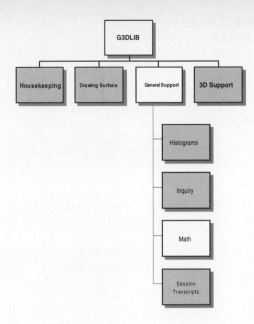

The C run-time libraries provide a bare minimum of support for numerical programmers. This will change in the future as C gets more serious about numerics. Right now, basic conversion and extended operations are supplied as is. If you have access to better functions, use them. The convenience of converting between radians and degrees and the like without impinging on the programming process (in addition to the desire to fill a couple of glaring holes) is all that motivated me to include these routines here.

Listing 5-49 contains the exported math API. Several details should catch your eye. Trig functions for both radians and degrees and the unit-conversion routines make for a very flexible trig function library. The coordinate-conversion routines also provide support for more than Cartesian coordinates.

Listing 5-49. General Math Functions in math.c

```
// general math
long        WINAPI G3D_Math_Round(double x);
long        WINAPI G3D_Math_Trunc(double x);
double      WINAPI G3D_Math_Sqr(double x);
double      WINAPI G3D_Math_CosD(double Angle);
double      WINAPI G3D_Math_CosR(double Angle);
double      WINAPI G3D_Math_ACosD(double Angle);
double      WINAPI G3D_Math_SinD(double Angle);
double      WINAPI G3D_Math_SinR(double Angle);
double      WINAPI G3D_Math_ASinD(double Angle);
double      WINAPI G3D_Math_TanD(double Angle);
double      WINAPI G3D_Math_TanR(double Angle);
```

Listing 5-49.   (cont.)

```
double     WINAPI G3D_Math_ATanD(double Angle);
double     WINAPI G3D_Math_Power(double Base, int Exponent);
double     WINAPI G3D_Math_Log(double x);
double     WINAPI G3D_Math_Exp10(double x);
int        WINAPI G3D_Math_Sign(double x);
// conversions
double     WINAPI G3D_Math_Radians(double Angle);
double     WINAPI G3D_Math_Degrees(double Angle);
void       WINAPI G3D_Math_Cylr2Cart(double R, double Theta, double Z,
                   LPDOUBLE x,
                   LPDOUBLE y,
                   LPDOUBLE z );
void       WINAPI G3D_Math_Cart2Cylr (DOUBLE   x,
                   DOUBLE   y,
                   DOUBLE   z,
                   LPDOUBLE R,
                   LPDOUBLE Theta,
                   LPDOUBLE Z);
void       WINAPI G3D_Math_Sphr2Cart(double R,
                   double Theta, double Phi,
                   LPDOUBLE x,
                   LPDOUBLE y,
                   LPDOUBLE z );
void       WINAPI G3D_Math_Cart2Sphr(DOUBLE   x,
                   DOUBLE   y,
                   DOUBLE   z,
                   LPDOUBLE R,
                   LPDOUBLE Theta,
                   LPDOUBLE Phi);
```

These functions come in three flavors:

- miscellaneous,
- transcendental, and
- conversion.

Miscellaneous

The three miscellaneous functions *G3D_Math_Round*, *G3D_Math_Trunc*, and *G3D_Math_Sign* are useful in dealing with conversions between real-valued systems and integer-valued systems. Listings 5-50 to 5-52 show the implementation of these functions. You should especially notice the help of the compiler in the *G3D_Math_Trunc* function as compared to the explicit coding of the *G3D_Math_Round* function; otherwise, they're simple enough to speak for themselves.

Listing 5-50. G3D_Math_Round

```
long  WINAPI G3D_Math_Round(double x)
{
    return (long)(x+0.5);
}
```

Listing 5-51. G3D_Math_Trunc

```
long  WINAPI G3D_Math_Trunc(double x)
{
    return (long)x;
}
```

Listing 5-52.   G3D_Math_Sign

```
int     WINAPI G3D_Math_Sign(double x)
{
    if (x < 0)
      return (-1);
    else
    {
      if (x > 0)
        return (1);
      else
        return (0);
    }
}
```

Transcendental

Transcendental function support includes trig, log, and exponential functions. Trig functions are all based on the ratio of the sides of a triangle, and are most often shown inscribed in a unit circle. Figure 5-14 shows this relationship with half the arc of the circle showing. The units used in this drawing are *radians*. There are 2 pi radians in 180 degrees. This library includes both radian and degree functions, as well as conversions between the two. This means that you can use whatever function fits your situation.

Figure 5-15 shows the cosine function over the interval [-pi/2, 2pi]. I included it here so you wouldn't have to go to a calculus text to see this graph; I've included the other transcendental functions for the same reason. It's a good idea for you to understand the behavior of these functions over the basic interval. This is not to say that you need to memorize the values of these functions around the unit circle; just get a feel for their behavior. Listing 5-53 shows the cosine pair implementation, *G3D_Math_CosD* and *G3D_Math_CosR*. You can see that they provide these functions by using the underlying radian and degree functions. Once again, the library is its own first customer.

Figure 5-14.   Sin, Cos, and Tan

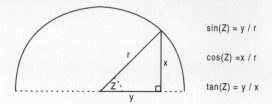

$$sin(Z) = y / r$$

$$cos(Z) = x / r$$

$$tan(Z) = y / x$$

Figure 5-15.   Cos Function Graph [-pi/2 to 2pi]

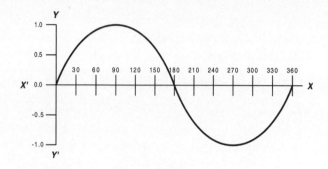

Listing 5-53.   Cosine Functions

```
double  WINAPI G3D_Math_CosD(double Angle)
{
    return (cos( Radians( Angle ) ));
}
double  WINAPI G3D_Math_CosR(double Angle)
{
    return (cos(  Angle ));
}
```

Figure 5-16 shows the sine function over the interval [-pi/2, 2pi]. The implementation of the two sine functions, *G3D_Math_SinD* and *G3D_Math_SinR*, is shown in Listing 5-54. Once again these are basic implementations and not a special treatment of the trig functions.

Figure 5-16.   Sin Graph Over Interval [-pi/2,2pi]

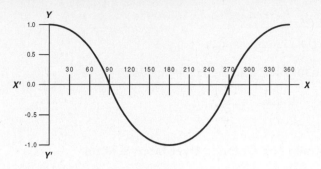

Listing 5-54.   Sine Functions

```
double  WINAPI G3D_Math_SinD(double Angle)
{
    return (sin( Radians( Angle ) ));
}
double  WINAPI G3D_Math_SinR(double Angle)
{
    return (sin( Angle  ));
}
```

Tangent is graphed in Figure 5-17. This function is provided in two flavors, radians or degrees, just like the others, so for *G3D_Math_TanD* or *G3D_Math_TanR* see Listing 5-55.

Figure 5-17.   Tangent Graphed Over Interval [-3/2pi,3/2pi]

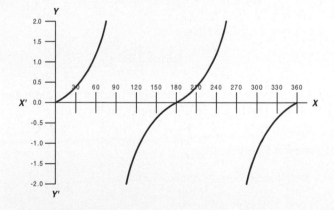

Listing 5-55.   Tangent Functions

```
double  WINAPI G3D_Math_TanD(double Angle)
{
    return (tan( Radians( Angle ) ));
}
double  WINAPI G3D_Math_TanR(double Angle)
{
    return (tan(  Angle  ));
}
```

Figure 5-18.   Common Log Graphed Over Interval [0,10]

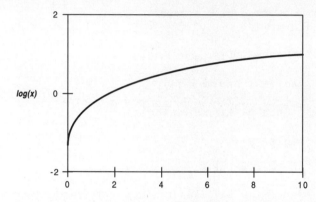

The natural logarithmic function, or *base 2 log* (Figure 5-18), is found in the run-time library. However, the common logarithm, or *base 10 log* function, isn't. This function follows from the equality for logarithms of bases other than e:

Equation 5-1.   Common Log Equality

$$logx = \frac{lnx}{lna}$$

Substitute the constant for *ln10* in the denominator as the new base, as shown in the implementation of *G3D_Math_Log10* in Listing 5-56.

Listing 5-56.   Common Log Function

```
double  WINAPI G3D_Math_Log10(double x)
{
    return (log(x) / Ln10);
}
```

Figure 5-19. Exponential Function Graphed in the Interval [-2,4]

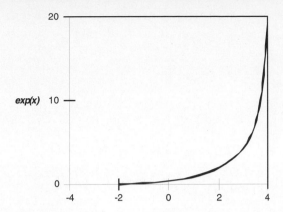

The exponential function, graphed in Figure 5-19, is also part of the run-time library, but its corresponding base 10 function is not. This function operates on the following equality:

Equation 5-2. Common Exponentiation Equality

$$y = e^{x \ln 10}$$

It is implemented in Listing 5-57 as function **G3D_Math_Exp10**.

Listing 5-57. Common Exponential Function

```
double  WINAPI G3D_Math_Exp10(double x)
{
    return (exp( x * Ln10 ));
}
```

The next function, **G3D_Math_Power**, provides the general capability to raise a value to an exponent, shown by the equality:

Equation 5-3. Power Equality

$$x = a^y$$

Thus, **G3D_Math_Power** takes two parameters: the *base number*, equivalent to *a* in Equation 5-3, and the *exponent*, which equates to *y* in Equation 5-3. See Listing 5-58 for the implementation.

Listing 5-58. Power

```
double  WINAPI G3D_Math_Power(double Base, int Exponent)
{
    double bP;
    int    t;

    if (Exponent == 0)
    {
        return (1);
    }
    else
    {
        bP = 1.0;
        for ( t  = 1;
              t <= Exponent;
              t++ )
        {
          bP = bP * Base;
        }
        return (bP);
    }
}
```

Conversions

Conversions depend on some important constants. The **ln10** constant has already been used in the *Log10* and *Exp10* functions. **PiUnder180** and **PiOver180** are used by the trigonometric conversion routines *G3D_Math_Radians* and *G3D_Math_Degrees*, which are found in Listings 5-60 and 5-61, respectively. Listing 5-59 shows the constants. These functions convert to the unit indicated by their name; thus, *G3D_Math_Radians* converts from a degree to a radian.

Listing 5-59. Conversion Constants

```
double Ln10       = 2.30258509299405E+000;
// Ln( 10 )  =  2.3025851
double PiOver180  = 1.74532925199433E-002;
//Pi  / 180 =  0.0174533
double PiUnder180 = 5.72957795130823E+001;
// 180 / Pi  = 57.2957795
```

Listing 5-60. Radians to Convert Degrees to Radians

```
double  WINAPI G3D_Math_Radians(double Angle)
{
    return (Angle * PiOver180);      //   { Angle * Pi / 180 }
}
```

Listing 5-61.   Degrees to Convert Radians to Degrees

```
double  WINAPI G3D_Math_Degrees(double Angle)
{
    return (Angle * PiUnder180);  //    { Angle * 180 / Pi }
}
```

The last two functions, *G3D_Math_Cylr2Cart* and *G3D_Math_Sphr2Cart*, convert from the cylindrical and spherical coordinate systems.

Figure 5-20.   Cylindrical Coordinates

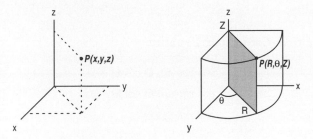

Cylindrical coordinates, shown in Figure 5-20, are related to Cartesian coordinates by the following equalities:

Equation 5-4.   Cylindrical and Cartesian Coordinate Equalities

$$x = r \cos \Theta, y = r \sin \Theta, z = z$$

$$r^2 = x^2 + y^2, \cos \Theta = \frac{x}{r}, \sin \Theta = \frac{y}{r}$$

Listing 5-62 shows the implementation of the cylindrical-to-Cartesian half of this system. The other half is easily implemented if you need it.

Listing 5-62.   cylr2cart Function

```
void WINAPI G3D_Math_Cylr2Cart(double Rho, double Theta, double d,
                 LPDOUBLE X, LPDOUBLE Y LPDOUBLE Z)
{
    double X, Y;
    Theta = Radians( Theta );
    X     = Rho * cos( Theta );
    Y     = Rho * sin( Theta );
    Z     = d;
}
```

Figure 5-21.   Spherical Coordinates

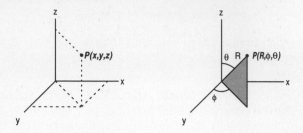

Spherical coordinates, graphically depicted in Figure 5-21, are related to Cartesian coordinates by this equality:

Equation 5-5.   Spherical-Coordinate Equality

$$x = rho\ sin\ \Theta\ cos\ \Theta$$
$$y = rho\ sin\ \Theta\ sin\ \Theta$$
$$z = rho\ cos\ \Theta$$

The function implementing this relationship, *G3D_Math_Sphr2Cart*, is shown in Listing 5-63.

Listing 5-63.   sphr2cart Function

```
void WINAPI  G3D_Math_Sphr2Cart(double R, double Theta, double Phi,
                     LPDOUBLE X, LPDOUBLE Y, LPDOUBLE Z )
{
    double X, Y, Z;
    Theta = Radians( Theta );
    Phi   = Radians( Phi );
    X     = R * sin( Theta ) * cos( Phi );
    Y     = R * sin( Theta ) * sin( Phi );
    Z     = R * cos( Theta );
}
```

Finally the last base component, the session transcript, is covered.

G3DLib General Support: Session Transcripting

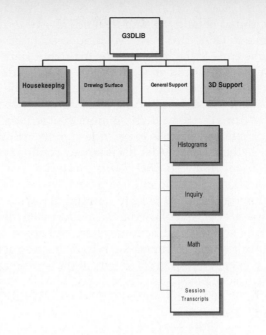

The session transcript is an important tool for both informational and debugging purposes. The basis of a session transcript is a text output window combined with service routines allowing applications to generate transcript output. The applications we'll develop will weave transcripting into their code, thereby exposing the processes involved. If you change the single-frame nature of the application to a many-frame nature (like a key-frame animation system using a script language), the parser can use the session transcript to provide script-error reporting. Once you have a tool like a general purpose text output window, you can use it for many things.

First things first—what are we constructing? We know we need to export a window class and provide service routines. Rather than recreate the wheel, we'll adopt the sound strategy of building on or borrowing from an existing piece of work. In this case, we'll borrow from Schulman, et al. ("Call Standard C I/O Functions from Your Windows Code Using the WINIO Library," *MSJ*, Vol. 6, Iss. 4, and *Undocumented Windows*, Addison-Wesley, 1992); their WINIO C-style text output window is a good, publicly available starting place that is well-documented in its own right.

WINIO in its pristine form gives Windows programmers access to the standard I/O of the C run-time library. It also provides a great deal more, but we need only a small part of the functionality of WINIO for our purposes. If you haven't examined WINIO, I recommend that you spend the time. It has quite a few interesting ideas, and will certainly start your programmer-juices stirring. WINIO also provides moveable, resizeable, scrollable text windows. This is why we're borrowing it as the basis of transcripts.

WINIO in its native form makes strategy and style assumptions that are slightly unpalatable for our system. First, it assumes that it owns the application; second, it forces an overall coding style. But while doing this it provides a stdio-like interface, which is a valuable feature. The style it enforces is tightly tied to WINIO's notion of ownership. It does many things behind the scenes, which allows you to use a stdio interface and code just like any other "DOS" program. The hidden-event handlers take over after your program goes over the edge of the main routine to provide persistence.

This is all well and good, but all we really needed was a simple text-transcription mechanism that is subservient to the application, not the other way around. Our first step, then, is to examine WINIO and prune those portions necessary for a TTY-style output window.

This turns out to be nothing more than writing a wrapper layer around the pruned version of WINIO internals to provide a public API that conforms to our defined model. Visibility in the public header file is strictly confined to the three functions *G3D_Trans_Create*, *G3D_Trans_Add*, and *G3D_Trans_Destroy*.

Examining the code in Listing 5-64, we see the visible header file and the limited API. It's important for you to keep in mind that what we're providing here is a globally available window class. Following the model in the MakeApp shells, we use a window instance structure and access function to store and access instance-specific data. Making this structure into a wrapper around the WINIO main structure and hiding the details of the WINIO code is as easy as Listing 5-65, which shows the structure that helps make this possible and an example of how to use the instance data structure access mechanism. This access mechanism is, in turn, built on the **GetWindowWord/GetWindowLong** functions of Windows itself.

Listing 5-64.   Transcript Functions in trans.c

```
// public declarations
BOOL          WINAPI G3D_Trans_Init(void);
HWND          WINAPI G3D_Trans_Create(HINSTANCE hInst, HWND hwP,    LPSTR
strTitle,RECT rcP);
void          WINAPI G3D_Trans_Add(WINIOWND*  pwiniownd,
BYTE FAR *pch, unsigned cch);
void          WINAPI G3D_Trans_Destroy(HWND hwnd);
BOOL          WINAPI G3D_Trans_Term(void);
```

Listing 5-65.   TRANS Structure

```
// instance data structure
typedef struct tagWINIOWND
{
   HWND           hwnd;
   LPWINIO_WNDDATA lpwd;
} WINIOWND;
typedef WINIOWND FAR *LPWINIOWND;
// instance data access
  WINIOWND * pwiniownd = WINIO_GetPtr(hwnd);
```

We only took those parts of WINIO that were necessary to construct this brain-dead transcripting version — the definitions needed for buffer, style, and display and the types needed for creation, scrolling, and internals; but all of these are hidden from view. I've treated the details of the WINIO implementation as a black box here. If you're really interested in comparing the subset to see how I extracted the code and converted it for use in a DLL, examine in detail the implementation on your source code disk.

For most purposes, all that's needed is knowledge of the public API and its usage policy. The public API includes the ability to create and destroy *Trans* windows, and add to the buffer contained in a *Trans* window. From these simple roots we'll construct a basic, but useful, logging tool.

We must create the meta-type or class before any instances can be created. By calling init functions in the *G3D_Main* function during DLL initialization, we have the opportunity to perform subsystem-specific initialization. For the transcripting layer, *G3D_Trans_Init* uses **RegisterClass** to register the transcript class with the CS_GLOBALCLASS attribute, which makes it publicly available. This example doesn't include any checking to see whether the class has already been registered. The class is deregistered in the subsystem-termination function, which is invoked by the **WEP**. Both of these functions are shown in Listing 5-66.

Listing 5-66.   Registering and Unregistering the Global Trans Class

```
BOOL WINAPI G3D_Trans_Init(void)
{
    WNDCLASS  wc;
    gcxScroll = GetSystemMetrics(SM_CXVSCROLL);
    gcyScroll = GetSystemMetrics(SM_CYHSCROLL);
    LoadString(hLibInst,IDS_TRANSCLASS,szBuffer,sizeof(szBuffer));
    if ( bInit )
        return TRUE;
    wc.style         = CS_GLOBALCLASS | CS_HREDRAW | CS_VREDRAW;
    wc.lpfnWndProc   = WINIO_WndProc;
    wc.cbClsExtra    = 0;
    wc.cbWndExtra    = 4;
    wc.hInstance     = hLibInst;
    wc.hIcon         = NULL;
    wc.hCursor       = LoadCursor(NULL, IDC_ARROW);
    wc.hbrBackground = GetStockObject(WHITE_BRUSH);
    wc.lpszMenuName  = NULL;
    wc.lpszClassName = szBuffer;
    return RegisterClass(&wc);
}
BOOL WINAPI G3D_Trans_Term(void)
{
    LoadString(hLibInst, IDS_TRANSCLASS,
      szBuffer,    sizeof(szBuffer));
    return UnregisterClass(szBuffer, hLibInst);
    return TRUE;
}
```

Once that's taken care, of the API is enabled. Calling *G3D_Trans_Create* as shown in Listing 5-67 creates an instance of a transcript window. Invoking *G3D_Trans_Destroy* terminates the life of a transcript window. Simple. Once again, these are just windows. A standard window handle is returned.

Listing 5-67. Sample Trans_Create and Trans_Destroy Calls

```
BOOL Trans_OnCreate(TRANSWND* ptranswnd, CREATESTRUCT FAR*
lpCreateStruct)
{
    RECT rcT;
    GetClientRect(ptranswnd->hwnd,&rcT);
    if (winio_hwnd = G3D_Trans_Create(g_app.hinst,
                                    ptranswnd->hwnd,
                                      (LPSTR) NULL,
                                   rcT))
    {
...
    }
    return TRUE;
}
void Trans_OnDestroy(TRANSWND* ptranswnd)
{
...
    G3D_Trans_Destroy(winio_hwnd);
}
```

The only external action required of the transcript window is to append text. Internally, it handles all details of scrolling, painting, etc. Listing 5-68 contains *G3D_Trans_Add*, which handles appending text to the specified transcript window.

Listing 5-68. Adding to a Transcript

```
WINIOWND* pww  = WINIO_GetPtr(hw);
    int            len;
    char           s[144];
// copy to displayable
    G3D_Trans_Add(pww, s,len);
```

Did you notice that the code fragment using *G3D_Trans_Add* does not address format-ted output like printf in the run-time library? There's a reason for this. In addition to the running transcripts in the window, the applications also log to a file. This is especially nice in the debugging phase; if the app crashes, you're not left totally in the dark. In most cases, the log file will contain at least a partial transcript, although this depends on how early you crashed (there are no guarantees for startup crashes). Crashes at startup have the potential of catching the system at a very vulnerable time. The transcript child window is typically the first one created to minimize this window of vulnerability, but this only minimizes the time without the ability to log; it doesn't really fix the problem.

In the interests of two types of code simplification, the printf-like function is defined in the application. First, from a file-handle point of view, it can be tricky to have the DLL attempt to deal with the file I/O for multiple clients. Second, from a coding point of view, the printf-like function needs to use variable arguments on the stack, which can prove troublesome in a DLL that depends on the application's stack. In any respect, wherever you decide to place this function, the variable argument function *Trans_Printf* handles formatted output just like printf. See Listing 5-69 for the code.

Listing 5-69.   Trans_Printf Formatted Output Function

```
int FAR _cdecl Trans_Printf(HWND hw, LPSTR strFmt, ...)
{
    va_list          marker;
    WINIOWND* pww  = WINIO_GetPtr(hw);
    int              len;
    char             szFileName[144];
    FILE*            out;
    va_start(marker, strFmt);
    len  = vsprintf(s, strFmt, marker);
// open the file
    if ( (out = fopen(ptw->szTransName,"a")) != NULL)
    {
// write the buffer
        fseek(out,0,SEEK_END);
        fprintf(out,"%Fs\n",(LPSTR)s);
// close the file
        fclose(out);
    }
// copy to displayable
    G3D_Trans_Add(pww, s,len)      return len;
}
```

Usage: Color Cube Demo II

When trying to learn something new, it's always wise to eliminate as many variables as you can. Following that general rule, re-implementing a known example with a new API is an obvious way to learn the usage pattern demanded by the new API. Throughout this book, we re-implement a known piece of code in new and interesting ways to illustrate how to use the building blocks we are making.

The RGBCube example from Chapter 4 is all we know at this point, and it is perfectly adequate to explore and instruct us on how to use canvases and *GENV* services. It should be obvious that the changes we need to make to convert to *GENV* usage are concentrated in the view module.

Regardless of whether we use a fixed-size or variable-size canvas policy in the application, there are certain actions we must take. We must create and destroy the graphics environment. We must do palette handling and painting. The drawing loop itself has to be accounted for. These code blocks comprise the latest edition of the RGB Color Cube, using *GENVs* and *CANVASES*. This large block of common code, in both a fixed-size and a variable-size canvas environment, points out the flexibility and generality of the interface. The differences between fixed- and variable-size canvas policy are limited to the window procedure, the sizing code, and the scrolling code.

Common Code

In the Chapter 4 example, we skipped the palette-handling policy; this allows our introduction of the graphics environment at this point to coincide with the exposure of our use of palettes. The window procedure is very similar for both fixed- and variable-size canvas handling. Changes occur in the WM_CREATE, WM_DESTROY, and WM_PAINT handlers of the view window procedure. All canvas-based view window procedures gain a WM_QUERYNEWPALETTE and WM_PALETTECHANGED handler, as shown in the code fragment in Listing 5-70.

Listing 5-70.   Generic New Handlers in View_WndProc

```
HANDLE_MSG(pvwwnd, WM_QUERYNEWPALETTE, View_OnQueryNewPalette);
HANDLE_MSG(pvwwnd, WM_PALETTECHANGED,  View_OnPaletteChanged);
```

In turn, let's examine these functions. In *View_OnCreate* you create a graphics environment with an arbitrary 400 x 400 lightweight canvas with the BLACK_CANV style. The previously shown palette code is invoked to create the palettes representing the mixing-model cubes. Then the default color mixing model is set and a message is posted to force an update. Note that this is an effective decoupling of the drawing logic from the screen-updating code. Drawing is responsible for performing calculations and updating the graphics environment. Screen updating simply displays a frame. Separating the act of drawing on the surface from that of displaying the surface will reappear many times in our discussions, and is critical to our 3D drawing strategy.

In *View_OnDestroy* you must deallocate the *GENV* instance and free the palettes. You must perform this in a last-in, first-out order, so the palettes are released before freeing the *GENV*. See Listing 5-71 for details on both the creation and destruction functions.

Listing 5-71.   View_OnCreate and View_OnDestroy

```
BOOL View_OnCreate(VWWND* pvwwnd,
                   CREATESTRUCT FAR* lpCreateStruct) {
    RECT rW,rV;
    HDC  hdc;
    rW.left   = 0;
    rW.top    = 0;
    rW.right  = 400;
    rW.bottom = 400;
    CopyRect((LPRECT)&rV,(LPRECT)&rW);
    CopyRect((LPRECT)&pvwwnd->rV,(LPRECT)&rW);
    pvwwnd->genv  = G3D_GEnv_Create(pvwwnd->hwnd,LIGHT,NULL,
        BLACK_CANV,rW,rV);
    if ( !(pvwwnd->genv) )
        return FALSE;
```

```
        G3D_GEnv_Clear(pvwwnd->genv,GetStockObject(BLACK_BRUSH));
        hprgb = InitRGBPalette();
        hpcmy = InitCMYPalette();
        if ( !hprgb || !hpcmy )
            return FALSE;
        Model = CMD_RGB;
        PostMessage(pvwwnd->hwnd,WM_COMMAND,CMD_RGB,0L);
        return TRUE;
}
void View_OnDestroy(VWWND* pvwwnd)
{
        G3D_GEnv_Reset(pvwwnd->genv,ID_SCREENPALETTE);
        FreePalette(hprgb);
        FreePalette(hpcmy);
        G3D_GEnv_Destroy(pvwwnd->genv);
}
```

Palette Handling

The palette routines that were included with the WLib from Chapter 4 implemented no policy. If you wish to "act nice" in the Windows environment it's critical that you handle the WM_QUERYNEWPALETTE and WM_PALETTECHANGED messages. While not much has been written about palettes beyond that in the SDK and Petzold, there are two other sources of information: "Palette Awareness" and "The Palette Manager: How and Why" by Ron Gery, which can be found on both CompuServe and the Microsoft Developer Network CD, and the article on palettes in *Andrew Schulmans' Undocumented Windows Corner*, "Exploring Windows Palettes," by Jeffrey M. Cogswell in *Dr. Dobbs Journal* (Vol.18, No. 5, May 1993).

The policy implemented here is similar to that discussed in these articles, the SDK examples, and Petzold, but I've modified it to work with the graphics environment and its canvas. Two DCs must be synchronized with the palette here:

- the DC associated with the canvas, and
- the DC to which the canvas will be blitted.

If these DCs are not in agreement as to their palette, strange things will happen.

It's a very nice feature of palettes that they can be selected into multiple DCs. This saves the resource cost of creating multiple palettes out of GDI's scarce local heap. This also reinforces the fact that the canvas does not really "own" the palette like it does the bitmap. In WM_QUERYNEWPALETTE, the palette is selected, realized, and deselected in both DCs in the standard manner. In WM_PALETTECHANGED, the window-handle check to avoid a recursive situation is also standard, and once again the palette is selected, realized, and deselected in both DCs to keep them in sync. See Listings 5-72 and 5-73 for the palette message handlers.

Listing 5-72.   QueryNew Palette Message Handler

```
BOOL View_OnQueryNewPalette(VWWND* pvwwnd){
  HPALETTE hOldP1;
  HPALETTE hOldP2;
  HDC      hdc;
  HWND     hwP;
  int      nc = 0;
  hdc   = GetDC(pvwwnd->hwnd);
  G3D_GEnvReset(pvwwnd->genv,ID_SCREENPALETTE);
  switch(Model){
      case CMD_RGB:
          hOldP1 = SelectPalette(hdc,hprgb,0);
          G3D_GEnvSetVal(pvwwnd->genv,
              ID_SCREENPALETTE,(DWORD)hprgb);
          break;
      case CMD_CMY:
          hOldP1 = SelectPalette(hdc,hpcmy,0);
          G3D_GEnvSetVal(pvwwnd->genv,
              ID_SCREENPALETTE,(DWORD)hpcmy);
          break;
      case CMD_CRT:
          break;
  }
  nc    = RealizePalette(hdc);
  G3D_GEnvUse(pvwwnd->genv,ID_SCREENPALETTE);
  InvalidateRect(pvwwnd->hwnd,NULL,FALSE);
  UpdateWindow(pvwwnd->hwnd);
  switch(Model) {
      case CMD_RGB:
      case CMD_CMY:
          SelectPalette(hdc,hOldP1,0);
          break;
  }
  ReleaseDC(pvwwnd->hwnd,hdc);
  return (nc != 0 );
}
```

Listing 5-73. PaletteChanged Palette Message Handler

```
void View_OnPaletteChanged(VWWND* pvwwnd,
                              HWND hwndPaletteChange){
   HPALETTE hOld,hOldP2;
   HDC      hdc;
   int      nc;

   if (( hwndPaletteChange != pvwwnd->hwnd ) &&
      ( hwndPaletteChange != g_app.hwndMain )) {
      hdc   = GetDC(pvwwnd->hwnd);
      G3D_GEnvReset(pvwwnd->genv,ID_SCREENPALETTE);
      switch(Model)   {
          case CMD_RGB:
              hOldP1 = SelectPalette(hdc,hprgb,0);
              G3D_GEnvSetVal(pvwwnd->genv,
              ID_SCREENPALETTE,(DWORD)hprgb);
              break;
          case CMD_CMY:
              hOldP1 = SelectPalette(hdc,hpcmy,0);
              G3D_GEnvSetVal(pvwwnd->genv,
              ID_SCREENPALETTE,(DWORD)hpcmy);
              break;
          case CMD_CRT:
              break;
      }
      nc    = RealizePalette(hdc);
      G3D_GEnvUse(pvwwnd->genv,ID_SCREENPALETTE);
      UpdateColors(hdc);
      switch(Model{
        case CMD_RGB:
        case CMD_CMY:
          SelectPalette(hdc,hOldP1,0);
          break;
      }
      ReleaseDC(pvwwnd->hwnd,hdc);
   }
}
```

This process could be simplified by making the view window an "owndc" window. You would do this when you register the window class by using the CS_OWNDC style; later, you'll get a chance to see the effect of "owndc."

Painting

We've finished the palette-handling policy, so next we need to nail down the details of painting.

First *View_Draw* draws the cube (using *CubePaint*) onto the memory bitmap and DC. *View_OnPaint* uses *G3D_GEnv_Paint* to render the bitmap to the screen, as shown in Listing 5-74. The actual drawing is slightly different than that shown in Chapter 4. Instead of depending on GDI's mapping modes to perform scaling, this one uses viewport-relative sizing calculations as input to the drawing code. This is shown in the code fragment in Listing 5-75.

Listing 5-74.   View_OnPaint

```
void View_OnPaint(VWWND* pvwwnd){
    PAINTSTRUCT ps;
    HPALETTE       hOldP1,hOldP2;
    RECT           rDst,rSrc;
    HDC            hdc;
    int            xScroll,yScroll;
    hdc = BeginPaint(pvwwnd->hwnd, &ps);
    GetClientRect(pvwwnd->hwnd, (LPRECT)&rDst);
    xScroll  = GetScrollPos  (pvwwnd->hwnd, SB_HORZ);
    yScroll  = GetScrollPos  (pvwwnd->hwnd, SB_VERT);
    GetClientRect(pvwwnd->hwnd, (LPRECT)&rSrc);
    rSrc.left     = xScroll;
    rSrc.top      = -yScroll;
    G3D_GEnv_Paint(pvwwnd->genv,
                    hdc,rDst, rSrc,
                    FALSE);
    EndPaint(pvwwnd->hwnd, &ps);
}
```

Listing 5-75.   Viewport-Relative Cube Calculations

```
xsize = min(rr.right-rr.left,rr.bottom-rr.top);
ySize = 0;
xSpot = xSize/10;
ySpot = xSpot;
xSpace = xSize/12;
ySpace = xSize/12;
xDiff = xSpace/3;
yDiff = ySpace/3;
xInit = xSpace/3;
yInit = ySpace/3;
```

Drawing

This version of the drawing loop shows direct access to the *GENV* structure to perform graphics using a GDI output primitive. In Chapter 6, our library will grow dedicated output primitives that will clean this up. This version, however, retrieves the DC to use for drawing from the *GENV*, as shown in Listing 5-76. Once again, using the *GENV* routines means that reading and writing the canvas as a bitmap, screen output (as in Listing 5-74), printer output, and clipboard sharing are all very easy.

Listing 5-76.   GENV-Based Drawing

```
for (g=0; g<5; g++)
  {
     HDC hDC = G3D_GEnv_GetVal(pvwwnd->genv,ID_DC);
        y = ySize + yInit + (g * yDiff);
        rgbColor.fGreen = (float)g * 1./4.;
        for (b=0; b<5; b++){
             x = xInit + (g * xDiff);
             rgbColor.fBlue  = (float)b * 1./4.;
             for (r=0; r<5; r++){
                 rgbColor.fRed   = (float)r * 1./4.;
// display palette colors
                 WL_Color_RGBtoCRT( &rgbColor, &crtValue );
                 lsClr = PALETTERGB(crtValue.cRed,
             crtValue.cGreen,crtValue.cBlue);
                 hBr       = CreateSolidBrush( *((DWORD*)&lsClr) );
                 hOldBrush = SelectObject(hDC,hBr);
                 PatBlt(hDC, po.x, po.y, ps.x, ps.y, PATCOPY);
             DeleteObject( SelectObject(hDC,hOldBrush) );

                 x += xSpot + xSpace;
             }
             y += ySpot + ySpace;
        }
  }
```

Now we need to look at the generic canvas-usage code. The specifics of fixed- and variable-size differences in implementation remain to be tackled. Make sure you follow what was done here, because it forms the basis for all the drawing yet to come.

Fixed Canvas Path

It should be obvious that a fixed canvas must implement some sizing and scrolling policy. The frame window must handle the WM_GETMINMAXINFO message to implement the fixed canvas policy. Handling this message allows you to communicate with the window manager about sizing policy, making it trivial to force a fixed size. This is shown in Listing 5-77; here the size is limited to an upper bound of 400 x 400, plus a little fudge factor for scrollbars and the like.

Listing 5-77.   WM_GETMINMAXINFO Handler in Frame_WndProc

```
void Frame_OnMinMax(FRAME* pfrm,MINMAXINFO FAR *lpMinMaxInfo)
{
    DWORD ilrPad;
    DWORD itbPad;
    ilrPad = 2 * G3D_Inq_Inquire(NULL,XFRAME) + 2;
    itbPad = 2 * G3D_Inq_Inquire(NULL,YFRAME) +
                 G3D_Inq_Inquire(NULL,YMENU) +
                 G3D_Inq_Inquire(NULL,YCAPTION) + 2;
    lpMinMaxInfo->ptMaxSize.x      = 400 + (int)ilrPad;
    lpMinMaxInfo->ptMaxSize.y      = 400 + (int)itbPad;
    lpMinMaxInfo->ptMaxTrackSize.x = 400 + (int)ilrPad;
    lpMinMaxInfo->ptMaxTrackSize.y = 400 + (int)itbPad;
}
```

This leaves the way for the view layer to manipulate the data within the fixed area. The fixed canvas view window procedure gains WM_SIZE, WM_HSCROLL, and WM_VSCROLL handlers as shown in the code fragment in Listing 5-78.

Listing 5-78.   New Handlers in Fixed Canvas View_WndProc

```
    HANDLE_MSG(pvwwnd, WM_SIZE,    View_OnSize);
    HANDLE_MSG(pvwwnd, WM_HSCROLL, View_OnHScroll);
    HANDLE_MSG(pvwwnd, WM_VSCROLL, View_OnVScroll)

    HANDLE_MSG(pvwwnd, WM_QUERYNEWPALETTE, View_OnQueryNewPalette);
    HANDLE_MSG(pvwwnd, WM_PALETTECHANGED,  View_OnPaletteChanged);
```

Scrolling is easy, as you saw in Chapter 2, given the canvas. Since the demo programs do not have multiple panes, they implement view-specific scrollers but their code is almost identical to that in Chapter 2. Sizing, during the WM_SIZE message, is identical to the Chapter 2 example blocks, which are not repeated here. Figure 5-22 shows a screenshot of the fixed-canvas demo application, sized so that the scrollbars are showing.

Figure 5-22. Fixed-Canvas RGBCube Screenshot

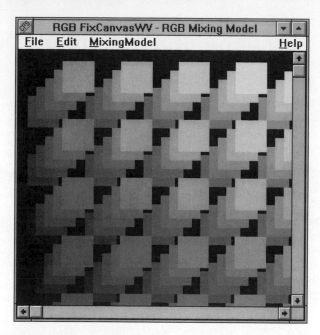

Variable Canvas Path

So what will it take to implement a variable canvas? At this point, it's quite trivial. First, modify the window procedure; then simply re-implement the size handler to resize the canvas instead of setting up the scroll bars.

The variable canvas view window procedure gains a WM_SIZE handler as shown in the code fragment in Listing 5-79. Instead of scrolling, it grows the bitmap so the WM_VSCROLL and WM_HSCROLL routines fall by the wayside.

Listing 5-79. New Handlers in Variable Canvas View_WndProc

```
HANDLE_MSG(pvwwnd, WM_SIZE,         View_OnSize);

HANDLE_MSG(pvwwnd, WM_QUERYNEWPALETTE, View_OnQueryNewPalette);
HANDLE_MSG(pvwwnd, WM_PALETTECHANGED,  View_OnPaletteChanged);
```

Listing 5-80 shows *View_OnSize* for this variation of our RGBCube demo application. Using the cx and cy parameters and *G3D_GEnv_Size*, it resizes the canvas. Then it forces an update and, voilà, the new cube appears. Figure 5-23 shows a variable-size canvas display and the RGBCube scaled to a smaller size.

Listing 5-80.   Variable Canvas Version of View_OnSize

```
void View_OnSize(VWWND* pvwwnd, UINT state, int cx, int cy)
{
   RECT rW,rV;
   RECT rect;
   HDC  hdcm;
   int  cxScroll, cyScroll, cxCANVAS = 0, cyCANVAS = 0;

   if ( fCreate )
      return;

   rW.left   = 0;
   rW.top    = 0;
   rW.right  = cx;
   rW.bottom = cx;
   CopyRect((LPRECT)&rV,(LPRECT)&rW);
   CopyRect((LPRECT)&pvwwnd->rV,(LPRECT)&rW);
  G3D_GEnv_Size(pvwwnd->genv,rW);
   PostMessage(pvwwnd->hwnd,WM_COMMAND, Model,0L);
   InvalidateRect (pvwwnd->hwnd, NULL, FALSE);
}
```

Figure 5-23.   Variable Canvas RGBCube Screenshot

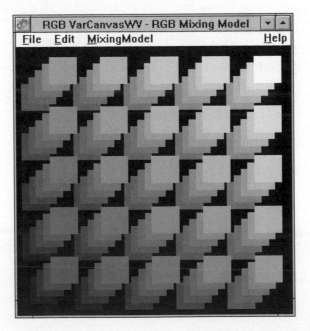

That's it! The ease with which we can change the policy in the demo application should indicate how powerful the building blocks are that we've created.

Summary

The G3DLib has three major sub-components:

- Drawing Surface services,
- General Support services, and
- 3D Support services.

This chapter implemented the Drawing Surface and General Support services. Drawing Surface services contains drawing-surface management, support, and utility. General Support services contains functions that handle:

- histogram,
- inquiry,
- math, and
- session transcripting.

Within 3D Support services, you are provided with:

- graphics output primitives and attributes (which we'll cover in Chapter 6), and
- vector, transform, and viewing system services (found in Chapter 7).

The graphics environment is our common thread. Using the Windows services of Chapter 4, we created the drawing surface and encapsulated a canvas, providing the graphics environment. This graphics environment is a framework that connects Windows to classical graphics, and all of this is built on the Windows services functions.

The graphics environment defines a useful policy for co-existing with a windowing system and a basis for creating the window-system-aware 3D applications like those we'll work on in Section III.

In accordance with the old saw "there is more than one way to skin a cat," this is not the only graphics environment that could be created. The underlying API allows definition and creation of a wide variety of useful primitives like the canvas and the graphics environment. Because of this, both the subsystem-level functions and the *G3D_GEnv_* functions are exported from the DLL. This lets you create other useful abstractions from these primitives as needed.

6

G3DLib Construction Part II: Primitives and Attributes

In This Chapter

- Build a layer on top of GDI that clients will use to draw 2D primitives in device coordinates.
- Enhance the primitives with attributes and attribute control.
- Understand issues behind attribute costs and methods to shift the cost burden.

Introduction

It's good to try to avoid any direct GDI calls. You may have to make exceptions in some cases, but it's still something to shoot for. Developing a graphics output primitive layer implies developing one that handles some form of graphics output attributes as well. PHIGS defines fancy attribute handling, including some very useful creatures like bundles. My approach, however, sticks to the basics and provides a much simpler attribute strategy for each graphics output primitive.

The output primitive functions expand on the access routines provided by the canvas. Canvas access routines allowed array-like access to a row, column location in the canvas. Output primitives enable more-natural drawing on the display surface and work at a higher level than the point-like mechanism of the access routines.

Table 6-1 shows the modules in the G3DLib to help you place the primitive functions in their context. It's useful to categorize them by the number of points needed, which breaks down into:

- one-point primitives,
- two-point primitives, and
- *n*-point primitives.

Listing 6-1 shows the primitive exported API in exactly this order.

Table 6-1. G3DLib Source Modules

Files	Description
G3DLib Housekeeping	
gl_init.c,gl_init.h	Library global initialization
gl_term.c,gl_term.h	Library global termination
gl_err.c,gl_err.h	Library error reporting
g3d_inc.h	Main include file, applications reference this
Drawing Surface	
glgenv.c,glgenv.h	Graphics environment,manages coords for canvas
canvas.c,canvas.h	Canvas provides offscreen drawing surface for genv
bmpbuff.c,bmpbuff.h	Light part of canvas, hidden
membuff.c,membuff.h	Heavy part of the canvas,hidden
coords.c,coords.h	Coordinate mapping
winview.c,winview.h	Window/viewport using coord layer
General Support	
inquiry.c,inquiry.h	System inquiry, hides GetDeviceCaps/GetSystemMetrics
hist.h,hist.h	Histogram support
math.c,math.h	General math functions
trans.c,trans.h	Session transcript global window class based on WINIO
3D Support	
prims.c,prims.h	Output to genv
vec4d.c,vec4d.h	Vector functions
matrix.c,matrix.h	Basic matrix functions
xform.c,xform.h	Matrix transforms
viewing.c,viewing.h	Viewing systems

Listing 6-1. Primitive Functions in prims.c

```
// prims
// one-point
BOOL      WINAPI G3D_GEnv_Point(LPGLGENV glgenv, long x, long y,
                    DWORD hbr);
BOOL      WINAPI G3D_GEnv_Text(LPGLGENV glgenv,
                        long      x1, long y1,
                        LPSTR     lpText,
                        LONG      tLen,
                        DWORD     hFont);
// two-point
BOOL      WINAPI G3D_GEnv_Line(LPGLGENV glgenv,
                        long x1,    long y1,
                        long x2,    long y2,
                        DWORD       hPen);
BOOL      WINAPI G3D_GEnv_Rect(LPGENV glgenv,
                        long      x1, long y1,
                        long      x2, long y2,
                        DWORD     hpen,DWORD    hbr);
```

```
// n-point
BOOL        WINAPI G3D_GEnv_Polyline(LPGENV  glgenv,
                                     LPPOINT  pPoly,
                                     long     nPnts,
                                     DWORD    hpen);
BOOL        WINAPI G3D_GEnv_Polygon(LPGENV  glgenv,
                                    LPPOINT  pPoly,
                                    long     nPnts,
                                    DWORD    hpen,
                                    DWORD    hbr);
BOOL        WINAPI G3D_GEnv_Polypolygon(LPGENV   glgenv,
                                        LPPOINT  pPoly,
                                        LPINT    pCounts,
                                        long     nPolys,
                                        DWORD    hpen,
                                        DWORD    hbr);
```

One other defining feature of output-primitive behavior remains; what is known as the drawing mode. There are two modes usually associated with output: *immediate* and *retained*.

In standard usage, immediate-mode graphics happen at the point of call. This means that using a client-area DC and a GDI primitive directly has immediate results. The graphic must also be completely respecified and redrawn every time window damage needs to be repaired. Retained-mode graphics, on the other hand, maintain some record of output (like the Central Structure Store in PHIGS), so it can more easily repair damage using this record.

Our system is somewhere in between. We buffer output primitives to the canvas, so it's certainly not an immediate-mode system; but hierarchies and a formal facility for manipulating them are outside of the scope of this system, so it's not truly retained-mode either. Because of its canvas-based output, it resembles retained-mode more than immediate though, so your decisions about output must be made with one key fact in mind: Until the next screen refresh, the effect of your output primitives won't be seen, unless you do some extra work on the client end.

The demo programs in this chapter and the usage examples in the rest of the application will show a working example of this type of functionality and its implications about output behavior and program-output architecture.

Once we've established the output primitives, attributes are our next target. Attributes are a necessary feature of graphics output, and control of them lets you manipulate appearance values to gain the desired effect. Attributes present an interesting design problem and can be implemented in a variety of ways. In our implementation, we avoid some of the more ambitious attribute strategies, like a central structure store that keeps a record in a special-purpose database of primitives and related information.

Both the canvas, with the slots you saw in Table 5-2, and the primitive functions reveal the attribute strategy. It is a two-part strategy consisting of a default attribute setting and an override capability. The default setting is in the canvas slots; the override is provided by the explicit attribute parameters in each output primitive. This approach supports two flavors of attribute specification and usage:

- *repetitive*, with each primitive call having the same attribute, and
- *single-shot*, with each primitive call having different attributes.

In this way, if you want repetitive drawing with a certain attribute, the slots are convenient. If the drawing changes so frequently that your drawing tools are also continually changed (a single-shot drawing), the API supports that as well. Besides flexibility, another nice side effect of this strategy is a measure of control over the performance costs associated with attribute selection. The costs are clearly associated with certain actions of the API (notably *SetVal/Use* and the output primitives in single-shot mode), and now you can decide how much to pay and when.

You'll also notice the minimal use of abstraction here. This wrapper layer is less concerned with portability and the like and more concerned with local management. GDI objects are used directly and are not hidden from the client programmer. This violation of the wrapper-layer rules gains some performance and control.

Another key feature of our attribute strategy is handle-size independence. Since GDI underlies this system and all attributes are constructed on top of GDI objects, the nature of the GDI objects is reflected in the attributes and their types. We want this to be as transparent as possible to 32-bit and 16-bit cards, so all GDI objects are treated as DWORD values rather than 16-bit handles. This greatly simplifies the use and maintenance of the API.

G3DLib 3D Support: Primitives

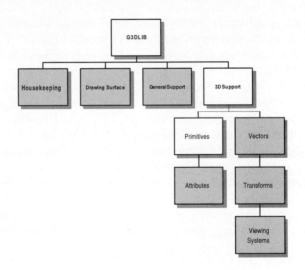

Primitives, decomposed into one-point, two-point, and *n*-point types, consist of:

- point and text output primitives,
- a line and rectangle output primitive, and
- a polyline, a polygon, and a polypolygon output primitive.

This basic set must meet the needs of:

- wireframe rendering, which uses line and polyline,
- simple hidden-line, solid-shaded, and flat-shaded rendering, which uses polyline and polygon, and
- ray-traced, which uses point- or pixel-level output.

In addition, text labels are nice, since a graph doesn't mean anything without a label. That rounds out the set of output primitives provided for your use. It's quite easy to extend this set of primitives, but for now these suffice.

One-Pointers—Point Output

The most basic output primitive is the pixel- or point-output primitive. The public graphics output primitive function, *G3D_GEnv_Point*, is shown in Listing 6-2. It provides a point primitive defined geometrically as shown in Figure 6-1. This function is implemented as shown in Listing 6-3 and you should especially note the usage of **PatBlt** and a brush to draw a pixel.

Listing 6-2.   Point-Output Primitive Declaration

```
BOOL        WINAPI G3D_GEnv_Point(LPGLGENV glgenv,
                                  long x, long y,
                                  DWORD hbr);
```

Figure 6-1.   Point Geometry

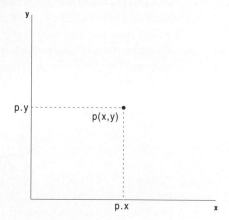

Listing 6-3.   G3D_GEnv_Point Implementation

```
BOOL  WINAPI G3D_GEnv_Point(LPGENV glgenv,
                            long x, long y,
                            DWORD hbr)
{
    HBRUSH  hOldBrush;
    HDC     hdc = (HDC)G3D_GEnv_GetVal(glgenv,ID_DC);
    if ( hbr )
    {
        hOldBrush = SelectObject(hdc, (HBRUSH)hbr);
    }
//
```

Listing 6-3.   (cont.)

```
    PatBlt(hdc, x, y, 1, 1, PATCOPY);
//
    if ( hbr )
    {
        SelectObject(hdc,hOldBrush );
    }
    return TRUE;
}
```

You might be asking yourself "What gives here? Why not use **SetPixel**?" Hearkening back to Petzold's article on color issues in Windows, if we always rely on a brush that was created using palette colors, the graphics library can maintain consistency within itself for color selection. This means that the color requested and drawn for point primitives and that for filled polygons is always based on the same representation, a brush. **SetPixel** uses a simple color-value specification, which won't accomplish this.

The next pertinent facts about this block of code are its usage of the brush parameter to override the contents of the underlying DC, and its return of the DC to the pristine state before function exit. This enables the dual-attribute behavior we've already discussed. If a NULL brush is passed in, we use the current style settings; if a valid brush handle is passed in, we use it to override the current settings. Again, we use GDI objects directly here to avoid any extra memory references, rather than introduce another abstraction above this layer and have the code here decoding and creating things. This makes these output functions very lightweight.

The final pertinent fact is the function's use of a DWORD value for the brush. This implementation detail allows the library not to care whether its base system is 32 bits or 16 bits.

One-Pointers—Text Output

We must be able to draw text. *G3D_GEnv_Text* provides this ability, and is also a single-point primitive. The public text output primitive function *G3D_GEnv_Text* declaration is shown in Listing 6-4. Figure 6-2 shows that this function uses the same geometrical definition as the point primitive, since it is also a one-point primitive, but it outputs a text string at the point rather than a color.

Listing 6-4.   Text Output Primitive Declaration

```
BOOL        WINAPI G3D_GEnv_Text(LPGLGENV glgenv,
                            long       x1, long y1,
                            LPSTR      lpText,
                            LONG       tLen,
                            DWORD      hFont);
```

Figure 6-2   Text Output Geometry

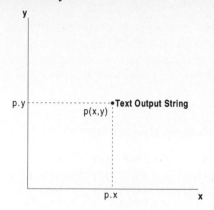

Attribute control lets you specify orientations. The output function only defines the starting location.

This function, implemented in Listing 6-5, shows the same attribute behavior—overrides and 32/16 transparency. The usage of **TextOut** instead of **ExtTextOut** is perhaps its most interesting feature. From a performance point of view, simply replacing the call to **TextOut** with **ExtTextOut**, maybe adding some default parameters so we don't clutter up the interface, can result in some performance gains. (See Dave Edsun's wonderful article "Dave's Top Ten List of Tricks, Hints, and Techniques for Programming in Windows" in *MSJ*, Vol. 7, No. 6.) This is foregone here simply because the additional features of **ExtTextOut** and the additional parameters it requires really requires a more complicated interface and our philosophy here is to keep it simple.

Listing 6-5.   G3D_GEnv_Text Implementation

```
BOOL  WINAPI G3D_GEnv_Text(LPGENV glgenv,
                           long    x1, long y1,
                           LPSTR   lpText,
                           LONG    tLen,
                           DWORD   hFont)
{
    HFONT   hfo;
    HDC     hdc = (HDC)G3D_GEnv_GetVal(glgenv,ID_DC);
    if ( hFont )
    {
       hfo = SelectObject(hdc, (HFONT)hFont);
    }
//
    TextOut(hdc,x1,y1,lpText,(int)tLen);
//
    if ( hFont )
    {
       SelectObject(hdc,hfo);
    }
    return TRUE;
}
```

Two-Pointers—Line Output

The ability to draw a line is the next step up in complexity. Lines are also a necessity in a graphics system. *G3D_GEnv_Line*, declared in Listing 6-6, provides this primitive. The implementation again follows the pattern of providing the attribute-override dualism and the 32/16 transparency. This function provides a line primitive using the geometry shown in Figure 6-3.

Listing 6-6.   **Line Output Primitive Declaration**

```
BOOL        WINAPI G3D_GEnv_Line(LPGLGENV glgenv,
                            long x1,    long y1,
                            long x2,    long y2,
                            DWORD       hPen);
```

Figure 6-3.   **Line Output Geometry**

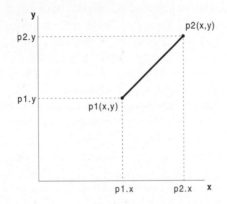

G3D_GEnv_Line, implemented in Listing 6-7, uses **MoveTo** and **LineTo** and assumes nothing about the current point. This means the graphics library really has no policy about where the pen is. The price of this simplicity is a loss of some performance increment. In repetitive drawing cases, the current point may not change, so **MoveTo** can be redundant. This is an obvious optimization, and if a real performance hot spot existed, this would be the first thing to change. As before, in keeping with the philosophy of simplicity and policy-free behavior, I've avoided this.

Other than the item I've already mentioned, this is not a really remarkable function. Another benefit of this extremely simple approach is that if you do get around to caring about optimizations it's easy to see the cost equation here. There's just not a lot to factor in. But be careful about extending this subsystem by adding a layer. Function calls cost on 486 machines, since any jump flushes the instruction cache and momentarily stalls the processor. It's best to keep this layer thin, since output functions get called a lot.

Listing 6-7.   G3D_GEnv_Line Implementation

```
BOOL  WINAPI G3D_GEnv_Line(LPGENV glgenv,
                          long x1, long y1,
                          long x2, long y2,
                          DWORD hpen)
{
    HPEN    hOldP;
    HDC     hdc = (HDC)G3D_GEnv_GetVal(glgenv,ID_DC);
    if ( hpen )
    {
        hOldP = SelectObject(hdc, (HPEN)hpen);
    }
//
    MoveTo(hdc,x1,y1);
    LineTo(hdc,x2,y2);
//
    if ( hpen )
    {
        SelectObject(hdc,hOldP );
    }
    return TRUE;
}
```

Two-Pointers—Rectangle Output

While the *n*-point polygon output to come may be used more, the need to draw only rectangles occurs often enough (and the functions for rectangles are simple enough) that the inclusion of a rectangle primitive is easy to justify. Listing 6-8 contains the declaration for the rectangle output primitive *G3D_GEnv_Rect*. It takes the expected two points, a pen for the outline, and a brush for the interior fill.

Listing 6-8.   G3D_GEnv_Rect Output Primitive Declaration

```
BOOL        WINAPI G3D_GEnv_Rect(LPGENV glgenv,
                        long     x1, long y1,
                        long     x2, long y2,
                        DWORD    hpen,
                        DWORD    hbr);
```

G3D_GEnv_Rect's implementation again follows the pattern of providing attribute-override dualism and 32/16 transparency. This function provides a rectangle primitive using the geometry shown in Figure 6-4.

Figure 6-4.   Rectangle Output Geometry

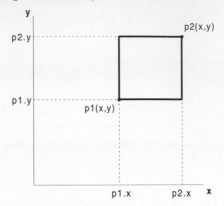

Listing 6-9, which contains the implementation, not only shows the attribute selection but again shows the use of **PatBlt** to lay down the color. Why use this instead of GDI's **Rectangle**? This approach simplifies the number of variables involved in color selection by using a minimum of GDI functions in the library. **PatBlt** is also fast and bug-free in most of the drivers out there because it is one of the lower-level routines. Various GDI functions have had known bugs over the years; however, if you prefer **Rectangle**, feel free to change it. That is all there is to this function.

Listing 6-9.   G3D_GEnv_Rect Implementation

```
BOOL  WINAPI G3D_GEnv_Rect(LPGENV glgenv,
                           long       x1, long y1,
                           long       x2, long y2,
                           DWORD      hpen,
                           DWORD      hbr)
{
    HBRUSH   hOldBrush;
    HPEN     hOldP;
    HDC      hdc = (HDC)G3D_GEnv_GetVal(glgenv,ID_DC);
    if ( hpen )
    {
        hOldP = SelectObject(hdc, (HPEN)hpen);
    }
    if ( hbr )
    {
        hOldBrush = SelectObject(hdc, (HBRUSH)hbr);
    }
//
    PatBlt(hdc, x1, y1, x2, y2, PATCOPY);
//
    if ( hbr )
    {
        SelectObject(hdc,hOldBrush );
    }
```

```
    if ( hpen )
    {
        SelectObject(hdc,hOldP );
    }
    return TRUE;
}
```

N-Pointers—Polyline Output

It's nice to be able to "batch up" or *packetize* a bunch of calls. In the Win-16 world, this is not quite as critical to performance as it is in the Win-32 world. Since the 32-bit NT environment is based on a client-server model like X-Windows, graphics output calls must cross the client-server boundary, which imposes some overhead. In this environment, the ability to packetize calls can be critical to performance. Our API reflects this *not* out of a desire to be NT-compatible, but because some of the output routines used in the 3D demo programs and the modeler can take advantage of this functionality as well. Even in the Win-16 world these calls provide some advantage, and here we'll use them to the library's benefit.

Providing a packetized routine, which admittedly forces some policy and is not a "simple" function, is not really in violation of our goals because surface plotting and modeling can put these functions to good use. The environment they live in requires repetitive line-drawing for some rendering techniques, so a function that provides this can leverage this application behavior into a small gain in performance.

Listing 6-10 contains the declaration for *G3D_GEnv_Polyline*. Figure 6-5 shows the geometrical view of the functionality provided by this routine.

Listing 6-10. Polyline Output Primitive Declaration

```
BOOL        WINAPI G3D_GEnv_Polyline(LPGENV   glgenv,
                                     LPPOINT  pPoly,
                                     long      nPnts,
                                     DWORD    hpen);
```

Figure 6-5. Polyline Output Geometry

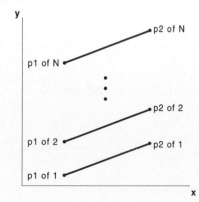

This function is, in turn, implemented in Listing 6-11. At the risk of being a bore, let me note again that the implementation follows the pattern of providing the attribute-override dualism and 32/16 transparency.

Listing 6-11.   G3D_GEnv_Polyline Implementation

```
BOOL  WINAPI G3D_GEnv_Polyline(LPGENV glgenv,
                              LPPOINT  pPoly,
                              long     nPnts,
                              DWORD    hpen)
{
   HPEN    hOldP;
   HDC     hdc = (HDC)G3D_GEnv_GetVal(glgenv,ID_DC);
   if ( hpen )
   {
      hOldP = SelectObject(hdc, (HPEN)hpen);
   }
//
   Polyline( hdc, pPoly,nPnts);
//
   if ( hpen )
   {
      SelectObject(hdc,hOldP );
   }
   return TRUE;
}
```

G3D_GEnv_Polyline uses the GDI function **Polyline** to work its magic. This governs the parameters in the API (an array of GDI-points and a count), since they must accommodate GDI's needs. The application assumes all responsibility for point-array setup. This function only performs output, and again is not really all that remarkable.

N-Pointers—Polygon Output

The next level of complexity in output primitives is that of closed figures, or polygons. GDI provides a routine to do this, so our library doesn't have to simulate this behavior internally by calling the line primitive itself. Listing 6-12 shows the function declaration for the polygon function.

Listing 6-12.   Polygon Output Primitive Declaration

```
BOOL        WINAPI G3D_GEnv_Polygon(LPGENV glgenv,
                              LPPOINT  pPoly,
                              long     nPnts,
                              DWORD    hpen,
                              DWORD    hbr);
```

Polygons are closed figures that can be described geometrically as a series of points, as illustrated in Figure 6-6.

Using what GDI provides is as easy as defining an API and implementing the function. Listing 6-13 performs the implementation, which is, again, a thin pass-through to GDI that enables the attribute and handle-size policies. The most important detail here is the use of both a pen and brush by the polygon output primitives. This is a closed figure that may be filled with a color, and that may have an outline. That's all that's really important here; once again, this function is quite simple.

Figure 6-6.   Polygon Output Geometry

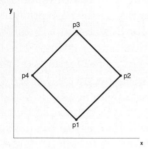

Listing 6-13.   Polygon Output Primitive Implementation

```
BOOL  WINAPI G3D_GEnv_Polygon(LPGENV glgenv,
                              LPPOINT  pPoly,
                              long     nPnts,
                              DWORD    hpen,
                              DWORD    hbr)
{
    HPEN     hOldP;
    HBRUSH   hOldBr;
    HDC      hdc = (HDC)G3D_GEnv_GetVal(glgenv,ID_DC);
    if ( hpen )
       hOldP = SelectObject(hdc, (HPEN)hpen);
    if ( hbr )
       hOldBr = SelectObject(hdc, (HBRUSH)hbr);
//
    Polygon( hdc, pPoly,nPnts);
//
    if ( hpen )
       SelectObject(hdc,hOldP );
    if ( hbr )
       SelectObject(hdc,hOldBr );
    return TRUE;
}
```

If you expected something more glamorous, this is a prime example of an implementation reality—many of the details of banging out an API are repetitive and boring once you've made the design decisions. Our hands are largely tied in the implementation of these functions, so the implementation almost drives itself. In most cases, if the design has been thorough and really covered the issues, this should be true.

N-Pointers —Polypolygon Output

The last output primitive we'll talk about is a polypolygon function. In a manner similar to the repetitive line drawing leveraged by the polyline function, we can leverage repetitive polygon drawing by including an API function providing this functionality. The geometry for this output primitive has the same relation to the base polygon primitive as the polyline primitive has to the base line primitive; for this reason, we don't need an illustration here.

Listing 6-14 contains the declaration and Listing 6-15 the implementation for *G3D_GEnv_Polypolygon*. It provides the expected features (attribute and handle-size handling), and in the course of doing so it uses, no surprise, the GDI function **PolyPolygon**. Again, we'll let GDI force the library's parameter set. In this case, the required parameters are an array of vertex GDI-points and an array of counts, as well as the number of polygons represented in these two arrays. The application assumes all responsibility for array setup and performs only output, just like the polyline function.

Listing 6-14.   Polypolygon Output Primitive Declaration

```
BOOL   WINAPI G3D_GEnv_Polypolygon(LPGENV    glgenv,
                                   LPPOINT   pPoly,
                                   LPINT     pCounts,
                                   long       nPolys,
                                   DWORD     hpen,
                                   DWORD     hbr);
```

Listing 6-15.   G3D_GEnv_Polypolygon Implementation

```
BOOL   WINAPI G3D_GEnv_Polypolygon(LPGENV    glgenv,
                                   LPPOINT   pPoly,
                                   LPINT     pCounts,
                                   long       nPolys,
                                   DWORD     hpen,
                                   DWORD     hbr)
{
    HPEN    hOldBr;
    HPEN    hOldP;
    HDC     hdc = (HDC)G3D_GEnv_GetVal(glgenv,ID_DC);
    if ( hpen )
    {
        hOldP = SelectObject(hdc, (HPEN)hpen);
    }
    if ( hbr )
```

```
    {
        hOldBr = SelectObject(hdc, (HPEN)hbr );
    }
//
    PolyPolygon( hdc, pPoly, pCounts, nPolys);
//
    if ( hpen )
    {
        SelectObject(hdc,hOldP );
    }
    if ( hbr )
    {
        SelectObject(hdc,hOldBr );
    }
    return TRUE;
}
```

This function again uses two GDI objects—a brush and a pen—to allow the attribute overrides. It might be more in keeping with the wrapper-layer philosophy to define this in terms of the structures provided in the attribute layer, but, in a bow to the dual gods of practicality and performance, we use the GDI objects directly. This means the library doesn't have to de-reference some structure at the point of drawing the primitive. The DC setup shown here, and the source in general, uses native types directly, rather than defining an attribute layer. Attributes are finessed here, but they're our next topic.

G3DLib 3D Support: Attributes

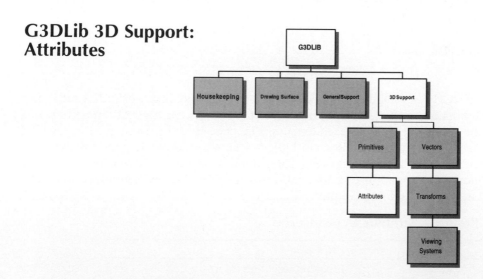

Attributes control the appearance of output primitives. Our attribute strategy is to use GDI attributes to control both the canvas and the output primitive functions. The output primitives each have a default attribute set; this means many drawing requirements can be satisfied without much attribute usage. Wireframe drawing, for example, can simply manipulate the canvas background styles and accept the default attributes. In the same vein, a monochrome hidden-surface renderer can also use this feature to gain performance by subtracting drawing-tool selection time from overall rendering time.

The pertinent fact about attributes should be immediately apparent—using attributes decreases performance. The amount of attribute use correlates directly to the performance cost. But with the library's policy of providing for defaults and overrides, we at least have a mechanism that allows fine-grain control, and we know the costs up front.

Remember that this is a two-part strategy of canvas defaults and primitive point-of-call overrides. Use whichever one suits your style. Each type of rendering uses different GDI attributes. See Table 6-2 for a list of this attribute usage.

Table 6-2.   Output Attribute Modification Granularity

Render Type	Attribute Action
Wireframe	Set some default line attribute and render the entire scene.
Solid	The fill brush must change only once per object.
Shaded color	Each polygon is potentially different gray.
Ray-traced	Each pixel is potentially different.

This attribute strategy of direct usage of the GDI object imposes the least possible overhead. All we need to do is categorize the GDI attributes with respect to the functions to clarify the dependencies.

The attribute categories parallel output primitive use in the API, which results in a categorization of attributes, as follows:

- point styles,
- line styles,
- polygon styles, and
- text styles.

Using the underlying GDI drawing tools for the canvas and output-primitive attributes has the advantage of simplicity. It adds no new data types and no new API functions. You simply use the GDI objects you're used to using. On a per-output-primitive basis, the GDI objects you need to deal with are shown in Table 6-3. This boils down to pens, brushes, and fonts. The hidden implication here is that in 256-color mode, you need a palette. You should now have enough information to understand the attribute strategy employed here and make use of it. It really is pretty simple.

Table 6-3.   Primitive Attribute Dependencies

Primitive	Attributes
Point	Brush representing color
Text	Font
Line	Color, width, and style (GDI LOGPEN)
Rectangle	Line attributes plus brush
Polyline	Line attributes
Polygon	Same as rectangle
Polypolygon	Same as rectangle

Demo 1: RGBCube, Round 3—Using the Rect Primitive

Our tried-and-true RGBCube demo will serve us one more time. Redoing this example with the primitive updates shows a simple primitive usage, and allows us to discuss only the changes, as I've described previously. This is the last time we'll re-implement the RGBCube, but not the last time we'll use this technique of repetitive and step-wise refinement of an implementation.

This version of the drawing loop uses the primitive function *G3D_GEnv_Rect* to refine the code from Chapters 4 and 5. This version is shown in Listing 6-16. Brush creation remains the same, but the selection is now handled within the rectangle function because, in this case, the fill color changes every rectangle in the RGB cube display. The primitive call is highlighted in the listing.

Listing 6-16. Primitive-Based Drawing

```
for (g=0; g<5; g++)
  {
    HDC hDC = G3D_GEnv_GetVal(pvwwnd->genv,ID_DC);

        y = ySize + yInit + (g * yDiff);
        rgbColor.fGreen = (float)g * 1./4.;
        for (b=0; b<5; b++){
            x = xInit + (g * xDiff);
            rgbColor.fBlue  = (float)b * 1./4.;
            for (r=0; r<5; r++){
                rgbColor.fRed   = (float)r * 1./4.;
// display palette colors
                WL_Color_RGBtoCRT( &rgbColor, &crtValue );
                lsClr = PALETTERGB(crtValue.cRed,
                crtValue.cGreen,crtValue.cBlue);
                hBr   = CreateSolidBrush( ((DWORD)lsClr));
                G3D_GEnv_Rect(pv->genv,
                                 po.x, po.y, ps.x, ps.y,
                                 NULL,hbr);
                DeleteObject( hbr );

                x += xSpot + xSpace;
            }
            y += ySpot + ySpace;
        }
  }
```

The only remarkable thing about this code is how much cleaner it reads than the original from Chapter 4. The API functions read like the actions they encapsulate, and the API usage helps to clarify what could easily be an unreadable code-clot of GDI activity. You use *G3D_GEnv_GetVal* to get the DC, *WL_Color_RGBtoCRT* and **PaletteRGB** to massage the color value, **CreateSolidBrush** to make a GDI object, *G3D_GEnv_Rect* to draw the rectangle, and finally **DeleteObject** to remove the GDI drawing tool. Just reading the names of these routines reveals a lot about what this complementary use of GDI and library routines is doing.

This code is a bad candidate for attribute access, since the fill color changes with each rectangle. But this example does show the one-shot attribute-override feature. The next example allows a closer look at attribute control using the attribute structures.

Demo 2: General Primitive and Attribute Tester

The RGBCube has served us well, but we need to move on to better things. An excellent primitive and attribute example program is a random-drawing program. Just combine all primitives drawn in a random way in one program with randomized attributes, and you get a general-purpose primitive and attribute thrasher.

This program uses the one-pointers and two-pointers in a set of routines that are completely random, and the n-pointers in a set of functions that are more regular (you might even say contrived; but they're closer to surface plotting than to random dots). The set of functions that perform this drawing consists of the following:

- One-pointers
  1. *Point_Draw* to draw a random point field
  2. *Text_Draw* to draw the string "Test Text" using a random font among the 10 default fonts

- Two-pointers
  1. *Line_Draw* to make a "superfuse" random kaleidoscope-like pattern
  2. *Rect_Draw* to draw random rectangles (Petzold -style)

- *N*-pointers
  1. *Polyline_Draw* to draw a grid of polylines with fixed attributes
  2. *Polygon_Draw* to draw a grid of rectangles with each row having fixed attributes

We'll ignore function *Polypolygon_Draw* for the moment, but it is very similar to the other repetitive drawing functions, and will get used in examples to come. You don't want to see too much silly drawing code at one sitting.

I'll discuss this set of drawing routines in turn, but before I get down to the details of the individual routines, you need to understand the global behavior of the library, which has some implications for the code of this demo program. First, this library implements a version of retained mode, so our drawing commands won't have an immediate effect. This isn't great in an interactive drawing routine like a superfuse. If this isn't clear, let me restate it: You see drawing output only on a canvas refresh. In a kaleidoscope program, this would mean a lot of **BitBlt**s—too many to make the program practical. Your dilemma, then, becomes how to bridge this gulf. The answer is to avoid the dilemma altogether. This kind of immediate-mode graphics is not what the canvas is good at. The canvas is best used to retain the results of drawing operations.

Our demo program is meant to exercise each primitive, so we just won't worry about this problem. We'll do some extra coding for a "directdraw" code block. This is a duplication of functionality, and, again, GDI is being used directly. This direct-draw mode makes our demo program feel snappy at the cost of *not* using all of our wonderful library routines.

In addition to the snappy output to the screen, the primitives are also output to the canvas. By double-drawing here, we *simulate* the effect of both reasonably fast interaction and double-buffering.

To lessen the cost of eliminating double-buffering, the canvas-based *G3D_GEnv* calls are bracketed with a Boolean variable *dbuffer*, which is carried to the interface in the Options menu. By disabling the double-buffering (really "double-drawing" here), you see the true drawing speed of GDI. The cost is that the off-screen bitmap no longer retains the image, thus preventing any effective redrawing, printing, saving to a file, or sharing on the clipboard through the graphics environment-canvas vehicle.

The typical usage pattern for a modeler application is single-frame drawing, which fits the abstraction provided by the canvas. This just goes to show that one tool seldom fits all, which explains the continuing popularity of the Swiss-Army knife. The lesson here is not to expect anything for free from your tools.

Point Output

Drawing a random field is really easy. Simply hook the x and y variables up to the **rand** function in the C Run-Time Library, and away you go. To make it really interesting, hook the three color components, red, green, and blue, up to the random-number generator as well. Again, the items chosen for randomization include the point's x, y location and its RGB value.

Figure 6-7 shows an example of the output with a low density; a random pattern of dots of random colors. Listing 6-17 shows the *Point_Draw* function. The code clearly shows the immediate-mode/retained-mode dichotomy. These demos may seem mindless (and they are), but they do thrash the API.

Listing 6-17. Point_Draw

```
void Point_Draw(HDC hdc){
    FRAME*      pfrm   = Frame_GetPtr(g_app.hwndMain);
    CLIENT*     pcli   = Client_GetPtr(pfrm->hwndClient);
    VWWND*      pvwwnd = View_GetPtr(pcli->hwView);
    HBRUSH      hBrush, hbro1;
    int         xleft,ytop,nRed,nGreen,nBlue;
    CRT         c;
    xleft     = rand() %cxClient;
    ytop      = rand() %cyClient;
    nRed    = rand() %255;
    nGreen  = rand() %255;
    nBlue   = rand() %255;
```

Listing 6-17.   (cont.)

```
//immediate
   hBrush = CreateSolidBrush(PALETTERGB(nRed,nGreen,nBlue));
   hbro1  = SelectObject(hdc,hBrush);
   PatBlt(hdc, xleft, ytop, 1, 1, PATCOPY);// retained mode
   if ( dbuffer ){
     G3D_GEnv_Point(pvwwnd->genv, xleft,ytop,hBrush);

   }
   SelectObject(hdc,hbro1);
   DeleteObject(hBrush);
//
}
```

Figure 6-7.   Point_Draw Output

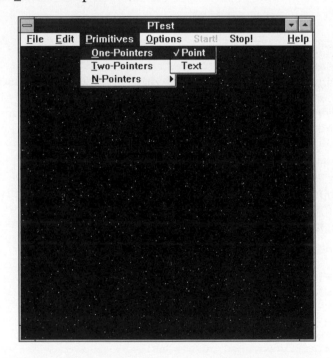

Text Output

The other single-point output primitive is the text primitive. The items picked for randomization include:

- font x, y location,
- font color,
- font width and height,

- font orientation, and
- font facename.

Figure 6-8 shows a smattering of random repetitions of the string "Test Text."

The block of code to do this is too large to show in its entirety, so I've opted instead to show you the key pieces in Listings 6-18 through 6-20: the randomizer code, then the retained mode code, and finally the immediate-mode code. See the source disk for all the code.

Figure 6-8   Random Text Output

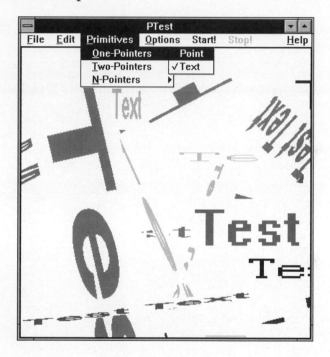

Listing 6-18.   Randomizing Chunks from Text_Draw

```
...
  x       = rand() %cxClient;
  y       = rand() %cyClient;
  nRed    = rand() %255;
  nGreen  = rand() %255;
  nBlue   = rand() %255;
  w       = rand () %128;
  h       = rand () %128;
  u       = rand () %3600;
  c       = PALETTERGB(nRed,nGreen,nBlue);
...
```

Listing 6-18.   (cont.)

```
ifname                      = rand () %10;
  switch(ifname){
    case 0:
      lstrcpy(lfCurrent.lfFaceName, "ARIAL");
      lstrcpy(ts.szFont, "ARIAL");
      break;
    case 1:
      lstrcpy(lfCurrent.lfFaceName, "COURIER");
      lstrcpy(ts.szFont, "COURIER");
      break;
    case 2:
      lstrcpy(lfCurrent.lfFaceName, "TIMES NEW ROMAN");
      lstrcpy(ts.szFont, "TIMES NEW ROMAN");
      break;
    case 3:
      lstrcpy(lfCurrent.lfFaceName, "MS SANS SERIF");
      lstrcpy(ts.szFont, "MS SANS SERIF");
      break;
    case 4:
      lstrcpy(lfCurrent.lfFaceName, "MS SERIF");
      lstrcpy(ts.szFont, "MS SERIF");
      break;
    case 5:
      lstrcpy(lfCurrent.lfFaceName, "ROMAN");
      lstrcpy(ts.szFont, "ROMAN");
      break;
    case 6:
      lstrcpy(lfCurrent.lfFaceName, "SCRIPT");
      lstrcpy(ts.szFont, "SCRIPT");
      break;
    case 7:
      lstrcpy(lfCurrent.lfFaceName, "MODERN");
      lstrcpy(ts.szFont, "MODERN");
      break;
    case 8:
      lstrcpy(lfCurrent.lfFaceName, "SYMBOL");
      lstrcpy(ts.szFont, "SYMBOL");
      break;
    case 9:
      lstrcpy(lfCurrent.lfFaceName, "SYSTEM");
      lstrcpy(ts.szFont, "SYSTEM");
      break;
  }
...
```

Listing 6-19.   Retained-Mode Code Chunks from Text_Draw

```
...
//immediate
...
// retained mode
   if ( dbuffer )
   {
      G3D_GEnv_Text(pvwwnd->genv,
                    x,y,
                    "Test Text",
                    lstrlen("Test Text"),
                    hf);

   }
/immediate
...
```

Listing 6-20.   Immediate-Mode Code Chunks from Text_Draw

```
...
//immediate
   lfCurrent.lfWidth        = w;
   lfCurrent.lfHeight       = h;
   lfCurrent.lfEscapement   = u;
...
//
// immediate mode
//
   SetTextColor(hdc,c);
   hf = CreateFontIndirect(&lfCurrent);
   if (hf)
   {
      hfo1 = SelectObject(hdc, hf);
      TextOut(hdc,x,y,"Test Text",lstrlen("Test Text"));
//retained mode
...
//
      SelectObject(hdc, hfo1);
      DeleteObject(hf);
   }
}
...
```

The randomizer operates on the elements shown in the earlier bullet list, and ends up creating a font for immediate mode. The immediate-mode code in Listing 6-20, or, more properly, the code that draws directly on the client DC, has control over font creation; the random font is passed to the retained-mode code and the *G3D_GEnv_Text* function, shown in Listing 6-19. The immediate-mode block simply uses **SetTextColor**, **CreateFontIndirect**, and **TextOut**. The two key details from the point function, immediate-mode versus retained-mode, and the resource handling, also stand out here.

Line Output

The line-drawing demo generates a superfuse or a random, spirographic-like display. Drawing a superfuse can be broken down into three parts:

- randomly regular line-segment calculations,
- randomly regular line-segment drawing, and
- undrawing the line segments.

The exact nature of the randomization is not quite as important as the gross nature of the routine. The method used here is only one way of doing this, and is not the primary focus of our discussion. The important thing is the primitive and attribute usage of the demo, not the cuteness of the program. If it really interests you, read the code on the disk to see exactly how to make kaleidoscope-like drawings similar to the one shown in Figure 6-9.

Figure 6-9.   Superfuse Line Output

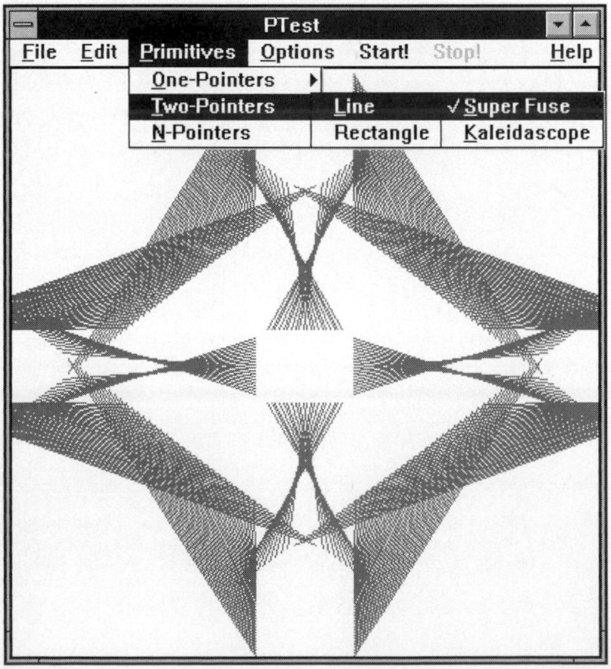

I've included only the briefest code block in Listing 6-21. It shows the basic pattern that is repeated in the core drawing loop, the immediate- and retained-mode usage. To clean up the internals of the line-drawing, I created demo function *DrawLine4* to encapsulate both **MoveTo** and **LineTo**. The double-buffer control variable is also used to allow the true GDI speed to show through. Once again this simply repeats the formula for line primitives and attributes.

Listing 6-21.   Code Blocks in Line_Draw

```
void FAR PASCAL DrawLine4( HDC hdc, int x1, int y1, int x2, int y2 )
{
   MoveTo(hdc, x1,y1);
   LineTo(hdc, x2,y2);
}



...

        DrawLine4( hdc,(CX-XA), (CY-Y1),(CX-XB), (CY-Y2) );
        if ( dbuffer )
           G3D_GEnv_Line(pv->genv,
                        (CX-XA), (CY-Y1),
                        (CX-XB), (CY-Y2),
                        (DWORD)hPen);

...
```

Rectangle Output

The random rectangle-drawing routine is a simple derivation of the code shown in Petzold. Figure 6-10 shows the mostly boring output of the rectangle routine *Rect_Draw*. The critical code block is shown in Listing 6-22. Once again, the code invokes *G3D_GEnv_Rect*. This basic code should show you exactly how to use these functions, so what it is doing with the functions should get in the way as little as possible. This example certainly does that.

Listing 6-22.   Code Block from Rect_Draw

```
//immediate
   hBrush = CreateSolidBrush(PALETTERGB(nRed,nGreen,nBlue));
   hbro1  = SelectObject(hdc,hBrush);
   hpo1   = SelectObject(hdc,hPen);
   PatBlt(hdc,
          min(xleft,xright),min(yTop,yBottom),
          max(xleft,xright),max(yTop,yBottom),
          PATCOPY);
   SelectObject(hdc,hbro1);
   SelectObject(hdc,hpo1);
```

Listing 6-22.   (cont.)

```
//retained
   if ( dbuffer ){

      G3D_GEnv_Rect(pvwwnd->genv,
                    min(xleft,xright),min(yTop,yBottom),
                    max(xleft,xright),max(yTop,yBottom),
                    (DWORD)hPen,
                    (DWORD)hBrush);
   }
   SelectObject(hdc,hbro1);
   SelectObject(hdc,hpo1);
   DeleteObject(hBrush);
   DeleteObject(hPen);
```

Figure 6-10.   Rect_Draw Output

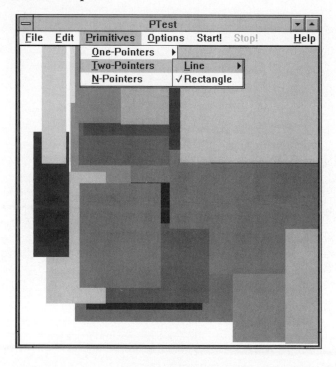

Polyline Output

Using the polyline primitive is really very easy. Instead of calling the line function with two points, an array of points collects the x, y values and maintains a count of array entries. Instead of sweating over what to draw, this demo draws a simple 2D grid. Lines in x and in y form a rectangular grid.

This can be drawn in a nested loop of two function calls. Simply batch up the x lines in one call for each row, then batch up the y lines in a second call for each column. This illustrates the simplifying power of these "multiple-draw" functions.

The retained-mode code block that generates a portion of this grid is shown in Listing 6-23. This is still line drawing, and only the call to **G3D_GEnv_Polyline**, along with some setup logic, is contained in Listing 6-23 so we keep repetition to a minimum.

Listing 6-23.   G3D_GEnv_Polyline Usage in Polyline_Draw

```
POINT xpts[100]; //GDI point struct
...
   for ( i = 0; i < 11; i++)
   {
     xpts[i].x = xo + xs*i;
     xpts[i].y = yo + ys*j;
   }
    G3D_GEnv_Polyline(pvwwnd->genv,xpts,11,(DWORD)hPen);
...
```

Polygon Output

The polygon-drawing code simply revisits the random rectangle-drawing routine and is simply a derivation of the earlier code, modified to fill the points of the polygon around the circuit of the rectangle instead of just passing the two points to the rectangle function. This function also takes advantage of GDI's ability to close the polygon from the last point to the first.

I'll show you two code blocks from **Polygon_Draw**, one for point setup and one for the actual output. **G3D_GEnv_Polygon** is in the second block, but there's nothing really remarkable here, just the standard invocation sequence you would expect from reading the function prototype. Listing 6-24 contains these code blocks, which concludes the second demo program of Chapter 6.

Listing 6-24.   Blocks from Polygon_Draw

```
//
...
   nRed    = rand() %255;
   nGreen  = rand() %255;
   nBlue   = rand() %255;
   crt.cRed   = nRed;
   crt.cGreen = nGreen;
   crt.cBlue  = nBlue;
   c         = PALETTERGB(nRed,nGreen,nBlue);
   switch(bckclr)
   {
     case CMD_WHITE:
        hPen  = CreatePen(PS_SOLID,1,RGB(0,0,0));
        break;
     case CMD_BLACK:
        hPen  = CreatePen(PS_SOLID,1,RGB(255,255,255));
        break;
   }

   hBrush = CreateSolidBrush(PALETTERGB(nRed,nGreen,nBlue));
   hbro1  = SelectObject(hdc,hBrush);
   hpo1   = SelectObject(hdc,hPen);
   Polygon(hdc,pts,4);
   SelectObject(hdc,hbro1);
   SelectObject(hdc,hpo1);
//
//retained
   if ( dbuffer )
   {
      G3D_GEnv_Polygon(pv->genv,
                       pts,4,
                  (DWORD)hPen,
                  (DWORD)hBrush);
   }
//
  DeleteObject(hBrush);
  DeleteObject(hPen);
...
```

Summary

Primitives can be categorized as:

- one-point,
- two-point, and
- *n*-point.

A suite of routines in those categories includes:

- pixel, text,
- Line, rect,
- polyline, polygon, and polypolygon.

An attribute strategy that uses stored defaults and invocation-level overrides provides for both repetitive- and single-invocation usage. Attributes use the underlying GDI objects, so no new data structures are developed to support this strategy.

Output in libraries is implemented in either immediate or retained mode. This library exhibits behavior closest to retained mode so the demo programs and API usage reflect this. The demo programs exhibit this behavior in both the revisited RGB cube example and the Primtest general primitive- and attribute-thrasher example.

7 G3DLib Construction Part III: Vectors, Transforms, and Viewing Systems

In This Chapter

- Introduction to the three components of this 3D system: vectors, matrix transforms, and viewing system primitives.
- A look at 4D homogeneous coordinates as the mathematical basis of this implementation.
- A lesson on how to build apps from all these wonderful pieces.

Introduction

You already know that the code in this chapter will result in your ability to generate 2D renderings of 3D geometrical representations. The modeler operates in terms of 3D-object geometry, which needs to be defined, generated, and manipulated.

The 3D support services define what can be generated and manipulated, and provide the routines to perform the generation and manipulation.

This system is based on a triad of components:

- vectors,
- matrix transforms, and
- viewing system primitives.

Vectors are synonymous with points, which allows us to treat values as parameters in a wide range of routines, at the cost of a point not always being a point. For instance, not only is a location in 3D-space represented as a vector, a row or column in a matrix can also be considered a vector.

A matrix is a rectangular array, or table, of numbers. Matrices are commonly described in terms of rows and columns, sometimes using $m \times n$ notation to concisely describe the components. Matrix representation has many uses, but in this library we'll use matrices to represent transformations in space that correspond to the operations required in the 3D geometrical world for positioning and viewing.

Once we lay the vector and matrix transform foundation, we can construct basic viewing systems. In this chapter, we'll develop two simple systems. The *4-parameter viewing system* allows specification of a viewing point. This system assumes you're looking at the origin. For scenes not clustered at the origin, this is obviously insufficient. A simple camera system that lets you specify a from and a lookat point provides better scene control. Our system lets you move the camera around and has the basics of interactivity, but it's still not virtual reality. An entire book could be written just on viewing systems and interactivity to cover the depth required by virtual reality and CAD systems. Still, the camera system is where it all begins.

Why provide both viewing systems? Simple efficiency. Surface plots and some other basic 3D-plotting applications do not really require the extra effort involved in setting up a camera system and hooking keyboard input to camera positioning. Having both viewing systems lets you choose which system is appropriate for a particular application — consistent with the tool-building and policy-free approach the libraries follow. Table 7-1 contains the ubiquitous G3DLib source listing, with the four modules covered in this chapter shown

Table 7-1.   G3DLib Source Modules

Files	Description
G3DLib Housekeeping	
gl_init.c,gl_init.h	Library global initialization
gl_term.c,gl_term.h	Library global termination
gl_err.c,gl_err.h	Library error reporting
g3d_inc.h	Main include file, applications reference this
Drawing 3	
glgenv.c,glgenv.h	Graphics environment,manages coords for canvas
canvas.c,canvas.h	Canvas provides offscreen drawing surface for genv
bmpbuff.c,bmpbuff.h	Light part of canvas, hidden
membuff.c,membuff.h	Heavy part of the canvas,hidden
coords.c,coords.h	Coordinate mapping
winview.c,winview.h	Window/viewport using coord layer
General Support	
inquiry.c,inquiry.h	System inquiry, hides GetDeviceCaps/GetSystemMetrics
hist.h,hist.h	Histogram support
math.c,math.h	General math functions
trans.c,trans.h	Session transcript global window class based on WINIO
3D Support	
prims.c,prims.h	Output to genv
vec4d.c,vec4d.h	Vector functions
matrix.c,matrix.h	Basic matrix functions
xform.c,xform.h	Matrix transforms
viewing.c,viewing.h	Viewing systems

in bold italic.

These actions can be done in 3D space, but are more conveniently done in the abstract 4D space known as *homogeneous coordinates.* You're probably asking yourself "What is this 4D here?" Don't worry, we are not going to cross the space-time warp or anything like it. We're simply using a mathematical abstraction or trick that helps with special treatment of "bad" cases in 3D systems (like lines to infinity). These cases are generally hard to represent, but become somewhat easier in 4D space.

Mathematical tricks often prove quite useful in dealing with little details like this. The notion of homogeneous coordinates is one of these tricks.

G3DLib 3D Support: Coordinates and Vectors

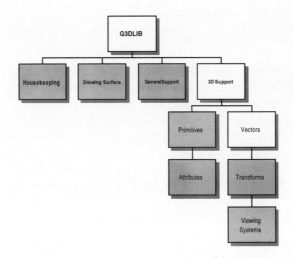

I've called this section "Coordinates and Vectors," but I could just as easily have called it "Coordinates Are Vectors." Objects are described by 3D coordinates, which in this system are vectors. In addition, the basic vector representation is the 4D homogeneous one.

Homogeneous Coordinates

Just what exactly are homogeneous coordinates? Earlier, I introduced the notions of an object in n-space and its representation in $(n+1)$-space, as well as the key fact that sometimes the solution in $(n+1)$-space is more tractable then its corresponding n-space solution. I described this as a "mathematical trick," which it is, but it is legal. There is a "mapping" from n-space to $(n+1)$-space, as well as an inverse mapping from $(n+1)$-space to n-space that (interestingly enough) is known as a projection. There are many of these mappings and inverses, but only one that's of concern to us. We'll use it to construct and convert n-space and $(n+1)$-space vectors.

Before we worry about constructing anything, however, let's get some notational details out of the way. Let's call 3D space *real space,* and use capital letters to represent real-space coordinates. Then 4D space is *homogeneous space,* represented by lowercase letters.

Real-space coordinates are mathematically described as a row, as shown in Equation 7-1.

Equation 7-1.   3D Vector in Row Notation

$$[XYZ]$$

This becomes a data structure, as shown in Listing 7-1. A 3D vector is simply described using three doubles. The only problem, as previously noted, is that certain edge cases are hard to handle, and can give you no end of headache once you reach a certain amount of complexity. You know this is insufficient if we want to provide for extensibility; even if you don't initially stress the 3D representation, you will.

Listing 7-1.   3D Vector Data Structure

```
typedef struct V3D
{
    double x,y,z;
} VECTOR3D;
```

In keeping with the extensible style, we use homogeneous notation as the basis for the vector class. A vector in homogeneous space can be viewed as a real-space vector with an added scale factor for four coordinates (hence the "4D" label).

Homogeneous space coordinates are mathematically described as a row, as shown in Equation 7-2. This row becomes a data structure, as shown in Listing 7-2.

Equation 7-2.   4D Vector in Row Notation

$$[xyzw]$$

Listing 7-2.   4D Vector Data Structure

```
typedef struct V4D
{
    double x,y,z,w;
} VECTOR4D;
```

A 4D vector is represented as four doubles. What, then, is the relationship between real space and homogeneous coordinates? Equation 7-3 shows the basis for converting homogeneous space to real space as well as the inverse relation.

Equation 7-3.   3D-to-4D Vector Relationships

homogeneous - to - real:

$[X, Y, Z] = [x \: / \: wy \: / \: wz \: / \: w]$

real-to-homogeneous:

$[X, Y, Z] * w = [xw, yw, zw, w]$ for any w $\neq$ 0

Mathematically, it's not important which w you choose, but in practice it is. In our case, by choosing $w = 1$, we make some simplifications possible in most cases. In this approach, the transformations produce the desired effect on the real-space coordinates and the fourth coordinate is ignored. Again, in practice, if we need more flexible navigation, fixed-point representations, or other additional features, we may need to revisit this simplifying decision.

So why do we even bother with the fourth coordinate? It might be ignored in the vector, but in the next element of the triad, matrices, it's a different story. When we carry the 4D representation forward into the matrix transformation services, the fourth coordinate's existence is justified. Let's look, for example, at the matrix transforms necessary to pipeline a point. Equation 7-4 shows the 3D equations necessary to scale, rotate, and translate. Rotation and scaling are both multiplication, so they can be easily combined. But translation is an addition that must be treated differently. Here's where 4D notation helps. Again referring to Equation 7-4, take a look at the companion 4D equation and you can see both the notational simplicity and the combination of the translation into the 4D matrix multiplication. This is the main reason for using 4D notation: simplicity at the matrix level.

First, though, we need to finish with vectors.

Equation 7-4.   3D Versus 4D Matrix Notation

$$P' = P^*M3D + T$$

$$P' = P^*M4D$$

P' is the new point

P is the old point

$M3D$ is the composite 3D matrix with both rotation and scaling

T is the 3D translation vector

$M4D$ is the composite 4D matrix with rotation, scaling, and translation

VECTOR4D API

Using the 4D vector data structure, Listing 7-3 defines the **VECTOR4D** API. It follows the general formula of instance-management routines, instance-generating operations, and in-place operations to give you maximum flexibility. Sometimes you want to create new vectors from old ones, and sometimes you want to adjust the value of an existing vector. In both cases, dynamically allocated memory is used for vector storage. This means you have access to as many vectors as the Windows memory manager allows access to.

Listing 7-3. VECTOR4D API Definition

```
typedef struct V4D
{
    DOUBLE  x,y,z,w;
} VECTOR4D, *PVECTOR4D, FAR *LPVECTOR4D;

#define VECTOR4DX(v) ((v).x)
#define VECTOR4DY(v) ((v).y)
#define VECTOR4DZ(v) ((v).z)
#define ONE4D        1
#define ZERO4D       0
#define DOUBLEINF4D  0x7FFFFFFF


// vector instance management
LPVECTOR4D   WINAPI G3D_V4D_VNew4D(DOUBLE a,DOUBLE b,DOUBLE c);
void         WINAPI G3D_V4D_VSet4D(LPVECTOR4D lpV,
                        DOUBLE x,DOUBLE y,DOUBLE z,DOUBLE W);
int          WINAPI G3D_V4D_VDel4D(LPVECTOR4D lpV);
//
DOUBLE       WINAPI G3D_V4D_VDot4D(VECTOR4D v1,VECTOR4D v2);
DOUBLE       WINAPI G3D_V4D_VMag4D(VECTOR4D v);

//new instance ops
LPVECTOR4D   WINAPI G3D_V4D_NVCross4D(VECTOR4D v1,VECTOR4D v2);
LPVECTOR4D   WINAPI G3D_V4D_NVNorm4D(VECTOR4D v);
LPVECTOR4D   WINAPI G3D_V4D_NVScale4D(DOUBLE s,VECTOR4D V);
LPVECTOR4D   WINAPI G3D_V4D_NVAdd(VECTOR4D V1,VECTOR4D V2);
LPVECTOR4D   WINAPI G3D_V4D_NVSub4D(VECTOR4D V1,VECTOR4D V2);
LPVECTOR4D   WINAPI G3D_V4D_NVDiv4D(VECTOR4D V,DOUBLE s);

//in place ops
void         WINAPI G3D_V4D_VCross4D(LPVECTOR4D lpV,
                        VECTOR4D v1, VECTOR4D v2);
void         WINAPI G3D_V4D_VNorm4D(LPVECTOR4D lpV, VECTOR4D v);
void         WINAPI G3D_V4D_VScale4D(LPVECTOR4D lpV,
                        DOUBLE s,VECTOR4D V);
void         WINAPI G3D_V4D_VAdd4D(LPVECTOR4D lpV,
                        VECTOR4D V1, VECTOR4D V2);
void         WINAPI G3D_V4D_VSub4D(LPVECTOR4D lpV,
                        VECTOR4D V1, VECTOR4D V2);
void         WINAPI G3D_V4D_VDiv4D(LPVECTOR4D lpV,
                        VECTOR4D V,DOUBLE s);
```

Let's consider this for a minute. Windows provides 8,192 selectors to the system. An application cannot hope for more than half that amount, according to the documentation. That's 4,096 selectors. Only four thousand vectors! That's no good, right? Well, not quite. Remember, the modeler uses 3D objects abstracted on top of the basic 3D support services. The question then becomes how many selectors each object uses and how it represents itself. At some point, we'll need to implement more sophisticated allocation strategies. For now, though, this system uses the simplistic approach. This illustrates the general principle

"The more you want to do, the more you have to do." You'll see the limitations imposed by this solution to the problem when we get to Part III. For now, even without sophisticated allocation strategies, several hundred objects are possible.

Here, we're concerned with the basic 3D support services and, more exactly, with the VECTOR4D API. In considering this API, we need to provide element-access routines in addition to the general formula of:

- instance-management routines,
- instance-generating operations, and
- in-place operations.

This allows you to create and delete instances of vectors, create new vectors as the result of operations, and change the value of an existing vector as the result of an operation.

Element Access

While the *GENV* and *CANVAS* APIs provided a suite of routines to operate on both the elements of the data structure (*GetVal/SetVal*) and elements of the underlying object (*GetPix/SetPix* and *GetMem/SetMem*), here we only need access to elements of the data structure. This is provided by the simple set of macros shown in Listing 7-4.

Listing 7-4.   VECTOR4D Element-Access Macros

```
#define VECTOR4DX(v) ((v).x)
#define VECTOR4DY(v) ((v).y)
#define VECTOR4DZ(v) ((v).z)
```

G3D_V4D_Vset4D performs the set part of the access functions as shown in Listing 7-5. This function sets the elements to the values passed in as parameters.

Listing 7-5.   G3D_V4D_VSet4D

```
void           WINAPI G3D_V4D_VSet4D(LPVECTOR4D lpV,
DOUBLE x,DOUBLE y,DOUBLE z,DOUBLE w)
{
    lpV->x = x;
    lpV->y = y;
    lpV->z = z;
    lpV->w = w;

    return ;
}
```

That is all we need for the element-access functions.

Instance Management

Instance management is easily performed with two operations: new and delete. These operations provide memory allocation and deallocation services to support instances. Occasionally a true copy and not an alias is needed.

Listing 7-6 contains **G3D_V4D_VNew4D**, the instance-creation function. This function uses the **TRY/CATCH** macros to guard the allocation. It uses **WL_Mem_Alloc** for memory allocation and **G3D_Error_Process** for error handling. As long as you check the return value when calling this function, this provides a robust service that is guaranteed to either return a pointer or generate an error and a NULL return. In a system designed to handle a lot of elements (like the environment in which a modeler executes), this kind of guarded-execution resource-allocation strategy is best. You must assume that the environment will fail to satisfy your requests for resources and that it basically wants to make your program deaf, dumb, and blind. If by chance it satisfies your requests for many objects with lots of polygons and coordinates, fine. But never assume that any scene you generate can be rendered on any machine.

Listing 7-6.   G3D_V4D_VNew4D

```
LPVECTOR4D    WINAPI   G3D_V4D_VNew4D(DOUBLE a,DOUBLE b,DOUBLE c)
{
    LPVECTOR4D lpV;
    TRY{
        lpV       = WL_Mem_Alloc(GHND,sizeof(VECTOR4D));
        if ( !lpV ) {
            Throw((LPCATCHBUF)&_ci.state,V4DERR_ALLOCFAILURE);
        }
        else {
                lpV->x = a;
                lpV->y = b;
                lpV->z = c;
                lpV->w = ZERO4D;
                return lpV;
        }
    }
    CATCH{
        switch(_exk){
           case V4DERR_ALLOCFAILURE:
           default:
              G3D_Error_Process(_exk);
              break;
        }
        return NULL;
    }
    END_CATCH
}
```

The corresponding delete operation, shown in Listing 7-7, is much simpler. Function *G3D_V4D_VDel4D* calls *WL_Mem_Free* to perform memory deallocation.

Listing 7-7.   G3D_V4D_VDel4D

```
int          WINAPI G3D_V4D_VDel4D(LPVECTOR4D lpV)
{
    WL_Mem_Free(lpV);

    return 1;
}
```

That concludes the instance-management functions — short and sweet. Next, we'll consider the instance-generating and in-place operations. These routines are grouped together because they implement the same operations on different sets of parameters. It is useful to see this side-by-side.

Instance Generation and In-Place Operations

This subsystem provides the following vector operations:

- addition,
- subtraction,
- division,
- scaling,
- magnitude,
- normalization,
- dot product, and
- cross product.

Addition, subtraction, and division are straightforward enough. Scaling and division by scalar values are reciprocals of each other; one multiplies a vector by a constant, the other divides. Magnitude is distance. The normal gives us the direction of a vector with its magnitude removed. Dot product and cross product are the final vector operations, comprising a full set.

Vector Addition
Vector addition, shown graphically for two dimensions in Figure 7-1, is a component-wise addition.

Figure 7-1.   Vector Addition

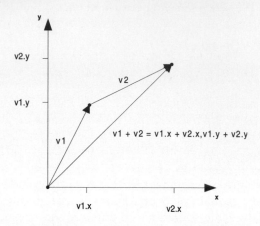

The extension to 4D is straightforward. Listing 7-8 contains the implementation of the instance-generating operation, and Listing 7-9 contains the in-place operation.

Listing 7-8.   G3D_V4D_NVAdd4D

```
LPVECTOR4D   WINAPI G3D_V4D_NVAdd4D(VECTOR4D V1, VECTOR4D V2)
{
    LPVECTOR4D lpV;

    lpV  = G3D_V4D_VNew4D( ZERO4D,ZERO4D,ZERO4D);
    lpV->x = V1.x + V2.x;
    lpV->y = V1.y + V2.y;
    lpV->z = V1.z + V2.z;
    lpV->w = ZERO4D;
    return lpV;
}
```

Listing 7-9.   G3D_V4D_VAdd4D

```
void         WINAPI G3D_V4D_VAdd4D(LPVECTOR4D lpV,
             VECTOR4D V1, VECTOR4D V2)
{
    lpV->x = V1.x + V2.x;
    lpV->y = V1.y + V2.y;
    lpV->z = V1.z + V2.z;
    lpV->w = ZERO4D;
    return ;
}
```

It should be obvious that *G3D_V4D_NVAdd4D* must perform memory allocation and should use workhorse *WL_Mem_Alloc*. The neat trick here is using the instance-creation function to encapsulate the memory call for us. We can use *G3D_V4D_VNew4D* instead of writing additional memory-allocation code; this is effective code reuse. Once an instance is created, its values must be initialized to the result of adding the components of V1 to the components of V2.

G3D_V4D_VAdd4D is even simpler; it sets the output parameter to the correct values — the sum of input vectors V1 and V2.

Vector Subtraction

Subtraction is, similar to addition, a component-wise operation. Figure 7-2 illustrates the 2D version of this operation, and Listings 7-10 and 7-11 contain the implementations of the 4D version we use here. Again, it's a straightforward extension of the instance-generating function *G3D_V4D_NVSub4D* and the in-place function *G3D_V4D_VSub4D*. Once again, we'll use *G3D_V4D_VNew4D* for instance creation.

Figure 7-2.   Vector Subtraction

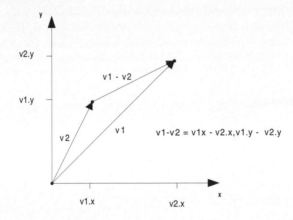

Listing 7-10.   G3D_V4D_NVSub4D

```
LPVECTOR4D   WINAPI G3D_V4D_NVSub4D(VECTOR4D V1, VECTOR4D V2)
{
    LPVECTOR4D lpV;

    lpV =  G3D_V4D_VNew4D( ZERO4D,ZERO4D,ZERO4D);
    lpV->x = V1.x - V2.x;
    lpV->y = V1.y - V2.y;
    lpV->z = V1.z - V2.z;
    lpV->w = ZERO4D;
    return lpV;
}
```

Listing 7-11.   G3D_V4D_VSub4D

```
void            WINAPI G3D_V4D_VSub4D(LPVECTOR4D lpV,
                    VECTOR4D V1, VECTOR4D V2)
{
    lpV->x = V1.x - V2.x;
    lpV->y = V1.y - V2.y;
    lpV->z = V1.z - V2.z;
    lpV->w = ZERO4D;
    return ;
}
```

Vector Scaling and Division

These functions are reciprocals of each other, so we'll look at them together. Figure 7-3 depicts 2D scaling of a vector; the divide operation is the inverse, so instead of extending the vector it contracts it. With that out of the way, Listings 7-12 and 7-13 contain the implementations of the scaling pair *G3D_V4D_NVScale4D* and *G3D_V4D_VScale4D*; Listings 7-14 and 7-15 contain the divide pair *G3D_V4D_NVDiv4D* and *G3D_V4D_VDiv4D*. These functions follow the same implementation methodology; use the *VNew4D* function for memory allocation and perform the member-wise operation.

Figure 7-3.   Vector Scaling

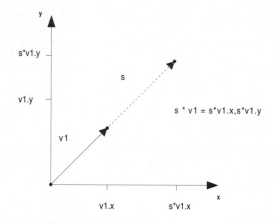

Listing 7-12.   G3D_V4D_NVScale4D

```
LPVECTOR4D    WINAPI G3D_V4D_NVScale4D(DOUBLE s,VECTOR4D V)
{
    LPVECTOR4D lpV;

    lpV  = G3D_V4D_VNew4D( ZERO4D,ZERO4D,ZERO4D);
```

Listing 7-16.   G3D_V4D_VMag4D

```
DOUBLE          WINAPI G3D_V4D_VMag4...
{
    return sqrt(v.x*v.x+v.y*v.y+v...
}
```

Listing 7-17.   G3D_V4D_NVNorm4D

```
LPVECTOR4D    WINAPI G3D_V4D_NVNo...
{
    LPVECTOR4D lpV;
    DOUBLE     l = G3D_V4D_VMag4...

    if (l == 0)
        return NULL;
    lpV = G3D_V4D_VNew4D( ZERO4...

    lpV->x = v.x/l;
    lpV->y = v.y/l;
    lpV->z = v.z/l;
    lpV->w = ZERO4D;

    return lpV;
}
```

Listing 7-18.   G3D_V4D_VNorm4D

```
void          WINAPI G3D_V4D_VNor...
{
    DOUBLE      l = G3D_V4D_VMag...

    if (l == 0)
        return ;
    lpV->x = v.x/l;
    lpV->y = v.y/l;
    lpV->z = v.z/l;
    lpV->w = ZERO4D;

    return ;
}
```

Vector Dot Product

The vector dot product produces a num...
point in the same direction, which is r...
polygon-shading calculations, and ray ...
cally in Equation 7-6.

```
    lpV->x = V.x * s;
    lpV->y = V.y * s;
    lpV->z = V.z * s;
    lpV->w = ZERO4D;

    return lpV;
}
```

Listing 7-13.   G3D_V4D_VScale4D

```
void            WINAPI G3D_V4D_VScale4D(LPVECTOR4D lpV,
                       DOUBLE s,VECTOR4D V)
{
    lpV->x = V.x * s;
    lpV->y = V.y * s;
    lpV->z = V.z * s;
    lpV->w = ZERO4D;
    return ;
}
```

Listing 7-14.   G3D_V4D_NVDiv4D

```
LPVECTOR4D     WINAPI G3D_V4D_NVDiv4D(VECTOR4D V,DOUBLE s)
{
    LPVECTOR4D lpV;

    lpV = G3D_V4D_VNew4D( ZERO4D, ZERO4D,ZERO4D);
    if ( s == 0.0 )
        s = FLT_EPSILON;
    lpV->x = V.x / s;
    lpV->y = V.y / s;
    lpV->z = V.z / s;
    lpV->w = ZERO4D;
    return lpV;
}
```

Listing 7-15.   G3D_V4D_VDiv4D

```
void            WINAPI G3D_V4D_VDiv4D(LPVECTOR4D lpV,
                       VECTOR4D V,DOUBLE s)
{
  if ( s == 0.0 )
      s = FLT_EPSILON;
    lpV->x = V.x / s;
    lpV->y = V.y / s;
    lpV->z = V.z / s;
    lpV->w = ZERO4D;

    return ;
```

Vector Magnitude and Unit Norr

Vectors have a length or magnitu
that translates to the square root c
The concept of a vector of magni
vector is calculated from it by first
shown in Equation 7-5.

Equation 7-5.   Magnitude and U

$$|v|$$

$$U$$

This process is also called *norm*
circle in two dimensions, as show

Figure 7-4.   Unit Vector

Unit circle with radius

It is most important to differe
generating a normal to a surface –
vectors are not the same, either. S
have a unit vector generated fron
in many places to describe directi

Listing 7-16 implements the r
creating operation, and Listing 7-

Equation 7-6.   Vector Dot Product;

$$V1 \cdot V2 = |V1||V2| \cos \theta$$

$$(\text{where } 0 <= \theta <= \pi)$$

or

$$V1 \cdot V2 = V1x * V2x + V1y * V2y + V1z * V2$$

If the two vectors are perpendicular, the dot product will be zero. If they are the same, the dot product equals the magnitude squared. If the two are unit vectors, the result represents the cosine of the angle between the two vectors. Listing 7-19 contains the implementation of the vector dot product function **G3D_V4D_VDot4D**.

Listing 7-19.   G3D_V4D_VDot4D

```
double      WINAPI G3D_V4D_VDot4D(VECTOR4D v1,VECTOR4D v2)
{
    return ((v1.x * v2.x) + (v1.y * v2.y) + (v1.z * v2.z));
}
```

It is calculated in the second manner from Equation 7-6; that is, as a sum of products of the vectors components. Figure 7-5 shows 2D dot-product geometry.

Figure 7-5.   The Dot Product

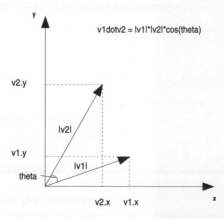

Vector Cross Product

The final vector operation is the cross product. This operation multiplies two vectors and returns a vector. Mathematically, a vector cross product is defined in Equation 7-7.

Equation 7-7.   Vector Cross Product

$$V3 = V1 \otimes V2 = |V1||V2| \sin \theta$$
$$(where \; 0 <= \theta <= \pi)$$
or
$$V3x = V1y * V2z - V1z * V2y$$
$$V3y = V1z * V2x - V1x * V2z$$
$$V3z = V1x * V2y - V1y * V2x$$

The operation proceeds component-wise from the trigonometric definition, as before. A cross product can only be illustrated in three dimensions, as in Figure 7-6. Where the angle between the two vectors is greater than 0 and less than 180, the new vector has a geometric interpretation where the magnitude of the cross-product vector equals the area of the parallelogram described by the original two vectors.

Figure 7-6.   Vector Cross Product

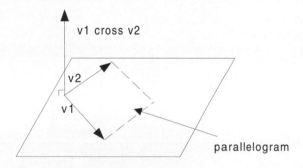

v1crossv2 is perpendicular to plane of v1 and v2
|v1crossv2| is equal to area of parallelogram

Listings 7-20 and 7-21 contain the two functions **G3D_V4D_NVCross4D** and **G3D_V4D_VCross4D**. These two functions complete the implementation of the vector subsystem.

Listing 7-20. G3D_V4D_NVCross4D

```
LPVECTOR4D    WINAPI G3D_V4D_NVCross4D(VECTOR4D v1, VECTOR4D v2)
{
    LPVECTOR4D lpV;

    lpV =  G3D_V4D_VNew4D( ZERO4D,ZERO4D,ZERO4D);
    lpV->x = v1.y * v2.z - v2.y * v1.z ;
    lpV->y = v1.z * v2.x - v2.z * v1.x ;
    lpV->z = v1.x * v2.y - v2.x * v1.y ;
    lpV->w = ZERO4D;
    return lpV;
}
```

Listing 7-21. G3D_V4D_VCross4D

```
void          WINAPI G3D_V4D_VCross4D(LPVECTOR4D lpV,
                     VECTOR4D v1, VECTOR4D v2)
{
    lpV->x = v1.y * v2.z - v2.y * v1.z;
    lpV->y = v1.z * v2.x - v2.z * v1.x;
    lpV->z = v1.x * v2.y - v2.x * v1.y;
    lpV->w = ZERO4D;
    return ;
}
```

G3DLib 3D Support: Matrices, Part I— Matrix Operations

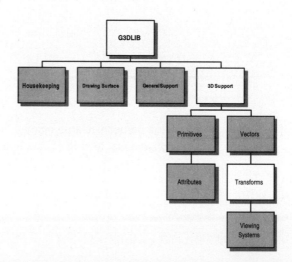

Once the vector layer is built, it is time to work on the matrix subsystem. In this suite of routines, the 4D matrix operations are captured. This is where we actually use the fourth parameter instead of throwing it away. The matrix subsystem is composed of two parts: simple matrix operations and matrix transformations.

Both parts of the matrix API follow the basic elements of the formula:

- element access,
- instance management,
- instance-generating operations, and
- in-place operations.

The simple operations include creating and deleting matrices, as well as generating simple rotation, scaling, and transformation matrices. In the process of generating these simple operations, we'll also provide the ability to zero out a matrix and make an identity matrix.

Once we've completed the basic operations, the next step is to handle *composite* operations (the repetitive application of transformations). Built from simple matrix operations like rotations, scalings, and translations, the viewing matrix is a composite matrix. In this manner, the 4D matrix is a convenient way to describe viewing transformations. It is the result of concatenating several different, simple operations together. You'll see, step-by-step, how this is done as we develop the *MATRIX4D* API.

MATRIX4D Operation API

Listing 7-22 contains the API definition of the underlying data structure for both the basic and transform API: the *MATRIX4D.* As you can see, the *MATRIX4D* structure is a 4x4 array of doubles. Consistent with the extensible API formula, we define a suite of routines built around a data structure as the basis of the subsystem. These routines fit the now-standard service areas:

- element access,
- instance management,
- instance-generating operations, and
- in-place operations.

Element-setting access functions let you set the value of any element of an array functionally. Extracting a value is left to using array notation. The instance-management functions create and delete instances of 4x4 matrices. In providing DLL-based services, it's critical that we allocate memory for this rather than depending on the stack. Instance-generating and in-place operations are built for each basic operation required, providing dual routines for each operation purely for your convenience.

Listing 7-22.   MATRIX4D API Definition

```
typedef struct M4D
{
    DOUBLE T[4][4];
} MATRIX4D,*PMATRIX4D, far *LPMATRIX4D;

// instance management
LPMATRIX4D   WINAPI G3D_M4D_MNew4D(void);
int          WINAPI G3D_M4D_MDel4D(LPMATRIX4D lpM);
```

Listing 7-22. *(cont.)*

```
// new instance ops
LPMATRIX4D    WINAPI G3D_M4D_NZero4D(void);
LPMATRIX4D    WINAPI G3D_M4D_NIdentity4D(void);
LPMATRIX4D    WINAPI G3D_M4D_NTranspose4D(LPMATRIX4D T);
LPMATRIX4D    WINAPI G3D_M4D_NTranslate4D(VECTOR4D V);
LPMATRIX4D    WINAPI G3D_M4D_NUniformScale4D(DOUBLE s);
LPMATRIX4D    WINAPI G3D_M4D_NScale4D(VECTOR4D);
LPMATRIX4D    WINAPI G3D_M4D_NRotateX(DOUBLE);
LPMATRIX4D    WINAPI G3D_M4D_NRotateY(DOUBLE);
LPMATRIX4D    WINAPI G3D_M4D_NRotateZ(DOUBLE);
LPMATRIX4D    WINAPI G3D_M4D_NMatrix4D(
                    DOUBLE m11,DOUBLE m12,DOUBLE m13,DOUBLE m14,
                    DOUBLE m21,DOUBLE m22,DOUBLE m23,DOUBLE m24,
                    DOUBLE m31,DOUBLE m32,DOUBLE m33,DOUBLE m34,
                    DOUBLE m41,DOUBLE m42,DOUBLE m43,DOUBLE m44);

// in place ops
void          WINAPI G3D_M4D_Zero4D(LPMATRIX4D lpZ);
void          WINAPI G3D_M4D_Identity4D(LPMATRIX4D lpI);
void          WINAPI G3D_M4D_Transpose4D(LPMATRIX4D lpTt,
                    LPMATRIX4D T);
void          WINAPI G3D_M4D_Translate4D(LPMATRIX4D lpT,VECTOR4D V);
void          WINAPI G3D_M4D_UniformScale4D(LPMATRIX4D lpS,
                        DOUBLE s);
void          WINAPI G3D_M4D_Scale4D(LPMATRIX4D lpT,VECTOR4D P);
void          WINAPI G3D_M4D_RotateX(LPMATRIX4D lpM,DOUBLE deg);
void          WINAPI G3D_M4D_RotateY(LPMATRIX4D lpM,DOUBLE deg);
void          WINAPI G3D_M4D_RotateZ(LPMATRIX4D lpM,DOUBLE deg);
void          WINAPI G3D_M4D_Matrix4D(LPMATRIX4D lpM,
                    DOUBLE m11,DOUBLE m12,DOUBLE m13,DOUBLE m14,
                    DOUBLE m21,DOUBLE m22,DOUBLE m23,DOUBLE m24,
                    DOUBLE m31,DOUBLE m32,DOUBLE m33,DOUBLE m34,
                    DOUBLE m41,DOUBLE m42,DOUBLE m43,DOUBLE m44);
```

Element Access

The element-access operations are slightly different from the *VECTOR4D* API, where we developed macros to extract the values and a set function. Here, only the set function has an equivalent. We provide two of these: *G3D_M4D_NMatrix4D* (Listing 7-23), which returns a new instance initialized as indicated; and *G3D_M4D_Matrix4D* (Listing 7-24), which sets the values of an existing instance. For now, ignore the call to *G3D_M4D_NIdentity* and *G3D_M4D_Identity*, and just look at the element-setting aspect of these two functions. We'll get to the identity functions soon enough.

Listing 7-23. G3D_M4D_NMatrix4D

```
LPMATRIX4D    WINAPI G3D_M4D_NMatrix4D(
                DOUBLE m11,DOUBLE m12,DOUBLE m13,DOUBLE m14,
                DOUBLE m21,DOUBLE m22,DOUBLE m23,DOUBLE m24,
                DOUBLE m31,DOUBLE m32,DOUBLE m33,DOUBLE m34,
                DOUBLE m41,DOUBLE m42,DOUBLE m43,DOUBLE m44)


{
    LPMATRIX4D lpM;

    lpM = G3D_M4D_NIdentity4D();
    lpM->T[0][0] = m11; lpM->T[0][1] = m12;
    lpM->T[0][2] = m13; lpM->T[0][3] = m14;

    lpM->T[1][0] = m21; lpM->T[1][1] = m22;
    lpM->T[1][2] = m23; lpM->T[1][3] = m24;

    lpM->T[2][0] = m31; lpM->T[2][1] = m32;
    lpM->T[2][2] = m33; lpM->T[2][3] = m34;

    lpM->T[3][0] = m41; lpM->T[3][1] = m42;
    lpM->T[3][2] = m43; lpM->T[3][3] = m44;

  return lpM;
 }
```

Listing 7-24. G3D_M4D_Matrix4D

```
void          WINAPI G3D_M4D_Matrix4D ( LPMATRIX4D lpM,
                    DOUBLE m11,DOUBLE m12,DOUBLE m13,DOUBLE m14,
                    DOUBLE m21,DOUBLE m22,DOUBLE m23,DOUBLE m24,
                     DOUBLE m31,DOUBLE m32,DOUBLE m33,DOUBLE m34,
                     DOUBLE m41,DOUBLE m42,DOUBLE m43,DOUBLE m44)

{
    lpM->T[0][0] = m11; lpM->T[0][1] = m12;
    lpM->T[0][2] = m13; lpM->T[0][3] = m14;

    lpM->T[1][0] = m21; lpM->T[1][1] = m22;
    lpM->T[1][2] = m23; lpM->T[1][3] = m24;

    lpM->T[2][0] = m31; lpM->T[2][1] = m32;
    lpM->T[2][2] = m33; lpM->T[2][3] = m34;

    lpM->T[3][0] = m41; lpM->T[3][1] = m42;
    lpM->T[3][2] = m43; lpM->T[3][3] = m44;

    return ;
}
```

Instance Management

We again use a creation and a deletion function to encapsulate memory management and provide heap-based instances. Listing 7-25 contains the implementation of the creation function *G3D_M4D_MNew4D*, and its comment describes the mapping of array element (i, j) to placement in the array.

Listing 7-25.   G3D_M4D_MNew4D

```
//
// Matrices are represented as 4x4 homogeneous
//
// 00 01 02 03
// 10 11 12 13
// 20 21 22 23
// 30 31 32 33
//
LPMATRIX4D   WINAPI  G3D_M4D_MNew4D(void){
    LPMATRIX4D lpM;
    TRY  {
       lpM        = WL_Mem_Alloc(GHND,sizeof(MATRIX4D));
       if ( !lpM ){
           Throw((LPCATCHBUF)&_ci.state,M4DERR_ALLOCFAILURE);
       }
       else {
            return lpM;
       }
    }
    CATCH{
       switch(_exk) {
          case M4DERR_ALLOCFAILURE:
          default:
             G3D_Error_Process(_exk);
             break;
       }
       return NULL;
    }
    END_CATCH
}
```

You should also recognize the familiar usage of the *TRY/CATCH* macros, *WL_Mem_Alloc*, and *G3D_Error_Process*, in the creation function.

Listing 7-26 contains the implementation of the corresponding destruction function *G3D_M4D_MDel4D*. This function simply uses *WL_Mem_Free* to deallocate the dynamic memory associated with that instance.

Listing 7-26.   G3D_M4D_MDel4D

```
int           WINAPI G3D_M4D_MDel4D(LPMATRIX4D lpM)
{
    WL_Mem_Free(lpM);

    return 1;
}
```

Instance-Generating and In-Place Operations

The set of operations provided here includes:

- zero,
- identity,
- transpose,
- translate,
- uniform and vector scale, and
- x, y, and z rotation.

This is the basis of the transform section, and also prepares us for even more advanced eventualities.

Zero

Zeroing a matrix does exactly what it sounds like. Every element of the matrix is set to zero. Listings 7-27 and 7-28 contain the instance-generating and in-place operations, respectively. The instance-generating function uses *G3D_M4D_MNew4D* to create an instance.

Listing 7-27.   G3D_M4D_NZero4D

```
LPMATRIX4D   WINAPI G3D_M4D_NZero4D(void)
{
    LPMATRIX4D lpZ;
    int        i,j;

    lpZ = G3D_M4D_MNew4D( );
    for (i = 0; i < 4; i++)
          for (j = 0; j < 4; j++)
                lpZ->T[i][j] = 0.0;
    return lpZ;
}
```

Listing 7-28.   G3D_M4D_Zero4D

```
void            WINAPI G3D_M4D_Zero4D(LPMATRIX4D lpZ)
{
    int      i,j;

    for (i = 0; i < 4; i++)
          for (j = 0; j < 4; j++)
              lpZ->T[i][j] = 0.0;
    return ;
}
```

Identity

The next operation, identity, sets the major diagonal to one. The comment in Listing 7-29 shows where the major diagonal is. Identity matrices are used in the concatenation process. Listing 7-29 contains *G3D_M4D_NIdentity* (the instance-generating function), and Listing 7-30 contains *G3D_M4D_Identity* (the in-place function). Both use the fact that on the major diagonal, i == j in the (i, j) notation for matrices.

Listing 7-29.   G3D_M4D_NIdentity4D

```
//
// returns identity Matrix :
//                               1    0    0    0
//                               0    1    0    0
//                               0    0    1    0
//                               0    0    0    1
//
//LPMATRIX4D    WINAPI G3D_M4D_NIdentity4D(void)
{
    LPMATRIX4D lpI;
    int        i,j;

    lpI = G3D_M4D_MNew4D( );
    for (i = 0; i < 4; i++)
          for (j = 0; j < 4; j++)
              lpI->T[i][j] = (i == j);
    return lpI;
}
```

Listing 7-30.   G3D_M4D_Identity4D

```
void            WINAPI G3D_M4D_Identity4D(LPMATRIX4D lpI)
{
    int      i,j;

    for (i = 0; i < 4; i++)
          for (j = 0; j < 4; j++)
              lpI->T[i][j] = (i == j);
    return ;
}
```

Transpose

The transpose operation is useful for developing inverses. Strictly speaking, we don't use inverses here. If you decide to add object hierarchies to the system, this is one area that would have to be revisited. As I already mentioned, you'd also have to work on the attribute handling. Still, we do what we can to prepare for the future, and we know transposes will be useful then, so we'll include them now. Listing 7-31 contains instance-generating function *G3D_M4D_NTranspose4D* and Listing 7-32 contains in-place function *G3D_M4D_Transpose4D*.

Listing 7-31.   G3D_M4D_NTranspose4D

```
//
// returns transpose row/column Matrix :
//
//LPMATRIX4D   WINAPI G3D_M4D_NTranspose4D(LPMATRIX4D T)
{
    LPMATRIX4D lpTt;
    int i,j;

    lpTt = G3D_M4D_MNew4D( );
    for (i=0; i<4; i++) {
        for (j=0; j<4; j++) {
            lpTt->T[i][j] = T->T[j][i];
        }
    }
    return lpTt;
}
```

Listing 7-32.   G3D_M4D_Transpose4D

```
void         WINAPI G3D_M4D_Transpose4D(LPMATRIX4D lpTt,LPMATRIX4D T)
{
    int i,j;

    for (i=0; i<4; i++) {
        for (j=0; j<4; j++) {
            lpTt->T[i][j] = T->T[j][i];
        }
    }
    return ;
}
```

Translation

The translation operation allows us to "move" or translate an object from one location to the next. Mathematically, we can express this as shown in Equation 7-8. The translation can also be represented outside of the matrix by a vector like [Tx, Ty, Tz, 1].

Equation 7-8. The Translation Transformation

$$[x', y', z', 1] = [x, y, z, 1] \begin{vmatrix} 1 & 0 & 0 & 0 \\ 0 & 1 & 0 & 0 \\ 0 & 0 & 1 & 0 \\ Tx & Ty & Tz & 1 \end{vmatrix}$$

Listings 7-33 and 7-34 contain the pair of functions, *G3D_M4D_NTranslate4D* and
G3D_M4D_Translate4D, that provide instance-generation and in-place operation. You'll
notice that *G3D_M4D_NTranslate4D* begins by using the identity instance-generating function to initialize the matrix. *G3D_M4D_Translate* has a simpler task, and simply sets the
correct elements of the array to the translation vector.

Listing 7-33.   G3D_M4D_NTranslate4D

```
//           .
// returns a translation ( by vector ) Matrix :
//
//                               1     0     0     0
//                               0     1     0     0
//                               0     0     1     0
//                             v.x   v.y   v.z     1
//
LPMATRIX4D   WINAPI G3D_M4D_NTranslate4D(VECTOR4D V)
{
    LPMATRIX4D lpT;

    lpT = G3D_M4D_NIdentity4D();
    lpT->T[3][0] = V.x;
    lpT->T[3][1] = V.y;
    lpT->T[3][2] = V.z;

    return lpT;
}
```

Listing 7-34.   G3D_M4D_Translate4D

```
void          WINAPI G3D_M4D_Translate4D(LPMATRIX4D lpT,VECTOR4D V)
{
    lpT->T[3][0] = V.x;
    lpT->T[3][1] = V.y;
    lpT->T[3][2] = V.z;

    return ;
}
```

Scaling

The scaling operation lets us adjust the size of an object in one of the x, y, z axes. We can express this mathematically as Equation 7-9.

Equation 7-9. The Scaling Transformation

$$[x', y', z', 1] = [x, y, z, 1] \begin{vmatrix} Sx & 0 & 0 & 0 \\ 0 & Sy & 0 & 0 \\ 0 & 0 & Sz & 0 \\ 0 & 0 & 0 & 1 \end{vmatrix}$$

Note also that the scaling can also be represented outside of the matrix by a vector like [Sx, Sy, Sz, 1]. It provides two kinds of scaling: uniform and non-uniform. *Uniform scaling* transforms each axis by the same value. *Non-uniform scaling* lets you specify a vector that may contain three different scaling factors.

Listings 7-35 and 7-36 contain the functions *G3D_M4D_NUniformScale4D* and *G3D_M4D_UniformScale4D*, which provide uniform-scaling instance generation and in-place operation. Listings 7-37 and 7-38 contain the non-uniform scaling functions *G3D_M4D_NScale4D* and *G3D_M4D_Scale4D*, providing instance generation and in-place operation.

Listing 7-35. G3D_M4D_NUniformScale4D

```
LPMATRIX4D   WINAPI G3D_M4D_NUniformScale4D(DOUBLE s)
{
    LPMATRIX4D lpS;
    VECTOR4D   p;

    G3D_V4D_VSet4D(&p,s,s,s,ONE4D);
    lpS = G3D_M4D_NScale4D(p);
    return lpS;
}
```

Listing 7-36. G3D_M4D_UniformScale4D

```
void         WINAPI G3D_M4D_UniformScale4D(LPMATRIX4D lpS,DOUBLE s)
{
    VECTOR4D   p;

    G3D_V4D_VSet4D(&p,s,s,s,ONE4D);
    G3D_M4D_Scale4D(lpS,p);
    return ;
}
```

Listing 7-37.   G3D_M4D_NScale4D

```
//
// returns a scaling Matrix :
//                                         sx    0     0     0
//                                         0     sy    0     0
//                                         0     0     sz    0
//                                         0     0     0     1
//
LPMATRIX4D   WINAPI G3D_M4D_NScale4D(VECTOR4D P)
{
    LPMATRIX4D lpT;

    lpT = G3D_M4D_NIdentity4D();
    lpT->T[0][0] = P.x;
    lpT->T[1][1] = P.y;
    lpT->T[2][2] = P.z;
    lpT->T[3][3] = P.w;
    return lpT;
}
```

Listing 7-38.   G3D_M4D_Scale4D

```
void         WINAPI G3D_M4D_Scale4D(LPMATRIX4D lpT,VECTOR4D P)
{
    lpT->T[0][0] = P.x;
    lpT->T[1][1] = P.y;
    lpT->T[2][2] = P.z;
    lpT->T[3][3] = P.w;
    return ;
}
```

The uniform-scaling operations use *G3D_V4D_VSet4D* to generate a vector from the scalar value, then use the non-uniform routines. Other than that, they completely defer to the non-uniform routines.

The non-uniform routines are more similar to what you've already seen. Listing 7-37 shows that the instance generating case begins, again, by using the identity function to initialize the matrix. The in-place and simpler case just assigns the values.

Rotations
Each axis needs a rotation. This means we need to define three rotations in all: x, y, and z. In dealing with three-dimensional rotations, you must be concerned with origins and alignments. Rotations take place around an axis, and if that axis passes through the coordinate origin and is aligned with the prime axes, you can us
e the simplest form. But in general, to rotate about an arbitrary point other than the origin, you need to perform the following three steps.

1. Translate to the origin.
2. Perform the rotation.
3. Translate back to the original position with the new orientation.

For purposes of simplification, this library provides only the primitive rotations. You can easily build on this by implementing this three-step process. It's mainly a matter of definition and convenience. As you'll see, we can implement simple local transforms without this haggling. Again, if you add object hierarchies, you'll need a transformation stack and a more general transformation capability, but this is sufficient for basic geometric modeling requirements.

Equations 7-10 through 7-12 contain the relations for x, y, and z rotation, respectively. Note that x and y rotation are a permutation of the z rotation.

Equation 7-10. The x-Rotation Transformation

$$[x',y',z',1] = [x,y,z,1] \begin{vmatrix} 1 & 0 & 0 & 0 \\ 0 & \cos\theta & -\sin\theta & 0 \\ 0 & \sin\theta & \cos\theta & 0 \\ 0 & 0 & 0 & 1 \end{vmatrix}$$

Equation 7-11. The y-Rotation Transformation

$$[x',y',z',1] = [x,y,z,1] \begin{vmatrix} \cos\theta & 0 & \sin\theta & 0 \\ 0 & 1 & 0 & 0 \\ -\sin\theta & 0 & \cos\theta & 0 \\ 0 & 0 & 0 & 1 \end{vmatrix}$$

Equation 7-12. The z-Rotation Transformation

$$[x',y',z',1] = [x,y,z,1] \begin{vmatrix} \cos\theta & -\sin\theta & 0 & 0 \\ \sin\theta & \cos\theta & 0 & 0 \\ 0 & 0 & 1 & 0 \\ 0 & 0 & 0 & 1 \end{vmatrix}$$

Look carefully and you'll see that each rotation affects only the *other* axes, not itself. Also, the rotation angle is measured clockwise about the origin, as though looking "down" at the origin from a point on the +z-axis. Figures 7-7 to 7-9 graphically illustrate the three rotation transformations. This should help to visually clarify the matrix equations in relation to the axes, and give you a feel for what is going on.

Figure 7-7.   X-Rotation Transformation

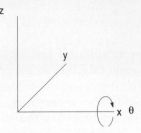

Figure 7-8.   Y-Rotation Transformation

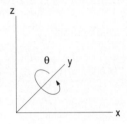

Figure 7-9.   Z-Rotation Transformation

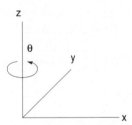

Again, look at the matrices and verify that each rotation leaves its own axis untouched. For instance, let's substitute the value for a 90-degree x-rotation into the matrix and see what happens (see Equation 7-13). The value of sin(90) is 1and the value of cos(90) is 0. Immediately, you should recognize that something is going on in columns 2 and 3.

Equation 7-13.   The x-Rotation Transformation for x=90

$$[x',y',z',1] = [x,y,z,1] \begin{vmatrix} 1 & 0 & 0 & 0 \\ 0 & 0 & -1 & 0 \\ 0 & 1 & 0 & 0 \\ 0 & 0 & 0 & 1 \end{vmatrix}$$

Compare this to the identity matrix in Listing 7-29 (and its comment), and you should see that the major diagonal has had its elements switched. This is basically what the x- rotation does. It interchanges y and z, and changes the sign of y.

Doing some simple substitutions of key values around the unit circle (like 90,180, etc.) into the various rotations shows a lot of the behavior of this transformation. It might be useful for you to spend a little time doing this, but I've avoided it here for both size and continuity reasons.

That leaves implementation. For each transformation, we'll implement the usual pair of instance-generating and in-place functions. The x-rotation implementations are contained in Listings 7-39 and 7-40, the y-rotations in Listings 7-41 and 7-42, and the z-rotations in Listings 7-43 and 7-44. This is a bit of code to digest at one sitting, but a couple of things help. First, the rotations follow a general formula of permutation of the z-rotation. Second, the implementation follows the formula of the API, so there is some regularity that should help you read the code.

As you read through this code, notice that the comments for the instance-generating functions repeat the matrix formulation for documentation purposes. Next, each function uses temporaries to store the results of the sin and cosine calculation, saving an extra call to each function. The instance-generating functions use *G3D_M4D_NMatrix4D* and the in-place functions use *G3D_M4D_Matrix4D* to set each element of the 4x4 matrix.

Listing 7-39.   G3D_M4D_NRotateX4D

```
//
// returns a Matrix to rotate about the x axis
// where           cp=Cos(p),  sp=Sin(p),
//
//                 1   0    0   0      pitch
//                 0   cp  -sp  0
//                 0   sp   cp  0
//                 0   0    0   1
//
LPMATRIX4D    WINAPI G3D_M4D_NRotateX (DOUBLE deg)
{
    double cp,sp;
    cp = G3D_Math_CosD(deg);
    sp = G3D_Math_SinD(deg);
    return G3D_M4D_NMatrix4D(ONE4D,     ZERO4D,  ZERO4D,    ZERO4D,
                             ZERO4D,     cp,      -sp,       ZERO4D,
                             ZERO4D,     sp,      cp,        ZERO4D,
                             ZERO4D,     ZERO4D,  ZERO4D,    ONE4D);
}
```

Listing 7-40.   G3D_M4D_RotateX4D

```
void            WINAPI G3D_M4D_RotateX (LPMATRIX4D lpM,DOUBLE deg)
{
    double cp,sp;
    cp = G3D_Math_CosD(deg);
    sp = G3D_Math_SinD(deg);
    G3D_M4D_Matrix4D( lpM,
                      ONE4D,       ZERO4D,       ZERO4D,       ZERO4D,
                      ZERO4D,      cp,           -sp,          ZERO4D,
                      ZERO4D,      sp,           cp,           ZERO4D,
                      ZERO4D,      ZERO4D,       ZERO4D,       ONE4D);
    return ;
}
```

Listing 7-41.   G3D_M4D_NRotateY4D

```
//
// returns a Matrix to rotate about the y axis
// where:         cy=Cos(y),   sy=Sin(y),
//
//             cy  0  sy   0       yaw
//              0  1   0   0
//            -sy  0  cy   0
//              0  0   0   1
//
LPMATRIX4D  WINAPI G3D_M4D_NRotateY(DOUBLE deg)
{
    double cy,sy;
    cy = G3D_Math_CosD(deg);
    sy = G3D_Math_SinD(deg);
    return G3D_M4D_NMatrix4D(cy,        ZERO4D,     sy,       ZERO4D,
                             ZERO4D,    ONE4D,      ZERO4D,   ZERO4D,
                             -sy,       ZERO4D,     cy,       ZERO4D,
                             ZERO4D,    ZERO4D,     ZERO4D,   ONE4D);
}
```

Listing 7-42.   G3D_M4D_RotateY4D

```
void            WINAPI G3D_M4D_RotateY (LPMATRIX4D lpM,DOUBLE deg)
{
    double cy,sy;
    cy = G3D_Math_CosD(deg);
    sy = G3D_Math_SinD(deg);
    G3D_M4D_Matrix4D( lpM,
                      cy,           ZERO4D,    sy,        ZERO4D,
                      ZERO4D,       ONE4D,     ZERO4D,    ZERO4D,
                      -sy,          ZERO4D,    cy,        ZERO4D,
                      ZERO4D,       ZERO4D,    ZERO4D,    ONE4D);
    return ;
}
```

Listing 7-43. G3D_M4D_NRotateZ4D

```
//
// returns a Matrix to rotate about the z axis
// where:        cr=Cos(r),  sr=Sin(r).
//
//            cr -sr  0  0      roll
//            sr  cr  0  0
//             0   0  1  0
//             0   0  0  1
//
LPMATRIX4D   WINAPI G3D_M4D_NRotateZ (DOUBLE deg)
{
    double cr,sr;
    cr = G3D_Math_CosD(deg);
    sr = G3D_Math_SinD(deg);
    return G3D_M4D_NMatrix4D(cr,    -sr,      ZERO4D, ZERO4D,
                             sr,     cr,      ZERO4D, ZERO4D,
                             ZERO4D, ZERO4D,  ONE4D,  ZERO4D,
                             ZERO4D, ZERO4D,  ZERO4D, ONE4D);
}
```

Listing 7-44. G3D_M4D_RotateZ4D

```
void          WINAPI G3D_M4D_Scale4D(LPMATRIX4D lpT,VECTOR4D P)
{
    lpT->T[0][0] = P.x;
    lpT->T[1][1] = P.y;
    lpT->T[2][2] = P.z;
    lpT->T[3][3] = P.w;
    return ;
}
```

This concludes our discussion of basic matrix operations. Next, we'll use matrix transformations to transform vectors and do other transformations, and we'll build composite transforms. This will round out the matrix services.

G3DLib Support:Matrices, Part II — Matrix Transformations

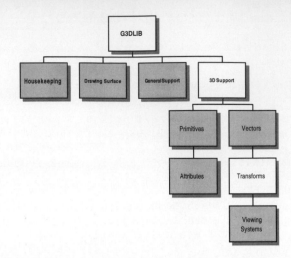

Once the simple 4D matrix operations are captured, it's time to build composite matrices and use transform matrices on both vectors and matrices. In addition, we'll tackle the projection step as a transformation-API function. Three key areas are the final elements we need to construct viewing systems:

- vector multiplication by transform and transform multiplication by transform,
- projection transformation, and
- transformation concatenation.

To do this, we need to construct the matrix transformation layer.

MATRIX4D Transform API

Whoever said "Consistency is the hobgoblin of small minds" wasn't an extensible-API programmer. We'll again follow the extensible-API formula (a suite of routines built around a data structure). Listing 7-45 contains the *MATRIX4D* transformation API definition.

Listing 7-45.   MATRIX4D Transformation API Definition

```
//  Transform constants
#define DEND       0
#define SCALE      1
#define TRANSLATE  2
#define ROTATEX    3
#define ROTATEY    4
#define ROTATEZ    5
#define PROJECT    10
//  Projection types
#define PARALLEL   20
#define PERSPECTIVE 21
// vector by matrix transforms
```

```
void                  WINAPI G3D_Xfrm_TransformPoint(LPVECTOR4D Pout,
                                                      VECTOR4D Pin,
                                                      LPMATRIX4D Tx);
void                  WINAPI G3D_Xfrm_TransformNPoints(LPVECTOR4D  lpP,
                                                       LPVECTOR4D  lpD,
                                                       int         cnt,
                                                       MATRIX4D    T);
// matrix by matrix transforms
void                  WINAPI G3D_Xfrm_TxT4D(LPMATRIX4D C,
                                            LPMATRIX4D A,LPMATRIX4D B);
// projection
void                  WINAPI G3D_Xfrm_ProjectPoint(LPVECTOR4D Pout,
                                                   VECTOR4D   Pin,
                                                   int        nType);
void                  WINAPI G3D_Xfrm_ProjectNPoints(LPVECTOR4D  lpP,
                                                     LPVECTOR4D  lpD,
                                                     int         cnt,
                                                     int         nType);
//generate arbitrary transform
int                   FAR cdecl G3D_Xfrm_MakeTM(LPMATRIX4D lpT,int a,...);
```

First, we need to define some important manifest constant, then the transformation usage, projection, and concatenation function prototypes define the transformation API. Transformations are most often applied to vectors (although they can be applied to matrices), and the API reflects this with the **G3D_Xfrm_TransformNPoints** function that parallels the repetitive functions of the output-primitive layer. It lets you "batch up" a bunch of vectors. Stringing a sequence of matrix operations together produces what is often called a *composite transform matrix* or CTM. The matrix-by-matrix transformation function is the basis of this functionality, and the transformation concatenation functions heavily use it as well.

Vector by Transform

As in the output-primitive layer, there are two actions accommodated in this API: one-point transformations and *n*-point transformations.

Each has its place, and it is wise for the API designer to allow the application programmers to choose between them. The functions **G3D_Xfrm_TransformPoint** and **G3D_Xfrm_TransformNPoints** apply transformations to vectors, assigning each component of the vector the result of the vector multiplied by a column. Equation 7-14 shows this operation.

Equation 7-14.   A Transform Applied to a Vector

$$
\begin{aligned}
x' &= \left| xT00 + XT01 + xT02 + xT03 \right| = [x,y,z,w] \\
y' &= \left| yT10 + yT11 + yT12 + yT13 \right| \\
z' &= \left| zT20 + zT21 + zT22 + zT23 \right| \\
w' &= \left| wT30 + wT31 + wT32 + wT33 \right|
\end{aligned}
\begin{vmatrix}
T00 & T01 & T02 & T03 \\
T10 & T11 & T12 & T13 \\
T20 & T21 & T22 & T23 \\
T30 & T31 & T32 & T33
\end{vmatrix}
$$

Listing 7-52. *(cont.)*

```
case TRANSLATE:
        x = *((DOUBLE far *)arg)++;
        y = *((DOUBLE far *)arg)++;
        z = *((DOUBLE far *)arg)++;
        G3D_V4D_VSet4D(&t,x,y,z,ZERO4D);
        G3D_M4D_Translate4D(&Temp,t);
        G3D_Xfrm_TxT4D(T, T,&Temp);
        break;

    case ROTATEX:
        x = *((DOUBLE far *)arg)++;
        G3D_M4D_RotateX(&Temp,x);
        G3D_Xfrm_TxT4D(T, T,&Temp)
        break;

    case ROTATEY:
        x = *((DOUBLE far *)arg)++;
        G3D_M4D_RotateY(&Temp,x);
        G3D_Xfrm_TxT4D(T, T, &Temp);
        break;

    case ROTATEZ:
        x = *((DOUBLE far *)arg)++;
        G3D_M4D_RotateZ(&Temp,x);
        G3D_Xfrm_TxT4D(T, T, &Temp);
        break;

    default:
        return 0;
    }
  }
  return 1;
}
```

The manifest constants that were defined back in Listing 7-45 provide "op-codes" for you to signify what basic matrix transformation you want. A master loop controls extracting repetitive op-codes, and tests for the DEND op-code. It also extracts the op-code parameter to allow it to decode the arguments. For each op-code, the temporary matrix is set up again, using *G3D_M4D_Zero4D* and *G3D_M4D_Identity4D*. Depending on the op-code, the value is extracted and a matrix constructed. Once the matrix is constructed, *G3D_Xfrm_TxT4D* multiplies the two matrices together. If more than one op-code is used, this process results in a concatenated matrix. The op-codes provided for are:

- scale,
- translate,
- rotatex,
- rotatey, and
- rotatez.

Scale sets up a vector from the three input values using *G3D_V4D_VSet4D*, then uses that vector with *G3D_M4D_Scale4D* to make a scaling matrix. *Translate* sets up a vector from the three input values using *G3D_V4D_VSet4D*, then uses it with *G3D_M4D_Translate4D* to make a translation matrix. The *rotations* require only one parameter each, the rotation angle, and they use it directly for x, y, and z rotation in *G3D_M4D_RotateX4D*, *G3D_M4D_RotateY4D*, and *G3D_M4D_RotateZ4D*, respectively.

This ends our consideration of matrices, so now we move to the final leg of the tripod: viewing systems.

G3DLib 3D Support: Viewing-System Primitives

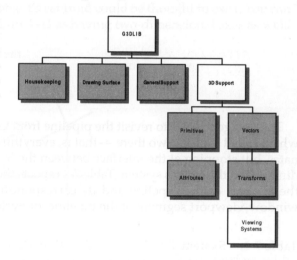

In Chapter 1, you learned that viewing parameters and the viewing transformation operate on the objects in a scene to generate images. The library provides two independent models for viewing that scene. The modeler we'll develop in Section III uses a pinhole camera viewing system, which is really nice for interactive applications, because moving the camera seems natural. But sometimes it's easier to use a simpler "world" for test programs, demos, and the like. Here, we'll develop what is commonly called a *four-parameter system*, which requires only an observer point and a distance to the viewing plane to specify the viewing geometry.

The viewing API, shown in Listing 7-53, defines two init and two move functions for the two viewing systems: 4-parameter and from-lookat.

Listing 7-53.   Viewing System Definition API

```
LPMATRIX4D    WINAPI G3D_View_InitEye(LPGENV    genv,
                                      VECTOR4D  vp,
                                      double    vs);
void          WINAPI G3D_View_MoveEye(LPGENV    genv,
                                      LPMATRIX4D Tx,
                                      VECTOR4D  vp,
                                      double    vs);
```

Figure 7-14. Step 3: Y-Rotation by Angle Theta Transformation

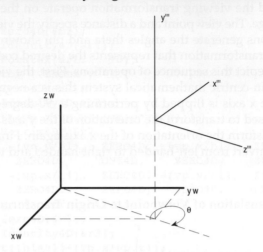

Figure 7-15. Step 4: X-Rotation by Angle Phi Transformation

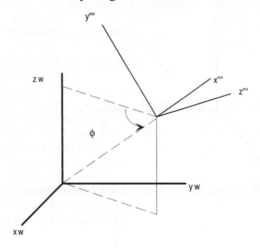

If you were reading carefully, you noticed the lack of sin and cosine calls in the implementation of *G3D_View_InitEye*. Once again, we use simple geometry, since trig functions are merely ratios of the lengths of the sides of a right triangle. This construction closely follows *Principles of Interactive Computer Graphics*, Second Edition, by William M. Newman and Robert F. Sproull (McGraw-Hill, 1979), which was the graphics programmer's bible before Foley and van Dam eclipsed it.

Equation 7-17 shows the sequence of matrix operations that produce a viewing system from point (6,8,7.5) with the viewing axis ze pointed at the origin. A D/S ratio of 4 for D=60 and S=15 is specified.

Figure 7-16. Step 5: Inversion of Z Axis by -1 Scaling Transformation

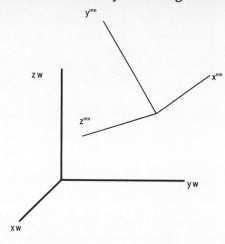

Equation 7-17. The 4-Parameter Sequence for (6,8,7.5)

$$
\underset{t1\ (-vp)}{\begin{bmatrix} 1 & 0 & 0 & 0 \\ 0 & 1 & 0 & 0 \\ 0 & 0 & 1 & 0 \\ -6 & -.8 & -7.5 & 1 \end{bmatrix}}
\underset{r1\ (90)}{\begin{bmatrix} 1 & 0 & 0 & 0 \\ 0 & 0 & -1 & 0 \\ 0 & 1 & 0 & 0 \\ 0 & 0 & 0 & 1 \end{bmatrix}}
\underset{r2\ ry}{\begin{bmatrix} -.8 & 0 & .6 & 0 \\ 0 & 1 & .0 & 0 \\ -.6 & 0 & -.8 & 0 \\ 0 & 0 & 0 & 1 \end{bmatrix}}
\underset{r3\ rx}{\begin{bmatrix} 1 & 0 & 0 & 0 \\ 0 & .8 & .6 & 0 \\ 0 & -.6 & .8 & 0 \\ 0 & 0 & 0 & 1 \end{bmatrix}}
\underset{sz\ scalexy}{\begin{bmatrix} 4 & 0 & 0 & 0 \\ 0 & 4 & 0 & 0 \\ 0 & 0 & -1 & 0 \\ 0 & 0 & 0 & 1 \end{bmatrix}}
$$

$$
\underset{tl}{\begin{bmatrix} 1 & 0 & 0 & 0 \\ 0 & 1 & 0 & 0 \\ 0 & 0 & 1 & 0 \\ -6 & -.8 & -7.5 & 1 \end{bmatrix}}
\overset{x}{\cdot}
\underset{r1}{\begin{bmatrix} 1 & 0 & 0 & 0 \\ 0 & 0 & -1 & 0 \\ 0 & 1 & 0 & 0 \\ 0 & 0 & 0 & 1 \end{bmatrix}}
=
\begin{bmatrix} 1 & 0 & 0 & 0 \\ 0 & 1 & -1 & 0 \\ 0 & 1 & 0 & 0 \\ -6 & -7.5 & 8 & 1 \end{bmatrix}
$$

$$
\underset{t1xr1}{\begin{bmatrix} 1 & 0 & 0 & 0 \\ 0 & 0 & -1 & 0 \\ 0 & 1 & 0 & 0 \\ -6 & -7.5 & 8 & 1 \end{bmatrix}}
\overset{x}{\cdot}
\underset{r2}{\begin{bmatrix} -.8 & 0 & .6 & 0 \\ 0 & 1 & 0 & 0 \\ -.6 & 0 & -.8 & 0 \\ 0 & 0 & 0 & 1 \end{bmatrix}}
=
\begin{bmatrix} -0.8 & 0 & 0.6 & 0 \\ 0.6 & 0 & 0.8 & 0 \\ 0 & 1 & 0 & 0 \\ 0 & -7.5 & -10 & 1 \end{bmatrix}
$$

$$
\underset{t1xr1xr2}{\begin{bmatrix} -0.8 & 0 & 0.6 & 0 \\ 0.6 & 0 & 0.8 & 0 \\ 0 & 1 & 0 & 0 \\ 0 & -7.5 & -10 & 1 \end{bmatrix}}
\overset{x}{\cdot}
\underset{r3}{\begin{bmatrix} 1 & 0 & 0 & 0 \\ 0 & .8 & .6 & 0 \\ 0 & -.6 & .8 & 0 \\ 0 & 0 & 0 & 1 \end{bmatrix}}
=
\begin{bmatrix} -0.8 & -0.36 & 0.48 & 0 \\ 0.6 & -0.48 & 0.64 & 0 \\ 0 & 0.8 & 0.6 & 0 \\ 0 & 0 & -12.5 & 1 \end{bmatrix}
$$

$$
\begin{array}{ccc}
\overset{\text{t1 xr1 xr2 xr3}}{\begin{bmatrix} -0.8 & -0.36 & 0.48 & 0 \\ 0.6 & -0.48 & 0.64 & 0 \\ 0 & 0.8 & 0.6 & 0 \\ 0 & 0 & -12.5 & 1 \end{bmatrix}} \cdot
\overset{\text{x} \quad \text{sz}}{\begin{bmatrix} 4 & 0 & 0 & 0 \\ 0 & 4 & 0 & 0 \\ 0 & 0 & -1 & 0 \\ 0 & 0 & 0 & 1 \end{bmatrix}} =
\begin{bmatrix} -3.2 & -1.44 & -0.48 & 0 \\ 2.4 & -1.92 & -0.64 & 0 \\ 0 & 3.2 & -0.6 & 0 \\ 0 & 0 & 12.5 & 1 \end{bmatrix}
\end{array}
$$

When this viewing system is used on a cube defined as in Table 7-3, it produces the output values in Table 7-4.

Table 7-3. Cube Definition

Point ID	x	y	z
Point1	−1	1	−1
Point2	1	1	−1
Point3	1	−1	−1
Point4	−1	−1	−1
Point5	−1	1	1
Point6	1	1	1
Point7	1	−1	1
Point8	−1	−1	1

Table 7-4. Cube Output Values

Point ID	x	y	z
Point1	5.6	−3.68	12.94
Point2	−0.8	−6.56	11.98
Point3	−5.6	−2.72	13.26
Point4	0.8	0.16	14.22
Point5	5.6	2.72	11.74
Point6	−0.8	−0.16	10.78
Point7	−5.6	3.68	12.06
Point8	0.8	6.56	13.02

And that finishes the basics of using the 4-parameter system. Two of the three examples at the end of this chapter will also use the 4-parameter system.

Transformations, Part II: The Pinhole Camera Viewing System

The from-lookat system is so named because it uses both a *from* point to position the viewpoint and a *lookat* point to specify the focus direction. This allows you to implement an arbitrary placement and focus type system from the simpler system built in the library.

Our system uses the from and lookat points, as well as an up vector and a twist angle, to further orient the camera. In addition, we also provide the D/S ratio for the final scaling transformation. This is a pretty elaborate system and allows for some pretty nice viewing. Figure 7-17 illustrates the viewing geometry supported by this system. Notice that there are three coordinate axes: the viewpoint, the focus point, and the world. If any object existed, an object coordinate system centered at its centroid could be thought to exist. The projection plane shown in Figure 7-17 could be thought to have a two-dimensional axis as well.

Figure 7-17   From-Lookat Viewing System

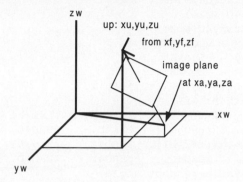

Listing 7-55 contains the central part of the implementation of *G3D_View_InitCamera*, with the guarding *TRY/CATCH* code removed. You can see the exact sequence of operations involved in building this CTM. The steps boil down to the following.

1. Translate the viewpoint to the origin.
2. Flip the x axis by a –90-degree rotation.
3. Rotate the y axis by a lookat-dependent angle.
4. Rotate the x axis again by a lookat-dependent angle.
5. Perform a z-rotate camera twist about the horizon.
6. Reverse the direction of z and scale.

This accomplishes a more-advanced version of the same process used in the 4-parameter viewing system — hence the similarity. In this implementation, the Up vector should be used to orient the camera; failing to do so eliminates special effects like flying upside-down.

As in the 4-parameter viewing system, the init function creates an instance of a *MATRIX4D* structure in which to build the transformation, while the move function generates a transform in an existing structure. Because the core block of code is the same, *G3D_View_MoveCamera* is not shown. Still, Listing 7-55 contains quite a block of code.

Listing 7-55.   Core Code of G3D_View_InitCamera

```
//translate viewpoint to origin
        G3D_M4D_Zero4D(&t1);
        G3D_M4D_Identity4D(&t1);
        G3D_V4D_VScale4D(&vFrom, -1.0,  vFrom);
        G3D_M4D_Translate4D(&t1, vFrom);
        G3D_V4D_VScale4D(&vFrom, -1.0,  vFrom);
```

Listing 7-55. (*cont.*)

```
//flip x axis
        G3D_M4D_Zero4D(&r1);
        G3D_M4D_Identity4D(&r1);
        G3D_M4D_RotateX(&r1,    90);
//rotate y axis by lookat dependent angle
        G3D_M4D_Zero4D(&r2);
        G3D_M4D_Identity4D(&r2);
        tfx = vFrom.x - vLookAt.x;
        tfy = vFrom.y - vLookAt.y;
        tfz = vFrom.z - vLookAt.z;
        h1  = sqrt((tfx*tfx) + (tfy*tfy));
        G3D_M4D_Matrix4D( &r2,
                        -(tfy/h1),   ZERO4D,    (tfx/h1),   ZERO4D,
                        ZERO4D,      ONE4D,     ZERO4D,     ZERO4D,
                        -(tfx/h1),   ZERO4D,    -(tfy/h1),  ZERO4D,
                        ZERO4D,      ZERO4D,    ZERO4D,     ONE4D);
//rotate x axis by lookat dependent angle
        G3D_M4D_Zero4D(&r3);
        G3D_M4D_Identity4D(&r3);
        h2  = sqrt((tfx*tfx) + (tfy*tfy) + (tfz*tfz));
        G3D_M4D_Matrix4D( &r3,
                        ONE4D,     ZERO4D,    ZERO4D,    ZERO4D,
                        ZERO4D,    h1/h2,     tfz/h2,    ZERO4D,
                        ZERO4D,    -tfz/h2,   h1/h2,     ZERO4D,
                        ZERO4D,    ZERO4D,    ZERO4D,    ONE4D);
//perform "twist" about the horizon (assumed 0-0-1, should use up )
        G3D_M4D_Zero4D(&r4);
        G3D_M4D_Identity4D(&r4);
        G3D_M4D_RotateZ(&r4, ang);
// final right/left/projection scaling
        G3D_M4D_Zero4D(&sc);
        G3D_M4D_Identity4D(&sc);
        G3D_V4D_VSet4D(&ps, vd/vs,  vd/vs,  -1.0, 1.0);
        G3D_M4D_Scale4D(&sc,ps);
// wipe it and build up the CTM
        G3D_M4D_Zero4D(Tx);
        G3D_M4D_Identity4D(Tx);
        G3D_Xfrm_TxT4D(Tx,Tx,&t1);
        G3D_Xfrm_TxT4D(Tx,Tx,&r1);
        G3D_Xfrm_TxT4D(Tx,Tx,&r2);
        G3D_Xfrm_TxT4D(Tx,Tx,&r3);
        G3D_Xfrm_TxT4D(Tx,Tx,&r4);
        G3D_Xfrm_TxT4D(Tx,Tx,&sc);

        return Tx;
```

Again, if you were reading carefully you noticed the lack of sine and cosine calls in the implementation of **G3D_View_InitEye**. As before, we only need to use simple geometry here.

Figures 7-18 to 7-23 depict the sequence of operations performed by the code in Listing 7-55. First, the viewpoint is translated to the origin. Again, this is a negative translation. Second, the direction of the x axis is flipped by performing a -90-degree rotation. Third, the y axis is rotated by a lookat-dependent angle, replacing the theta rotation of the 4-parameter system. Fourth, the x axis is again rotated, this time by a lookat-dependent angle, replacing the phi rotation from the 4-parameter system. Fifth, the camera is twisted about z (the horizon). Again note that to be truly accurate, the Up vector should be taken into account. Finally, the z axis flipping and D/S scaling transformation occurs exactly like that in the 4-parameter system. The two lookat-dependent angles use the sides of the triangles, the trigonometric relations, and the Pythagorean formula to compute sine and cosine values rather than using the library functions.

Figure 7-18.   Step 1: Translation of Viewpoint to Origin Transformation

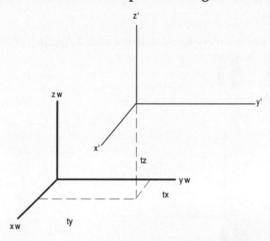

Figure 7-19.   Step 2: X-Rotation by -90-Degree Transformation

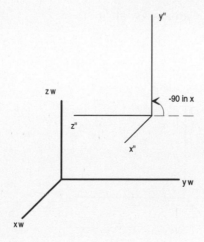

Figure 7-20. Step 3: Y-Rotation by Lookat-Dependent Angle Transformation

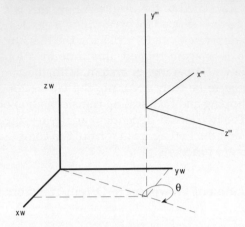

Figure 7-21. Step 4: X-Rotation by Lookat-Dependent Angle Transformation

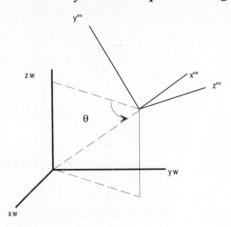

Figure 7-22. Step 5: Z-Rotation Camera Twist

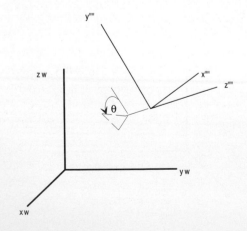

Figure 7-23. Step 6: Inversion of Z Axis by -1 Scaling Transformation

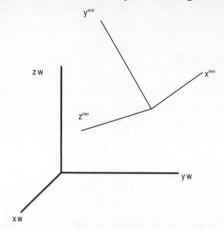

At this point, I could produce another sample sequence of calculations showing a simple example, but the proof is in the pudding, so let's get on to the real examples and see this work in some demo programs.

Demos

As I've said before, demo programs are the life of the graphics programmer, especially the graphics library provider. Here are three demo programs that introduce the viewing systems:

1. A simple rotating cube using 4-parameter viewing.
2. A simple surface plot using 4-parameter viewing.
3. A simple camera system using the cube again.

This set of demos clearly illustrates object representation, world generation, and world manipulation issues.

In general, the additions to the shell demo program provide two sets of new functionality: 3D and canvas-based graphics.

System Two, if you remember, is the 3D graphics system of object-to-world-to-eye coordinates. This basically follows object instantiation and world generation, as well as viewing transformation. The interface between System Two and System One is the projection transformation. It generates "sw" or "screen window" floating-point coordinates. System One provides the mapping to "sv" or "screen viewport" coordinates and output, as well as the display surface to which the output is destined. So, briefly, this is what we need to do to take care of System-Two usage:

1. Define a 3D object.
2. Define a viewing transformation.
3. Transform the object vertex coordinates.
4. Draw the object.

Drawing services are where System One comes into play. A graphics environits canvas must exist, the window-viewport mapping must be specified, and the
projection points must be mapped to device coordinates using System-One routi

Variation: Rotating Single Cube

For the simple cube demo, we'll follow the process I've just described. It is bes
reverse order starting with canvas creation and window-viewport mapping be
ceeding to object-representation and instantiation, transformation, projection, a
ing.

Graphics Environment and the Canvas
The lifetime of the graphics environment and its canvas includes creation, sizing,
and destruction. First, at creation, the window-viewport values are defined and t
is instantiated, as shown in Listing 7-56. I haven't included the sizing code here, ev
it is required for a fixed canvas, since it is implemented exactly as in the Chapter
The painting logic is shown in Listing 7-57, followed by the *GENV* destruction
7-58.

Listing 7-56.   Creation

```
...
   pv->rW.left   = -15.0;
   pv->rW.bottom = -15.0;
   pv->rW.top    =  15.0;
   pv->rW.right  =  15.0;
   pv->rV.left   = 0;
   pv->rV.top    = 0;
   pv->rV.right  = 400;
   pv->rV.bottom = 400;
...

pv->genv = G3D_GEnv_Create(pv->hwnd,LIGHT,NULL,BLACK_CANV,
                           pv->rW,pv->rV);
...
```

Listing 7-57.   Painting

```
...
     rDst.left    = 0;
     rDst.right   = rV.right;
     rDst.top     = 0;
     rDst.bottom  = rV.bottom;
     rSrc.left    = xScroll;
     rSrc.top     = -yScroll;
...
```

```
G3D_GEnv_Paint(pv->genv,
               hValidDC,
               rDst,
               rSrc,
               FALSE);
...
```

Listing 7-58. Destruction

```
...
G3D_GEnv_Destroy(pv->genv);
...
```

Window-Viewport Mapping and User-to-Device Coordinate Mapping

The window-viewport mapping allows us to use a few cute tricks. By manipulating the ratios of window extent to viewport extent and paying attention to the fact that the perspective divide shrinks the range of values, we can somewhat maintain the apparent size of parallel and perspective projected objects.

Listing 7-59 shows how the window range is manipulated, depending on the projection, while the viewport is left constant. Function *G3D_Coords_UsertoDevice* uses the window-viewport mapping; this function maps window coordinates to viewport coordinates for us as shown in Listing 7-60.

Listing 7-59. Window-Viewport Tricks

```
switch(vtype)
    {
    case CMD_ORTHO:
        pv->rW.left   = -15.0;
        pv->rW.bottom = -15.0;
        pv->rW.right  =  15;
        pv->rW.top    =  15;
        break;
    case CMD_PERSP:
        pv->rW.left   = -1.2;
        pv->rW.bottom = -1.2;
        pv->rW.right  =  1.2;
        pv->rW.top    =  1.2;
        break;
    }
//  reset wv
    G3D_WV_SetWindow(pv->genv,
                     pv->rW.left,  pv->rW.bottom,
                     pv->rW.right, pv->rW.top);
    G3D_WV_SetViewport(pv->genv,
                  pv->rV.left, pv->rV.top,
              pv->rV.right,pv->rV.bottom);
```

Listing 7-60.   User-to-Device Mapping Before Primitive Output

```
G3D_Coords_UsertoDev(pv->genv,p1.x,p1.y,&xv1,&yv1);
 G3D_Coords_UsertoDev(pv->genv,p2.x,p2.y,&xv2,&yv2);
 G3D_GEnv_Line(pv->genv,(long)xv1,(long)(long)yv1,
                        (long)xv2,(long)yv2,NULL);
 G3D_GEnv_Text(pv->genv,(long)xv2,(long)yv2,"x",1,NULL);
```

Object Representation and Instantiation

The cube demo does not require a sophisticated representation scheme like the modeler. The cube requires eight points to define it. These eight points are shared among six faces. Listing 7-61 shows the representation as a *VECTOR4D* array.

Listing 7-61.   Cube Representation

```
/* define 3d origin */
int       nXOrg = 0;
int       nYOrg = 0;
int       nZOrg = 0;
/* define default cube size */
int       nXLen = 2;
int       nYLen = 2;
int       nZLen = 2;
/* cube */
VECTOR4D  Edges[9];
```

This is sufficient for this program. Listing 7-62 shows the cube-initialization internals sequence. Since this cube lives at the origin, the initialization and world instantiation steps can be collapsed here. Listing 7-63 then shows an invocation of initialization function *SetVertexes*.

Listing 7-62.   Object Initialization

```
void SetVertexes( void )
{
   Edges[1].x = nXOrg - (nXLen/2.);
   Edges[2].x = Edges[1].x;
   Edges[3].x = nXOrg + (nXLen/2.);
   Edges[4].x = Edges[3].x;
   Edges[5].x = Edges[1].x;
   Edges[6].x = Edges[1].x;
   Edges[7].x = Edges[3].x;
   Edges[8].x = Edges[4].x;

   Edges[1].y = nYOrg + (nYLen/2.);
   Edges[2].y = nYOrg - (nYLen/2.);
   Edges[3].y = Edges[2].y;
```

```
    Edges[4].y = Edges[1].y;
    Edges[5].y = Edges[1].y;
    Edges[6].y = Edges[2].y;
    Edges[7].y = Edges[3].y;
    Edges[8].y = Edges[4].y;

    Edges[1].z = nZOrg - (nZLen/2.);
    Edges[2].z = Edges[1].z;
    Edges[3].z = Edges[1].z;
    Edges[4].z = Edges[1].z;
    Edges[5].z = nZOrg + (nZLen/2.);
    Edges[6].z = Edges[5].z;
    Edges[7].z = Edges[5].z;
    Edges[8].z = Edges[5].z;

    Edges[1].w = 1;
    Edges[2].w = 1;
    Edges[3].w = 1;
    Edges[4].w = 1;
    Edges[5].w = 1;
    Edges[6].w = 1;
    Edges[7].w = 1;
    Edges[8].w = 1;
}
```

Listing 7-63.   SetVertexes Invocation

```
//init 3d world
    SetVertexes();
```

Viewing Transformation: Generation

The viewing transformation generation is very straightforward. Define the viewpoint, in this case the point (6,8,7.5). Define the D/S ratio. Then invoke *G3D_View_InitEye* to receive the CTM in the return value. Listing 7-64 contains the sequence that produces the desired result.

Listing 7-64.   Viewing Transformation Generation

```
//viewpoint in cartesian
    vp.x   = 6.0;
    vp.y   = 8.0;
    vp.z   = 7.5;
//scaling
    vs     = 3;

//init cumulative local or rotate transform
    G3D_M4D_Identity4D(&T);
//build two viewing transforms
    tParaProj  = G3D_View_InitEye(pv->genv,vp,vs);
    tPerspProj = G3D_View_InitEye(pv->genv,vp,vs);
```

Viewing Transformation: Usage

Using the viewing transform is also quite easy. Listing 7-65 defines function *TransformEdges*, which loops and calls *G3D_Xfrm_TransformPoint* for each point in the cube. This function takes the viewing matrix as an argument and uses *G3D_Xfrm_TransformPoint* to apply it repetitively to the cube vertexes.

Listing 7-65.   Viewing Transformation Acting on Cube Edges

```
void  TransformEdges( VWWND * pv,int vtype, LPMATRIX4D Tx )
{
    int       i,j;

    for ( i = 1; i <= 8; i++ )
    {
        G3D_Xfrm_TransformPoint((LPVECTOR4D)&Edges[i],Edges[i],Tx);
    }
    return;
}
```

At this point, instead of transforming a point at a time, this code is "batched up" by calling *G3D_Xfrm_TransformNPoints*. In addition, a "local" transformation rotates the object continuously. This is called a *local* transformation because it affects only the object's orientation (local) coordinates — not the camera or the global coordinate system (See Listing 7-66).

Listing 7-66.   Local Transformation Acting on Cube Edges

```
...
//  transform n degrees around an axis
    G3D_M4D_Identity4D(&Temp);
    switch(nWhichTrans)
    {
     case ROTATEX:
         G3D_M4D_RotateX(&Temp,CurDegrees);
         break;
     case ROTATEY:
         G3D_M4D_RotateY(&Temp,CurDegrees);
         break;
     case ROTATEZ:
         G3D_M4D_RotateZ(&Temp,CurDegrees);
         break;
 }
...
//  build cumulative local transform
    G3D_Xfrm_TxT4D(&T,&T,&Temp);
//  do local
    TransformEdges(pv,vtype, &T);
...
```

Projection Transformation: Usage

Remember the transformation operation that defined function *TransformEdges*? The projection operation defines function *ProjectEdges*, which produces screen coordinates for us in a very similar way. Note that *G3D_Xfrm_ProjectPoint*; which this function encapsulates, takes only the manifest constant indicating the projection, not a matrix. Listing 7-67 contains this function.

Listing 7-67.   ProjectEdges

```
void  ProjectEdges( VWWND * pv,int vtype, LPMATRIX4D Tx )
{
   int      i,j;

   for ( i = 1; i <= 8; i++ )
   {
      G3D_Xfrm_ProjectPoint((LPVECTOR4D)&Edges[i],Edges[i],
                   vtype == CMD_PERSP ?  PERSPECTIVE : PARALLEL);
   }
   return;
}
```

Drawing: Wireframe, Hidden-Line, and Solid-Color

There are three drawing routines we'll cover here: wireframe, hidden-line, and solid-color. For our cube, wireframe simply draws the bottom rectangle, top rectangle, and four lines connecting them to minimize drawing. This is shown in Listing 7-68 in function *DrawEdges*. It uses a sequence of two calls to *G3D_Coords_UsertoDevice*, coupled to a line draw by function *G3D_GEnv_Line*. This is performed for each line segment as I've previously discussed and shown in the code.

Listing 7-68.   Wireframe Cube Drawing

```
void  DrawEdges( VWWND* pv,HDC hDC )
{
   long      xv1,xv2,yv1,yv2;
    // 1-2
   G3D_Coords_UsertoDev(pv->genv,Edges[1].x,Edges[1].y,&xv1,&yv1);
   G3D_Coords_UsertoDev(pv->genv,Edges[2].x,Edges[2].y,&xv2,&yv2);
   G3D_GEnv_Line(pv->genv,(long)xv1,(long)yv1,
                         (long)xv2,(long)yv2,NULL);
    // 2-3    front face
   G3D_Coords_UsertoDev(pv->genv,Edges[2].x,Edges[2].y,&xv1,&yv1);
   G3D_Coords_UsertoDev(pv->genv,Edges[3].x,Edges[3].y,&xv2,&yv2);
   G3D_GEnv_Line(pv->genv,(long)xv1,(long)yv1,
                         (long)xv2,(long)yv2,NULL);
    // 3-4
   G3D_Coords_UsertoDev(pv->genv,Edges[3].x,Edges[3].y,&xv1,&yv1);
   G3D_Coords_UsertoDev(pv->genv,Edges[4].x,Edges[4].y,&xv2,&yv2);
   G3D_GEnv_Line(pv->genv,(long)xv1,(long)yv1,
                         (long)xv2,(long)yv2,NULL);
```

Listing 7-68. (*cont.*)

```
// 4-1
  G3D_Coords_UsertoDev(pv->genv,Edges[4].x,Edges[4].y,&xv1,&yv1);
  G3D_Coords_UsertoDev(pv->genv,Edges[1].x,Edges[1].y,&xv2,&yv2);
  G3D_GEnv_Line(pv->genv,(long)xv1,(long)yv1,
                         (long)xv2,(long)yv2,NULL);
  // connect front to back at 1-5
  G3D_Coords_UsertoDev(pv->genv,Edges[1].x,Edges[1].y,&xv1,&yv1);
  G3D_Coords_UsertoDev(pv->genv,Edges[5].x,Edges[5].y,&xv2,&yv2);
  G3D_GEnv_Line(pv->genv,(long)xv1,(long)yv1,
                         (long)xv2,(long)yv2,NULL);
  // 5-6
  G3D_Coords_UsertoDev(pv->genv,Edges[5].x,Edges[5].y,&xv1,&yv1);
  G3D_Coords_UsertoDev(pv->genv,Edges[6].x,Edges[6].y,&xv2,&yv2);
  G3D_GEnv_Line(pv->genv,(long)xv1,(long)yv1,
                         (long)xv2,(long)yv2,NULL);
  // 6-7    back face
  G3D_Coords_UsertoDev(pv->genv,Edges[6].x,Edges[6].y,&xv1,&yv1);
  G3D_Coords_UsertoDev(pv->genv,Edges[7].x,Edges[7].y,&xv2,&yv2);
  G3D_GEnv_Line(pv->genv,(long)xv1,(long)yv1,
                         (long)xv2,(long)yv2,NULL);
  // 7-8
  G3D_Coords_UsertoDev(pv->genv,Edges[7].x,Edges[7].y,&xv1,&yv1);
  G3D_Coords_UsertoDev(pv->genv,Edges[8].x,Edges[8].y,&xv2,&yv2);
  G3D_GEnv_Line(pv->genv,(long)xv1,(long)yv1,
                         (long)xv2,(long)yv2,NULL);
  // 8-5
  G3D_Coords_UsertoDev(pv->genv,Edges[8].x,Edges[8].y,&xv1,&yv1);
  G3D_Coords_UsertoDev(pv->genv,Edges[5].x,Edges[5].y,&xv2,&yv2);
  G3D_GEnv_Line(pv->genv,(long)xv1,(long)yv1,
                         (long)xv2,(long)yv2,NULL);
  // connect front to back at 2-6
  G3D_Coords_UsertoDev(pv->genv,Edges[2].x,Edges[2].y,&xv1,&yv1);
  G3D_Coords_UsertoDev(pv->genv,Edges[6].x,Edges[6].y,&xv2,&yv2);
  G3D_GEnv_Line(pv->genv,(long)xv1,(long)yv1,
                         (long)xv2,(long)yv2,NULL);


// connect front to back at 3-7
  G3D_Coords_UsertoDev(pv->genv,Edges[3].x,Edges[3].y,&xv1,&yv1);
  G3D_Coords_UsertoDev(pv->genv,Edges[7].x,Edges[7].y,&xv2,&yv2);
  G3D_GEnv_Line(pv->genv,(long)xv1,(long)yv1,
                         (long)xv2,(long)yv2,NULL);
// connect front to back at 4-8
  G3D_Coords_UsertoDev(pv->genv,Edges[4].x,Edges[4].y,&xv1,&yv1);
  G3D_Coords_UsertoDev(pv->genv,Edges[8].x,Edges[8].y,&xv2,&yv2);
  G3D_GEnv_Line(pv->genv,(long)xv1,(long)yv1,
                         (long)xv2,(long)yv2,NULL);
```

```
//draw x on front face
   G3D_Coords_UsertoDev(pv->genv,Edges[1].x,Edges[1].y,&xv1,&yv1);
   G3D_Coords_UsertoDev(pv->genv,Edges[3].x,Edges[3].y,&xv2,&yv2);
   G3D_GEnv_Line(pv->genv,(long)xv1,(long)yv1,
                          (long)xv2,(long)yv2,NULL);

   G3D_Coords_UsertoDev(pv->genv,Edges[4].x,Edges[4].y,&xv1,&yv1);
   G3D_Coords_UsertoDev(pv->genv,Edges[2].x,Edges[2].y,&xv2,&yv2);
   G3D_GEnv_Line(pv->genv,(long)xv1,(long)yv1,
                          (long)xv2,(long)yv2,NULL);

   return;
}
```

Hidden-line drawing uses a cheap trick here. By subtracting opposite corners of the cube, we can get an idea of the orientation of the cube. This defines which of a pair of faces should be drawn for each of the three pairs comprising the six faces of the cube. This is *not* a general technique for hidden-line removal and will only work on a cube. Listing 7-69 shows the implementation of **DrawHiddenEdges**. This function differs from **DrawEdges** in its consideration of the cube as a group of faces instead of unrelated line segments.

Listing 7-69. Hidden-Line Cube Drawing

```
void  DrawHiddenEdges( VWWND * pv,HDC hDC ){
 long      xv1,xv2,yv1,yv2;

 if ( Edges[5].z - Edges[1].z < 0 ){
    // 5-6
    G3D_Coords_UsertoDev(pv->genv,Edges[5].x,Edges[5].y,&xv1,&yv1);
    G3D_Coords_UsertoDev(pv->genv,Edges[6].x,Edges[6].y,&xv2,&yv2);
    G3D_GEnv_Line(pv->genv,(long)xv1,(long)yv1,
                           (long)xv2,(long)yv2,NULL);
    // 6-7     back face
    G3D_Coords_UsertoDev(pv->genv,Edges[6].x,Edges[6].y,&xv1,&yv1);
    G3D_Coords_UsertoDev(pv->genv,Edges[7].x,Edges[7].y,&xv2,&yv2);
    G3D_GEnv_Line(pv->genv,(long)xv1,(long)yv1,
                           (long)xv2,(long)yv2,NULL);
    // 7-8
    G3D_Coords_UsertoDev(pv->genv,Edges[7].x,Edges[7].y,&xv1,&yv1);
    G3D_Coords_UsertoDev(pv->genv,Edges[8].x,Edges[8].y,&xv2,&yv2);
    G3D_GEnv_Line(pv->genv,(long)xv1,(long)yv1,
                           (long)xv2,(long)yv2,NULL);
    // 8-5
    G3D_Coords_UsertoDev(pv->genv,Edges[8].x,Edges[8].y,&xv1,&yv1);
    G3D_Coords_UsertoDev(pv->genv,Edges[5].x,Edges[5].y,&xv2,&yv2);
    G3D_GEnv_Line(pv->genv,(long)xv1,(long)yv1,
                           (long)xv2,(long)yv2,NULL);
 }
 else {
```

Listing 7-69.   (*cont.*)

```
// 1-2
   G3D_Coords_UsertoDev(pv->genv,Edges[1].x,Edges[1].y,&xv1,&yv1);
   G3D_Coords_UsertoDev(pv->genv,Edges[2].x,Edges[2].y,&xv2,&yv2);
   G3D_GEnv_Line(pv->genv,(long)xv1,(long)yv1,
                          (long)xv2,(long)yv2,NULL);
   // 2-3     front face
   G3D_Coords_UsertoDev(pv->genv,Edges[2].x,Edges[2].y,&xv1,&yv1);
   G3D_Coords_UsertoDev(pv->genv,Edges[3].x,Edges[3].y,&xv2,&yv2);
   G3D_GEnv_Line(pv->genv,(long)xv1,(long)yv1,
                          (long)xv2,(long)yv2,NULL);
   // 3-4
   G3D_Coords_UsertoDev(pv->genv,Edges[3].x,Edges[3].y,&xv1,&yv1);
   G3D_Coords_UsertoDev(pv->genv,Edges[4].x,Edges[4].y,&xv2,&yv2);
   G3D_GEnv_Line(pv->genv,(long)xv1,(long)yv1,
                  (long)xv2,(long)yv2,NULL);
   // 4-1
   G3D_Coords_UsertoDev(pv->genv,Edges[4].x,Edges[4].y,&xv1,&yv1);
   G3D_Coords_UsertoDev(pv->genv,Edges[1].x,Edges[1].y,&xv2,&yv2);
   G3D_GEnv_Line(pv->genv,(long)xv1,(long)yv1,(
                          long)xv2,(long)yv2,NULL);//
// draw x on front face
   G3D_Coords_UsertoDev(pv->genv,Edges[1].x,Edges[1].y,&xv1,&yv1);
   G3D_Coords_UsertoDev(pv->genv,Edges[3].x,Edges[3].y,&xv2,&yv2);
   G3D_GEnv_Line(pv->genv,(long)xv1,(long)yv1,
                          (long)xv2,(long)yv2,NULL);
   G3D_Coords_UsertoDev(pv->genv,Edges[4].x,Edges[4].y,&xv1,&yv1);
   G3D_Coords_UsertoDev(pv->genv,Edges[2].x,Edges[2].y,&xv2,&yv2);
   G3D_GEnv_Line(pv->genv,(long)xv1,(long)yv1,
                          (long)xv2,(long)yv2,NULL);
}
if ( Edges[2].z - Edges[1].z < 0 )
{
   // 2-3     front face
   G3D_Coords_UsertoDev(pv->genv,Edges[2].x,Edges[2].y,&xv1,&yv1);
   G3D_Coords_UsertoDev(pv->genv,Edges[3].x,Edges[3].y,&xv2,&yv2);
   G3D_GEnv_Line(pv->genv,(long)xv1,(long)yv1,
                          (long)xv2,(long)yv2,NULL);
   // connect front to back at 3-7
   G3D_Coords_UsertoDev(pv->genv,Edges[3].x,Edges[3].y,&xv1,&yv1);
   G3D_Coords_UsertoDev(pv->genv,Edges[7].x,Edges[7].y,&xv2,&yv2);
   G3D_GEnv_Line(pv->genv,(long)xv1,(long)yv1,
                          (long)xv2,(long)yv2,NULL);
   // 7-6
   G3D_Coords_UsertoDev(pv->genv,Edges[7].x,Edges[7].y,&xv1,&yv1);
   G3D_Coords_UsertoDev(pv->genv,Edges[6].x,Edges[6].y,&xv2,&yv2);
   G3D_GEnv_Line(pv->genv,(long)xv1,(long)yv1,
                          (long)xv2,(long)yv2,NULL);
   // 6-2
   G3D_Coords_UsertoDev(pv->genv,Edges[6].x,Edges[6].y,&xv1,&yv1);
   G3D_Coords_UsertoDev(pv->genv,Edges[2].x,Edges[2].y,&xv2,&yv2);
```

```
G3D_GEnv_Line(pv->genv,(long)xv1,(long)yv1,
                        (long)xv2,(long)yv2,NULL);
}
else
{
    // 1-4
    G3D_Coords_UsertoDev(pv->genv,Edges[1].x,Edges[1].y,&xv1,&yv1);
    G3D_Coords_UsertoDev(pv->genv,Edges[4].x,Edges[4].y,&xv2,&yv2);
    G3D_GEnv_Line(pv->genv,(long)xv1,(long)yv1,
                            (long)xv2,(long)yv2,NULL);
    // 4-8    top face
    G3D_Coords_UsertoDev(pv->genv,Edges[4].x,Edges[4].y,&xv1,&yv1);
    G3D_Coords_UsertoDev(pv->genv,Edges[8].x,Edges[8].y,&xv2,&yv2);
    G3D_GEnv_Line(pv->genv,(long)xv1,(long)yv1,
                            (long)xv2,(long)yv2,NULL);
    // 8-5
    G3D_Coords_UsertoDev(pv->genv,Edges[8].x,Edges[8].y,&xv1,&yv1);
    G3D_Coords_UsertoDev(pv->genv,Edges[5].x,Edges[5].y,&xv2,&yv2);
    G3D_GEnv_Line(pv->genv,(long)xv1,(long)yv1,
                            (long)xv2,(long)yv2,NULL);
    // 5-1
    G3D_Coords_UsertoDev(pv->genv,Edges[5].x,Edges[5].y,&xv1,&yv1);
    G3D_Coords_UsertoDev(pv->genv,Edges[1].x,Edges[1].y,&xv2,&yv2);
    G3D_GEnv_Line(pv->genv,(long)xv1,(long)yv1,
                            (long)xv2,(long)yv2,NULL);
}
if ( Edges[4].z - Edges[1].z > 0 )
{
    // 1-2
    G3D_Coords_UsertoDev(pv->genv,Edges[1].x,Edges[1].y,&xv1,&yv1);
    G3D_Coords_UsertoDev(pv->genv,Edges[2].x,Edges[2].y,&xv2,&yv2);
    G3D_GEnv_Line(pv->genv,(long)xv1,(long)yv1,
                            (long)xv2,(long)yv2,NULL);
    // 2-6    left face
    G3D_Coords_UsertoDev(pv->genv,Edges[2].x,Edges[2].y,&xv1,&yv1);
    G3D_Coords_UsertoDev(pv->genv,Edges[6].x,Edges[6].y,&xv2,&yv2);
    G3D_GEnv_Line(pv->genv,(long)xv1,(long)yv1,
                            (long)xv2,(long)yv2,NULL);
// 6-5
    G3D_Coords_UsertoDev(pv->genv,Edges[6].x,Edges[6].y,&xv1,&yv1);
    G3D_Coords_UsertoDev(pv->genv,Edges[5].x,Edges[5].y,&xv2,&yv2);
    G3D_GEnv_Line(pv->genv,(long)xv1,(long)yv1,
                            (long)xv2,(long)yv2,NULL);
 // 5-1
    G3D_Coords_UsertoDev(pv->genv,Edges[5].x,Edges[5].y,&xv1,&yv1);
    G3D_Coords_UsertoDev(pv->genv,Edges[1].x,Edges[1].y,&xv2,&yv2);
    G3D_GEnv_Line(pv->genv,(long)xv1,(long)yv1,
                            (long)xv2,(long)yv2,NULL);
}
else
{
```

Listing 7-69.   *(cont.)*

```
// 4-3
   G3D_Coords_UsertoDev(pv->genv,Edges[4].x,Edges[4].y,&xv1,&yv1);
   G3D_Coords_UsertoDev(pv->genv,Edges[3].x,Edges[3].y,&xv2,&yv2);
   G3D_GEnv_Line(pv->genv,(long)xv1,(long)yv1,
                          (long)xv2,(long)yv2,NULL);
     // 3-7     right face
   G3D_Coords_UsertoDev(pv->genv,Edges[3].x,Edges[3].y,&xv1,&yv1);
   G3D_Coords_UsertoDev(pv->genv,Edges[7].x,Edges[7].y,&xv2,&yv2);
   G3D_GEnv_Line(pv->genv,(long)xv1,(long)yv1,
                          (long)xv2,(long)yv2,NULL);
     // 7-8
   G3D_Coords_UsertoDev(pv->genv,Edges[7].x,Edges[7].y,&xv1,&yv1);
   G3D_Coords_UsertoDev(pv->genv,Edges[8].x,Edges[8].y,&xv2,&yv2);
   G3D_GEnv_Line(pv->genv,(long)xv1,(long)yv1,
                          (long)xv2,(long)yv2,NULL);
     // 8-4
   G3D_Coords_UsertoDev(pv->genv,Edges[8].x,Edges[8].y,&xv1,&yv1);
   G3D_Coords_UsertoDev(pv->genv,Edges[4].x,Edges[4].y,&xv2,&yv2);
   G3D_GEnv_Line(pv->genv,(long)xv1,(long)yv1,
                          (long)xv2,(long)yv2,NULL);
   }
   return;
}
```

Finally, in a variation of the face-drawing code, *DrawSolidEdges* replaces line drawing with polygon drawing to enable solid filling of the polygons. A segment of this function is shown in Listing 7-70.

Listing 7-70.   DrawSolidEdges Code Segment

```
...

   // 5-6
   // 6-7     TOP face
   // 7-8
   // 8-5
   G3D_Coords_UsertoDev(pv->genv,Edges[5].x,Edges[5].y,&xv1,&yv1);
   pgdi[0].x = xv1;
   pgdi[0].y = yv1;
   G3D_Coords_UsertoDev(pv->genv,Edges[6].x,Edges[6].y,&xv1,&yv1);
   pgdi[1].x = xv1;
   pgdi[1].y = yv1;
   G3D_Coords_UsertoDev(pv->genv,Edges[7].x,Edges[7].y,&xv1,&yv1);
   pgdi[2].x = xv1;
   pgdi[2].y = yv1;
   G3D_Coords_UsertoDev(pv->genv,Edges[8].x,Edges[8].y,&xv1,&yv1);
   pgdi[3].x = xv1;
```

```
    pgdi[3].y = yv1;
    G3D_Coords_UsertoDev(pv->genv,Edges[5].x,Edges[5].y,&xv1,&yv1);
    pgdi[4].x = xv1;
    pgdi[4].y = yv1;
    hbr    = CreateSolidBrush(PALETTERGB(128,0,0));
    G3D_GEnv_Polygon(pv->genv,(LPPOINT)&pgdi,5,NULL,(DWORD)hbr);
    DeleteObject(hbr);
...
```

Drawing Attributes

Now that we've covered the basics of drawing, we need to consider the kinds of lines
and polygons and their attributes. The attributes involved here are:

- background color,
- pen color, and
- fill color.

Listing 7-71 shows the appropriate attribute code and Figure 7-24 shows the grayscaled
result for solid-color drawing.

Listing 7-71. Attribute Code Segments

```
//background attributes
 switch(bckclr)
   {
    case CMD_WHITE:
        FillRect(hDC, &rV, GetStockObject(bckclr-CMD_BCKBASE));
        break;
    case CMD_BLACK:
        FillRect(hDC, &rV, GetStockObject(bckclr-CMD_BCKBASE));
        break;
   }
// drawing pen
  switch(bckclr)
   {
    case CMD_WHITE:
        SelectObject(hDC, hBlackPen);
        break;
    case CMD_BLACK:
        SelectObject(hDC, hWhitePen);
        break;
   }
// solid colors red,green,blue
  hbr    = CreateSolidBrush(PALETTERGB(128,0,0));
  hbr    = CreateSolidBrush(PALETTERGB(0,128,0));
  hbr    = CreateSolidBrush(PALETTERGB(0,0,128));
```

Figure 7-24.   Grayscaled Solid-Color Cube Screenshot

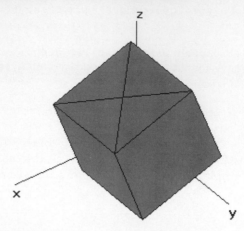

Variation: Simple Surface Plot

As in the cube demo, we can easily summarize the System-Two surface plot changes:

1. Define a contour grid object to accept the z values.
2. Define z = f(x, y) grid functions.
3. Define a viewing transform.
4. Transform the contour coordinates.
5. Draw the contour coordinates.

As mentioned previously, it's at the point of drawing services that System One comes into play. We need to create the graphics environment and its canvas must exist, specify the window-viewport mapping, and map the resultant projection points to device coordinates using System-One routines.

The graphics environment and canvas code that handles System-One details is identical to the cube demo, so I haven't repeated it here. The window-viewport mapping is slightly different, so I've repeated the discussion sequence from the cube example starting at this point. The viewing transformation generation is identical, using the Newman-Sproull sample viewpoint. Viewing transformation usage and projection are slightly changed, though. Here's the order of topics:

- window-viewport mapping,
- object-representation and instantiation,
- surface plot functions,
- transformation usage,
- projection, and
- drawing.

Window-Viewport Mapping and User-to-Device Coordinate Mapping

The range of values for the surface plot is greater than the range for the cube, which is reflected in the window-viewport code. In the parallel case, a range from [-50,-50] to [50,50] is chosen. In the perspective case, we choose [-6,-6] to [6,6]. Once again, the differential is about a factor of 10; the image is being scaled by about an order of magnitude to account for the effect of the perspective division. See Listing 7-72 for the code.

Listing 7-72.   Window-Viewport Hacking for Appearance's Sake

```
switch(vtype)
   {
    case CMD_ORTHO:
        pv->rW.left   = -50.0;
        pv->rW.bottom = -50.0;
        pv->rW.top    =  50.0;
        pv->rW.right  =  50.0;
        G3D_WV_SetWindow(pv->genv,
                         pv->rW.left,  pv->rW.bottom,
                         pv->rW.right, pv->rW.top);
        G3D_WV_SetViewport(pv->genv,
                           pv->rV.left, pv->rV.top,
                           pv->rV.right,pv->rV.bottom);
        break;
    case CMD_PERSP:
        pv->rW.left   = -6.0;
        pv->rW.bottom = -6.0;
        pv->rW.top    =  6.0;
        pv->rW.right  =  6.0;
        break;
   }
   G3D_WV_SetWindow(pv->genv,
                    pv->rW.left,  pv->rW.bottom,
                    pv->rW.right, pv->rW.top);
   G3D_WV_SetViewport(pv->genv,
                      pv->rV.left, pv->rV.top,
       pv->rV.right,pv->rV.bottom);
```

Object Representation and Instantiation

The surface plot defines a rectangular array to match the (i, j) grid to the extent of the function evaluation. Then, for every (i, j), we evaluate a function of (x, y), substituting x and y. This generates a series of values, typically called z values, as a result. These are stored in the array as "elevations" in the contour grid array *contourMap*. This defines the set of (x, y, z)s needed to graph a surface plot. Listing 7-73 contains the function *SetEdges*. It sets up multiple surface plots based on various equations, which I'll cover in more detail in the next section. Listing 7-74 contains a sample invocation.

Listing 7-73.   SetEdges

```
VECTOR4D    contourMap[31][31];    /* -15 to 15*/

void WINAPI SetEdges( int nObj, int vtype)
{
   int  i,j;
   int s,t;

   switch(nObj) {
      case 0:
         CreateSExpFunction();
         break;
      case 1:
         CreateSCosFunction();
         break;
      case 2:
         CreateSSinFunction();
         break;
      case 3:
         CreateLExpFunction();
         break;
      case 4:
         CreateLCosFunction();
         break;
      case 5:
         CreateLSinFunction();
         break;
   }
   return;
}
```

Listing 7-74.   SetEdges Invocation

```
//set surface
   SetEdges(nCurObject, vtype);
```

Surface Plot Functions

Here we look at three basic functions: exp, cosine, and sine. There are two variants, *simple* and *large*, that can be generated for any of these functions.

Each function generator iterates across the (i, j) grid and calculates and assigns the "z-elevation" to the contour grid array. The functions plotted include the following.

- SExp = exp(-.1 * x2)+1
- SCos = 2*cos(i+1) + 1
- SSin = 2*sin(i+1) + 1
- LExp = 7*exp(-.1*x2*y2) + 1
- LCos =cos(x*y) + 1
- LSin = 2 * sin(sqrt(x2*y2))+1

Listing 7-75 contains one of these generator functions as an example. For the rest of the code, see your examples disk.

Listing 7-75. LSin Function Generator

```
void CreateLSinFunction()
{
int  i,j;
int s,t;
double x,y,z,c;

  for (i = -15; i<= 15; i++)  {
    x = i/2.0;
    for (j = -15; j<= 15; j++) {
      y = j/2.0;
      c = x*x + y*y;
      z = 2 * (sin( sqrt( c ) ) + 1) + 1;
      s = i+15;
      t = j+15;
      contourMap[s][t].x = x;
      contourMap[s][t].y = y;
      contourMap[s][t].z = z;
      contourMap[s][t].w = 1;
    }
  }
}
```

Viewing Transformation: Usage

In a manner similar to the cube demo, the main transformation process shown in Listing 7-76 sets the edges, transforms them, projects them, and draws them.

Listing 7-76. Basic Viewing Usage

```
//  reset vertices
   SetEdges(nCurObject, vtype);
//  do wc-ec,project
   TransformEdges(nCurObject,vtype,
              vtype == CMD_PERSP ? tPerspProj : tParaProj);
   ProjectEdges(nCurObject,vtype,
              vtype == CMD_PERSP ? tPerspProj : tParaProj)
//  draw it
   DrawSurfaceEdges( pv,rtype,nCurObject,hDC);
  nCurObject++;
```

Listing 7-77 shows the internals of *TransformEdges*. It invokes *G3D_Xfrm_TransformPoint* on its own behalf. The twist is iterating across the grid rather than across each point of the cube.

Listing 7-77. TransformEdges

```
void WINAPI TransformEdges( int nObj, int vtype, LPMATRIX4D Tx )
{
   int  i,j;
   int  s,t;

   for (i = -15; i<= 15; i++)  {
     x = i/2.0;
     for (j = -15; j<= 15; j++) {
         s = i+15;
         t = j+15;
         G3D_Xfrm_TransformPoint((LPVECTOR4D) &contourMap[s][t],
                                       contourMap[s][t],
                                       Tx);
     }
   }
   return;
}
```

Projection Transformation: Usage
The projection operation is also very similar to the cube example. It invokes
G3D_Xfrm_ProjectPoint, as shown in Listing 7-78, across the grid.

Listing 7-78. ProjectEdges

```
void WINAPI ProjectEdges( int nObj, int vtype, LPMATRIX4D Tx )
{
   int  i,j;
   int  s,t;

   for (i = -15; i<= 15; i++)  {
     x = i/2.0;
     for (j = -15; j<= 15; j++) {
         s = i+15;
         t = j+15;
         G3D_Xfrm_ProjectPoint((LPVECTOR4D) &contourMap[s][t],
                                     contourMap[s][t],
                       vtype == CMD_PERSP ? PERSPECTIVE : PARALLEL);
     }
   }
   return;
}
```

Drawing: Wireframe, Hidden-Line, and Solid-Color
Drawing the surface plot again takes three forms: wireframe, hidden-line, and solid-color.
   Again, we use a trick for hidden-line. By painting the surface from back to front, we can
approximate the "painters" algorithm. Since the viewpoint doesn't change, it is easy to do
this with no checking code.

Listing 7-79 contains wireframe drawing function *DrawSurfacePlot*. It iterates down the rows and draws a sequence of lines using polyline, then iterates down the columns doing likewise. This results in a rectangular grid. It also means that the minimum number of lines is drawn.

Listing 7-79.   DrawSurfacePlot

```
void DrawSurfacePlot(VWWND* pv,HDC hDC)
{
VECTOR4D  p,p1,p2;
POINT     pgdi[30];
int       i,j;
long      xv1,xv2,yv1,yv2;

  for (i = -14; i <= 15; i++)
  {
      for (j = -14; j<= 15; j++)
      {
          G3D_Coords_UsertoDev(pv->genv,
                          contourMap[i-1+15][j-1+15].x,
                          contourMap[i-1+15][j-1+15].y,
                          &xv1,&yv1);
          pgdi[j-1+15].x = xv1;
          pgdi[j-1+15].y = yv1;
      }
      G3D_GEnv_Polyline(pv->genv,(LPPOINT)&pgdi,30,NULL);
      if (PeekMessage(&g_app.msg, NULL, 0, 0, PM_REMOVE))
      {
            TranslateMessage(&g_app.msg);
            DispatchMessage(&g_app.msg);
      }
  }
  for (j = -14; j<= 15; j++)
  {
      for (i = -14; i <= 15; i++)
      {
          G3D_Coords_UsertoDev(pv->genv,
                          contourMap[i-1+15][j-1+15].x,
                          contourMap[i-1+15][j-1+15].y,
                          &xv1,&yv1);
          pgdi[i-1+15].x = xv1;
          pgdi[i-1+15].y = yv1;
      }
      G3D_GEnv_Polyline(pv->genv,(LPPOINT)&pgdi,30,NULL);
      if (PeekMessage(&g_app.msg, NULL, 0, 0, PM_REMOVE))
      {
            TranslateMessage(&g_app.msg);
            DispatchMessage(&g_app.msg);
      }
  }
}
```

Listing 7-80 contains the hidden-line (another cheating way) function *DrawHiddenSurfacePlot*. Instead of drawing x, y lines, it draws polygons. In this case the polygons are filled with a default white brush to give a "monochrome" effect, but I'll talk more on that in the attribute section. It again cheats to determine surface visibility. By drawing the polygons in a back-to-front order, we can approximate a "painters" algorithm, with no checking, for a scene that doesn't move.

Listing 7-80.   DrawHiddenSurfacePlot

```
void DrawHiddenSurfacePlot(VWWND* pv,HDC hDC)
{
VECTOR4D p,p1,p2;
POINT    pgdi[5];
int      i,j;
long     xv1,xv2,yv1,yv2;

  for (i = -14; i <= 15; i++)
  {
    for (j = -14; j<= 15; j++)
    {
      G3D_Coords_UsertoDev(pv->genv,
                     contourMap[i-1+15][j-1+15].x,
                     contourMap[i-1+15][j-1+15].y,
                     &xv1,&yv1);
      pgdi[0].x = xv1;
      pgdi[0].y = yv1;

      G3D_Coords_UsertoDev(pv->genv,
                     contourMap[i+15][j-1+15].x,
                     contourMap[i+15][j-1+15].y,
                     &xv1,&yv1);
      pgdi[1].x = xv1;
      pgdi[1].y = yv1;

      G3D_Coords_UsertoDev(pv->genv,
                     contourMap[i+15][j+15].x,
                     contourMap[i+15][j+15].y,
                     &xv1,&yv1);
      pgdi[2].x = xv1;
      pgdi[2].y = yv1;

      G3D_Coords_UsertoDev(pv->genv,
                     contourMap[i-1+15][j+15].x,
                     contourMap[i-1+15][j+15].y,
                     &xv1,&yv1);
      pgdi[3].x = xv1;
      pgdi[3].y = yv1;
```

```
        G3D_Coords_UsertoDev(pv->genv,
                              contourMap[i-1+15][j-1+15].x,
                              contourMap[i-1+15][j-1+15].y,
                              &xv1,&yv1);
        pgdi[4].x = xv1;
        pgdi[4].y = yv1;

        G3D_GEnv_Polygon(pv->genv,(LPPOINT)&pgdi,5,NULL,NULL);
      }
      if (PeekMessage(&g_app.msg, NULL, 0, 0, PM_REMOVE))
      {
            TranslateMessage(&g_app.msg);
            DispatchMessage(&g_app.msg);
      }
   }
}
```

Finally, the solid-color drawing routine *DrawShadedSurfacePlot* is exactly like *DrawHiddenSurfacePlot*, differing only in attribute usage. Because of this similarity and for space reasons, I'm not going to show you *DrawShadedSufacePlot* here. For the code, see your examples disk.

Drawing Attributes

There are two parts to attribute strategy: polygon outlines and interiors.

Depending on the canvas style, the pen that either draws or outlines the polygon (determined by rendering method) is chosen based on the canvas background style. A white pen is used for a black background and a black pen is used for a white background. Listing 7-81 contains a code segment that illustrates pen selection.

Listing 7-81.   Line Attribute Code — Pen Determination and Selection

```
...
   switch(bckclr)
   {
      case CMD_WHITE:
          FillRect(hDC, &rV, GetStockObject(bckclr-CMD_BCKBASE));
          SelectObject(hDC, hBlackPen);
          break;
      case CMD_BLACK:
          FillRect(hDC, &rV, GetStockObject(bckclr-CMD_BCKBASE));
          SelectObject(hDC, hWhitePen);
          break;
   }
...
```

The polygon fill attribute is a little trickier. For monochrome hidden-line plots, the default brush (white) is used to fill. This means that the white pen against the white brush, in the case of a black background, disappears into nothingness. For that case, the black pen is used instead and is overridden with code similar to Listing 7-81 but testing for rendering type instead of background color type.

We now have monochrome handled sufficiently, but what about color? At this point, all we can implement without resorting to an illumination model (which we've only talked about on the high level so far) is a "gradient" of a particular color. By carefully cycling through the gradient, we can achieve the appearance of shading, because from one far corner (say left, top) to the other (say right, bottom), the colors will appear to change in shade. The trick here is generating and using the gradient of colors. Three actions, coupled together, make this possible:

- arbitrary gradient color palette generation,
- brush array creation using gradient colors, and
- gradient color cycling during drawing.

The gradient colors are arbitrarily assigned red, magenta, blue, aqua, green, and orange as shown in Listing 7-82.

Listing 7-82.   Gradient Palette Colors

```
#define RED      RGB(255,0,  0)
#define MAGENTA RGB(255,0,  255)
#define BLUE     RGB(0,0,255)
#define AQUA     RGB(0,  255,255)
#define GREEN    RGB(0,  255,0)
#define ORANGE   RGB(255,128, 0)
#define NUMSHADECOL 15
```

Listing 7-83 contains *InitRGBPalette*, which uses these definitions to build a Windows GDI Palette object using *WL_Pal_Create* when the palette specification is complete.

Listing 7-83.   InitRGBPalette

```
HPALETTE InitRGBPalette(void){
    HPALETTE    hp;
    CRT         crtValue;
    int         run, shade,n;
// setup palette for NUMSHADECOL shades of 6 colors
    pPal = (LOGPALETTE *)LocalAlloc(LPTR,sizeof(LOGPALETTE) +
 (NUMSHADECOL*6)* sizeof(PALETTEENTRY));
    if ( !pPal )
        return 0;
    pPal->palNumEntries = NUMSHADECOL*6;
    pPal->palVersion    = 0x300;
    n                   = 0;
    for (run=0; run<6; run++) {
```

```
                 COLORREF crTableEntry;
                 COLORREF c;
                 crTableEntry   = ColorMapTable[run];
                 crtValue.cGreen = GetGValue(crTableEntry);
                 crtValue.cBlue  = GetBValue(crTableEntry);
                 crtValue.cRed   = GetRValue(crTableEntry);
                 for (shade=0; shade<NUMSHADECOL; shade++){
                     switch(run){
                         case 0:
                             crtValue.cRed   -= 8;
                             break;
                         case 1:
                             crtValue.cRed   -= 8;
                             crtValue.cBlue  -= 8;
                             break;
                         case 2:
                             crtValue.cBlue  -= 8;
                             break;
                         case 3:
                             crtValue.cGreen -= 8;
                             crtValue.cGreen -= 8;
                             break;
                         case 4:
                             crtValue.cGreen -= 8;
                             break;
                         case 5:
                             crtValue.cRed   -= 8;
                             crtValue.cGreen -= 4;
                             break;
                     }
                     /* assign into palette */
                     pPal->palPalEntry[n].peRed   = crtValue.cRed;
                     pPal->palPalEntry[n].peGreen = crtValue.cGreen;
                     pPal->palPalEntry[n].peBlue  = crtValue.cBlue;
                     pPal->palPalEntry[n].peFlags = PC_NOCOLLAPSE;
                     /* bump pointer */
                     n++;
                 }
             }
         }
         hp = WL_Pal_Create(pPal);
         return hp;
}
```

The usual application palette policy that handles WM_QUERYNEWPALETTE and WM_PALETTECHANGED messages holds here as well, but we can't rely on our usual blitheness about the WM_PAINT message and palette selection if we want palette animation. Remember, since the canvas permanently selects the palette into the memory DC and the palette message handlers synchronize the client DC and the memory DC, if the palette message handlers do their job, the usual paint logic ignores palettes. If the palette is animated, though, it is not a static beast, and the canvas then needs updating. Also, for ease-of-use, palettes to be animated should not be identity palettes. Identity palettes contain the system colors at either end. Animating cycles entries from end-to-end. Adding the system colors breaks the smoothness of the gradient animation. Within the range of the defined colors, 15 shades are stepped off by increments of 8 in the 0-256 CRT color-space range.

Instead of freeing the palette memory immediately, as most code examples show, the palette specification is then retained and used to create an array of brushes. Listing 7-84 contains *InitBrushArray* and *FreeBrushArray*, which implement a "pre-creation" brush strategy. This strategy of pre-creating all brushes achieves a major performance improvement over "at-need" creation strategy.

Listing 7-84.   Brush Array Functions

```
BOOL WINAPI InitBrushArray(void)
{
    int      n;
    COLORREF c;

    for (n=palpad; n<NUMSHADECOL*6+palpad; n++)
    {
        c = PALETTERGB(pPal->palPalEntry[n].peRed,
                       pPal->palPalEntry[n].peGreen,
                       pPal->palPalEntry[n].peBlue);
        rgbPal[n-palpad] = CreateSolidBrush(c);
    }

    return TRUE;
}
//
// release a "reserved" palette
//
BOOL WINAPI FreeBrushArray(void)
{
    int         n;

    for (n=0; n<NUMSHADECOL*6; n++)
        if ( rgbPal[n] )
            DeleteObject(rgbPal[n]);
    LocalFree((HANDLE)pPal);

    return TRUE;
}
```

Strictly speaking, we also need to note that animating the palette will introduce an alignment problem for drawing. For that reason, we'll add a reset command to the palette vocabulary.

Once the brushes are created, we select an offset in the brush array, depending on the polygon's place in the grid. Listing 7-85 shows the relevant code blocks extracted from *DrawShadedSurfacePlot*.

Listing 7-85.   Brush and Shade Selection

```
...
for (i = -14; i <= 15; i++)
{
  run   = nCurObject*NUMSHADECOL;
  shade = (i-1+15)/2;
  hOldBrush = SelectObject(hDC, rgbPal[run + shade]);
...
```

This relatively crude system means that in the original palette placement, each grid iterates across a color that slowly changes in shade. Figure 7-25 shows a grayscale rendition of the LExp grid.

Figure 7-25.   Grayscaled Surface Plot of LExp Function

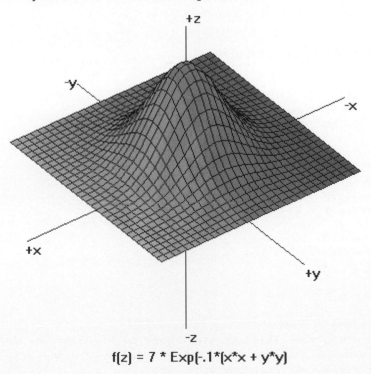

$$f[z] = 7 * Exp[-.1*(x*x + y*y)]$$

Variation: Simple Camera Viewing System

The simple camera system is like the original cube demo with the viewing-system construction changed. Once the from-lookat system is implemented, it's natural for you to want to move the camera. Hooking up the keyboard to manipulate camera positioning is quite easy at this point. The changes for the simple camera cube demo are summarized in two steps:

1. Define a from-lookat viewing transformation.
2. Enable interactivity by allowing the camera to be moved under keyboard control.

We've already covered the other elements of this demo, including the rest of Systems One and Two. None of our object representation, object generation, or attribute manipulation changes either.

Viewing Transformation: Generation

The main differences in this viewing transformation setup are the number and form of the parameters — there are more and they are slightly different. We use helper functions liberally. The first code block shown in Listing 7-86 actually comes from function *InitViewpoint*. It, in turn, uses helpers *setAt* and *setFrom*, which simply set the components of the desired vector to the input parameters (they're not shown here).

Listing 7-86.   From-Lookat Generation

```
...
//clipping/scaling
  pv->vd     = 60;
  pv->vs     = 15;
//viewing
  setAt(pv,0,0,0);
  setFrom(pv,
          pv->at.x + 2 * pv->vd/pv->vs,
          pv->at.y + 2 * pv->vd/pv->vs,
          pv->at.z + 2 * pv->vd/pv->vs);
//
  pv->up.x   = 0;
  pv->up.y   = 0;
  pv->up.z   = 1;
//
  pv->hrzR   = 0;
...
//init 3d viewing system
  tParaProj  = G3D_View_InitCamera(pv->genv,pv->from,pv->at,pv->up,
                                   pv->hrzR,pv->vd,pv-.vs);
  tPerspProj = G3D_View_InitCamera(pv->genv,pv->from,pv->at,pv->up,
                                   pv->hrzR,pv->vd,pv->vs);
...
```

All of this simply feeds *G3D_View_InitCamera*, and receives a viewing transformation matrix or CTM in return. That matrix is used in the transformation phase of the pipeline. The pipeline uses the usual pair of *G3D_Xfrm_TransformPoint* and *G3D_Xfrm_ProjectPoint* to generate screen coordinates and *G3D_Coords_UsertoDevice* to map them to canvas coordinates before using an output primitive. You have already seen it all so I've not repeated it here. The important detail here is the ability to move the camera and generate multiple views of a single scene.

Camera Positioning: Keyboard Control

Hooking the keyboard up to the camera is as simple as defining a key-binding and writing the code to modify the from x, y, and z values based on those keys.

Listing 7-87 contains the code block extracted from the WM_KEYDOWN handler *View_OnKey*.

Listing 7-87.   Key Handling Code Block

```
...

   switch ( vk ) {
     case VK_UP:
        pv->from.y += t_inc;
        if ( !bFixed )
          pv->at.y   += t_inc;
        break;
     case VK_DOWN:
        pv->from.y -= t_inc;
        if ( !bFixed )
          pv->at.y   -= t_inc;
        break;
     case VK_LEFT:
        pv->from.x -= t_inc;
        if ( !bFixed )
          pv->at.x   -= t_inc;
        break;
     case VK_RIGHT:
        pv->from.x += t_inc;
        if ( !bFixed )
          pv->at.x   += t_inc;
        break;
     case VK_PRIOR:
     case VK_NUMPAD9:
        pv->from.z += t_inc;
        if ( !bFixed )
          pv->at.z   += t_inc;
        break;
     case VK_NEXT:
```

Listing 7-87.   (*cont.*)

```
case VK_NUMPAD3:
        pv->from.z -= t_inc;
        if ( !bFixed )
          pv->at.z   -= t_inc;
        break;
    default:
        return;
        break;
  }
...
```

Remember how, in the cascaded MakeApp architecture, the frame layer handed this message to the client layer, which then directed it to the proper (in this case only) child pane? The key-binding used is shown in Table 7-5.

Table 7-5.   Camera Control Key-Bindings

VK Key	Action	Note
VK_LEFT	-x	
VK_RIGHT	+x	
VK_UP	+y	
VK_DOWN	-y	
VK_NEXT	-z	Page-down key
VK_NUMPAD3		Same with numlock on
VK_PRIOR	+z	Page-up key
VK_NUMPAD9		Same with numlock on

This allows for basic scene positioning. If you want to take advantage of more advanced features that remain dormant, you're now ready. For instance, you could pull the horizon rotation angle out to the interface, allowing you to twist the camera as you fly.

Camera Positioning: Viewing System Regeneration

Viewing system regeneration, again, turns out to be quite simple. The result of modifying the from position from Listing 7-87 is fed into *G3D_View_MoveCamera* to return an updated CTM.

Based on this, we can render a new image. Listing 7-88 contains a code block illustrating this action.

Listing 7-88.   Camera-Positioning Code Block

```
...
//
// move the camera
//
  G3D_View_MoveCamera(pv->genv,tParaProj, pv->from,pv->at,pv->up,
        pv->hrzR,pv->vd,pv->vs);
```

```
      G3D_View_MoveCamera(pv->genv,tPerspProj,pv->from,pv->at,pv->up,
          pv->hrzR,pv->vd,pv->vs);
//
// rewalk objects
//
  hDC   = (HDC)G3D_GEnv_GetVal(pv->genv,ID_DC);
  PaintCube(pv,hDC);
  InvalidateRect(pv->hwnd,NULL,TRUE);
...
```

The output of all of this is much the same as the rotating cube, but you can change the viewpoint. Figure 7-26 shows a distant view of the cube to illustrate the effect of moving the viewpoint further away, receding it, if you will.

Figure 7-26.   Distant From-Lookat Cube Screenshot

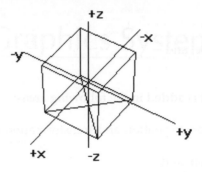

Summary

Geometry needs to be defined, generated, and manipulated.
    Our system is based on a triad of components:

- vectors,
- matrix transformations, and
- viewing system primitives.

We use a "pseudo-homogeneous" representation for coordinates, mainly for the convenience of 4x4 matrix representation.
    We've followed, wherever appropriate, the API implementation formula of element-access routines, in addition to:

- instance-management routines,
- instance-generating operations, and
- in-place operations.

8

Modeling, Modeling Support Services, and Description Languages

In This Chapter

- Discussion of WinMod3D modeling architecture and the M3D modeler support services at the next level of detail.
- Expansion of the conceptual MVC triad into implementation, unifying the four phases of the modeler.
- Another look at the M3D contents, leading to the development of the M3D front-end support for the description languages.
- Discussion of translation issues and the benefits of applying formal language skills and tools to the problem. This includes a discussion of front-end features in general, including separation into modeling and scene languages.
- Description of the modeling language elements, and their parser shell and general tokenizer.
- Description of the scene-description language elements.

Introduction

With the development of the DLL service libraries behind us, we'll continue our quest for a 3D modeling application by implementing the M3D Support Services. We'll also do some further construction on the WinMod3D modeler itself. The construction of the modeler and development of the support routines are tightly coupled. The phases and needs of the WinMod3D modeling application dictate the content of the M3D support services much like the general requirements for performing vector graphics in a raster windowing environment force the contents of the WLib and the G3DLib.

This chapter consists of two main sections. The first is concerned with architecture; the second starts the implementation. There are three parts to describing the architecture. Part one describes the strategic plan from which the construction process of both the modeler and the support services is guided. Part two goes into detail about WinMod3D construction and the MVC internals implemented here. Part three partitions the support services to correspond to the phases of the modeler. Once we've dealt with the architecture, implementation begins with the front-end and description languages.

Modeler Architecture Part I: WinMod3D Strategic Plan

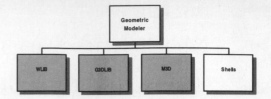

This discussion centers around six architectural concepts:

1. Separate modeling and scene description languages,
2. User-definable color and material lookup tables with binary search by name,
3. "Glue" provided by the dual representation of objects and a viewing system based on a single specification for both polygon and ray-trace modes,
4. Process flow support using repetitive data structures and mapping functions,
5. MVC support with a state machine "controlling" the "model" (or internal data structures), multiple views, and the user interface, and
6. M3D support services that provide helper functions for each phase of the modeler.

Modeling and Scene-Description Language

Scene geometry is not enough to drive the modeler; there are certain control parameters at a higher level than the geometry. We explicitly recognize this in our design and separate these parameters out into a ".mod" modeling script. With the .mod file, both these additional control parameters and the scene-geometry file are specified. The scene-geometry file contains the typical viewpoint, background, lights, and individual object definitions. The modeling script sets up the scene description, which, in turn, describes the object list. Both of these script languages are what Jon Bently calls *little languages* in *More Programming Peals* (Addison-Wesley, 1988). They share this property, and with a simplification can share a tokenizer to ease the process of parsing language elements.

Color and Material Lookup Tables

A user-defined lookup scheme for color and material specification enhances the extensibility of the modeler, but this is not the only reason to take this extra effort. Hard-coding two large tables for these specifications would take more space in the data segment than is currently available or even prudent to use. The DS (Data Segment) memory usage alone would dictate this action, but considered with the benefit of extensibility, this is an easy decision.

Object Representation and Viewing System

The glue holding this together is the combination of a dual viewing system and a dual object representation scheme derived from a common source. The 3D object and its dual representation and the pipeline and its dual representation are equally important. The polygon-mode pipeline is represented by a 4x4 (or 4D) matrix, sometimes known as a

Composite Transformation Matrix (CTM), that uses the pinhole camera specification contained in the scene description. The ray-trace pipeline is represented by a set of 4D vectors that also use the pinhole camera specification.

The scene description is translated to build the 3D object list. The underlying 3D object-list data structure provides a dual representation based on the single specification contained in the scene description. We use this directly in polygon mode, and we can also use it with a round-robin geometrical approach to derive the ray-trace representation.

The finishing touch is the use of the single viewing system specification to build the polygon and ray-trace mode pipelines. At this point, both the objects that result in the image and the operations necessary to create that image exist in memory.

Process-Flow Support

Whenever a process must be applied to a repetitive data structure like a list or a tree, mapping functions can simplify the code by delegating to each object the responsibility of performing the action. Adding these mapping functions to a data structure definition gives us some of the benefits of object-oriented programming, albeit in a crude sense. This, in essence, allows us to invert loops across a list by moving the code within the mapping function. The looping control structure then simply invokes the appropriate mapping function and each object operates on itself.

There are two major benefits to this approach. First, the pipeline process is now captured in the mapping functions and the control loops. Second, each 3D object is a self-contained entity, which minimizes the effort required to add a new object.

MVC Support

The overall organizing principle is the very simple MVC implementation you first saw (in some detail) in Chapter 2. It gives us a way to handle the task of managing internal data structures, output, and user input, and is a dominant feature in the changes to the MakeApp shell that result in WinMod3D. The entire MVC scheme consists of a formal controller that manages the presentation of a rendering (view) of internal data (model).

A common implementation method for controllers is the *state machine* or, more properly, the *Finite State Machine (FSM)*. Using an FSM along with internal-control variables makes it easy to arbitrate when an action may take place, greatly simplifying your management of the user interface. For instance, it is nice to be able to prevent the user from opening a new file while the modeler is pipelining thousands of polygons. Since the transformation process operates on the current model and its scene, and opening a file deletes that memory and allocates a new model and a new scene, this action is a potential catastrophe.

M3D Support Services

The Modeler Support Services, or M3D, are a group of functions that are separate from the core WinMod3D code, but, due to their direct dependence on the modeler, are not completely general. While not as nice as a DLL, this is not a complete hardship. The M3D contains the following subsystems:

- Front-End, Part I   Description language support,
- Front-End, Part II   3D object instantiation support,
- Core Functions, Part I   World manipulation support,
- Core Functions, Part II   World rendering support, and
- Post-Processing   Color analysis support.

Front-end actions begin with the need to specify a 3D world and end with the instantiation of the 3D objects that make up the desired scene. The front end provides a parser and translates from an external disk representation into the internal representation used by the modeler. This happens in the model and scene specification phases.

The separation into two specification phases enables growth toward a multi-scene capability. Once the front end has finished its I/O task and provided the "food" for world generation, its tasks are over. Functions that support both general-language parsing actions and 3D object instantiation enable assembly of the front end.

The guts of the modeler, supported by the core functions, come into play next, using the data structures that represent the objects from world generation to feed the viewing pipeline. This includes both the world manipulation and world rendering phases. "Manipulation" here means camera movement and world transformation since, if you remember, we're not supporting editing functions. The user can manipulate the camera position and the view of the computer-simulated world. A geometry engine takes in world coordinates and generates eye coordinates. Rendering means output, including:

- wireframe,
- monochrome hidden line,
- solid-color hidden line,
- flat-shaded, and
- ray-traced.

This wide range of output helps support picture generation by enabling an incremental approach to picture composition. First, generate a wireframe rendition to make sure the image (in general) appears as you wish. Then use the solid-color and flat-shaded modes to verify basic color and lighting details. When all of the elements of your image are ready, you use ray-trace mode to generate your final images.

This is well and good, but there's another purpose lurking behind this system: dual representation and the range of drawing modes is also a testbed for 3D modelers. Following the process of designing and implementing a system like this forces you to think through the issues, see the limitations, and realize where you can tweak this system to get a little more out of it. Making pretty pictures and learning about modeler internals at the same time — what more could you ask for?

Color — that's what! Remember, 256-color mode needs some assistance before we can display the images in color. Our image is grayscaled "on-the-fly," and then we do basic color analysis on the data. There are two color-analysis methods supported: the popularity algorithm and the median-cut algorithm.

With the support of the geometry library, you're now ready to begin constructing the modeler.

Key facts about the modeler include the following:

- The modeler supports two representations, explicit and analytic, to enable both polygon drawing and object tracing.
- Color and material tables are user-definable.
- Polygon-based objects and ray objects share surface properties.
- Both shading and tracing are done using a common viewing definition.
- The polygon visibility determination uses a huge block of memory and quicksort.
- Histograms, intensity buffers, and color analysis combine with the use of off-screen bitmaps to enable color image generation, even on 256-color displays.

The dual representation scheme allows both polygon drawing and object tracing to be performed in the same modeler. In this respect, it is a critical element of the modeler, the effects of which are apparent in a great deal of the internals.

Surface properties depend on three concepts: color, surface property coefficients, and texture definitions. In this implementation, objects are defined in terms of a color and a material. A material is then composed of surface-property coefficients and a texture definition, which allows a powerful surface-property descriptive capability.

Both ways of looking at the world, polygon-based and ray-object-based, use this surface-property definition scheme and a common definition for the viewing system, but they diverge quickly from there. Polygon drawing uses the G3DLib to generate a matrix representing a camera and transforms the explicit vertex points using that matrix. The object tracer uses the viewpoint definition to create the initial ray, and then uses that to generate the image.

Visibility determination is another area of divergence. Polygons undergo a visibility determination process using the viewpoint and the surface normal. This is known as *backface culling*. The visible polygons are then collected in a separate list and further manipulated. This is a two-step process consisting of first sorting and then drawing the polygons. Usually, we use a bubble sort to order the polygons. A bubble sort is extremely simple and uses minimal memory, making it a clear choice for the DOS environment. This is Windows, though. With a little bit of work, we can handle blocks of memory larger than 64K, and up-to-date runtime libraries from compiler vendors handle these blocks. So in Windows we can use the RTL quicksort and save both coding and execution time. We save coding time since we're employing reuse. We save execution time, since the quicksort algorithm is an $O(NlogN)$ algorithm, where bubble sort is an $O(N^2)$ (the dreaded quadratic). You might not think this is such a big deal, but when you're rendering 20,000 or more polygons you start to regard such details a bit differently. And, yes, this modeler will handle that many polygons, provided the machine you are executing on has enough memory (16MB for models of that size). All of this is to determine visibility for polygons, while the ray-tracing process itself determines visibility.

Finally, this whole quest is all about generating color images. On machines with at least 32K colors, we can use direct color assignment. But in case you're not so lucky, we'll make provisions for the 256-color adapters by using color analysis and post-processing.

That, in a nutshell, is what it's all about. Looking ahead, the next two sections present more in-depth discussions of both the architecture and the library. Once that is out of the way, we'll start all over again with implementation. Table 8-1 maps the M3D to the phases of the modeler and the chapters and topics of Part III.

Table 8-1.   Modeler and Support Services, by Chapter and Topic

M3D	Modeler	Chapter and Topic
	State machine	Ch 8, Architecture
	Mapping functions	
Front End Part I	Tokenizing,Parsing	Ch 8, Description Languages
	World generation	
Front End Part II	World generation	Ch 9, Object Instantiation
	Mapping functions	
Core Functions Part I	World manipulation	Ch10, Polygons and Objects
	Mapping functions	
Core Functions Part II	World rendering	Ch 10, Shading and Texturing
	Mapping functions	
	State machine	Ch 11, Architecture
Post-Processing	Post-processing	Ch 11, Color Analysis

There's a lot of material to cover. With the complete source on your disk, though, you can take your time to go through it at your own speed. In this book, I'll cover each topic in detail, but I haven't included every line of code. The discussions of each topic are to help you understand the process, not just the code; so I've only included the critical blocks in the text.

Modeler Architecture Part II: WinMod3D and MVC

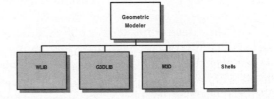

Chapter 2 introduced you to the basics of MVC-style architecture. There we extended the foundation MakeApp code to implement a layered-view architecture. By adding a controller to this base and allowing the controller to arbitrate between the user interface (menus, keyboard), the display area (main image view and alternate views), and the modeling data structures, we can implement a simple MVC.

Figure 8-1 shows the relationships within this infrastructure. The controller is central to this scheme, even if it is only one leg of the tripod. It arbitrates the user interface, handles ownership of key internal data structures, and drives the display. You're probably thinking that we'll need some truly gnarly code to perform all this magic. Wrong. The beauty of a state machine is that the code is extremely simple. All it takes is a couple of data structure definitions, one table containing internal logic, and about a page of code for the main driver function.

First, though, you need some definitions:

- State   The current activity or process of machine.
- Event   An input to the machine.
- Transition   A change of state based on valid input.

Figure 8-1.   MVC Relationships in Detail

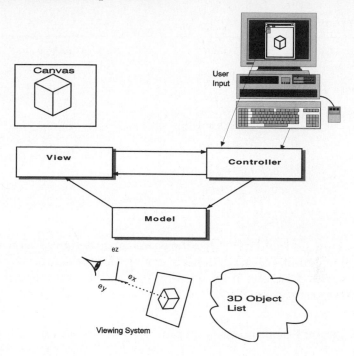

Instead of controlling a device or parsing process, this state machine controls the activity of the modeler. State machines are defined by a table consisting of valid states, valid events for each state, the next state, and the transition from one state to the next, together with the main driver. In our implementation, the transition logic is contained in functions represented by function pointers invoked by the driver on the transition.

Once you've implemented a state machine, you move to the task of hooking up the pieces to it, in other words, allowing it to assume control, which provides a logical ordering of the necessary steps for the construction process. How you build the state machine becomes the primary question.

The basics of developing a state machine are taken straight from parsing theory. Parsing, or *syntax analysis,* uses a state machine as its mechanism for extracting tokens from an input stream, including checking the validity of a particular token. This is similar to what the modeler needs. It has an input stream of events, and needs to determine if that event is "legal" in the current state.

This type of problem is well-suited to a *State Transition Diagram* (or STD), which can be "solved" using a Finite State Machine or FSM. An STD contains states, arcs, and labeled events like Figure 8-2. An FSM is a machine (in this case, a process or function) that controls the execution of code through a sequence of well-defined actions for each state. Practically speaking though, the nice thing about STDs and FSMs is that it's particularly easy to implement an FSM to act on an STD as a simple table-driven executive or driver function that takes as its input an event and changes the machine state to the next state if the transition is legal. A sample table entry is shown in Listing 8-1.

Listing 8-1.　State Table Fragment

```
// State       Event          Next_State          F_List
// ─────────────────────────────────────────────────────────
   S_OFF,      E_POWER,       S_POWER,            power_state,0,0,0,
```

Figure 8-2.　State Transitions

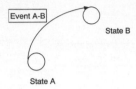

This table uses function definitions, like the power_state definition shown in Listing 8-2. The driver function definition is also shown in Listing 8-2. It takes an event, scans the table entries for the current state, and if the event is legal in that state executes the indicated functions and changes the state.

Listing 8-2.　Example Transition Logic and Main Driver Function Definitions

```
int FAR power_state(STATE * cur);
int FAR driver(int ev, STATE * cur);
```

That briefly covers the "how"; the "what" is introduced with a list of the events supported by this state machine, as shown in Listing 8-3. These can be broken down as follows:

- machine and table control,
- ready state control,
- transformation and rendering control,
- save, print, and quantize — image buffer operations, and
- rendering run control (interrupt and done).

Listing 8-3.　State Machine Valid Events

```
//events
#define E_POWER          1
#define E_SCENE_IN       2
#define E_SCENE_OUT      3
#define E_CALC_VIEW      4
#define E_CHANGE_VIEW    5
#define E_CHANGE_RENDER  6
```

```
#define E_CHANGE_OPTIONS 7
#define E_IMAGE_QUANT    8
#define E_IMAGE_SAVE     9
#define E_IMAGE_PRINT    10
#define E_STOP           11
#define E_TIMEOUT        12
#define E_DONE           13
#define E_LAST           14
```

This follows a cradle-to-grave philosophy for machine control: the machine is in control almost from the beginning of application startup until just before shutdown. It makes sense to make as much use as possible of the state machine's resources.

The bootstrap process powers up, or *boots*, the machine. Whenever a model is created by opening a file, the machine goes into "ready" state, which automatically starts a rendering run, kicking the machine into "calc" state; when the machine is quiescent it returns to "ready" state. At that point, the state machine has assumed its role as controller — it manages the data state of the modeling data structures and drives the screen updates of the model. In a limited form, this is the MVC paradigm.

The support functions of the M3D can be categorized into three broad areas, which correspond to our scheme for considering the modeler:

- front-end support,
- core function support, and
- post-processing support.

Now, we'll take a more detailed look at each of them.

Modeler Architecture Part III: WinMod3D and the M3D Support Services

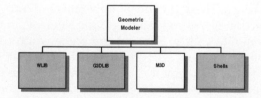

Now that we've created the two DLL support libraries and you understand the basics of the modeler architecture, it's time to take another look at the contents of the M3D. You know that it has five parts:

1. Front-End Part I,
2. Front-End Part II,
3. Core Functions Part I,
4. Core Functions Part II, and
5. Post-Processing.

This breakdown is shown in Figure 8-3. The basic makeup of each part should be clear as well — description languages, object instantiation, world manipulation, world rendering, and color analysis/support.

Figure 8-3.   M3D Contents

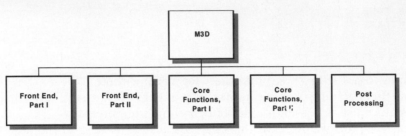

We've ploughed this field once already in Chapter 3, but we'll go over it again to refresh your memory before we dive into implementation details in Part II.

Front-End Part I

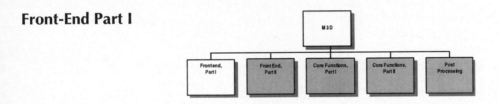

Part I support of the front end is clearly aimed at language and translation issues. Functions in this area ease the translation burden, but don't create any component of our models or scenes. These functions cooperate in identifying tokens in the control-file input stream. Function *gettoken* identifies basic elements in the input stream, then the parsers for both the model control file and the scene control file do the actual recognition. The model control-file token identification is the responsibility of *parse_model*, which, in turn, identifies the scene geometry control file and invokes the scene parser function *parse_scene*. Function *parse_scene* then identifies scene description tokens in the scene control file.

The action taken when a token is recognized in either control file is the responsibility of the Front-End Part II functions. Still, having three functions that do most of the work — *gettoken, parse_scene*, and *parse_model* — pays the rent for this section of the library. As you'll see in the last half of this chapter, these three functions make the translation process both manageable and explainable. Table 8-2 shows the source files that provide these functions.

Figure 8-4 shows the three areas of responsibility — tokenizing, model script parsing, and scene script parsing — that make up the Front-End Part I routines.

Table 8-2.   M3D Front-End Part I Source Modules

M3D Subsystems	Description
Front End Part I	Provides script language support
token.c,token.h	Description tokenizing
parse.c,parse.h	Model and scene description parsing

Figure 8-4.   M3D Front-End Part I

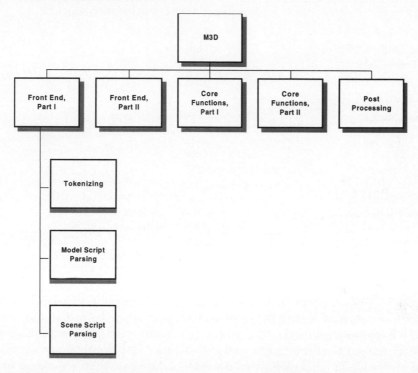

Front-End Part II

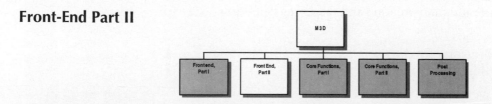

Once we have a color table specification, material table specification, and common object definition, the instantiation process begins. The color table specification is read and *MakeColorLookupTable* builds a color table. The material table specification is likewise handled by *MakeMaterialLookupTable*. Last, but not least, are the objects themselves. A set of *Makexxx* object-instantiation functions create objects.

In addition to *MakeColorLookupTable*, *MakeMaterialLookupTable*, and the *Makexxx* object-instantiation functions the behind-the-scenes functions create lights, surface definitions, and the camera representing the viewpoint. Table 8-3 lists the source modules containing the relevant functions.

Table 8-3.   M3D Front-End Part II

M3D Subsystems	Description
Front End Part II	Provides 3D object instantiation support
Surface Properties	
ccolor.c,ccolor.h	Color lookup
material.c,material.h	Material lookup
Object Support	
Polygon Objects	
explicit..c,explicit.h	Face-vertex polygon helpers
Ray-trace Objects	
sphere.c,sphere.h	Perfect sphere
plane.c,plane.h	Infinite plane
simples.c,simples.h	Circle,rectangle,triangle helpers
simquad.c,simquad.h	Simplified quadratic helpers
cylinder.c,cylinder.h	Uses simplified quadratic and circle
cone.c,cone.h	Uses simplified quadratic and circle
box.c,box.h	Uses rectangles
pyramid.c,pyramid.h	Uses a rectangle and triangles

Figure 8-5 (opposite) depicts the functional areas in Front-End Part II. In terms of modeler actions, the second part of the front-end support adds the functions necessary to respond to the tokens identified in the control-file input stream. The actions represented by these functions result in the building of the modeling database. When the front-end actions are done, the modeler has a populated database. Likewise, when we conclude our discussion of the second part of front-end support, you'll understand the elements in the modeler and the instantiation process. Once the modeling database is built, the machine can enter ready state, and manipulation and rendering can begin.

Core Functions Part I — World Manipulation

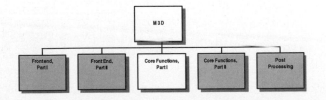

Camera positioning starts the image-generation process, which is supported by the manipulation functions. The camera is initially generated as part of the scene parsing pro-

Figure 8-5.   M3D Front-End Part II

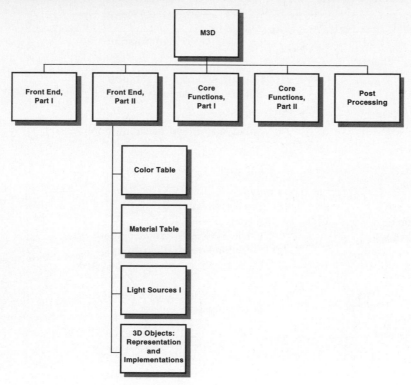

cess. In addition, the state machine that forms the core of the modeler can modify the camera based on user input. The manipulation process uses the camera to operate on the object list.

In particular, for each object the transformation method supports polygon mode, while the intersect method supports ray-trace mode. The list of objects is the backbone of this process. The object list is a simple single-linked list. The best way to think about this is to say that the system contains 3D objects with the "listable" property mixed in, resulting in the ability to make linked lists of 3D objects. Table 8-4 lists the source modules that implement the manipulation functions, and Figure 8-6 displays the logical breakdown.

This leads us to the whole point of what we're doing: the projection, mapping, and drawing process, with shading thrown in for good measure. These actions are part of the rendering process, which also depends on the 3D object list. In addition, rendering results in output, so awareness of pipeline and coordinate issues rears its head again. These details are important for using these functions and the rendering support covered next.

Table 8-4.   Core Functions Part I

M3D Subsystems	Description
Core Functions Part I	Provides world manipulation
Generic Object Support	
object.h	Generic +3D object definition
linklist.c,linklist.h	Linklist routines for type 'object'
3D Object Support	
polysurf.h,raysurf.h	Polygon and ray-trace definitions
Polygon Objects	
face.c,face.h	Face-vertex polygon helpers
Ray-trace Objects	
sphere.c,sphere.h	Perfect sphere
plane.c,plane.h	Infinite plane
simples.c,simples.h	Circle,rectangle,triangle helpers
simquad.c,simquad.h	Simplified quadratic helpers
cylinder.c,cylinder.h	Uses simplified quadratic and circle
cone.c,cone.h	Uses simplified quadratic and circle
box.c,box.h	Uses rectangles
pyramid.c,pyramid.h	Uses a rectangle and triangles

Figure 8-6.   M3D Core Functions Part I

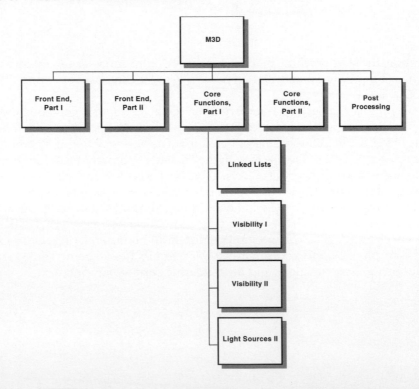

Core Functions Part II— World Rendering

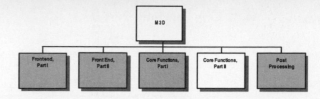

After transformation comes projection, mapping, and drawing. Shading occurs somewhere in between. Shading uses eye coordinates to generate intensity values, affects but uses screen coordinates (or post-projection-mapping-drawing values) as output. This affects the internals. The 3D object list is the backbone around which the Core Functions (Parts I and II) operate and this, too, defines the appearance of the internals.

The object list provides a simple way to iterate and apply a function. The ***drawedges***, ***drawface***, and ***normal*** object function-pointer methods provide a good deal of the rendering code, but the rest comes from rendering support, in terms of implementation of line/polygon drawing for polygon mode, ray generation for ray-trace mode, lights, illumination, and grayscaling.

The results of rendering are twofold. In polygon mode, the face values are stored while an immediate grayscale is performed. In ray-trace mode, the pixel values are stored while the grayscale process is performed to provide immediate feedback. Table 8-5 illustrates the components of the rendering support. Figure 8-7 shows the logical decomposition of the Core Functions Part II.

Table 8-5.   Core Functions Part II

M3D Subsystems	Description
Core Functions Part II	Provides world rendering
Polygon Objects	
polydraw.c,polydraw.h	Polygon drawing modes
face.c,face.h	Face-vertex polygon helpers
Ray-trace objects	
bound.c,bound.h	Bounding volumes
trace.c,trace.h	Ray-trace drawing mode
sphere.c,sphere.h	Perfect sphere
plane.c,plane.h	Infinite plane
simples.c,simples.h	Circle,rectangle,triangle helpers
simquad.c,simquad.h	Simplified quadratic helpers
cylinder.c,cylinder.h	Uses simplified quadratic and circle
cone.c,cone.h	Uses simplified quadratic and circle
box.c,box.h	Uses rectangles
pyramid.c,pyramid.h	Uses a rectangle and triangles
Lights	
light.c,light.h	Light sources
Shading,Surface Properties	
illume.c,illume.h	Illumination model
surfprop.c,surfprop.h	Surface property definition
Texturing	
textures.c,textures.h	Procedural texturing

Figure 8-7.   M3D Core Functions Part II

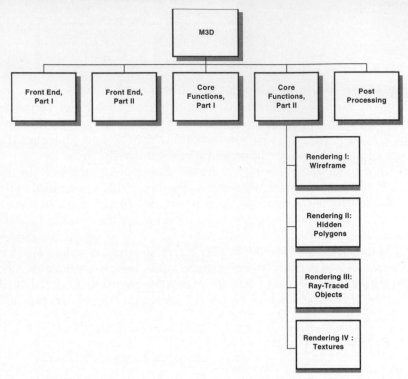

The results, the stored values, are used by the final component: the post-processing phase. In the post-processing step, the stored values are converted to color information and used to replace the grayscale.

Post-Processing

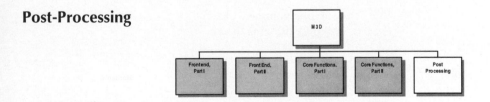

The rendering process leaves a legacy of intensity values on either a face or a pixel basis. This legacy must be processed to produce color images. The post-processing routines provide that support in three areas:

1. *popularity quantization* method for 256-color support,
2. *median cut quantization* method for 256-color support, and
3. *direct color assignment* for 32K- (or higher) color support.

This caps off a wide range of routines supporting color. Starting with the color and palettes you met in Chapter 4, and carrying through to the canvas attribute slot support, intensity memory buffers, and histogram data structures of Chapter 5, our quest for color concludes with these quantization routines and the rough plot of the histogram bin structure in the modeler (in Chapter 11). Table 8-6 lists the source modules that are part of the post-processing phase, and the logical breakdown is shown in Figure 8-8.

Table 8-6.   Post-Processing Support

M3D Subsystems	Description
Post-Processing	Provides color post-processing support
quantize.c,quantize.h	Quantization control
mcut.c,mcut.h	Median cut
popular.c,popular.h	Popularity

Figure 8-8.   M3D Post-Processing

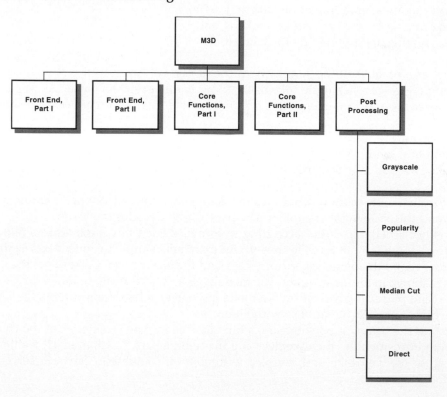

That concludes the recap of M3D, its contents, and its purpose. When you consider this with the other library routines and the modeler itself, you'll realize that we've examined the entire nature of this system. Referring again to Table 8-1, you should now know exactly what to expect from each chapter in Part III.

M3D Front-End Support Part I: Description Languages

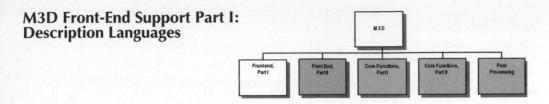

Our first step is to implement the parsers for the model and scene control files. Developing a parser usually includes all of the following steps:

- finding a parsing rule,
- constructing a State Transition Diagram (STD),
- constructing a table of states and tokens, and
- normalizing and optimizing the table.

In our case, because of the simplicity of the parser, we can skip this formalism. These script languages share a simple tokenizer. "How is this possible?" you ask. It's possible because there are only three things this tokenizer must recognize for either script language:

- white space,
- comments, and
- unknown but valid tokens.

This tokenizer returns only when a valid token is encountered, but performs no recognition beyond the occurrence of a token. The parser itself decodes the token.

This is not strictly "correct" according to formal theory, but it maximizes reusability. What we're doing is similar to Figure 8-9. Our extremely simple tokenizer acts as the lexer in Figure 8-4, and the modeling script parser and the scene script parser take the place of the parser shown in the same figure. The modeling parser is directly under control of main, but the scene parser is invoked by the modeling parser when it encounters the 'SCENE' token, which is slightly at variance with Figure 8-4.

Those are the basics of parsing, so it's time to dive in. The remainder of the chapter is devoted to implementing the tokenizer and the two parsers. In Chapter 11, we'll connect the parser to the controller and, coupled with object instantiation, carry ourselves to the ready state.

Figure 8-9. Parsing Architecture

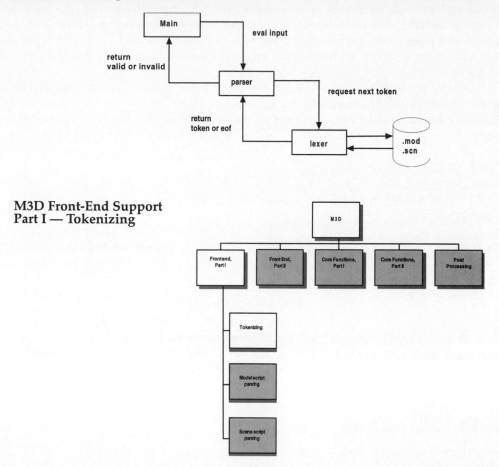

M3D Front-End Support
Part I — Tokenizing

We use two elements to construct the tokenizer and hook it to the parsers. The data structure definition shown in Chapter 3 (and repeated here in Listing 8-4) and the implementation of *gettoken* are all that is required.

Listing 8-4 defines an enum of three elements, representing *word, newline,* and *EOF* (End-Of-File). The word token represents a valid but unknown token. Nil and EOF are housekeeping, internals-type tokens, important for both termination and comment handling.

Listing 8-4. TOKEN Enum

```
typedef enum
{
    WORD_t, NL_t, EOF_t
}
TOKEN;
```

The implementation of *gettoken* is not too tough, especially when broken into two chunks to ease digestion. First, we'll look at the overall structure of the tokenizing process. Then we move on to the guts of handling each element type — white space, comments, and valid tokens — along with the housekeeping. This two-pass approach makes it easy to see what is happening globally with the input stream before examining the handling of any particular element.

Routine *gettoken* is shown in Listing 8-5, missing the core of each case statement. This is really the "husk" of the function, with the kernels to follow. Details you should be paying attention to here are the definition of another enum and a while loop. The enum defines elements:

- NEUTRAL,
- INCOMMENT,
- INANSICOMMENT, and
- WORD.

The main body of the program is centered around the use of the while loop

```
while ((c = getc (in_file)) != EOF)
{
}
```

and use of the state to arbitrate the classification of input from **getc**. This amounts to another state machine, one that has four states corresponding to the enum. Important actions are taken only if a WORD is found (more on that in a bit), but the main thing is that this provides a way to easily classify characters from the input stream one at a time.

Listing 8-5.   Tokenizer Husk

```
TOKEN WINAPI gettoken (char FAR * word, FILE FAR * in_file)
{
     enum
     {
          NEUTRAL, INWORD, INCOMMENT, INANSICOMMENT
     }
     state = NEUTRAL;
     int c, c2;
     char *w;

     w = word;
     while ((c = getc (in_file)) != EOF)
     {
          switch ((int) state)
          {
```

```
                         case NEUTRAL:
                         {
 ...
                         }
/*Stay in this state,tossing chars,until closing marker.*/
                         case INCOMMENT:
                         {
 ...
                         }
/*Stay in this state,tossing chars,until newline closing marker.*/
                         case INANSICOMMENT:
                         {
 ...
                         }

/* Gather up the word. */
                         case INWORD:
                         {
 ...
                         }
                }
        }

        return EOF_t;
}
```

Now you need to know some details on each state. The NEUTRAL state provides an easy mechanism to discard any characters we do not want. This is how we process white space and other noise. States INCOMMENT and INANSICOMMENT, as their names suggest, allow processing of comments in the description languages. This turns out to be a critical feature for large scene files. Defining tens or hundreds of objects in a scene file can get large and cryptic if you don't have comments. Handling the comment types separately simplifies things — each block of code is simpler than the whole. Finally, WORD is what it is all about. The WORD token simply checks to make sure this is really alphanumeric, but otherwise assumes that the only thing that could get here is a valid word for the parser.

Details on NEUTRAL handling are in Listing 8-6. This code looks at the character, and if it's a newline it returns that token, if it is a slash ('/'), it does a lookahead using **getc** to see if the next character confirms a comment. If so, it does a state transition to one of the comment states. If not, it uses the routine **ungetc** to restore the lookahead character to the input stream — an important detail. The default handling uses **isalnum** to check for a transition to the WORD state. Note that if a word is found, the entire word is constructed character-by-character for return (remember, the process calling *gettoken* must do the determination post-tokenizing to finish the process) and the NEUTRAL state is careful to not lose the first character.

Listing 8-6. NEUTRAL Handling

```
switch (c)
{
      case '\n':
            return NL_t;
      case '/':      /* start of comment? */
            c2 = getc (in_file);
            if (c2 == '*')
            {
                  state = INCOMMENT;
                  continue;
            }
            else if ( c2 == '/')
          {
                  state = INANSICOMMENT;
                  continue;
            }
            else
            {
                  ungetc (c2, in_file);
                  continue;
            }
      default:
            if (isalnum (c) || c == '_')
            {
                  state = INWORD;
                  *w++ = (char)c;
            }
            continue;
}
```

The COMMENT state, shown in Listing 8-7, performs a similar action, testing for '*', looking ahead using **getc**, and restoring the input stream using **ungetc**, if necessary. This use of **getc** and **ungetc** and examination of the input stream is characteristic of the translation process.

Listing 8-7. COMMENT Handling

```
switch (c)
{
      case '*':      /* end of comment? */
            if ((c2 = getc (in_file)) == '/')
            {
                  state = NEUTRAL;
                  continue;
            }
            else
```

```
                  {
                          ungetc (c2, in_file);
                          continue;
                  }
          default:
                  continue;

}
```

ANSICOMMENT handling, supporting one-line ANSI comments, is similar and is shown in Listing 8-8. It must actually test for newline, since this is a one-line comment. Instead of explicitly handling the newline, it defers the handling to the NEUTRAL state and restores the input stream using **ungetc**.

Listing 8-8.   ANSICOMMENT Handling

```
switch (c)
{
        case '\n':    /* end of commentline */
//ungetc here and let neutral handle
                  state = NEUTRAL;
                  ungetc (c, in_file);
                  continue;
        default:
                  continue;
}
```

The last element, WORD, is handled by the code block shown in Listing 8-9. As previously mentioned, it tests for alphanumeric using **isalnum**. If valid, the character is stored into the constructed string. If invalid, it restores the input stream using **ungetc**, and terminates the constructed string with a NULL — again, very important.

Listing 8-9.   WORD Handling

```
if (isalnum (c) || c == '_')
{
        *w++ = (char)c;
        continue;
}
else
{
        ungetc (c, in_file);
        *w = NULL;
        return WORD_t;
}
```

That's all there is to it. These four blocks, within the husk, allow easy shredding of the input description file into element strings. From that point, the description language parser simply has to determine which WORD was returned by looking at the constructed string, and then initiate the correct action.

**M3D Front-End Support Part I —
Model Description**

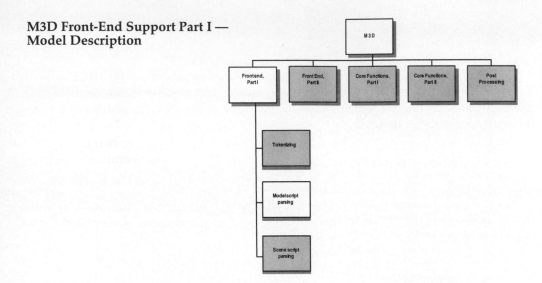

The script languages provide the content that makes possible the tokenizer's blind recognition of words. We've already discussed the separation of scripting into modeling and scene components. Chapter 3 introduced the tokens in the modeling script, and Table 8-7 adds to that discussion with a brief description of the actions taken when *parse_model* encounters a token.

Table 8-7. Modeling Element and Effect

Modeling Script Element	Effect
Canvas size	Changes canvas size
Initial rendering type	Inits global
Color lookup table specification	Builds color lookup table
Material lookup table specification	Builds material lookup table
Shading and tracing environment variables	Inits globals
Scene geometry description file	Loads scene

The structure of the data file is next on our agenda. The data content of each token or WORD takes a common form, as shown in Listing 8-10 for the .MOD modeling script file.

Listing 8-10. Modeling Script Element General Form

```
TOKEN
   NAME    = VALUE
```

The contents are essentially NAME/VALUE pairs separated by an '=' sign (and optional white space). The NAME element and the '=' are not strictly necessary, but the resulting script would be exceptionally terse, especially for numeric entries like the rendering type, as signified by the 'RENDER' token. Remember, these options basically connect to a menu choice and, thus, must equate to a #define somewhere, somehow, which implies an integer-valued scheme. Simply putting the number 2 in the projection slot to indicate perspective, instead of a 1 for parallel, would be very terse. Using the NAME makes it a little easier to remember, and easier for someone else to read as well. Full details on each token will be given in turn, for now it is enough to see the general form.

It's important that you understand the general structure of the parsing phase before we move on to implementing *parse_model*. The same information holds true for *parse_scene* as well, so this is doubly important. Function *parse_script*, shown in Listing 8-11, contains the important details. Again, as in *gettoken*, the use of an enum and a while loop stand out. This enum shows only the NEUTRAL state, since we'll be developing two flavors of this function, one in this section and one in the next. The while loop now employs *gettoken* to manage the input stream, then uses the expected switch statement to handle the state logic. This is, obviously, a case of nested state machines: the tiny one, handling the input stream by character; and the small one of *parse_script*. Remember that the tokenizer performs no recognition, so the NEUTRAL state in the *parse_script*-style functions must perform this task.

Listing 8-11.   Function parse_script Pseudo-Code

```
void  WINAPI parse_script(...,char FAR *filename FILE FAR *infile)
{

    TOKEN    curr_token;
    int      n,nf;
    char     szBuffer[256];
    enum
    {
      NEUTRAL,...
    }
    state = NEUTRAL;
    char word[132], element[132];

    while ((curr_token = gettoken (word, infile)) != EOF_t)
    {
        switch ((int) state)
        {
                    /*
            The "home" state. If a "word" is found,
               a )assume that it is an element name,
               b )set the state appropriately.
               c )fall through to element parsing block
                    */
              case NEUTRAL:
...

                break;
```

Listing 8-11.   (*cont.*)

```
...


      }
  }
} /* end parse_script */
```

Now it's time to examine *parse_model*, shown in "husk" form in Listing 8-12. This function repeats *parse_script* with the blanks filled in as far as the enum and the other case statements within the switch.

Listing 8-12.   Function parse_model in "Husk" Form

```
void  WINAPI parse_model (FRAME * pfrm,VWWND * pv,
        LPMODEL theModel,
        char FAR  * filename, FILE FAR * infile)
{
   LPSCENE   lpt;
   TOKEN     curr_token;
   int       n,nf;
   char      szBuffer[256];
   enum
   {
     NEUTRAL,RES,RENDER,COLORS,MATERIALS,ENVIRONMENT,SCENE
   }

   char word[132], element[132];

   while ((curr_token = gettoken (word, infile)) != EOF_t)
   {
       switch ((int) state)
       {
             case NEUTRAL:
...
           case RES:
...             state = NEUTRAL;
               break;
           case RENDER:
...             state = NEUTRAL;
               break;
           case COLORS:
...             state = NEUTRAL;
               break;
           case MATERIALS:
...             state = NEUTRAL;
               break;
           case ENVIRONMENT:
...             state = NEUTRAL;
               break;
```

```
            case SCENE:
...                 state = NEUTRAL;
                    break;
...


        }
    }
} /* end parse_model */
```

We'll consider the seven blocks of code, six modeling elements, and neutral-block token recognition step individually. The helper functions discussed in Chapter 3, providing the lower-level support, come into play here as well.

The NEUTRAL state handling code in Listing 8-13 only performs an action if a WORD was recognized. First, it does some setup using *Clear_Buffers* and saves the token for comparison. It then simply uses **_strcmpi** to test for the ASCII representation of the element name. If it finds a match, a state transition occurs and the flow of control drops through the code below the NEUTRAL case. Order is, therefore, important here. For this to work properly, the NEUTRAL case must be first. Helper function *Clear_Buffers*, shown in Listing 8-14, clears out the string variables used for handling the three terms.

Listing 8-13. NEUTRAL State Code

```
...
switch ((int) curr_token)
{
    case WORD_t:
        Clear_Buffers();
        strcpy (element, word);
        if(!_strcmpi(element, "RES"))
        {
                state = RES;
        }
        else if(!_strcmpi(element, "RENDER"))
        {
                state = RENDER;
        }
        else if(!_strcmpi(element, "COLORS"))
        {
                state = COLORS;
        }
        else if(!_strcmpi(element, "MATERIALS"))
        {
                state = MATERIALS;
        }
        else if(!_strcmpi(element, "ENVIRONMENT"))
        {
                state = ENVIRONMENT;
        }
        else if(!_strcmpi(element, "SCENE"))
        {
                state = SCENE;
```

Listing 8-13. *(cont.)*

```
    }
    continue;

  default:
    break;
}
...
```

Listing 8-14.   Clear_Buffers

```
void WINAPI Clear_Buffers()
{
    _fstrset(Buf1, 0);
    _fstrset(Buf2, 0);
    _fstrset(Buf3, 0);
}
```

The next states actually make things happen. They do this around the *MODEL* data structure, shown in Listing 8-15. As you can see, most of the elements contained there are directly derived from the tokens. There are also a few extras, and we'll discuss those in turn as well, but, by and large, the six tokens define the elements of the *MODEL* data structure. There are members for canvas resolution, rendering type, color and material lookups, shading and tracing environment variables, and the scene itself.

Listing 8-15.   MODEL Data Structure

```
typedef struct tagMODEL
{
//canvas res,rendering type
   int  nxVRes;
   int  nyVRes;
   int  Rendering;
// scene properties
   char          szColorsFileName[144];
   LPCOLORARRAY     Colors;
   char          szMaterialsFileName[144];
   LPMATERIALARRAY Materials;
   char          szTexturesFileName[144];
   LPNOISEDATA     Noise;
// 5 shade weights,trace depth
   VECTOR4D        LoclW,ReflW,TranW;
   VECTOR4D        MinW,MaxW;
   int             RayDepth;
//scene scriptfile
   char          szSceneFileName[144];
   LPSCENE     Scene;
```

```
// object extents to "autoframe" the scene
   EXTENTS      Extents;
} MODEL;
typedef MODEL FAR * LPMODEL;
```

Let's look at the details of these six tokens.

First is the RES state. This one handles canvas-resolution details and is shown in Listing 8-16. It uses helper *LoadWord*, shown in Listing 8-17, to get integer values for both the x and y canvas resolution. If they are different from the current size, it uses *G3D_GEnv_SetViewport* to both update the current viewport size and resize the canvas. Later, when the extents of the objects in the scene are known, it calculates the window size and the *G3D_WV_* routines are used to manipulate just the window-viewport mapping and not the canvas size. Notice that the transcript log is updated using *Trans_Printf*.

Listing 8-16. RES Code Block

```
LoadWord(infile,&n);
  theModel->nxVRes = n;
  width            = n;
  LoadWord(infile,&n);
  theModel->nyVRes = n;
  height           = n;
  Trans_Printf(winio_hwnd,
             (LPSTR)"loading x,y canvas res %d,%d...\n",
             theModel->nxVRes,theModel->nyVRes);
// reset viewport ie size canvas with call to genv_setviewport
// after get all object data will force reset of w-v mapping
 if ( theModel->nxVRes != pv->rV.right ||
       theModel->nyVRes != pv->rV.bottom )
  {
          rV.left   = 0;
          rV.top    = 0;
          rV.right  = theModel->nxVRes;
          rV.bottom = theModel->nyVRes;
          pv->rV.left   = 0;
          pv->rV.top    = 0;
          pv->rV.right  = theModel->nxVRes;
          pv->rV.bottom = theModel->nyVRes;
          G3D_GEnv_SetViewport(pv->genv,
                                 pv->rV.left, pv->rV.top,
                   pv->rV.right,pv->rV.bottom);
  }
```

Listing 8-17. LoadWord

```
void WINAPI LoadWord(FILE * InFile,WORD *a)
{
   Clear_Buffers();
   fscanf(InFile, "%s %s %s", Buf1, Buf2, Buf3);
   *a=atoi(Buf3);
}
```

Next, the RENDER state assigns the current rendering type. This extremely simple block is shown in Listing 8-18. It contains a call to *LoadWord* to retrieve the value part of a name/value pair, then uses a little trick to calculate the value of the global variable based on the #define value with a little subtraction used to match the simple integer to the #define value indicating the rendering type. In addition, this is logged by some code for the running transcript. The available rendering types are:

1. wireframe,
2. monochrome hidden line,
3. solid-color hidden line,
4. flat-shaded, and
5. ray-traced.

This function is characterized by the use of *LoadWord*, the little subtraction trick, and the switch-statement/*Trans_Printf* logging code style. See Listing 8-18 for this block.

Listing 8-18. RENDER Block

```
LoadWord(infile,&n);
 theModel->Rendering  = CMD_WIRE - 1 + n;
 switch(n)
 {
     case 1:
                 lstrcpy(szBuffer,"Wireframe");
                 break;
     case 2:
                 lstrcpy(szBuffer,"Hidden");
                 break;
     case 3:
                 lstrcpy(szBuffer,"Solid");
                 break;
     case 4:
                 lstrcpy(szBuffer,"Flat");
                 break;
     case 10:
                 lstrcpy(szBuffer,"Raytraced");
                 break;
 }
 Trans_Printf(winio_hwnd,
(LPSTR)"loading render type (%s)...\n",szBuffer);
```

The next two blocks, COLOR and MATERIAL, require the instantiation functions *MakeColorLookupTable* and *MakeMaterialLookupTable* that are covered in Chapter 9. Both routines, however, use *LoadText* to retrieve a specification file name. Listing 8-19 contains the *LoadText* helper. The COLOR block in Listing 8-20 shows how it and *MakeColorLookupTable* are used. The run-time library function **_getcwd** is also used here.

Listing 8-19. LoadText

```
void WINAPI LoadText(FILE * InFile,LPSTR a)
{
   Clear_Buffers();
   fscanf(InFile, "%s %s %s", Buf1, Buf2, Buf3);
   strcpy(a, Buf3);
}
```

Listing 8-20. COLOR Block

```
char     szName[144];
 LoadText(infile,(LPSTR)szName);
 lstrcpy((LPSTR)theModel->szColorsFileName,(LPSTR)szName);
  Trans_Printf(winio_hwnd,
  (LPSTR)"scene colors file %Fs...in the queue to parse\n",
  theModel->szSceneFileName);
//
// then load colors
//
   _getcwd (szBuffer, sizeof (szBuffer));
    lstrcat(szBuffer,"\\");
    lstrcat(szBuffer,theModel->szColorsFileName);
    theModel->Colors = MakeColorLookupTable(szBuffer);
    hprgb = InitRGBPalette(theModel->Colors);
    InitRGBBrushArray(theModel->Colors);
```

We'll hold the details of the color specification file and *MakeColorLookupTable* until Chapter 9. The first thing this block does after creating the color table is to use it to create an RGB palette using *InitRGBPalette*. It follows that up by creating the GDI brush array, *InitRGBBrushArray*, we use as a performance enhancer. I'll cover these functions and the color handling in Chapter 11 when we assemble the modeler.

The MATERIAL block is parallel, using *LoadText* and **_getcwd** to support *MakeMaterialLookupTable* this time. See Listing 8-21.

Listing 8-21.   MATERIAL Block

```
char       szName[144];
 LoadText(infile,(LPSTR)szName);
 lstrcpy((LPSTR)theModel->szMaterialsFileName,(LPSTR)szName);
 Trans_Printf(winio_hwnd,
   (LPSTR)"scene materials file %Fs...in the queue to parse\n",
   theModel->szSceneFileName);
//
// then load materials
//
 _getcwd (szBuffer, sizeof (szBuffer));
 lstrcat(szBuffer,"\\");
 lstrcat(szBuffer,theModel->szMaterialsFileName);
 theModel->Materials = MakeMaterialLookupTable(szBuffer);
```

The ENVIRONMENT block loads shading weights and ray-recursion depth control, both of which are important. When using multiple lights, you need a scheme to avoid light intensity overflow. Think about it. With a single light, you only do your shading calculations once; with multiple lights, you do them for each light in a loop — a summation. You need some value clamping to the range [0,1], and these control variables help. Of course, this does not mean you cannot overexpose an object. It simply restricts the resulting values to 1 to avoid bad calculations later. In a similar manner, while the ray tracer lets you model the interaction of light between objects, you should not permit recursion to infinity: you need some depth control. Listing 8-22 shows the ugly details involved. It uses *LoadVector*, which kindly removes the NAME and '=' then uses *ReadVector* to actually perform the file I/O. These helper functions are shown in Listing 8-23.

Listing 8-22.   ENVIRONMENT Block

```
VECTOR4D v;
//total, reflective and transmissive components
 LoadVector(infile, &v);
 theModel->LoclW = v;
 LoadVector(infile, &v);
 theModel->ReflW = v;
 LoadVector(infile, &v);
 theModel->TranW = v;
//min and max
 LoadVector(infile, &v);
 theModel->MinW  = v;
 LoadVector(infile, &v);
 theModel->MaxW  = v;
//trace depth
  LoadWord(infile,&n);
  theModel->RayDepth = n;
```

Listing 8-23.   LoadVector and ReadVector

```
void WINAPI LoadVector(FILE * InFile,LPVECTOR4D v)
{
   Clear_Buffers();
   fscanf(InFile, "%s %s", Buf1, Buf2);
   ReadVector(InFile, v);
}
void WINAPI ReadVector(FILE *InFile,LPVECTOR4D v)
{

   double x,y,z;

   fscanf(InFile,"%lf %lf %lf",&x, &y, &z);
   v->x = x;
   v->y = y;
   v->z = z;
   return;
}
```

That leaves the SCENE block, shown in Listing 8-24. This block specifies the file containing the scene geometry of interest for this rendering run. It uses *parse_scene* to load the scene data. But before it does that, you see this curious function called *InitNoise*. This function is part of the procedural texturing scheme for the ray tracer, and will be covered as part of texturing in Chapter 10. For now, all we need to be concerned with is that it initializes a data pointer.

Listing 8-24.   SCENE Block and LoadScene

```
...
// init noise lattice,load scene file name
  theModel->Noise      = InitNoise();
  LoadText(infile,(LPSTR)szName);
  lstrcpy((LPSTR)theModel->szSceneFileName,(LPSTR)szName);
// then parse scene for single frame modeler
  _getcwd (szBuffer, sizeof (szBuffer));
  lstrcat(szBuffer,"\\");
  lstrcat(szBuffer,theModel->szSceneFileName);
  theModel->Scene = LoadScene(pv,theModel,szBuffer);
...
//
LPSCENE WINAPI LoadScene(VWWND * pv,LPMODEL mWorld,
                         LPSTR szFileName)
{
    FRAME*        pfrm = Frame_GetPtr(g_app.hwndMain);
    SURFPROPS     surfprops;
    LPSCENE       lpsFrame;
    COLORREF      c;
    FILE *        infile;
    char          szSceneFile[MAXBUFFERLEN];
    int           i,x,y;
```

Listing 8-24. *(cont.)*

```
// open the scene file
    lstrcpy((LPSTR)szSceneFile,szFileName);
    if ( (infile = fopen(szSceneFile,"rt")) == NULL) {
        ProcessError(pfrm,GENERR_OPENSFILEFAIL);
        return 0;
    }
    TRY
    {
        lpsFrame = WL_Mem_Alloc(GHND,sizeof(SCENE));
        if ( !lpsFrame ) {
            Throw((LPCATCHBUF)&_ci.state,GENERR_ALLOCFAILURE);
        }
        else {
            _fmemset((char far *) lpsFrame,'\0',sizeof(LPSCENE));
// cheat and init visface here,parse the scene,close scene file
// return the frame ( scene ) pointer
            InitViewpoint(lpsFrame);
            InitVisFace(lpsFrame);
            parse_scene(pfrm,pv,mWorld,lpsFrame,szFileName, infile);
            fclose(infile);
            return lpsFrame;
        }
    }
    CATCH
    {
        switch(_exk) {
        case GENERR_LOADSFILEFAIL:
        case GENERR_ALLOCFAILURE:
        default:
            ProcessError(pfrm,_exk);
            break;
        }
        return NULL;
    }
    END_CATCH
}
```

Next, it uses *LoadText* to load the scene file name from the model description file stream; *LoadScene* then opens the scene-description file stream and parses it. *LoadScene* is also shown in Listing 8-24, where it simply opens the scene file, calls *parse_scene* on the file, and closes the scene file.

This loading of the scene geometry ends our discussion of the modeling parser. It's now time to continue front-end translation with the scene script language.

**M3D Front-End Support Part I —
Scene Description**

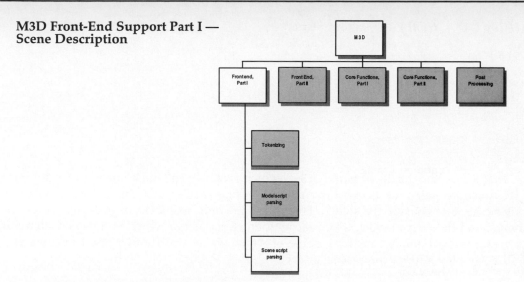

As the model script and *parse_model* control the scene file and the invocation of *parse_scene*, so does *parse_scene* control scene generation of the camera, background information, lights, and, most important, 3D objects. The elements of the scene script and their corresponding actions are shown in Table 8-8. I'll defer the details of the common object definition until the discussion of that block.

Table 8-8.   Scene Element and Effect

Token	Effect
v - viewing vectors and angles	Defines camera (transform matrix)
b - background color	Defines background color/brush
a - global ambient background light	Global ambient component, used with above background to paint background of scene
l - positional light location	Create instance of light and add to light list
o - common object definition	Create instance of 3D object and add to object list

As you can see, the actions taken here complete the translation process. Chapter 9 completes the front end by binding the creation of various key entities, like the specification tables, and the two lists: lights and 3D objects. This will leave the modeler on the brink of its true purpose — image creation — which is covered in Chapters 10 and 11.

Function *parse_scene* does the scene parsing. It resembles *parse_script* in form, but has a different data file structure. Listing 8-25 shows the basic structure of entries in an .SCN scene file.

Listing 8-25.   .SCN File Element Structure

```
TOKEN
   VALUE(S)
except for 3D objects ( o )

o
...
end
```

That leaves the details of *parse_scene*, which is shown in "husk" form in Listing 8-26. This function again repeats *parse_script* with the blanks filled in as far as the enum and the other case statements in the switch. Here, there are only six blocks of code, five scene elements, and the neutral-block token recognition step, each of which will be considered in turn. Additional helper functions, some of which we've already discussed in Chapter 3, will again play a supporting role.

Listing 8-26.   Function parse_scene in "Husk" Form

```
void  WINAPI parse_scene (FRAME * pfrm,VWWND * pv,
   LPMODEL theModel, LPSCENE theScene,
   char FAR  * filename, FILE FAR * infile)
{
   TOKEN         curr_token;
   enum
   {
      NEUTRAL,VIEWDEF,AMBIENT,BACKDEF,LITEDEF,OBJDEF,ENDOBJECT
   }

   char word[132], element[132];

   while ((curr_token = gettoken (word, infile)) != EOF_t)
   {
      switch ((int) state)
      {
           case NEUTRAL:
...
         case VIEWDEF:
...            state = NEUTRAL;
               break;
         case AMBIENT:
...            state = NEUTRAL;
               break;
         case BACKDEF:
...            state = NEUTRAL;
               break;
```

```
               case LITEDEF:
...                state = NEUTRAL;
                   break;
               case OBJDEF:
...                state = NEUTRAL;
                   break;
...


       }
   }
} /* end parse_scene */
```

The NEUTRAL-state handling code in Listing 8-27, like the others, only performs an action if a valid token or WORD is recognized.

Listing 8-27.   NEUTRAL State Code

```
...
switch ((int) curr_token)
{
   case WORD_t:
       strcpy (element, word);
       if(!_strcmpi(element, "V"))
       {
               state = VIEWDEF;
       }
       else if(!_strcmpi(element, "A"))
       {
               state = AMBIENT;
       }
       else if(!_strcmpi(element, "B"))
       {
               state = BACKDEF;
       }
       else if(!_strcmpi(element, "L"))
       {
               state = LITEDEF;
       }
       else if(!_strcmpi(element, "O"))
       {
               state = OBJDEF;
       }
       else if(!_strcmpi(element, "END"))
       {
               state = NEUTRAL;
       }
   default:
       break;
}
...
```

Again, we use **_strcmpi** to test for an ASCII representation of the element name, to find a match and force a state transition. The requirement that the NEUTRAL case be first, allowing a match to "fall through" on a state transition, exists here as well. However, the scene does not use the NAME/VALUE pair and '=' sign approach; it also doesn't need the *Clear_Buffer* function or the functions that use the three-buffer system. Instead, these blocks directly load the values like *ReadVector* from the last section.

This leads our discussion to the five scene-element blocks.

The five blocks all operate on the *SCENE* data structure, shown in Listing 8-28. This is a large structure, containing both control and information elements (all the counters). Most of the actions taken here directly populate this data structure, so you need to be familiar with it. As the five scene blocks are handled, you'll see elements of the *SCENE* structure involved.

Listing 8-28.   SCENE Structure

```
typedef struct tagSCENE
{
// scan res
   int          scanX;
   int          scanY;
// eye and transforms
   VIEWPOINT    Eye ;
// background
   Color             BackgrndColor ;
   char              szBackColor[64];
   CRT               bc;
   HBRUSH            hbc, ho;
//objects
   LPOBJECT          ObjectList;
   int        nObjs;
//poly
   long              NumFaces;
   long              NumVerticies;
//analytic
   int        nPlanes ;
   int        nSpheres ;
   int        nCubes ;
   int        nPyramids ;
   int        nCones ;
   int        nCylinders ;
   int        nQuadrics ;
// HLHSR
   LPFACELIST VisFaces;
//shading
   LPOBJECT          LightList;
   int               nLights;
```

```
//tracing
   int          nRays;
   int          nShadows;
   int          nReflected;
   int          nRefracted;
} SCENE;

typedef SCENE FAR * LPSCENE;
```

The VIEWDEF block is next. The viewing system can be modified in two ways: by the definition in the scene file and by the arrow keys through the keyboard interface. The simple camera system in Chapter 7 showed you how to do this from the keyboard; we'll use almost the same viewing definition here. Table 8-9 shows the format and description of the VIEWDEF elements corresponding to the elements of the from-lookat viewing system from Chapter 7.

Table 8-9. VIEWDEF Elements

Token/Element		Description
v		
%g %g %g	(from)	3 floating-point values -XYZ position
%g %g %g	(at)	""
%g %g %g	(up)	""
%g %g %g	(twistangle, vd,vs)	Angle unused, vd and vs used in both modes
%d %d	(scan resolution)	Allows quick rendering pass in ray-trace mode

The addition of the scan res really helps your prototyping in ray-trace mode. Even with flat-shaded previews, it can take a bit of fiddling until your image looks "just right." Decoupling the scan resolution from the canvas resolution lets you specify "lo-res" mode for prototyping. The VIEWDEF block is shown in Listing 8-29. It loads the *VIEWPOINT* structure that was previewed in Chapter 3 and that is shown complete in Listing 8-30.

Listing 8-29. VIEWDEF Block

```
Trans_Printf(winio_hwnd,"loading viewpoint...\n");
fscanf(infile,"%lf %lf %lf",
                &theScene->Eye.view_from.x,
                &theScene->Eye.view_from.y,
fscanf(infile,"%lf %lf %lf",
                &theScene->Eye.view_at.x,
                &theScene->Eye.view_at.y,
fscanf(infile,"%lf %lf %lf",
                &theScene->Eye.view_up.x,
                &theScene->Eye.view_up.y,
                &theScene->Eye.view_up.z);
```

Listing 8-29. (*cont.*)

```
fscanf(infile,"%lf %lf %lf",
                   &theScene->Eye.view_horzangle,
                   &theScene->Eye.view_vd,
                   &theScene->Eye.view_vs);
Trans_Printf(winio_hwnd,"loading scan resolution...\n");
fscanf(infile,"%d %d",&theScene->scanX,&theScene->scanY);
Trans_Printf(winio_hwnd,"——————————————————————————————————\n");
```

Listing 8-30.   VIEWPOINT Structure

```
typedef struct t_viewpoint
{
//viewing
VECTOR4D view_from ;
VECTOR4D view_at ;
VECTOR4D view_up ;
double view_horzangle;
//clipping/scaling
double view_vd ;
double view_vs ;
} VIEWPOINT;
```

The *VIEWPOINT* structure is very straightforward. It consists of three vectors and three doubles representing the viewing definition elements. The scan resolution is not part of *VIEWPOINT*, but an attribute of the *SCENE* data structure. This makes sense, because the scan resolution must somehow adjust the ray scanning size and is really unrelated to the camera viewpoint. I'm not going to show you the process of transforming this VIEWDEF, as captured in the *VIEWPOINT* structure, yet. As we put the modeler together in Chapter 11, we'll fill in the gaps like this in the parsing phase and creation actions. For now, though, it's important for you to know that both polygon and ray-trace mode use this structure.

The next two blocks, AMBIENT and BACKDEF, cooperate in defining background color. Table 8-10 shows formatting information for them.

Table 8-10.   AMBIENT and BACKDEF elements

Token/Element	Description
a %g %g %g (ambient)	RGB intensity level range [0,1]
b %s (background)	Background color, ASCII name in color table

Global ambient illumination is controlled by the AMBIENT definition, and is used to calculate the background color (in conjunction with the BACKDEF) and the ambient lighting term in the illumination model. The AMBIENT block calls *ReadVector* to load a single vector representing the red, green, and blue components of the ambient lighting intensity. It does more transcripting than anything else, and is shown in Listing 8-31.

Listing 8-31. AMBIENT Block

```
Trans_Printf(winio_hwnd,
      (LPSTR)"Setting global ambient term...\n");
ReadVector(infile, &Ia);
Trans_Printf(winio_hwnd,"Ambient      %+lf   %+lf   %+lf\n",
    Ia.x,Ia.y,Ia.z);
```

The BACKDEF block is not as clean as the other blocks we've been looking at. The background color acts directly on the background of the image view. The Options menu also allows the user to switch between the standard BLACK_CANV and WHITE_CANV and the user-defined canvas background colors. This is, of necessity, application oriented. What you see here is not the intrusion of View pane code, but rather Hist pane code. Curious, hmmm? This will become more clear in Chapter 11 as we construct the modeler, but let me just say that we can't update the View pane right now because the model and scene data structures are "under construction."

The point at which we know the background color is the first point when a "wipe" could take place. At some point, both the Hist and the View panes will be wiped, so here we'll wipe the Hist pane to give a "progress report" to the user interface. If you see the Hist pane clear, you know the parse has gotten this far. As soon as the scene is constructed and attached to the model, the global state will "know" about the new model and the View pane will get wiped.

The rest of the code is pretty straightforward. If it finds a BACKDEF, it overrides the current background color option. Menu mucking using **CheckMenuItem** keeps the menu in sync with regard to informing the user about the current background. It loads the color by name and uses *LookupColorByName* to match the name to a color. This is a simple binary search, and will be discussed in more detail in Chapter 9. As soon as it knows the color value for that name *WL_Color_RGBtoCRT* converts the RGB color to the GDI CRT color space. It then creates a brush using macro **PALETTERGB** and **CreateSolidBrush**. See Listing 8-32 for details.

Listing 8-32. BACKDEF Block

```
CLIENT   *  pcli  = Client_GetPtr(pfrm->hwndClient);
HISTWND  * ph     = Hist_GetPtr(pcli->hwHist);
int     piClr;
LONG    lsClr;

hfM = GetMenu(GetParent(GetParent(pv->hwnd)));
CheckMenuItem(hfM,bckclr, MF_UNCHECKED);
bckclr = CMD_USER;
Trans_Printf(winio_hwnd,"Loading background color...\n");
fscanf(infile,"%s",theScene->szBackColor);
piClr = LookupColorByName((theModel->Colors),
theScene->szBackColor, theScene->BackgrndColor );
```

Listing 8-32. (*cont.*)

```
Trans_Printf(winio_hwnd,"Background color        %s\n",
theScene->szBackColor);
WL_Color_RGBtoCRT((RGB FAR *)&theScene->BackgrndColor,
                  (CRT FAR *)&(theScene->bc));
c     = PALETTERGB(theScene->bc.cRed,
                   theScene->bc.cGreen,
                   theScene->bc.cBlue);
theScene->hbc = CreateSolidBrush(c);
SetupHistCanvas( ph,bckclr,theScene);
Plot_Hist(ph,(HDC)G3D_GEnv_GetVal(ph->henv,ID_DC));
Trans_Printf(winio_hwnd,"————————————————\n");
```

The next-to-last block is the LITEDEF block, for which the formatting information is shown in Table 8-11. The code for extracting this from the input stream is in Listing 8-33.

Table 8-11.   LITEDEF Elements

Token/Element		Description
l		
%g %g %g	(position)	XYZ coordinates
%s	(color)	Light color, ASCII name in color table

Listing 8-33.   LITEDEF Block

```
Trans_Printf(winio_hwnd,(LPSTR)"Loading light source data...\n");
ReadLight(theModel,infile, &light);
this = MakeLight(theScene,
                 light);
if ( this )
{
   AddToList(&theScene->LightList,this);
   PrintLightInfo((LPLIGHTSRC)this->o_edata,winio_hwnd);
   theScene->nLights ++ ;
   Trans_Printf(winio_hwnd,"————————————————\n");
}
else
{
   Trans_Printf(winio_hwnd,"————————————————\n");
}
```

This block defines a light. A light definition contains two entries: a position and a color. The external representation is realized as an instance of a *LIGHTSRC* structure, shown in Listing 8-34. Light intensity, used as a multiplier for brightness, is assumed here to be 1, so it is not expected to be in the script file. The color is specified by name, and is based on the color-table values. The lookup function maps from name to value, and a copy of the color value in RGB format is stored to minimize lookups. A vector is defined to store the light position. The polygon shader and the ray-tracer use the same light coordinates for lighting calculations.

Listing 8-34.   LIGHTSRC Structure

```
typedef struct t_light
{
      VECTOR4D o_light_pos;
      VECTOR4D light_rgb;
      char     szLiteColor[64];
      double   light_brightness;
} LIGHTSRC;
```

Four interesting functions are used here: three light functions and one list function. First, *ReadLight* extracts values from the input stream. Then we use *MakeLight* to create a new instance matching the specification that was just read in. If the instantiation succeeds, the light is attached to the light list using *AddToList*, and a "dump" of the light data is sent to the transcript using *PrintLightInfo*. The three light functions all operate on the *LIGHTSRC* data structure from Listing 8-34.

The *MakeLight* function is covered in Chapter 9, where we go in-depth into object instantiation. *AddToList* is in Chapter 10 with the other list functions. Both *ReadLight* and *PrintLightInfo* are shown here, and can be seen in Listings 8-35 and 8-36.

ReadLight simply reads in the position and the ASCII name of the light color, then calls *LookUpColorByName* and stores the returned color RGB values in the *LIGHTSRC* structure.

Listing 8-35.   ReadLight

```
void  WINAPI ReadLight(LPMODEL theModel,FILE *InFile,LPLIGHTSRC l)
{
  double x,y,z;
  char    szBuff[128];
  Color  color;
  fscanf(InFile,"%lf %lf %lf",&x, &y, &z);
  l->o_light_pos.x = x;
  l->o_light_pos.y = y;
  l->o_light_pos.z = z;
  fscanf(InFile,"%s",szBuff);
  lstrcpy(l->szLiteColor,szBuff);
  LookupColorByName((theModel->Colors),szBuff, color );
  l->light_rgb.x = color[0];
  l->light_rgb.y = color[1];
  l->light_rgb.z = color[2];
  l->light_brightness = 1.0;
  return;
}
```

PrintLightInfo uses *Trans_Printf* to dump the eye coordinates of the light.

Listing 8-36. PrintLightInfo

```
int WINAPI PrintLightInfo(LPLIGHTSRC l,HWND hw)
{

    Trans_Printf(hw,
                "a %s light at %lf %lf %lf\n of brightness %lf\n",
                l ->szLiteColor,
                l ->o_light_pos.x,
                 l ->o_light_pos.y,
                 l ->o_light_pos.z,
                 l ->light_brightness);
    return 1;
}
```

We're now finished with all of the code blocks except the common object definition block.

The common object definition is used internally to generate both forms of a 3D object: the explicit face and vertex representation, which reads a series of "points" and "connections"; and the analytic representation, which derives the information required from the geometry of the explicit representation and the local transformation. Table 8-12 contains formatting information for the OBJDEF block.

Table 8-12.   OBJDEF Elements

Token/Element	Description
o	
%s	Object type (Sphere,plane,cube,pyramid,cylinder,cone)
%s	Object database filename (typically "type".dat in cwd)
%s	Color name
%s	Material name
%g %g %g	Scale factors (x y z)
%g %g %g	Rotate factors (x y z)
%g %g %g	Translate factors (x y z)

This is the most complex definition we've seen yet, which means that dealing with it is a little more complicated than the other blocks. Because of this, the object definition contains an "end" token to signify the end of the object definition block. This makes it easy to code another while loop, this one "while not end of object." The "husk" of the OBJDEF block is shown in Listing 8-37.

Listing 8-37.   OBJDEF Block Husk

```
// read type and dat file, assemble dat path
fscanf(infile,"%s",Buf1); //type
fscanf(infile,"%s",Buf2); //dat file
if ( nExtOffset == 0 || nFileOffset == 0 ){
    LPSTR lp;
    int   Ext = '.';
    int   fN  = '\\';
    lp  = strchr(filename,Ext);
    nExtOffset  = lp - filename + 1;
    lp  = strrchr(filename,fN);
    nFileOffset  = lp - filename + 1;
}
SplitPath(filename,szDrive,szPath,szFile,nFileOffset,szExt,
nExtOffset);
lstrcpy(szBuff,szDrive);
lstrcat(szBuff,szPath);
lstrcat(szBuff,Buf2);
lstrcpy(Buf2,szBuff);
// read rest of object block
while ( (fscanf(infile,"%s",szBuff) != EOF) )
{
    if (!_fstricmp((LPSTR)szBuff,(LPSTR)"END") )
                    break;
    if (!_fstricmp((LPSTR)szBuff,(LPSTR)"COLOR") )
    {
...
    }
    if (!_fstricmp((LPSTR)szBuff,(LPSTR)"MATERIAL") )
    {
...
    }
    if (!_fstricmp((LPSTR)szBuff,(LPSTR)"SCALE") )
    {
...
    }
    if (!_fstricmp((LPSTR)szBuff,(LPSTR)"ROTATE") )
    {
...
    }
    if (!_fstricmp((LPSTR)szBuff,(LPSTR)"TRANSLATE") )
    {
...
    }
```

Listing 8-37.   (cont.)

```
// now build local transform for it
...
// perform local transforms and then add to list
   if ( this )
   {
      TransformEdges(pv,this,&eT);
      AddToList(&theScene->ObjectList,this);
   }
}
```

This large block has nine parts, which fill in the *OBJECT* structure shown in Listing
8-38. This structure is the basic linked-list element around which the 3D object and light
lists are built.

Listing 8-38.   The OBJECT Structure

```
typedef struct t_object
{
   struct t_object FAR *next;
   unsigned short      o_type ;
   unsigned short      o_id ;
//
   struct t_objectprocs
   {
//debugging
           int    (*print) () ;
//polygon-(explicit)
           int    (*transform) () ;
           int    (*drawedges) () ;
           int    (*drawface) () ;
//quadric-(analytic)
           int    (*intersect) () ;
           int    (*normal) () ;
//shading
           int    (*shade) () ;
//cleanup
           int    (*free) () ;
   } * o_procs ;
//
//color,coefficients,texture
//
   SURFPROPS            o_surfprops;
//
//explicit and analytic data
```

```
//
   LPVOID                o_edata;
   LPVOID                o_adata;
} OBJECT ;

typedef OBJECT FAR * LPOBJECT;
```

Notice the function-pointer structure, the **SURFPROPS** member, and the two LPVOID parameters. The **SURFPROPS** member lets us associate a surface property definition with each object. The void pointers form the basis of the dual representation. The linked-list level does not know or care about any underlying 3D object representation. To that level, this is simply a list element. To some of the "guts" code, however, these members provide the information to perform the manipulation and rendering of the object.

Let's get back to the nine parts of the object definition block. You saw the extraction of the first part in Listing 8-37. The type and data files that contain the explicit face and vertex information are extracted from the input stream and saved. They will be used again in a bit. Next, we do a little path hacking using *SplitPath*, then the while loop extracts the remaining object definition tokens until an end is encountered. The while loop completes the blocks for data controlling color, material, scaling, rotation, and translation. At this point, only the actual object instantiation remains.

Here, we consider the code up to the point of instantiation. Only two blocks then remain to be covered: the one that generates the local transformation and the block that not only does the local transformation of the 3D object but also adds the object to the object list.

The color handling is similar to what has gone before. We load the ASCII name and *LookupColorByName* finds the corresponding RGB values that are used to populate the **SURFPROPS** structure. **SURFPROPS** works in conjunction with the object-type specific structure to make a 3D object. Listing 8-39 contains this block of code.

Listing 8-39. Block for Object Color

```
fscanf(infile,"%s ", &szBuff);
lstrcpy((LPSTR)surfprops.szColor,(LPSTR)szBuff);
LookupColorByName((theModel->Colors),(LPSTR)szBuff, surfprops.surf_color);
```

We'll get into more details of the **SURFPROPS** structure in Chapter 10 when we talk about shading and texturing, but this set of values is important now, so let's spend a minute on them.

The surface properties, shown in Listing 8-40, consist of:

- color,
- k_a, k_d, k_s, shine, k_t, and ior coefficients, and
- texture.

They are each specified in the OBJDEF block by name. This naming is nice, because we can now identify a surface as a "red shinycountertop," where "red" is the base color and "shinycountertop" indicates a combination of coefficients and a texture — in this case, a surface with visible highlights but no texture (in other words, smooth). The color is simply an entry from the color lookup table, and, for convenience, we store both ASCII and RGB.

The coefficients describe the components of the illumination model: k_a is the ambient component; k_d is the diffuse component. Both k_a and k_d are used by the flat-shader. The coefficient k_s is the specular component, and shine is the Phong cosine power for highlights. These two components control the existence and size of highlighting. Usually, $0 <= k_a <= 1$, $0 <= k_d <= 1$, and $0 <= k_s <= 1$, though it is *not* required that $k_a + k_d + k_s = 1$. The coefficients k_t and ior are intended for general transmittance (the fraction of light passed per unit) in both reflection and refraction, but are used here only for reflectance, since refraction is not supported. We're not supporting refraction here, because the ray tracer generates nice images anyway, and refraction adds to the complexity of both the shading and the intersecting. The complexity increases because refractive objects need to be considered as having two sides for both of the shading and intersection algorithms; normally, objects have only one side, which is a basic assumption of our modeler (more on this in Chapter 10).

Listing 8-40.   SURFPROPS Structure

```
typedef struct t_surfprops
{
 //name
   char        szName[64];
 //color
   char        szColor[64];
   Color       surf_color ;
 //coefficients
   VECTOR4D    surf_ka ;    //ambient
   VECTOR4D    surf_kd ;    //diffuse
   VECTOR4D    surf_ks ;    //specular
   double      surf_shine ; //phong shine factor
   VECTOR4D    surf_kt ;    //transmissive ( refl and refr )
   double      surf_ior ;   //index of refraction
 //texture
   char        szTexture[64];
   int         surf_tid;
   LPVOID      surf_texdata;
} SURFPROPS ;

typedef SURFPROPS FAR *LPSURFPROPS;
```

Listing 8-41 contains a block for the material name that is similar to the block for color, but using *LookupMaterialByName*. This block also uses *PrintSurfPropInfo* to display the current surface properties as the object is constructed.

Listing 8-41.   Block for Object Material

```
fscanf(infile,"%s ", &szBuff);
lstrcpy((LPSTR)surfprops.szName,(LPSTR)szBuff);
LookupMaterialByName((theModel->Materials),(LPSTR)szBuff, &surfprops);
PrintSurfPropInfo(surfprops,winio_hwnd);
```

PrintSurfPropInfo is shown in Listing 8-42. This block hints at many things to come: the usual ASCII color, texture, name, and coefficients. The last block is the teaser. This is where some of the details of texturing show through, at least as far as the CHECKER texture. Again, we'll use a void pointer to store instance-specific data in a general structure, as seen in the access of the "texdata" member.

Listing 8-42.   PrintSurfPropInfo

```
int WINAPI PrintSurfPropInfo(SURFPROPS o_surfprops,HWND hw)
{

    Trans_Printf(hw,"%Fs %Fs %Fs surface\n",
                o_surfprops.szColor,
                o_surfprops.szTexture,
                o_surfprops.szName);
    Trans_Printf(hw, "surf props ka = %lf %lf %lf\n",
                o_surfprops.surf_ka.x,
                o_surfprops.surf_ka.y,
                o_surfprops.surf_ka.z);
    Trans_Printf(hw,"surf props kd = %lf %lf %lf\n",
                o_surfprops.surf_kd.x,
                o_surfprops.surf_kd.y,
                o_surfprops.surf_kd.z);
    Trans_Printf(hw,"surf props ks = %lf %lf %lf\n shine = %lf\n",
                o_surfprops.surf_ks.x,
                o_surfprops.surf_ks.y,
                o_surfprops.surf_ks.z,
                o_surfprops.surf_shine);
    Trans_Printf(hw,"surf props kt = %lf %lf %lf\n ior = %lf\n",
                o_surfprops.surf_kt.x,
                o_surfprops.surf_kt.y,
                o_surfprops.surf_kt.z,
                    o_surfprops.surf_ior);
if ( o_surfprops.surf_texdata)
    {
        switch(o_surfprops.surf_tid)
        {
            LPCHECKDATA lpcd;
            case CHECKER:
                lpcd = o_surfprops.surf_texdata;
                Trans_Printf(hw,
                            "checker color 1 = %lf %lf %lf\nchecker
```

Listing 8-42.   (*cont.*)

```
color 2 = %lf %lf %lf\n period = %lf\n",
                            lpcd->ch_color1.x,
                            lpcd->ch_color1.y,
                            lpcd->ch_color1.z,
                            lpcd->ch_color2.x,
                            lpcd->ch_color2.y,
                            lpcd->ch_color2.z,
                            lpcd->ch_period);
            break;
        }
    }
    Trans_Printf(hw,"————————\n");
    return 1;
}
```

With the surface properties in hand, the remaining code blocks construct the object trans-formation and the object-specific structure, finally transforming the object and attaching it to the 3D object list.

Remember the "type".dat element from Table 8-12? It specifies the object database file in the current working directory *(cwd)*. This file contains the explicit face and vertex represen-tation values. Think of it as a pristine version of each object (sphere, plane, box, pyramid, cylinder, cone) of size 1 located at the origin. These are *object coordinates*. Constructing the local transformation lets you easily take this prototypical object definition and "instance" it into world coordinates with a scaling, a translation, and a rotation transformation. Each instance of the 3D object is then attached to a list and manipulated by the controller. List-ings 8-43 through 8-45 contain the scaling, translation, and rotation blocks. All of these blocks use the *EX3DOBJECT* structure, shown in Listing 8-46, for variable oe3d.

Listing 8-43.   SCALE Block

```
fscanf(infile,"%lf ", &sx);
fscanf(infile,"%lf ", &sy);
fscanf(infile,"%lf\n",&sz);
oe3D.l_transforms.S.x = sx;
oe3D.l_transforms.S.y = sy;
oe3D.l_transforms.S.z = sz;
Trans_Printf(winio_hwnd,"scale        %+lf  %+lf  %+lf\n",sx,sy,sz);
```

Listing 8-44. TRANSLATE Block

```
fscanf(infile,"%lf ", &tx);
fscanf(infile,"%lf ", &ty);
fscanf(infile,"%lf\n",&tz);
oe3D.l_transforms.T.x = tx;
oe3D.l_transforms.T.y = ty;
oe3D.l_transforms.T.z = tz;
Trans_Printf(winio_hwnd,"translate  %+lf  %+lf  %+lf\n",tx,ty,tz);
```

Listing 8-45. ROTATE Block

```
fscanf(infile,"%lf ", &rx);
fscanf(infile,"%lf ", &ry);
fscanf(infile,"%lf\n",&rz);
oe3D.l_transforms.R.x = rx;
oe3D.l_transforms.R.y = ry;
oe3D.l_transforms.R.z = rz;
Trans_Printf(winio_hwnd,"rotate     %+lf  %+lf  %+lf\n",rx,ry,rz);
```

Listing 8-46. EX3DOBJECT Structure

```
// An explicit 3d object is a face/vertex object
// the structure here is used as edata on the generic object struct

typedef struct t_explicit_3Dobject
{
//explicit [face/vertex]
   char                 szDatFile[MAXNAMELEN];
   int                  nV,nF,nVinF;
   POLYSURFACE          o_psurf ;
   struct t_localtransforms
   {
      VECTOR4D R;
      VECTOR4D S;
      VECTOR4D T;
   } l_transforms;
} EXPLICIT3DOBJECT
```

For now, ignore the *POLYSURFACE* structure — it's the core of the polygon mode, and we'll cover it in Chapter 9. Here, we're concerned with the local transformation member. This comes together in Listing 8-47, using *G3D_M4D_Identity4D* and *G3D_Xfrm_MakeTM* to form an identity matrix and then to concatenate the various transformations and build a CTM for the local transformation.

Listing 8-47.   Building the Local Transformation

```
// now build local transform for explicit
G3D_M4D_Identity4D(&eT);
G3D_Xfrm_MakeTM(&eT,
                    SCALE,       sx,sy,sz,
                    ROTATEX,     rx,
                    ROTATEY,     ry,
                    ROTATEZ,     rz,
                    TRANSLATE,  tx,ty,tz,DEND);
//now build local rotation for rayobject
G3D_M4D_Identity4D(&aT);
G3D_Xfrm_MakeTM(&aT,
                ROTATEX,     rx,
                ROTATEY,     ry,
                ROTATEZ,     rz,DEND);
```

The G3DLib makes this a two-call operation. Note the use of two transformations, with the second one only using the rotation. The ray tracer forces us into this little bit of asymmetry. The scaling and translation information are all the ray tracer needs to instance most objects; the rotation is used for a subset. However, the explicit object uses a composite transformation, which is the difference.

The *PLANE* data structure and object block show much the same treatment.

The creation of the various object-type specific instances is next. We'll look at both the construction block and the helper for each of the six objects (sphere, plane, box, pyramid, cylinder, and cone). Notice that these structures are not necessarily the permanent structure associated with the underlying representation. These are simply used to tell the *Makexxx* layer how to instance a particular object. *Makexxx* is free to perform some indirection of its own as it constructs the explicit and analytic information from this data. Still, the end result cannot be too different, and you'll see in Chapter 9 that even though things change, they mostly stay the same. Also, in these blocks we'll update the counters that the info pane uses to display scene content information.

The *SPHERE* structure and object block, shown in Listings 8-48 and 8-49, confirm the simplicity of the sphere object. A center and a radius are sufficient to describe the sphere mathematically, although, for performance, we often cache in the structure the radius-squared term that is frequently used as well. The setup uses the scaling and translation to size the radius and position the center (spheres are rotationally invariant — well, perfect ones are, anyway) and invokes *MakeSphere* to construct the instance that will be added to the list.

Listing 8-48.   SPHERE Structure

```
// Define sphere specific info ( center, radius )
typedef struct t_sphere
{
  VECTOR4D   sph_center;           /* It's location */
  double     sph_radius;           /* It's radius */
  double     sph_radius2;          /* It's radius squared */
} SPHERE;
typedef SPHERE FAR *LPSPHERE;
```

Listing 8-49.   SPHERE Code Block

```
// sphere,center and radius
// only one that doesnt need explicit data to build
//translated
            sphere.sph_center.x = oe3D.l_transforms.T.x;
            sphere.sph_center.y = oe3D.l_transforms.T.y;
            sphere.sph_center.z = oe3D.l_transforms.T.z;
//scaled
            sphere.sph_radius   = oe3D.l_transforms.S.x;
            sphere.sph_radius2  = sphere.sph_radius *
sphere.sph_radius;
//no rotation - perfect sphere
//instanced
            this = MakeSphere(theScene,
                              sphere,
                              Buf2,oe3D);
            this->o_type = T_SPHERE;
            theScene->nSpheres++;
```

The infinite plane object is defined by a distance and a normal, and the vector dot product of the normal and the view vector is cached for performance. The block of code sets the infinite plane in the default orientation and uses the ray-tracer rotation transformation and *G3D_Xfrm_TransformPoint* to orient it. *MakePlane* then performs the actual creation duties. See Listings 8-50 and 8-51.

Listing 8-50.   PLANE Structure

```
// Define infinite plane specific info, normal and distance
typedef struct t_plane
{
  VECTOR4D   pl_normal;            /* It's normal */
  double     pl_distance;          /* It's pythagorean distance */
  double     pl_NdotV;             /* cached visibility   */
} PLANE;
typedef PLANE FAR *LPPLANE;
```

Listing 8-51.   PLANE Code Block

```
//translated
                plane.pl_distance = oe3D.l_transforms.T.z;
//no scaling - infinite in rayspace
//rotated
                G3D_V4D_VSet4D(&plane.pl_normal,
                             0,0,-1,
                             ONE4D);
                G3D_Xfrm_TransformPoint((LPVECTOR4D)&plane.pl_normal,
                             plane.pl_normal,
                             &aT);
//instanced
                this = MakePlane(theScene,
                             plane,
                             Buf2,oe3D);
                this->o_type = T_PLANE;
                theScene->nPlanes++;
```

There are a variety of tricks to the next four objects. They are all composite objects, not simple ones like the sphere and infinite plane. The cylinder and cone need endcaps, or they would be "infinite" surfaces — a circle, in other words. And the box and pyramid have to be a collection of "faces" that are rectangles or triangles. This is hidden from the *Makexxx* layer, but you still need to be aware of it. All this boils down to three plane figures (circle, rectangle, and triangle) projected on a plane — but more on that in Chapter 9.

The *BOX* structure and code block, shown in Listings 8-52 and 8-53, show signs of these tricks. The *SIMPLEPOLY* member of the structure is designed for the plane figure information that will be covered in detail in Chapter 9. Other than that, it uses the same sequence of the scaling and translation followed by a make function, *MakeBox* here, and finishes up by incrementing the counter.

Listing 8-52.   BOX Structure

```
// Define box specific info
typedef struct t_box
{
  VECTOR4D     c_center;              /* It's location */
  VECTOR4D     c_w;                   /* width  vec */
  VECTOR4D     c_h;                   /* height vec */
  VECTOR4D     c_d;                   /* depth  vec */
  SIMPLEPOLY   c_faces[6];            /* each face */
} BOX;
typedef BOX FAR *LPBOX;
```

Listing 8-53. BOX Code Block

```
//translated
                box.c_center = oe3D.l_transforms.T;
//scaled
                G3D_V4D_VSet4D(&box.c_w,
                               oe3D.l_transforms.S.x,
                               0,0,ONE4D);
                G3D_V4D_VSet4D(&box.c_h,
                               0,
                               oe3D.l_transforms.S.y,
                               0,ONE4D);
                G3D_V4D_VSet4D(&box.c_d,
                               0,0,
                               oe3D.l_transforms.S.z,
                               ONE4D);
//no rotation - not implemented
//instanced
                this =  MakeBox(theScene,
                               box,
                               Buf2,oe3D,&aT);
                this->o_type = T_BOX;
                theScene->nCubes++;
```

The *PYRAMID* structure and code blocks in Listings 8-54 and 8-55 show the same signature. Scaling, translation, the *MakePyramid* invocation, and counter incrementing are all performed.

Listing 8-54. PYRAMID Structure

```
// Define pyramid specific info
typedef struct t_pyramid
{
  VECTOR4D    p_center;            /* its location */
  VECTOR4D    p_v1,p_v2;           /* v1,c,v2 - vertex 1 and 2 around
corner c */
  VECTOR4D    p_height;            /* altitude */
  SIMPLEPOLY  p_faces[5];          /* each face */
} PYRAMID;
typedef PYRAMID FAR *LPPYRAMID;
```

Listing 8-55.   PYRAMID Code Block

```
//translated
                pyramid.p_center = oe3D.l_transforms.T;
//scaled
                G3D_V4D_VSet4D(&pyramid.p_v1,
                                oe3D.l_transforms.S.x,
                                0,0,ONE4D);
                G3D_V4D_VSet4D(&pyramid.p_v2,
                                0,
                                oe3D.l_transforms.S.y,
                                0,ONE4D);
                G3D_V4D_VSet4D(&pyramid.p_height,
                                0,0,
                                oe3D.l_transforms.S.z,
                                ONE4D);
//no rotation - not implemented
//instanced
                this =  MakePyramid(theScene,
                                pyramid,
                                Buf2,oe3D,&aT);
                this->o_type = T_PYR;
                theScene->nPyramids++;
```

The coverage of the cylinder — the *CYLINDER* structure and the *MakeCylinder* invocation block — is contained in Listings 8-56 and 8-57. They hold no surprises at this point, just the standard altitude and radius approach used in the data structure, and the now-familiar sequence of scaling, translation, *MakeCylinder* invocation and counter incrementing.

Listing 8-56.   CYLINDER Structure

```
// Define cylinder specific info
typedef struct t_cylinder
{
  VECTOR4D   c_bcenter;              /* bottom location */
  double     c_radius;              /* radius*/
  VECTOR4D   c_tcenter;              /* top location */
  double     c_altitude;
} CYLINDER;
typedef CYLINDER FAR *LPCYLINDER;
```

Listing 8-57.   CYLINDER Code Block

```
//scaled
   cylinder.c_altitude   - oe3D.l_transforms.S.z;
   G3D_V4D_VSet4D(&cylinder.c_bcenter,
                        0,0,0,
                        ONE4D);
```

```
  cylinder.c_radius       = oe3D.l_transforms.S.x;
  cylinder.c_tcenter     = cylinder.c_bcenter;
  cylinder.c_tcenter.z += cylinder.c_altitude;
//rotated
  G3D_Xfrm_TransformPoint((LPVECTOR4D)&cylinder.c_bcenter,
                                      cylinder.c_bcenter,
                                      &aT);
  G3D_Xfrm_TransformPoint((LPVECTOR4D)&cylinder.c_tcenter,
                                      cylinder.c_tcenter,
                                      &aT);
//hack
  G3D_V4D_VSet4D((LPVECTOR4D)&temp,
                 0.0,0.0,cylinder.c_altitude,ONE4D);
  G3D_Xfrm_TransformPoint((LPVECTOR4D)&temp,
                                      temp,
                                      &aT);
//translated
  cylinder.c_bcenter.x += oe3D.l_transforms.T.x;
  cylinder.c_bcenter.y += oe3D.l_transforms.T.y;
  cylinder.c_bcenter.z += oe3D.l_transforms.T.z;
  cylinder.c_tcenter.x += oe3D.l_transforms.T.x;
  cylinder.c_tcenter.y += oe3D.l_transforms.T.y;
  cylinder.c_tcenter.z  = cylinder.c_bcenter.z + temp.z;
//instanced
  this =  MakeCylinder(theScene,
                       cylinder,
                       Buf2,oe3D,&aT);
  this->o_type = T_CYL;
```

The last object, the cone, is shown in Listings 8-58 and 8-59. The *CONE* structure and the *MakeCone* invoking code block should, again, be free of surprises. The *CONE* structure contains both a top and a bottom radius. The top radius is unused and exists in case you wish to expand the modeler in the future to handle objects, like funnels or ice-cream cones, that are not closed at the top like a standard cone. The code block should be highly familiar (but hopefully not tiresome; this is, after all, creating 3D objects).

Listing 8-58   CONE Structure

```
//define cone specific info
 typedef struct t_cone
{
  VECTOR4D  c_bcenter;              /* bottom location */
  double    c_bradius;
  VECTOR4D  c_tcenter;              /* top location */
  double    c_tradius;
  double    c_altitude;
} CONE;
typedef CONE FAR *LPCONE;
```

Listing 8-59. CONE Code Block

```
//scaled
   cone.c_altitude   = oe3D.l_transforms.S.z;
   G3D_V4D_VSet4D(&cone.c_bcenter,
                      0,0,0,
                      ONE4D);
   cone.c_tcenter    = cone.c_bcenter;
   cone.c_tcenter.z += cone.c_altitude;
   cone.c_tradius    = 0;
   cone.c_bradius    = oe3D.l_transforms.S.x;
//rotated
   G3D_Xfrm_TransformPoint((LPVECTOR4D)&cone.c_bcenter,
                                        cone.c_bcenter,
                                        &aT);
   G3D_Xfrm_TransformPoint((LPVECTOR4D)&cone.c_tcenter,
                                        cone.c_tcenter,
                                        &aT);
//hack
   G3D_V4D_VSet4D((LPVECTOR4D)&temp,
                             0.0,0.0,cone.c_altitude,ONE4D);
   G3D_Xfrm_TransformPoint((LPVECTOR4D)&temp,
                                        temp,
                                        &aT);
//translated
   cone.c_bcenter.x += oe3D.l_transforms.T.x;
   cone.c_bcenter.y += oe3D.l_transforms.T.y;
   cone.c_bcenter.z += oe3D.l_transforms.T.z;
   cone.c_tcenter.x += oe3D.l_transforms.T.x;
   cone.c_tcenter.y += oe3D.l_transforms.T.y;
   cone.c_tcenter.z  = cone.c_bcenter.z + temp.z;
//instanced
   this =  MakeCone(theScene,
                    cone,
                    Buf2,oe3D,&aT);
   this->o_type = T_CONE;
   theScene->nCones++;
```

That leaves the final initialization, transforming the object, and inserting it into the 3D object list. Listing 8-60 contains a brief code chunk (not even a block) that uses functions *SetSurfProps*, *TransformEdges*, and *AddToList* to do this. *SetSurfProps* simply takes the *SURFPROPS* structure that was built from the object definition and sets the appropriate elements of the *OBJECT* structure represented by the *this* variable. I've not included *SetSurfProps* here, but it is on your disk.

Listing 8-60. Code for Transformation and List Actions

```
// perform local transform on explicit and then add to list
if ( this )
{
    SetSurfProps(this,surfprops);
    ...
    TransformEdges(pv,this,&T);
    AddToList(&theScene->ObjectList,this);
}
```

That only leaves *TransformEdges* and *AddToList* uncovered, which is an auspicious place to end Chapter 8, because the function *TransformEdges* operates on the internals generated by the *Makexxx* calls which, as promised, is a Chapter 9 topic. *AddToList*, the list functions, and operations on existing objects are covered in Chapter 10.

Summary

We went into more detail on the architectural concepts of the modeler:

- separate modeling and scene description languages,
- user-definable color and material lookup tables with binary search by name,
- process flow support using repetitive data structures and mapping functions, and
- MVC support with a state machine controlling the modeling data structures, the multiple views, and the user interface.

This led us into more information on the simple MVC implementation, especially the state machine controller.

We then went on to a brief overview of the M3D, to remind you of its contents:

- Front End Part I   Description language support,
- Front End Part II   3D object instantiation support,
- Core Functions Part I   World manipulation support,
- Core Functions Part II World rendering support, and
- Post-Processing   Color analysis support.

The bulk of this chapter was devoted to the Front-End Part I functions. It presented the split of description chores into two distinct script languages: modeling and scene geometry. To handle translation tasks we implemented a general tokenizer and two parsers, functions *gettoken, parse_scene*, and *parse_model*. The discussion of the implementation of Front-End Part I led into Front-End Part II, over the bridge of the *Makexxx* functions.

What's Next?

The remaining chapters and topics are shown in Table 8-13. As you can see, we still have a lot to do.

Table 8-13. Remaining Chapters and Topics

M3D	Modeler	Chapter and Topic
Front End Part II	World generation Mapping functions	Ch. 9, Object Instantiation
Core Functions Part I	World manipulation Mapping functions	Ch.10, Polygons and Objects
Core Functions Part II	World rendering Mapping functions	Ch. 10, Shading and Texturing
Post-Processing	State machine Post-Processing	Ch. 11, Architecture Ch. 11, Color Analysis

Chapter 9 will finish the instantiation of objects, leading into lists in Chapter 10. There we will implement the list API and cover the key loops across the object list for visibility and shading. Chapter 11 puts it all together and completes the 3D modeler.

9 3D Objects and Scenes

In This Chapter

- Development of functions in the Front End Part II subsystems of the M3D support services:

  — color lookup table,
  — material lookup table,
  — light source objects, and
  — 3D objects.

- Instantiation, usage, and destruction of the color and material lookup tables, including a binary search by name.
- RGB palette and GDI brush array performance enhancement techniques.
- Construction of a light instance from a light source definition.
- Definition of the object representation and implementation of the object database.
- Implementation of programmatic object data generation and construction of an object instance from an object definition. This includes sample instantiations to demystify scene creation.
- Explanation and examples of test pictures. Discussion of scene composition and introduction to algorithmic scene generation.

Introduction

It may seem obvious that a scene is nothing without objects, but, in reality, there are four components working together with the viewpoint and background components (global ambient light and background color) to give a scene its appearance: the color lookup table, the material lookup table, the list of light sources, and the list of the 3D objects. The color and material lookup tables define the range of appearances and colors an object may take. The list of light sources, together with the global ambient illumination, define the lighting portion of the shading process. Finally, the 3D objects and their surface properties interact with the other components to generate the image.

The color specification is very simple. It is made up of two parts: ASCII name and RGB value. A memory representation of a block of these colors is used as a database by a binary search algorithm to provide name matching.

Material specification is a little more involved. It is a three-part specification: two names and a set. The material itself is named for easy usage, like "shinycountertop." It also contains a texture name and a set of surface coefficients that combine with the object color to make an object surface property specification.

We implement light sources in minimal fashion here. We'll implement both a position and a color, but assume that intensities are unity and support only point light sources.

You've seen the parser up to the point of individual object files, so now it's time to define the objects themselves in terms of geometry. This involves two forms of representations for objects:

1. explicit face and vertex representation, and
2. implicit analytic, based on equations for intersections of basic surfaces.

This dualism is reflected in the implementation. There is another layer of code beneath the *Makexxx* layer you saw in Chapter 8. This layer uses the two void pointers contained in the object structure, as was also shown in Chapter 8. If you remember, I deferred the discussion of the guts of object implementation then, leaving the picture incomplete. I'll fill in the blanks in that picture here. When you're done with Chapter 9, you'll be ready to manipulate and render these objects — the main topic of Chapter 10.

Color Specifications

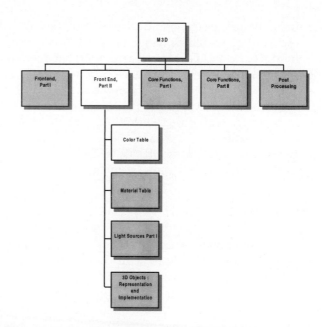

The color table is externally defined. The modeling script contains an entry that lets the user define a color table. The lookup-by-ASCII name service is enabled using this definition and, as you've already seen, *LookupColorByName* is used in several places. You should be aware of the difference between color table values and Windows' GDI color. The color table and the color lookup define color as the RGB [0,1] real-valued space; GDI regards it as the [0,255] integer-valued space discussed in Chapter 4. This is where the conversion routines like *WL_Color_RGBtoCRT* pay off. Being able to provide a loadable definition implies memory management as well, and the color table functions also include this support. In addition, solid-color rendering uses the raw RGB color so we'll provide palette and brush support for this, too.

Still, what exactly is a color table? Listing 9-1 shows the data structure definitions for the color table entries. We define a string for the name and space for the three floating-point values in the *COLORENTRY*. The *COLORARRAY* structure is a variable-sized array of *COLORENTRIES* consistent with the standard extensible API techniques we've already discussed.

Listing 9-1.   Color Table Data Structures

```
typedef double Color[3] ;

typedef struct t_color_entry {
      char    ce_name[64] ;
      Color   ce_color ;
} COLORENTRY;

typedef COLORENTRY FAR *LPCOLORENTRY;
typedef struct t_color_array
{
  int        iEntries;
  COLORENTRY ceColors[1];
} COLORARRAY;

typedef COLORARRAY FAR *LPCOLORARRAY;
```

It's now time to discuss formatting details.

Color Table Format

The file colors.dat, provided on the source disk, contains the default color table. There is nothing special about this set of colors; they are based on a similar set provided with X-11 and PEX. Listing 9-2 contains the token/name/value block from a typical modeling script. The format of the colors.dat file is of more interest. Table 9-1 contains the elements found in the color table.

Listing 9-2.   COLORTABLE Modeling Script Entry

```
COLORS
   Color   = colors.dat
```

Table 9-1.   COLORTABLE Elements

Element	Description
%d	Total colors (A convenience)
% s %g %g %g	ASCII name followed by the 3 RGB values

You can see that this is quite simple. A count is the first element, which eases the memory-management burden. Instead of looping and allocating as each entry is encountered, this lets you preallocate all table entries at the cost of maintaining the count entry. This is followed by count entries of a string of up to 64 characters followed by three floating-point values. This string is the ASCII name and the RGB value assigned to it.

Listing 9-3 contains the color definitions in colors.dat. This is a good range of colors, and a wide range of scene coloration is possible by using it. Remember, when an object is flat-shaded, each polygon has its color calculated based on the original color, object position, and light position; likewise, when an object is ray-traced, each pixel has its color calculated. Obviously, many colors result from this process. Each object, the background, and each light may have a color. The light color is used for highlights in ray-traced mode.

Listing 9-3.   RGB Color Table colors.dat

```
71
Aquamarine          .439216   .858824   .576471
Black               0.0       0.0       0.0
Blue                0.0       0.0       1.0
BlueViolet          .623529   .372549   .623529
Brown               .647059   .164706   .164706
CadetBlue           .372549   .623529   .623529
Coral               1.0       .498039  0.0
CornflowerBlue      .258824   .258824   .435294
Cyan                0.0       1.0       1.0
DarkGreen           .184314   .309804   .184314
DarkOliveGreen      .309804   .309804   .184314
DarkOrchid          .6        .196078   .8
DarkSlateBlue       .419608   .137255   .556863
DarkSlateGray       .184314   .309804   .309804
DarkSlateGrey       .184314   .309804   .309804
DarkTurquoise       .439216   .576471   .858824
DimGray             .329412   .329412   .329412
DimGrey             .329412   .329412   .329412
Firebrick           .556863   .137255   .137255
ForestGreen         .137255   .556863   .137255
Gold                .8        .498039   .196078
Goldenrod           .858824   .858824   .439216
Gray                .752941   .752941   .752941
Green               0         1         0
GreenYellow         .576471   .858824   .439216
Grey                .752941   .752941   .752941
IndianRed           .509804   .184314   .184314
Khaki               .623529   .623529   .372549
LightBlue           .74902    .847059   .847059
LightGray           .658824   .658824   .658824
LightGrey           .658824   .658824   .658824
LightSteelBlue      .560784   .560784   .737255
LimeGreen           .196078   .8        .196078
Magenta             1         0         1
```

```
Maroon              .656863  .137255  .419608
MediumAquamarine    .196078  .8       .6
MediumBlue          .196078  .196078  .8
MediumForestGreen   .419608  .556863  .137255
MediumGoldenrod     .917647  .917647  .678431
MediumOrchid        .576471  .439216  .858824
MediumSeaGreen      .258824  .435294  .258824
MediumSlateBlue     .498039 0         1
MediumSpringGreen   .498039 1         0
MediumTurquoise     .439216  .858824  .858824
MediumVioletRed     .858824  .439216  .576471
MidnightBlue        .184314  .184314  .409804
Navy                .137255  .137255  .556863
NavyBlue            .137255  .137255  .556863
Orange              .8       .196078  .196078
OrangeRed           1       0         .498039
Orchid              .858824  .439216  .858824
PaleGreen           .560784  .737255  .560784
Pink                .837255  .360784  .660784
Plum                .917647  .678431  .917647
Red                 1       0         0
Salmon              .435294  .258824  .258824
SeaGreen            .137255  .556863  .419608
Sienna              .556863  .419608  .137255
SkyBlue             .196078  .6       .8
SlateBlue           0        .498039 1
SpringGreen         0        1        .498039
SteelBlue           .137255  .419608  .556863
Tan                 .858824  .576471  .439216
Thistle             .847059  .74902   .847059
Turquoise           .678431  .917647  .917647
Violet              .409804  .184314  .409804
VioletRed           .8       .196078  .6
Wheat               .847059  .847059  .74902
White               .988235  .988235  .988235
Yellow              1        1        0
YellowGreen         .6       .8       .196078
```

Now that you understand the format of the data, it's time to implement the functions that support the color table.

Color Table Functions

There are four functions in the color table API, three visible and one internal:

1. MakeColorLookupTable,
2. FreeColorLookupTable,
3. LookupColorByName, and
4. BinaryColorSearch.

The make and free functions provide construct and destroy tables, while the lookup function provides the name service and uses (internally) *BinaryColorSearch* to perform a binary search.

MakeColorLookupTable, in Listing 9-4, uses the count value to allocate memory (using *WL_Mem_Alloc* from the WLib) and an extremely simple **fscanf** loop to read in the values. It returns a long pointer to the color table. Its companion function, *FreeColorLookupTable* (shown in Listing 9-5), simply deallocates the memory using *WL_Mem_Free*.

Listing 9-4.   MakeColorLookupTable

```
LPCOLORARRAY WINAPI MakeColorLookupTable(LPSTR SrcFile)
{
    FILE          *objfile;
    int           i,nCols;
    LPCOLORARRAY  LoadColors;
    long          asb;
    double        x,y,z;
    lstrcpy((LPSTR)szBuff,(LPSTR)SrcFile);
    /* object db file */
    if ( (objfile = fopen(szBuff,"r+t")) == NULL)
    {
        MessageBox(NULL,"object dat file open failure!",
                   "scene package",MB_OK);
        return NULL;
    }
    fscanf(objfile,"%d",&nCols);
    LoadColors = (LPCOLORARRAY)WL_Mem_Alloc(GHND,
        sizeof(COLORARRAY) + (nCols)*sizeof(COLORENTRY));
    LoadColors->iEntries = nCols;
        for ( i = 0; i < LoadColors->iEntries; i++ )
    {
        fscanf(objfile,"%s",
               LoadColors->ceColors[i].ce_name);
        fscanf(objfile,"%lf %lf %lf",&x,&y,&z);
        LoadColors->ceColors[i].ce_color[0] = x;
        LoadColors->ceColors[i].ce_color[1] = y;
        LoadColors->ceColors[i].ce_color[2] = z;
    }
    fclose(objfile);
    return LoadColors;
}
```

Listing 9-5.   FreeColorLookupTable

```
int WINAPI FreeColorLookupTable(LPCOLORARRAY Colors)
{
   WL_Mem_Free(Colors);
   return 1;
}
```

The lookup function *LookupColorByName*, implemented in Listing 9-6, uses the binary search function *BinaryColorSearch*. If it finds a color, it copies the value, using the macro *ColorCopy*, into the far pointer provided in the parameter list, and returns the color table index. If it doesn't find a color, it returns a zero.

Listing 9-6. LookupColorByName

```
int WINAPI LookupColorByName(LPCOLORARRAY Colors,char * name,
                             Color color)
{
     int rc ;
     rc = BinaryColorSearch(name,0,Colors->iEntries - 1 ,Colors) ;
     if (rc < 0) {
           return(0) ;
     }

     ColorCopy(Colors->ceColors[rc].ce_color, color) ;
     return rc;
}
```

Functions *BinaryColorSearch* and *ColorCopy* are shown in Listing 9-7. *BinaryColorSearch* implements a standard binary search algorithm. Any search operation, if you remember, identifies a specific element in a set; that's just what it does here as well. Even though this table is small, it can be expanded, so it's important that you understand the search algorithm.

Listing 9-7. BinaryColorSearch

```
int BinaryColorSearch(char * name,int l,int h,LPCOLORARRAY Colors)
{
     int m, rc ;
     if (l > h)
           return(-1) ;

     m = (l + h) / 2 ;

     rc = strcmp(name, Colors->ceColors[m].ce_name) ;
     if (rc == 0)
           return m ;
     else if (rc < 0)
           return BinaryColorSearch(name, l, m-1, Colors) ;
     else
           return BinaryColorSearch(name, m + 1, h, Colors) ;
}

#define ColorCopy(a,b)      (b)[0]=(a)[0];(b)[1]=(a)[1];(b)[2]=(a)[2];
```

In general, the cost of a search depends on the structure of the records being searched and the nature of the key, but Table 9-2 lists some common searches and the O(n) time complexity for them.

Table 9-2.   Search Algorithms and Time Complexity

Name	Structure of Records	Knuth Vol III page	O(n)
sequential	unordered	393	N
sequential	ordered table	393	N/2
binary search	ordered table	406	log N
binary tree	ordered tree	422	log N

Notice that the binary search entry describes the structure of the records as "ordered." What does that mean here? If you look back at Listing 9-2 and the color table entries, you'll notice that they are sorted alphabetically. It is this sorting that "ordered" refers to, because the name is used as the search key.

Again, it may be overkill to worry about algorithmic performance in a color table containing only 71 entries, but it's important that you understand the table order so that you can extend it successfully when you want to. You must alphabetize as you add entries. As for performance, now that you know the details, you can decide for yourself.

Now let's move on to the internals of the search — it uses **strcmp** to perform an alphabetic comparison and uses the result to continue the search by using recursion. A *recursive function* is one that calls itself; this is not the only one we use in this application. In this search, we use the result of the **strcmp** to determine the new set of parameters and call *BinaryColorSearch* again. At the front of the function, you'll see an "l and h" test that prevents a bad search.

That concludes the color table API. The modeler first uses the color table to construct an "RGB" palette exactly matching the color table for the solid-color rendering scheme. These functions are next on our list.

Color Support

Three functions provide the solid-color rendering support:

1. InitRGBPalette,
2. InitRGBBrushArray, and
3. FreeRGBBrushArray.

As discussed before, the brush array concept redistributes brush creation/destruction time to a point outside the main rendering loop. Remember, there are two phases to the strategy for brush arrays — the retained palette specification and the brush array itself.

InitRGBPalette provides the first phase — the retained palette specification. Its body is shown in Listing 9-8. Two details stand out here. First is the use of variable palpad and skipping slots in the specification to enable the use of *WL_Pal_MakeIdentityPal*, which makes this palette an identity palette. Any time a color mapping needs to occur (for example, the DDB-to-DIB translation for file I/O), this speeds things up and keeps GDI from perturbing anything.

Second, the use of global memory with *WL_Mem_Alloc* means that we don't need to use the local heap for palette memory. Several palettes will be allocated, as you will see, and the data segment will be crowded with other data, so depending on the local heap here would be a bad idea. Within the loop conversion routine, *WL_Color_RGBtoCRT* transforms the RGB specification in the color table entries into the GDI form. Finally, *WL_Pal_CreatePal* performs the GDI-related rituals to receive a palette handle.

Listing 9-9 shows the implementation of *InitRGBBrushArray*, which is the second phase of our strategy here — the brush cache. It carefully adjusts for the identity palette entries and uses the macro **PALETTERGB** and **CreateSolidBrush**. If you remember, macro **PALETTERGB** simply returns the RGB value if a palette does not exist in the current graphics mode; thus, it works well in both 256-color and high-color modes. The results are stored in a global brush array — rgbPal. You'll see this array used in Chapter 10 in the rendering sections.

Listing 9-8. InitRGBPalette

```
HPALETTE WINAPI InitRGBPalette(LPCOLORARRAY LoadColors)
{
    HPALETTE       hp;
    CRT                      crtValue;
    int            run;
    DWORD          size;
// setup palette for x-11 colors
    size = (MAXPALCOL + 2* palpad) * sizeof(PALETTEENTRY);
    size = sizeof(LOGPALETTE) + size;
    prgbPal = (LOGPALETTE *)WL_Mem_Alloc(GHND,size);
    if ( !prgbPal )
       return 0;
    prgbPal->palNumEntries = MAXPALCOL + 2 * palpad;
    prgbPal->palVersion    = PALVERSION;
    for (run = palpad;run <= (LoadColors->iEntries) palpad; run++)
    {
        WL_Color_RGBtoCRT((RGB FAR *)&(LoadColors->
                           ceColors[run-palpad].ce_color),
                      (CRT FAR *)&crtValue);

                      /* assign into palette */
        prgbPal->palPalEntry[run].peRed   = crtValue.cRed;
        prgbPal->palPalEntry[run].peGreen = crtValue.cGreen;
        prgbPal->palPalEntry[run].peBlue  = crtValue.cBlue;
        prgbPal->palPalEntry[run].peFlags = PC_RESERVED;
    }
```

Listing 9-8. *(cont.)*

```
WL_Pal_MakeIdentityPal(prgbPal);

hp = WL_Pal_Create(prgbPal);

return hp;
}
```

The corresponding free function, *FreeRGBBrushArray*, is shown in Listing 9-10. It actually performs two tasks — brush array and RGB palette cleanup. Since the palette cleanup is a two-liner this is not a real burden. First, we delete the brushes using **DeleteObject**. Then the palette handle is deleted using **WL_Pal_Destroy** and the palette specification released using **WL_Mem_Free**. These last two lines are the ones related strictly to palettes.

Listing 9-9.   InitRGBBrushArray

```
BOOL WINAPI InitRGBBrushArray(LPCOLORARRAY LoadColors)
{
    int      n;
    COLORREF c;

    for (n=palpad; n<=(LoadColors->iEntries+palpad); n++)
    {
        c = PALETTERGB(prgbPal->palPalEntry[n].peRed,
                       prgbPal->palPalEntry[n].peGreen,
                       prgbPal->palPalEntry[n].peBlue);
        rgbPal[n-palpad] = CreateSolidBrush(c);


    }
    Trans_Printf(winio_hwnd,"%s\n",
            (LPSTR)"built the rgb palette...");
    return TRUE;
}
```

Listing 9-10.   FreeRGBBrushArray

```
BOOL WINAPI FreeRGBBrushArray(LPCOLORARRAY LoadColors)
{
    int        n;

    for (n=0; n<= (LoadColors->iEntries); n++)
        if ( rgbPal[n] )
            DeleteObject(rgbPal[n]);
```

```
    if ( hprgb )
    {
        WL_Pal_Destroy(hprgb);
        WL_Mem_Free(prgbPal);
        hprgb = NULL;
        prgbPal  = NULL;
        Trans_Printf(winio_hwnd,"%s\n",(
                    LPSTR)"freed the rgb palette...");
    }

    return TRUE;
}
```

That finishes color and leads to materials.

Material Specifications

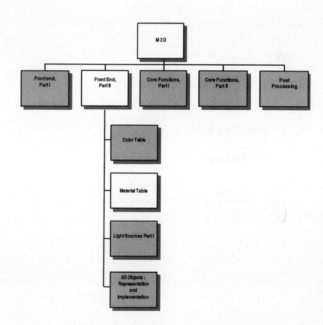

The material table is the second externally defined rendering resource. Again, the modeling script lets you define your own table as long as you adhere to the format. While the format of this table is a little more complex, it provides an easy way to name a set of surface coefficients and a texture. This, together with color, defines the surface properties of a 3D object.

While extending this table is a little more work than extending the color table, the ability to have more than a simple color attached to a surface means you can trace a wider range of images. Having a named material makes it trivial to try out a new set of surface coefficients to see how changing the coefficients will change the shading. Just duplicate an entry, create a new name, and make the appropriate modifications to the table and new entry.

What is a material? Listing 9-11 contains the data-structure definitions for the basic entity— the *MATERIALENTRY*. The *MATERIALARRAY* structure is simply a variable-sized array of *MATERIALENTRIES* using the extensible-API rules. While the color table simply defines RGB values, the material table and its *MATERIALENTRY* components define surface coefficients in the *SURFCOEFFS* structure and a texture in three parts: a name, an ID, and a void pointer. I've already mentioned, in passing, the surface coefficients in the parsing phase. I'm going to defer the details on what they mean a little longer, until Chapter 10. The important thing about their usage here is the naming and management of sets of coefficients.

Listing 9-11.   Materials Data Structures

```
typedef struct t_material
{
 //name
   char          m_name[64];
 //coefficients
   SURFCOEFFS   m_surfprops;
 //texture
   char          m_texture[64];
   int           m_tid;
   LPVOID        m_texdata;
} MATERIALENTRY;

typedef struct t_material_array
{
    int             iEntries;
    MATERIALENTRY meMaterials[1];
}MATERIALARRAY;

typedef MATERIALARRAY FAR *LPMATERIALARRAY;
```

I'm also deferring the detailed discussion of textures until Chapter 10, but I'll cover the data structures for individual texturing functions here. Briefly, the name and ID identify the texture function and the void pointer is a mechanism to cache any information that might be needed by a texturing function. The materials data file then contains extra records for certain texture functions. Again, without going into detail: five textures are supported, as shown in Table 9-3, which lists the textures and indicates which ones have a supporting data structure. From this you can see there are three additional structures to be considered.

Listing 9-12 contains the texturing data structures. *CHECKDATA*, *WOODDATA*, and *MARBLEDATA* support their textures as shown in Table 9-3. We'll use these structures in *MakeMaterialLookupTable* and again in the shading and texturing process (in Chapter 10).

Table 9-3. Textures and Data

Texture Name	Description	Supporting Data
Smooth	Default — no texture	no
Grit	Simple random	no
Checker	Periodic	yes
Wood	Cyclic	yes
Marble	Noise-based	yes

Listing 9-12. Texture Data Structures

```
typedef struct t_checker
{
    VECTOR4D    ch_color1;
    VECTOR4D    ch_color2;
    double      ch_period;
} CHECKDATA;

typedef CHECKDATA FAR *LPCHECKDATA;
//
typedef struct t_wood
{
    VECTOR4D    wd_dark;
    VECTOR4D    wd_light;
} WOODDATA;

typedef WOODDATA FAR *LPWOODDATA;
//
typedef struct t_marble
{
    double  m_cyclewidth;
} MARBLEDATA;

typedef MARBLEDATA FAR *LPMARBLEDATA
```

You're now ready for the implementation. *LookupMaterialByName* provides an interface that is almost identical to *LookupColorByName* and shamelessly duplicates *BinaryColorSearch* as *BinaryMaterialSearch*. If you add another external resource table, for instance to extend the shader and add shader definitions, you'll need to explore some more general table/search implementation.

Memory cleanup is performed by *FreeMaterialLookupTable*. Before we examine these functions, we'll need to go more into the details of the material table format.

Material Table Format

The current working directory must contain a materials file referenced in the script file as shown in Listing 9-13, with the usual token/name/value block from a typical script.

Listing 9-13. MATERIALTABLE Modeling Script Entry

```
MATERIALS
  Material   = material.dat
```

The elements of the material table are defined in Table 9-4. Once again, you'll see the counter at the front to ease memory management. These blocks borrow the beginning/end token pairing from the OBJDEF block to allow a nested while-loop approach. The name is used as a search key, which implies another alphabetic table organization. You saw the texture names when we defined the texture support data structures. The various surface coefficients determine the intensity of the various terms in the shading equations you saw in Chapter 2. Don't worry, we'll cover surface properties, textures, and shading extensively in Chapter 10, so hold any lingering questions a little longer.

Table 9-4.   MATERIALTABLE Elements

Token/Element		Description
count		Number of entries in table
m		Start definition
name	%s	ASCII name
texture %s		TEXTURE name
k_a	%g %g %g	Ambient component
k_d	%g %g %g	Diffuse component
k_s	%g %g %g	Specular component (highlights)
shine	%g	Specular shininess value
k_t	%g %g %g	Transmission component
ior	%g	Index of refraction
end		End definition

Listing 9-14 contains the default material table entries. This gets to be a lot of data, and it is much easier to remember "shinycountertop" for a smooth surface with medium-sized highlights (specular term) than it would be to remember 14 floating-point values. This lets you easily combine shapes and textures to produce a variety of appearances in a scene.

A couple of problems exist with this scheme. First, it's difficult to make small changes to colors or materials. The best way to fix this is to add user interface widgets that let the user modify values with a slider or a scrollbar. (You could easily add this to the code.) Second, the total count entry in the tables makes maintenance tedious. You could, if you want, make the color and material table smarter to fix this. Finally, you need to realize that these "tweaks" for making slight changes and adding new values can have a bad effect on already-finished model/scene descriptions. Since the modeling script defines the color and material table filename, there is no reason to try a "one size fits all" approach with these tables. Make new tables when you need to. By a clever use of naming conventions, you can make obvious associations between model/script and color/material tables. The downside of this is the proliferation of data files, but there is no such thing as a free lunch.

Listing 9-14.   Default Material Table Values

```
15
m
NAME     anodized
TEXTURE smooth
KA       1. 1. 1.
KD       0. 0. 0.
KS       0. 0. 0.
SHINE    0
KT       0 0 0
IOR      0
end
m
NAME     basicmarble
TEXTURE marble
KA       .1 .1 .1
KD       .4 .4 .4
KS       .2 .2 .2
SHINE    25
KT       0 0 0
IOR      0
MARBLEDATA
C 125
end
m
NAME     brass
TEXTURE smooth
KA       .1 .1 .1
KD       .3 .3 .3
KS       .6 .5 .25
SHINE    30
KT       0 0 0
IOR      1
end
m
NAME     cement
TEXTURE grit
KA       .2 .2 .2
KD       .8 .8 .8
KS       .0 .0 .0
SHINE    0
KT       0 0 0
IOR      0
end
m
NAME     chessboard
TEXTURE checker
KA       .2 .2 .3
KD       .6 .6 .6
KS       .4 .4 .4
```

Listing 9-14. *(cont.)*

```
SHINE    25
KT       0  0  0
IOR      .5
CHECKDATA
C1   1   0   0
C2  .1  .1  .1
P   .05
end

m
NAME     chrome
TEXTURE  smooth
KA       .1 .1 .1
KD       .1 .1 .1
KS       .6 .6 .6
SHINE    30
KT       0  0  0
IOR      1
end
m
NAME     countertop
TEXTURE  smooth
KA       .7 .7 .7
KD       .5 .5 .5
KS       .2 .2 .2
SHINE    10
KT       0  0  0
IOR      0
end
m
NAME     ebony
TEXTURE  smooth
KA       .1 .1 .1
KD       .35 .35 .35
KS       .1 .1 .1
SHINE    1
KT       0  0  0
IOR      1
end
m
NAME     grass
TEXTURE  grit
KA       .2 .2 .2
KD       .6 .8 .25
KS       .0 .0 .0
SHINE    0
KT       0  0  0
IOR      0
end
m
```

```
NAME      matte
TEXTURE smooth
KA        .7 .7 .7
KD        .5 .5 .5
KS        .0 .0 .0
SHINE     0
KT        0 0 0
IOR       0
end
m
NAME      mirror
TEXTURE smooth
KA        .1 .1 .1
KD        .4 .4 .4
KS        .5 .5 .5
SHINE     50
KT        0 0 0
IOR       1
end
m
NAME      oak
TEXTURE wood
KA        .1 .1 .1
KD        .4 .35 .35
KS        .1 .1 .1
SHINE     5
KT        0 0 0
IOR       0
WOODDATA
WD .435 .258 .248
WL .556 .419 .137
end
m
NAME      plastictile
TEXTURE checker
KA        .1 .1 .3
KD        .7 .7 .7
KS        .2 .2 .2
SHINE     4
KT        0 0 0
IOR       0
CHECKDATA
C1  1  0  0
C2 .2 .2 .2
P   .1
end
m
NAME      shinycountertop
TEXTURE smooth
```

Listing 9-14. (*cont.*)

```
KA          .5 .5 .5
KD          .5 .5 .5
KS          .3 .3 .3
SHINE       20
KT          0 0 0
IOR         0
end
m
NAME        water
TEXTURE     grit
KA          .1 .1 .3
KD          .1 .3 .3
KS          .1 .1 .4
SHINE       3
KT          0 0 0
IOR         0
end
```

From here, we'll go to the implementation of the material API.

Material Table Functions

There is a great deal of regularity in the API; this is apparent here because once again we use four functions, and again three are visible and one is internal. The material table functions are:

1. MakeMaterialLookupTable,
2. FreeMaterialLookupTable,
3. LookupMaterialByName, and
4. BinaryMaterialSearch.

The make and free functions construct and destroy the table; while the lookup function provides the name service and uses *BinaryMaterialSearch* to perform the same kind of binary search you just saw in the previous section.

MakeMaterialLookupTable, in Listing 9-15, uses the count value to allocate memory (using *WL_Mem_Alloc* from the WLib) just like its companion color-table generator; this time, however, the I/O loop is a bit more complex.

Describing the complexity of this nested loop sequence is best handled by the "husk" approach I've used previously. There are thirteen blocks here, as shown in Listing 9-15.

Listing 9-15.   MakeMaterialLookupTable

```c
LPMATERIALARRAY WINAPI MakeMaterialLookupTable(LPSTR SrcFile)
{
    FILE            *infile;
    int             i,nMats;
    LPMATERIALARRAY LoadMats;
    long            asb;
    double          x,y,z;
    lstrcpy((LPSTR)szBuff,(LPSTR)SrcFile);
    /* object db file */
    if ( (infile = fopen(szBuff,"r+t")) == NULL)
    {
        MessageBox(NULL,"object dat file open failure!",
           "scene package",MB_OK);
        return NULL;
    }
    fscanf(infile,"%d",&nMats);
    LoadMats = (LPMATERIALARRAY)WL_Mem_Alloc(GHND,
               sizeof(MATERIALARRAY) +
               (nMats)*sizeof(MATERIALENTRY));
    LoadMats->iEntries = nMats;
    i = 0;
    while ( (fscanf(infile,"%s",szBuff) != EOF) )
    {
        if (!_fstricmp((LPSTR)szBuff,(LPSTR)"M") )
        {
            while ( (fscanf(infile,"%s",szBuff) != EOF) )
            {
                if (!_fstricmp((LPSTR)szBuff,(LPSTR)"END") )
                {
                    PrintMaterialInfo(LoadMats->meMaterials[i],
                                   winio_hwnd);
                    i++;
                    break;
                }
                if (!_fstricmp((LPSTR)szBuff,(LPSTR)"NAME") )
                {
                    fscanf(infile,"%s", &szBuff);
                    lstrcpy((LPSTR)LoadMats->meMaterials[i].m_name,
                           (LPSTR)szBuff);
                }
                if (!_fstricmp((LPSTR)szBuff,(LPSTR)"TEXTURE") )
                {
...
                }
                if (!_fstricmp((LPSTR)szBuff,(LPSTR)"KA") )
                {
...
                }
                if (!_fstricmp((LPSTR)szBuff,(LPSTR)"KD") )
                {
```

Listing 9-15. (cont.)

```
...
                }
                if (!_fstricmp((LPSTR)szBuff,(LPSTR)"KS") )
                {
...
                }
                if (!_fstricmp((LPSTR)szBuff,(LPSTR)"SHINE") )
                {
...
                }
                if (!_fstricmp((LPSTR)szBuff,(LPSTR)"KT") )
                {
...
                }
                if (!_fstricmp((LPSTR)szBuff,(LPSTR)"IOR") )
                {
...
                }
                if (!_fstricmp((LPSTR)szBuff,(LPSTR)"CHECKDATA") )
                {
 ...
                }
                if (!_fstricmp((LPSTR)szBuff,(LPSTR)"WOODDATA") )
                {
...
                }
                if (!_fstricmp((LPSTR)szBuff,(LPSTR)"MARBLEDATA") )
                {
...
                }
            }
        }
    }
    fclose(infile);
    return LoadMats;
}
```

The END and NAME blocks are shown in Listing 9-15, the texture name block
TEXTURE in Listing 9-16, the surface coefficient blocks KA, KD, KS, SHINE, KT, and IOR
in Listings 9-17 through 9-21, and the texture data blocks CHECKDATA, WOODDATA,
and MARBLEDATA are in Listings 9-22 to 9-24.

Listing 9-16. TEXTURE Block

```
fscanf(infile,"%s ", &szBuff);
lstrcpy((LPSTR)LoadMats->meMaterials[i].m_texture,
        (LPSTR)szBuff);
if (!_fstricmp((LPSTR)szBuff,(LPSTR)"SMOOTH") )
    LoadMats->meMaterials[i].m_tid = 1;
if (!_fstricmp((LPSTR)szBuff,(LPSTR)"CHECKER") )
    LoadMats->meMaterials[i].m_tid = 2;
if (!_fstricmp((LPSTR)szBuff,(LPSTR)"WOOD") )
    LoadMats->meMaterials[i].m_tid = 3;
if (!_fstricmp((LPSTR)szBuff,(LPSTR)"GRIT") )
    LoadMats->meMaterials[i].m_tid = 4;
if (!_fstricmp((LPSTR)szBuff,(LPSTR)"MARBLE") )
    LoadMats->meMaterials[i].m_tid = 5;
if !_fstricmp((LPSTR)szBuff,(LPSTR)"TURBULENTMARBLE") )
    LoadMats->meMaterials[i].m_tid = 6;
```

Listing 9-17.   Ka and Kd Block

```
...
fscanf(infile,"%lf %lf %lf",&x,&y,&z);
LoadMats->meMaterials[i].m_surfprops.surf_ka.x = x;
LoadMats->meMaterials[i].m_surfprops.surf_ka.y = y;
LoadMats->meMaterials[i].m_surfprops.surf_ka.z = z;
...
//
...
fscanf(infile,"%lf %lf %lf",&x,&y,&z);
LoadMats->meMaterials[i].m_surfprops.surf_kd.x = x;
LoadMats->meMaterials[i].m_surfprops.surf_kd.y = y;
LoadMats->meMaterials[i].m_surfprops.surf_kd.z = z;
...
```

Listing 9-18.   Ks Block

```
fscanf(infile,"%lf %lf %lf",&x,&y,&z);
LoadMats->meMaterials[i].m_surfprops.surf_ks.x = x;
LoadMats->meMaterials[i].m_surfprops.surf_ks.y = y;
LoadMats->meMaterials[i].m_surfprops.surf_ks.z = z;
```

Listing 9-19.   SHINE Block

```
fscanf(infile,"%lf",&x);
LoadMats->meMaterials[i].m_surfprops.surf_shine = x;
```

Listing 9-20. Kt Block

```
fscanf(infile,"%lf %lf %lf",&x,&y,&z);
LoadMats->meMaterials[i].m_surfprops.surf_kt.x = x;
LoadMats->meMaterials[i].m_surfprops.surf_kt.y = y;
LoadMats->meMaterials[i].m_surfprops.surf_kt.z = z;
```

Listing 9-21. IOR Block

```
fscanf(infile,"%lf",&x);
LoadMats->meMaterials[i].m_surfprops.surf_ior = x;
```

Listing 9-22. CHECKDATA Block

```
LPCHECKDATA lpchkd;

lpchkd = (LPCHECKDATA)WL_Mem_Alloc(GHND,sizeof(CHECKDATA));
fscanf(infile,"%s", &szBuff);
if (!_fstricmp((LPSTR)szBuff,(LPSTR)"C1") )
{
    fscanf(infile,"%lf %lf %lf",&x,&y,&z);
    lpchkd->ch_color1.x = x;
    lpchkd->ch_color1.y = y;
    lpchkd->ch_color1.z = z;
}
fscanf(infile,"%s", &szBuff);
if (!_fstricmp((LPSTR)szBuff,(LPSTR)"C2") )
{
    fscanf(infile,"%lf %lf %lf",&x,&y,&z);
    lpchkd->ch_color2.x = x;
    lpchkd->ch_color2.y = y;
    lpchkd->ch_color2.z = z;
}
fscanf(infile,"%s", &szBuff);
if (!_fstricmp((LPSTR)szBuff,(LPSTR)"P") )
{
    fscanf(infile,"%lf",&x);
    lpchkd->ch_period = x;
}
LoadMats->meMaterials[i].m_texdata = (LPVOID)lpchkd;
```

Listing 9-23. WOODDATA Block

```
LPWOODDATA lpwd;

lpwd = (LPWOODDATA)WL_Mem_Alloc(GHND,sizeof(WOODDATA));
fscanf(infile,"%s", &szBuff);
if (!_fstricmp((LPSTR)szBuff,(LPSTR)"WD") )
{
```

```
        fscanf(infile,"%lf %lf %lf",&x,&y,&z);
        lpwd->wd_dark.x = x;
        lpwd->wd_dark.y = y;
        lpwd->wd_dark.z = z;
}
fscanf(infile,"%s", &szBuff);
if (!_fstricmp((LPSTR)szBuff,(LPSTR)"WL") )
{
        fscanf(infile,"%lf %lf %lf",&x,&y,&z);
        lpwd->wd_light.x = x;
        lpwd->wd_light.y = y;
        lpwd->wd_light.z = z;
}
LoadMats->meMaterials[i].m_texdata = (LPVOID)lpwd;
```

Listing 9-24. MARBLEDATA Block

```
LPMARBLEDATA lpmd;

lpmd = (LPMARBLEDATA)WL_Mem_Alloc(GHND,sizeof(MARBLEDATA));
fscanf(infile,"%s", &szBuff);
if (!_fstricmp((LPSTR)szBuff,(LPSTR)"C") )
{
        fscanf(infile,"%lf",&x);
        lpmd->m_cyclewidth = x;
}
LoadMats->meMaterials[i].m_texdata = (LPVOID)lpmd;
```

In this code, you'll see two while loops. The outer performs a "while not EOF" loop. Note that, strictly speaking, I could have used a for loop since we know the count. This approach, however, makes it easier to remove the counter and size on the fly — a possible enhancement. The END block terminates the inner while loop that extracts the parameters for one material block from the input stream. It also invokes *PrintMaterialInfo* to dump a copy of the material data to the transcript log. This way, it's easy to identify what material an image used and what needs to be recreated. The NAME block is equally simple. It uses the expected **fscanf** to retrieve the name.

The surface coefficient blocks and the texture data blocks also use **fscanf**, according to the formatting information, to extract the parameter values. I'm not going to cover them in detail, since they're like the others — if you want to take a look at them, refer to the code on your disk.

Companion function *FreeMaterialLookupTable*, shown in Listing 9-25, performs the check for supporting texture data and deallocates that before deallocating the *MATERIALENTRY*. In both cases, the deallocation uses *WL_Mem_Free*.

Listing 9-25.　FreeMaterialLookupTable

```
int WINAPI FreeMaterialLookupTable(LPMATERIALARRAY Materials)
{
    int i;
  for ( i = 0; i < Materials->iEntries; i++ )
  {
        if (!_fstricmp((LPSTR)Materials->meMaterials[i].m_texture,
                   (LPSTR)"CHECKER") )
        {
          WL_Mem_Free(Materials->meMaterials[i].m_texdata);
 }
        if (!_fstricmp((LPSTR)Materials->meMaterials[i].m_texture,
                   (LPSTR)"WOOD") )
        {
          WL_Mem_Free(Materials->meMaterials[i].m_texdata);
        }
        if (!_fstricmp((LPSTR)Materials->meMaterials[i].m_texture,
                   (LPSTR)"MARBLE") )
        {
          WL_Mem_Free(Materials->meMaterials[i].m_texdata);
        }
    }
    WL_Mem_Free(Materials);
    return 1;
}
```

The lookup function *LookupMaterialByName* is presented in Listing 9-26, and uses the binary search function *BinaryMaterialSearch*. If the material is matched, a rather tedious copy occurs — you could easily define a macro or other function to clean this up; the important detail is the target of the copy.

Listing 9-26.　LookupMaterialByName

```
int WINAPI LookupMaterialByName(LPMATERIALARRAY Materials,char * name, LPSURFPROPS
match)
{
  int rc ;
  rc = BinaryMaterialSearch(name,0,
                        Materials->iEntries - 1, Materials);
  if (rc < 0) {
             return(0) ;
        }
  match->surf_ka = Materials->meMaterials[rc].m_surfprops.surf_ka;
  match->surf_ks = Materials->meMaterials[rc].m_surfprops.surf_ks;
  match->surf_kd = Materials->meMaterials[rc].m_surfprops.surf_kd;
  match->surf_shine =
     Materials->meMaterials[rc].m_surfprops.surf_shine;
  match->surf_kt = Materials->meMaterials[rc].m_surfprops.surf_kt;
```

```
match->surf_ior =
   Materials->meMaterials[rc].m_surfprops.surf_ior;
 match->surf_tid     = Materials->meMaterials[rc].m_tid;
 match->surf_texdata = Materials->meMaterials[rc].m_texdata;
 lstrcpy(match->szTexture, Materials->meMaterials[rc].m_texture);     return 1 ;
}
```

The return parameter type for the matched value is a *SURFPROPS* pointer. Our material strategy clears a little more at this point. While the material array uses the *SURFCOEFFS* structure, this structure does not appear in the 3D objects themselves — it is internal to the material table. By the time an object specification is finished, the underlying material table definition has been transformed and is not visible. Other than that, it is very similar to its COLORTABLE cousin.

Function *BinaryMaterialSearch* is contained in Listing 9-27. It depends on alphabetic table ordering and uses **strcmp** for comparisons and the same checking and recursion algorithm.

Listing 9-27.   BinaryMaterialSearch

```
int BinaryMaterialSearch(char * name, int l, int h,
                         LPMATERIALARRAY Materials)
{
    int m, rc ;
    if (l > h)
            return(-1) ;

    m = (l + h) / 2 ;

    rc = strcmp(name, Materials->meMaterials[m].m_name) ;
    if (rc == 0)
            return m ;
    else if (rc < 0)
        return BinaryMaterialSearch(name, l, m-1, Materials) ;
    else
        return BinaryMaterialSearch(name, m + 1, h, Materials) ;
}
```

That finishes our discussion of the material API, with the exception of *PrintMaterialInfo*. This helper function uses *Trans_Printf* to dump exactly the information you have just seen, so I'm not going to repeat it here. If you need to see the implementation, look at the source code on your disk.

With that, we're on to light sources.

Light Sources I: Instantiation

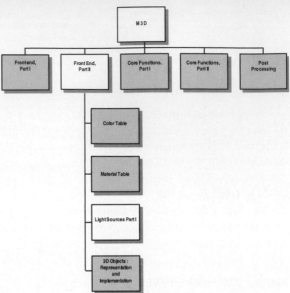

Light sources are created and inserted in the light list, and are used in the rendering process to generate shaded images. We're now going to look at the creation and insertion phases; rendering usage will keep until Chapter 10.

You've already seen the light source data structure LIGHTSRC, but it is repeated in Listing 9-28 to refresh your memory. The critical elements are the position and color, with the brightness included for growth potential.

Listing 9-28.   LIGHTSRC Structure

```
typedef struct t_light
{
    VECTOR4D  w_light_pos;
    VECTOR4D  o_light_pos;
    VECTOR4D  light_rgb;
    char      szLiteColor[64];
    double    light_brightness;
} LIGHTSRC;
```

The coordinates are used, if you remember, to provide values for both polygon and ray shading calculations. The light coordinates are shared between the two modes for these calculations. Notice the storage of both ASCII and RGB values for color. The ASCII and RGB dualism is a convenience: once we have looked up the name, we never have to do so again.

Using the data structure as a template, the creation of a light source object in memory happens during the parse phase, when the light token is extracted from the input stream. Back in Chapter 8, we deferred the implementation of function *MakeLight*, which was invoked in Listing 8-34, the LITEDEF block, to Chapter 9. We'll now tidy up that loose thread: *MakeLight* is implemented in Listing 9-29.

Listing 9-29.   MakeLight

```
LPOBJECT WINAPI MakeLight (LPSCENE    theScene,
                           LIGHTSRC   lsrc)
{
  LPOBJECT this = NULL;
  LPLIGHTSRC  l ;

  this = WL_Mem_Alloc(GHND, sizeof(OBJECT));
  if (this != NULL)
  {
    this->o_type   = LightSource;
    this->o_procs  = & LightProcs ;
    l              = (LPLIGHTSRC) WL_Mem_Alloc(GHND,
                                        sizeof(LIGHTSRC)) ;
//copy light data
    *l             = lsrc;
    this->o_edata = (LPVOID) l ;
//set surface data color for convenience ( a dupe )
    this->o_surfprops.surf_color[0] = lsrc.light_rgb.x;
    this->o_surfprops.surf_color[1] = lsrc.light_rgb.y;
    this->o_surfprops.surf_color[2] = lsrc.light_rgb.z;
  }
  return(this);
}
```

The light source object is used within a list, so the *MakeLight* function shows the footprint of the *OBJECT* structure and its function-pointer structure. *MakeLight* also shows the void pointer usage, here storing light data as "explicit" data. The husk of the *OBJECT* structure supports generic list manipulations, and the "internal" void pointer supports the object-specific data used by object-specific actions, such as light source data. Finally, the WLib allocator, *WL_Mem_Alloc*, is used to allocate the memory, continuing the standard API usage.

Every *Makexxx* function has a corresponding free function. *FreeLight* fulfills that purpose here and is shown in Listing 9-30.

Listing 9-30.   FreeLight

```
int FreeLight(LPOBJECT this)
{
  WL_Mem_Free(this->o_edata);
  return 1;
}
```

It simply uses *WL_Mem_Free* to return the light objects' memory to the global heap. Three important light functions remain—*MakeLightVec, MakeLightRay,* and *GetLightColor* — as well as the specific usage of light sources by the polygon drawing code and the object tracing code. Those functions and details will be revealed in the in-depth coverage of polygons and rays in Chapter 10. First, we need to define the 3D objects themselves.

3D Objects: Representation and Implementation

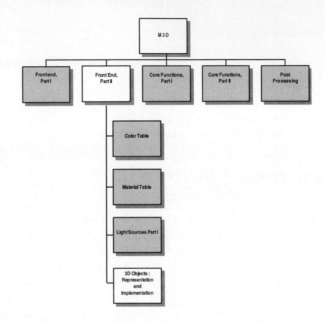

A 3D graphics system must support a basic set of objects to be considered a modeling system. Without that minimum set of objects and the ability to manipulate a group of them, the system could not be described as a modeler. All this means is that a modeling system must provide something to model with. The color and material tables, the list of light sources, the viewpoint, and the background components (ambient light and background color) all contribute to the modeling system; without 3D objects, however, this is all pointless.

As previously discussed, our modeler provides the following 3D objects:

- sphere,
- plane,
- cylinder,
- cone,
- box, and
- pyramid.

A wireframe version of these objects is shown in Figure 9-1. The objects provided and their use are your primary concerns as an API programmer. As an implementer, you're concerned with the details of the internals. In this case, you play both roles.

Figure 9-1. 3D Objects

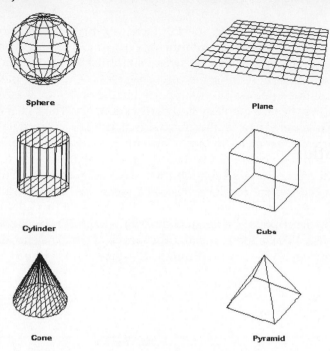

First, I'll cover the internals so you can see into the core of the system. Once you understand how everything is implemented (covered here in the second part of Chapter 9), we'll consider the usage from an external viewpoint in Chapter 10. At that point, you will not only know how to perform actions with the system, but, more important, you'll know the limits of these tools; it will be clear to you exactly where these limits are in the code.

Internals start with representation. *Representation* here means both the abstract of the approach and what it implies about data structures and the implementation. Two representations are used: an explicit face/vertex representation of face lists and vertex lists supplying a polygonized view of the world, and, coupled to that, an analytic, equation-based representation used in the ray-traced rendering mode. This description, however, says nothing about implementation.

Implementation of the explicit face and vertex form is supported by an "object database" containing the face and vertex data for each object. The format of the OBJDEF record discussed in Chapter 8 explained the slot for the data file briefly; it is this "database" file that I was referring to there. Once the face and vertex information has been assimilated, we can derive the analytic representation from the geometry of the object. This is convenient, because the database need only support the one representation on disk. Internally, we'll need a suite of routines for each form. The two ways of describing the same object and the API support the two rendering methods: polygon-based and ray-based. The dualism and form of these representations imply a great deal, as do the details of the respective APIs and the limits of the system.

Representation Part I: Explicit Object Geometry

Face and vertex representation uses a list of faces, together with a list of the actual vertex points, to describe the topology or ordering of vertices. Separating these two lists accomplishes two important goals: vertex reuse and simplification of the surface visibility process. With the list of faces describing the vertex used for each "point" of the face, it becomes trivial to reuse common points; this is supported in the object database generation.

Figure 9-2 shows the face topology and vertex geometry. The face data contains a quad of the face indices, ordered in a counterclockwise circuit. The vertex data contains the three-dimensional Cartesian geometry in (x,y,z) form for each distinct point. Notice that the face data is truly an index into the vertex data, as in a database. They are stored separately, which allows the vertex data-generation process to independently cull duplicate vertex data without disturbing the resultant object's appearance. This also means that the face data contains the absolute minimum amount of data needed to fully describe the object (or to recreate the description), so the data describing each 3D object is thus "normalized," in a database sense. What's more, because the face data contains enough descriptive data, the visibility sort process can manipulate the face data without ever touching the vertex data.

Figure 9-2.   Explicit Form

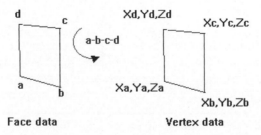

This is all nice, but it does beg the question of where this data comes from. Yes, as you suspected, three-dimensional data does not fall manna-like out of the heavens to feed the rendering engine. You must write a program. Actually, you can generate the simplest two objects, the box and pyramid, easily using simple manual techniques. Spheres, planes, cylinders, and cones are another story, though. You can use some of the same mathematics the ray tracer will use to provide both the internals of the object database generation process and an opportunity to use the mathematics of the analytic representation in a practical way for the first time. But before you get to database-generation, you can't avoid the math any longer.

Representation Part II: Analytic Object Geometry

First, this mathematical approach is based on lines, planes, and plane figures in three-space and quadric surfaces in three-space. These are part of what is known as *analytic geometry*, and even though they are typically taught in freshman calculus, they only require algebra

— no integral or differential calculus. We use these equations, along with the techniques of parametric equations and the more common substitution method for a system of equations.

Parametric equations are a way to use a variable (parameter) as the "seed" to drive a system of equations. For example, Equation 9-1 shows the standard equation of a right-opening parabola.

Equation 9-1.   Right-to-Left Parabola Standard Form

$$y^2 = 4px$$

Equation 9-2 would produce a parabola as described in Figure 9-3. In other words, the parabola is tangent to the y-axis at (0,-3) and has a principal axis ("is symmetrical about") at the line y = -3.

Equation 9-2.   Parabola Equation for Graph in Figure 9-3

$$(y + 3)^2 = x$$

Figure 9-3.   Parabola (y+3)$^{2=x}$

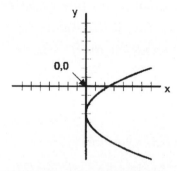

Parameterizing this by t yields, in Equation 9-3:

Equation 9-3.   Parameterized Parabola

$$x = t^2, y = t - 3, -\infty < t < \infty$$

This defines the parabola for all t, and effectively traces out the graph by generating both the independent and dependent axes of a graph from iterating across one variable (parameter). This example in two-dimensions shows how trivial the parabola should be to implement as a loop.

The system of equations in Equation 9-3 is called the *parametric equations* of the parabola in parameter t. You can think of t as either time or distance. Basically this replaces one equation in two unknowns with two equations in one unknown.

The Cartesian equation of the parabola can be found by eliminating the parameter t. First, find the value of t in terms of one of the other variables (either x or y). Then substitute this value in one of the equations to eliminate one of the variables. For example, doing this for the previous equation results in Equation 9-4.

Equation 9-4.   Substitution

$$t = y + 3, \text{ substituted in the } x\text{ - equation gives } x = (y + 3)^2$$

We now have an equation in x and y — we're back to where we started. This parameterizing and substituting is a critical part of the entire process, and you should be able to go back and forth between either form; after all, this is only algebra.

With the basics of parameterization and substitution behind us, it's time to discuss lines and rays. A *ray* is a parameterized line. Lines, remember, are defined by two points. Rays are infinite lines, and can be defined in terms of an origin point, and the current point on the line in the line's direction. Equation 9-5 mathematically defines this ray for us.

Equation 9-5.   Rays Defined as a Parameterized Line

$$origin \ = Ro = [Xo, \ Yo, \ Zo]$$

$$direction \ = Rd = [Xd, \ Yd, \ Zd], \ where$$

$$Xd^2 + Yd^2 + Zd^2 = 1 \ (normalized \ point)$$

$$defines \ a \ ray \ as \ the \ set \ of \ points \ on \ the \ line$$

$$R(t) = Ro + Rd * t \ where \ t \ > \ 0.$$

With that in hand, it is time to discuss the representation of the basic objects. While the sphere and plane are simpler surfaces, the most general approach, as discussed in Chapter 2, is based on Equation 9-6.

Equation 9-6.   Generalized Quadric Formula

$$AX^2 + BY^2 + CZ^2 + DXY + EXZ + FYZ + GX + HY + IZ + J = 0$$

This is the family of infinite quadrics, and can be used for cylinders and cones. As I noted at the time, this suffers from too much generality, and using this family implies the use of some technique to bound the extents. Table 9-5 shows these equations and parameters of the common quadric surfaces for your reference.

We'll use a simpler approach here, describing each object as follows:

- the sphere and plane are described by their specific equations,
- a subset of this equation describes the cone and cylinder, and
- the box and pyramid use an extension of the infinite plane.

The box and pyramid use rectangles and triangles together to form their faces. These are defined mathematically as you would expect in three-space, with an origin and extents for the sides. A normal describes their orientation. The endcaps for the cylinder and cone are treated as circles and fit in with the rectangle that constructs the box and the triangle that

Table 9-5.   Quadric Surfaces, Equations, and Parameters

Quadric Surface	Equation	Parameters									
		A	B	C	D	E	F	G	H	I	J
Sphere	$X^2 + Y^2 + Z^2 - 1 = 0$	1	1	1	0	0	0	0	0	0	-1
Cylinder along											
X	$Y^2 + Z^2 - 1 = 0$	0	1	1	0	0	0	0	0	0	-1
Y	$X^2 + Z^2 - 1 = 0$	1	0	1	0	0	0	0	0	0	-1
Z	$X^2 + Y^2 - 1 = 0$	1	1	0	0	0	0	0	0	0	-1
Cone along											
X	$-X^2 + Y^2 + Z^2 = 0$	-1	1	1	0	0	0	0	0	0	0
Y	$X^2 - Y^2 + Z^2 = 0$	1	-1	1	0	0	0	0	0	0	0
Z	$X^2 + Y^2 - Z^2 = 0$	1	1	-1	0	0	0	0	0	0	0
Plane in											
YZ	$X = 0$	0	0	0	0	0	0	1	0	0	0
XZ	$Y = 0$	0	0	0	0	0	0	0	1	0	0
XY	$Z = 0$	0	0	0	0	0	0	0	0	1	0
Paraboloid along											
X	$Y^2 + Z^2 - X = 0$	0	1	1	0	0	0	-1	0	0	0
Y	$X^2 + Z^2 - Y = 0$	1	0	1	0	0	0	0	-1	0	0
Z	$X^2 + Y^2 - Z = 0$	1	1	0	0	0	0	0	0	-1	0
Hyperboloid (one sheet) along											
X	$-X^2 + Y^2 + Z^2 - 1 = 0$	-1	1	1	0	0	0	0	0	0	-1
Y	$X^2 - Y^2 + Z^2 - 1 = 0$	1	-1	1	0	0	0	0	0	0	-1
Z	$X^2 + Y^2 - Z^2 - 1 = 0$	1	1	-1	0	0	0	0	0	0	-1

completes the pyramid. These plane figures can be considered to be within an infinite plane, and we then need to test for point inside/point outside the polygon.

Now you have a mathematical definition for each 3D object. You still need more information. You also need to solve for the intersection of the parameterized line and the 3D object. This is the ray/object intersection problem. The substitution and elimination technique reduces this and solves the system of equations for each ray-object intersection type.

The sphere is first on the list. The equation of a sphere is given in Equation 9-7, and should make clear the sphere is dependent only on the position of its origin and its radius. Using this equation, the ray equation is substituted and the result is solved for t. To do this, express the ray equation as a set of equations for the set of points [X Y Z] in terms of t.

Equation 9-7.   Sphere Formula

$$X^2 + Y^2 + Z^2 - R^2 = 0$$

After the appropriate simplification, this yields Equation 9-8:

Equation 9-8.   Sphere Coefficients

$$At^2 + Bt + c = 0, where$$
$$A = Xd^2 + Yd^2 + Zd^2 = 1$$
$$B = 2(Xd(Xo - Xc) + Yd(Yo - Yc) + Zd(Zo - Zc))$$
$$C = (Xo - Xc)^2 + (Yo - Yc)^2 + (Zo - Zc)^2 - Sr^2 \ (Sr = sphere\ radius)$$

There are two important details here: A is always 1, and the radius squared term can be pre-computed, as I mentioned previously. This is a quadratic and can be solved using the standard form simplified, because A = 1.

Remember your quadratic rules: the discriminant is the part under the square root — when it is less than zero, no valid root exists outside of the complex plane. So solve the discriminant first; if it is less than zero, no intersection occurs. If the discriminant is greater than zero, continue to solve. The smaller positive real root is the closest intersection. Use intelligent checking that T0 is greater than zero and, if not, switching to T1 to save some time. If no such point exists, no intersection occurs. If such a point does exist and the distance t is found, you can calculate the actual intersection point, but I won't get into that until Chapter 10 and the section on ray tracing and visibility.

Equation 9-9 contains the equations of the roots. Here, the goal is simply to introduce you to the process.

Equation 9-9.   Sphere Roots in B and C

$$T_0 = -B - sqrt(B^2 - 4C) / 2$$
$$T_1 = -B + sqrt(B^2 - 4C) / 2$$

That concludes the discussion of the sphere.

The plane is a little simpler, since the equation for a plane in space has no squared terms. Equation 9-10 contains the plane equation.

Equation 9-10.   Plane Formula

$$AX + BY + CZ + D = 0\ where,$$
$$A^2 + B^2 + C^2 = 1$$

Based on this, the plane normal Pn is simply [A B C] and the distance from the coordinate origin is D. The sign of D determines the side of the plane on which the origin is located. Again, we calculate the distance by substituting the ray equation into the plane equation. The variable t is then as shown in Equation 9-11.

Equation 9-11.   Distance T to Intersection Point on Plane

$$t = -(AXo + BYo + CZo + D) / (AXd + BYd + CZd)$$

The resulting value is used to calculate various intermediate values that test for the validity of this point. I'll say more on this issue when I cover the implementation of the intersection in Chapter 10; for now, this is sufficient.

The plane and sphere are described solely in terms of these equations, and could thus be considered "simple" objects. The cylinder, cone, box, and pyramid cannot be described quite so simply. They are not true "composite" objects (like a teapot or a table), but they consist of a combination of simple objects — hence, we'll call them "combo" objects instead of "compo."

We define cylinders and cones in two parts: the *sheet* (or main part) and the *endcap(s)*.

The endcaps of both cylinders and cones are circles. So our question really is: how do we describe a circle? Thankfully, a circle is a plane figure contained on an infinite plane. Once the infinite plane has been solved for as I've already described, you need only test whether the intersection point is within the circle. There are a number of ways to do point/polygon inside/outside testing. The main body of the cylinder or cone, here called the *sheet*, is described by the subset of the quadric equation shown in Equation 9-12.

Equation 9-12.   Simpler Subset of Quadric Formula

$$AX^2 + BY^2 + CZ^2 + Ey = D$$

Using the same substitution technique results in two equations, depending on which parameters have non-zero values. The result is, again, a quadratic equation, as shown in Equation 9-13, and non-complex roots represent the intersection point(s). The usual checking for the non-interesting cases will save some calculations.

Equation 9-13.   Quadratic Surface Intersection Equations in t

$$t^2(AXd^2 + BYd^2 + CZd^2) + 2t(AXoXd + BYoYd + CZoZd) +$$
$$(AXo^2 + BYo^2 + CZo^2 - D) = 0, and$$
$$t^2(AXd^2 + CZd^2) + 2t(AXoXd - EYd + CZoZd) +$$
$$(AXo^2 - EYo^2 + CZo^2) = 0$$

There is another question of the order of evaluation, but that also will wait until we implement the intersection test code for cylinders and cones.

That leaves just the box and the pyramid. It may seem counter-intuitive, but the simplest objects in the polygon form — the box and pyramid — require the most work in analytic form and are the hardest for the ray tracer. The box and pyramid are really a collection of rectangles and triangles making up faces. The rectangle and the triangle, like the circle, are plane figures contained on an infinite plane. The pyramid is a little bit trickier, since it is a combination of a rectangle base and triangle sides. This makes it the only "combo" object *not* composed of one plane figure type. (This is true for both polygon mode and ray trace mode.) Still, these are only extensions of the plane intersection code you've already seen: it may be tricky, but it's still not rocket science.

Taken together, we'll need to support three plane figures in the code as far as definition and intersection. This will be controlled by the individual object; the main rendering loop will have no idea that a box is really a combination of discrete components or that a sphere is a single analytic body.

Now you've seen more of the details of the analytic representation, and it should be clear how you can generate a parametric version of the equations from the basic algebraic equations. Substituting the ray equation into the parametric equation, simplifying until an equation equal to zero is generated, and using the quadratic formula to solve for the roots that represent the intersection points are the basic techniques employed here.

Now that you know the how, you need to generate the prototypical objects. These pristine originals will be the templates that the *OBJDEF* blocks use to create a specific instance of an object; the front-end then translates and instantiates that "spec" into reality. This leads us to the object database and the object database generation process.

Representation Part III: The Object Database

This chapter is certainly not to be compared to Genesis, but there is a parallel: the object database is the beginning of all creation to the modeler. Here, the archetypes are defined; these are the templates that can specify an instance and feed the world-generation process. Without these archetypes the modeler could only model the void. There might be light, but nothing else would exist.

In many simple 3D graphics texts, the rendering and viewing process ends about where I ended Chapter 7: with a simple cube or box in general, and if you're lucky a pyramid. One of the reasons for this is that the database of points and vertices must come from somewhere. These types of texts don't want to stop to consider geometry again and write another program or two, so the set of points and vertices remains visibly out of our grasp. Writing more code, while not a panacea, fixes this problem.

We need to cover several details first, though. We generated the box and the pyramid manually because they are so simple. The remaining objects — sphere, plane, cylinder, and cone — need "programmatic" generation. This amounts to building a face and vertex representation mathematically with trig and geometry, and writing this information to a disk file. This process is essentially the same for all four of these objects.

Instead of doing this within the modeler, we'll do it here since the object database programs are simplest to consider as command-line DOS programs. It would be easy for you to change this and add interactive creation into the modeler, but then you'd want to edit the scenes also, instead of just the "template" objects, and then.... As you can see, this becomes a never-ending story. In the interest of having an ending, we'll treat these generators extremely simply and externally. We'll construct a small API for face/vertex creation and face/vertex storage instead of using some ad hoc code; we'll also use some of the math functions from the G3DLib here. Instead of worrying about it and wasting time because these are DOS programs and G3DLIb is a Windows DLL, some code is duplicated here.

Listing 9-31 contains the definition of the API.

Listing 9-31.   3D Object Database Helpers

```
long    WINAPI Round(double x);
double  WINAPI Radians(double Angle);
double  WINAPI CosD(double Angle);
double  WINAPI SinD(double Angle);
void    WINAPI CheckForRepeatedVertices(double x,double y,
                                        double z );
void    WINAPI AddVertex(double x, double y,double z);
void    WINAPI SaveData(LPSTR FileName);
```

This code has three parts:

1. Math helpers,
2. Add API for creation, and
3. Save function for disk file storage.

The math helpers are duplicates of the routines from G3DLib with the naming convention removed to avoid confusion. Functions *Round*, *Radians*, *CosD*, and *SinD* are provided in this form. The add API includes functions to test for repeated vertices. Remember, since the face topology and the vertex geometry are stored separately, and since the face topology is in control, only the unique points need to be contained in the vertex list to allow a description to be generated by the face list. The function *CheckForRepeatedVertices* supports *AddVertex* by performing a check for duplicate points. Once the face and vertex lists are built, *SaveData* iterates across the lists and saves the object database.

This brings us to the format of the save file.

The format of the object database is a header record of counts, then the vertex data followed by the face data. The counts describe the number of vertices, number of faces, and number of vertices per face (triangle or rectangle). This is shown in **printf**-style formats in Table 9-6.

Table 9-6. Object Database Save File Elements

Element	Description
%d %d %d	Vertices,faces,number of points in a face
%g %g %g	Vertices count float triples of [X Y Z] coords
...	
%d %d %d (%d)	Number of points values repeated numfaces times

As you can see, this is pretty straightforward. The header record contains the number of vertex records, the number of face records, and how many vertex records a face record describes. This last is either 3 or 4 here. Only triangles and rectangles are supported as polygon building blocks.

Before implementing these functions, the entire process could use some explanation. The manual generation of the box and the pyramid gives me the opportunity. The general procedure, including conceptualization and the logical arrangement of steps, is shown in these two manual generation processes. Once you have the basics, the programmatic generation of the more complex 3D objects seems like a natural progression. As a side note, the programmatic generation is an extension of the simpler generators shown in Roger T. Stevens' and Christopher D. Watkins' books *Advanced Graphics Programming in Turbo Pascal* (M&T Books) and *Advanced Graphics Programming in C and C++* (M&T Books), as well as *Programming in 3 Dimensions* by Christopher D. Watkins and Larry Sharp (M&T Books).

Manual Generation I: The Box

The box, because of its simplicity, is the basic face/vertex object. It consists of six faces and eight unique vertex points. These are rectangles, so we use the points in groups of four. If our only criteria for object creation were the needs of wireframe mode, no ordering would be necessary. This modeler provides hidden-line/hidden-surface removal (HLHSR) using a z-sort and painters algorithm along with multiple rendering types: hidden monochrome, hidden solid color, and hidden flat-shaded. This means that we need to consider the details of HLHSR in building the object database.

This means we have to order the faces. Remember that in Chapter 2 and earlier in this chapter I described the faces in terms of a counterclockwise circuit. This circuit supports the creation of the surface normal, which is critical to the visibility process. Figure 9-4 shows the box's faces in relation to the viewpoint and the surface normals.

Figure 9-4.   Box Visibility Geometry

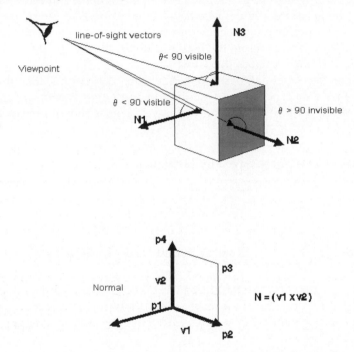

The surface normal is produced by performing a cross-product of two vectors formed from the vertices of the face in question. Remember from Chapter 7 that the result of the cross-product is also a vector. The normal and the viewpoint, as shown by Figure 9-4, define an angle. Again from Chapter 7, remember that the dot product represents the co-sine of the angle between two vectors if they are unit vectors. This means that the result of the dot product of N dot V tells us whether a face is visible: if the angle is less than or equal to 90 degrees (as shown) the face is visible; if the angle is greater than 90 degrees, the face is invisible.

The key thing then is generating the surface normal, because the dot product and cross-product are provided in the G3DLib by *G3D_V4D_VDot4D* and *G3D_V4D_VCross4D*, and the viewpoint is built on top of the G3D camera routines. The surface normal is generated from vectors that are built from the vertex points. If you change the ordering, you change the direction of the normal. Figure 9-5 shows this for the single face that you saw in Figure 9-4.

Figure 9-5.   Ordering and Surface Normals

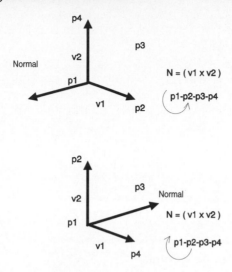

Here, you see both a counterclockwise circuit and a clockwise circuit. The direction of the v1 and v2 vectors built from the vertex points changes, as does the direction of the normal. The key thing here is consistency. From Figure 9-5 you should deduce that either circuit can describe a face, but that each face should be defined in the same order to ensure that the normals are all generated in the proper fashion to accurately indicate visibility. For this modeler, all circuits are defined counterclockwise, as seen from the outside of the object. This is a critical detail: the visibility test and HLHSR rendering modes will fail if this is not faithfully adhered to. Fortunately, it is easy to do this in the manual generation process, and the programmatic generation process is also easy to control.

With all the ordering details out of the way, we need to discuss the vertex coordinate values. The vertex coordinates are simple 3D coordinates — no fourth coordinate is stored on disk because homogeneous coordinates are a mathematician's (actually a geometer's) device and need only be stored in the calculation process. This makes object database generation even easier.

Before discussing the box itself, though, you need to know the details of positioning and sizing. The positioning of the prototypical object should be about the origin to make the translation process in the modeler seem natural. An object is then instantiated at the origin, and the translation terms stored in the OBJDEF move the prototype to its desired final location. The size of the prototypical object is typically taken as 1 or 2. Each face edge is then of size 1 or 2, and a single face straddling the origin does so between either [-.5,.5] or [1,1].

The general details of ordering, positioning, and sizing have all been addressed. That leaves the values of the vertex points themselves. The box vertex points used in Chapter 7 are similar to the ones used here. Listing 9-32 contains the box database of faces and vertices. Figure 9-6 supports this definition. Figure 9-6 does not contain face ID numbers, but it should be obvious. Compare Listing 9-32 to the format information in Table 9-6 and see the expansion of the ellipses into the eight vertex triplets and the six face quadruplets.

Listing 9-32. Box Database in box.dat

```
8  6  4
  1.0   1.0   1.0
 -1.0   1.0   1.0
 -1.0  -1.0   1.0
  1.0  -1.0   1.0
  1.0   1.0  -1.0
 -1.0   1.0  -1.0
 -1.0  -1.0  -1.0
  1.0  -1.0  -1.0
 4  3  2  1
 3  7  6  2
 8  7  3  4
 5  8  4  1
 6  5  1  2
 6  7  8  5
```

Figure 9-6.   Box and Box Database Points

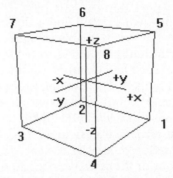

While the box and the pyramid are relatively easy to consider by direct examination, the other four 3D objects are not easily treated like this. Typically, they have many vertices and many faces, several being defined as some number greater than 20. Twenty vertices is 60 floating-point numbers (without considering homogeneous coordinates). Twenty faces is 80 face-identifying integers. You can see that hand-checking these quickly gets rather interesting. It is easier to check the sphere, plane, cylinder, and cone definitions by viewing them graphically than by inspecting the values. The pyramid, however, is still simple enough to generate and follow manually.

Manual Generation II: The Pyramid
The pyramid used here consists of four triangles and one rectangle. The base is a rectangle instead of two triangles for one important purpose that will become clear in Chapter 10: to illustrate in the code where a perturbation must take place to accommodate objects that are not uniformly constructed of one polygon type. Every other polygon-mode 3D object is formed of only rectangles. While this uniformity is nice, it tends to obscure important details like where the code depends on it until extension and expansion force you to reacquaint yourself and remember these details. The pyramid points out, at least within this system, key points that assume certain things about object and face geometry.

Beyond that, it uses the same visibility and ordering rules in its construction. All circuits are counterclockwise as seen from the outside. The sizing rules are the same as well, a size of 1 or 2. The prototypical pyramid is positioned about the origin as shown in Figure 9-7. Listing 9-33 contains the corresponding pyramid database of face and vertex values.

Listing 9-33.   Pyramid Database in pyramid.dat

```
5  5  3
1.0  0.0  0.0
1.0  1.0  0.0
0.0  1.0  0.0
0.0  0.0  0.0
0.5  0.5  1.0
2  1  5
3  2  5
4  3  5
1  4  5
1  2  3  4
```

Figure 9-7.   Pyramid and Pyramid Database Points

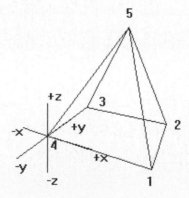

The base is a rectangle of edge-size 1, defined in the [+x,+y] quadrant. The altitude is defined as 1, and the apex is at [.5,.5,1], in the [+x,+y] quadrant. Once again face IDs are not included in Figure 9-7.

That takes care of the manual creation of the pyramid, and, with the box, covers the extent of what it is convenient to generate by hand. The programmatically generated objects come next. You will further explore the geometry of the remaining objects, and write code that describes your exploration.

Programmatic Generation I: MakeSphere

The sphere, plane, cylinder, and cone are too complex for manual generation of the database of face and vertex values. When the going gets too tough for hand calculation, the tough write code. This is where the mini-API defined in Listing 9-31 comes into play. We'll use that API to develop small DOS programs to do the hard work for us. First, we'll look at the sphere.

The main for the sphere program is contained in Listing 9-34. Starting here lets us consider the justification for the mini-API routines. The sphere generator breaks down into three discrete steps:

1. Read values from user.
2. Generate database.
3. Save database.

A sphere is described in terms of latitudinal and longitudinal, or horizontal and vertical, bands. The intersections of these bands form rectangles, and the intersection points are the vertices.

Figure 9-8 shows two views of an extremely crude sphere — it is 6 bands horizontal (around the sphere) and 6 bands vertical (pole to pole). By way of contrast, the sphere shown in Figure 9-9 has been used in most of the images you have seen and will see; it is 12 bands vertical and 20 bands horizontal. These values must divide evenly into 360 because they are used to "segmentize" the horizontal and vertical into bands. It would be tedious and pointless to attempt to label the points of the 12 x 20 sphere, and even with the 6 x 6 sphere there are 36 rectangles to consider. No, coding is the way here.

That returns us to consideration of the sphere main in Listing 9-34. Using the values for the horizontal and vertical bands, the function *SetupSphere* is invoked followed by *MakeSphereDatabase*. Finally, *SaveData* dumps the database to the save file.

Figure 9-8.   Sphere of Six Bands Vertical by Six Bands Horizontal

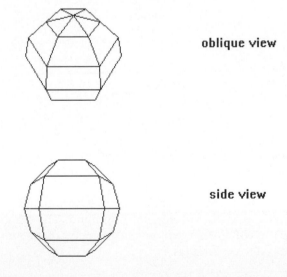

oblique view

side view

Figure 9-9.   Sphere of Twelve Bands Vertical by Twenty Bands Horizontal

Listing 9-34.   Sphere Generator Main Body

```
main (int argc, char **argv)
{
    FILE *out_file;
    int h,v;

    fprintf (stdout, "3DDB Sphere Generator .1 \n");
    fprintf (stdout, "\n");
    fprintf (stdout, "\n");
//
    fprintf (stdout, "enter horizontal bands ( even into 360 ): ");
    fscanf (stdin, "%d",&h);
    fprintf (stdout, "enter vertical bands  ( even into 360 ): ");
    fscanf (stdin, "%d",&v);
//
    SetupSphere(h,v);
    MakeSphereDatabase();
//
    fprintf (stdout, "generating sphere.dat ...%d by %d \n",h,v);
    fprintf (stdout, "\n");
    fprintf (stdout, "\n");
    SaveData("sphere.dat");

}
```

Now we specify what is being saved. The form of the object database is a list of vertices and a list of faces. An array of vectors and an array of face IDs are sufficient to represent those values. Next we must determine the size of any individual object and the form of these arrays. At this point we're not trying anything fancy. Each object generator is a separate DOS program, and each has an entire 64K data segment. This means we can specify a large static array. Dynamic memory allocation is slight overkill for these simple programs. How big of an array do we need? Listing 9-35 answers that question by defining the face array to be of size 800 and the vertex array to be twice as big, with 1600 elements. Why not 4 times the size, since each face has a maximum of 4 vertex points? The code for the programmatic generation of objects includes a check for repeated vertices. Any vertex that is reused appears only once. It might not be true in all cases, but the vertex count is unlikely to be more than twice the face count, and in most cases it will be even less. Think about the box and sphere. Each vertex point is an element in the four faces in the sphere and three faces in the box (see Figure 9-10). This makes it impossible to have 4 times (or even 3 times) the vertices per face.

Figure 9-10.   Sphere and Box Vertex Reuse

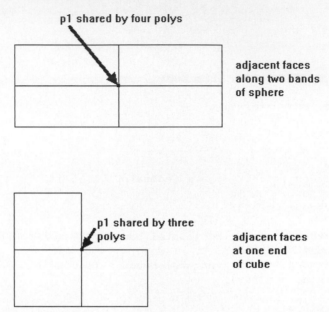

With that out of the way, let's consider *SaveData* first since this function is identical for all four programmatic generators. It also clarifies the makeup of the face and vertex arrays.

Listing 9-35 contains *SaveData*. It first dumps the header record, then writes the vertices and the face list, and finally closes the file. Key control variables used here are LastVertex, LastFace, and LastVertexNumInFace. These are used as the header record values and the control variables for the vertex and face loops. Once the lists are defined, it really is this simple. The vertex array is one-based here, but note the addressing calculation used to find the proper face IDs. This provides for zero-based addressing in the face list by subtracting 1 from the face number (taken sequentially in list order).

Listing 9-35.   SaveData

```
void WINAPI SaveData(LPSTR FileName)
{
    FILE*   OutFile;
    double  x, y, z;
    int     fn, fid;

    OutFile=fopen(FileName, "w+t");

    fprintf(OutFile,"%d ", LastVertex);
    fprintf(OutFile,"%d ", LastFace);
    fprintf(OutFile,"%d\n",LastVertexNumInFace);
```

```
    for(VertexNum=1; VertexNum<=LastVertex; VertexNum++)
    {
        x = Vertex[VertexNum].x;
        y = Vertex[VertexNum].y;
        z = Vertex[VertexNum].z;
        fprintf(OutFile,"%lf ", x);
        fprintf(OutFile,"%lf ", y);
        fprintf(OutFile,"%lf\n",z);
    }

    for(fn=1; fn<=LastFace; fn++)
    {
        for(VertexNumInFace=1;
            VertexNumInFace<=LastVertexNumInFace;
            VertexNumInFace++)
        {
            fid = (int)Face[((fn-1)*5)+VertexNumInFace];
            fprintf(OutFile,"%d ",fid);
        }
        fprintf(OutFile,"\n");
    }

    fclose(OutFile);
}
```

This leads us back to the generation phase performed by functions *SetupSphere* and *MakeSphereDatabase*. As expected, these functions result in the vertex and face lists that *SaveData* uses. *SetupSphere* is shown in Listing 9-36. It initializes various variables, including the previous three header-record count variables.

Listing 9-36. SetupSphere

```
void SetupSphere(int Horz, int Vert)
{
//
    VertexNum             = 1;
    VertexNumInFace       = 1;
    H                     = Horz;
    V                     = Vert;
    LastFace              = H*V;
    LastVertexNumInFace   = MaxVertexNumInFace;
    LastVertex            = LastFace * LastVertexNumInFace;
    DTheta                = 360 / H;
    HalfDTheta            = DTheta / 2;
    Theta                 = HalfDTheta;
    DPhi                  = 180 / V;
    HalfDPhi              = DPhi / 2;
    Phi                   = HalfDPhi;
}
```

The most important new variables here are the horizontal and vertical control variables. DTheta and HalfDTheta control the horizontal and DPhi and HalfDPhi control the vertical. The number of horizontal and vertical bands are stored in globals H and V, respectively. This prepares to iterate around the circles that form the bands, generating the segments that describe the circle. Remember your geometry again. You can describe a circle by a series of line segments inscribed within the circle's boundary. As the number of line segments increases, the accuracy of the representation of the circle increases as well. Notice that here is where we calculate the values for the header control variables, used in *SaveData.* LastVertex, LastFace, and LastVertexNumInFace are all calculated here, too.

That leaves function *MakeSphereDatabase*, shown in Listing 9-37. In a master loop for all faces, it calculates the values for the four vertices for each face using sine and cosine to increment around the circle in discrete segments.

Listing 9-37.   MakeSphereDatabase

```
void MakeSphereDatabase()
{
   int     T;
   double  x, y, z;

   Horz = 1;
   Vert = 1;
   for( FaceNum = 1; FaceNum <= LastFace; FaceNum++)
   {
        sinPhi = SinD(Phi-HalfDPhi);
        cosPhi = CosD(Phi-HalfDPhi);
        AddVertex( sinPhi*CosD(Theta-HalfDTheta),
                   sinPhi*SinD(Theta-HalfDTheta), cosPhi );
        AddVertex( sinPhi*CosD(Theta+HalfDTheta),
                   sinPhi*SinD(Theta+HalfDTheta), cosPhi );

        sinPhi = SinD(Phi+HalfDPhi);
        cosPhi = CosD(Phi+HalfDPhi);
        AddVertex( sinPhi*CosD(Theta+HalfDTheta),
                   sinPhi*SinD(Theta+HalfDTheta), cosPhi );
        AddVertex( sinPhi*CosD(Theta-HalfDTheta),
                   sinPhi*SinD(Theta-HalfDTheta), cosPhi );

        Theta -= DTheta;
        VertexNumInFace = 1;
        ++Horz;
        if ( Horz>H)
        {
           Horz=1;
           ++Vert;
           Theta=HalfDTheta;
           Phi +=DPhi;
        }
   }
}
```

The triplet produced by this calculation is then passed to *AddVertex*, which does checks to make sure the segment count does not exceed the number of bands the user specified. If they are exceeded, the requisite resets are performed.

AddVertex, shown in Listing 9-38, also performs a check for repeated vertices using *CheckForRepeatedVertices* (Listing 9-39). If the check passes, the values are added to the current vertex list and the face list is updated. It uses an addressing calculation similar to what you saw in *SaveData.*

Listing 9-38.   AddVertex

```
void    WINAPI AddVertex(double x, double y,double z)
{
    int offs;

    RepeatedVertex = FALSE;
    if ( RepeatedVertexCheck )
        CheckForRepeatedVertices(x,y,z);
    else
        RepeatedVertex = FALSE;
    if ( !RepeatedVertex )
    {
        Vertex[VertexNum].x = x;
        Vertex[VertexNum].y = y;
        Vertex[VertexNum].z = z;

        offs=((FaceNum-1)*5)+VertexNumInFace;
        Face[offs]=VertexNum;
        LastVertex = VertexNum;
        ++VertexNum;
    }
    else
    {
        offs=((FaceNum-1)*5)+VertexNumInFace;
        Face[offs]=OldVertexNum;
    }
    ++VertexNumInFace;
}
```

Listing 9-39.   CheckforRepeatedVertices

```
void    WINAPI CheckForRepeatedVertices(double x, double y, double z )
{
    RepeatedVertex = FALSE;
    if ( FaceNum >  1 )
    {
        for(OldVertexNum  = VertexNum-1;
            OldVertexNum >= 1;
            OldVertexNum—)
```

Listing 9-39. (cont.)

```
    {
        if (( Vertex[OldVertexNum].x == x ) &&
            ( Vertex[OldVertexNum].y == y ) &&
            ( Vertex[OldVertexNum].z == z ))
        {
            RepeatedVertex = TRUE;
            break;
        }
    }
  }
}
```

That wraps up both the completion of the sphere-generator application and the mini-API for all of the generators. As I cover the remaining 3D objects I'll use these functions again and again. So let's move on to the plane.

Programmatic Generation II: MakePlane
With the object-generation mini-API out of the way, we can focus on the main body and its user querying, setup, and calculation functions for our remaining objects.

The main body for the plane generator is shown in Listing 9-40. Instead of querying the user for a number of horizontal and vertical contours (although x and y would probably be better terms here), these numbers are hardcoded.

Listing 9-40. Plane Generator Main Body

```
main (int argc, char **argv)

{
 FILE *out_file;

 fprintf (stdout, "3DDB Plane Generator .1 \n");
 fprintf (stdout, "\n");
 fprintf (stdout, "\n");
//
     SetupPlane(-Span, Span, -Span, Span, Contour, Contour, Offset);

     MakePlaneDatabase();
//
 fprintf (stdout, "generating plane.dat ... \n");
 fprintf (stdout, "\n");
 fprintf (stdout, "\n");
     SaveData("plane.dat");
}
```

The size of the plane is, in general, controlled by the scaling of the OBJDEF. The plane used by ray-trace mode is infinite, so whatever happens here and in the OBJDEF for a plane is an approximation in polygon mode. The plane as we use it here is one-sided as well, which means that if you "fly" to -z numbers in hidden-line mode, the plane disappears. Think about it — this is the result you should expect based on our definitional scheme. If you want a two-sided plane, either change the code to take this into account (very ugly) or define two planes that are 180-degree reflections of each other. This forces the "underneath" plane to have circuits in the desired direction.

With that said about the initial values, the trail of code crumbs leads us back to *SetupPlane* and *MakePlaneDatabase*.

SetupPlane is shown in Listing 9-41. It, like all the setup functions, initializes variables, including the three header-record count variables. The most important new variables here are the plane horizontal and vertical control variables: Dx, Dy, HalfDx, and HalfDy.

Listing 9-41.   SetupPlane

```
void SetupPlane(double Xlft, double Xrgt,
                double Ybot, double Ytop,
                int HorzContours, int VertContours,
                double offset)
{
  VertexNum=1;
  VertexNumInFace=1;
  LastFace=HorzContours*VertContours;
  LastVertexNumInFace=MaxVertexNumInFace;
  LastVertex=LastFace*LastVertexNumInFace;
  sx=1;
  sy=1;

  Dx=(Xrgt-Xlft)/(double)(HorzContours-1);
  Dy=(Ybot-Ytop)/(double)(VertContours-1);
  HalfDx=Dx/((offset+1.0)*2.0);
  HalfDy=Dy/((offset+1.0)*2.0);

  ix=Xlft;
  iy=Ytop;
  ex=Xrgt;
  ey=Ybot;
}
```

From Figure 9-11 you can see how the contour values define Dx and Dy. This is a pretty simple geometry. HalfDx and HalfDy are calculated from Dx and Dy as helpers.

MakePlaneDatabase (Listing 9-42) is the final plane-generation function. In a while loop, the value of the stepping calculations is fed to *AddVertex*. Note that the z value is always 0.0, which indicates a prototypical plane in the x-y plane at z = 0.0. This becomes the standard orientation of a plane. From this orientation the OBJDEF contents instance a plane object.

Figure 9-11. Plane Horizontal Generation Geometry

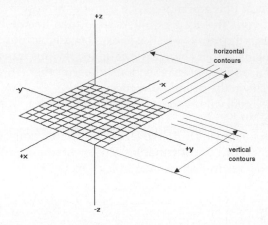

Listing 9-42. MakePlaneDatabase

```
void MakePlaneDatabase(){
  double XMinus, XPlus;
  double YMinus, YPlus;
  VertexNum=1;
  FaceNum=1;
  VertexNumInFace=1;
  x=ix;
  do {
    XMinus=sx*(x-HalfDx);
    XPlus =sx*(x+HalfDx);
    y=iy;
    do{
      YMinus=sy*(y-HalfDy);
      YPlus =sy*(y+HalfDy);
      AddVertex(FaceNum,XMinus, YMinus, 0.0);
      AddVertex(FaceNum,XPlus,  YMinus, 0.0);
      AddVertex(FaceNum,XPlus,  YPlus,  0.0);
      AddVertex(FaceNum,XMinus, YPlus,  0.0);
      ++FaceNum;
      VertexNumInFace=1;
      y+=Dy;
    }
    while( (long)y >= (long)ey);
    x+=Dx;
  }
  while( x <= ex);
}
```

That completes the plane and leaves just the cylinder and the cone.

Programmatic Generation III: MakeCyl

The cylinder is defined as an *altitude*, or height, and a number of *sweeps*, or segments, around the circles that describe the endcaps. This geometry is shown in Figure 9-12. In the prototypical cylinder, the altitude is 1. The number of sweeps is determined by querying the user. Since the approximation is more accurate with more sweeps, even with the scaling defined in the OBJDEF record for each instance of an object it makes sense to query again here. This advantage is less for the plane.

Figure 9-12.   Cylinder-Generation Geometry

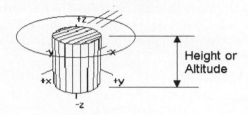

We're up to the main body and parallel functions *SetupCylinder* and *MakeCylinderDatabase.*

The cylinder generator main body is shown in Listing 9-43. You'll see the query, setup/ generate, and save signature shown by the generators. *SetupCylinder* and *MakeCylinderDatabase* are the meat. The main body is simply a shell that asks the user for the number of sweeps, calls these two functions, and invokes *SaveData* to save the result to file cylinder.dat.

Listing 9-43.   Cylinder Generator Main Body

```
main int argc, char **argv)
{

    FILE *out_file;
    int  s;

    fprintf (stdout, "3DDB Cylinder Generator .1 \n");
    fprintf (stdout, "\n");
    fprintf (stdout, "\n");
//
    fprintf (stdout,
      "enter sweeps around the cylinder( even into 360 ): ");
     fscanf (stdin, "%d",&s);
```

Listing 9-43. *(cont.)*

```
//
    SetupCylinder(s);
    MakeCylinderDatabase();

    fprintf (stdout, "generating cylinder.dat ...%d sweeps\n",s);
    fprintf (stdout, "\n");
    fprintf (stdout, "\n");
    SaveData("cylinder.Dat");

}
```

SetupCylinder is shown in Listing 9-44. It also initializes global variables. Because of the circular nature of the cylinder (and the cone, as well) the code again uses the control variables DTheta and HalfDTheta to control stepping around the circumference of the cylinder (in this case, a horizontal circle).

Listing 9-44.   SetupCylinder

```
void SetupCylinder(int NumOfFaces)
{
//
    VertexNum           = 1;
    VertexNumInFace     = 1;
    LastFace            = NumOfFaces;
    LastVertexNumInFace = 4;
    LastVertex          = LastFace * LastVertexNumInFace;
    DTheta              = 360 / LastFace;
    HalfDTheta          = DTheta / 2;
    Theta               = HalfDTheta;
}
```

That leaves *MakeCylinderDatabase* (Listing 9-45). It generates rectangles that connect the two ends of the cylinders. The circle is stepped around using Theta, incremented by DTheta. The face is created by connecting the two points at angles (Theta + HalfDTheta), (Theta - HalfDTheta) on the top at z = 1 with the ones at the bottom at z = -1. This is all done within a loop, using *AddVertex* to store the values in the global face and vertex arrays. Once again, we do this counterclockwise.

Listing 9-45.   MakeCylinderDatabase

```
void MakeCylinderDatabase()
{
//
  for ( FaceNum = 1; FaceNum <= LastFace; FaceNum++)
  {
```

```
   AddVertex(CosD(Theta-HalfDTheta) SinD(Theta-HalfDTheta), 1.0 );
   AddVertex(CosD(Theta+HalfDTheta),SinD(Theta+HalfDTheta), 1.0 );
   AddVertex(CosD(Theta+HalfDTheta),SinD(Theta+HalfDTheta),-1.0 );
   AddVertex(CosD(Theta-HalfDTheta),SinD(Theta-HalfDTheta),-1.0 );

   Theta += DTheta;
   VertexNumInFace = 1;
 }
 EndCaps();
}
```

Finally, function *EndCaps* generates the two circles that cap the cylinder at its top and bottom. The circles are defined by connecting opposite segments. Figure 9-13 shows the endcap geometry. *EndCaps* itself is in Listing 9-46. *EndCaps* loops around the circle defining the circumference of the cylinder and spitting out trapezoids for the top and bottom interleaved. The modeler uses the GDI function **Polygon**, wrapped by *G3D_GEnv_Polygon*, to draw modeler faces, so this doesn't matter to the rendering phase. As usual, *AddVertex* saves the face/vertex values for *SaveData.*

Figure 9-13.   Endcap Geometry for Cylinders and Cones

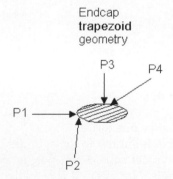

Listing 9-46.   EndCaps

```
void EndCaps()
{
    int tmp;
//
    NumFacesonEndCap = LastFace / 2 - 1;
    tmp = NumFacesonEndCap & 1;
    if ( tmp == 1 )
       Theta = -90 + HalfDTheta;
    else
       Theta = -90 + DTheta;
    if ( LastFace == 4 )
      NumFacesonEndCap = 2;
    for ( T = 0; T <= NumFacesonEndCap; T++)
    {
```

Listing 9-46. *(cont.)*

```
        AddVertex( CosD(180-Theta-HalfDTheta),
                   SinD(180-Theta-HalfDTheta), -1.0);
        AddVertex( CosD(180-Theta+HalfDTheta),
                   SinD(180-Theta+HalfDTheta), -1.0);
        AddVertex( CosD(Theta-HalfDTheta),
                    SinD(Theta-HalfDTheta),    -1.0);
        AddVertex( CosD(Theta+HalfDTheta),
                   SinD(Theta+HalfDTheta),     -1.0);
        ++FaceNum;
        ++LastFace;
        VertexNumInFace = 1;
        AddVertex( CosD(Theta+HalfDTheta),
                   SinD(Theta+HalfDTheta),      1.0);
        AddVertex( CosD(Theta-HalfDTheta),
                   SinD(Theta-HalfDTheta),      1.0);
        AddVertex( CosD(180-Theta+HalfDTheta),
                   SinD(180-Theta+HalfDTheta), 1.0);
        AddVertex( CosD(180-Theta-HalfDTheta),
                   SinD(180-Theta-HalfDTheta), 1.0);
        ++FaceNum;
        ++LastFace;
        VertexNumInFace = 1;
        Theta += DTheta;
    }
}
```

That leaves just the cone generator.

Programmatic Generation IV: MakeCone

The final object generator, the cone, is similar to the cylinder but with a twist. Figure 9-14 contains two views of the prototypical cone. From this, it would seem obvious that the "sheet" part of the cone is a triangle. Not quite. It is actually defined as a rectangle, but a *degenerate* one, meaning that two of its points are *co-incident* (in other words, at the same location). This means that the four points actually only describe a triangle.

GDI handles this nicely for us, making the code for the cone oblivious to the distinction between triangle and rectangle. The pyramid handling code, on the other hand, must know (in its present incarnation) about its oddity. Actually, you have already encountered this, in the sphere, but I didn't mention it because it is easier to see what is going on here. You will encounter degenerate rectangles again, so please remember this fact of the cone and sphere prototype definitions. If, at some point, GDI no longer handled this, for instance, you would have to change this implementation.

On to the generator itself. Listing 9-47 displays the main body of the cone database generator. This has the typical three parts of user query, setup/calculation, and saving. The number of sweeps is again queried from the user, using the RTL function **fscanf**. Once that's out of the way, *SetupCone* and *MakeConeDatabase* do the setup and calculation that feeds *SaveData* and the output file cone.dat.

Figure 9-14.   Cone Generator Geometry

top-side view

bottom-side view

Listing 9-47.   Cone Generator Main Body

```
main (int argc, char **argv)
{
    FILE *out_file;
    int   s;

    fprintf (stdout, "3DDB Cone Generator .1 \n");
    fprintf (stdout, "\n");
    fprintf (stdout, "\n");
//
    fprintf (stdout,
      "enter sweeps around the cone ( even into 360 ): ");
    fscanf (stdin, "%d",&s);

// Num Faces => 360 / Even Number = Integer (180 is max)
    SetupCone(s);
    MakeConeDatabase();
//
    fprintf (stdout, "generating cone.dat ...%d sweeps \n",s);
    fprintf (stdout, "\n");
    fprintf (stdout, "\n");
    SaveData("Cone.Dat");
}
```

SetupCone is shown in Listing 9-48. It should be very familiar, since it initializes variables that you've seen several times now: the header record variables and the Theta and DTheta pair for stepping around the circumference of the defining circle. Similarly, *MakeConeDatabase* in Listing 9-49 should hold no surprises at this point. It looks very similar to the cylinder function except for two details.

Listing 9-48.   SetupCone

```
void SetupCone(int NumOfFaces)
{
//
    VertexNum            = 1;
    VertexNumInFace      = 1;
    LastFace             = NumOfFaces;
    LastVertexNumInFace = 4;
    LastVertex           = LastFace * LastVertexNumInFace;
    DTheta               = 360 / LastFace;
    HalfDTheta           = DTheta / 2;
    Theta                = HalfDTheta;
}
```

Listing 9-49.   MakeConeDatabase

```
void MakeConeDatabase()
{
//
    for ( FaceNum = 1; FaceNum <= LastFace; FaceNum++)
    {
        AddVertex( 0.0, 0.0, 1.0 );
        AddVertex( 0.0, 0.0, 1.0 );
        AddVertex( CosD(Theta+HalfDTheta),
                   SinD(Theta+HalfDTheta), -1.0 );
        AddVertex( CosD(Theta-HalfDTheta),
                   SinD(Theta-HalfDTheta), -1.0 );

        Theta -= DTheta;
        VertexNumInFace = 1;
    }
    EndCap();
}
```

The first set of *AddVertex* calls are all to the same point — defining the apex. The other difference is that the call to *EndCaps* is substituted with a call to *EndCap*. *EndCap* is shown in Listing 9-50, and is a simpler cousin of *EndCaps*. The same for-loop is used, but only one cap is made with the group of calls to *AddVertex*.

Listing 9-50.   EndCap for the Cone Generator

```
void EndCap()
{
    int tmp;
//
    NumFacesonEndCap = LastFace / 2 - 1;
    tmp = NumFacesonEndCap & 1;
```

```
    if ( tmp == 1 )
       Theta = -90 + HalfDTheta;
    else
       Theta = -90 + DTheta;
    if (  LastFace == 4 )
      NumFacesonEndCap = 2;
    for ( T = 1; T <= NumFacesonEndCap; T++)
    {
        AddVertex(CosD(180-Theta-HalfDTheta),
                  SinD(180-Theta-HalfDTheta),  -1.0);
        AddVertex( CosD(180-Theta+HalfDTheta),
                   SinD(180-Theta+HalfDTheta), -1.0);
        AddVertex( CosD(Theta-HalfDTheta),
                   SinD(Theta-HalfDTheta),      -1.0);
        AddVertex( CosD(Theta+HalfDTheta),
                   SinD(Theta+HalfDTheta),      -1.0);

        ++FaceNum;
        ++LastFace;
        VertexNumInFace = 1;
        Theta += DTheta;
    }
}
```

That wraps it up. At this point, you've seen both manual and programmatic generation. It should be easy to take the mini-API and make new generators. Then you would have to extend both polygon and ray modes to deal with your new object type. The world-generation phase, and specifically the object instantiation part of it, is the first area of the modeler that will need changes. The world-manipulation phase also needs some touchup, but we can wait on that until Chapter 10.

Next, we'll tackle the instantiation sequences, starting with the explicit object loading. That coverage exposes the code that is dependent on object-specific details, and finishes our effort to provide what is necessary; it's also a good place to begin the coverage of the manipulation code.

Implementation Part I: Loading Explicit Objects

With all of that explanation out of the way, it is time to actually do something: load a 3D object. Here we deal with the explicit form. Once that's finished, we'll cover the details of the analytic form, leading us back to the object instantiation thread left from Chapter 8.

The explicit form is really quite simple to handle. Listing 9-51 contains *MakeExObject*, which controls this process. It allocates an *EX3DOBJECT* structure and invokes *Load3DObject* to populate it.

Listing 9-51.   MakeExObject

```
LPEX3DOBJECT WINAPI MakeExObject(LPSCENE     theScene,
                                 LPOBJECT    theMaster,
                                 LPSTR       szObjFileName,
                                 EX3DOBJECT  ex3DObj )
{
    FRAME  *  pfrm   = Frame_GetPtr(g_app.hwndMain);
    LPEX3DOBJECT     this = NULL;

    TRY {
        this = (LPEX3DOBJECT)WL_Mem_Alloc(GHND,sizeof(EX3DOBJECT));
        if ( !this )
        {
            Throw((LPCATCHBUF)&_ci.state,GENERR_ALLOCFAILURE);
        }
        else
        {
            Load3DObjectFile(theScene,theMaster,szObjFileName,this);
            this->l_transforms = ex3DObj.l_transforms;
            lstrcpy((LPSTR)this->szDatFile,(LPSTR)szObjFileName);
            return(this);
        }
    }
    CATCH{
        switch(_exk)
        {
            case GENERR_ALLOCFAILURE:
            default:
                ProcessError(pfrm,_exk);
                break;
        }
        return 0;
    }
    END_CATCH
}
```

The *EX3DOBJECT* structure is shown in Listing 9-52. It uses the *TRY/CATCH* macros to guard the allocation of the *EX3DOBJECT*.

Listing 9-52.   EX3DOBJECT Structure

```
typedef struct t_explicit_3Dobject
{
//explicit [face/vertex]
    char                szDatFile[MAXNAMELEN];
    int                 nV,nF,nVinF;
    POLYSURFACE         o_psurf ;
    struct t_localtransforms
    {
```

```
      VECTOR4D R;
      VECTOR4D S;
      VECTOR4D T;
   }  l_transforms;
} EXPLICIT3DOBJECT ;
typedef EXPLICIT3DOBJECT FAR *LPEX3DOBJECT;
typedef EXPLICIT3DOBJECT EX3DOBJECT;
```

This structure is a repository for the local transformation information and the face and vertex information. Also note, as I mentioned before, the usage of two sets of vertices. This allows "working storage" of the current eye-coordinate values, as well as "original storage" of the world coordinates. If you didn't have the memory facilities of Windows enhanced mode, your alternate approach would be to develop inverse transformations and back-transform the data. This would work as follows: take world coordinates; transform them to eye coordinates and do the rest of the pipeline manipulations; then inverse-transform. You can see that this requires two transformations for every view — a performance cost.

The two-vertices approach takes the space trade-off, a natural in this environment. Table 9-7 displays the two approaches and their steps for your comparison. From this, you can clearly see the memory trade-off versus the time trade-off. Simply by using duplicate coordinates as we do here, we avoid the worry about inverse transformations and avoid the time-consuming inverse transformation step. This inverse step isn't insignificant; it takes approximately as long as the forward transformation step, since it does basically the same matrix operations on exactly the same number of points. This step makes the app seem faster but it makes an already memory-hoggish application even piggier.

Table 9-7. Duplicate Coordinates Versus Inverses

Action	WinMod3D	Alternate Approach
	(Duplicate coords,no inverses)	*(Single coords with inverses)*
Memory use	Two copies of memory	One copy of memory
Pipeline 1	Transform original into working	Transform original in place
Pipeline 2	Perform other steps	Perform other steps
Pipeline 3	N/A	Inverse tranform points back

That leads to Listing 9-53 and *Load3DObject*. This function has responsibility for performing the file open and close using **fopen** and **fclose**. If the open succeeds, it saves the header record counts and then allocates memory for the face and vertex lists, with the TRY/CATCH macros providing the usual guard. If this fails, a tragic error occurs and is thrown using Throw. If it succeeds, it updates various scene counts for the info pane, then populates the *POLYSURFACE* itself. The face and vertex counts are updated, then *LoadData* is called to retrieve the actual values of the face and vertex lists.

Listing 9-53. Load3DObjectFile

```c
void WINAPI Load3DObjectFile(LPSCENE      theScene,
                             LPOBJECT     theMaster,
                             LPSTR        ObjFileName,
                             LPEX3DOBJECT theObject){
   FRAME  *  pfrm  = Frame_GetPtr(g_app.hwndMain);
   FILE *objfile;
   int   nVerts,nFaces,nVinF;
   char  szBuffer[128];
   lstrcpy((LPSTR)szBuffer,(LPSTR)ObjFileName);
   if ( (objfile = fopen(szBuffer,"r+t")) == NULL)
   {
      MessageBox(NULL,"object dat file open failure!",
                  "scene package",MB_OK);
      return ;
   }
   fscanf(objfile,"%d %d %d ",&nVerts, &nFaces, &nVinF);
...
   theObject->nV    = nVerts;
   theObject->nF    = nFaces;
   theObject->nVinF = nVinF;
   TRY{
      theObject->o_psurf.prm_verticies  =
          (LPVERTEX)WL_Mem_Alloc(GHND,sizeof(VERTEX) +
                              (nVerts+1)*sizeof(VECTOR4D));
      theObject->o_psurf.wrk_verticies  =
          (LPVERTEX)WL_Mem_Alloc(GHND, sizeof(VERTEX) +
                              (nVerts+1)*sizeof(VECTOR4D));
      theObject->o_psurf.faces.fi       =
          (LPFACE)WL_Mem_Alloc(GHND,(nFaces+2)*sizeof(FACE));
      if ( !theObject->o_psurf.prm_verticies ||
           !theObject->o_psurf.wrk_verticies ||
           !theObject->o_psurf.faces.fi){
         fclose(objfile);
         Throw((LPCATCHBUF)&_ci.state,GENERR_ALLOCFAILURE);
      }
      else{
         theScene->NumFaces                     += nFaces;
         theScene->NumVerticies                 += (long)nVerts;
         theObject->o_psurf.faces.fiNum         = nFaces;
         theObject->o_psurf.prm_verticies->vpNum = nVerts;
         theObject->o_psurf.wrk_verticies->vpNum = nVerts;
         LoadData(objfile,theMaster,theObject,
               nVerts,nFaces,nVinF);
         fclose(objfile);
         return;
      }
   }
   CATCH  {
      switch(_exk) {
```

```
                case GENERR_ALLOCFAILURE:
                default:
                    ProcessError(pfrm,_exk);
                    break;
            }
        return ;
        }
    END_CATCH
}
```

Listing 9-54 contains the *POLYSURFACE* structure and Listing 9-55 contains *LoadData*. The *POLYSURFACE* structure contains the definition of both sets of vertices in support of the dual-coordinate approach. The header record data has already been extracted, so *LoadData* loops across all the vertices and **fscanf**'s them in, using *G3D_V4D_VSet4D* to populate each vertex. *LoadData* then loops across all the faces, loading the indices into the vertex list that define each face's circuit.

Listing 9-54.   POLYSURFACE Structure

```
typedef struct t_polysurface
{
   FACELIST    faces;
   LPVERTEX    prm_verticies;
   LPVERTEX    wrk_verticies;
} POLYSURFACE ;
typedef POLYSURFACE FAR *LPPOLYSURFACE;
```

Listing 9-55.   LoadData

```
void WINAPI LoadData(FILE          *objfile,
                     LPOBJECT      theMaster,
                     LPEX3DOBJECT this,
                     int           LastVertex,
                     int LastFace,int VertexNumInFace)
{
    LPVERTEX   lpvtx;
    FACELIST   fl;
    FACE       ft;
    double     x, y, z;
    int        f, v, VertexNum,FaceNum;

    for(VertexNum=1; VertexNum<=LastVertex; VertexNum++) {
      fscanf(objfile,"%lf ", &x);
      fscanf(objfile,"%lf ", &y);
      fscanf(objfile,"%lf ",&z);
      G3D_V4D_VSet4D((LPVECTOR4D)
                     &this->o_psurf.prm_verticies->vp[VertexNum],
                     x, y, z, 1);
    }
```

Listing 9-55. (*cont.*)

```
for(FaceNum=1; FaceNum<=LastFace; FaceNum++) {
  this->o_psurf.faces.fi[FaceNum].fi = FaceNum;
  this->o_psurf.faces.fi[FaceNum].oi = theMaster->o_id;
  this->o_psurf.faces.fi[FaceNum].ni = VertexNumInFace;
  ft                        = this->o_psurf.faces.fi[FaceNum];
  for(v=1; v<=VertexNumInFace; v++) {
    fscanf(objfile,"%d ", &f);
    ft.indx[v] = f;

    SetFace((LPFACE)&this->o_psurf.faces.fi[FaceNum],v,f) ;
  }
}
if ( theMaster->o_type == T_PYR )
{
  this->o_psurf.faces.fiNum            = 5;
  this->o_psurf.faces.fi[LastFace].ni = VertexNumInFace + 1;
  ft                        = this->o_psurf.faces.fi[LastFace];
  fscanf(objfile,"%d ", &f);
  ft.indx[VertexNumInFace+1] = f;
  SetFace((LPFACE)&this->o_psurf.faces.fi[LastFace],
          VertexNumInFace+1,f) ;
}
}
```

The *SetFace* helper function, shown in Listing 9-56, helps all this along.

Listing 9-56. SetFace

```
void WINAPI SetFace( LPFACE fi, int Index, int Value)
{
    fi->indx[Index] = Value;
    return;
}
```

I've covered the point of having the prototypical object face and vertex values loaded into a block of memory. We still have not scaled and translated them by the specification in the OBJDEF. The next step is to take these prototypical values and the OBJDEF specification and create the instance. The analytic representation derives what it needs from the prototypical values and the OBJDEF specification. Before we're done, we'll transform the explicit representation.

Implementation Part II: Deriving Analytic Objects

Deriving the values needed by the ray-tracing mode is critical to the success of the modeler. Each object, instanced by the OBJDEF, has its analytic representation calculated from the elements of the OBJDEF. This process is also slightly complicated by the "combo" objects:

the cylinder, cone, box, and pyramid. They make it necessary to construct the analytic representation piecewise. The sphere and infinite plane are completely described by one equation, which is very convenient but also extremely limiting. By extending the reach of the modeler to handle these "combo" analytic objects and performing piecewise construction, we expand the range of scenes that can be generated, which, in turn, produces much nicer images as our end result.

I gave you a hint of how this occurs when I described the math behind the plane. There I noted that the plane coefficients when squared sum to one; in other words, a vector constructed from the plane coefficients is both a normal used to describe orientation and a normalized, or unit magnitude, vector. This is convenient since it saves us a magnitude call.

Each object in its turn will contain the code for its version of this. While the coverage in Chapter 10 will again use the ray equation and parameterized versions of the individual object equations, the derivation is mostly geometrical. For an example, with a known location of one edge, and a known size of the edge, the next edge can be determined. This will be repeated for each of the objects:

- sphere,
- infinite plane,
- cylinder,
- cone,
- box, and
- pyramid.

At this point, we've covered the internals of the object instantiation phase in great detail and the remaining loose thread in the front-end coverage will be back in *parse_scene* — the object-instantiation *Makexxx* functions visible to the parse phase.

Objects: The Sphere

The analytic sphere is instanced by function *MakeAnSphere*. This function allocates a *SPHERE* structure using *WL_Mem_Alloc* and is guarded by the ubiquitous TRY/CATCH block. Listing 9-57 contains the implementation of *MakeAnSphere* and Listing 9-58 presents the *SPHERE* structure for you. The sphere, like the plane, is relatively simple. The elements of the allocated *SPHERE* structure are assigned the values of the passed-in *SPHERE* structure elements. Remember from Chapter 8 that *parse_scene* constructed a static *SPHERE* structure from the local transform data and passed it to *MakeSphere*. *MakeSphere*, in turn, invokes *MakeAnSphere*; we'll talk more on this in the next section.

Listing 9-57.   MakeAnSphere

```
LPSPHERE MakeAnSphere(SPHERE sphere)
{
     FRAME  *   pfrm   = Frame_GetPtr(g_app.hwndMain);
     LPSPHERE sp ;

     TRY
     {
         sp = (LPSPHERE) WL_Mem_Alloc(GHND, sizeof(SPHERE)) ;
         if ( !sp )
         {
            Throw((LPCATCHBUF)&_ci.state,GENERR_ALLOCFAILURE);
         }
         else
         {
            sp -> sph_center.x = sphere.sph_center.x;
            sp -> sph_center.y = sphere.sph_center.y;
            sp -> sph_center.z = sphere.sph_center.z;
            sp -> sph_radius   = sphere.sph_radius;
            sp -> sph_radius2  = sphere.sph_radius2;

            return(sp);
         }
     }
     CATCH
     {
         switch(_exk)
         {
           case GENERR_ALLOCFAILURE:
           default:
              ProcessError(pfrm,_exk);
              break;
         }
         return 0;
     }
     END_CATCH
}
```

Listing 9-58.   SPHERE Structure

```
typedef struct t_sphere
{
  VECTOR4D  sph_wcenter;           /* It's location */
  VECTOR4D  sph_center;            /* It's location */
  double    sph_radius;            /* It's radius */
  double    sph_radius2;           /* It's radius squared */
} SPHERE;

typedef SPHERE FAR *LPSPHERE;
```

MakeAnSphere is the target here. As you can see, the allocated structure is simply assigned the values of the structure passed by parameter. The code won't always be this simple; once past the plane, the details get more interesting, so breathe easy while you can. Let's move on to the infinite plane.

Objects: The Plane

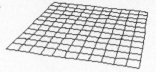

The plane is the second of the two simple analytic objects (those described completely by one equation). Here, the plane is instanced by function *MakeAnPlane*. This function performs allocation of a *PLANE* structure again using *WL_Mem_Alloc* and guarded by the ubiquitous TRY/CATCH block. Listing 9-59 contains *MakeAnPlane* and Listing 9-60 has the *PLANE* structure. The plane is even simpler than the sphere, being defined by two values: the normal and the distance. Once again, the elements of the allocated structure are assigned the value of the passed-in structure; here, a *PLANE* in both cases.

Listing 9-59. MakeAnPlane

```
LPPLANE MakeAnPlane(PLANE plane)
{
        FRAME  *   pfrm   = Frame_GetPtr(g_app.hwndMain);
        LPPLANE pl ;

        TRY
        {
            pl = (LPPLANE) WL_Mem_Alloc(GHND, sizeof(PLANE)) ;
            if ( !pl )
            {
                Throw((LPCATCHBUF)&_ci.state,GENERR_ALLOCFAILURE);
            }
            else
            {

                pl->pl_distance = -plane.pl_distance;
                pl->pl_normal   = plane.pl_normal;

                G3D_V4D_VNorm4D((LPVECTOR4D)&pl->pl_normal,
                                          pl->pl_normal);

                return(pl);
            }
        }
        CATCH
        {
```

Listing 9-59. *(cont.)*

```
        switch(_exk)
        {
            case GENERR_ALLOCFAILURE:
            default:
                ProcessError(pfrm,_exk);
                break;
        }
        return 0;
    }
    END_CATCH
}
```

Listing 9-60. PLANE Structure

```
typedef struct t_plane
{
  VECTOR4D  pl_normal;          /* It's normal */
  double    pl_distance;        /* It's pythagorean distance */
  double    pl_NdotV;           /* cached visibility     */
} PLANE;

typedef PLANE FAR *LPPLANE;
```

Think back to Chapter 8 and *parse_scene*, with its construction of local structure variables for each object type. These variables are used to populate permanent, allocated structures destined for the 3D object list. This pattern will be repeated, so expect to see it again.
As you can see, this was pretty simple. The "combo" objects remain and they require a
more involved derivation process.

Objects: The Cylinder

The analytic cylinder object is instanced by function *MakeAnCylinder*. There are no surprises, just the allocation of a *CYLINDER* structure using *WL_Mem_Alloc* and guarded by
a TRY/CATCH block. *MakeAnCylinder* is shown in Listing 9-61; Listing 9-62 shows the
CYLINDER structure. The elements of the *CYLINDER* structure should be obvious at this
point. The *CYLINDER* structure is copied into an allocated *QUADRIC* structure, and this
permanent structure is shown in Listing 9-93. The structure copy in *MakeAnCylinder* starts
the setup of the analytic representation for the later phases.

Don't miss the innocuous call to *OrientQuadric*, however. This function forces you to
notice that the structure setup is not quite as it was before. The *QUADRIC* contains elements that are copied from the original *CYLINDER* structure and calculated elements. The

OrientQuadric function, shown in Listing 9-64, initializes the calculated elements for *MakeAnCylinder* and *MakeAnCone.* This little bit of indirection lets us use the similarity between the cylinder and the cone.

Listing 9-61.   MakeAnCylinder

```
LPQUADRIC MakeAnCylinder(CYLINDER cylinder)
{
      FRAME  *   pfrm   = Frame_GetPtr(g_app.hwndMain);
      LPQUADRIC c ;

      TRY
      {
         c = (LPQUADRIC) WL_Mem_Alloc(GHND, sizeof(QUADRIC)) ;
         if ( !c )
         {
            Throw((LPCATCHBUF)&_ci.state,GENERR_ALLOCFAILURE);
         }
         else
         {
//
//     get base and apex info
//
               c-> q_altitude =cylinder.c_altitude;
               c-> q_bcenter  =cylinder.c_bcenter;
               c-> q_bradius   =cylinder.c_radius;
               c-> q_tcenter  =cylinder.c_tcenter;
               c-> q_tradius  =cylinder.c_radius;

               OrientQuadric(c);
               return(c);
         }
      }
      CATCH
      {
         switch(_exk)
         {
            case GENERR_ALLOCFAILURE:
            default:
               ProcessError(pfrm,_exk);
               break;
         }
         return 0;
      }
      END_CATCH
}
```

Listing 9-62. CYLINDER Structure

```
typedef struct t_cylinder
{
  VECTOR4D  c_bcenter;              /* bottom location */
  double    c_radius;              /* radius*/
  VECTOR4D  c_tcenter;             /* top location */
  double    c_altitude;
} CYLINDER;

typedef CYLINDER FAR *LPCYLINDER;
```

Listing 9-63. QUADRIC Structure

```
typedef struct t_quadric
{
  VECTOR4D  q_bcenter;              /* bottom location */
  double    q_bradius;
  double    q_bdot;
  VECTOR4D  q_tcenter;                 /* top location */
  double    q_tradius;
  double    q_altitude;
  VECTOR4D  q_u,q_v,q_w;
  double    q_slope, q_mind, q_maxd;
  CIRCLE    q_endcaps[2];           /* cone,cylinder ends */
  double    q_dm1,q_dm2;
} QUADRIC;

typedef QUADRIC FAR *LPQUADRIC;
```

Listing 9-64. OrientQuadric

```
void WINAPI OrientQuadric(LPQUADRIC quadric)
{
   VECTOR4D t;
   double   rt;

   G3D_V4D_VSub4D(&quadric->q_w,quadric->q_tcenter,
                  quadric->q_bcenter);
   G3D_V4D_VNorm4D(&quadric->q_w,quadric->q_w);
   quadric->q_slope = (quadric->q_tradius - quadric->q_bradius)
                      /quadric->q_altitude;
   quadric->q_bdot  = -G3D_V4D_VDot4D(quadric->q_bcenter,
                                      quadric->q_w);
   G3D_V4D_VSet4D(&t,0,0,1,ONE4D);
   rt = dabs(dabs(G3D_V4D_VDot4D(t,quadric->q_w))-1.0);
   if ( rt < SMALL )
     G3D_V4D_VSet4D(&t,0,1,0,ONE4D);
```

```
     G3D_V4D_VCross4D(&quadric->q_u,quadric->q_w,t);
     G3D_V4D_VCross4D(&quadric->q_v,quadric->q_u,quadric->q_w);
     G3D_V4D_VNorm4D(&quadric->q_u,quadric->q_u);
     G3D_V4D_VNorm4D(&quadric->q_v,quadric->q_v);
     quadric->q_mind = G3D_V4D_VDot4D(quadric->q_w,
                                       quadric->q_bcenter);
     quadric->q_maxd = G3D_V4D_VDot4D(quadric->q_w,
                                       quadric->q_tcenter);
     if ( quadric->q_maxd < quadric->q_mind)
     {
        rt              = quadric->q_maxd;
        quadric->q_maxd = quadric->q_mind;
        quadric->q_mind = rt;
     }
}
```

Both the cylinder and the cone are represented by a sheet and endcap(s) components in combination. The difference between the sheets is basically a simple slope calculation. The *QUADRIC* structure is the union of all of the elements needed for the cylinder and the cone, and allows us to use one set of intersection testing and normal generation code for both object types.

The *QUADRIC* structure contains a raft of new variables. The most important are the slope (q_slope), the base dot product (q_bdot), and the orientation vectors (q_u, q_v, and q_w). These three vectors represent a local coordinate system that will be used for intersection calculations.

The q_w vector is defined along the long axis as seen from the subtraction of the two center locations using *G3D_V4D_VSub4D*. Then a little trick ensures that the other two vectors are at right angles to the q_w vector. This involves using a unit z-vector (either positive or negative depending on the dot product being checked for) to first cross with q_w, forming q_u. Then, to complete the orthogonal trio, cross q_w and q_u, Library function *G3D_V4D_VCross4D* is used for the cross operation, and *G3D_V4D_VDot4D* is used for the dot operation.

This critical trio is then normalized and used to generate other stored values that are used in the intersection test for visibility and normal generation for shading. The usage of these parameters will become clear in Chapter 10 when I discuss visibility, intersection, shading, and normals. The *CIRCLE* element of the *QUADRIC* structure is used to generate the endcaps. Here, we only handle the sheet. Next, you will see the invocation of *OrientCircle*, shown in Listing 9-65, twice for the cylinder and once for the cone. The cone, our next object, also uses the *QUADRIC* structure and the *OrientCircle* and *OrientQuadric* functions.

Listing 9-67 shows the *CONE* structure. It differs from the *CYLINDER* structure because a cone has two different radii. The upper radius is usually 0, indicating a closed cone. Both the polygon and ray-traced renderings depend on objects being closed.

Listing 9-67.   CONE Structure

```
typedef struct t_cone
{
  VECTOR4D  c_bcenter;                   /* bottom location */
  double    c_bradius;
  VECTOR4D  c_tcenter;                   /* top location */
  double    c_tradius;
  double    c_altitude;
} CONE;

typedef CONE FAR *LPCONE;
```

The problem is the one-sided nature of plane figures and normal directions. Shading uses the normal direction, as does the hidden-line algorithm. Remember that the plane object shows this one-sided nature more than any other object; this was discussed in the programmatic-generation section. This means that you'd need to do some work to extend the system to open objects. That leaves the box and the pyramid, which use the rectangle and triangle; these are companion plane figures to the circle used for endcaps.

Objects: The Box

The box is composed completely of plane figures. The six faces of the box are six plane figures projected on a properly-oriented plane. This is actually more tedious than it is truly difficult, so don't get scared — the math is not that hard.

This analytic object is instanced by function *MakeAnBox*. This sets up the extent vectors and the center location. This information is cached in a *BOX* structure in *parse_scene* and copied into a *SIMPLENGON* structure that exploits the commonality between the box and the pyramid. The function *MakeAnBox* is shown in Listing 9-68, with the two data-structure definitions shown in Listings 9-69 and 9-70. *MakeAnBox* uses *WL_Mem_Alloc* and guards the allocation with a TRY / CATCH block.

Listing 9-68.   MakeAnBox

```
LPSIMPLENGON MakeAnBox(BOX box)
{
    FRAME   *       pfrm    = Frame_GetPtr(g_app.hwndMain);
    LPSIMPLENGON c ;
```

```
        TRY
        {
            c = (LPSIMPLENGON) WL_Mem_Alloc(GHND, sizeof(NGON)) ;
            if ( !c )
            {
                Throw((LPCATCHBUF)&_ci.state,GENERR_ALLOCFAILURE);
            }
            else
            {
             c->ng_center = box.c_center;
             G3D_V4D_VSet4D(&c->ng_w,
                            box.c_w.x,
                            0,0,ONE4D);
             G3D_V4D_VSet4D(&c->ng_h,
                               0,
                               box.c_h.y,
                               0,ONE4D);
             G3D_V4D_VSet4D(&c->ng_d,
                               0,0,
                               box.c_d.z,ONE4D);
//
                return(c);
            }
        }
        CATCH
        {
            switch(_exk)
            {
                case GENERR_ALLOCFAILURE:
                default:
                    ProcessError(pfrm,_exk);
                    break;
            }
            return 0;
        }
        END_CATCH

}
```

Listing 9-69. BOX Structure

```
typedef struct t_box
{
  VECTOR4D    c_center;             /* It's location */
  VECTOR4D    c_w;                  /* width  vec */
  VECTOR4D    c_h;                  /* height vec */
  VECTOR4D    c_d;                  /* depth  vec */
} BOX;

typedef BOX FAR *LPBOX;
```

Listing 9-70. SIMPLENGON Structure

```
typedef struct t_ngon
{
  VECTOR4D    ng_center;           /* It's location */
  VECTOR4D    ng_w;                /* width  vec */
  VECTOR4D    ng_h;                /* height vec */
  VECTOR4D    ng_d;                /* depth  vec */
  SIMPLEPOLY  ng_faces[7];         /* each face */
} NGON;

typedef NGON FAR * LPSIMPLENGON;
```

The orientation function *OrientRectangle*, implemented in Listing 9-71, works with a
SIMPLEPOLY structure, defined in Listing 9-72. It takes the *SIMPLEPOLY* elements from
a *SIMPLENGON* and, for each face in a box (along with the base of the pyramid broken
out as a special case), orients the vertex and normal elements and caches the dot product
for visibility.

Listing 9-71. OrientRectangle

```
void   WINAPI OrientRectangle(LPSIMPLENGON lpng, int which,
                     LPSIMPLEPOLY pgram,EX3DOBJECT ex3DObj)
{
   VECTOR4D t;
   double   rt;

   switch(which){
      case 1:               // back
         G3D_V4D_VSet4D(&pgram->sp_center,
                     lpng->ng_center.x - lpng->ng_w.x,
                     lpng->ng_center.y, lpng->ng_center.z,
                     ONE4D);
         pgram->sp_v1 = lpng->ng_w; //1
         pgram->sp_v2 = lpng->ng_d; //3
         break;
      case 2:               // right
         G3D_V4D_VSet4D(&pgram->sp_center,
                     lpng->ng_center.x,lpng->ng_center.y,
                     lpng->ng_center.z,
                     ONE4D);
         pgram->sp_v1 = lpng->ng_d;  //3
         pgram->sp_v2 = lpng->ng_h;  //2
         break;
      case 3:               // left
         G3D_V4D_VSet4D(&pgram->sp_center,
                     lpng->ng_center.x - lpng->ng_w.x,
                     lpng->ng_center.y,lpng->ng_center.z,
                     ONE4D);
```

```
              pgram->sp_v1 = lpng->ng_d;    //3
              pgram->sp_v2 = lpng->ng_h;    //2
              break;
      case 4:                   //front
         G3D_V4D_VSet4D(&pgram->sp_center,
                        lpng->ng_center.x - lpng->ng_w.x,
                        lpng->ng_center.y + lpng->ng_h.y,
                        lpng->ng_center.z,
                        ONE4D);
         pgram->sp_v1 = lpng->ng_d;   //3
         pgram->sp_v2 = lpng->ng_w;   //1
         break;
   }
```

Listing 9-72.   SIMPLEPOLY Structure

```
typedef struct t_simplepolygon
{
  VECTOR4D   sp_center;  /* a corner */
  VECTOR4D   sp_v1,sp_v2;/*v1,v2 - vertex 1 and 2 around corner c */
  VECTOR4D   sp_normal;  /* normal  vec */
  double     sp_NdotV;   /* cached visibility    */
} SIMPLEPOLY;

typedef SIMPLEPOLY FAR *LPSIMPLEPOLY;
```

That is the extent of this part of the instantiation process. The overall *Makexxx* functions remain. First, we need to cover the pyramid to finish off this level of coverage.

Objects: The Pyramid

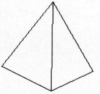

The pyramid completes the cycle. The last object we'll consider in this section is constructed from both triangles and rectangles. You've seen the rectangle; the triangle is very similar. It also follows the lead of the box and, in a round-robin manner, defines the plane figures that make up each instance of a pyramid.

The *PYRAMID* structure is shown in Listing 9-73. It, too, should hold no surprises by this point.

Listing 9-73. PYRAMID Structure

```
typedef struct t_pyramid
{
  VECTOR4D     p_center; /* its location */
  VECTOR4D     p_v1,p_v2;/*v1,v2 - vertex 1 and 2 around corner c */
  VECTOR4D     p_height; /* altitude */

} PYRAMID;

typedef PYRAMID FAR *LPPYRAMID;
```

The pyramid is instanced by function *MakeAnPyramid,* contained in Listing 9-74. This is the allocation function repeated (ad nauseam, by now). The pyramid is described by two vectors (two vectors describe a plane and the base is a plane) and a height to the plane of the apex in the overall terms.

Listing 9-74. MakeAnPyramid

```
LPSIMPLENGON MakeAnPyramid(PYRAMID pyramid,EX3DOBJECT ex3DObj)
{
      FRAME  *   pfrm  = Frame_GetPtr(g_app.hwndMain);
      LPSIMPLENGON p ;

      TRY
      {
         p = (LPSIMPLENGON) WL_Mem_Alloc(GHND, sizeof(NGON)) ;
         if ( !p )
         {
             Throw((LPCATCHBUF)&_ci.state,GENERR_ALLOCFAILURE);
         }
         else
         {
// translate center
         p->ng_center =  pyramid.p_center;
         G3D_V4D_VSet4D(&p->ng_w,
                         pyramid.p_v1.x,
                         pyramid.p_v1.y,
                         pyramid.p_v1.z,
                         ONE4D);
         G3D_V4D_VSet4D(&p->ng_d,
                         pyramid.p_v2.x,
                         pyramid.p_v2.y,
                         pyramid.p_v2.z,
                         ONE4D);
         G3D_V4D_VSet4D(&p->ng_h,
                         pyramid.p_height.x,
                         pyramid.p_height.y,
                         pyramid.p_height.z,
                         ONE4D);
```

```
//
                return(p);
            }
        }
        CATCH
        {
            switch(_exk)
            {
                case GENERR_ALLOCFAILURE:
                default:
                    ProcessError(pfrm,_exk);
                    break;
            }
            return 0;
        }
        END_CATCH
}
```

These values are then used to define the pyramid piecewise, using *OrientTriangle* for the sides and *OrientRectangle* for the base. When we cover the last piece of the puzzle, the *Makexxx* function *MakePyramid*, this will become clearer. *OrientTriangle* is shown in Listing 9-75. You can inspect it and see the piecewise definition of the four triangle sides.

Listing 9-75.   OrientTriangle

```
void    WINAPI OrientTriangle(LPSIMPLENGON lpng, int which,
                              LPSIMPLEPOLY tri,EX3DOBJECT ex3DObj){
    VECTOR4D t;
    double    rt;
    switch(which) {
        case 1:
            G3D_V4D_VSet4D(&tri->sp_center,
                        lpng->ng_center.x + lpng->ng_w.x,
                        lpng->ng_center.y + lpng->ng_d.y,
                        lpng->ng_center.z,
                        ONE4D);
            G3D_V4D_VScale4D(&tri->sp_v1,-1.0,lpng->ng_w); //1
            G3D_V4D_VSet4D(&tri->sp_v2,                    //centertop
                        -.5*lpng->ng_w.x, -.5*lpng->ng_d.y,
                        lpng->ng_h.z,ONE4D);
            break;
        case 2:
            G3D_V4D_VSet4D(&tri->sp_center,
                        lpng->ng_center.x,
                        lpng->ng_center.y, lpng->ng_center.z,
                        ONE4D);
            G3D_V4D_VSet4D(&tri->sp_v1,                    //centertop
                        .5*lpng->ng_w.x, .5*lpng->ng_d.y,
                        lpng->ng_h.z,ONE4D);
            tri->sp_v2 = lpng->ng_d;                       //2
            break;
```

Listing 9-75. (*cont.*)

```
    case 3:
      G3D_V4D_VSet4D(&tri->sp_center,
                    lpng->ng_center.x,
                    lpng->ng_center.y, lpng->ng_center.z,
                    ONE4D);
      tri->sp_v1 = lpng->ng_w;                          //3
      G3D_V4D_VSet4D(&tri->sp_v2,                       //centertop
                    .5*lpng->ng_w.x,
                    .5*lpng->ng_d.y,
                    lpng->ng_h.z,ONE4D);
      break;
    case 4:
      G3D_V4D_VSet4D(&tri->sp_center,
                    lpng->ng_center.x + lpng->ng_w.x,
                    lpng->ng_center.y + lpng->ng_d.y,
                    lpng->ng_center.z,
                    ONE4D);
      G3D_V4D_VSet4D(&tri->sp_v1,                       //centertop
                    -.5*lpng->ng_w.x, -.5*lpng->ng_d.y,
                    lpng->ng_h.z,ONE4D);
      G3D_V4D_VScale4D(&tri->sp_v2,-1.0,lpng->ng_d); //4
      break;
  }
  G3D_V4D_VCross4D(&tri->sp_normal,
                  tri->sp_v1,
                  tri->sp_v2);
  G3D_V4D_VNorm4D(&tri->sp_normal,
                  tri->sp_normal);

  tri->sp_NdotV = G3D_V4D_VDot4D(tri->sp_normal,tri->sp_center);
}
```

That concludes the internals of the main part of the analytic portion of the initialization for each object. With the *Makexxx* functions that are next, you'll see the combination of the *MakeAnxxx* and the explicit function *MakeExObject* acting together to make the 3D object.

Implementation Part III: Object Instantiation

Instantiating the objects takes us back to Chapter 8. Instead of forcing you to flip pages, I'll repeat the important blocks, the *Makexxx* ones. Inside the *Makexxx* functions, we construct the explicit and analytic dual representation using the techniques and functions described in the last several sections.

The block from *parse_scene* that uses the object type to determine the type of 3D object to create is shown in Listing 9-76. The discussion of each object repeats both the details of this block and the contents of each *Makexxx* function. The first time you saw this block, it may not have been clear exactly what was going on, but this time you should have no problem following the code.

Listing 9-76.   Makexxx Block from parse_scene

```
if (!_fstricmp((LPSTR)Buf1,(LPSTR)"plane") )
{
...
}
if (!_fstricmp((LPSTR)Buf1,(LPSTR)"sphere") )
{
...
}
if (!_fstricmp((LPSTR)Buf1,(LPSTR)"box") )
{
...
}
if (!_fstricmp((LPSTR)Buf1,(LPSTR)"pyramid") )
{
...
}
if (!_fstricmp((LPSTR)Buf1,(LPSTR)"cylinder") )
{
...
}
if (!_fstricmp((LPSTR)Buf1,(LPSTR)"cone") )
{
...
}
```

Objects: The Sphere

The contents of the sphere *Makexxx* block from *parse_scene* are repeated in Listing 9-77. Here you can clearly see the analytic *SPHERE* structure being populated from the explicit *EX3DOBJECT* structure. Then *MakeSphere* creates an instance of an *LPOBJECT* structure to add to the linked list of 3D objects. The *LPOBJECT* is used as a shell around the two representation structures.

Listing 9-77.   Sphere Makexxx Block from parse_scene

```
// sphere,center and radius
// only one that doesnt need explicit data to build
//translated
                sphere.sph_center.x = oe3D.l_transforms.T.x;
                sphere.sph_center.y = oe3D.l_transforms.T.y;
                sphere.sph_center.z = oe3D.l_transforms.T.z;
```

Listing 9-77. *(cont.)*

```
//scaled
                sphere.sph_radius    = oe3D.l_transforms.S.x;
                sphere.sph_radius2   = sphere.sph_radius *
sphere.sph_radius;
//no rotation - perfect sphere
//instanced
                this = MakeSphere(theScene,
                                  sphere,
                                  Buf2,oe3D);
                this->o_type = T_SPHERE;
                theScene->nSpheres++;
```

Listing 9-78 provides the implementation of *MakeSphere*. You should notice the assignment of the object ID to support retrieval from the list by ID and the assignment of the object-function pointers. This assignment of the function pointers is one place our implementation would have to change if the M3D support services were to become a DLL. In that case, you would have to adjust the interface to a fair number of functions and remove the accompanying dependencies, but that is another topic.

Listing 9-78.   MakeSphere

```
LPOBJECT WINAPI MakeSphere(LPSCENE theScene, SPHERE sphere,
                LPSTR szObjFileName,EX3DOBJECT ex3DObj )
{
      FRAME   *    pfrm    = Frame_GetPtr(g_app.hwndMain);
      LPOBJECT     this = NULL;
      LPSPHERE     spA ;
      LPEX3DOBJECT spE ;

      TRY
      {
          this = (LPOBJECT)WL_Mem_Alloc(GHND,sizeof(OBJECT));
          if (!this) {
             Throw((LPCATCHBUF)&_ci.state,GENERR_ALLOCFAILURE);
          }
          else{
             this -> o_id      = theScene->nObjs;
             this -> o_type    = T_SPHERE;
              this -> o_procs   = & SphereProcs ;

             spE = MakeExObject(theScene,this,szObjFileName,
                           ex3DObj);
             if (!spE) {
                Throw((LPCATCHBUF)&_ci.state,GENERR_ALLOCFAILURE);
             }
```

```
            else {
               this -> o_edata   = (LPVOID) spE ;
            }
            spA              = MakeAnSphere(sphere);
            if (!spA){
               Throw((LPCATCHBUF)&_ci.state,GENERR_ALLOCFAILURE);
            }
            else {
               this -> o_adata   = (LPVOID) spA ;
            return(this);
            }
         }
      }
   }
   CATCH
   {
      switch(_exk)
      {
         case GENERR_ALLOCFAILURE:
         default:
            ProcessError(pfrm,_exk);
            break;
      }
      return 0;
   }
   END_CATCH
}
```

You should also notice both the invocation of *MakeExObject* with the filename to extract the explicit face and vertex values, and the invocation of *MakeAnSphere* to derive the values needed to describe the sphere in ray-trace mode. Also noteworthy are the void pointer elements of the ***OBJECT*** structure, which provide the mechanism for attaching the dual representation to the "listable" shell data structure.

That wraps up the sphere object. We've talked about the basics of explicit representation, including face topology and vertex geometry. You've seen the analytic basis of the sphere object and its derivation from the explicit values. And finally, I've shown you the main instantiation function, *MakeSphere*, invoked by the parser. Next object on deck is the plane.

Objects: The Plane

The plane object is more affected by the switch from polygon to ray modes than any of the other objects. The analytic plane is infinite; this causes obvious problems in polygon mode, which depends on finite polygon definitions. The solution is to ignore the problem and do whatever is practical. The polygon-mode plane is a finite plane controlled by the scaling values in the ***OBJDEF.*** The ray-mode plane is infinite, and if you aim the camera correctly you can get an artificial horizon. In polygon mode, if the scaling is large enough that the rest of the objects are contained within the extent of the plane, for most purposes we achieve the same effect.

In polygon mode, the objects rest on a plane, and it's possible that the edge of the plane can be seen from some camera angles. In ray-trace mode, the objects rest on a plane, and from some camera angles you can see an artificial horizon, due to the maximum distance limit rather than the "edge of the world" seen in polygon mode. This is a definitional oddity, true, but it is not unlivable if you define your scenes accordingly.

Listing 9-79 contains the source for the *Makexxx* block that performs plane handling. Again, this code should be understandable as it sets up the *MakePlane* call.

Listing 9-79.   Makexxx Block for Plane Object from parse_scene

```
//translated
                plane.pl_distance = oe3D.l_transforms.T.z;
//no scaling - infinite in rayspace
//rotated
                G3D_V4D_VSet4D(&plane.pl_normal,
                              0,0,-1,
                              ONE4D);
                G3D_Xfrm_TransformPoint((LPVECTOR4D)&plane.pl_normal,
                                        plane.pl_normal,
                                        &aT);
//instanced
                this = MakePlane(theScene,
                                 plane,
                                 Buf2,oe3D);
                this->o_type = T_PLANE;
                theScene->nPlanes++;
```

The *MakePlane* function is implemented in Listing 9-80. It again shows the signature of memory allocation, TRY/CATCH, and explicit and analytic creation. The analytic action is performed by *MakeAnPlane*, and the explicit work is again performed by *MakeExObject*. The same void-pointer usage is also visible.

Listing 9-80.   MakePlane

```
LPOBJECT WINAPI MakePlane (LPSCENE theScene, PLANE plane,
                LPSTR szObjFileName,EX3DOBJECT ex3DObj)
{
   FRAME  *   pfrm   = Frame_GetPtr(g_app.hwndMain);
   LPOBJECT      this = NULL;
   LPPLANE       plA;
   LPEX3DOBJECT plE ;
//
     TRY
     {
```

```
            this = (LPOBJECT)WL_Mem_Alloc(GHND,sizeof(OBJECT));
            if (!this){
                Throw((LPCATCHBUF)&_ci.state,GENERR_ALLOCFAILURE);
            }
            else {
                this -> o_id       = theScene->nObjs;
                this -> o_type     = Plane;
                this -> o_procs    = & PlaneProcs ;

                plE = MakeExObject(theScene,this,szObjFileName,
                                   ex3DObj);
                if (!plE) {
                    Throw((LPCATCHBUF)&_ci.state,GENERR_ALLOCFAILURE);
                }
                else{
                    this -> o_edata   = (LPVOID) plE ;
                }

                plA              = MakeAnPlane(plane);
                if (!plA) {
                    Throw((LPCATCHBUF)&_ci.state,GENERR_ALLOCFAILURE);
                }
                else {
                    this -> o_adata   = (LPVOID) plA ;
                    return(this);
                }
            }
        }
        CATCH
        {
            switch(_exk)
            {
                case GENERR_ALLOCFAILURE:
                default:
                    ProcessError(pfrm,_exk);
                    break;
            }
            return 0;
        }
        END_CATCH
    }
```

It is critical to set the object ID (as we do here), because the 3D object list is traversed in several different ways, one of which is by ID. Again, we initialize the object function-pointer group. These are all static functions, since they are in an object library and are included in the executable at link time. If you examine the addresses of these functions, you can see that they reside in the .exe itself unlike the functions in either the WLib or G3DLib DLLs.

The general form of these *Makexxx* functions should be getting clearer now. The cylinder is next on our list.

Objects: The Cylinder

Cylinders are formed from the raw materials you've already seen, with a twist of the individual plane figures for the endcaps. Listing 9-81 shows the code block that invokes *MakeCylinder*. Once again, the use of the temporary *CYLINDER* structure should be clear.

Listing 9-81.   Makexxx Block for Cylinders in parse_scene

```
//scaled
   cylinder.c_altitude   = oe3D.l_transforms.S.z;
   G3D_V4D_VSet4D(&cylinder.c_bcenter, 0,0,0,ONE4D);
   cylinder.c_radius     = oe3D.l_transforms.S.x;
   cylinder.c_tcenter    = cylinder.c_bcenter;
   cylinder.c_tcenter.z += cylinder.c_altitude;
//rotated
   G3D_Xfrm_TransformPoint((LPVECTOR4D)&cylinder.c_bcenter,
                                       cylinder.c_bcenter,&aT);
   G3D_Xfrm_TransformPoint((LPVECTOR4D)&cylinder.c_tcenter,
                                        cylinder.c_tcenter, &aT);
//hack
   G3D_V4D_VSet4D((LPVECTOR4D)&temp,0.0,0.0,
                   cylinder.c_altitude,ONE4D);
   G3D_Xfrm_TransformPoint((LPVECTOR4D)&temp, temp,&aT);
//translated
   cylinder.c_bcenter.x += oe3D.l_transforms.T.x;
   cylinder.c_bcenter.y += oe3D.l_transforms.T.y;
   cylinder.c_bcenter.z += oe3D.l_transforms.T.z;
   cylinder.c_tcenter.x += oe3D.l_transforms.T.x;
   cylinder.c_tcenter.y += oe3D.l_transforms.T.y;
   cylinder.c_tcenter.z  = cylinder.c_bcenter.z + temp.z;
//instanced
   this =  MakeCylinder(theScene,cylinder,Buf2,oe3D,&aT);
   this->o_type = T_CYL;
```

That leads us to *MakeCylinder*, shown in Listing 9-82. Besides all of the key details you have seen already, you now see the invocation of *OrientCircle*, after the allocation of the memory for the analytic circle. Then and only then do we create the two endcaps.

Listing 9-82.   MakeCylinder

```
LPOBJECT WINAPI MakeCylinder(LPSCENE theScene, CYLINDER Cylinder,
           LPSTR szObjFileName,EX3DOBJECT ex3DObj )
{
     FRAME  *   pfrm   = Frame_GetPtr(g_app.hwndMain);
     LPOBJECT      this = NULL;
```

```
      LPQUADRIC   cA ;
      LPEX3DOBJECT cE ;

      TRY
      {
          this = (LPOBJECT)WL_Mem_Alloc(GHND,sizeof(OBJECT));
          if (!this)
          {
             Throw((LPCATCHBUF)&_ci.state,GENERR_ALLOCFAILURE);
          }
          else
          {
             this -> o_id      = theScene->nObjs;
             this -> o_type    = T_CYL;
             this -> o_procs   = & CylinderProcs ;

             cE   = MakeExObject(theScene,this,szObjFileName,
                     ex3DObj);
             if (!cE) {
                Throw((LPCATCHBUF)&_ci.state,GENERR_ALLOCFAILURE);
             }
             else{
                this -> o_edata   = (LPVOID) cE ;
             }

             cA                = MakeAnCylinder(Cylinder);
             if (!cA) {
                Throw((LPCATCHBUF)&_ci.state,GENERR_ALLOCFAILURE);
             }
             else {
                OrientCircle(cA,0,&cA->q_endcaps[0],ex3DObj,T);
                OrientCircle(cA,1,&cA->q_endcaps[1],ex3DObj,T);
                this -> o_adata   = (LPVOID) cA ;
                return(this);
             }
          }
      }
      CATCH
      {
         switch(_exk)
         {
            case GENERR_ALLOCFAILURE:
            default:
               ProcessError(pfrm,_exk);
               break;
         }
         return 0;
      }
      END_CATCH
}
```

That's the only twist in the cylinder code, one you will see repeated in the cone object. The cone object (next on our list) exposes an instantiation implementation very similar to what you've just seen with the cylinder.

Objects: The Cone

The cone object completes the simple quadrics. You'll quickly see that the source is virtually identical to the cylinder code, except for the name change and the use of only one endcap. Remember from the previous discussion of cones that the cone is usually used with a zero upper radius; this implies no upper endcap.

From the implementation view, Listing 9-83 contains the cone block from *parse_scene*. This block sets up the call to *MakeCone*.

Listing 9-83.   Makexxx Block for Cones in parse_scene

```
//scaled
   cone.c_altitude   = oe3D.l_transforms.S.z;
   G3D_V4D_VSet4D(&cone.c_bcenter,0,0,0,ONE4D);
   cone.c_tcenter    = cone.c_bcenter;
   cone.c_tcenter.z += cone.c_altitude;
   cone.c_tradius    = 0;
   cone.c_bradius    = oe3D.l_transforms.S.x;
//rotated
   G3D_Xfrm_TransformPoint((LPVECTOR4D)&cone.c_bcenter,
                                       cone.c_bcenter,&aT);
   G3D_Xfrm_TransformPoint((LPVECTOR4D)&cone.c_tcenter,
                                       cone.c_tcenter,&aT);
//hack
   G3D_V4D_VSet4D((LPVECTOR4D)&temp,
                              0.0,0.0,cone.c_altitude,ONE4D);
   G3D_Xfrm_TransformPoint((LPVECTOR4D)&temp,temp,&aT);
//translated
   cone.c_bcenter.x += oe3D.l_transforms.T.x;
   cone.c_bcenter.y += oe3D.l_transforms.T.y;
   cone.c_bcenter.z += oe3D.l_transforms.T.z;
   cone.c_tcenter.x += oe3D.l_transforms.T.x;
   cone.c_tcenter.y += oe3D.l_transforms.T.y;
   cone.c_tcenter.z  = cone.c_bcenter.z + temp.z;
//instanced
   this =  MakeCone(theScene,cone, Buf2,oe3D,&aT);
   this->o_type = T_CONE;
   theScene->nCones++;
```

The source for *MakeCone* is shown in Listing 9-84. The sequence used here should be clear enough for you to recite it by heart: Allocate within a TRY/CATCH block; set up explicit data with *MakeExObject*; set up analytic data with *MakeAnCone*; and, finally, set up the endcap with *OrientCircle*. Don't forget the void-pointer usage, the object ID assignment, and the function-pointer setup.

Listing 9-84.   MakeCone

```
LPOBJECT WINAPI MakeCone(LPSCENE theScene, CONE Cone,
                    LPSTR szObjFileName,EX3DOBJECT ex3DObj)
{
     FRAME   *   pfrm   = Frame_GetPtr(g_app.hwndMain);
     LPOBJECT     this = NULL;
     LPQUADRIC    cA ;
     LPEX3DOBJECT cE ;

     TRY
     {
         this = (LPOBJECT)WL_Mem_Alloc(GHND,sizeof(OBJECT));
         if (!this)
         {
            Throw((LPCATCHBUF)&_ci.state,GENERR_ALLOCFAILURE);
         }
         else
         {
            this -> o_id        = theScene->nObjs;
            this -> o_type      = T_CONE;
            this -> o_procs     = & ConeProcs ;

            cE     = MakeExObject(theScene,this,szObjFileName,
                            ex3DObj);
            if (!cE) {
               Throw((LPCATCHBUF)&_ci.state,GENERR_ALLOCFAILURE);
            }
            else {
               this -> o_edata   = (LPVOID) cE ;
            }

            cA                = MakeAnCone(Cone);
            if (!cA) {
               Throw((LPCATCHBUF)&_ci.state,GENERR_ALLOCFAILURE);
            }
            else{
               OrientCircle(cA,0,&cA->q_endcaps[0],ex3DObj,T);
               this -> o_adata   = (LPVOID) cA ;
               return(this);
            }
         }
     }
}
```

Listing 9-84. (*cont.*)

```
CATCH
{
   switch(_exk)
   {
      case GENERR_ALLOCFAILURE:
      default:
         ProcessError(pfrm,_exk);
         break;
   }
   return 0;
}
END_CATCH
}
```

As you can see (even if this coverage seems repetitive), a lot happens in these functions. Once one of these objects is instantiated, it can be added to the linked list of objects. Once it's in the list, the rendering engine controls it and the other objects by invoking the various object functions through the function pointers as needed. The rendering engine is, in turn, controlled by the state machine. The state machine, in its turn, is embedded in the application; but that's what I'll cover in Chapter 11. There's plenty more to do before that; first, the rest of object instantiations here in Chapter 9, then all of Chapter 10, dealing with visibility and shading.

Objects: The Box

The box and the pyramid are the last two objects, and are the only two composed solely of plane figures. Their construction reflects this fact, which is really the only new implementation detail here (just like the use of the circle was the only addition for the cylinder and then the cone after it).

The block from *parse_scene* that invokes *MakeBox* (shown in Listing 9-85) is pretty familiar at this point. Obvious details — like the usage of vector function *G3D_V4D_VSet4D* to initialize the size vectors, which illustrates the dominance of API usage in general — are just not that relevant.

Listing 9-85.   Makexxx Block for Boxes in parse_scene

```
//translated
            box.c_center = oe3D.l_transforms.T;
//scaled
            G3D_V4D_VSet4D(&box.c_w,
                         oe3D.l_transforms.S.x,
                         0,0,ONE4D);
```

```
                G3D_V4D_VSet4D(&box.c_h,
                               0,
                               oe3D.l_transforms.S.y,
                               0,ONE4D);
                G3D_V4D_VSet4D(&box.c_d,
                               0,0,
                               oe3D.l_transforms.S.z,
                               ONE4D);
//no rotation - not implemented
//instanced
                this =  MakeBox(theScene,box,Buf2,oe3D,&aT);
                this->o_type = T_BOX;
                theScene->nCubes++;
```

The *MakeBox* function is where the action is. Shown in Listing 9-86, it does the usual sequence. The new additions are the six calls to *OrientRectangle*. This performs the round-robin initialization of the faces of the ray-traced representation.

Listing 9-86.   MakeBox

```
LPOBJECT WINAPI MakeBox(LPSCENE theScene, BOX Box,
                   LPSTR szObjFileName,EX3DOBJECT ex3DObj ){
     FRAME  *   pfrm   = Frame_GetPtr(g_app.hwndMain);
     LPOBJECT      this = NULL;
     LPSIMPLENGON cA ;
     LPEX3DOBJECT cE ;

     TRY
     {
         this = (LPOBJECT)WL_Mem_Alloc(GHND,sizeof(OBJECT));
         if (!this) {
            Throw((LPCATCHBUF)&_ci.state,GENERR_ALLOCFAILURE);
         }
         else{
          this -> o_id       = theScene->nObjs;
          this -> o_type     = T_BOX;
         this -> o_procs   = & BoxProcs ;
         cE = MakeExObject(theScene,this,szObjFileName,ex3DObj);
          if (!cE){
             Throw((LPCATCHBUF)&_ci.state,GENERR_ALLOCFAILURE);
          }
          else {
              this -> o_edata   = (LPVOID) cE ;
          }
          cA               = MakeAnBox(Box);
          if (!cA){
              Throw((LPCATCHBUF)&_ci.state,GENERR_ALLOCFAILURE);
          }
          else{
```

Listing 9-86.   *(cont.)*

```
            OrientRectangle(cA,1,&cA->ng_faces[1],ex3DObj);
            OrientRectangle(cA,2,&cA->ng_faces[2],ex3DObj);
            OrientRectangle(cA,3,&cA->ng_faces[3],ex3DObj);
            OrientRectangle(cA,4,&cA->ng_faces[4],ex3DObj);
            OrientRectangle(cA,5,&cA->ng_faces[5],ex3DObj);
            OrientRectangle(cA,6,&cA->ng_faces[6],ex3DObj);
            this -> o_adata   = (LPVOID) cA ;
            return(this);
        }
      }
   }
   CATCH
{
      switch(_exk) {
        case GENERR_ALLOCFAILURE:
        default:
          ProcessError(pfrm,_exk);
          break;
      }
      return 0;
   }
   END_CATCH
}
```

That does it for the box. One more object and the instantiation phase will be complete. Pyramids will do for us what they did for the Pharaohs of Ancient Egypt—mark an ending.

Objects: The Pyramid

You have reached the final object section of this chapter. The treatment of the pyramid instantiation process is completed here. We take a peek, again, at the instantiation block from *parse_scene.* We'll also consider *MakePyramid* now that you know the details of the explicit and analytic representations, as well as the implementation of the representations for each object.

The block from *parse_scene* that invokes *MakePyramid* is shown in Listing 9-87. As you can see, nothing exciting is happening here, especially now that the underlying details are clear.

Listing 9-87.   Makexxx Block for Pyramids in parse_scene

```
//translated
                pyramid.p_center = oe3D.l_transforms.T;
//scaled
                G3D_V4D_VSet4D(&pyramid.p_v1,
                                oe3D.l_transforms.S.x,
                                0,0,ONE4D);
                G3D_V4D_VSet4D(&pyramid.p_v2,
                                0,
                                oe3D.l_transforms.S.y,
                                0,ONE4D);
                G3D_V4D_VSet4D(&pyramid.p_height,
                                0,0,
                                oe3D.l_transforms.S.z,
                                ONE4D);
//no rotation - not implemented
//instanced
                this =  MakePyramid(theScene,
                                    pyramid,
                                    Buf2,oe3D,&aT);
                this->o_type = T_PYR;
                theScene->nPyramids++;
```

When you saw this block in Chapter 8, you probably wondered exactly what it did, but by now, I'm sure you don't even need to see *MakePyramid* to guess at the implementation.

Still, instead of making you guess, the implementation of *MakePyramid* is displayed in Listing 9-88. The usual sequence is broken by the *OrientTriangle* sequence for each of the four side faces, followed by a single call to *OrientRectangle* for the base.

Listing 9-88.   MakePyramid

```
LPOBJECT WINAPI MakePyramid(LPSCENE theScene, PYRAMID Pyramid,
                        LPSTR szObjFileName,EX3DOBJECT ex3DObj)
{
  FRAME  *   pfrm   = Frame_GetPtr(g_app.hwndMain);
  LPOBJECT     this = NULL;
  LPSIMPLENGON pA ;
  LPEX3DOBJECT pE ;

  TRY
  {
      this = (LPOBJECT)WL_Mem_Alloc(GHND,sizeof(OBJECT));
      if (!this){
         Throw((LPCATCHBUF)&_ci.state,GENERR_ALLOCFAILURE);
      }
      else {
         this -> o_id     = theScene->nObjs;
         this -> o_type   = T_PYR;
         this -> o_procs  = & PyramidProcs ;
```

Listing 9-88. *(cont.)*

```
            pE = MakeExObject(theScene,this,szObjFileName,ex3DObj);
            if (!pE) {
               Throw((LPCATCHBUF)&_ci.state,GENERR_ALLOCFAILURE);
            }
            else {
               this -> o_edata   = (LPVOID) pE ;
            }

            pA                    = MakeAnPyramid(Pyramid,ex3DObj);
            if (!pA){
               Throw((LPCATCHBUF)&_ci.state,GENERR_ALLOCFAILURE);
            }
            else{
                OrientTriangle(pA,1,&pA->ng_faces[1],ex3DObj);
                OrientTriangle(pA,2,&pA->ng_faces[2],ex3DObj);
                OrientTriangle(pA,3,&pA->ng_faces[3],ex3DObj);
                OrientTriangle(pA,4,&pA->ng_faces[4],ex3DObj);
                OrientRectangle(pA,7,&pA->ng_faces[5],ex3DObj);

                this -> o_adata   = (LPVOID) pA ;
                return(this);
            }
         }
      }
   }
   CATCH
   {
        switch(_exk)
        {
           case GENERR_ALLOCFAILURE:
           default:
             ProcessError(pfrm,_exk);
             break;
        }
        return 0;
     }
     END_CATCH
}
```

That wraps up the coverage of the pyramid, the *Makexxx* functions, and the details of
the instantiation phase for 3D objects. Before ending the chapter, though, it's time to consider scenes since we have all of these nice objects. First, we'll look at scenes from a standpoint of testing and debugging the objects themselves, and next from the standpoint of
making interesting pictures.

Scene Generation

There are two parts to scene generation: test scene generation and programmatic scene generation.

Test scenes let you easily verify the correctness of your rendering code. If changes to the rendering code make the test scenes appear as expected, the likelihood of the changes being correct is high. The test scenes thus act as a validation suite.

Programmatic scene generation makes it possible to write code that writes scenes. This can work well with recursive or iterative techniques that use parameters to drive the generation process. For instance, certain types of interesting scenes and objects can be generated recursively. The depth of recursion is, thus, an obvious parameter of a recursive scene generator. The other parameters depend on the nature of the scene being generated.

Test Scene Generation

Whenever something changes, you need to run tests. It doesn't matter if your change is adding a new object, changing a shader, adding a new shader, adding a new rendering mode, or whatever. If you change it, you should test it.

The basic set of tests starts with each object in a scene by itself. These scenes test general geometry in the wireframe, hidden-surface, and ray-traced modes. With only one object, it's simple to debug the geometry if something is wrong. It also makes hidden-line debugging easier. One-object scenes are also quick. You can cycle many times to test without really noticing the rendering overhead. This is especially true in polygon mode; ray-trace mode costs more by its nature.

The next set of scenes tests shading, light sources, and surface properties. This tests the illumination models, the surface properties and lookups, the light source list, and the environment variables to clamp intensity values. This set starts to take longer because both wireframe and hidden-surface modes are useless here. These tests are designed to stress the flat shader and the ray tracer.

Finally, you should keep around tests for specific features of the ray tracer; run these tests whenever the source is changed. Good candidates for this set are mirrored surfaces next to each other to test ray cutoff depth, different textures, and other variations. The specific form of your test scenes does not matter as much as which feature they're designed to stress.

Another testing measurement is *coverage*. How much coverage of the feature set does this group of scenes give? When you consider the entire set of tests, you should be able to put at least one check in every function's box.

While this is not complete by any means, this does provide a good base of test scenes for the modeler. Scenes that provide tests for geometry, general shading, and ray-trace mode features provide enough coverage that you can be sure when you add a new feature that the entire system won't fall apart like a house of cards.

These categories are covered by the default test scene suite shown in Table 9-8. This includes the basic object test, a more-advanced geometry test, and general shading/ray-trace mode testers rolled into the third set.

Table 9-8.   Test Scenes Provided on Your Disk

Simple Geometry (Single object)	Object out Each Axis (6 objects of each type)	Objects Above Floor (5 objects above plane)
scone.mod,.scn	crnrcone.mod,.scn	gridcone.mod,.scn
scube.mod,.scn	crnrcube.mod,.scn	gridcube.mod,.scn
scyl.mod,.scn	crnrcyl.mod,.scn	gridcyl.mod,.scn
splane.mod,.scn	N/A	N/A
spyr.mod,.scn	crnrpyr.mod,.scn	gridpyr.mod,.scn
ssph.mod,.scn	cnrnrsph.mod,.scn	gridsph.mod,.scn

The filenames starting with the prefix "s" contain a single object definition. This is the simplest geometry test. The filenames that begin with "crnr" each contain six objects translated out the axes. This "six corners" effect lets us look at each object in many locations, validating the translation operation. Finally, the filenames that begin with "grid" all contain five objects arranged above a plane. Objects defined out the negative z axis are not visible in a scene like this and are not carried over from the crnr scenes. The main difference is the definition of textures in the grid files. They begin to flesh out the tests by exercising features of the tracer.

Programmatic Scene Generation

Once the test scenes are out of the way, the renderer is debugged enough that you can let your imagination design whatever scenes you want, as long as they contain only the basic building blocks. It is sometimes possible to generate interesting scenes programmatically.

Before we can consider that topic, however, we need the ability to generate a model description, a scene description header, and OBJDEF blocks that are part of a scene description and can be appended to a scene description header. Listings 9-89 to 9-91 contain utility routines that perform these valuable services.

DumpModelFile in Listing 9-89 lets you generate a .mod description file that references the scene file passed in as a parameter. A simple *fprintf* with a formatting string to generate the SCENE block gives us a bit of generalism. When we add the ability to specify each element of the model description as a parameter, we add to the flexibility of this routine; this is left as an exercise.

Listing 9-89.   DumpModelFile for Programmatic Scene Generation

```
void WINAPI DumpModelFile(FILE* OutFile,LPSTR SceneFile)
{
    double x, y, z;
    int    fn, fid;
//canvas res
    fprintf(OutFile,"RES\n");
    fprintf(OutFile,"    XRES      = 200\n");
    fprintf(OutFile,"    YRES      = 200\n");
```

```
//render - initial drawing
    fprintf(OutFile,"RENDER\n");
    fprintf(OutFile,"   WIREFRAME = 1\n");
//color table
    fprintf(OutFile,"COLORS\n");
    fprintf(OutFile,"   COLORS    = colors.dat\n");
//materials
    fprintf(OutFile,"MATERIALS\n");
    fprintf(OutFile,"   MATERIALS = material.dat\n");
//ENV weights for adaptive depth control + depth control
    fprintf(OutFile,"ENVIRONMENT\n");
    fprintf(OutFile,"   LOCLWGT   = .55    .55     .55\n");
    fprintf(OutFile,"   REFLWGT   = .45    .45     .45\n");
    fprintf(OutFile,"   TRANWGT   = 0.0    0.0     0.0\n");
    fprintf(OutFile,"   MINWGT    = 0.0003 0.0003 0.0003\n");
    fprintf(OutFile,"   MAXWGT    = 1.0    1.0     1.0\n");
    fprintf(OutFile,"   RDEPTH    = 5\n");
//SCENE = .scn scene geometry description file
    fprintf(OutFile,"SCENE\n");
    fprintf(OutFile,"   GEOMETRY  = %s\n",SceneFile);
}
```

Listing 9-90 holds the implementation for *DumpSceneHeader*. The purpose of *DumpSceneHeader* is to write a VIEWDEF block, an AMBIENT block, a BACKDEF block, and two LITEDEF blocks to the specified file. It takes the at viewing point as a parameter. Implementation of more flexibility is left to you.

Listing 9-90. DumpSceneHeader for Programmatic Scene Generation

```
void WINAPI DumpSceneHeader(FILE* OutFile,VECTOR4D at)
{
    double x, y, z;
    int    fn, fid;
//viewpoint
    fprintf(OutFile,"v\n");
    fprintf(OutFile,"250.0    0.0 250.0\n");
    fprintf(OutFile," %lf    %lf    %lf\n",at.x,at.y,at.z);
    fprintf(OutFile," 0.0    0.0    1.0\n");
    fprintf(OutFile," 0      40     10  \n");
    fprintf(OutFile,"200 200\n");
//ambient
    fprintf(OutFile,"a\n");
    fprintf(OutFile,".25 .25 .25\n");
//background
    fprintf(OutFile,"b\n");
    fprintf(OutFile,"White\n");
```

Listing 9-90.   (*cont.*)

```
//lights
    fprintf(OutFile,"l\n");
    fprintf(OutFile,"800   800 800\n");
    fprintf(OutFile,"White\n");
    fprintf(OutFile,"l\n");
    fprintf(OutFile,"800 -800 800\n");
    fprintf(OutFile,"White\n");
}
```

The scene description remains incomplete; we need objects to populate the scene.

This leaves the writing of the OBJDEF block. Listing 9-91 contains *MakeObject*, which takes the object type, color, material, and local transformation then writes out an OBJDEF. This function is more parameterized than the previous functions because it has to be. With these functions in hand, we are ready to further consider programmatic scene generation.

Listing 9-91.   Making OBJDEF Blocks for Programmatic Scene Generation

```
void WINAPI MakeObject(FILE* OutFile,LPSTR object,
                       LPSTR color,LPSTR material,
                       VECTOR4D S,VECTOR4D R,VECTOR4D T)
{
    double x, y, z;
    int    fn, fid;
//header,type,.datname
    fprintf(OutFile,"o\n");
    fprintf(OutFile,"%s\n",object);
    fprintf(OutFile,"%s.dat\n",object);
//color,material
    fprintf(OutFile,"COLOR    %s\n",color);
    fprintf(OutFile,"MATERIAL %s\n",material);
//local transforms
    fprintf(OutFile,"SCALE     %lf %lf %lf\n",S.x,S.y,S.z);
    fprintf(OutFile,"ROTATE    %lf %lf %lf\n",R.x,R.y,R.z);
    fprintf(OutFile,"TRANSLATE %lf %lf %lf\n",T.x,T.y,T.z);
//end
    fprintf(OutFile,"END\n");
}
```

A good place to start is the SPD again. I mentioned the SPD, or Standard Procedural Database, in connection with the NFF (Neutral File Format) description language way back in the discussion of description language elements in Part I. The SPD version 2.2 package contains several standard scenes; Table 9-9 lists the contents of that release.

Table 9-9.   SPD Release Version 2.2 Contents

Scene	Description
Balls	Recursive 9-sphere system generator
Gears	Meshed triangular gears generator
Mountain	Fractal mountain with refractive spheres generator
Rings	Pyramid of dodecahedral rings generator
Tetra	Recursive tetrahedral pyramid system generator
Tree	Cone and sphere tree generator

In addition to these scene generators, the SPD release contains a module of utility routines. Any of those scene generators would have to be converted to this system using *DumpModelFile*, *DumpSceneHeader*, and *MakeObject*.

The ball generator from SPD 2.2 can be subsumed easily into this system, but a more interesting scene is the "sphereflake" defined in the original article (*IEEE Computer Graphics & Applications*, November 1987). Figure 9-15 shows a sphereflake. It is another recursive sphere-based scene. The source for the sphereflake was not included in the SPD 2.2 release, so choosing it here seems natural.

Figure 9-15.   Sphereflake

Listing 9-92 is the main program for the sphereflake generator. It asks for recursion levels, initial radius, shrink factor for each recursion, and an initial position. This defines the sphereflake. You can see the use of the three utility routines.

Listing 9-92.   Main for Sphereflake Generator

```
main (int argc, char **argv)
{
    FILE      *out_file;
    int       levels;
    VECTOR4D S,R,T;

    fprintf (stdout, "3D Scene SphereFlake Generator .1 \n");
    fprintf (stdout, "\n");
    fprintf (stdout, "\n");
//
    fprintf (stdout, "enter levels ( 1-4 ): ");
    fscanf (stdin, "%d",&levels);
    fprintf (stdout, "enter initial radius : ");
    fscanf (stdin, "%lf",&globalrad);
    fprintf (stdout, "enter shrink factor  : ");
    fscanf (stdin, "%lf",&globaldiv);
    fprintf (stdout, "enter initial pos    : ");
    fscanf (stdin, "%lf %lf %lf",&T.x,&T.y,&T.z);
    fprintf (stdout, "\n");
    fprintf (stdout, "\n");
//
    fprintf (stdout, "generating sflake.mod...\n");
    fprintf (stdout, "\n");
    fprintf (stdout, "\n");
//
    out_file=fopen("sflake.mod", "w+t");
    DumpModelFile(out_file,"sflake.scn");
    fclose(out_file);
//
```

In addition, *MakeFlakes* (Listing 9-93) hides the recursion. It recurses three times, once around the equator and once around each pole. Other than that, this code speaks for itself.

Listing 9-93.   MakeFlakes Sphereflake Helper

```
void MakeFlakes(FILE* OutFile,VECTOR4D ParentOrg,
               int level,double rad,double div)
{
    double    newrad,newgap,theta,costheta,sintheta,o,a,h;
    int       i;
    VECTOR4D S,R,T;
```

```
//
//set smaller rad size
//set other constant data
//
    newrad = rad/div;
    o      = rad * G3D_Math_SinD(G3D_Math_ACosD((7.0*rad/8.0)/rad));
    S.x    = S.y = S.z = newrad;
    R.x    = R.y = R.z = 0.0;
    newgap = newrad/2.0 + 1.0;
//test recursion
    if ( level <= 1 )
        return;
    level—;
//
//output subs around
//
    fprintf(OutFile,"\\\\ equator at level %d\n",level);
    for ( i = 0; i < 6; i++)
    {
        double  xs,ys;
        xs  = G3D_Math_CosD(i*60) * rad;
        ys  = G3D_Math_SinD(i*60) * rad;
        if ( xs >= 0.0 )
            T.x     = ParentOrg.x + xs + newgap;
        else
            T.x     = ParentOrg.x + (xs - newgap);
        if ( ys >= 0.0 )
            T.y     = ParentOrg.y + ys + newgap;
        else
            T.y     = ParentOrg.y + (ys - newgap);
        T.z     = ParentOrg.z;
        MakeObject(OutFile,"sphere","SkyBlue","mirror",
                   S,R,T);
        MakeFlakes(OutFile,T,level,newrad,div);
    }
}
```

This example serves two important purposes: first, it generates a nice scene; second, it illustrates the use of the programmatic scene-generation utility functions. Either hand-cranked or programmatic scene generation is possible now. From this, you can see that it is easy to start building real-world objects with the set of primitive 3D objects provided by the modeler. Have at it!

Summary

Four components of world generation are provided here:

1. color,
2. materials,
3. light sources, and
4. 3D objects.

Color is supported by the user-defined lookup table and lookup function *LookupColorByName*. This provides a solid-color capability, built on top of the WLib color routines and supported by the palette routines of the G3DLib. The convenience of ASCII names for colors is the result of building this subsystem.

Materials are provided by the user-defined lookup table and lookup function *LookupMaterialByName*. While the name and technique are the same, materials are drastically different. They consist of a set of surface properties and a texture. They are also known by their ASCII names.

Light sources are instantiated and placed in a list to support the illumination model and the two rendering types that use an illumination model: flat-shaded mode and ray-traced mode.

The other half of the light API, which supports the rendering process directly, awaits in Chapter 10.

That leaves 3D objects. 3D objects are a major part of what it is all about. Without them, all the work on color, material, and light is wasted. With them, scenes come alive. The objects provided in this modeler include:

- sphere,
- plane,
- cylinder,
- cone,
- box, and
- pyramid.

I discussed the implementation of the *Makexxx* functions and the internal details of both representations in detail. Both explicit face and vertex representation and the analytic equation-based representation should be familiar by now. I've also discussed exactly how the *LPOBJECT* hides the details of the dual representation.

Once the object definition is complete, the issue of scene generation arises. Scene generation was examined from the standpoint of both test scenes and programmatic generation. This provides some basic scenes for using the modeler without much effort.

At this point, you should have a good understanding of the objects used in the modeler from a definition and representation standpoint. At this, the process of adding these objects to the object lists and using them in the manipulation and rendering phase is all that remains between you and the implementation of the modeler.

10

Polygon Drawing and Object Tracing

In This Chapter

- Revelation of the application/library dichotomy by consideration of the application-oriented topics of algorithms and control architecture, leading into the manipulation and rendering phases. This includes techniques to:

  1. determine surface visibility, and
  2. perform surface shading.

- Placement of the algorithms and techniques you've previously learned into their context according to classical graphics.
- Brief coverage of HLHSR (Hidden-Line, Hidden-Surface Removal) taxonomy, leading back to sorting and algorithms, memory usage, and upper bounds on the size of a model.
- Finish of the discussion of control and control architecture, including the list API, the mapping functions, and more on the internals of the manipulation and rendering process itself.
- Discussion of visibility in two parts: one for polygon mode and one for ray-trace mode.
- Discussion of shading, shading geometry, and shader calculations.
- Presentation of texture mapping and procedural texturing. Show textures as the finishing touch to object and scene appearance in this modeler.

Introduction

Chapters 8 and 9 introduced the world generation phase, and took us from the point of an ASCII script file to objects in memory. In this chapter, we take control over those objects, placing them into a list that will allow manipulation and rendering, and performing the manipulation and rendering. In Chapter 11, we will assemble these pieces into a coherent whole and do the color post-processing.

The transformation of the light list and the 3D object list are the only manipulations supported in this modeler. Object or scene editing must happen at the script level. Still, moving the camera around is enough to let you make an AVI-format (Audio Video Interleaved) movie, for instance (although this gets tedious with no automatic support). You need to be able to manipulate the list itself to get to the list element that needs to be transformed or rendered. The linked list support and the function pointers stored in the *OBJECT* shell structure are central architectural features.

Once you get to a 3D object and it has been transformed, the next steps are visibility and rendering. Two visibility methods are supported here: the backface-culling z-sort visibility of polygon mode and the ray/object intersection test visibility of the ray tracer. These are two techniques among many that can be used to solve the hidden-line, hidden-surface removal (HLHSR) problem.

Once visibility is determined, we have to determine the color of the object. This is called *rendering* and there are five different rendering types supported:

1. wireframe,
2. monochrome hidden,
3. solid-color hidden,
4. flat-shaded, and
5. ray-traced.

This range of types allows you not only to have some fun but also to see how a wide variety of pieces work together. Wireframe mode doesn't need HLHSR; monochrome, solid color, and flat-shaded renderings, on the other hand, all require HLHSR. These are all polygon-based renderings. Ray-traced rendering uses a different technique to determine visibility, but it's still just another way of determining visibility.

The techniques used here are only two of many ways to determine visibility. The polygon method depends heavily on a sort, and this is where the boundary between computer graphics and computer science blurs; you, the programmer, should understand the algorithms you are using; you need to know what they can do and what they can't. For this reason, we'll take a brief side trip to explore the algorithmic basis of "what is."

Once we determine visibility, our work turns to shading. Both polygon-based and ray-traced methods use an illumination model. The ray-traced illumination model is simply a superset of the flat-shaded model. The two illuminaton models share terms in the shading equation. We can look at the entire process as one of incremental improvement in image quality as we add and evaluate terms in the shading equation. Understanding the basics of shading means you understand it all. There is no discontinuity or sudden change of gears. Understand one, and the next should be a logical progression.

While flat-shaded and ray-traced models share the basics of an illumination model, additional opportunities exist in ray-traced mode to determine the final pixel color. We'll take advantage of one such opportunity by adding simple procedural texturing. This enables us to further define the appearance of an object (for example, to specify that a plane should look like a chessboard instead of having a plain, boringly even appearance). I'll oversimplify many of the details of texturing (both text and code) in the interests of time and space. We need the ability to perform operations like rotation in texture space for robust texturing, but I'll skip them in the name of brevity here. This is not the only shortcut, but I'll give you a clear path to fix these problems. Rotation forces us to add the ability to specify a rotation relative to the texture space for each point, then generate the transformation and use it. This set of operations shouldn't be foreign to you by this juncture. I'll point out where in the code you should take what action, so you should be able to make just about any modifications or enhancements with little trouble.

The stage is now set for this chapter. First, we'll tackle a bit of algorithms, then the main course of visibility and rendering. We'll follow that up with a wee taste of texture for dessert. Once you have digested this meal, there's one more feast and you are done. So let's get on with some algorithmic explorations.

Algorithms

In Chapter 1, I introduced the basic classification of algorithms by time complexity, along with the O-notation for describing algorithms. Chapter 9, in the lookup-table sections, presented the basic searches in terms of algorithms and time complexity, but did not explore how to relate this to runtime. I did this, basically, because the tables for both color and materials are generally small and have no major effect on overall modeler performance, since the world load time is minimal compared to manipulation and rendering time. The transformation, visibility, and shading processes consume a lot of time. It's critical that you understand where and why if you wish to improve and extend the modeler.

This means that a little study of algorithms in general (and the ones used here in particular) will produce practical results. Besides the standard definition of an algorithm as "a method of solution," it's useful to categorize an algorithm as:

- a problem to solve,
- a range of values and environments, and
- a step-by-step sequence of actions.

Taken together, this defines an algorithm. It misses the point if we exclude the problem statement, range of values over which the problem is defined, and the environment it executes in, as well as the step-by-step sequence of actions (what is usually thought of as "the algorithm"). By the way, this categorization is similar to Tom Swan's in "Algorithm Alley," (*Dr. Dobbs Journal*, May1993). Instead of his use of beginning and ending, though, I use range of values and environment. The range of values implicitly determines a beginning and ending. An example is that in a square root the negative values are not defined. This can be defined as:

$$y = sqrt(x), where\ 0 <= x < MAX\ (MAXINT, MAXFLOAT, etc.)$$

Thus, the statement of the problem and the range do determine beginning and end (at least in this example). If you think about it, this holds true in general — range determines domain. The environment in the square root example would be integer, double, or whatever, and that would further fix the values. Finally, the step-by-step sequence of actions is perhaps the dominant member of the set.

Besides this basic definition of an algorithm and the classifications of time complexity, several new concepts help us zero in on algorithms. Here is a non-numerical examination of algorithms; this considers precision and accuracy issues and the ascendancy of one approach over another in those terms. This makes for a more general evaluation.

First, you must understand the problem's dimensions. In order to determine the best solution, you must know which properties or details of the problem are important to this application and this solution. Is it time-constrained? Is it space-constrained? What are the approximate costs? What do the average and worst-case analyses reveal? What upper/lower bounds issues exist? All of this defines the concepts of algorithms and algorithm design.

Time and space analysis examines how the two most important resources — time (in CPU cycles) and space (in memory bytes) are used. Obviously, it's desirable for running time to be minimized. The usual trade-off is to use space, or memory, to compensate for the performance cost. This usually takes the form of pre-calculating values and storing them, or saving the calculated values as long as possible to avoid repetitive calculations. For example, some floating-point libraries use pre-calculated lookups for transcendentals. Our modeler saves intensities in polygon mode to feed the color post-processing step, for another example.

The time and space analysis does a simple cost-benefit evaluation. The cost of space is traded off against the benefit of speed. How much speed and benefit we want for what cost becomes our next issue. This examination of algorithmic cost and the approximate analysis are what O-notation was designed for. It was first introduced in 1892 by Paul G. H. Bachman in *Analytische Zahlentheorie*, according to Donald E. Knuth (*The Art of Computer Programming*, Vol. 1, 2nd Ed., "Fundamental Algorithms," Addison-Wesley, 1973). It allows a symbolism to support approximate analysis, and reduces consideration to "values on order of" or "values approaching." This is also known as an *asymptote*, so this is sometimes referred to as *asymptotic* behavior. Simple O-notation is represented by:

$$y = O(n), \text{ or}$$

$$y = O(n)^2$$

This is read as "y is then said to be of order n," or "of order n-squared." This is a way of discussing the computing costs of y in terms of n. Thus, in the n-squared case, you could say that a 2-fold increase in data will result in a 4-fold increase in work (time), and that a 4-fold increase in data results in a 16-fold increase in work. There are often constant factors involved as well, but here the topic of functional dominance and cost functions arises. That is the beauty of the O-notation; the dominant term in any cost function determines the order of complexity of the function.

This cost function and its approximation let us build a model of computation, and from that we can perform average or worst-case analysis. As a result, we can find at least an upper bound, if not a lower bound as well.

Algorithms and Functional Dominance

Functional dominance is simple to understand, and is a good, quick-and-dirty guesstimate of execution time. Regardless of the cost function, some term dominates. For instance, Wilbon Davis in "Time Complexity," *The C User's Journal*, (Vol. 10, No. 9, September 1992) shows a table of values for various sorts, along with quadratic functions that fit the empirical data from testing. The interesting thing about such empirically derived formulas is that they can be reduced to the dominant term.

Consider an $O(n^2)$ function as an example. At a value of n = 100, the n-squared term represents a factor on the order of 10,000. This is 100 times larger than the n term in the quadratic, which has a value on the order of 100. The n-squared term clearly dominates.

A couple of handy rules make using this practical; Table 10-1 shows various functions and rules. This uses the terminology *dom(f,g)* where, given functions f and g, *dom(f,g)* represents the dominant function.

Table 10-1. O-Notation Simplification Rules

Function	Rules
$Akn_k + Ak\text{-}1n_{k-1} + ... + A1n + A0$	$O_{(nk)}$(polynomial)
$f+g$	$O(dom(f,g))$
kf	$O(f)$ where k is constant
$f*g$	$O(f)*O(g)$

Between this and the classifications from Chapter 1, we're establishing a basis for making a quick-and-dirty estimate. This remains, though, a theoretical approximation. The amount of time for any particular input is unknown, we only know its *order of magnitude* or $O(n)$.

Using this approximation, we get both a pessimistic view of worst-case running time over all inputs and a realistic view of average running time. This gives a good "feel" for the behavior of a program when you clearly understand its internals. We rarely, if ever, discuss best-case performance — in algorithms, as in project management, there are no optimists.

We can investigate the upper and lower bounds. This is even more theoretical in some respects, but it has one important aspect — the lower bound tells us that if we want to perform some action faster, we'll need a fundamentally different approach.

Still, this is a generally applicable process, and it has two redeeming features: it is relatively easy to apply, and the asymptotic run-time estimate is often good enough for what Jon Bentley calls "back-of-the-envelope" calculations. In other words, these calculations are sufficient to make sure we won't require 120-second minutes to handle message load or 26-hour days to perform daily backups or an overly large increment of rendering time. That leads us to consider the algorithmic basis of the polygon mode and the ray-trace mode.

Algorithms and HLHSR

Let's look at the modeler. Algorithms like matrix multiplication are data-independent; their cost is simply the sum of the mathematical operations. The transformation process — basically, each point multiplied by a matrix — is not susceptible to asymptotic analysis. However, to render in any mode other than wireframe, you need to determine which surfaces (or parts of surfaces) are visible. That process is a different story.

Figure 10-1 is a tree diagram of different visible-surface algorithms: a *taxonomy*, if you will. Broadly categorized into object/world space and screen space algorithms, these represent a wide range. In this application, we'll use the two algorithms at the far end of the spectrum. Explicit polygon-based objects use back-face culling/z-sorting and the painter's algorithm to determine visibility. Analytic equation-based objects use ray/object intersections or ray-tracing to determine visibility.

We also need to analyze the sorting of the polygon-based objects. Sorting, like the searching from Chapter 9, is a well-researched topic. Basic sorts and their $O(n)$ times are shown in Table 10-2.

Figure 10-1.   Taxonomy of Visible Surface Algorithms

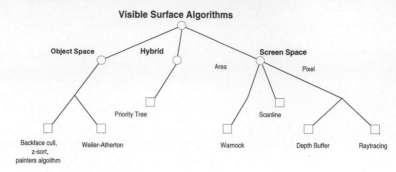

Table 10-2.   Sorting Algorithms and Running Time

Sort Name	Knuth Page	Time
Bubble	106	N^2
Shell	84	$N^{3/2}$
Quick	114	NLogN
Tree	422–451	NLogN

Many currently available implementations use Bubble Sort because of its simplicity and minimal memory requirements. Quicksort, however, is a much better-behaved algorithm, having O(NlogN) behavior. An excellent place to learn about quicksort, besides Knuth, is P. J. Plauger's *The Standard C Library* (Prentice-Hall, 1992).

Quicksort prevents the z-sort from dominating the cost equation. When we use the quadratic form, as we increase the number of objects, the sort time responds according to the square rule — this term will not go away in the cost function unless a cubic ($O(n^3)$) appears. Since the rest of the process involves evaluating either data-independent functions like matrix multiplication or constant functions like drawing a rectangle for each face, the only answer there is faster hardware.

Despite the desirable performance characteristics of quicksort, it does have one problem. It requires you to pass it a single block containing what amounts to an array of structures, the structure size, and a comparison function. Quicksort chugs through the array knowing the size, and, according to its logic, passes two elements to the comparison function at a time. The result of this further drives the sort.

The key detail to us is the single block of memory. This necessitates a little careful thought about memory usage and adjustment to your coding practices and memory models. The face data structure is the sortable unit. It contains enough information to be sorted, and, through its direction, the retrieval of the correct geometry.

Listing 10-1 shows the hierarchy of scene, facelist, and face. The scene contains a facelist. This facelist, in turn, contains a huge pointer to an array of face structures. The interlocking nature of the data structures should be obvious. Remember that each object is meticulous about setting its ID to support the search-for-element-by-ID requirement.

Listing 10-1. Face Visibility Data Structures

```
//face
typedef struct t_face
{
      //id
    int             oi;
      //visibility
    double          z;
      //shading
    VECTOR4D        i;
      //topology
    int             fi;
    int             ni;
    int             indx[5];
      //extra
    double          pad;
}FACE;

typedef FACE huge *HPFACE;

//facelist
typedef struct t_facelist
{
    DWORD           fiNum;
    HPFACE          fi;
}FACELIST;

//scene
typedef struct tagSCENE
{
...
// HLHSR
    LPFACELIST      VisFaces;
...
}
```

The face structure uses the object ID internally by storing and using it to "index" into the object list. Once the object itself is accessible, the face topology lets you retrieve the correct vertex values. What this means is that the sort process can get away with sorting topology only, which (at least) minimizes space for the sort. Exactly how much space it saves, though, is a good question.

The face data structure is 64 bytes. It works out this evenly because of the 8-byte pad variable. This lets all moves work on quadword boundaries and is critical for huge pointer operating. This also means that 1024 faces can be stored in 64K, with only 8K of wasted space — the 8-byte pad again. On average, it seems that no more than two-thirds of any individual object's polygons can ever be visible. Indeed, for a cube, the actual fractions could be one-half (three faces visible), one-third (two faces visible), or one-sixth (one face visible and the degenerate case). This means that a scene consisting of 100 spheres of 240 faces each — in other words, 24,000 polygons — results in a worst case of 18,000 visible polygons, requiring a 1152K block of memory. This is, of course, in addition to the smaller blocks required for each object.

By the way, our upper limit here is the size of the largest memory block that can be allocated. On a 80386 machine, that is 16MB minus 64K. Working out the numbers goes like this: (1024*1024*16) - 65536 = 16,711,580 bytes. This result divided by 64 is 261,120. This means that on a 80386 with no changes to the algorithm, you can hope to render over 260,000 polygons.

That leads us to the need to know how many blocks are taken by an object. A 3D object is represented by the *OBJECT* structure and its two void pointers. Polygon-mode adds three selectors — the facelist and the two vertex lists (original and working) — resulting in six selectors per object. The modeler uses a few others: the color and material lookup, the visible facelist (a huge pointer), and the noise data covered later in this chapter — these all cost. Because of this cost, the number of objects in the system is limited more by selectors and selector usage than any other factor.

It's time for a brief review of Windows and selectors. The System Virtual Machine (SVM) owns the WinApps, as shown in Figure 10-2. The Virtual Machine Manager (VMM) presents the SVM and all WinApps with one Local Descriptor Table (LDT) from which to allocate selectors. An LDT, by definition, contains 8,192 selectors. We consider half of these available selectors as the maximum a single task can allocate, so 4,096 is the maximum possible. Taking out some for the overhead (say, 100 in the worst case) leaves enough for 650 objects (650*6 = 3900). With 650 as the maximum, if we use a sphere with 240 faces, the modeler will support scenes of at least 156,000 polygons. Using a sphere with more faces increases the number of polygons in the scene, decreasing the number of objects that can be used. On average, 650 objects of up to 400 faces each will fit under the upper bound on a block of memory, which is the limiting factor on this implementation of the polygon-based visibility algorithm.

Figure 10-2.   Windows Virtual Machine Layout and Memory Management

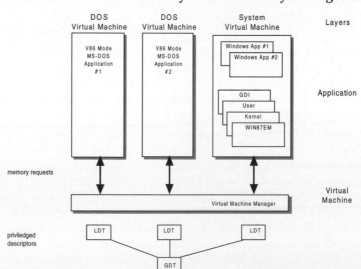

All this talk about algorithms leads us into the discussion of the details of the polygon-based visibility techniques used here — back-face culling, z-sorting, and the painter's algorithm. Those details show that a major factor in considering the algorithm in relation to the application and its environment is memory and memory usage: a resource-utilization issue. Besides the object list, there are: each object and its five dependent selectors, the overhead allocations, the graphics environment and canvas memory requirements, and the color post-processing memory requirements (canvas memory buffer and histogram bins); you can see that this (and most any 3D modeling) application has a serious appetite for memory. You can also see why it was so important to pave the way for sub-allocation, the driving force behind wrapping the Windows memory routines.

With that out of the way, it is back to the taxonomy.

The taxonomy of the algorithms displayed in Figure 10-1 can be viewed from the vantage point of a few general principles. Intersections are used when two surfaces are thought to be visible and one partially occludes the other. The intersection of the surface projections on the viewing plane, depending on the method, will have to resolve surface-surface, plane-surface, line-surface, and/or line-line intersections. All visible-surface algorithms sort objects, surfaces, or surface boundaries. In most cases, the sort key is some coordinate value (z-sort here) of each member (face) of a collection of geometric primitives (object list). All of the visible-surface algorithms try to perform as efficiently as possible. Although all are constrained to some degree by the nature of the problem (to calculate intersections and sort), they differ in the steps they use to optimize the process. Optimization is a topic unto itself.

Algorithms and Optimization

The previous section dealt with polygon mode and HLHSR, but optimization crosses the boundaries between the modes. Therefore it is best considered separately from the points of view of polygon and ray-trace modes. In both cases, though, the effort concentrates on making calculations more efficient and reducing the number of calculations required to generate an image.

A partial list of possible polygon-mode optimizations includes:

- *Coherence*, which allows information computed for one location to be incrementally updated to give information about a nearby location.
- *Transformations*, which separate the transformation and projection operations, perform visibility testing, and only project visible objects/surfaces/lines.
- *Reduction in Dimension*, which was defined earlier in reverse. Instead of treating 3-space as 4-space like homogeneous coordinates do, this technique treats 3-space as 2-space. For instance, the determination of polygon overlap can be simplified by projecting first, reducing from 3-space to 2-space by the projection transformation.
- *Culling Back-Faces*, which eliminates all backward-facing surfaces, as determined by the normal direction. This speeds up not only projection, but also the mapping, shading, and drawing processes by reducing the number of items that must be manipulated.
- *Clipping*, which is another technique for eliminating from further consideration any surfaces that lie completely behind the viewpoint and that lie outside the viewing pyramid (or *frustum*).

This system uses the transformation and culling optimizations in polygon rendering. If you decide to add anything to polygon mode, clipping is the next logical choice. This optimization is not trivial (on the difficulty scale), because you need both line and polygon clippers. As a side note, back-face culling and clipping operations in their simplest form depend on an important limitation: no reflection in the polygon modeler.

Coherence and reduction are more appropriate for other algorithms and other representations. (Note that the representation has crept back into our discussion.) Coherence, for example, is of the most use in scan-line algorithms. The real use of a scan-line algorithm is to rasterize polygons for incremental shading, like true Phong shading. In addition, Phong shading needs adjacency information, which moves you toward considering a change of the polygon-mode representation to some form that maintains the "nextness" property. That's a big change. Still, all this is driven by considering the algorithms and the representations.

Ray-trace mode has its own set of techniques. Figure 10-3 is a graphical representation of the possible ray-tracing acceleration techniques; Table 10-3 shows some examples for each category. This gives you many choices for speeding up the trace.

Figure 10-3.   Ray-Tracing Acceleration Techniques Taxonomy

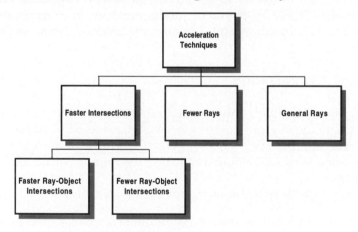

Table 10-3.   Example Algorithms by Category

Faster Intersections	Fewer Intersections	Fewer Rays	General rays
Object bounding volumes	Bounding volume hierarchies	Adaptive tree-depth control	Beam tracing
Efficient intersectors	Space subdivision		Cone tracing
			Pencil tracing

The first category, "Faster Intersections," has two subcategories, one concerned with reducing the number of necessary intersection tests by using bounding volumes, and the other concerned with achieving the fastest possible intersection calculations by using efficient intersectors. The category "Fewer Rays" describes techniques that reduce the number of rays that have to be intersected with the environment. The last category, "complex rays," includes techniques that define a more general ray that contains the basic ray used here as a special (degenerate) case. This has both advantages and disadvantages. The advantages include faster calculations, anti-aliasing, and additional optical effects. Disadvantages can include limitations on primitives in a scene and inaccurate intersection results.

Most procedural objects are based on some technique for efficiently calculating the intersection that makes the distinction between object definition and acceleration somewhat vague. Efficient intersection calculations are certainly our goal, and, as you will see, the code used here is not bad. In this case, your attempt to squeeze the last possible bit of speed out of this code by changing to a cleverer algorithm is (probably) an acceleration technique; the original code is (most certainly) a representation/definition.

This ray tracer uses bounding volumes. These are volumes that surround an object and allow simpler intersection calculations. This technique boils down to using a simple approximation as a first test for intersection: for example, surround a more complex object with a sphere, which makes the initial bounding intersection test simpler and faster. If the ray does not intersect the bounding volume, it will definitely not intersect the object the bounding volume represents.

Using a sphere as a bounding box can easily be incorporated into the ray tracer, since we've already implemented spheres. We would need a way to initialize the bounding box, keep track of its presence, and use it, but the pieces are all there. Spheres are not the best bounding volume object, but they are simple and perfectly adequate for this tracer.

One example of a sphere's deficiency in this role is for bounding a long, thin object. In this case, the area of the sphere that generates false hits is large. Figure 10-4 shows this arrangement after projection; you can easily see how bad the worst case can be. This leads us back to algorithms and cost functions.

Figure 10-4.   Problem Areas of Bounding Spheres

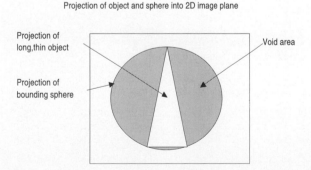

As with this example, bounding volumes all have a cost associated with them. The simplicity of the intersection calculation is not a sufficient criteria for picking bounding volumes. The wasted, or *void* area, where an intersection with the bounding volume generates false hits is also a consideration. This can be expressed in a cost function in terms of the original object and the bounding volume, as shown in Equation 10-1 where:

Equation 10-1.   Bounding Box Cost Function

$T = b * B + i * I,$ where

T = total cost
b = bounding volume intersection test count
B = cost of testing the bounding volume
i = number of times the object or item in question is tested for intersection
I = cost of testing the object or item in question

From this you can see that the bounding volume is a winner for misses. False hits really cost, since they cause two calculations to be done instead of one (the bounding-volume hit that was "positive" and the object intersection that was "negative"). The percentage of bounding volume hits to object hits needs to be high to achieve value from the bounding volume, because if it's not, you'll be computing both the bounding and original object calculations in many cases where they are not needed. In that case, it would be quicker to perform only the original object calculation without the bounding volume. False hits are bad for performance, and a bounding-volume geometry that results in lots of false hits will have a very measurable cost in this area.

Fewer ray techniques include adaptive depth control, which we implement here. Adaptive tree-depth control lets you set criteria for controlling the recursion based on the materials within the scene. Coupled with a maximum-depth check, adaptive depth control prevents the propagation of low-intensity rays that contribute very small amounts to a pixel's color. Listing 10-2 shows the simple depth check that is standard for ray tracing.

Listing 10-2.   Recursion Depth Maximum Limits Alone

```
//
// Recursion limit check
//
    if (Depth > pv->mWorld->RayDepth)
{
//
// depth check failed, set color to backgrund
//
     Color->x = Ia.x;
     Color->y = Ia.y;
     Color->z = Ia.z;
     return;
}
else
{
// continue trace
...
}
```

Listing 10-3 shows the improved version with the adaptive depth check using a weighting system. In Chapter 8, you saw the environment block define a set of weights along with a depth value. The ray tracer uses these modeling parameters to provide a combination of adaptive depth control based on the materials in the scene, and a recursion-depth maximum.

Listing 10-3. Adaptive Depth Control with Recursion Depth Maximum Limits

```
//
// Adaptive depth and recursion limit check
//
if ((TotW < pv->mWorld->MinW) && (Depth > pv->mWorld->RayDepth))
{
//
// depth check failed, set color to backgrund
//
     Color->x = Ia.x;
     Color->y = Ia.y;
     Color->z = Ia.z;
     return;
}
else
{
// continue trace
...
}
```

General rays subsume the techniques of beam, cone, and pencil tracing. Those techniques extend the simple parametric ray with the idea of tracing many rays simultaneously. Beams, cones, and pencils are used as "bundles" of rays. The family of rays that represent these figures are used in calculations. By restricting these techniques to simpler primitives with faster intersection calculations, we can use advanced techniques without losing too much speed. In that respect, this can be considered an acceleration technique for advanced rendering results like fuzzy shadows (penumbrae) and dull reflections (cone tracing), the ability to use spatial coherence and easier anti-aliasing (beam tracing), and motion blurring, transparent-object dispersion, and creating movies with a continuously moving point of view (pencil tracing). While these techniques use multiple rays, they make trade-offs elsewhere to get better results without all the cost that we might normally need to pay for better results.

Control Architecture, Manipulation, and Rendering

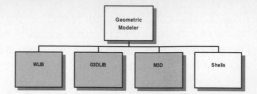

It is important to remember the "prime directive" here — build the modeler and images will come. All of this support-library code is well and good, as are the discussions of topics like algorithms. Our occasional return to topics directly related to the modeler architecture reminds us of our main goal: building the modeler. This section concentrates on control architecture, specifically that of lists and list-mapping functions.

Lists are used by the state machine, under control of the application, to direct the modeler's operations. The list of lights and the list of 3D objects help you with the manipulation and rendering operations because they contain their own manipulation and rendering methods. Under the state machine's control, the list is traversed and the correct method is executed. The loop doing this doesn't need to know any internal details of either the operation or the object; it simply invokes the correct method.

The name of the function, which hopefully corresponds to the action it takes is all the procedural knowledge needed here. This almost guarantees that minimum maintenance will be required, because there's almost nothing in this loop. In addition, this style is highly readable. The code is arranged in relatively tight loops that look like the code in Listing 10-4.

Listing 10-4.   On-Demand Object Retrieval and Method Invocation

```
...

 ot    = GetElement(pv->mWorld->Scene->ObjectList,i+1);
(ot->o_procs->transform(ot,vtype==CMD_PERSP?tPerspProj:tParaProj));
...
```

An object is retrieved from the list using **GetElement** and its ID. When the object is retrieved its transformation method is automatically invoked. This is possible because the **OBJECT** structure includes both a self-referential declaration (making it "listable") and the object ID. Listing 10-5 shows a partial data structure definition for the **OBJECT** structure.

Listing 10-5.   OBJECT Internals

```
typedef struct t_object
{
    struct t_object FAR *next;
    unsigned short   o_type ;
    unsigned short   o_id ;
...

} OBJECT ;
```

This lets us use a transparent coding style and makes it harder to hide an important fact — the different rendering techniques use different granularities for object access and output. This influences the set of functions that the 3D objects must support. Specifically, wireframe rendering always considers the world at the 3D object level. To the wireframe loops, it is enough to traverse the object list and perform operations on the entire object — transformation, projection, mapping, and drawing. Hidden polygon and ray-trace rendering modes require a different access mechanism at a different granularity than the entire object.

The hidden polygon mode starts by transforming every vertex in an object. So at the transformation level, the object remains the granularity of access. The visibility process, however, generates a list of faces. The faces in this list define the topology and are sorted for visibility, allowing the sort process to move around a minimum of data. Thus, the faces must stand alone and remain unconnected to the object, at least in any direct way. But the faces must still relate to the object in some way, which drives the retrieval process. Using and retrieving by an index is a common technique that we'll use here.

In a similar manner, ray-trace mode uses the object intersection to determine which object was hit. This object then contributes to the current pixel color and its properties are used. Again, this requires an access by object ID. This is summarized in Table 10-4.

Table 10-4. Rendering and Granularity

Rendering Mode	Access/Draw	Access Granularity	Functions Mechanism
Wireframe	Object/line	Next-pointer	Transform,drawedges
Hidden polygon	Visible face/rectangle	Obj-id	Transform,drawface
Ray tracing	Intersected obj/pixel	Obj-id	Intersect,normal

The ID and type in Listing 10-4 are critical supporting elements. Without them, the next pointer and the listable property would not allow the proper access. This supports the wireframe drawing loop, using simple "list order" for drawing. This also supports hidden polygon drawing, where the drawing loop after transformation only knows the visible face and must use the object ID to index into the object list before it can use the face topology to index into the vertex list. Finally, the ray tracer is supported, with its need for object-level access, but by object ID, not "list-order." Here, a hidden requirement of the visibility algorithms forces our hand in the linked-list services.

Lists and Mapping Functions

The result is an API function supporting the retrieve-by-ID requirement, supplementing the typical next-pointer access of list-order. Listing 10-6 contains the linked-list API.

Listing 10-6.   Linked-List API

```
void     AddToList(LPOBJECT FAR *ListPtr, LPOBJECT Item);
unsigned FreeList (LPOBJECT FAR *ListPtr);
LPOBJECT GetElement(LPOBJECT ListPtr,unsigned short Object_id);
unsigned PrintList(LPOBJECT ListPtr,HWND hw);
```

The **OBJECT** structure, the linked-list API, and the two active **OBJECT** lists (lights and 3D objects) provide scaffolding around the function pointers that define object behavior.

The function pointers (Listing 10-7) control the basic behavior of each object. This "encapsulation" makes it possible to rewrite the control loops as shown, in the "inside-out" manner of object-oriented programming. The loop knows only what it is supposed to do — retrieve an object and operate on it — not how to do it. The objects themselves are responsible for the how. This more-equitable distribution of procedural knowledge hopefully localizes the effects of any particular change.

Listing 10-7.   Function Pointers for Object Behavior

```
struct t_objectprocs
   {
//debugging
     int    (*print) () ;
//polygon-(explicit)
     int    (*transform) () ;
     int    (*drawedges) () ;
     int    (*drawface) () ;
//quadric-(analytic)
     int    (*intersect) () ;
     int    (*normal) () ;
//cleanup
     int    (*free) () ;
   } * o_procs ;
```

We manipulate the light source using an **OBJECT** list. The light source has a much smaller set of behaviors when compared to the 3D objects that are also manipulated using an **OBJECT** list. Listing 10-8 contains an o_procs structure with the valid light functions. Only the print and free functions are necessary. The light source is "piggybacking" on the listable property of the **OBJECT** structure to make it easy to manipulate lights — the same interface manipulates both the light and the 3D object lists. Without the **OBJECT** structure and this crude inheritance of the listable attribute (traceable to using the **OBJECT** structure, a common shell data structure with a next pointer), we would need two sets of functions; one for lights and one for 3D objects.

Listing 10-8.   Light Source Function Pointers

```
ObjectProcs LightProcs =
{
LightPrint,
NULL,
NULL,
NULL,
NULL,
NULL,
FreeLight,
} ;
```

The 3D objects are as different from each other as they are from the light list, but the **OBJECT** structure and the function pointers simplify it again. By changing the group of pointers (which ones depends on the object) to something similar to Listing 10-9, each 3D object type fully populates the function-pointer group and defines itself. Once this is done, each object construction simply assigns the group of function pointers in the static structure (Listing 10-9) to the function-pointer structure element you saw in Chapter 9 during the discussion of object instantiation.

Listing 10-9.   Sphere Function-Pointer Static Structure Assignment

```
ObjectProcs SphereProcs =
{
        SpherePrint,
        SphereTransform,
        SphereDrawEdges,
        SphereDrawFace,
        SphereIntersect,
        SphereNormal,
        FreeSphere,
} ;
```

The content of this function-pointer structure is not arbitrarily defined. The *print* function does simple debugging. The *transform* function manipulates the vertex list. Functions *drawedges* and *drawface* support wireframe and hidden-polygon modes. That leaves *intersect* and *normal* for ray-trace mode. The *free* function is far from "just" a housekeeping convenience, as you'll see at the end of the chapter.

The best way to get a feel for these functions is to see them used. The next several sections take high-level views of the manipulation and rendering processes, in preparation for the details.

Wireframe

Much earlier, in Chapter 2 to be exact, I gave you a pseudo-code definition for the wireframe process. A simple refinement of that will start clearing the fog around the function pointers for mapping. Our first *in situ* examination begins here, with a description of the core of wireframe mode. (Ellipses indicate where I'm skipping some code.)

Listing 10-10 shows the expanded pseudo-code for wireframe mode, and, for the first time, the elegance of this style should be apparent to even the jaundiced eye. You can read this loop easily for all objects, get an object using *GetElement*, transform it using *transform*, then render it using *drawedges*. That is the essence of wireframe mode.

Listing 10-10.   Refined Generalized Wireframe Vertex Drawing Process

```
...
for ( i = 0; i < pv->mWorld->Scene->nObjs;i++)
{
        LPOBJECT     ot;
//retrieve from list
        ot    = GetElement(pv->mWorld->Scene->ObjectList,i+1);
//transform
        (ot->o_procs->transform(ot,
                     vtype==CMD_PERSP? tPerspProj:tParaProj));
...
//project,map, and draw
        (ot->o_procs->drawedges(ot,pv->genv,phist,hDC));

}
```

You saw the details of the function pointers for the sphere object in Listing 10-9, and all the other 3D objects use a parallel construction. The operation of the *transform* function *SphereTransform*, implemented in Listing 10-11, simply uses *G3D_Xfrm_TransformPoint* within a for loop to transform each vertex point. Again, all the other 3D objects have a similar construction.

Listing 10-11.   SphereTransform

```
int
SphereTransform(LPOBJECT this, LPMATRIX4D Tx)
{
   LPEX3DOBJECT lp3DObj;
   LPSPHERE     sp;
   LPVERTEX     lpvt_o,LPVERTEX      lpvt_w;
   int          j;

   lp3DObj = this->o_edata;
   lpvt_w  = lp3DObj->o_psurf.wrk_verticies;
   lpvt_o  = lp3DObj->o_psurf.prm_verticies;
```

```
    for ( j = 0; j < lp3DObj->nV; j++)
    {
        G3D_Xfrm_TransformPoint((LPVECTOR4D)&lpvt_w->vp[j+1],
                                            lpvt_o->vp[j+1],
                             (LPMATRIX4D)Tx);
    }
    return 1;
}
```

The rendering segment remains; here, the term "rendering" encompasses projecting, mapping, and drawing. The *SphereDrawEdges* mapping function has this duty, and it immediately delegates to the *DrawSurfaceEdges* function, as you can see in Listing 10-12. The implementation of *DrawSurfaceEdges* later in this chapter will conclude the coverage of wireframe mode.

Listing 10-12.   SphereDrawEdges

```
SphereDrawEdges(LPOBJECT this, LPGENV genv,HISTWND * ph,HDC hDC)
{
    DrawSurfaceEdges( this,genv,ph,hDC);
    return 1;
}
```

Conceptually, this small set of functions does these obvious (hopefully) and well-understood operations. The other modes add shading to this process, so the next set of pseudo-code (for hidden polygon and ray-traced modes) requires a brief divergence on visibility and shading.

Visibility and Shading Overview

The basics of the visibility and shading process were briefly covered in Chapter 2. Visibility was discussed again in Chapter 9 with the development of the 3D object geometry. Now it is time to consider both visibility and shading.

The section of Chapter 9 that dealt with the object database discussed visibility and normals. Figure 10-5 repeats part of Figure 9-4, to reinforce the geometry involved in visibility.

Visibility uses the two vectors defined by the face normal and the viewpoint. The angle between the normal and the viewpoint defines orientation. If the angle is obtuse (that is greater than 90), the face is invisible. If the angle is acute (that is 90 or less), the face is visible. The dot product, introduced in Chapter 7, is geometrically interpreted as the cosine of the angle between two vectors. Examining cosine, you know that in the range 0<=theta<=90 cosine is between [1,0]. In the range above 90, cosine turns negative. This geometric interpretation is the basis of using the dot product to test for visibility in polygon mode. Simply put, an acute angle corresponds to a visible face, and an obtuse angle corresponds to an invisible face.

Figure 10-5.   Polygon-Mode Visibility Geometry

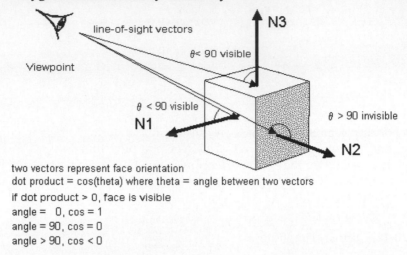

Ray-trace mode uses a different approach to determine visibility. The parametric equation of a line is used to extend the ray through a particular pixel on the image plane into the scene. Either the ray hits something, or it doesn't. If the ray hits something, the parameter t gives the distance to the line-object intersection point. Substituting that distance back into the ray (line) equation gives the intersection point. Figure 10-6 shows sample rays shooting out and going through each pixel and into the scene. Some rays hit or intersect objects and some just go on "forever" or until a reasonable maximum distance is reached.

Figure 10-6.   Ray-Tracing Visibility Process

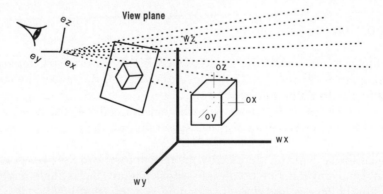

The interesting thing is that the shading process uses the same test in a symmetry of operations, but it's not really mentioned. Most texts treat the process of visibility and shading in different places, often separated by many pages, and the connection between the geometry of visibility and the geometry of shading is often not made. Figure 10-7 presents information similar to the shading geometry image used in Chapter 2. Here, the similarity should be clear between the visibility test and the evaluation of the diffuse term for the flat shader.

Figure 10-7. Shading and Visibility Geometry Compared

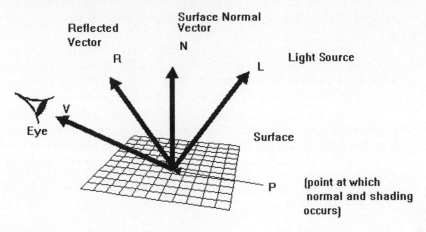

The visibility test uses the dot product of the surface normal and the viewpoint. This is shown in Equation 10-2. Conversely, Equation 10-3 shows the flat-shading equation. It uses ambient lighting components and diffuse lighting components to produce basic lighting. The specular term that produces highlights uses the reflected vector to evaluate that term, again with a dot product.

Equation 10-2.   Visibility Test

$$cos(\theta) = NdotV$$

Equation 10-3.   Flat-Shading Illumination Model

$$diffuse\ term = kd \sum_{j=1}^{j=ls} I_l(\overline{N}dot\overline{L}j)$$

Equation 10-4 contains the specular term. The reflected vector that it uses, once more with the viewpoint, is determined as shown in Equation 10-5. This is, again, based on the dot product of the light-source's position and the normal.

Equation 10-4.   Specular Term

$$specular\ term = ks \sum_{j=1}^{j=ls} I_l(\overline{R}_{j'} * V)^n$$

Equation 10-5.   Reflected Vector

$$reflected\ vector\ R = 2 * N * (LdotN) - L$$

Now all the vectors shown in Figure 10-7 are in their place for the visibility and shading calculations. It's well and good to know the vectors and calculations involved in shading, but you can't extrapolate the interaction of the surface-property parameters and the geometry of the surface directly from the equations. A description of shading must include a discussion of what the surface definition means, and, in turn, what the calculations are really doing.

You saw the components of the surface property description in Chapter 3, but they're repeated in Listing 10-13 to refresh your memory. This discussion centers around the surface coefficients k_a, k_d, and k_s represented by surf_ka, surf_kd, and surf_ks. The surf_ka coefficient represents the net contribution from *ambient* light — the light that is everywhere in a scene, sometimes called *background* light. Coefficient surf_kd represents the net contribution from *diffuse* lighting or *scattering*. The coefficient surf_ks represents *specular* lighting or *highlights,* and represents the net contribution of highlights to an object's color. Remember that k_t (for *refraction*) is included in the definition, but is currently unimplemented.

Listing 10-13.   Surface Properties

```
typedef struct t_surfprops
{
 //name
   char        szName[64];
 //color
   char        szColor[64];
   Color       surf_color ;
 //coefficients
   VECTOR4D    surf_ka ;     //ambient
   VECTOR4D    surf_kd ;     //diffuse
   VECTOR4D    surf_ks ;     //specular
   double      surf_shine ; //phong shine factor
   VECTOR4D    surf_kt ;//(reflection and refraction )
   double      surf_ior ;   //index of reflectionn/refraction
 //texture
   char        szTexture[64];
   int         surf_tid;
   LPVOID      surf_texdata;
} SURFPROPS ;
```

These coefficients control the way light interacts with a surface. They define the amount of light (by component) that is propagated or reflected (*not* absorbed) by the surface. In either case, this describes the light that the human eye sees. The coefficients range from [0,1] with 0 indicating absence of the component and 1 indicating saturation.

Ambient light is defined as light everywhere in a scene, or global background illumination. The idea is that, except in a pitch-black cave, some "global" light indirectly illuminates surfaces. For instance, if you place a box in a room with a single light on one side, it is still visible on all sides due to the ambient light reflecting from the walls, floor, and ceiling. The side away from the light is shown in Figure 10-8 without ambient lighting and inFigure

10-9 with ambient lighting. In Figure 10-8, the black face is visible but not illuminated (or "in the light"). This is very unrealistic, because the ambient light in a room always illuminates the face. True, it might not be bright, but it will not be completely black. Figure 10-9 shows the face with the minimal illumination provided by the ambient term.

Figure 10-8.   Face Without Ambient Lighting

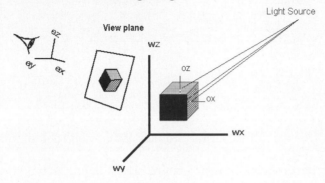

Figure 10-9.   Face with Ambient Lighting

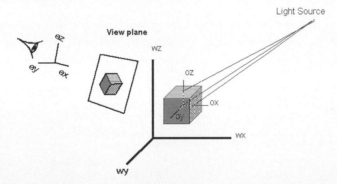

You should intuitively understand the effect here — ambient light makes sure that faces to the "off" side of the light don't just disappear. The ambient coefficient, surf_ka, controls this. Surf_ka ranges from [0,1]: at 0, the face has no ambient illumination and is not visible; as the value increases toward 1 the face goes from faint to strong illumination.

A word about ambient, saturation, and other light sources is in order. If you saturate ambient, don't expect to see the effect of other light sources; highlights, for instance, won't appear. Think about it. The intensity of a pixel ranges from [0,1], which maps to [0,255] in 256-color CRT space. The k-values, ranging from [0,1], control the contribution of the components of the light. Highlighting actually means adding enough light to make a white spot at just the right point. Raising one of the other components, approaching saturation, makes it harder and harder to discern the highlight.

That leads us to consider the diffuse term. While ambient light is simply the amount of global background that is bounced, the diffuse component describes the amount of direct lighting that the surface propagates. Coefficient surf_kd controls this component, and Figure 10-10 describes this diffuse propagation. It can be thought of as a uniform, regular scattering of light.

Figure 10-10.   Diffuse Component of Light

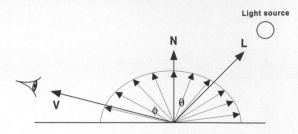

You've already seen the diffuse term in Equations 10-3 and 10-4, so this puts a face to the math.

The specular reflection component remains. The shading geometry shown in Figure 10-7 showed the use of R, the reflected vector, in the overall picture. Equation 10-5 defined the calculation of vector R, which is used in Equation 10-4 to calculate the specular highlight value.

Figure 10-11 shows vector R and the lobe-shaped surface representing the highlight, superimposed on the diffuse reflection. While coefficient surf_ks ultimately controls how much of this is seen, the shine factor also plays a major part. Values of the shininess coefficient, surf_shine, affect the shape of the highlight surface. A larger value of surf_shine results in a small, tight highlight; a small value of surf_shine makes a flatter, less-intense highlight. As surf_shine goes to 0, the highlight disappears.

Figure 10-11.   Specular Reflection Component

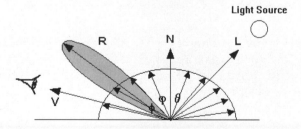

We don't use the coefficient surf_kt, which controls the transmittance of light, so we can't model refractive materials. However, we can model mirrored surfaces by using a simple recursion. This is a form of transmittance and does allow us to make some very nice images. Figure 10-12, for example, contains a raytracing of a simple mirrored image.

This hints at the capabilities and limitations of the modeler. Besides the equations and the controlling geometry, I've talked about the surface coefficients and their physical basis. Next, it is time to examine the details of the process to build on this overview of the geometry and equations involved in visibility and shading.

Figure 10-12.   Ray-Tracing of Mirrored Sphere

Polygon-Based Visibility and Rendering

The basic process for hidden-polygon mode was described briefly in Chapter 2. There, the simple transformation/drawing sequence of wireframe mode was extended with two new steps: building and z-sorting the visible list. Now it is time to explore that process a little further.

Listing 10-14 contains an expanded version of the pseudo-code from Chapter 2. The transformation loop is shown here as a separate loop. The wireframe discussions you saw in both Chapter 2 and earlier in this chapter oversimplified the implementation. Wireframe and hidden-polygon share the transformation operation by the simple method of breaking it out into a separate loop. This means that *GetElement* is called an extra time in hidden-polygon mode.

Listing 10-14.   Generalized Hidden-Polygon Drawing Process

```
...
//transform to eye
for ( i = 0; i < pv->mWorld->Scene->nObjs;i++){
        LPOBJECT    ot;
//retrieve from list
        ot    = GetElement(pv->mWorld->Scene->ObjectList,i+1);
```

Listing 10-14. *(cont.)*

```
//transform
        (ot->o_procs->transform(ot,
                    vtype==CMD_PERSP? tPerspProj:tParaProj));
}
...
// begin visibility
for ( i = 0; i < pv->mWorld->Scene->nObjs;i++){
        LPOBJECT    ot;
        LPEX3DOBJECT lp3DObj;
        ot      = GetElement(pv->mWorld->Scene->ObjectList,i+1);
        lp3DObj = ot->o_edata;
        for ( j = 0; j < lp3DObj->nF && pfrm->bDraw;j++)
        {
            if ( IsFaceVisible(...) )
            {
               if ( AddVisFace(...,
                            pv->mWorld->Scene->VisFaces,
                            pv->mWorld->Scene->VisFaces->fiNum,
                            ...) )
            }
        }
}
...
//z-sort the visible face list
SortFaces(pv->mWorld->Scene->VisFaces->fi,
          pv->mWorld->Scene->VisFaces->fiNum);
...
// project,map,draw visible list
...
 for ( i = 0; i < pv->mWorld->Scene->VisFaces->fiNum ; i++){
...
      ot      = GetElement(pv->mWorld->Scene->ObjectList,pfi->oi);
...
      (ot->o_procs->drawface(ot,pfi,lpvt,pv,phist,hDC));
...
}
...
```

Once the transformation process is done, hidden-polygon mode is quite different. The face visibility process creates a potentially huge dynamic array of face structures. The *IsFaceVisible* function performs the visibility test using the normal. When visibility is determined to be true, *AddVisibleFace* places this face structure into the list of visible faces. This list of faces must be sorted in the z or depth-sorted, which is done by *SortFaces*.

When that is done, the list is in back-to-front order, and a traversal and draw in that order produces a painter's algorithm drawing process. More-distant objects are painted over by closer objects in the process of the traversal and draw, in a way similar to how an artist paints a picture. Listing 10-9 showed *SphereDrawFace* assigned to the *drawface* mapping function. The other objects all contain parallel functions for hidden-polygon mode. *SphereDrawFace* is shown in Listing 10-15 and, like *SphereDrawEdges*, it delegates immediately; in this case to *DrawFace*.

Listing 10-15.   SphereDrawFace

```
int
SphereDrawFace(LPOBJECT this,HPFACE fi,LPVERTEX lpvt,
               VWWND * pv,HISTWND * ph,HDC hDC)
{
   DrawFace( this,fi,lpvt,pv,ph,rtype,hDC);
   return 1;
}
```

DrawFace, in Listing 10-16, is a big switch where the rendering subtype of hidden-polygon mode is taken into consideration. Later in this chapter, I'll pencil in the blanks I'm leaving here and in the internals of the mapping functions. With all of the operations and processing in the bag at that point, the remaining steps amount to intelligently assembling the pieces, which is done in Chapter 11.

Listing 10-16.   DrawFace

```
void WINAPI DrawFace( LPOBJECT this,HPFACE fi,LPVERTEX lpvt,
                      VWWND * pv,HISTWND * ph,int rtype,HDC hDC )
{

   switch(rtype)
   {
     case CMD_HIDDEN:
          DrawHiddenFace(this,fi,lpvt,pv->genv,ph,hDC);
          break;
     case CMD_SOLID:
          DrawSolidFace(this,fi,lpvt,pv->genv,ph,hDC);
          break;
     case CMD_FLAT:
          DrawFlatShadedFace(this,fi,lpvt,pv,ph,hDC);
          break;
   }
   return;
}
```

Visibility and Rendering Based on Ray Objects

The discussion in Chapter 2 is again our launching point. There, the pseudo-code description of raytracing introduced you to the process flow. There, I described the entire process in one piece. But here it is better to separate this process into three main processes that map into the three main functions: main tracing loop, individual ray trace, and pixel shade. These operations map into functions *RayRenderObjectList*, *Trace*, and *Shade*.

The main tracing loop, presented in more detailed pseudo-code in Listing 10-17, has three features you should particularly notice (they'll get more coverage later): the generation of the root ray, construction of pixel rays, and the application of the illumination model and procedural texturing.

Listing 10-17. Main Ray-trace Loop

```
...
//generate the root ray
..MakeEyeRay (pv,
          pv->mWorld->Scene->Eye.view_from,
          pv->mWorld->Scene->Eye.view_at,
          pv->mWorld->Scene->Eye.view_up,
          &rS,&rU,&rV,&Ray);
   ...
   for ( iy = 0 ; iy <= pv->mWorld->Scene->scanY-1; iy++)
   {
// render each pixel across horizontal scan line
      for ( ix = 0; ix <= pv->mWorld->Scene->scanX-1; ix++)
      {
         MakePixelRay (pv,Ray.r_origin,rS,rU,rV,ix,iy,&Ray);
// calculate eye ray for this pixel
         Trace (pv,&pv->mWorld->MaxW,depth,
               &Ray,&Intensity);
      ...
   }
 }
...
```

Function *MakeEyeRay* generates the root ray and uses the viewpoint in from/lookat form to generate vectors that will be used to construct the ray that goes through each pixel of the image plane, our next step.

MakePixRay takes the components created in the root generation process and the current image plane location and generates a pixel ray. The image plane corresponds to the canvas, and the nested for loop across the x and y pixel extents feeds *MakePixelRay*.

Using the ray, function *Trace* traces the rays, testing for intersection with the object list and invoking *ShadePoint* to calculate pixel intensities. Listing 10-18 raises the portion of the pseudo-code from Chapter 2 that represented *Trace* to the next level of detail. Here, you can see the depth check, the object loop to check for intersection using the *intersect* mapping function, and the storing of the intersection. This sets up the shading process.

Listing 10-18.   Trace Pseudo-Code

```
...
if (Depth > pv->mWorld->RayDepth)
{
    return;
}
...
Object     = pv->mWorld->Scene->ObjectList;
while(Object)
{
   (Object->o_procs->intersect(Object,Ray,&hit));
// Save ptr to closest object intersected
   if ((hit.isect_t > EPSILON) && (hit.isect_t < MinT))
   {
       MinT        = hit.isect_t;
       NearestObj = Object;
       Nearesthit = hit;
   }
      Object = Object->next;    if ( hit )

}
...
if intersection
{
//
//   If we get here, we know that Ray has intersected an object
//   use the parameter MinT to calculate point of intersection.
//
      GetIsectPt(Ray->r_origin,Ray->r_direction,MinT,&Point);

//
//   Now find the normal to the intersected object at the point
//   of intersection.
//
      NearestObj->o_procs->normal(NearestObj,&Nearesthit,
                                  Point,&Normal);
...
//
//   shade and apply procedural texture
//
      ShadePoint(pv,TotW,Depth,
                 NearestObj,Ray,Normal,Point,&Nearesthit,
                 Color);
}
...
```

If no intersection exists, the color is set to the background, which is not shown here. If an intersection exists, its point is calculated using *GetIsectPt*. In addition to the point of intersection, the shading process requires the normal at the point. The mapping function

normal retrieves the normal for each object. These are passed to *ShadePoint*, which formally applies the illumination model at point P with normal N.

Function *ShadePoint*, the third leg of the tripod supporting tracing, is shown in Listing 10-19. This function hides the details of applying the illumination model and the procedural texturing. *LocalReflShader* applies the local illumination model at the point, including reflection as its name suggests. *Texture* applies a procedural texture if one is defined for the surface; otherwise it applies the default "smooth" texture that really is no texture at all.

Listing 10-19.   ShadePoint Implementation

```
void WINAPI ShadePoint( VWWND     * pv,
                        LPVECTOR4D TotW,int Depth,
                        LPOBJECT   Object,
                        LPRAY      Ray,
                        VECTOR4D   Normal,
                        VECTOR4D   Point,
                        LPISECT    hit,
                        LPVECTOR4D Color)
{
   VECTOR4D  TxtrColor = {ZERO4D,ZERO4D,ZERO4D,ONE4D};
   VECTOR4D  LoclColor = {ZERO4D,ZERO4D,ZERO4D,ONE4D};

//get color from local illumination model(a,d,s,and reflection)
   LocalReflShader(pv,TotW,Depth,
                Object,Ray,Normal,Point,
                &LoclColor);
//add texture
   Texture(pv,
           Object,Ray,Normal,Point,
            &TxtrColor);
   G3D_V4D_VAdd4D(Color,TxtrColor,LoclColor);
//clamping
   G3D_V4D_VSet4D(Color,
                   min(1.0,Color->x),
                   min(1.0,Color->y),
                   min(1.0,Color->z),
                   ONE4D);
   return;
}
```

That concludes our brief romp through the visibility and rendering processes. You are now ready for the next level of detail; you've even had time for a quick look at the transformation process. We used the mapping functions at various points in this process without calling special attention to them, but you can see how the supporting scaffolding of the linked lists and the mapping functions makes operating on the elements of a scene quite easy — for both 3D objects and lights. Add to this the controlling hand of the state machine, and managing all these 3D abstractions and processes becomes a little less daunting.

This is the divide-and-conquer approach: I split the problem of building a modeler into simple engineering and 3D issues. The implementation techniques and architectural features help with the management task and make it easy to incrementally add 3D graphics functionality. The lists and mapping functions present a general form that, if followed by additional 3D objects, will not disturb the scaffolding. You'll have to change the front-end to accommodate additional instantiations, but the transformation and rendering processes support extension as long as you use the same basic formula for how an object is built, what it must do, and what is expected of it.

The list functions are the next item on our agenda. They are (finally) covered in detail to put them to bed. Don't worry, this list API is very simple — only what's needed and not much more. Once we have that out of the way, we'll go to the next level of detail on the visibility and rendering process.

Linked Lists

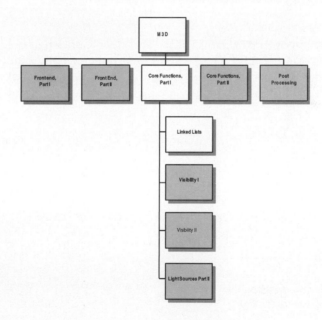

The linked list API, repeated in Listing 10-20 for your convenience, is extremely simple. You can add an element to a list, you can print the contents of the list, you can retrieve an element by object ID, and you can free the entire list. Four operations make up the entire API — what could be simpler?

Listing 10-20.   List API Revisited

```
void     AddToList(LPOBJECT FAR *ListPtr, LPOBJECT Item);
unsigned FreeList (LPOBJECT FAR *ListPtr);
LPOBJECT GetElement (LPOBJECT ListPtr,unsigned short Object_id);
unsigned PrintList(LPOBJECT ListPtr,HWND hw);
```

The basics of linked lists should be clear, and you don't need to waste a lot of time on introductory topics. Figure 10-13 shows the basic idea behind linked lists: the next pointer and "hooking up" a set of related items. You move to the next item in the list by simply de-referencing the next pointer. That leads us to the implementation of the individual API functions.

Figure 10-13.   Linked-List General Structure

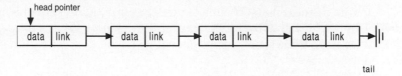

Add

The implementation of *AddToList* is simple and clear. Contained in Listing 10-21, you can see the two parts of *AddToList*. The first part determines whether this is the initial element to be added, and, if so, acts accordingly by setting the list pointer itself. Every element after the first simply "hooks" in to the existing list by adjusting next pointers appropriately.

Listing 10-21.   AddToList

```
//
//Given a ptr to the ptr to the list and a ptr to an object,
//add the object at the head of the list.
//
void AddToList (LPOBJECT FAR *ListPtr, LPOBJECT Item)
{

  if (*ListPtr == NULL)
  {
    *ListPtr   = Item;
    Item->next = NULL;
  }
  else
  {
    Item->next = *ListPtr;
    *ListPtr   = Item;
  }
}
```

The modeler does not need insert and relink functionality, and it doesn't need to do any of the other actions that can be done with a list. Small and simple is the rule here. Having said that, it's time to move on.

GetElement

Retrieval by object ID, as you saw in Table 10-4, is critical to both hidden-polygon and ray-trace modes. At some point all you will know, or all you can find out, will be the object ID. When you need something and you're a programmer, the answer is often to write a function.

Function *GetElement*, shown in Listing 10-22, provides this valuable service. Again, this function is really simple. It iterates across the list and does a simple test. If the test succeeds, the object has been found and is returned. If not, the object ID requested doesn't exist and a NULL pointer is returned. What could be more obvious?

Listing 10-22.   GetElement

```
LPOBJECT GetElement (LPOBJECT ListPtr, unsigned short Object_id)
{
  unsigned Number = 0;

  while (ListPtr)
  {
    Number++;
    if ( ListPtr->o_id == Object_id )
        return ListPtr;
    ListPtr = ListPtr->next;
  }
  return (NULL);
}
```

PrintList

When engineering a system this large, a modicum of debugging is a good thing. From that perspective, I've included the *PrintList* function in the API. As you will see in Chapter 11, we dump the contents of the light and 3D object lists by using a Lists menu.

PrintList, implemented in Listing 10-23, is straightforward, with a twist. *PrintList* uses the mapping functions to do its work. Each object function-pointer structure contains a print function, so *PrintList* uses this fact: it iterates across the list and invokes each object's print functions.

Delegating responsibility for printing down a level to the individual objects has a nice effect. First, because of its mapping function use, the *PrintList* function exhibits the nice, tight little loops you are coming to know so well and that we used in the manipulation and rendering processes. Second, you can add objects to the list and use the *PrintList* debugging facility simply by providing this print function. This may only be a simple-minded dump, but this facility is enough to see, for instance, whether the latest change to the material table was picked up correctly in the current scene, by examining the scene and the properties of a particular object.

Listing 10-23.   PrintList

```
unsigned PrintList (LPOBJECT ListPtr,HWND hw)
{

  unsigned Number = 0;

  while (ListPtr)
  {
    Number++;
    ListPtr->o_procs->print(ListPtr,hw);
    ListPtr = ListPtr->next;
  }
  return (Number);
}
```

Free

That leaves the free operation, performed by function *FreeList*. Remember, if this operation doesn't perform correctly, major memory leaks will accumulate or, worse yet, crashes will occur. It's a wise use of time to bring up the scaffolding code like *AddToList* and *FreeList* independent of actually rendering images. Testing these basic architectural components saves a lot of grief. This same philosophy resulted in the inclusion of the *PrintList* function for debugging. It doesn't matter how nicely you render if your application eats memory and brings your system down.

The code for *FreeList* is a little more involved, so read it carefully in Listing 10-24. The entire list is iterated across in a while loop and the free operation takes place in a two-step process. The first step is to ask each object to free itself. This is why the mapping functions included free.

Listing 10-24.   FreeList

```
unsigned FreeList (LPOBJECT FAR *ListPtr)
{

  LPOBJECT TempPtr;
  unsigned Number = 0;

  while (*ListPtr)
  {
//first free object specific memory by asking itself to do it
    (ListPtr)->o_procs->free(*ListPtr);
    TempPtr  = *ListPtr;
    *ListPtr = (*ListPtr)->next;
```

```
//then free "listable" object structure
    WL_Mem_Free (TempPtr);
    Number++;
  }
  ListPtr = NULL;
  return (Number);
}
```

This is *not* an amenity. With the addition of multiple representations and the dual void pointer within the **OBJECT** structure, the **FreeList** function really has no way of knowing how to do its job without really getting into the questionable code practice of defeating modularity and encapsulation. My approach, while less direct, is nicer in that respect.

The twist about step one is the little dance it does with the pointers. If you are not careful, the free operation can leave you holding nothing — in other words, it can leave dangling references. After the free mapping function is invoked, the pointer to the object is retained in the temporary variable. It then traverses the list to the next location, and uses the temporary to accomplish the second step: freeing the **OBJECT** structure memory. **WL_Mem_Free** accomplishes this for us, and the function returns (as a safety check) the number of items freed.

This concludes the list API. You are now about to enter the visibility and rendering sections. From here to the modeler construction in Chapter 11 is graphics and more graphics.

Visibility I:
Culling and Sorting

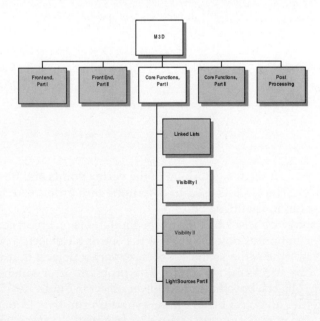

Visible surface determination, as implemented here, has two parts:

- back-face culling, and
- visible-face sorting in z-depth.

Visible surface comparisons occur in eye space before the perspective transformation to screen space. This makes it both easier (since the perspective divide has not taken place) and faster. Projection only occurs on the visible surfaces (in other words, only after visibility has been determined), which saves quite a few operations.

Just saying this is not enough, though. There are several important details about objects and scenes that affect what can be an object and what can be a scene.

This discussion starts with the object definition given in Chapter 9 and continues with a hard look at the face/vertex method. The object and its representation is one limiting factor, but it is not the only one. The visibility process itself imposes certain limitations on the construction of scenes. Understanding this is critical to understanding internals; without it, you have little chance of successfully extending the system.

The Physical Basis of Polygon-Mode Visibility

First, we need to look back to the object definition. The face and vertex representation is depicted in Figure 10-14, which is similar to Figure 2-5 (Chapter 2).

Figure 10-14.   Face/Vertex Representation and Visibility Support

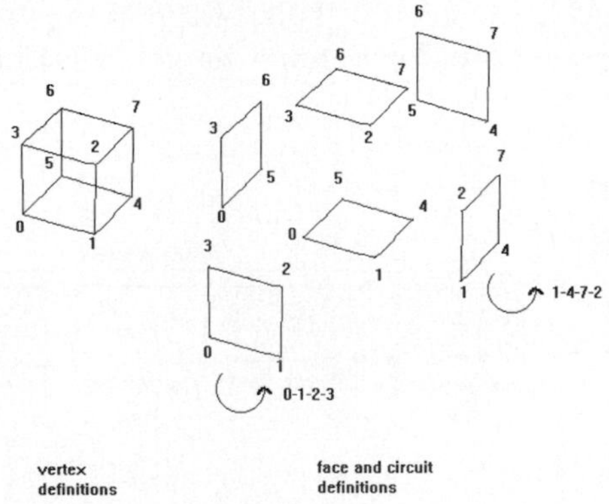

vertex
definitions

face and circuit
definitions

Here you can see the definition of the vertex points and how faces are determined from the vertices. The circuits used to determine face order also define normal direction. This should be obvious at this point.

What may not be so obvious are the limitations on object construction. Restrictions exist on the formation of objects because the set of all objects you can construct using face/vertex is not the same as the set of face/vertex objects that this visibility and rendering method can successfully handle. The problem, in a nutshell, is the existence of self-obscuring objects. Specifically, the lower object in Figure 10-15 shows the effect of "throwing" together an object based on the cylinder primitive. Depending on the viewing angle, this may (or may not) work. Figures 10-16 and 10-17 show a sequence similar to what an animation might contain. The viewpoint is receding away, and, as the angle changes, the horizontal cylinder "seeps" through. This happens because the nature of sampling in hidden-polygon mode is the face, and a single z-value per face, at that. The simplicity of this approach generates these "artifacts."

Figure 10-15.   Physical Basis of Visibility: Restrictions on Objects

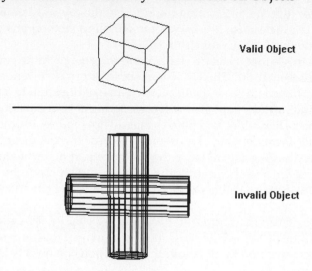

Valid Object

Invalid Object

Figure 10-16.   Acceptable View of Two-Cylinder Object

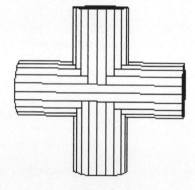

Figure 10-17.   Unacceptable View of Two-Cylinder Object

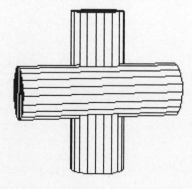

The solution is maintaining adjacency information and extending the data structures and visibility test for this. The interesting thing is that the ray-trace mode renders the two-cylinder object correctly, because it uses a point-sampling method and will, therefore, determine the correct value for each pixel.

From this, you can see that it can be challenging to generate more complex shapes with polygon-mode representation. This is where some alternate-boundary representation (b-rep) format like winged-edge, or a complete change of direction to a Constructive Solid Geometry representation (CSG-rep), is worth considering at your next major overhaul point. Still, composite objects like tables and houses that do not require complex intersections are representable. While changing the polygon-mode representation, the nice thing about dual representation is that as long as you leave the ray-trace part of it (the dual representation), the *OBJECT* list system, and the scaffolding around undisturbed, the modeler won't be completely dead during such momentous changes. This can help somewhat with debugging.

Make no mistake, changing representations is a big change. The good news is that I'll give you enough of the details on the what, how, and why of this representation for you to write that code. Now that you know about the restrictions on objects for this modeler, it's time to look at scenes.

The polygon mode imposes a few other restrictions. In constructing a scene, we can't resolve the same kind of problems we just discussed. For instance, objects cannot intersect other objects. This is an obvious extension of the rule for making composite objects like the two-cylinder object. Figure 10-18 shows a plane and a sphere, with the sphere defined as being embedded in the plane. This won't work correctly from all angles.

Figure 10-18.   Poorly Defined Sphere and Plane

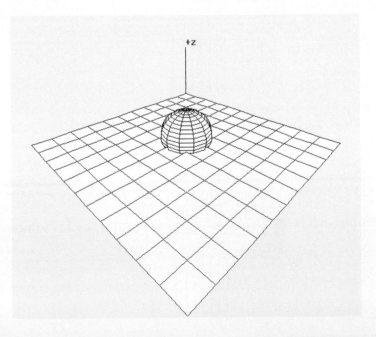

You can "fake" out the visibility process at certain angles, but, as before, trying to generate a series of images always exposes the fakery. It is better to try to live within the rules this modeler imposes. Figure 10-19 shows a better scene. Here, the sphere is translated up just enough to sit on top of the plane. If you really wanted the effect shown in Figure 10-18, a better approach would be to implement a hemisphere or partial-sphere object. That begs the question of specifying the amount of arc, but those are questions that are handled by the object generator code. Writing an object generator and then adding the object and its mapping functions implements a new object. Once a set of face and vertex values are generated into a .dat file, the polygon mode really does not (with the exception of the pyramid) take much notice of the object type. It simply plugs and chugs its way through the face and vertex list, applying the desired functions.

Figure 10-19.   Well-Defined Sphere and Plane

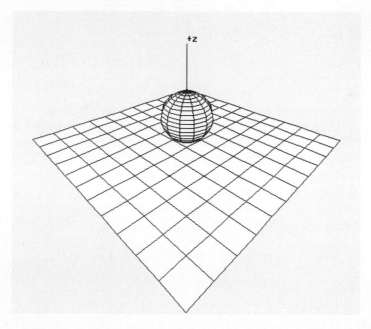

Within those limitations, you're free to define a scene as you wish, which allows for a wide range of possibilities. Figure 10-20 shows in two parts what can be accomplished with an economy of objects. Both a monochrome hidden line and a ray-traced image of a simple table and sphere are shown. It's difficult to do many tables because the support for defining composite objects is limited, but a simple scene like this is manageable by manual means.

Figure 10-20.   Simple Scene of Table, Sphere, and Plane in Two Renditions

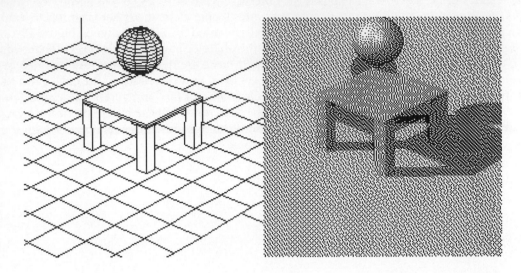

You now know what can and cannot be accomplished, so it is time to go back to the code mines and continue digging at the visibility and rendering veins. We'll now expand the pseudo-code of Listing 10-14. I'll cover the internals of the transformation, visible face list generation, and face list sorting, leaving the projection, mapping, and drawing of the rendering phase until later in the chapter. This way, we can examine the visible process for the ray tracer and compare visibility more easily.

Visibility Process

There are four main parts to generating a hidden-polygon image:

- transformation,
- visible list generation,
- visible list sorting, and
- visible list rendering.

We'll consider the first three now and defer the rendering until later. While the transformation process is relatively simple and builds on material shown in Chapter 7, the visible list generation process generates and uses the surface normal. The sorting process uses the visible list and quicksort to perform a depth sort in the z-direction. This manipulates the visible list to prepare it for the rendering algorithm.

The transformation process is shared between the wireframe and hidden-polygon modes. Each vertex point is simply transformed in turn. It could not be clearer or easier. After the three examples in Chapter 7, performing the transformation step across a set of points is old hat.

Listing 10-9 showed you *SphereTransform* and its explanation stated that the transformation functions are all similar. Listing 10-25 contains another representative transformation function, *ConeTransform*, showing how the object-mapping function hides the individual object function name. In the global name space, all that's visible is the **transform** function. These functions are all the same, even the pyramid (made up of both triangles and a rectangle). Remember that in the explicit object load process, the last face of the pyramid had its face vertex count incremented to account for the asymmetry of components.

Listing 10-25.   Cone Object Transform Function ConeTransform

```
int
ConeTransform(LPOBJECT this, LPMATRIX4D Tx)
{
    LPEX3DOBJECT lp3DObj;
    LPVERTEX     lpvt_o;
    LPVERTEX     lpvt_w;
    int          j;

    lp3DObj = this->o_edata;
    lpvt_w  = lp3DObj->o_psurf.wrk_verticies;
    lpvt_o  = lp3DObj->o_psurf.prm_verticies;

    for ( j = 0; j < lp3DObj->nV; j++)
    {
        G3D_Xfrm_TransformPoint((LPVECTOR4D)&lpvt_w->vp[j+1],
                                          lpvt_o->vp[j+1],
                              (LPMATRIX4D)Tx);
    }
    return 1;
}
```

In a for loop across all the vertex points, each point is transformed from the "original" world coordinates (wc) to the "working" eye-coordinate values (ec) and saved for later use. The transformation uses the Tx *LPMATRIX4D* pointer parameter and function *G3D_Xfrm_TransformPoint.*

All objects are now in eye coordinates. Next, it's time to cull back-faces using the surface normal test, the first step in the visibility process. This amounts to a two-step process of checking the face and its surface normal, and, if it is visible, adding it to the visible face list. Listing 10-26 contains the block of code in *PolyRenderObjectList* that performs this.

Listing 10-26.   Visible Face List Generation

```
...
//cull backfaces
for ( i = 0; i < pv->mWorld->Scene->nObjs && pfrm->bDraw;i++)
{
    LPOBJECT     ot;
    LPEX3DOBJECT lp3DObj;

    ot      = GetElement(pv->mWorld->Scene->ObjectList,i+1);
    lp3DObj = ot->o_edata;
    for ( j = 0; j < lp3DObj->nF && pfrm->bDraw;j++)
    {
        FACELIST   fl;
        FACE       ft;
        LPVERTEX   lpvt;

        fl   = lp3DObj->o_psurf.faces;
        lpvt = lp3DObj->o_psurf.wrk_verticies;

        if ( IsFaceVisible(&(fl.fi[j+1]),lpvt) )
        {
            if ( AddVisFace(pfrm,pv,
                            pv->mWorld->Scene->VisFaces,
                            pv->mWorld->Scene->VisFaces->fiNum,
                            (HPFACE)(&(fl.fi[j+1])) ) )
            {
                pv->mWorld->Scene->VisFaces->fiNum++;
                ...
            }
        }
    }
}
...
```

This code depends on two functions. *IsFaceVisible* does the surface normal generation and test, and feeds *AddVisibleFace*, which builds the visible face list. The use of the term list here is a little generous. This is not a linked list but an array of structures in memory, accessible by simply incrementing by the structure size to reach the next element. It is a list in concept, though, and that is what's important — not the implementation detail. This block of code also uses *GetElement* to retrieve the object, then uses the edata void pointer to access the explicit data. This is relatively "deep" before representation-specific details like the contents of a face are needed.

The *IsFaceVisible* and *AddVisibleFace* functions operate specifically on faces. Listing 10-1 showed the entire visibility data structure hierarchy. The key component here is the double value for the minimum z-value of the face. Instead of calculating a centroid, the preferable approach, we use one edge. This can, occasionally, make for some annoying artifacts. The benefit is simplicity.

IsFaceVisible is shown in Listing 10-27 and *GetFaceNorm* is in Listing 10-28. Notice the check to make sure the first choice of vertices are not coincident. Remember that the sphere and cone depend on degenerate rectangles; in other words, they really contain triangles that are, lazy us, left to GDI to sort out. While this is perfectly acceptable, it does have a side effect on the visibility process. If you do not check for this, you'll generate invalid normals. This is all encapsulated in function *GetFaceNorm.*

Listing 10-27. IsFaceVisible

```
BOOL WINAPI IsFaceVisible(HPFACE fi, LPVERTEX lpvt)
{
   VECTOR4D   vV,vN;
   double     dot;
//
// get vector for P
// get the surface normal
//
   GetFaceNorm(*fi,lpvt,&vV,&vN);

//
// N dot V normal dot view for visibility
//
   dot   = G3D_V4D_VDot4D(vN,vV);
//
// if > 0 then visible
//
   if ( dot >= 0.0 )
      return TRUE;
   else
      return FALSE;
}
```

Listing 10-28. GetFaceNorm

```
void WINAPI GetFaceNorm(FACE fi,LPVERTEX lpvt,
                    LPVECTOR4D P,LPVECTOR4D vNa)
{
   VECTOR4D   vt0a,vt1a,vt2a;
//
// get vectors for edges v3-v0,v1-v0
//
   vt0a = lpvt->vp[fi.indx[1]];
   vt1a = lpvt->vp[fi.indx[2]];
   vt2a = lpvt->vp[fi.indx[3]];
//
```

Listing 10-28.   (*cont.*)

```
// if ng try opposite corner first
//
   if ((vt0a.x==vt1a.x && vt0a.y==vt1a.y && vt0a.z==vt1a.z) ||
       (vt2a.x==vt1a.x && vt2a.y==vt1a.y && vt2a.z==vt1a.z))
   {
      vt0a = lpvt->vp[fi.indx[3]];
      vt1a = lpvt->vp[fi.indx[4]];
      vt2a = lpvt->vp[fi.indx[1]];
   }
   G3D_V4D_VSub4D(&vt0a,vt0a,vt1a);
   G3D_V4D_VSub4D(&vt2a,vt2a,vt1a);
//
// do cross to get normal, make unit vector
//
   G3D_V4D_VCross4D(vNa,vt0a,vt2a);
   G3D_V4D_VNorm4D(vNa,*vNa);
   *P    = vt1a;
}
```

I hope you didn't miss the big, midstream change that just occurred. There was a change in the fundamental unit. Previously, the granularity used was a complete object. Now, we make a mid-process switch to concentrate on faces. You might even say that, from here on out, we have a face-centric view of the universe. The face data structure has element oi, which contains the object ID, so the granularity switch can be reversed if desired. Indeed, we can think of the face as being at the middle of the data structure hierarchy. Figure 10-21 shows this.

Figure 10-21.   Explicit Data Structure Hierarchy

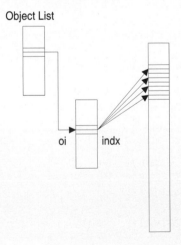

Object List

oi   indx

Face List   Vertex List

The oi object ID element indexes up into the object list, while the indx array contains vertex ID numbers and points into the vertex list. Once past *AddVisibleFace*, the hidden-polygon process never looks back, remains face-oriented to the end.

With that introduction, *AddVisibleFace* is shown in Listing 10-29. It uses the TRY/CATCH block to guard the reallocation of the face list. This is perhaps one of the most vulnerable spots in the modeler. Once the sizing and reallocating, using *WL_Mem_Realloc*, are out of the way and a valid block is in hand, a straightforward offsetting calculation feeds **hmemcpy** to copy the data from the source pointer into the destination list.

Listing 10-29. AddVisibleFace

```
BOOL WINAPI AddVisFace(FRAME * pfrm,VWWND  * pv,LPFACELIST pfl,
                     long fiNum,HPFACE fi)
{
    OBJECT        ot;
    DWORD         vfsize;
    TRY   {
       HPVOID       temp;
       LPOBJECT     this;
       LPEX3DOBJECT lp3DObj;

       vfsize = (DWORD)((DWORD)sizeof(FACE) *
               (DWORD)((DWORD)fiNum+(DWORD)2));
       temp   = (HPFACE)WL_Mem_Realloc(pfl->fi,vfsize,GHND);
       if ( !temp ){
           Throw((LPCATCHBUF)&_ci.state,GENERR_ALLOCFAILURE);
       }
       else{
           HPVERTEX     lpvt;
           HPFACE       pfi,test;
           char _huge * p;
           long         offset;
           double       zmin;
           int          i,o_id;
//
// update list and list entry
//
           pv->mWorld->Scene->VisFaces->fi = (HPFACE)temp;
           p         = (char _huge *)pv->mWorld->Scene->VisFaces->fi;
           offset    = (DWORD)((DWORD)fiNum * (DWORD)sizeof(FACE));
           p        +=offset;
           hmemcpy((HPVOID)p,(HPVOID)fi,sizeof(FACE));
//
// index back into object list to get verticies
//
           this      = GetElement(pv->mWorld->Scene->ObjectList,
                             fi->oi);
           lp3DObj = this->o_edata;
           lpvt    = lp3DObj->o_psurf.wrk_verticies;
//
```

Listing 10-29.   *(cont.)*

```
// update list entry's z value
//
        zmin    = 1E77;
        for ( i = 0; i < fi->ni; i++)  {
            if ( lpvt->vp[(fi->indx[i+1])].z < zmin )
                zmin = lpvt->vp[(fi->indx[i+1])].z;
        }
        pv->mWorld->Scene->VisFaces->fi[
            pv->mWorld->Scene->VisFaces->fiNum].z = zmin;
        return TRUE;
    }
  }
  CATCH
  {
...
  }
  END_CATCH
}
```

There are several things to note here. The face list can get very large, 16MB minus 16K maximum, which means huge pointers. Huge pointers mean a large or huge memory model, and explain the use of the huge copy function **hmemcpy**. The last important detail is the z-value manipulations. It is convenient at this point to go ahead and calculate the face's minimum z value. This also is the first point at which the visible faces are known, so doing this calculation here (at the point of placement into the huge list) saves an extra-huge, and potentially costly, memory access later.

That brings us to the final step in the visibility process: the depth sort. This visibility and rendering process requires polygons to be in z-order prior to actual drawing. The painter's algorithm fails if this is not true.

The quicksort algorithm, already heavily discussed, does the depth sort here. The C RTL provides a quicksort implementation in function **qsort**. This is defined in stdlib.h, as shown in Listing 10-30. Basically, you pass it the block of memory, the size of an element in the block (the structure size), the number of elements, and a comparison function. Disregarding the comparison function for a moment, that simply maps to the visible face list, the size of a face, and the visible face list count.

Listing 10-30.   Function qsort Prototype from stdlib.h

```
void __cdecl qsort(void *, size_t, size_t,
                   int (__cdecl *)(const void *, const void *));
```

The function *SortFace*, shown in Listing 10-31, invokes **qsort** on your behalf with those parameters and comparison function *zSort* (Listing 10-32). The comparison function is easy to understand. It checks the minimum z value placed in each face structure by *AddVisibleFace*. Function *zSort* does a "collating order" comparison between two faces: if face 1 is less than face 2, it returns the value 1; if the faces have identical z values, it returns the value 0; and if face 1 has a z value that is larger than face 2, it returns the value -1.

Listing 10-31.   SortFaces Invoking qsort with zSort

```
void WINAPI SortFaces(HPFACE pvFaces,long fiNum)
{
   qsort( (pvFaces),
          (size_t)((unsigned)fiNum),
          sizeof(FACE),
          zSort);
}
```

Listing 10-32.   Comparison Function zSort

```
int zSort(const void __huge *pf1, const void __huge *pf2)
{
   FACE __huge *pFace1 = pf1;
   FACE __huge *pFace2 = pf2;

   if ( pFace1->z < pFace2->z )
      return 1;
   else if ( pFace1->z > pFace2->z )
      return -1;
   else
      return 0;
}
```

The visibility process ends here and segues, almost indiscernibly, into the rendering phase. Before considering polygon-mode rendering, though, we need to look at this visibility process's analogue in ray-trace mode.

Visibility II: Tracing and Intersecting

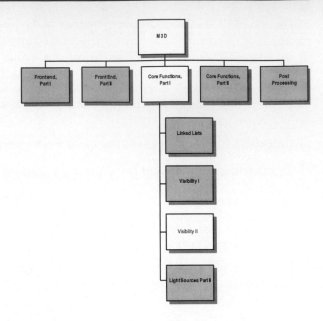

The ray-tracing process takes a different approach to visible surface determination. Referring back to Figure 10-1 (the taxonomy of visible surface algorithms), you can see that ray tracing is at the far right — a point-sampling algorithm. Visibility determination fits into the overall ray-tracing process, which has three parts:

- main ray-trace loop,
- single pixel trace (Function *Trace*), and
- single pixel shade (Function *ShadePoint*).

The main ray-trace loop controls ray generation and feeds function *Trace* to handle the details of each pixel, which, in turn, calls *ShadePoint* to apply the illumination model. This boils down to the following four steps:

1. root ray generation,
2. pixel ray generation,
3. tracing using *Trace*, and
4. gray/color calculations.

Trace here performs several valuable functions: it sets up the visible surface calculations, performs them, and uses the result to feed *ShadePoint*, which performs the pixel-color calculations. This section only considers the visibility sub-problem; the shading and gray process are not considered. This leaves the main ray-tracing loop and a good part of function *Trace* to unravel.

Physical Basis of Ray-Tracing Visibility

Raytracing is fundamentally different from polygon mode. There, the face data structure captured the information we needed to determine visibility, to connect the object to the face, and to connect the face to the vertices. Here, the granularity of consideration returns to the object level. You need to be concerned with objects, rays, intersections, and the image plane. Figure 10-22 describes the players you saw in Figure 10-6 and that you will become familiar with here.

Figure 10-22. Ray-Tracing Visibility Process Repeated

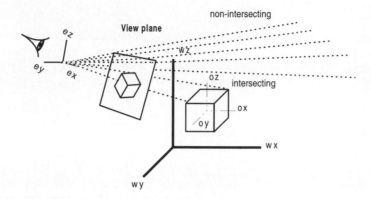

Let's take a moment to discuss objects and scenes in terms of limitations and restrictions, and follow a development parallel to the polygon mode. Ray tracing is a point-sampling algorithm. As its name implies, point-sampling algorithms calculate every point; other classes of algorithms use different granularities. Point-sampling processes give the scene compositor more freedom in combining objects and forming scenes. The restrictions on objects and limitations of scenes forced by polygon mode disappear. For instance, the two-cylinder object will behave as desired, because the mathematics are evaluated at each point instead of depending on one value per face. In the same vein, the sphere embedded in the plane will also behave better. With that out of the way, back to rays and visibility.

The first step in this process is root ray generation. As shown before, rays are implemented as parametric lines, with the two end-points typically named the *origin* and the *direction* of the ray. The parameter t is used to generate a new direction point until some maximum distance is reached. Reviewing the equations for the parametric line, Equation 10-6 restates this for you, with the mathematical definition of a ray. You see the origin and direction, along with the constraint on the components of the direction. Note that the ray is implemented as two vectors: an origin vector and a direction vector.

Equation 10-6. Rays Defined as a Parameterized Line

$$origin = Ro = [Xo, Yo, Zo]$$
$$direction = Rd = [Xd, Yd, Zd], \text{ where}$$
$$Xd^2 + Yd^2 + Zd^2 = 1 \text{ (normalized point)}$$
defines a ray as the set of points on the line
$$R(t) = Ro + Rd * t \text{ where } t > 0.$$

The *RAY* data structure, representing this parameterized line, is shown in Listing 10-33. It contains two vectors to represent the origin and direction.

Listing 10-33.   RAY Data Structure

```
//define parameterized line structure for ray
typedef struct  t_ray
{
  VECTOR4D r_origin;       /* a ray has an origin and direction */
  VECTOR4D r_direction;
} RAY;
typedef RAY FAR * LPRAY;
```

This defines a ray for us, so now we need two other pieces of information. First, the initial ray must be generated. This, in turn, depends on the viewing parameters from/lookat/up. Second, the root ray sets up the imaging process, which uses the pixel extents and the root ray to generate rays through each pixel — a sweeping of the image plane if you will.

Visibility Process

The main tracing loop with the root-ray generation called out is contained in Listing 10-34, and the particulars of root-ray generation are shown in Listing 10-35 in function *MakeEyeRay*. As advertised, this process uses the viewing parameters. Here, it generates a triple of vectors, all at right angles. This is usually referred to as an *orthogonal basis* in terms of linear algebra. This set of mutually perpendicular vectors can be used to form the basis of a new coordinate system.

Listing 10-34.   Root or Eye Ray Generation in Relation to the Main Trace Loop

```
...
//   calculate eye ray
  MakeEyeRay (pv,
              pv->mWorld->Scene->Eye.view_from,
              pv->mWorld->Scene->Eye.view_at,
              pv->mWorld->Scene->Eye.view_up,
               &rS,&rU,&rV,&Ray);
...
  for ( iy = 0 ; iy <= pv->mWorld->Scene->scanY-1; iy++)   {
// render each pixel across horizontal scan line
    for ( ix = 0; ix <= pv->mWorld->Scene->scanX-1; ix++)   {
// calculate eye ray for this pixel
        MakePixRay (pv,Ray.r_origin,rS,rU,rV,ix,iy,&Ray);
        Trace (pv,&pv->mWorld->MaxW,depth,
               &Ray,&Intensity);
        ...
    }
  }
...
```

Listing 10-35.   MakeEyeRay and Generation of rD, rU, and rV

```
void  WINAPI MakeEyeRay(VWWND * pv,
                        VECTOR4D from,VECTOR4D at,  VECTOR4D up,
                        LPVECTOR4D rS,LPVECTOR4D rU,LPVECTOR4D rV,
                        LPRAY Ray)
{
    VECTOR4D  rD;
    double    dist, mag;
//   important constant values
    halfx = ( pv->mWorld->Scene->scanX / 2.0);
    halfy = ( pv->mWorld->Scene->scanY / 2.0);
    f     = pv->mWorld->Scene->Eye.view_vd /
            pv->mWorld->Scene->Eye.view_vs;
    xaspf = 1/f;
    yaspf = 1/f;
    dist = G3D_V4D_VMag4D(pv->mWorld->Scene->Eye.view_from);
    Magnitude(&mag,dist);
//   viewfrom
    G3D_V4D_VSet4D(&(Ray->r_origin),
                      pv->mWorld->Scene->Eye.view_from.x,
                      pv->mWorld->Scene->Eye.view_from.y,
                      pv->mWorld->Scene->Eye.view_from.z,ONE4D);
//   orthogonal axes to sweep image plane
    G3D_V4D_VSub4D(&rD,pv->mWorld->Scene->Eye.view_at,
                      pv->mWorld->Scene->Eye.view_from);
    G3D_V4D_VNorm4D(&rD,rD);
    G3D_V4D_VSet4D(rV,
                      pv->mWorld->Scene->Eye.view_up.x,
                      pv->mWorld->Scene->Eye.view_up.y,
                      pv->mWorld->Scene->Eye.view_up.z,ONE4D);
    G3D_V4D_VCross4D(rU, rD, *rV);
    G3D_V4D_VScale4D(rS,halfx/((mag+3)*2),rD);
}
```

Just like the straightforward matrix multiplication transformation performed on the polygon vertices, the ray-tracing process does a coordinate transformation using these vectors. Objects defined in world coordinates are directly transformed by this process into screen viewport space. The result is pixels on the canvas. There is no real "in-between" point where coordinates are in eye space, or screen window space, as in polygon mode. It's an all-or-nothing process. Figure 10-23 shows the three vectors — rD, rU, and rV — created to define this basis. This is not quite enough, though. The magnitude of the rD vector places the image plane in relation to the scene. By moving this closer or farther from the objects in the scene, you control the appearance of the image in terms of relative sizes.

Figure 10-23.   Basis Geometry

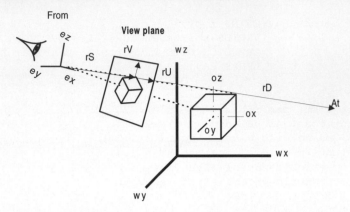

This scaling of the rD vector into the rS vector is shown in Listing 10-36. Note the centering calculation along with the scale by a factor of distance. This is different than the D/S scaling we'll use later. If you do not modify rD, the pixel-ray generation process places the image plane right on the at point because the magnitude of rD is the from/at distance. Modifying this by the magnitude of the distance moves the image plane away from the at point, which is what you would expect (since the camera moved). This is basically modifying what is called the *field of view*. The rS vector is then used along with the rU and rV vectors as parameters to *MakePixRay*.

Listing 10-36.   Generation of rS

```
...
  halfx = ( pv->mWorld->Scene->scanX / 2.0);
  halfy = ( pv->mWorld->Scene->scanY / 2.0);

  dist = G3D_V4D_VMag4D(pv->mWorld->Scene->Eye.view_from);
  Magnitude(&mag,dist);
...
  G3D_V4D_VScale4D(&rS,
                   halfx/((mag+1)*2),
                   rD);
...
```

Function *MakePixRay* takes these three vectors and the current pixel and generates a ray through the pixel that is fed to the trace process and function *Trace*. *MakePixRay*, shown in Listing 10-37, combines the current pixel x, y location and the vector triple of rS, rU, and rV into the direction vector for the pixel ray, and uses the view from point as the origin vector. It also uses a "focal length" to modify the x and y extents. This focal length does not directly relate to any similar value for lenses, but it works on the same principle. Large values give telephoto effects and distance compression, while small values give wide-angle effects and distortion.

Listing 10-37. MakePixRay and Focal Length Calculations

```
...
f = pv->mWorld->Scene->Eye.view_vd/pv->mWorld->Scene->Eye.view_vs;
xaspf = 1/f;
yaspf = 1/f;
...
void  WINAPI MakePixRay(VWWND * pv,VECTOR4D from,VECTOR4D at,
                    VECTOR4D rU,VECTOR4D rV,int rx, int ry,
                    LPRAY Ray)
{
  VECTOR4D TV1, TV2;
  double   sx, sy, f;

  sx = (rx     - halfx) * xaspf;
  sy = (halfy - ry) * yaspf;
  G3D_V4D_VScale4D (&TV2, sx, rU);
  G3D_V4D_VScale4D (&TV1, sy, rV);
  G3D_V4D_VAdd4D((LPVECTOR4D)&(Ray->r_direction),
                        TV1,TV2);
  G3D_V4D_VAdd4D((LPVECTOR4D)&(Ray->r_direction),
                         at,Ray->r_direction);

  G3D_V4D_VNorm4D((LPVECTOR4D)&(Ray->r_direction),
                        Ray->r_direction);
}
```

In the interests of reusing parameters, we use the D/S ratio contained in view_vd and view_vs to specify the focal length. Using the 60/15 ratio from Newman and Sproull gives an f of 4, and since roughly 3.4 corresponds to a 35mm camera lens, this approach gives acceptable results. This also means that changing the D/S parameters affects both polygon and ray-trace modes. This does not even begin to touch what can be done with the viewing parameters. Reversing left and right gives a through-the-looking-glass effect, for instance. Still, the manipulation of this minimum set of parameters is enough to adjust the focal length and the field of view.

Now that the root ray and the rays that will be "shot" through every pixel are understood, it is time to follow a ray on its journey. Listing 10-38 contains the block from *Trace* that pertains to visibility. It sets the initial color to black, and does a recursion check. This is necessary because the modeling of interactions between objects, basically reflections, occurs by way of recursion. Modeling reflection generates a new ray and *Trace* is called recursively to apply the whole process over again. If the trace is permitted, all the objects are iterated across, and the ***intersect*** mapping function is invoked. This function takes the object and the ray and generates a hit. It is this hit that then feeds the rest of the process.

Listing 10-38. Code Block Containing Visibility Segment of Trace

```
...
f = pv->mWorld->Scene->Eye.view_vd/pv->mWorld->Scene->Eye.view_vs;
xaspf = 1/f;
yaspf = 1/f;
...
void  WINAPI MakePixRay(VWWND * pv,VECTOR4D from,VECTOR4D at,
                        VECTOR4D rU,VECTOR4D rV,int rx, int ry,
                        LPRAY Ray)
{
  VECTOR4D TV1, TV2;
  double   sx, sy, f;

  sx = (rx    - halfx) * xaspf;
  sy = (halfy - ry) * yaspf;
  G3D_V4D_VScale4D (&TV2, sx, rU);
  G3D_V4D_VScale4D (&TV1, sy, rV);
  G3D_V4D_VAdd4D((LPVECTOR4D)&(Ray->r_direction),
                             TV1,TV2);
  G3D_V4D_VAdd4D((LPVECTOR4D)&(Ray->r_direction),
                             at,Ray->r_direction);

  G3D_V4D_VNorm4D((LPVECTOR4D)&(Ray->r_direction),
                             Ray->r_direction);
}
```

The *ISECT* data structure represents the hit. The data structure definition is shown in Listing 10-39. It stores the distance, the object, the face ID, and surface information. In point of fact, the *isect_enter* element prepares for transmittance and glass, allowing a ray to enter an object and leave. In any event, an instance of this structure stores hit information and passes it down to the normal generation and *ShadePoint* function. We'll get to more of that in a bit.

Listing 10-39. ISECT Data Structure Definition

```
// ray intersection

typedef struct t_isect
{
     double isect_t ;
     int          isect_enter ;
     VECTOR4D     isect_normal ;
     LPOBJECT     isect_prim ;
     int          isect_face_id ;
     SURFPROPS    isect_surfprops ;
} ISECT ;

typedef ISECT FAR *LPISECT;
```

Each object has an intersect mapping function. The intersect function finds the distance t, and the *GetIsectPt* function uses that value to calculate the point of intersection, represented as a vector. The six objects and their respective functions, plus the plane figure intersections (the circle used by the cylinder and cone, rectangle used by the box and pyramid, and triangle used by the pyramid) add up to nine intersection-related functions. Add the intersection-calculation function and you have a total of ten functions to finish out the visibility process. You can see that this is significantly more work than the polygon mode process, but the results are worth it.

Sphere intersection is handled by *SphereIntersect* (Listing 10-40), which is invoked by the generic *intersect* mapping function.

Listing 10-40   SphereIntersect

```
int SphereIntersect(LPOBJECT this, LPRAY  ray, LPISECT  hit)
{

    double      b, c, disc, t, d1,d2;
    VECTOR4D    V ,t1,t2;
    LPSPHERE    sp ;

    sp = (LPSPHERE) this -> o_adata ;

    G3D_V4D_VSub4D(&t1,sp->sph_center,ray->r_origin);

    b = G3D_V4D_VDot4D(ray->r_direction,t1) * -2.0;

    c = G3D_V4D_VDot4D(t1,t1) - sp->sph_radius2;

    disc = (b * b) - 4.0 * c;

    hit->isect_t = -1.0;
    if (disc < 0.0)
    {
            return(0);
    }

    disc = sqrt(disc);

    d1 = (-b - disc ) * .5;
    d2 = (-b + disc ) * .5;

    QIsectCheck(&t,d1,d2);_
    if (t > -1.0 )
    {
```

Listing 10-40 (*cont.*)

```
    hit->isect_t              = t;
    hit -> isect_prim       = this ;
    hit -> isect_enter = G3D_V4D_VDot4D(t1, t1) >
                            sp->sph_radius2 + EPSILON ? 1 : 0 ;
    hit -> isect_surfprops = this -> o_surfprops ;
    return(1);
  }
  return(0);
}
```

Function *intersect* turns out to be just a shell for the individual intersection functions, just like *transform* was for polygon mode. This allows the upper-level code to have one visible name for a single operation across disparate data types — a crude form of polymorphism, as well as name-space management.

The implementation shows the transformation of the equation for the sphere, shown in Equation 10-7.

Equation 10-7.   Sphere Formula

$$X^2 + Y^2 + Z^2 - R^2 = 0$$

To solve this equation, first move the r-squared term across the equals sign. Next, use the substitution technique, which eventually reduces to the result shown in Equation 10-8.

Equation 10-8.   Sphere/Ray Reduction

$$At^2 + Bt + c = 0, where$$
$$A = Xd^2, Yd^2, Zd^2 = 1$$
$$B = 2(Xd(Xo - Xc) + Yd(Yo - Yc) + Zd * (Zo - Zc))$$
$$C = (Xo - Xc)^2 + (Yo - Yc)^2 + (Zo - Zc)^2 - Sr^2 (Sr = sphere\ radius)$$

This is a quadratic, and coefficient a is equal to 1 because the direction vector was normalized (magnitude of 1). This means the quadratic root formula, shown in Equation 10-9, reduces to Equation 10-10.

Equation 10-9.   General Quadratic Roots

$$T_0, T_1 = -B \pm sqrt(B^2 - 4AC)/2A$$

Equation 10-10.   Sphere Quadratic Roots

$$T_0 = -B - sqrt\ (B^2 - 4C)/2$$
$$T_1 = -B + sqrt\ B^2 - 4C)/2$$

At this point, the code in Listing 10-40 should be a little less mysterious. The coefficients b and c are calculated, the discriminant check for valid roots is made, and if valid roots exist they are calculated. The hit *ISECT* parameter is updated accordingly. The general form here is:

1. Calculate coefficients.
2. Check discriminant.
3. If valid, calculate roots.
4. Use valid roots to update *ISECT* data structure.

You'll see this general form, in one variant or another, in most object-intersection functions. You should be able to pick out the parts of *SphereIntersect* that correspond to these steps. You also see the usage of *QIsectCheck*, which does a helpful check-and-swap to place the closer root in t2. Listing 10-41 shows the implementation for this function.

Listing 10-41.   QIsectCheck Helper

```
void QIsectCheck(double far * isect, double t1, double t2)
{

   if ((!( t1 > SMALL)) && (!(t2 > SMALL )))
      *isect = -1.0;
   else
   {
      if ( t1 > t2 )
      {
         if ( t2 < SMALL )
            t2 = t1;
      }
      else
      {
         if ( t1 > SMALL )
            t2 = t1;
      }
      *isect = t2;
   }
   return ;
}
```

The plane intersection calculations, invoked by mapping function *intersect* for objects of type plane, are performed by function *PlaneIntersect*. Equation 10-11 restates the plane formula, along with the constraints on the coefficients. Using the substitution technique with the plane equation and the ray equation yields the t resultant shown in Equation 10-12. This result is shown in both equation and vector notation, from which it is easy to read Listing 10-42.

Equation 10-11. Plane Formula

$$AX + BY + CZ + D = 0 \ where$$
$$A^2 + B^2 + C^2 = 1 \ and \ Pn = [a, \ b, \ c]$$

Equation 10-12. Distance to Intersection Point on Plane in Two Forms

$$t = -(aXo + bYo + cZo + d) / (aXd + bYd + cZd), or$$
$$t = -(Pn \ dot \ Ro + d) / (Pn \ dot \ Rd) \ in \ vector \ notation$$

Listing 10-42. PlaneIntersect

```
int PlaneIntersect(LPOBJECT this, LPRAY  ray, LPISECT  hit)
{
   LPPLANE  pl ;
   double   Vd, Vo, t;
//

   pl = (LPPLANE) this -> o_adata ;
//
//  Calculate the dot product of the planes normal and the
//  rays direction.
//
   Vd = G3D_V4D_VDot4D(pl->pl_normal,ray->r_direction);

   if (Vd <= EPSILON)  // ray is parallel to plane No intersection
   {
     hit->isect_t = 0.0;
     return(0);                   // return t=0
   }

   Vo  = G3D_V4D_VDot4D(pl->pl_normal,ray->r_origin);
   Vo += pl->pl_distance;
   Vo *= -1.0;
   hit->isect_t = Vo/Vd;
   if (hit->isect_t < 0.0)     // intersection behind ray origin
   {
     hit->isect_t = -1.0;
     return(0);                   // return t=0
   }
   hit -> isect_surfprops  = this -> o_surfprops;
   hit -> isect_prim  = this ;
   hit -> isect_enter = 0 ;
   return 1;                   // else return 1, t in isect
}
```

First, it makes a parallel check on the divisor term Vd = Pn dot Rd. Then it calculates the dot product of Pn and the origin ray Ro to begin the calculation of the Vo term. The distance D is added to this and a negation occurs to finish calculating Vo. Finally, these two terms are divided, yielding t. Once again, the hit parameter is updated to retain the important information.

That leaves the cylinder and cone (simple quadratics) and the box and pyramid (which are assembled from rectangles and triangles). These objects use bounding volumes to enhance performance. In this implementation, they use the sphere object, already covered, as the bounding volume. This requires two steps:

1. Construct the bounding volume at object instantiation time.
2. Use the bounding volume for intersection testing.

The first step is extremely easy. Listing 10-43 contains *MakeBoundingSphere* used in the construction process. It simply gets the Pythagorean distance based on the x,y,z scaling and uses it for a maximum radius. The o_bound element in the object that is passed in as a parameter is initialized to be this sphere.

Listing 10-43.   MakeBoundingSphere

```
void MakeBoundingSphere(LPOBJECT curObj,EX3DOBJECT oe3D)
{
    SPHERE sphere;
    double maxedge;

    maxedge = sqrt(SQR(oe3D.l_transforms.S.x) +
                   SQR(oe3D.l_transforms.S.y) +
                   SQR(oe3D.l_transforms.S.z));

    sphere.sph_center.x = oe3D.l_transforms.T.x;
    sphere.sph_center.y = oe3D.l_transforms.T.y;
    sphere.sph_center.z = oe3D.l_transforms.T.z;
    sphere.sph_radius    = maxedge + 1.0;
    sphere.sph_radius2   = sphere.sph_radius * sphere.sph_radius;

    curObj->o_bound      = sphere;
}
```

Listing 10-44 repeats Listing 8-60 and fills in the "blank" left there by the ellipses.

Listing 10-44.   Block at Parse Time to Create Bounding Sphere

```
// perform local transform on explicit and then add to list
    if ( this )
    {
        SetSurfProp(this, surfprops);
        MakeBoundingSphere(this,oe3D);
        TransformEdges(pv,this,&eT);
        AddToList(&theScene->ObjectList,this);
    }
```

That leaves the crucial function *BoundingSphereIntersect* (Listing 10-45). It performs the all-important test that boosts performance. It is a simplified version of *SphereIntersect*. It does not have to deal with the *ISECT* structure and returning hit information. Here, success or failure is sufficient. Listing 10-46 contains an example of its invocation so you can see the influence on object intersection function structure. As you can see, *BoundingSphereIntersect* is used here within an if test that brackets the normal intersection code. If the bound test succeeds, everything proceeds normally; but if the bound test fails, the function can terminate now and save execution time.

Listing 10-45.   BoundingSphereIntersect

```
int  BoundingSphereIntersect(LPOBJECT this, SPHERE BoundingSphere,
                             LPRAY  ray)
{
   double      b, c, disc, t, d1,d2;
   VECTOR4D    V ,t1,t2;

   G3D_V4D_VSub4D(&t1,BoundingSphere.sph_center,ray->r_origin);
   b   = G3D_V4D_VDot4D(ray->r_direction,t1) * -2.0;
   c   = G3D_V4D_VDot4D(t1,t1) - BoundingSphere.sph_radius2;
   disc = (b * b) - 4.0 * c;
   if (disc < 0.0)
   {
      return(0);
   }
   disc = sqrt(disc);
   d1 = (-b - disc ) * .5;
   d2 = (-b + disc ) * .5;

   QIsectCheck(&t,d1,d2);
   if (t > 0.0 )
   {
      return(1);
   }
   return(0);
}
```

Listing 10-46.   Example BoundingSphereIntersect Invocation

```
int SomeObjIntersect(LPOBJECT this, LPRAY  ray, LPISECT  hit)
{
   if (!BoundingSphereIntersect(this,this->o_bound,ray) )
      return 0;
//perform normal intersection calculations
   ...
}
```

With that behind us, we move on to the cylinder object. This is the first of the objects that require multiple pieces to provide the desired behavior. The cylinder and cone share two key facts and code blocks. First is the fact that they use the circle plane figure to provide endcaps; solving this is a variant of the plane intersection already shown. Second is the subset of the general quadric code (represented by Equation 10-13) used to represent the sheet of the cylinder and cone.

Equation 10-13.   Simpler Subset of Quadric Formula

$$AX^2 + BY^2 + CZ^2 + Ey = D$$

CylinderIntersect, shown in Listing 10-47, is the cylinder version of the intersect mapping function. It clearly shows this dependency by its use of *IsectCircle*, representing the plane figure intersections, and *IsectQuadric*, representing the subset of the general quadric. First, of course, it uses *BoundingSphereIntersect* to make sure it is worth doing the remaining calculations. If so, then *CylinderIntersect* finds out which side is up to determine which circle to test first. It does this by subtracting the centers of the top and bottom from the ray origin. By comparing the results, the top or bottom circle is tested for intersection using *IsectCircle*. These two tests bracket the test against the sheet using *IsectQuadric*. Again, these tests provide the distance t and the hit parameter is updated with this all-important intersection information.

Listing 10-47.   CylinderIntersect

```
int CylinderIntersect(LPOBJECT this, LPRAY  ray, LPISECT  hit){
   LPQUADRIC c ;
   ISECT     hit1;
   VECTOR4D  d1,d2;
   double    t;
   int       rv = 0;

   if (!BoundingSphereIntersect(this,this->o_bound,ray) )
      return 0;
   c = (LPQUADRIC) this -> o_adata ;
   if ( c->q_dm1 == 0.0 && c->q_dm2 == 0.0 ) {
      G3D_V4D_VSub4D(&d1,c->q_bcenter,ray->r_origin);
      G3D_V4D_VSub4D(&d2,c->q_tcenter,ray->r_origin);
      c->q_dm1 = G3D_V4D_VMag4D(d1);
      c->q_dm2 = G3D_V4D_VMag4D(d2);
   }
   hit->isect_t = -1.0;
   if ( c->q_dm2 > c->q_dm1 ) {              // base closer
      t = IsectCircle(&(c->q_endcaps[1]),ray->r_origin,
                   ray->r_direction,hit);  // do top first
      if ( t > 0.0 )     {
         hit -> isect_t          = t;
         hit -> isect_prim       = this;
         hit -> isect_face_id    = 1;
         hit -> isect_surfprops  = this -> o_surfprops ;
         rv = 1;
      }
   }
```

Listing 10-47.   (*cont.*)

```
      else   {                         // base further
        t = IsectCircle(&(c->q_endcaps[0]),ray->r_origin,
          ray->r_direction,hit);  // do base first
        if ( t > 0.0 )      {
           hit -> isect_t          = t;
           hit -> isect_prim       = this;
           hit -> isect_face_id    = 0;
           hit -> isect_surfprops = this -> o_surfprops ;
           rv = 1;
        }
      }
// sheet itself, hit_isect_t valid after isectquadric
    t = IsectQuadric(c,ray->r_origin,ray->r_direction,hit);
    if ( t > 0.0 ) {
        hit -> isect_prim       = this;
        hit -> isect_face_id     = 2;
        hit -> isect_surfprops = this -> o_surfprops ;
        rv = 1;
    }
    if ( c->q_dm2 > c->q_dm1 )  {
        t = IsectCircle(&(c->q_endcaps[0]),ray->r_origin,
                        ray->r_direction,&hit1);  // do top first
        if ( t > 0.0 ) {
           hit -> isect_t          = t;
           hit -> isect_prim       = this;
           hit -> isect_face_id    = 0;
           hit -> isect_surfprops = this -> o_surfprops ;
           rv = 1;
        }
    }

    else  {
        t = IsectCircle(&(c->q_endcaps[1]),ray->r_origin,
              ray->r_direction,&hit1);  // do top first_
        if ( t > 0.0 )
        {
           hit -> isect_t          = t;
           hit -> isect_prim       = this;
           hit -> isect_face_id    = 1;
           hit -> isect_surfprops = this -> o_surfprops ;
           rv = 1;
        }
    }
      return(rv);
}
```

The circle intersection is based on the plane, but the quadric intersection is based on a reduction of Equation 10-13 by the standard method (substitution and elimination) into a quadratic equation, as shown in Equation 10-14. The non-complex roots represent the intersection point(s). The quadric intersection calculations in *IsectQuadric* are shown in Listing 10-48.

Equation 10-14.   Quadratic Surface Intersection Equations in t

$$t^2(AXd^2 + BYd^2 + CZd^2) + 2t(AXoXd + BYoYd + CZoZd) +$$
$$(AXo^2 + BYo^2 + CZo^2 - D) = 0, \text{ and}$$
$$t2\ (AXd^2 + CZd^2) + 2t(AXoXd - EYd + CZoZd) +$$
$$(AXo^2 - EYo2 + CZo^2) = 0$$

Listing 10-48.   IsectQuadric

```
double WINAPI IsectQuadric(LPQUADRIC q, VECTOR4D P, VECTOR4D D, LPISECT
hit)
{
   VECTOR4D t, nP, nD;
   double    t1,t2, ss, a, b, c, dc, disc, sr, one_div_a;

   G3D_V4D_VSub4D(&t,P,q->q_bcenter);
   nP.x = G3D_V4D_VDot4D(t,q->q_u);
   nP.y = G3D_V4D_VDot4D(t,q->q_v);
   nP.z = G3D_V4D_VDot4D(t,q->q_w);
   nD.x = G3D_V4D_VDot4D(D,q->q_u);
   nD.y = G3D_V4D_VDot4D(D,q->q_v);
   nD.z = G3D_V4D_VDot4D(D,q->q_w);

   ss    = q->q_slope * q->q_slope;
   a     = (nD.x*nD.x)+(nD.y*nD.y)-(nD.z*nD.z)*ss;
   b     = 2.0 * ( (nP.x*nD.x)+(nP.y*nD.y)-(nD.z*nP.z*ss) -
      (q->q_bradius*q->q_slope*nD.z));
   c     = (nP.x*nP.x)+(nP.y*nP.y)-((nP.z*q->q_slope +
      q->q_bradius)*(nP.z*q->q_slope+q->q_bradius));

   if ( a == 0.0 )    {
      if ( b == 0.0 ) {
         hit->isect_t = -1.0;
         return hit->isect_t;
      }
      t2 = -c/b;
      if ( t2 < SMALL ) {
         hit->isect_t = -1.0;
         return hit->isect_t;
      }
      else{
         t1 = -1.0;
      }

   }
```

Listing 10-48. *(cont.)*

```
    else{
        disc = (b*b)-4.0*a*c;
        if ( disc < 0.0) {
          hit->isect_t = -1.0;
          return hit->isect_t;
        }
        else {
          sr        = sqrt(disc);
          one_div_a = 1.0 / (a+a);
          t1        = (-b - sr)*one_div_a;
          t2        = (-b + sr)*one_div_a;
          if ( (t1<0.0) && (t2<0.0) )
          {
             hit->isect_t = -1.0;
             return hit->isect_t;
          }
          else
          {
             if( t1 > t2 )        /* make t1 the nearest root */
             {
                double swap;
                swap = t1;
                t1   = t2;
                t2   = swap;
             }
          }
        }
    }
//2 roots
    if ( t1 > SMALL)
    {
       VECTOR4D ip;

       GetIsectPt(P,D,t1,&ip);
       dc = G3D_V4D_VDot4D(q->q_w,ip);
       if ( (!(dc < q->q_mind )) && (!(dc > q->q_maxd)) )
       {
          hit->isect_t = t1;
           hit -> isect_enter      = 1;
          return 1;
       }
       else
       {
          GetIsectPt(P,D,t2,&ip);
          dc = G3D_V4D_VDot4D(q->q_w,ip);
```

```
            if ( (!(dc < q->q_mind )) && (!(dc > q->q_maxd)) )
            {
                hit->isect_t = t2;
                 hit -> isect_enter       = 0;
                return 1;
            }
        }
    }
    if ( t2 > SMALL)
    {
        VECTOR4D ip;

        GetIsectPt(P,D,t2,&ip);
        dc = G3D_V4D_VDot4D(q->q_w,ip);
        if ( (!(dc < q->q_mind )) && (!(dc > q->q_maxd)) )
        {
            hit->isect_t = t2;
             hit -> isect_enter      = 0;
            return 1;
        }
    }
    hit->isect_t = -1.0;
    return hit->isect_t;
}
```

This function first re-orients the ray into the u,v space of the cylinder itself, seen in the nP and nD vector calculations. Once that is out of the way, you can see a slope calculation and the A, B, and C coefficient calculations. The sheet of the cone differs from the sheet of the cylinder solely by this slope value. This use of slope in the calculations (falling out for cylinders and remaining for cones) makes it possible to use this function for both the cone and cylinder. Again, we do some simple checks on the coefficients to avoid useless calculations. Then the standard discriminant check and calculation lead to the actual root calculation and determination of the intersection. Following that, the nearest root is moved into t1 here, and the hit parameter is updated. The helper function *GetIsectPt* is used again to set up the hit *ISECT* structure.

We still need to tackle the function *IsectCircle* before we can declare the cylinder done. This function is shown in Listing 10-49. It calculates what amounts to the same Vd and Vo values, but instead of stopping there, it generates the point for the t result using *GetIsectPt*. This is then used to get a distance from the circle's center for the intersection point. That is compared against the radius to determine point-in/point-out status. In the point-in case, the hit parameter is updated.

Listing 10-49. IsectCircle

```
double WINAPI IsectCircle(LPCIRCLE lpc, VECTOR4D P, VECTOR4D D, LPISECT
hit)
{
    VECTOR4D diff;
    double   p1,p2, t, r, dot;

    dot = G3D_V4D_VDot4D(lpc->c_normal,D);
    if ( dabs(dot) < SMALL ) {
        hit->isect_t = -1.0;
        return hit->isect_t;
    }
    else {
        VECTOR4D ip;

        p1 = lpc->c_NdotV;
        p2 = G3D_V4D_VDot4D(lpc->c_normal,P);
        t  = (p1-p2)/dot;
        GetIsectPt(P,D,t,&ip);
        G3D_V4D_VSub4D(&diff,ip,lpc->c_center);
        r = G3D_V4D_VMag4D(diff);
        if ( r > lpc->c_radius)
        {
            hit->isect_t = -1.0;
            return hit->isect_t;
        }
        else
        {
            hit->isect_t = t;
            return hit->isect_t;
        }
    }
    hit->isect_t = -1.0;
    return hit->isect_t;
}
```

The cone is similar to the cylinder but it has only one circle, which represents the base. Listing 10-50 presents the implementation of *ConeIntersect.*

Listing 10-50. ConeIntersect

```
int ConeIntersect(LPOBJECT this, LPRAY  ray, LPISECT  hit) {
    LPQUADRIC  c ;
    ISECT      hit1;
    VECTOR4D   d1,d2;
    double     dm1,dm2, t;
    int        rv = 0;
```

```
//
   if (!BoundingSphereIntersect(this,this->o_bound,ray) )
      return 0;
   c = (LPQUADRIC) this -> o_adata ;
   if ( c->q_dm1 == 0.0 && c->q_dm2 == 0.0 ) {
      G3D_V4D_VSub4D(&d1,c->q_bcenter,ray->r_origin);
      G3D_V4D_VSub4D(&d2,c->q_tcenter,ray->r_origin);
      c->q_dm1 = G3D_V4D_VMag4D(d1);
      c->q_dm2 = G3D_V4D_VMag4D(d2);
   }
   hit->isect_t = -1.0;
   if ( c->q_dm2 < c->q_dm1 ) {
      t = IsectCircle(&(c->q_endcaps[0]),ray->r_origin,
                      ray->r_direction,&hit1);  // do base first
      if ( t > 0.0 )
      {
         hit -> isect_t          = t;
         hit -> isect_prim       = this;
         hit -> isect_face_id    = 0;
         hit -> isect_surfprops = this -> o_surfprops ;
         rv = 1;
      }
   }
//
// sheet itself
//
   t = IsectQuadric(c,ray->r_origin,ray->r_direction,&hit1);
   if ( t > 0.0 )
   {
      hit -> isect_t          = t;
      hit -> isect_prim       = this;
      hit -> isect_face_id    = 2;
      hit -> isect_surfprops = this -> o_surfprops ;
      rv = 1;
   }
   if ( c->q_dm2 > c->q_dm1 )   {
      t = IsectCircle(&(c->q_endcaps[0]),ray->r_origin,
                      ray->r_direction,&hit1);  // do top first
      if ( t > 0.0 )
      {
         hit -> isect_t          = t;
         hit -> isect_prim       = this;
         hit -> isect_face_id    = 0;
         hit -> isect_surfprops = this -> o_surfprops ;
         rv = 1;
      }
   }
   return(rv);
}
```

This function shows a signature similar to *CylinderIntersect*, using *BoundingSphereIntersect* first, and then, if necessary, retrieving the analytic data from the adata void pointer, and doing both sheet and endcap calculations using *IsectQuadric* and *IsectCircle*. The difference is the way it figures out which of the two endcaps it needs, and the setting of the face ID. The cylinder had three potential face ID values (two endcaps and one sheet) — you'll see in the shading section that the choice of face ID actually makes a difference. The cone has two face IDs (one endcap and one sheet).

The orientation calculation determines whether the endcap representing the base is closer or farther than the sheet. It checks the farthest object first, determining the order you see in the implementation. Last, the *ISECT* structure is again used for value transmission.

As we move on to the box and the pyramid, the last two objects, the plane figure mathematics and the face ID become even more important. These two objects are completely built from primitive faces that are either rectangles or triangles. This extends the plane figure intersection code you saw in *IsectCircle* a little further.

The implementation of *BoxIntersect*, Listing 10-51, shows the unmistakable signs of piecewise assembly. It delegates all its work to *IsectRectangle*. If this illustrious function returns true, the t value is again used to update the *ISECT* structure. As a performance enhancer, the dot product for visibility was stored at scene-generation time and is recalculated when the camera moves. This means that we can ignore unnecessary calls to *IsectRectangle*, since they won't affect the run-time performance of the system for cubes. This is worth its cost in storage space and recalculation time.

Listing 10-51.   BoxIntersect

```
int BoxIntersect(LPOBJECT this, LPRAY  ray, LPISECT  hit)
{
    LPSIMPLENGON cA ;
    ISECT        hit1;
    double       d1,d2,d_tb,d_bf,d_lr,t;
    int          i,rv = 0;
//
    if (!BoundingSphereIntersect(this,this->o_bound,ray) )
       return 0;
    cA           = (LPSIMPLENGON) this -> o_adata ;
    hit->isect_t = -1.0;
    t            = BIG;
    for ( i = 1; i <= 6; i++)
    {
       if ( cA->ng_faces[i].sp_NdotV >= 0.0 )
       {
          double t1;
          t1 = IsectRectangle(&(cA->ng_faces[i]),
                     ray->r_origin,ray->r_direction,&hit1);
          if ( t1 > 0.0 && t1 < t ) //closer face
          {
             t                         = t1;
             hit -> isect_t            = t1;
```

```
            hit -> isect_prim    = this;
            hit -> isect_face_id  = i;
            hit -> isect_surfprops = this -> o_surfprops ;
            rv = 1;
         }
      }
   }
   return(rv);
}
```

Function *IsectRectangle*, Listing 10-52, again shows its plane intersection lineage. Once the familiar plane calculations have gotten us part of the way, helper functions *SetupRectangle* and *EvenCrossings* help in ray/object coordinate shuffling and point-in/point-out determination. The usual technique of reorienting the ray in the object's own u-v coordinate system is helped by *SetupRectangle*. Depending on the orientation of the face itself, the call to *SetupRectangle* changes. This is then fed into *EvenCrossings* to determine point-in/point-out.

Listing 10-52.   IsectRectangle

```
double WINAPI IsectRectangle(LPSIMPLEPOLY p,
                             VECTOR4D P, VECTOR4D D,
                             LPISECT hit)
{
   VECTOR4D nP, nD, gU,gV;
   double   p1,p2, t, r, dot;

   hit->isect_t = -1.0;
   dot = G3D_V4D_VDot4D(p->sp_normal,D);
   if ( dabs(dot) < SMALL )
   {
      hit->isect_t = -1.0;
      return hit->isect_t;
   }
   else
   {
      VECTOR4D ip, diff;

      p1 = p->sp_NdotV;
      p2 = G3D_V4D_VDot4D(p->sp_normal,P);
      t  = (p1-p2)/dot;
      GetIsectPt(P,D,t,&ip);
      G3D_V4D_VSub4D(&diff,ip,p->sp_center);
      if ( ( dabs(p->sp_normal.x) > dabs(p->sp_normal.y) ) &&
           ( dabs(p->sp_normal.x) > dabs(p->sp_normal.z) ) )
      {
```

Listing 10-52. (*cont.*)

```
            SetupRectangle(1,2,
                              (double far *)&p->sp_v1,
                              (double far *)&p->sp_v2,
                              (double far *)&diff,
                              &gU,&gV);
        }
        else if ( dabs(p->sp_normal.x) >= dabs(p->sp_normal.z) )
        {
            SetupRectangle(0,2,
                              (double far *)&p->sp_v1,
                              (double far *)&p->sp_v2,
                              (double far *)&diff,
                              &gU,&gV);
        }
        else
        {
            SetupRectangle(0,1,
                              (double far *)&p->sp_v1,
                              (double far *)&p->sp_v2,
                              (double far *)&diff,
                              &gU,&gV);
        }
    }
    if ( EvenCrossings(4,(double far *)&gU,(double far * )&gV) )
        hit->isect_t = -1.0;
    else
        hit->isect_t = t;
    return hit->isect_t;

}
```

Function *SetupRectangle*, shown in Listing 10-53, provides the u-v coordinate space that is then used in the final intersection calculations of *IsectRectangle*, which uses *EvenCrossings*.

Listing 10-53. **SetupRectangle**

```
void SetupRectangle(BYTE p1, BYTE p2,
                    double far * v1, double far * v2,
                    double far *delta,
                    LPVECTOR4D gu,LPVECTOR4D gv)
{
  gu->x=-delta[p1];
  gv->x=-delta[p2];
  gu->y= v1[p1] - delta[p1];
  gv->y= v1[p2] - delta[p2];
```

```
  gu->z= v2[p1] + v1[p1] - delta[p1];
  gv->z= v2[p2] + v1[p2] - delta[p2];
  gu->w= v2[p1] - delta[p1];
  gv->w= v2[p2] - delta[p2];
}
```

The *EvenCrossings* function implements, in Listing 10-54, what is known as the *Jordan curve theorem* for determining in/out. This theorem states that by constructing a line away from the intersection point and intersecting that with the polygon itself, if the number of intersections with itself is odd, the point is inside; otherwise, it is outside. Figure 10-24 shows this.

Figure 10-24.   Jordan Curve Theorem

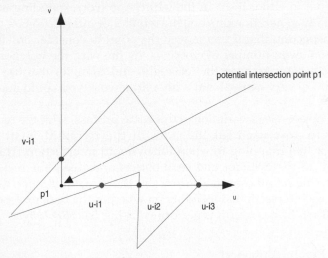

Listing 10-54.   EvenCrossings

```
BOOL EvenCrossings(BYTE Sides, double far * gu, double far * gv)
{
  BYTE i, j;
  WORD crossings;

  crossings=0;
  for(i=0; i<Sides; i++){
    j=(i+1) % Sides;
    if(((gv[i]<0) && (gv[j]>=0)) || ((gv[j]<0) && (gv[i]>=0)))
    {
      if((gu[i]>=0) && (gu[j]>=0))
         ++crossings;
      else
      {
       if((gu[i]>=0) || (gu[j]>=0))
       {
```

Listing 10-54. *(cont.)*

```
        if((gu[i]-gv[i]*(gu[j]-gu[i])/(gv[j]-gv[i]))>0)
          ++crossings;
      }
    }
  }
}
if((crossings%2)==0)
  return(TRUE);
else
  return(FALSE);
}
```

You can see that in either the u or the v direction (corresponding to the same u and v directions in the ray generation process) the number of intersections is odd. You should be able to tell by inspection that if you moved the point to consider outside the polygon the result would be an even number of crossings. By the way, the polygon in Figure 10-24 is considerably more complex than the rectangles and triangles that use this theorem here; but our algorithm is very general and with a little work you could adapt it to more complex figures.

The pyramid object uses a variation of this same process, with the twist that the triangle plane figures are now used for the sides of the pyramid. Listing 10-55 contains *PyramidIntersect*, the mapping function for pyramid intersection. This function uses an approach similar to the cylinder and cone objects and treats the rectangle base like the endcaps of the cylinder and cone; it also brackets the core intersection determination of the triangles. The base intersection, depending on whether the base is closer or further, either happens last or first. Either way, it is performed using *IsectRectangle*.

Listing 10-55. PyramidIntersect

```
int PyramidIntersect(LPOBJECT this, LPRAY  ray, LPISECT  hit){
   LPSIMPLENGON cA ;
   VECTOR4D     d1,d2,a;
   ISECT        hit1;
   double       dm1,dm2,d_tb,d_bf,d_lr,t,t1;
   int          i,rv = 0;
//
   if (!BoundingSphereIntersect(this,this->o_bound,ray) )
      return 0;
   cA           = (LPSIMPLENGON) this -> o_adata ;
   hit->isect_t = -1.0;
   t            = BIG;
   G3D_V4D_VSub4D(&d1,cA->ng_center,ray->r_origin);
   G3D_V4D_VAdd4D(&a, cA->ng_center,cA->ng_h);
   G3D_V4D_VSub4D(&d2,a,ray->r_origin);
   dm1 = G3D_V4D_VMag4D(d1);
   dm2 = G3D_V4D_VMag4D(d2);
```

```
     if ( dm2 < dm1 )  {
        t1   = IsectRectangle(&(cA->ng_faces[5]),ray->r_origin,
                    ray->r_direction,&hit1);  // do top first
       if ( t1 > 0.0 && t1 < t ) { //closer face
          hit -> isect_t        = t1;
          hit -> isect_prim      = this;
          hit -> isect_face_id   = 5;
          hit -> isect_surfprops = this -> o_surfprops ;
          rv = 1;
       }
     }
     for ( i = 1; i <= 4; i++) {
        if ( cA->ng_faces[i].sp_NdotV >= 0 ) {
           double t1;
           t1 = IsectTriangle(&(cA->ng_faces[i]),ray->r_origin,
                   ray->r_direction,&hit1);  // do top first
          if ( t1 > 0.0 && t1 < t ) { //closer face
             t                      = t1;
             hit -> isect_t         = t1;
             hit -> isect_prim      = this;
             hit -> isect_face_id   = i;
             hit -> isect_surfprops = this -> o_surfprops ;
             rv = 1;
          }
        }
     }
     if ( dm2 > dm1 )  {
        t1 = IsectRectangle(&(cA->ng_faces[5]), ray->r_origin,
               ray->r_direction,&hit1);  // do top first
       if ( t1 > 0.0 && t1 < t ) { //closer face
          hit -> isect_t        = t1;
          hit -> isect_prim      = this;
          hit -> isect_face_id   = 5;
          hit -> isect_surfprops = this -> o_surfprops ;
          rv = 1;
       }
     }
        return(rv);
}
```

The core of the calculation logic simply loops across the four triangles and calls *IsectTriangle*. The *ISECT* structure receives the results and transmits them back to the caller. Plane figure intersection function *IsectTriangle* in turn depends on *SetupTriangle*, *EvenCrossings*, and the Jordan curve theorem. The implementation of *IsectTriangle*, shown in Listing 10-56, closely resembles *IsectRectangle*. *SetupTriangle* also holds no surprises, as Listing 10-57 informs you. It implements a similar u-v mapping.

Listing 10-56.   IsectTriangle

```
double WINAPI IsectTriangle(LPSIMPLEPOLY tri,
                            VECTOR4D P, VECTOR4D D,
                            LPISECT hit)
{
   VECTOR4D nP, nD, gU,gV;
   double   p1,p2, t, r, dot;

   hit->isect_t = -1.0;
   dot = G3D_V4D_VDot4D(tri->sp_normal,D);
   if ( dabs(dot) < SMALL )
   {
      hit->isect_t = -1.0;
      return hit->isect_t;
   }
   else
   {
      VECTOR4D ip, diff;

      p1 = tri->sp_NdotV;
      p2 = G3D_V4D_VDot4D(tri->sp_normal,P);
      t  = (p1-p2)/dot;
      GetIsectPt(P,D,t,&ip);
      G3D_V4D_VSub4D(&diff,ip,tri->sp_center);
      if ( ( dabs(tri->sp_normal.x) > dabs(tri->sp_normal.y) ) &&
           ( dabs(tri->sp_normal.x) > dabs(tri->sp_normal.z) ) )
      {
         SetupTriangle(1,2,
                       (double far *)&tri->sp_v1,
                        (double far *)&tri->sp_v2,
                       (double far *)&diff,
                       &gU,&gV);
      }
      else if ( dabs(tri->sp_normal.x) >= dabs(tri->sp_normal.z) )
      {
         SetupTriangle(0,2,
                       (double far *)&tri->sp_v1,
                       (double far *)&tri->sp_v2,
                       (double far *)&diff,
                       &gU,&gV);
      }
      else
      {
         SetupTriangle(0,1,
                       (double far *)&tri->sp_v1,
                       (double far *)&tri->sp_v2,
                       (double far *)&diff,
                                  &gU,&gV);
      }
   }
}
```

```
    if ( EvenCrossings(3,(double far *)&gU,(double far * )&gV) )_
       hit->isect_t = -1.0;
    else
       hit->isect_t = t;
    return hit->isect_t;
}
```

Listing 10-57.   SetupTriangle

```
void SetupTriangle(BYTE p1, BYTE p2, double far * v1, double far * v2,
double far *
delta,LPVECTOR4D gu,LPVECTOR4D gv)
{
  gu->x=-delta[p1];
  gv->x=-delta[p2];
  gu->y= v1[p1] - delta[p1];
  gv->y= v1[p2] - delta[p2];
  gu->z= v2[p1] - delta[p1];
  gv->z= v2[p2] - delta[p2];
}
```

That leaves helper function *GetIsectPt*, shown in Listing 10-58. This function was used in many places to do the parametric calculation using the ray equation and the distance parameter that all of the intersection calculations yielded.

Listing 10-58.   GetIsectPt

```
void  WINAPI GetIsectPt(VECTOR4D Eye, VECTOR4D Dir, double Dist,
LPVECTOR4D Isect)
{
//
  Isect->x = Dist * Dir.x + Eye.x;
  Isect->y = Dist * Dir.y + Eye.y;
  Isect->z = Dist * Dir.z + Eye.z;
  Isect->w = 1.0;
}
```

That wraps up the treatment of ray-tracing visibility. You've seen the ray generation process and followed that ray through the intersection calculations for the six top-level objects and the plane figure helpers, circle, parallelogram, and triangle. Before we start on the rendering sections, the second installment of the light source code needs to be introduced.

Light Sources II: Manipulation

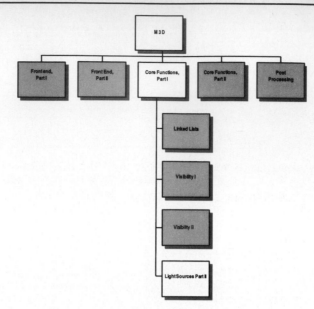

In Chapter 9, I introduced the light source, its data structures, and the instance management functions for creation and deletion. Here, I'll present the functions that operate on an instance of a light source, to complete the coverage of lights. The manipulation capability here is minimal, but it conforms to the requirements of the rendering phase of the modeler.

The capabilities presented here include the ability to generate vectors or rays between the current polygon/point and the light source, with functions *MakeLightVec* and *MakeLightRay*, as well as the ability to determine the color of a light with *GetLightColor*. The final function is the utility print function *PrintLightInfo*. The support for the shading process, at least as far as the light source is concerned, will be complete at that point.

The polygon mode uses *MakeLightVec* to generate the vector between the current polygon and the light source used to calculate color. Listing 10-59 contains the implementation of this function. You can see that it accesses the light source data using the void pointer, then simply uses the difference between the point P and the light source location, using function *G3D_V4D_VSub4D* to generate the vector used at calculation time.

Listing 10-59.   MakeLightVec

```
double   WINAPI MakeLightVec(LPOBJECT Light, VECTOR4D Point, LPVECTOR4D
LightVec)
{
  double     dist;
  LPLIGHTSRC l ;
//
  l = (LPLIGHTSRC)Light->o_edata;
//
//create vector from light source data structure
```

```
//
  G3D_V4D_VSub4D((LPVECTOR4D)LightVec,l->o_light_pos,Point);
//
//   return the distance
//
  dist = G3D_V4D_VMag4D(*LightVec);
  return(dist);
}
```

Function *MakeLightRay* is a parallel function providing exactly the same service for ray-tracing mode. It accesses the light position using the void pointer, and builds the direction vector portion of the ray. Of course, it also builds the origin. Listing 10-60 implements *MakeLightRay*. Both functions return the distance as a convenience.

Listing 10-60.   MakeLightRay

```
double WINAPI MakeLightRay (LPOBJECT Light, VECTOR4D Point, LPRAY Ray)
{
  double     dist;
  LPLIGHTSRC l ;
//
//   Create a ray from the point of intersection to light source.
//   Ray origin is the point. Ray direction is ray from center
//   of light source to point.
//
  Ray->r_origin = Point;

  l = (LPLIGHTSRC)Light->o_edata;

  G3D_V4D_VSub4D((LPVECTOR4D)&(Ray->r_direction),
                 l->o_light_pos,Point);
//
//   return the distance of this ray.
//   make unit vector of direction.
//
  dist = G3D_V4D_VMag4D(Ray->r_direction);
  G3D_V4D_VNorm4D(&Ray->r_direction,Ray->r_direction);
  return(dist);
}
```

Ray-trace mode implements a local illumination model that provides shadows. It does this by sending out a "shadow feeler" to determine, once there is an intersection, whether some object obscures the light. *GetLightColor* supports this task by looping across the 3D object list one more time. It does this by comparing the known intersection distance with the potentially obscuring distance. If the light is completely obscured, black is returned; otherwise the color of the light is returned. Listing 10-61 implements *GetLightColor*.

Listing 10-61. GetLightColor

```
VECTOR4D WINAPI GetLightColor (LPSCENE  Scene,
                               LPOBJECT Light,
                               LPOBJECT Object,
                               LPRAY    Ray,
                               double   Distance)
{

  LPOBJECT ShadowObj;
  VECTOR4D Color;
  double   TrialDist;
  ISECT    hit;
//
// Assume light source is obscured by some object
//
  Color.x = Color.y = Color.z = Color.w = 0.0;
//
//Test for object obscuring light source. Do not test
//to see if the object itself is obscuring the light source.
//
  ShadowObj = Scene->ObjectList;
  while (ShadowObj)
  {
    if (ShadowObj != Object)
    {
      TrialDist = ShadowObj->o_procs->intersect(ShadowObj,
                                                Ray,&hit);
//
//  If an intersection is found and it shadows the point ( ie is
//  between the light and the object ) then return black for color.
//
      if ((TrialDist > EPSILON) && (TrialDist < Distance))
        return(Color);
    }
    ShadowObj = ShadowObj->next;
  }
//
// Return the color specified for the light source.
//
  Color.x  = Light->o_surfprops.surf_color[0];
  Color.y  = Light->o_surfprops.surf_color[1];
  Color.z  = Light->o_surfprops.surf_color[2];
  return(Color);
}
```

That just leaves the print utility function *PrintLightInfo*. See Listing 10-62 for this simple dump of the light color, position, and brightness. The intensity of all lights is set to unity. This is another area of the system that can be extended with minimal effort.

Listing 10-62.   PrintLightInfo

```
int WINAPI PrintLightInfo(LPLIGHTSRC l,HWND hw)
{

    Trans_Printf(hw,
          "a %s light at %lf %lf %lf\n of brightness %lf\n",
                l ->szLiteColor,
                l ->w_light_pos.x,
    l ->w_light_pos.y,
    l ->w_light_pos.z,
    l ->light_brightness);
    return 1;
}
```

That finishes the second (and final) installment of light sources and light source functions. The polygon and ray-trace rendering modes remain, along with the texturing process. With the wireframe and the hidden-polygon renderings for rough views and the ray-trace mode for final imaging presented here, all that Chapter 11 will have to do is a final bit of architectural work around which all of this visibility and rendering functionality will drop into place.

Rendering I:
Wireframe Drawing

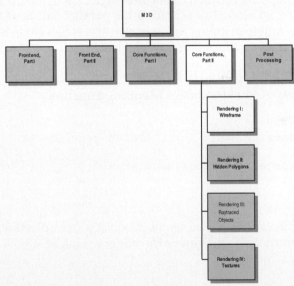

I've already described most of the wireframe drawing process and presented most of its code. By now, you should have a clear picture in your head of wireframe drawing. Just in case, though, I'll run through the entire process one more time.

Listing 10-63 contains both loops of the wireframe process. Previously, I showed this block as a single loop, but as the polygon-mode code explained, this was an oversimplification. The transformation mapping function and its internals at the object level are old news.

Listing 10-63. Both Loops in Wireframe Process

```
...
for ( i = 0; i < pv->mWorld->Scene->nObjs;i++)
{
        LPOBJECT    ot;
//retrieve from list
        ot    = GetElement(pv->mWorld->Scene->ObjectList,i+1);
//transform
        (ot->o_procs->transform(ot,
                    vtype==CMD_PERSP? tPerspProj:tParaProj));
}
...
for ( i = 0; i < pv->mWorld->Scene->nObjs;i++)
{
//project,map, and draw
        (ot->o_procs->drawedges(ot,pv->genv,phist,hDC));


}
```

That leads to the *drawedges* mapping function. Listing 10-12 contained the sphere *drawedges* mapping function **SphereDrawEdges**, and Listing 10-64 here shows the cone *drawedges* mapping function **ConeDrawEdges**. Compare the two and you will see an identical interface; all along I've espoused the parallel nature of the mapping functions. Basically, for any single mapping function, all objects behave in a similar manner. Indeed they even go so far as to depend on a single underlying function in some cases, including this one.

Listing 10-64. Cone drawedges Mapping Function

```
int
ConeDrawEdges(LPOBJECT this, LPGENV genv,HISTWND * ph,HDC hDC)
{
   DrawSurfaceEdges( this,genv,ph,hDC);
   return 1;
}
```

DrawSurfaceEdges is used by all 3D objects to implement wireframe rendering mode. The implementation of *DrawSurfaceEdges*, Listing 10-65, shows the somewhat-busy nature of this function.

Listing 10-65. DrawSurfaceEdges

```
void WINAPI DrawSurfaceEdges(LPOBJECT this,LPGENV genv,
                             HISTWND * ph,HDC hDC) {
   LPEX3DOBJECT lp3DObj;
   POINT    pgdi[5];
   int      i,j;
   long     xv1,yv1;
```

```
    lp3DObj = this->o_edata;
    for ( i = 0; i < lp3DObj->nF;i++){
        FACELIST  fl;
        FACE      ft;
        LPVERTEX  lpvt;
        VECTOR4D  vpt;

        fl   = lp3DObj->o_psurf.faces;
        ft   = fl.fi[i+1];
        lpvt = lp3DObj->o_psurf.wrk_verticies;
        for ( j = 0; j < lp3DObj->nVinF; j++) {
            vpt = lpvt->vp[ft.indx[j+1]];
            G3D_Xfrm_ProjectPoint((LPVECTOR4D)&vpt, vpt,
                      vtype == CMD_PERSP ? PERSPECTIVE : PARALLEL );
            G3D_Coords_UsertoDev(genv,
                                 vpt.x,vpt.y, &xv1,&yv1);
            pgdi[j].x = (int)xv1;
            pgdi[j].y = (int)yv1;
        }
        switch(bckclr)  {
            case CMD_BLACK:
            case CMD_USER:
                G3D_Hist_Set(ph->lph,1+NUMGRAYCOL);
                break;
            case CMD_WHITE:
                G3D_Hist_Set(ph->lph,0);
                break;
        }
        switch(this->o_type) {
            default:
            case T_PLANE:
            case T_SPHERE:
            case T_CONE:
            case T_CUBE:
            case T_CYL:
            case T_PYR:
// close the poly, no need to transform 1st point again
                pgdi[ft.ni].x = (int)pgdi[0].x;
                pgdi[ft.ni].y = (int)pgdi[0].y;
                break;
        }
        G3D_GEnv_Polyline(genv,(LPPOINT)&pgdi,
                          (long)lp3DObj->nVinF+1,NULL);
    }
}
```

The process contains three main parts:

- projection,
- mapping, and
- drawing.

The projection transformation is handled by *G3D_Xfrm_ProjectPoint*. The explicit values are extracted from the edata void pointer and plugged into the projection operation. This yields values in screen space, but in screen window space (sw), not screen viewport space (sv). Remember that screen viewport space directly corresponds to the canvas, while screen window space is an arbitrary floating-point valued range.

Window-viewport mapping is handled by *G3D_Coords_UsertoDev*. If you think about it, this naming makes more sense than confusing the issue by trying to use window or viewport again. The window coordinates are an arbitrary floating-point valued range that is specified by the user. The viewport coordinates are an integer-valued range corresponding to the device or canvas. The user and device nomenclature is more descriptive here.

That leaves us with values in sv coordinate space that can be used with the output primitive routines to generate output. *DrawSurfaceEdges* uses *G3D_GEnv_Polyline* to draw each face with a single call. The histogram calls maintain the illusion by setting up a "black and white" histogram. A "b&w" histogram has two entries — black and white — and an extremely simple graph. The other interesting feature is the reuse of the first vertex value to save a set of operations. The polygon must be closed to look right, which means a final line from the last vertex to the first. For a rectangle, this means a draw sequence like (1-to-2, 2-to-3,3-to-4,4-to-1). We don't need to repeat the projection and mapping operations on the first point, and the assignment of the value of the first point to the nth takes care of this. The switch statement alerts us that the possibility exists that this strategy might break as objects are added. Figure 10-25 contains a sample wireframe image, with each object supported by this system represented. Wireframe is done at this point, and it's on to the hidden-polygon mode. The projection, mapping, and drawing operations you saw here are also part of hidden-polygon mode, albeit slightly modified.

Figure 10-25.   Wireframe Rendition

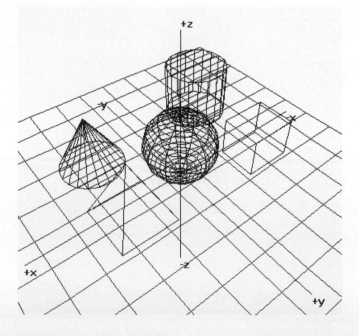

Rendering II: Shading and Drawing Polygons

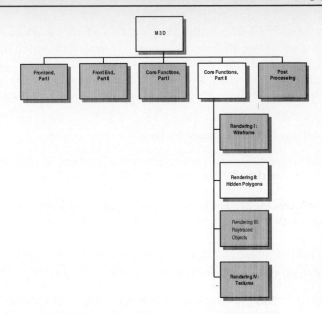

The rendering phase of hidden-polygon mode picks up where the transformation and visibility manipulations leave off. The transformation process is actually shared with wireframe mode. The visibility process is the driving force behind the hidden-polygon mode. It is during the visibility process that the switch in granularity occurs and our preoccupation with faces and a face-centric view dominates.

Listing 10-66 contains the bottom portion of Listing 10-14, the part that is relevant here. This code block contains the loop that operates on the visible face list and invokes mapping function *drawface* to do the projection, mapping, and drawing operations. Linked-list access function *GetElement* uses the stored object ID to retrieve the object containing the vertex data for this face. This allows *drawface* to concern itself solely with faces and vertices, and face and vertex value access, ignoring the details of object-level access.

Listing 10-66. Projection, Mapping, and Drawing in Hidden Polygon Mode

```
...
// project,map,draw visible list
...
 for ( i = 0; i < pv->mWorld->Scene->VisFaces->fiNum ; i++){
...
      ot      = GetElement(pv->mWorld->Scene->ObjectList,pfi->oi);
...
      (ot->o_procs->drawface(ot,pfi,lpvt,pv,phist,hDC));
...
}
...
```

Listing 10-67 contains the *ConeDrawFace* function, and, like the *SphereDrawFace* function of Listing 10-15, it delegates to *DrawFace*. Again, instead of forcing you to page backwards, the *DrawFace* function is repeated, here in Listing 10-68. This function uses the rendering type in a switch and invokes the individual polygon-drawing functions *DrawHiddenFace*, *DrawSolidFace*, and *DrawFlatShadedFace*.

Listing 10-67. ConeDrawFace

```
int ConeDrawFace(LPOBJECT this,HPFACE fi,LPVERTEX lpvt,
         VWWND * pv,HISTWND * ph,HDC hDC)
{
   DrawFace( this,fi,lpvt,pv,ph,rtype,hDC);
   return 1;
}
```

Listing 10-68. DrawFace

```
void WINAPI DrawFace( LPOBJECT this,HPFACE fi,LPVERTEX lpvt,
                  VWWND * pv,HISTWND * ph,int rtype,HDC hDC )
{

   switch(rtype)
   {
     case CMD_HIDDEN:
         DrawHiddenFace(this,fi,lpvt,pv->genv,ph,hDC);
         break;
     case CMD_SOLID:
         DrawSolidFace(this,fi,lpvt,pv->genv,ph,hDC);
         break;
     case CMD_FLAT:
         DrawFlatShadedFace(this,fi,lpvt,pv,ph,hDC);
         break;
   }
   return;
}
```

While the previous discussion ended at this point, it's now time to tackle these functions. They provide the three hidden-polygon renderings:

- monochrome HLHSR,
- solid-color HLHSR, and
- flat-shaded HLHSR.

The draw operation works a little differently with each function. Previously, the processing could simply be broken down as:

- projection,
- mapping, and
- drawing.

Now the draw operation includes the additional concern of what color to fill the polygon.

Monochrome HLHSR

The first task behind developing one of these rendering functions is deciding on a color scheme. Even in shaded renderings that depend on the mathematical formulation of an illumination model based on surface physics and optics, you need to decide which illumination model to use. The first step is our most important.

Monochrome mode provides a simple black-and-white rendition. Listing 10-69 contains *DrawHiddenFace*, but of equal interest is the attribute handling and monochrome drawing.

Listing 10-69. DrawHiddenFace

```
void DrawHiddenFace(LPOBJECT this,HPFACE fi,LPVERTEX lpvt,
                    LPGENV genv,HISTWND * ph,HDC hDC)
{
   LPEX3DOBJECT lp3DObj;
   VECTOR4D vpt;
   POINT    pgdi[5];
   int      i;
   long     xv1,yv1;

   for ( i = 0; i < fi->ni; i++)
   {
        vpt = lpvt->vp[fi->indx[i+1]];
        G3D_Xfrm_ProjectPoint((LPVECTOR4D)&vpt, vpt,
                vtype == CMD_PERSP ? PERSPECTIVE : PARALLEL );
        G3D_Coords_UsertoDev(genv,
                             vpt.x,vpt.y,
                             &xv1,&yv1);
        pgdi[i].x = (int)xv1;
        pgdi[i].y = (int)yv1;
   }

   lp3DObj = this->o_edata;
   switch(bckclr)
   {
      case CMD_BLACK:
      case CMD_USER:
         G3D_Hist_Set(ph->lph,1+NUMGRAYCOL);
         break;
```

Listing 10-69. *(cont.)*

```
   case CMD_WHITE:
      G3D_Hist_Set(ph->lph,0);
      break;
}
switch(this->o_type)
{
   default:
   case T_PLANE:
   case T_SPHERE:
   case T_CONE:
   case T_CUBE:
   case T_CYL:
   case T_PYR:
// close the poly, no need to transform 1st point again
      pgdi[fi->ni].x = pgdi[0].x;
      pgdi[fi->ni].y = pgdi[0].y;
      break;
}
G3D_GEnv_Polygon(genv,(LPPOINT)&pgdi,(long)fi->ni+1,NULL,NULL);
}
```

This rendering method means that you make no decision about color. The default attributes of the canvas, based on the canvas style and its background color, are enough for the pen and brush attributes of this mode. How this is provided is an important question as well. Listing 10-70 shows a block of code from the internals of the image-view window class. It sets both the client DC and the graphics environment attributes as the user changes the background color option, ignoring the background color in the scene description for the moment. This includes setting the text background color with **SetBkColor**, so that any labeling occurs with the inter-character region filled with the current background. The client DC uses a set of GDI calls, while the graphics environment can use *G3D_GEnv_SetVal* and the canvas style codes WHITE_CANV or BLACK_CANV to accomplish the same effect. I showed you the code that performs that action in the graphics environment in Chapter 5, and it closely resembles that in Listing 10-70.

Listing 10-70.   Attribute Control for Monochrome Hidden-Line Rendering

```
...
   case CMD_BLACK:
      SetTextColor(hdc1,RGB(255,255,255));
      SetBkMode(hdc1,OPAQUE);
      SetBkColor(hdc1,RGB(0,0,0));
      SelectObject(hdc1, hWhitePen);
      FillRect(hdc1, &rV, GetStockObject(BLACK_BRUSH));
      G3D_GEnv_SetVal(pv->genv,BLACK_CANV,NULL);
      G3D_GEnv_Clear(pv->genv,
                     GetStockObject(BLACK_BRUSH));
      break;
```

```
. . .
   case CMD_WHITE:
       SetTextColor(hdc1,RGB(0,0,0));
       SetBkMode(hdc1,OPAQUE);
       SetBkColor(hdc1,RGB(255,255,255));
       SelectObject(hdc1, hBlackPen);
       FillRect(hdc1, &rV, GetStockObject(WHITE_BRUSH));
       G3D_GEnv_SetVal(pv->genv,WHITE_CANV,NULL);
       G3D_GEnv_Clear(pv->genv,
                      GetStockObject(WHITE_BRUSH));
       break;
. . .
```

Other than the details of attribute selection, the monochrome mode implements the same projection, mapping, and drawing sequence. Note that the draw call to primitive function **G3D_GEnv_Polygon** accepts the default attributes as signified by the NULL parameter usage. That dovetails with the attribute control block, shown in Listing 10-70, that does the attribute manipulation out of the scope of the rendering run. This removes potential performance overhead cost in monochrome hidden-line mode. The only reason this is possible is that the implementation of a monochrome look can be accomplished by simply doing nothing — resulting in a lack of color. The other hidden-polygon modes are not so trivial. A sample monochrome image is shown in Figure 10-26.

Figure 10-26.   Monochrome HLHSR Image

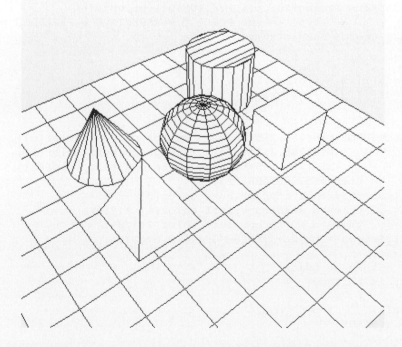

Solid-Color HLHSR

The solid color rendition closely resembles the monochrome rendition. They both use the projection, mapping, and drawing sequence. The difference is that solid-color mode uses the RGB palette created by *InitRGBPalette*. The color contained in the *OBJDEF* specification is used to draw each object in that "solid" color.

Listing 10-71 contains *DrawSolidFace*. As you can see, the implementation exactly parallels *DrawHiddenFace*, except for the color determination.

Listing 10-71.   DrawSolidFace

```
void DrawSolidFace(LPOBJECT this,HPFACE fi,LPVERTEX lpvt,
                LPGENV genv,HISTWND * ph,HDC hDC)
{
   LPEX3DOBJECT lp3DObj;
   VECTOR4D vpt;
   POINT    pgdi[5];
   HBRUSH   hbr,hOldBrush;
   COLORREF cr;
   int      i;
   long     xv1,yv1;
   long     avg;

   for ( i = 0; i < fi->ni; i++)
   {
        vpt = lpvt->vp[fi->indx[i+1]];
        G3D_Xfrm_ProjectPoint((LPVECTOR4D)&vpt,vpt,
                 vtype == CMD_PERSP ? PERSPECTIVE : PARALLEL );
        G3D_Coords_UsertoDev(genv,
                             vpt.x,vpt.y,
                             &xv1,&yv1);
        pgdi[i].x = (int)xv1;
        pgdi[i].y = (int)yv1;
   }

   cr = PALETTERGB(min(255,255*this->o_surfprops.surf_color[0]),
               min(255,255*this->o_surfprops.surf_color[1]),
               min(255,255*this->o_surfprops.surf_color[2]) );
   hbr      = CreateSolidBrush(cr);
   avg = ((255*this->o_surfprops.surf_color[0] + 255*
            this->o_surfprops.surf_color[1] + 255*
            this->o_surfprops.surf_color[2])/3);
   G3D_Hist_Set(ph->lph,1 + min(NUMGRAYCOL,avg));

   lp3DObj = this->o_edata;
   switch(this->o_type)
   {
      default:
      case T_PLANE:
```

```
        case T_SPHERE:
        case T_CONE:
        case T_CUBE:
        case T_CYL:
        case T_PYR:
// close the poly, no need to transform 1st point again
            pgdi[fi->ni].x = pgdi[0].x;
            pgdi[fi->ni].y = pgdi[0].y;
            break;
    }
    G3D_GEnv_Polygon(genv,(LPPOINT)&pgdi,(long)fi->ni+1,NULL,hbr);
    DeleteObject(hbr);
}
```

The object surface properties, a hardcoded RGB to CRT conversion (similar to the intensity-to-grayscale mapping to come), and the **PALETTERGB** macro combine to create a brush. The RGB palette must be selected into the DC of both the client area and the offscreen canvas for this to function correctly. Finally, the brush and the passed-in DC that corresponds to the offscreen canvas feed the *G3D_GEnv_Polygon* output primitive. Even though the color space conversion is hardcoded here instead of using *WL_Color_RGBtoCRT*, this is not necessarily as bad as it looks. Remember this does depend on the RGB palette, so an implied coupling of this function to the color space, palette, and conversion already existed. Plus we get one less function call. This is bypassing the API, but again as long as you understand what you are doing and why, the impact at this level is approximately three lines of code.

Listing 10-72 shows another block of code from the internals of the image view window class; this one is concerned with palette settings. You see the dual specifications, the client DC and the offscreen canvas, that keep attributes in sync. There are three different palette settings. The RGB palette is used for the solid rendering type indicated by value CMD_SOLID. If color post-processing has created or "genned" a palette, that palette is used. The default for all other modes is the gray palette that you will see later in more detail. Figure 10-27 contains an example solid-color image that has been grayscaled in an image editor and touched up with the statistics.

Listing 10-72. Attribute Control for Solid-Color Hidden Line Rendering

```
...
   if ( rtype == CMD_SOLID )
   {
      G3D_GEnv_SetVal(pv->genv,ID_SCREENPALETTE,(DWORD)hprgb);
      pv->hpOld = SelectPalette(hDC,hprgb,0);
   }
   else if ( bPosts && hpgen != NULL)
   {
      G3D_GEnv_SetVal(pv->genv,ID_SCREENPALETTE,(DWORD)hpgen);
      pv->hpOld = SelectPalette(hDC,hpgen,0);
   }
   else
   {
```

Listing 10-72. *(cont.)*

```
    G3D_GEnv_SetVal(pv->genv,ID_SCREENPALETTE,(DWORD)hpprn);
    pv->hpOld = SelectPalette(hDC,hpprn,0);
  }
  G3D_GEnv_Use(pv->genv,ID_SCREENPALETTE);
  RealizePalette(hDC);
...
```

Figure 10-27.   Solid-Color HLHSR Touched Up

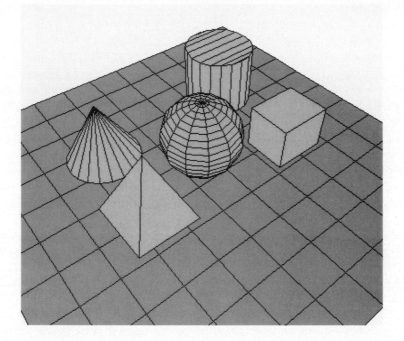

Flat-Shaded HLHSR

Flat-shaded rendering depends on a subset of the mathematical formulation of the illumination model, based on surface physics and optics, that is implemented in ray-trace mode. Flat shading is also called diffuse shading, after the dominant term in this model, the diffuse term. This is a simple model, easy to understand and implement.

Earlier, Equation 10-3 contained the diffuse term but didn't show the ambient one. Equation 10-15 contains both terms that the flat shader uses, the ambient and the diffuse. The ambient term is simply the global ambient illumination Ia times the k_a surface coefficient for the surface. The summation simply implies a loop, as you will see.

Equation 10-15.   Flat Shading with Both Terms

$$I = I_a k_a + kd \sum_{j=l}^{j=ls} I_l(\overline{N} * \overline{L}j)$$

Listing 10-73 implements *DrawFlatShadedFace*. It follows the same projection, mapping, and drawing process, but the edges are filled in. First, the face normal is retrieved using *GetFaceNorm* before the projection step. Once the mapping step is done, function *ShadePoly* implements the illumination model. Once an intensity is calculated, *PerformGray* takes the current grayscale method and generates the grayscale value used to select a gray brush. The grayscale is supported by an *InitGrayPalette*, *InitGrayBrushArray*, and *FreeGrayBrushArray* triplet much like the RGB support. *PerformGray* uses the gray method to generate a grayscale intensity that is used with the gray brush array rgbGray variable to feed *G3D_GEnv_Polygon*. Chapter 11 covers grayscaling and colorizing in detail.

Listing 10-73.   DrawFlatShadedFace

```
void DrawFlatShadedFace(LPOBJECT this,HPFACE fi,LPVERTEX lpvt,
                        VWWND * pv,HISTWND * ph,HDC hDC) {
    HBRUSH       hbr, hOldBrush;
    POINT        pgdi[5];
    COLORREF     cr;
    int          i,run;
    long         col,xv1,xv2,yv1,yv2;
    LPEX3DOBJECT lp3DObj;
    LPOBJECT     LightSource;
    VECTOR4D     vpt,P,vN,vL;
    LPLIGHTSRC   l ;
//
// get vertex normal at p
// project and map
//
    GetFaceNorm(*fi,lpvt,&P,&vN);
    for ( i = 0; i < fi->ni; i++)    {
        vpt = lpvt->vp[fi->indx[i+1]];
        G3D_Xfrm_ProjectPoint((LPVECTOR4D)&vpt,vpt,
                 vtype == CMD_PERSP ? PERSPECTIVE : PARALLEL );
        G3D_Coords_UsertoDev(pv->genv,
                             vpt.x,vpt.y, &xv1,&yv1);
        pgdi[i].x = (int)xv1;
        pgdi[i].y = (int)yv1;
    }
    switch(this->o_type)    {
      default:
      case T_PLANE:
      case T_SPHERE:
      case T_CONE:
      case T_CUBE:
      case T_CYL:
      case T_PYR:
```

Listing 10-73. (*cont.*)

```
// close the poly, no need to transform 1st point again
        pgdi[fi->ni].x = pgdi[0].x;
        pgdi[fi->ni].y = pgdi[0].y;
        break;
    }
//
// apply illumination model
// map to gray, draw flat shaded polygon
//
    ShadePoly(pv,&pv->mWorld->LoclW,this,vN,P,&Intensity);
    PerformGray(&Intensity,&col,gtype);
    fi->i = Intensity;
    run    = max( 0,col);
    run    = min( NUMGRAYCOL,col);
    G3D_GEnv_Polygon(pv->genv,(LPPOINT)&pgdi, (long)fi->ni+1,
                    (DWORD)hNullPen,(DWORD)rgbGray[max(run,0)]);
// force a render of the hist alternate view draw buffer
    if ( bHists ){
        G3D_Hist_Set(ph->lph,1 + run);
    }
}
```

The colorizing process is supported by the histogramming, and *G3D_Hist_Set* retains this face's value for use by the quantizing code. This is based on a 236-slot histogram, fitting into the Windows palette limitations. A final detail is the use of the NULL brush to eliminate edge lines. This makes the shading appear smoother, since it is unbroken by underlying structural lines.

Listing 10-74 shows the implementation of *ShadePoly*. *ShadePoly* conveniently hides the necessity of iterating across the light list and applying the illumination model. You then see the light source access by next-pointer, the usage of *MakeLightVec* to get the light input to the diffuse term, and the invocation of *FlatIntensityCalc* in the loop, culminating in the summation of values.

Listing 10-74. ShadePoly

```
void WINAPI ShadePoly(VWWND    * pv,
                      LPVECTOR4D TotW,
                      LPOBJECT   Object,
                      VECTOR4D   Normal, VECTOR4D   Point,
                      LPVECTOR4D Color)
{
    LPOBJECT   LightSource;
    VECTOR4D   vpt,P,vN,vL;
    LPLIGHTSRC l ;
//
```

```
// use p to calculate vector from light to face
// use l,n to calculate vertex intensity
//
   LightSource  = pv->mWorld->Scene->LightList;
   while (LightSource)                /* for each source */
   {
      VECTOR4D ti = {0.0,0.0,0.0,1.0};
      l          = (LPLIGHTSRC) LightSource-> o_edata ;
      MakeLightVec(LightSource,Point,&vL);
//
      FlatIntensityCalc(pv,Object->o_surfprops,
                        vL,l->light_rgb,Normal,&ti);
      Color->x  += (TotW->x*ti.x);
      Color->y  += (TotW->y*ti.y);
      Color->z  += (TotW->z*ti.z);
//
      LightSource = LightSource->next;
   }
}
```

That brings us to *FlatIntensityCalc*. See Listing 10-75 for the implementation of this function. Using the normal and the viewpoint, it does the NdotL light visibility test to determine whether the face gets ambient-only or ambient-plus-diffuse illumination. Remember, even if the face is turned away from the light but visible (it had to be visible to get here) it gets ambient. If it is visible and turned toward the light, it gets ambient plus diffuse illumination.

Listing 10-75.   FlatIntensityCalc

```
void WINAPI FlatIntensityCalc(VWWND * pv,SURFPROPS o_surfprops,
            VECTOR4D L,VECTOR4D LCol,VECTOR4D vN,LPVECTOR4D vI)
{
  VECTOR4D Ambient,Diffuse,Specular;
  VECTOR4D Color = {0.0,0.0,0.0,1.0};
  double   dist,CosTheta,CosAlpha;
  VECTOR4D Ref,temp;

  dist = G3D_V4D_VMag4D(L);
  G3D_V4D_VNorm4D(&L,L);
  CosTheta=G3D_V4D_VDot4D(vN, L);
// ambient only
  if(CosTheta <= 0.0){
    CalcAmbient(o_surfprops,&Ambient);
  }
  else{
//
// ambient and diffuse component
```

Listing 10-75. *(cont.)*

```
//

    CalcAmbient(o_surfprops,&Ambient);
    CalcDiffuse(o_surfprops,LCol,vN,CosTheta,&Diffuse);
//
// sum components
//
    G3D_V4D_VAdd4D(&Color,Ambient,Diffuse);
    G3D_V4D_VAdd4D(vI,*vI,Color);
  }
}
```

The ambient term is implemented by function *CalcAmbient*. The Ia global illumination in the scene description is multiplied by the surf_ka coefficient value. The diffuse term is implemented by function *CalcDiffuse*. This is a little more complicated, but if you read Equation 10-15 over again I think you'll see what's happening. The NdotL term is used, along with the surf_kd coefficient, the surface color, and the light color to calculate the intensity. Listing 10-76 contains this code. Figure 10-28 shows the result in a grayscaled, flat-shaded image. The difference between this and the solid-color image in grayscale is significant, but nothing when compared to the quality of the ray-traced images.

Listing 10-76.   Shading Term Functions

```
void WINAPI CalcAmbient(SURFPROPS o_surfprops, LPVECTOR4D vI)
{
   G3D_V4D_VSet4D(vI,
            o_surfprops.surf_ka.x*Ia.x*o_surfprops.surf_color[0],
            o_surfprops.surf_ka.y*Ia.y*o_surfprops.surf_color[1],
            o_surfprops.surf_ka.z*Ia.z*o_surfprops.surf_color[2],
            ONE4D);
}
void WINAPI CalcDiffuse(SURFPROPS o_surfprops, VECTOR4D LCol,
                        VECTOR4D vN, double NdotL,LPVECTOR4D vI)
{
   G3D_V4D_VSet4D(vI,
            LCol.x*o_surfprops.surf_kd.x*o_surfprops.surf_color[0],
            LCol.y*o_surfprops.surf_kd.y*o_surfprops.surf_color[1],
            LCol.z*o_surfprops.surf_kd.z*o_surfprops.surf_color[2],
            ONE4D);
   G3D_V4D_VScale4D(vI, NdotL, *vI);
}
```

You have now finished the manipulation and rendering of polygons. Visibility boils down to "NdotV"; while shading boils down to "NdotL." Just say "NdotV" for visibility and "NdotL" for lighting; it is almost mnemonic. Hidden-polygon mode also involves a granularity switch from the object-centric to the face-centric, huge pointers and blocks of memory, sorting, palettes, output, attributes, and shading.

Figure 10-28. Flat-Shaded Image in Grayscale

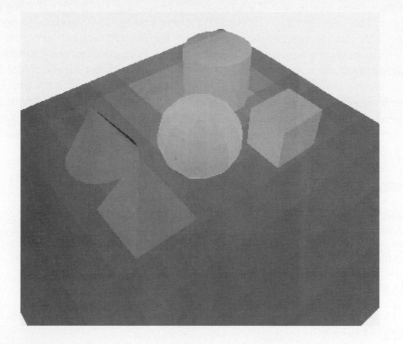

Rendering III: Shading and Drawing Ray-Traced Objects

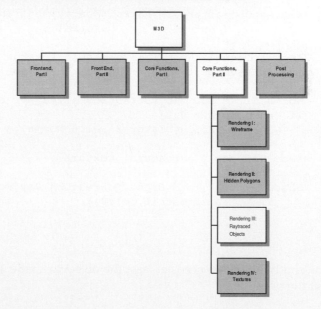

The ray-trace rendering process ends our consideration of the basic illumination model; all that remains after this is to examine procedural texturing. The ray-tracing process has been split into two parts, visibility and rendering, and is enhanced by the texturing process. I covered the visibility process earlier; now it's time to complete the circle.

The visibility process left us with an object and an intersection, in the NearestObj and NearestHit variables. Listing 10-77 picks up where Listing 10-38 left off with the code in function *Trace*. The process from *GetIsectPt* (where Listing 10-38 ended) to *ShadePoint* is shown here. Once the intersection is known from *GetIsectPt*, we can generate the normal using the *normal* mapping function. Each object contains its own normal function accessed from the mapping function. With the normal in hand, after a direction check, the *ShadePoint* function applies the illumination model. This is conceptually similar to the process for polygons, where *ShadePoly* was used. Within the *ShadePoint* function, the simple application of the ambient, diffuse, and specular terms is combined with the recursive simulation of "bounces" between objects, if they are reflective. The final touch of textures makes the pictures even prettier.

Listing 10-77.   Trace—The Rest of the Story

```
...
//
//    If we get here, we know that Ray has intersected an object
//    use the parameter MinT to calculate point of intersection.
//
      GetIsectPt(Ray->r_origin,Ray->r_direction,MinT,&Point);
//
//    Now find the normal to the intersected object at the point
//    of intersection.
//
       NearestObj->o_procs->normal(NearestObj, &Nearesthit, Point,
                                   &Normal);
//
//    Check to see if Normal is pointing towards Ray. If not
//    we must reverse the direction of the Normal.
//
       NormalDir = G3D_V4D_VDot4D(Normal,Ray->r_direction);
       if (NormalDir > 0.0)
          G3D_V4D_VScale4D(&Normal,-1.0,Normal);
//
//    shade and apply procedural texture
//
       ShadePoint(pv,TotW,Depth,NearestObj,Ray,Normal,Point,
                 &Nearesthit,Color);
    }
}
```

The shading process needs at least the object to shade, the point to shade, and the normal at the point.

Normal Generation

Normal generation provides a surface normal vector for the shading process. The normals are, in turn, made into unit vectors by using the *G3D_V4D_Mag4D* function. You should again notice the distinction between the normal vector of a surface and the process of "normalizing" a vector to make it of unit magnitude. The normal is used in shading calculations; the normalizing process is used to make the resultant vector be of magnitude 1. This unit vector can then be used in any calculations, including iterative, without worrying about multiplication or division causing floating-point overflow or underflow. This is a very important property when you're doing numerical calculations on a machine with limited range. While the pure mathematics may be able to deal with large numbers, there is a limit on the size of a number your machine may be able to handle. Chapter 5 dealt with this issue, in relation to the memory buffer and value storage.

With that out of the way, the *normal* mapping function is easy to read at the *Trace* function level. Each object contains a normal function, and the function-pointer technique gives the name space some uniformity. Within each normal function either a calculation is performed or a pre-stored value is returned. We now need to consider each object in turn: sphere, plane, cylinder, cone, box, and pyramid.

The sphere normal function, *SphereNormal* (Listing 10-78), calculates the normal as the vector from the center to the point of intersection, as shown in Figure 10-29. This is calculated using a simple subtraction and *G3D_V4D_VSub4D*, then "normalized" using *G3D_V4D_VNorm4D*.

Listing 10-78.   SphereNormal

```
int SphereNormal(LPOBJECT this,LPISECT hit,VECTOR4D P,LPVECTOR4D N)
{
   LPSPHERE sp ;

   sp = (LPSPHERE) this -> o_adata ;

   G3D_V4D_VSub4D(N, P, sp -> sph_center);
   G3D_V4D_VNorm4D(N, *N);
   return 1;
}
```

The plane normal is the same across an infinite plane, so we can pre-calculate it. This is only possible because no editing operations are supported in the manipulation process. If the plane moved, we would have to recalculate the normal, but it would remain constant across the surface. Listing 10-79 contains *PlaneNormal*, the plane version of the *normal* mapping function. It uses the void pointer o_adata to access and return the stored plane normal. Figure 10-30 shows the geometry involved; you can see from this that the normal vector is a constant.

Figure 10-29. **Sphere Normal Calculation**

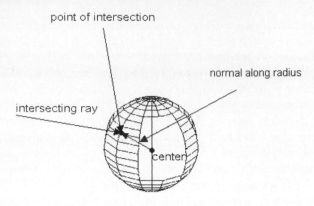

Listing 10-79. **PlaneNormal**

```
int PlaneNormal(LPOBJECT this,LPISECT  hit,VECTOR4D P,LPVECTOR4D N)
{
   LPPLANE  pl ;
//
   pl  = (LPPLANE) this -> o_adata ;
   N->x = pl->pl_normal.x;
   N->y = pl->pl_normal.y;
   N->z = pl->pl_normal.z;
   return 1;
}
```

Figure 10-30. **Plane Normal Geometry**

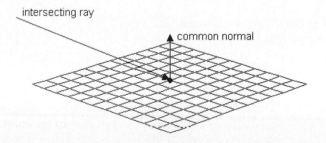

The cylinder normal is calculated by *CylinderNormal*, shown in Listing 10-80. As you would expect, it depends on the sub-components that make up the cylinder object — the two endcaps and the sheet. If the ray intersects one of the endcaps, as identified by the face ID, then *GetCircleNormal* is invoked; otherwise, it uses *GetQuadricNormal* to get the sheet normal at the point. The cone object likewise shares these two functions. Figures 10-31 and 10-32 depict the sheet and endcap situation.

Listing 10-80. CylinderNormal

```
int CylinderNormal(LPOBJECT this, LPISECT  hit, VECTOR4D P,
                   LPVECTOR4D N) {
   LPQUADRIC c ;
   double    t;
//
   c = (LPQUADRIC) this -> o_adata ;
   switch(hit->isect_face_id) {
      case 0:
         t = GetCircleNormal(&(c->q_endcaps[0]),P,N);
         break;
      case 1:
         t = GetCircleNormal(&(c->q_endcaps[1]),P,N);
         break;
      case 2:
         t = GetQuadricNormal(c,P,N);
         break;
   }
   return 1;
}
```

Figure 10-31.   Cylinder Normal Geometry

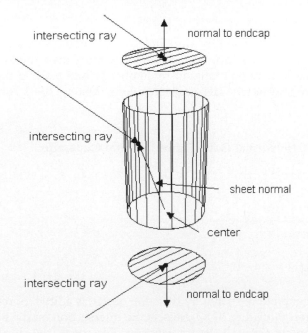

Figure 10-32.   Cone Normal Geometry

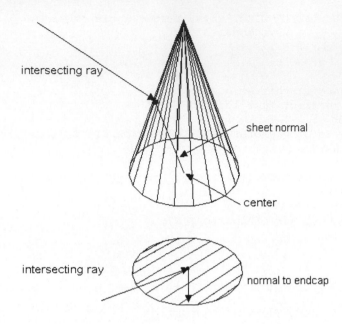

The endcap normal as generated by *GetCircleNormal* uses exactly the same code as *PlaneNormal*. These five lines are duplicated for clarity more than anything. We maintain a separate name space so we don't have to remember (while reading the code) that the circle is a plane figure and nearly identical to a plane. Listing 10-81 contains these five lines.

Listing 10-81.   GetCircleNormal Plane Figure Normal Generation

```
double WINAPI GetCircleNormal(LPCIRCLE c, VECTOR4D P, LPVECTOR4D N)
{
    N->x = c->c_normal.x;
    N->y = c->c_normal.y;
    N->z = c->c_normal.z;
    return 1;
}
```

The sheet normal generation, shared by the cone object, is a little more complex. Function *GetQuadricNormal* in Listing 10-82 projects the intersection on the base. The normal is a vector from this point through the intersection. For cones, the slope of the sheet is factored in; for cylinders, this term evaluates to 0. Figure 10-31 shows the cylinder with its endcaps and sheet exploded to show the individual normal processes.

Listing 10-82.   GetQuadricNormal

```
double WINAPI GetQuadricNormal(LPQUADRIC q, VECTOR4D P, LPVECTOR4D N)
{
    VECTOR4D vt;
    double   dt;

    dt = - (G3D_V4D_VDot4D(P,q->q_w)+q->q_bdot);
    G3D_V4D_VScale4D(&vt,dt,q->q_w);
    G3D_V4D_VAdd4D(&vt,vt,P);

    G3D_V4D_VSub4D(N,vt,q->q_bcenter);
    G3D_V4D_VNorm4D(N,*N);

    G3D_V4D_VScale4D(&vt,q->q_slope,q->q_w);
    G3D_V4D_VAdd4D(N,vt,*N);
    G3D_V4D_VNorm4D(N,*N);
    return 1;
}
```

The cone object normal function is *ConeNormal*. As advertised, this function uses *GetCircleNormal* and *GetQuadricNormal*. Remember *OrientQuadric*? It calculated the slope parameter used by *GetQuadricNormal* for cones. Listing 10-83 contains this code. You can see the similarity of geometry between Figures 10-32 and 10-31, the difference between them is in the code of *GetQuadricNormal* when the cone slope adjusts the result.

Listing 10-83.   ConeNormal

```
int
ConeNormal(LPOBJECT this, LPISECT  hit, VECTOR4D P, LPVECTOR4D N)
{
    LPQUADRIC  c ;
    double     t;
//

    c = (LPQUADRIC) this -> o_adata ;

    switch(hit->isect_face_id)
    {
        case 0:
            t = GetCircleNormal(&(c->q_endcaps[0]),P,N);
            break;
        case 2:
            t = GetQuadricNormal(c,P,N);
            break;
    }
    return 1;
}
```

That brings us to the box object. Boxes are built of six rectangles. The rectangle is an extension of the infinite plane; it's another plane figure like the circle. The base cube *normal* mapping function, *BoxNormal*, is shown in Listing 10-84. It delegates all normal generation to *GetRectangleNormal* and uses the face ID to decide which normal to return.

Listing 10-84.   BoxNormal

```
int BoxNormal(LPOBJECT this,LPISECT hit,VECTOR4D P,LPVECTOR4D N)
{
   LPSIMPLENGON cA ;
   double       t;
//

   cA  = (LPSIMPLENGON) this -> o_adata ;
   switch(hit->isect_face_id)
   {
      case 1:
         t = GetRectangleNormal(&(cA->ng_faces[1]),P,N);
         break;
      case 2:
         t = GetRectangleNormal(&(cA->ng_faces[2]),P,N);
         break;
      case 3:
         t = GetRectangleNormal(&(cA->ng_faces[3]),P,N);
         break;
      case 4:
         t = GetRectangleNormal(&(cA->ng_faces[4]),P,N);
         break;
      case 5:
         t = GetRectangleNormal(&(cA->ng_faces[5]),P,N);
         break;
      case 6:
         t = GetRectangleNormal(&(cA->ng_faces[6]),P,N);
         break;
   }
   return 1;
}
```

GetRectangleNormal is shown in Listing 10-85; it simply restates the *PlaneNormal* code in a rectangle wrapper. The same five lines of code (three assignments, the return, and the formal function declaration itself) are repeated here. We don't need the geometry figure here, since the plane figure code for rectangles, like that for circles, repeats the infinite-plane geometry. As an aside, this implementation of a cube in ray-trace mode resembles the polygon mode quite a bit in its face-centric approach. This "polygonalization" strategy can actually be quite valuable and general.

Listing 10-85. GetRectangleNormal

```
double WINAPI GetRectangleNormal(LPSIMPLEPOLY p, VECTOR4D P,
                                         LPVECTOR4D N)
{

  N->x = p->sp_normal.x;
  N->y = p->sp_normal.y;
  N->z = p->sp_normal.z;
  return 1;
}
```

This brings us to the last object in the normal generation process: the pyramid.

Listing 10-86 presents the pyramid normal function *PyramidNormal*. This function in turn depends on *GetRectangleNormal* and *GetTriangleNormal*.

Listing 10-86. PyramidNormal

```
int
PyramidNormal(LPOBJECT this,LPISECT hit,VECTOR4D P,LPVECTOR4D N)
{
      LPSIMPLENGON cA ;
  double        t;
//
  cA  = (LPSIMPLENGON) this -> o_adata ;
  switch(hit->isect_face_id)
  {
    case 1:
       t = GetTriangleNormal(&(cA->ng_faces[1]),P,N);
       break;
    case 2:
       t = GetTriangleNormal(&(cA->ng_faces[2]),P,N);
       break;
    case 3:
       t = GetTriangleNormal(&(cA->ng_faces[3]),P,N);
       break;
    case 4:
       t = GetTriangleNormal(&(cA->ng_faces[4]),P,N);
       break;
    case 5:
       t = GetRectangleNormal(&(cA->ng_faces[5]),P,N);
       break;
  }
  return 1;
}
```

With the face ID guiding the way, *PyramidNormal* invokes the correct sub-function. The supporting function *GetTriangleNormal* is shown in Listing 10-87. This is the last time you'll see these five lines repeated. The pyramid normal process again needs no figure to depict the geometry involved; this is a straightforward duplication of the infinite-plane code. The approach depends on the intersection code using the Jordan curve theorem to correctly limit the intersections to those inside the plane figure. Once that detail is out of the way, the constant normal can then be returned.

Listing 10-87. GetTriangleNormal

```
double WINAPI GetTriangleNormal(LPSIMPLEPOLY tri,VECTOR4D P,
                                LPVECTOR4D N)
{

   N->x = tri->sp_normal.x;
   N->y = tri->sp_normal.y;
   N->z = tri->sp_normal.z;
   return 1;
}
```

The shading process itself remains. The intersection point provided by *GetIsectPt*, the normal generated by the **normal** mapping function, and the intersected object in NearestObj all combine to feed the shading process.

Shading

Now that we're done with the preliminaries, the *ShadePoint* function comes under our scope. This function, introduced in Listing 10-19 and repeated here in Listing 10-88, applies the local illumination model, does simple procedural texturing, and clamps the intensity values to the range [0,1].

Listing 10-88. ShadePoint

```
void WINAPI ShadePoint( VWWND     * pv,
                        LPVECTOR4D TotW,int Depth,
                        LPOBJECT   Object,
                        LPRAY      Ray,
                        VECTOR4D   Normal, VECTOR4D   Point,
                        LPISECT    hit,
                        LPVECTOR4D Color)  {
   VECTOR4D  TxtrColor = {ZERO4D,ZERO4D,ZERO4D,ONE4D};
   VECTOR4D  LoclColor = {ZERO4D,ZERO4D,ZERO4D,ONE4D};
//get color from local illumination model(a,d,s,and reflection)
   LocalReflShader(pv,TotW,Depth,
                   Object,Ray,Normal,Point,
                   &LoclColor);
//add texture
   Texture(pv,
           Object,Ray,Normal,Point,
            &TxtrColor);
   G3D_V4D_VAdd4D(Color,TxtrColor,LoclColor);
```

```
//clamping
   G3D_V4D_VSet4D(Color,
                     min(1.0,Color->x),
                     min(1.0,Color->y),
                     min(1.0,Color->z),
                     ONE4D);
   return;
}
```

The local illumination model is similar to the Phong model (with specular highlights) and simulates reflective objects using recursion. There are five textures supported here:

1. smooth (no texture),
2. grit,
3. checkerboard,
4. wood, and
5. marble.

These are known as *procedural textures*: a mathematical texturing function, dependent on the coordinates of the surface being texturized, assures perspective validity and requires a minimal database size. In addition, there is usually a necessary texture transformation that maps the texture to a specific surface.

In our case, these textures are applied by function *Texture* without a texture transformation. This is simpler to understand, but has a drastic side effect. Any change to the object changes the texture appearance. The desired effect is for the texture to stay in a constant relationship to the object, independent of any changes to the object. This is known as *transformation invariance*. The checkerboard, which is the simplest texture (besides smooth or no texture), is, by its nature, the closest to being invariant. The other textures are not quite so nice. For any single frame, this is acceptable, but any attempt at serious animation will have to contend with this issue.

The clamping step is critical, because the intensity value at some point is converted to a grayscale value in the range [0,255] by a simple multiplication. The result is used to index into the brush array and the histogram bin structure. A negative value, or a positive value greater than 255, will result in a serious program error.

The illumination model is implemented by *LocalReflShader*, Listing 10-89, which I will deal with at length.

Listing 10-89.   LocalReflShader

```
void WINAPI LocalReflShader(VWWND     * pv,
                            LPVECTOR4D TotW,int Depth,
                            LPOBJECT   Object,
                            LPRAY      Ray,
                            VECTOR4D   Normal,VECTOR4D   Point,
                            LPVECTOR4D Color)
{
   LPOBJECT   LightSource;
   RAY        LightRay,ReflectedRay;
```

Listing 10-89. (*cont.*)

```
    VECTOR4D  Ambient, Diffuse, Specular, LightColor, ReflColor, W;
    double    DistanceT,ldist,CosTheta,VdotL,CosAlpha,Shine;
//  Calculate the reflected ray R from normal N and incoming ray V.
    ReflectedRay.r_origin = Point; /* structure copy */
    MakeReflRay(&ReflectedRay.r_direction,Ray->r_direction,Normal);
//  Start the calculation of the color with ambient.
    CalcAmbient(Object->o_surfprops,&Ambient);
    G3D_V4D_VAdd4D(Color,Ambient,*Color);
    LightSource=pv->mWorld->Scene->LightList;
    while (LightSource)              /* for each source */
    {
//     Generate a ray from Point to light source of interest.
       DistanceT  = MakeLightRay(LightSource,Point,&LightRay);
       LightColor = GetLightColor(pv->mWorld->Scene,LightSource,
                                  Object,&LightRay,DistanceT);
       ldist      = G3D_V4D_VMag4D(LightRay.r_origin);
// Check to see if our object faces the light
       CosTheta = G3D_V4D_VDot4D(Normal,LightRay.r_direction);
       if ( ( CosTheta > 0.0) )      {
// diffuse component
          CalcDiffuse(Object->o_surfprops,LightColor,Normal,
                      CosTheta,&Diffuse);
          G3D_V4D_VAdd4D(Color,Diffuse,*Color);
       }

       CosAlpha = G3D_V4D_VDot4D(ReflectedRay.r_direction,
                                 LightRay.r_direction);
// add highlight
    if ((CosAlpha > 0.0) && (isSpecular(Object)) )  {
       CalcSpecular(Object->o_surfprops,LightColor,Normal,
                    CosAlpha,Specular);
       G3D_V4D_VAdd4D(Color, Specular,*Color);
    }
    LightSource = LightSource->next;
    }
// Now consider reflection
    if (Object->o_surfprops.surf_ior > 0.0)  {
       G3D_V4D_VMul4D(&W,pv->mWorld->ReflW,*TotW);
       Trace(pv,&W,Depth+1,&ReflectedRay,&ReflColor);
       Color->x += ReflColor.x * Object->o_surfprops.surf_ior * W.x;
       Color->y += ReflColor.y * Object->o_surfprops.surf_ior * W.y;
       Color->z += ReflColor.z * Object->o_surfprops.surf_ior * W.z;
    }
}
```

First, it generates the reflected vector R that is used in the specular and reflection calculations, using *MakeReflRay*. The formula for the reflected vector, shown in Equation 10-16, scales by -1 to account for the fact the L vector is in the opposite direction of the usual form of this equation, as shown before in Equation 10-5.

Equation 10-16.   Reflected Vector R

$$R = -2 * N * (LdotN) + L$$

Listing 10-90 implements this for you.

Listing 10-90.   MakeReflRay

```
void  WINAPI MakeReflRay(LPVECTOR4D ReflRDir,VECTOR4D Dir,
                         VECTOR4D N)
{
   double   t;
   VECTOR4D tN;

   t = -2.0 * G3D_V4D_VDot4D(Dir,N);
   G3D_V4D_VScale4D(&tN,t,N);
   G3D_V4D_VAdd4D(ReflRDir,tN,Dir);
}
```

The ambient term is evaluated next, using the same *CalcAmbient* function as the flat-shaded polygon mode rendering. This term is added into the intensity value using *G3D_V4D_VAdd4D.* The next step is to loop across the light source list and apply the rest of the local illumination model.

It uses the light source functions *MakeLightRay* and *GetLightColor*: first, to retrieve a ray describing the current light; then, to check for obscuring objects. This check for obscuring objects is sometimes called the "shadow feeler," because if the light is obscured a dark value will be used. With the light ray and color, the same visibility test of the dot product determines whether to add the diffuse term. If the object is visible at this point, the diffuse term is evaluated using *CalcDiffuse*; the same function that was used for the second part of the flat-shaded calculation. These calculations are why the flat-shader illumination model is a subset of ray-trace illumination. The light source loop and visibility test are the same as well, although *MakeLightVec* is used there and there are no light color, shadow feeler, or specular calculations.

The specular calculation here uses the dot product to test the reflected vector R for visibility, because the highlight may not be visible from certain camera/light combinations. If the test succeeds, the specular term is evaluated using *CalcSpecular*. This function is shown in Listing 10-91.

Listing 10-91.   CalcSpecular

```
void WINAPI CalcSpecular(SURFPROPS o_surfprops, VECTOR4D LCol,
                  VECTOR4D vN, DOUBLE CosAlpha,LPVECTOR4D vI)
{
    double   Shine;
    if ( CosAlpha < BIG )
       Shine = G3D_Math_Power(CosAlpha,o_surfprops.surf_shine);
    else
       Shine = o_surfprops.surf_shine;
```

Listing 10-91. (*cont.*)

```
G3D_V4D_VSet4D(vI,
               LCol.x * Shine * o_surfprops.surf_ks.x,
               LCol.y * Shine * o_surfprops.surf_ks.y,
               LCol.z * Shine * o_surfprops.surf_ks.z,ONE4D);
}
```

The *G3D_Math_Power* function and the surf_shine exponent raise the CosAlpha value according to the relation shown in Equation 10-17. This is similar to Equation 10-4 with the RdotV term replaced with the CosAlpha term to correspond to this implementation. There's a trick here that was used by Craig Lindley in *Practical Ray Tracing in C* (Wiley, 1992). He uses the reflected ray R that was just calculated, because the angle between it and the light source happens to be equivalent to the angle between the calculated incident vector. The nice thing about this is that it saves calculation time.

Equation 10-17.   Specular Term Revisited

$$specular\ term\ = ks \sum_{j=1}^{j=ls} I_l(cos(a))$$

The local illumination model is complete at this point. Now it is time to add the component of color that is due to the contribution of reflections. The surf_ior component is used (or misused, since this is really supposed to be for true transmission) as a test for reflective or not reflective. If the object is reflective, we use the reflective weight from the modeling environment with the total weight to calculate a new weight. We then call *Trace* in a recursive manner with this new weight and a depth of one greater than the current depth. This is how the ray-trace mode simulates the interaction of objects with each other. If the object has a property (that of a mirror) that dictates interaction, recursion is used to model the bounces. The weight and depth allow the depth-recursion test at the top of the *Trace* function to terminate the recursion and the weights help to clamp and avoid overdriving the lighting.

An indication of lighting overdrive is when an object gets extremely bright or even all-white. An even worse indication of overdrive is floating-point overflow. The power function is particularly vulnerable to this. The modeler, at a higher level, takes steps to limit the damage from overflow and other floating-point errors, but they are still disconcerting. This will become even more important if you extend the functionality of lights to support individual intensities (right now, they are all intensity 1), cone-shaped lights, or other directional lights.

Once the recursion returns, the color value is used to add into the intensity value. The illumination model ends there without performing refraction, or even supporting the more detailed consideration of other transport modes. For the last detailed word on transport modes if you are interested in exploring and extending, see Andrew Glassner's article "Surface Physics for Ray Tracing" in *An Introduction to Ray Tracing* (Academic Press, 1989), which covers the different transport modes and the formal physics behind illumination models.

That finishes the basic shading and leads back to *ShadePoint* and the procedural texturing step. If we omitted texturing, the world would appear as in Figure 10-33. Figure 10-34 shows the effect of textures, even simple ones. Every object except the plane has the smooth texture, and the plane has the checkerboard texture. The checkerboard pattern makes the image much more pleasing, and is an indication of what is next.

Figure 10-33.   Ray-Traced Rendition of Simple Scene

Figure 10-34.   Ray-Traced with One Texture — The Textured Infinite Plane

Rendering IV: Textures

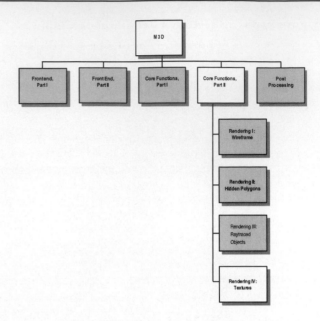

This section will introduce you to texturing in general, and then to the specific implementation details of the simple texturing provided by the modeler. The addition of even simple texturing, like that shown here, makes your images so much more pleasing that it's worth it — even without the ability to generate transformation-invariant textures.

Texture mapping includes a wide variety of techniques. They can be broadly categorized as:

- color perturbation using repeated patterns,
- color modulation using bitmaps, and
- surface perturbation using bump mapping.

The process of applying a bitmap is what we usually think of as texture mapping, but, as you can see, there's more to it than that. The color perturbation that occurs by using repeated patterns (the technique I use here) can range from the simple checkerboard and grit, to the more complex wood and marble that use a noise function, to even more esoteric patterns that are typically generated using a function. In a sense, the term itself is misleading because, with the exception of the bump mapping technique, the color values — not the surface shape or texture in the physical sense — are what is modified.

In addition, there are three concerns you must address for texture mapping:

1. What attribute of the object is to be modulated?
2. How is the texture mapping to be carried out? Or what is the mapping?
3. How should we handle artifacts (the issue of anti-aliasing)?

The texturing presented here deals with only the first concern, the attribute used to generate the texture. It carries out such a simple mapping that it generates artifacts. Bump mapping and the surface attribute that it modifies are not implemented here. To add bump mapping, you would typically do something like perturb the surface normal before *LocalReflShader* applies the illumination model. To add bitmap-based texture mapping, you would extend the texturing presented here to include a new type of material, with new material-specific data. This material is type "PIXMAP" (or some such) and the name of the bitmap to use would be specified either in the material file or by extending the OBJDEF record.

That leaves the process of using repeating patterns to modify or perturb the color of the surface. This process amounts to the use of small functions that generate values (procedures). These values are then used to perturb the existing color value. The [X,Y,Z] position is used in these calculations to generate a value in the texture space, which is then used to modify the color value that was calculated by the *LocalReflShader*. This is known as *procedural texturing*. As I've already mentioned, the whole issue of transformation invariance is ignored.

The [X,Y,Z] position should first be modified instead of being used directly to calculate color. The texture transformation allows a course correction to maintain an invariant appearance. This means that the texture transformation does the necessary operations to make a rotation/translation/scale-invariant texture mapping from the texture space to the object in world/eye coordinate space. If the object rotates, the texture should rotate. If the object is scaled, you have several choices: the patterns can get larger, or they can be repeated more times across the extent of the object.

In some cases, translation is not much of a problem, but in other cases it will significantly affect the appearance. For instance, when using a bitmap pattern, the application of the pattern could always begin at one edge. This would mean that object translation would not affect the texture mapping, since texture mapping occurs in the u-v space of the object. It is the u-v orientation of the object in relation to the orientation of the scene and the camera that, as well as scaling factors, affect the application of the bitmap in that case. On the other hand, the procedurally generated textures are heavily dependent on position; so translation does have an effect, after all. Without handling this transformation, it's futile to worry about artifacts and attempt any anti-aliasing.

This discussion barely scratches the surface of texture mapping. If you want more information, I'd suggest that you consult *Fundamentals of Three-Dimensional Computer Graphics* (Addison-Wesley, 1989) by Alan Watt and *Advanced Animation and Rendering Techniques* (Addison-Wesley, 1993) by Alan and Mark Watt. I can't say enough about these books. While Foley and van Dam cover the breadth of graphics, these books cover three-dimensional graphics for both the explorer and the practitioner. The article "Survey of Texture Mapping" by Paul Heckbert (*IEEE Computer Graphics and Applications*, November 1986) provides an older but still-valuable treatment and some very valuable references. Between all of these sources, you can find some real value if you wish to explore further and enhance your implementation.

With all that said and done, it is time to examine the texture implementation. As you already know, the textures provided here are:

- smooth,
- checkerboard,

- grit,
- wood, and
- marble.

The material table already defines a variety of textures with at least one of each type represented.

The smooth texture is really no texture at all. These objects have no perturbation applied to their color. Occasionally, an object may need a smooth appearance, and it is as easy to implement as the default case of a switch statement.

The checkerboard is a periodic texture. The pattern is repeated at a specified interval or period. Periodic textures also include, for example, waves. For the checkerboard, this is as simple as determining whether the point in/out of a test is in a dark or light checker. This is periodic based on position.

The grit texture is also extremely simple. A random number perturbs the surface to produce a slight variation across it, giving the appearance of surfaces like cement, dirt, or grass. The drawback is that it is too regular for realistic grass, but it does just fine for cement.

The wood and marble textures are based on a class of function known as *noise* functions. This produces a solid texture that, when applied to an objects' surface, makes it appear that the object was sculpted out of the material. Two authors (Darwyn R. Peachey with the paper "Solid Texturing of Complex Surfaces" and Ken Perlin with the paper "An Image Synthesizer," both in *SIGGRAPH Conference Proceedings*, 1985) are credited with independent and simultaneous proposals of this technique. Perlin, however, is usually the only one cited, probably because he provides enough of the math for the adventurous reader to see an implementation approach. This noise function needs to have three properties:

1. It is continuously defined in three-space — feed it [X,Y,Z] and a value comes back.
2. If two points are near in three-space, their values are "close."
3. If two points are far apart in three-space, their values are not correlated.

These last two create patterns that look like wood and marble, not a chaotic mess.

The master control function *Texture*, invoked by *ShadePoint*, is shown in Listing 10-92. It uses the texture ID and a switch statement to invoke the correct procedural texture. Notice the void-pointer access to get to the texture-specific data.

Listing 10-92. Texture Function

```
void WINAPI Texture(VWWND * pv,LPOBJECT Object, LPRAY IRay,
                VECTOR4D N, VECTOR4D IPt,LPVECTOR4D TexCol)
{
  LPEX3DOBJECT lp3DObj;
  VECTOR4D     OPt;
  int          x, y, z, rt;
  double       r;
```

```
lp3DObj = Object->o_edata;
switch(Object->o_surfprops.surf_tid)
{
  default:
  case SMOOTH:
      return;
      break;
  case CHECKER:
      Checker(pv->mWorld->Scene->scanX*10,
              (Object->o_surfprops.surf_texdata),
               IPt,TexCol);
      return;
      break;
  case WOOD:
      r = max(lp3DObj->l_transforms.S.x,
              lp3DObj->l_transforms.S.y);
      r = max(r,lp3DObj->l_transforms.S.z);
      Wood(r,(Object->o_surfprops.surf_texdata),
           IPt,TexCol);
      break;
  case GRIT:
      Grit(IPt,TexCol);
      break;
  case MARBLE:
      r = max(lp3DObj->l_transforms.S.x,
              lp3DObj->l_transforms.S.y);
      r = max(r,lp3DObj->l_transforms.S.z);
      Marble(pv,r,(Object->o_surfprops.surf_texdata),
             IPt, TexCol);
      break;
  case TURBULENTMARBLE:
      G3D_V4D_VSub4D(&OPt,IPt,pv->mWorld->Scene->Eye.view_from);
      r = max(lp3DObj->l_transforms.S.x,
              lp3DObj->l_transforms.S.y);
      r = max(r,lp3DObj->l_transforms.S.z);
      TurbulentMarble(pv,r,(Object->o_surfprops.surf_texdata),
                      OPt, TexCol);
      break;
  }
}
```

For the smooth texture (the default), no action is done.

The checkerboard texture invokes function *Checker*, using the texture-specific data and the current point.

The grit texture is implemented by the *Grit* function. This one is so simple that it has no texture-specific data but is dependent on the current point.

The wood texture is implemented by function *Wood*. It, too, uses texture-specific data and the current point.

There are two forms of marble — basic and turbulent. The material table supports entries with the "basicmarble" and "italianmarble" keywords to implement this. Functions *Marble* and *TurbulentMarble* provide the procedural textures. They have the same texture-specific data usage and current-point dependency that marks the wood and checkerboard textures.

The checkerboard texture is very simple. It uses the current point and some very simple logic to determine the color of square, dark or light, a given point belongs to. This is shown in Listing 10-93, which implements the *Checker* function. It uses texture-specific data depending on the result of the test for light or dark square. For the checkerboard texture, it contains the color values to use for light and dark colors. Figure 10-35 illustrates this texture.

Figure 10-35.   Checkerboard Plane

Listing 10-93.   Checker Function for Checkerboard Texture

```
void Checker(long scale,LPCHECKDATA cd,VECTOR4D Pt, LPVECTOR4D TexCol)
{
  long period;
  double x, y, z;
//
    x=((long)((Pt.x+scale)*cd->ch_period));
    y=((long)((Pt.y+scale)*cd->ch_period));
```

```
  period = (long)(x+y);
  if( (period%2) == 1)
    G3D_V4D_VSet4D(TexCol,
                    cd->ch_color1.x,
                    cd->ch_color1.y,
                    cd->ch_color1.z,ONE4D);
 else
    G3D_V4D_VSet4D(TexCol,
                    cd->ch_color2.x,
                    cd->ch_color2.y,
                    cd->ch_color2.z,ONE4D);
}
```

The grit texture is even easier to understand. It uses random numbers to generate a value that is added to the underlying color. The *Grit* function in Listing 10-94 shows this implementation. You can see the use of the **rand** RTL routine and the simple calculation involved. This is forced into the range of [.8,1] by the addition of. 8 to whatever the random-number calculation generates. Figure 10-36 shows an example of this texture.

Figure 10-36. Grit Sphere

Listing 10-94. Grit Function for Grit Texture

```
void Grit(VECTOR4D Pt, LPVECTOR4D TexCol)
{
  double d,r,rt;
//
    rt=rand()%32767;
    rt =rt/32768.0;
    d = r*.17;
    TexCol->x = d;
    TexCol->y = d;
    TexCol->z = d;
}
```

The wood texture and the function that implements it, like marble, depend on a noise function. This function provides a pseudo-random value for an [X,Y,Z] triple. This value is used to generate the perturbed color. The noise function is implemented as a lookup in an array. The array is allocated and initialized by function *InitNoise*. The memory for the array is deallocated by function *FreeNoise*. These are shown in Listings 10-95 and 10-96.

Listing 10-95. InitNoise Noise Array Allocator and Initializer

```
LPNOISEDATA FAR PASCAL InitNoise()
{
   LPNOISEDATA lpNoise;
   long ix, iy, iz;
   long xx, yy, zz;
//
   lpNoise = (LPNOISEDATA)WL_Mem_Alloc(GHND,sizeof(NOISEDATA));
   if ( !lpNoise )
      return FALSE;
// set seed, initialize lattice
  srand(GetTickCount());
   for(ix=0;ix<=MAXNOISE;ix++)
   {
for(iy=0;iy<=MAXNOISE;iy++)
      {
   for(iz=0;iz<=MAXNOISE;iz++)
         {
lpNoise->noise[ix][iy][iz] = (ROUND(rand()%12000));
xx = (ix==MAXNOISE) ? 0L : ix;
yy = (iy==MAXNOISE) ? 0L : iy;
zz = (iz==MAXNOISE) ? 0L : iz;
lpNoise->noise[ix}[iy][iz]=lpNoise->noise[xx][yy][zz];
         }
       }
   }
   return lpNoise;
}
```

Listing 10-96.   Noise Array Memory Deallocation

```
void FAR PASCAL FreeNoise(LPNOISEDATA lpN)
{
   WL_Mem_Free(lpN);
}
```

Function *Noise*, shown in Listing 10-97, uses the array allocated and initialized by *InitNoise*. It calculates a value based on code contained in Alan Watt's *Fundamentals of Three-Dimensional Computer Graphics* (Addison-Wesley, 1989), as the comment indicates. This is a line-by-line copy of the example implementation contained there.

Listing 10-97.   Noise

```
//
double FAR PASCAL Noise(LPNOISEDATA lpN,
                        double x, double y, double z) {
//
// based on Perlin's (1985) noise function - ideas found in Alan
// Watt's Fundamentals of Three-Dimensional Computer Graphics
//
   int     ix, iy, iz;
   double  ox, oy, oz;
   double  n00,n01,n10,n11;
   double  n0,n1,rnoise;
   int     n;
// offset to positive
   x=dabs(x);
   y=dabs(y);
   z=dabs(z);
// find lattice coords and offset (fractional part)
   ix=G3D_Math_Trunc(x)%MAXNOISE;
   iy=G3D_Math_Trunc(y)%MAXNOISE;
   iz=G3D_Math_Trunc(z)%MAXNOISE;
   ox=x-(int)x;
   oy=y-(int)y;
   oz=z-(int)z;
//interpolate
   n    = lpN->noise[ix][iy][iz];
   n00  = n + ox*(lpN->noise[ix+1][iy][iz] - n);

   n    = lpN->noise[ix][iy][iz+1];
   n01  = n + ox*(lpN->noise[ix+1][iy][iz+1] - n);

   n    = lpN->noise[ix][iy+1][iz+1];
   n10  = n + ox*(lpN->noise[ix+1][iy+1][iz] - n);

   n    = lpN->noise[ix][iy+1][iz+1];
   n11  = n + ox*(lpN->noise[ix+1][iy+1][iz+1] - n);
```

Listing 10-99. *(cont.)*

```
else {
    if (( dd < 9 ) || ( dd >= 12 )) {
        d = dabs(d - G3D_Math_Trunc(d/17)*17-10.5)*0.1538462;
        i = .4 +.3 *d + .2*Noise(pv->mWorld->Noise,Pt.x/(scale*10),
                            Pt.y/(scale*10),Pt.z/(scale*10));
    }
    else
        i = .2 + .2 * Noise(pv->mWorld->Noise,Pt.x/(scale*10),
                            Pt.y/(scale*10),Pt.z/(scale*10));
}
TexCol->x = .9 * i;
TexCol->y = .8 * i;
TexCol->z = .6 * i;
}
```

The wood texture uses this same scheme to account for scale. This means that there are several bands of texture on a sphere, for instance, instead of just one band. And the band sizes are sensitive to the scaling of the sphere instead of just growing in width. This is true both for wood grain and marble swirls. This scheme, while simple, does have its limits. For instance, it would be difficult to give adjacent objects of different size the same texture.

Going back to the basic marble, the bad thing about it is that it's basically just several bands of varying widths, seventeen to be exact, that are yanked around randomly to simulate swirls. While this is okay, as illustrated in Figure 10-38, there is a better method. The Perlin paper cited previously mentions a turbulence function and a method of "turbulating" a color using the *Noise* function. The *Turbulence* function in Listing 10-100 does this turbulating and the *TurbulentMarble* function of Listing 10-101 uses it to create better-looking swirls. See Figure 10-39 for the turbulent look.

Listing 10-100.   Turbulence

```
void Turbulence(VWWND * pv,VECTOR4D Pt,double far * t)
{
    double scale;

    scale = 1.0;
    while (scale > 1/64.0)
    {
        *t += dabs(Noise(pv->mWorld->Noise,Pt.x/scale,
                        Pt.y/scale,Pt.z/scale)*scale);
        scale /= 2.0;
    }
    return ;
}
```

Figure 10-38. **Basic Marble Sphere**

Figure 10-39. **Turbulent Marble Sphere**

Listing 10-101.   TurbulentMarble

```
void TurbulentMarble(VWWND *pv,double r,LPMARBLEDATA md,
                     VECTOR4D Pt, LPVECTOR4D TexCol){
  double dd;
//
  Pt.x+=1000;
  Pt.y+=1000;
  Pt.z+=1000;
  Turbulence(pv,Pt,&dd);
  Pt.x-=1000;
  Pt.y-=1000;
  Pt.z-=1000;
  TexCol->x = dabs(G3D_Math_SinR(Pt.x + dd));
  TexCol->y = dabs(G3D_Math_SinR(Pt.y + dd));
  TexCol->z = dabs(G3D_Math_SinR(Pt.z + dd));

}
```

Figure 10-40.   Checker, Wood, Both Marble Variants, and Smooth Mirror Textures

That concludes textures. They really do let you do a lot. The basic table scene you saw in Figure 10-20 is here again in Figure 10-40, with only some minor changes and the textures added. The difference is quite dramatic.

Now all our graphics pieces are in place, so let's construct the modeler!

Summary

At this point, we can view images that show a three-dimensional world. The images can be generated in five renditions:

- wireframe,
- monochrome hidden line,
- solid-color hidden line,
- flat-shaded hidden line, and
- ray-traced.

This chapter focused on ways to accomplish all of these renderings.

In all modes, the transformation, visibility, and rendering processes were dominated by the architectural technique of the mapping functions and the linked lists, across which the mapping functions are applied. The choice of algorithm for the polygon visibility process (the z-sort using the quicksort algorithm) implies a hard limitation on the maximum size of a scene, upwards of a quarter-of-a-million polygons.

The gory details of the polygon-mode visibility and shading process were explored, following up on the high-level view presented in Chapter 2. In the same manner, I covered ray-tracing visibility and the shading process. Light sources and the remaining light-source functions got thrown in the middle somewhere, and, finally, a discussion of simple procedural texturing put the finishing touches on our imaging capabilities.

That leaves only the process of building an application out of all these code blocks and related processes. Conceptually, you are now ready to see how all these pieces are assembled. Remember that the modeler returns us to a focus on application-level details and includes more coverage of architecture and robustness.

There are still some technical details to cover, notably the color post-processing and its supporting grayscale and histogram partners. Chapter 11 returns us to the application-construction process now that our library components are almost complete.

11 Implementing the 3D Modeler

In This Chapter

- Final implementation of the modeler.
- A look at robustness and error handling for the application, combining floating-point and Toolhelp error handling.
- Design of the state machine controller and construction of the state machine scaffolding.
- Connection of the four phases of the modeler to the controller, building the modeler in the process.
- Colorization of the final images.

Introduction

I've previously described the phases of the WinMod3D modeler as:

- world generation (front-end),
- world manipulation (core),
- world rendering (back-end), and
- color post-processing.

Both the support libraries and the architectural techniques employed in the modeler construction process are designed to support these four phases. These techniques include:

- a simple tokenizer to support the front end,
- user-definable lookup tables for color and materials, with capabilities for binary search by name,
- lists, mapping functions, and function pointers embedded in data structures in an object-oriented style to support many core functions, and
- a simple controller to manage all of this diversity.

The support libraries provide routines for:

- front-end language and object instantiation support,
- world manipulation and rendering support, and
- post-processing support.

Chapter 8 gave you the modeling and scene description languages, the tokenizer, and two parsers (one for each language). Chapter 9's coverage of object instantiation tied the front end to the core and put to rest any remaining Phase 1 concerns. That left consideration of the core functions: transformation, projection, and shading for polygons; intersection, normal generation, and shading for ray objects. Chapter 10 presented the details of handling these two representations during Phase 2 — world manipulation. But even with all this material, plus the WLib topics and the G3DLib topics of Part II, we still haven't gotten into the internals of a modeler. This chapter will take care of that.

I'll guide you through the stages of constructing a simple state machine that implements a table-driven FSM (finite state machine) automaton. In other words, we'll implement a function that dictates when an action may take place and when it can't. Once the state machine is in place, we can start the construction process in earnest.

Our first task is hooking up the front end. Once you can create a world, you'll want to manipulate it, so our next action will be to rope in menu and keyboard actions. We'll set up the file, options, painting, and post-processing menus, and the close function from the system menu.

At that point, we have a closed system. Once the state machine is up, a user must interact with the application in a manner determined by the state transition logic. This makes it trivial, for example, to prevent the user from opening a new file while in the middle of a pipeline run. We can easily trap and disable even the nonsensical (but probably safe) events like trying to print the off-screen buffer while in the middle of a pipeline run, which will print an incomplete image and waste paper. But if you wanted, you could certainly do more than simply disable these actions. For instance, you could buffer the print request until the image is complete; an action that probably makes sense, given the situation. This is easy to do by creating a FIFO (First-In, First-Out) stack of commands and executing them at the next ready cycle; you can graft this onto the state machine foundation.

With the code for a state machine, you can construct the guts of the MVC system. The various phases are connected around the central hub, and as each phase is hooked up, the modeler begins to come alive.

The key here is recognizing the big picture. The world generation phase is a two-part process: the first part is parsing the model script and instantiating the supporting color and material tables; the second part parses the scene script and the viewpoint, background (ambient and color), lights, and 3D objects. The lights and 3D objects are both contained in lists. The lists are managed by the controller in the manipulation and rendering phases. This consists of a set of five parallel steps in either polygon or ray-trace mode. Table 11-1 contains the parallel steps.

All drawing occurs in grayscale until the post-processing step. There, you are given two methods of quantization in 256-color mode. In 32K-color and higher modes, the retained intensity values are used to generate 24-bit color values — here, direct color assignment occurs. Table 11-2 shows the mapping from action and color mode to capability. As you can see, in 256-color mode a fair amount of work goes into color generation. In the 32K-color or higher modes, certain additional optimizations can be taken. I'll cover this in more detail in the section on color post-processing.

I'll also cover the grayscale process. To this point, the discussions on the modeler and rendering have made a lot of noise about grayscale. In this section, I'll talk about the design decisions that resulted in my choice of grayscale as the initial imaging, thus handling color as a post-processing step.

Table 11-1   Manipulation and Rendering Actions

Phase	Process	Polygon Mode	Ray Mode
Manipulation	Generate viewing system	Generate transform matrix	Generate root ray
	Transform	Loop across objects	Generate pixel ray
		Transform vertex points	Trace pixel ray
Rendering	Visibility	Cull back faces	Ray-object intersections
		Perform a z-sort*	
	Imaging I	Project and map vertex points	Generate intersection point
			Generate normal
	Imaging II	Shade** and draw poly	Shade pixel

*only in hidden poly modes
**only in flat-shaded poly mode

Table 11-2   Grayscaling and Color Post-Processing

Color Mode	Step	Render Mode	Action
Gray process	Calc values	Poly	Retained face intensities
		Ray	Retained intensity buffer values (MEMBUFF of CANVAS)
	Image & analyze	Poly & ray	Use histogram bins/ draw histogram graph
	Analyze support	Poly & ray	Invoke gray methods
	Draw	Poly & ray	Generate image in gray
256-color	Colorize	Poly & ray	Quantization and algorithmic generation of palettes I & II (Popularity & Median Cut)
		Poly	Reimage with retained intensities in the face data structure and new palette
		Ray	Reimage with retained intensities in the intensity buffer and new palette
>256-color	Colorize	Poly & ray	Direct color assignment with retained values

For both 8-bit and 24-bit modes, grayscale is a winner. In either mode, it lets you do color analysis to produce the best palette for a particular image, rather than using a fixed uniform palette for all images. By using a common gray brush array and palette, the gray brushes and palette can be created before drawing and "cached," thus eliminating creation/destruction overhead every time you need to draw. Of course, this means that the post-processing phase has to pay for it, because nothing is for free; the real benefit is that you only pay when you're at your final stage and have decided that it's worthwhile. In 8-bit mode, this is an optimization both for color usage and performance. In 24-bit mode (which also handles 15- and 16-bit modes), the reasoning behind grayscaling in 32K-color and higher is simply to avoid the GDI object creation/destruction overhead.

In both cases, this approach means you only pay the cost of creating color brushes when you ask for them. In the average polygon-mode scene, each polygon is a different color. With a worst case of two-thirds of the faces being visible, a scene of 2,000 cubes has 12,000 faces, about 8,000 of which are visible. That means 8,000 distinct colors — in 32K-color mode for polygon drawing, that's 8,000 brushes. This is a GDI cost; it adds up and only gets worse as the number of polygons and colors increases.

Fortunately, ray-trace mode uses point drawing, which does not require brushes. Imagine a 512x512 ray-trace: it contains 262,144 pixels and, in its worst case, can require a unique color for each pixel. If that required brushes, or if a polygon-mode drawing used that many distinct colors, GDI in its 16-bit incarnation would require us to be more creative in handling output attributes.

Efficient performance means using grayscaling in this environment of limited color resources. It removes this potential resource burden and provides a "preview" mode. When an image is nice, that's when you color it.

Similarly, if you're doing animation it can be desirable to match palettes across all images in a sequence to avoid artifacts. You can do this by saving a grayscale storyboard of the animation sequence and batch post-processing the entire sequence of images at once to reduce them to a common palette. This process is known as *color reduction* and is similar to the color quantization that supports our color post-processing.

Examining this optimization, Tables 11-3 and 11-4 contain GDI resource cost information.

Table 11-3.   GDI Logical Object Costs

Object Type	GDI Heap Usage (in bytes)	Global Memory Use (in bytes)
Pen	10 + sizeof(LOGPEN)	0
Brush	10 + sizeof(LOGBRUSH) + 6	0
Pattern brush	Same as brush + copy of bitmap	
Font	10 + sizeof(LOGFONT)	0
Bitmap	10 + 18	32 + room for bits
Palette	10 + 10	4 + (10 * numentries)
Rectangular region	10 + 26	0
Solid complex region	Rect region + (6 * (num scans - 1))	0
Region with hole	Region + (2*num scans with hole)	0

Table 11-4.   GDI Physical (Realized) Object Costs

Object Type	GDI Heap Usage (in bytes)	Global Memory Use (in bytes)
Pen	10 + 8 + device info	0
Brush	10 + 14 + device info	0
Font	55 (per realization)	Font data (per physical font)
Bitmap	0	0
Palette	0	0
Region	Intersection of region with visible region	0

Listings 11-1 and 11-2 contain profiler information so you can get an idea of performance benefits for a relatively simple scene.

Listing 11-1. Cacheless Performance of Mono Versus Flat-Shaded HLHSR

```
------------------------------------
Program Statistics - without gray brush cache
----------
Func            Func+Child      Hit
Time      %     Time       %    count  Function
------------------------------------------------------------
5920.900  9.1  8729.006  13.5  883    DrawFlatShadedFace (polydraw.c:327)
5728.806  8.8  5728.806   8.8  883    DrawHiddenFace (polydraw.c:197)
```

Listing 11-2. Cached Performance of Mono Versus Flat-Shaded HLHSR

```
Program Statistics -  with gray brush cache

Func            Func+Child      Hit
Time      %     Time       %    count Function

6068.118  9.6  6068.118   9.6  883   DrawHiddenFace    (polydraw.c:197)
5989.491  9.5  8626.633  13.7  883   DrawFlatShadedFace (polydraw.c:327)
```

From Tables 11-3 and 11-4 you can see that pens, brushes, fonts, and regions have both logical and physical costs in GDI's scarce local heap. Fonts cost global memory in both logical and physical cases; bitmaps and palettes have a sizable global memory cost for each logical object. Thus, the brush cache strategy does have a significant cost. The footprint presented by the modeler can use as much as 10K of GDI's heap.

The performance gain from the brush cache is small, but cumulative. For a small scene and only 883 draws, the difference between the actual function time for *DrawHiddenFace* and *DrawFlatShadedFace* can be accounted for by the elimination of the brush creation and destruction overhead in the cached performance numbers. The difference in the function-plus-child time is due to the illumination model overhead. This comparison shows a reversal in the relation due to the optimization, which is expected; otherwise, the optimization is not worthwhile.

Two quantization methods put the final touch on the grayscaling and colorizing processes. Quantization, and the reduction that was just mentioned in passing, are parts of color analysis in general, as are the color system and conversion routines of Chapter 4. The 32K and higher color modes all map into 24-bit color in the support libraries. That makes it possible to make one bitmap that will work across all the upper modes, since the 15- and 16-bit color modes simply ignore the additional information and truncate the color values. It also makes it possible to use direct assignment of the red, green, and blue information calculated by the modeler. While this must still be in the CRT space of [0,255], that is a simple step from the [0,1] intensities.

Before we explore the controller architecture and the grayscaling/colorizing, we need to address the issue of floating-point, integer, and exception error-handling. While Chapter 10 showed how to do many wonderful things with math, life for the numerical programmer is not quite so simple. In any mostly open-ended system that involves repeated calculations, it is possible to make "bad things" happen. Floating-point overflow or underflow from a calculation getting too large (in multiplication and addition) or too small (in division or subtraction) are a real problem. To this end, the C language provides signal handlers in the RTL. The installation of signal handlers for this application gives us some protection from fatal errors. This is still not foolproof, but the addition of one more light source causes an exception to be thrown and caught, in most cases without the application crashing.

This is not just a convenience; the modeler uses quite a bit of resources, including scarce and valuable GDI resources. Off-screen bitmaps, palettes, brushes and the brush cache, pens, and fonts all add up. A crash with this much of GDI allocated is like taking a shotgun to the guts of the graphics engine that drives all of Windows. For example, if GDI resources get too low, in the worst case, Windows cannot even paint an error box to inform you of this sad and overwhelming fact. The signal handlers for floating-point calculation errors and the Toolhelp exception handlers for integer calculation and general errors are worth your time to install in your application, and your users will thank you.

Modeler Architecture I: Robustness

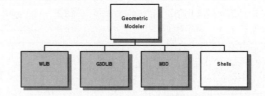

Floating point and the Windows environment have a unique relationship. Usually, performance and precision are the reasons to use a coprocessor — in other words, faster and better. Either way, the use of special hardware for floating-point means an increase in speed. This is valid here, as well, but the rules are a little more complicated. This discussion is based on the article "Floating-Point in Microsoft Windows" by David Long, which is included on the MSDN CD.

Windows and the multi-tasking world are not quite as straightforward as single-tasking environments like DOS. Figure 11-1 is a repeat of Figure 1-8. It shows the virtual machine architecture of Windows, with special attention to the VMCPD virtual math coprocessor device and multiple applications. It should be clear from this diagram that there are two levels between you and the coprocessor.

The first level is the 32-bit virtual device. The coprocessor device VxD allows the coprocessor to be shared between multiple virtual machines. This lets DOS applications in a DOS box and the system Virtual Machine share access to the one chip. All WinApps "live" in the system VM.

Within the system VM, the Windows emulator library WIN87EM.DLL works at the 16-bit level to virtualize the coprocessor among multiple Windows applications. This is the

Figure 11-1.   Windows Virtual Machine Layout and Floating Point

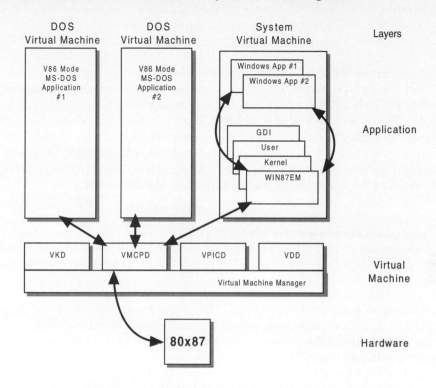

second level. These two layers account for the fact that floating-point performance under Windows is between two and three times slower than under a straight DOS program.

This approach is necessary to reflect the correct coprocessor state into each virtual machine, and then, within the system VM, to each WinApp. In addition to the coprocessor state, it also needs to reflect the exception state.

While context switches typically signify a coprocessor state, in actuality the floating-point context is not saved and restored automatically at task-switch time. Instead, it is demand-swapped by coprocessor usage. This strategy has important and beneficial effects on background computations: they can continue without incurring the additional overhead of a floating-point save/restore for each processing slice allotted by the **PeekMessage** technique. Remember that idle-loop code that executes in the background causes a task switch. It's very nice that the background application can hold the floating-point context like this.

Exceptions, on the other hand, require polling in this environment. Beneath the first layer of redirection by the VMCPD into the correct VM, WIN87EM.DLL both virtualizes the coprocessor (if one exists) or provides emulator support (if one does not). WIN87EM provides:

- software emulation of the coprocessor using the interrupt 3x interface,
- run-time checking for floating-point exceptions,
- default exception handling,

- per-task instancing of application-installed exception handlers,
- proper exception-interrupt returns for the VMCPD,
- coprocessor initialization and exception recovery, and
- an interface for Windows debuggers.

You can see the use of per-task, application-installed exception handlers. While WIN87EM properly handles exception handlers on an instance basis, the floating-point control word is not instanced. The sample application that accompanies the floating-point article on the MSDN CD illustrates this, and it leads to a bizarre situation. While one approach to floating-point exceptions is to avoid them by masking them out, if an application that uses WIN87EM does control-word masking, and then another application also does control-word masking and changes the setting, the first application is affected because of the lack of instancing. I'm now going to quote the statement about this from the Microsoft article because what it says is so important:

> "This is an undesirable and unavoidable situation that means you can neither expect to receive exceptions; nor can you expect not to receive them. Therefore, if you do floating-point math and use WIN87EM, you should install a signal handler on the assumption that you may need it!"

The exclamation point is in the original. That is quite a statement, and it means if you use one float or double variable, you should definitely think about installing a signal handler. In addition, you should be aware that the documentation to **_fpmath** is incomplete and incorrect. While the modeler does not invoke this function, documentation errors are always worth noting and the corrections are in the Microsoft article in addition to a wealth of additional information on floating-point and Windows.

Before discussing exception handlers, we need to cover the choice of math package (which, strangely enough, affects the handler). Three choices exist: emulator, alternate, and coprocessor math libraries that are linked with your application. Emulator generates code that will use the math coprocessor if present or emulate it if it's not. This is either the fastest or slowest choice.

Alternate math sacrifices emulator precision for speed in software. Altmath does this by avoiding the IEEE 80-bit long doubles, but still cannot compete with hardware. The coprocessor option will only run with a coprocessor. To use this option, you must check for the presence of the coprocessor and, if it's not there, gracefully exit the program after informing the user that they must purchase a chip to run your program — not a wise choice. The emulator package is the preferred choice here. If you have an x87 coprocessor or a 486 machine, you'll get fast floating-point. If you don't, the emulator library will still let you execute the program by doing floating-point in the software.

Sometimes, programmers use fixed-point arithmetic to avoid depending on hardware or an emulatr library. This arithmetic manages a floating-point number with an integer and decimal-point management. Typically, a long is used, giving 32-bits, and the decimal is placed in one of two places, giving 16.16 or 24.8 numbers (16 bits before the decimal and 16 after, or 24 before the decimal and 8 after, respectively) in a fixed form; hence the name fixed-point. From the range calculations discussed earlier, you should see that this severely limits what values can be represented. There are ways out of even that trap, but they include yet another scheme, this one built on top of the fixed-point decimal-point-management scheme. That's one scheme too many. No, the lesson is to avoid fixed-point and buy the hardware. If you are serious about graphics, invest in a machine with floating-point hardware.

Installing a signal handler for either a DLL or an application is done with the C RTL routine signal. The results depend on two factors:

1. Whether alternate math or emulator math is used.
2. Whether the routine is called by an application or DLL.

The emulator has more-complex behavior than Altmath, because Altmath exists in software. Thus, there are no hardware interrupts, VxDs, and system level details to get in the way. With the inclusion of WIN87EM in the picture, the handling follows this scenario.

1. Default handling is done by WIN87EM.DLL.
2. MSC and the BC RTL startup register a handler for you that becomes the default.
3. An application-installed handler overrides the default.
4. If the application calls into a DLL that registers a handler, the DLL's signal handler is called to handle any exceptions generated by it or by the application.
5. If the DLL uses **_fpinit** and **_fpterm** on exported functions' entry and exit points, then the DLL handler is only invoked when the DLL generates the exception.

Even the Microsoft article admits that this is confusing. The DLLs are the problem here. There are two approaches really: no signal handler in the DLL, and the **_fpinit** and **_fpterm** approach for each function. If the DLL will only dynalink to applications compiled for WIN87EM (hard to guarantee), then the DLL can assume the following:

- There is no need to initialize and terminate WIN87EM since the application already did.
- If both the DLL and application can accept the default exception handler, then again there's no need for DLL to do anything.
- If applications dynalinked to the DLL register a signal handler that behaves in a manner consistent with the handling and reporting needs of the DLL, then the DLL can "piggyback" on the application handler.

The code here forsakes the DLL handling because the application is tightly coupled to these DLLs and can provide the handling. This is consistent with these three assumptions. If these assumptions change, the floating-point segment of the API should receive the additional treatment it needs to work with unknown applications.

In any case, the default behavior of most applications is to post a WM_QUIT message to the current application queue — this is clearly unacceptable here because of the resource load the modeler gobbles up. The trail taken here is to hit the user interface with a dialog. This is shown in Figure 11-2 with a GP13 error showing. In this case, recovery is not possible, and you are best off using the "Kill Task" button; but in the case of most floating-point errors it is possible to restart. This dialog is invoked from the two handler functions: *FPExceptionInfo* for floating-point classes of errors and *THExceptionInfo* for all others.

Figure 11-2.   WinMod3D, Fault Handling, and Death

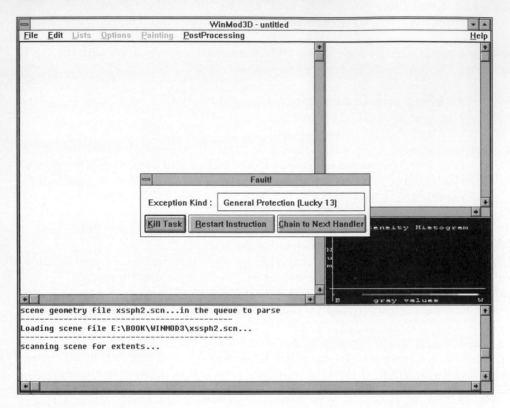

These two functions depend on the fault handler dialog *FaultDialogProc*, shown in Listing 11-3.

Listing 11-3.   FaultDialogProc

```
BOOL CALLBACK _export FaultDialogProc(HWND hDlg, WORD wMessage,
                                      WORD wParam, DWORD dwParam)
{
    switch (wMessage)      {
     case WM_INITDIALOG:
        SetDlgItemText(hDlg, IDC_FAULTNUM, (LPSTR)szExceptionType);
        Center(hDlg, CTR_PARENT);
        return TRUE;
     case WM_COMMAND:
      switch (wParam)      {
        case IDC_KILL:
           FreeAllResources();
           TerminateApp(0,NO_UAE_BOX);
           EndDialog(hDlg, wParam-IDC_KILL);
           return TRUE;
```

```
        case IDC_RESTART:
        case IDC_CHAIN:
            EndDialog(hDlg, wParam-IDC_KILL);
            return TRUE;
        default:
            return FALSE;
        }
    default:
        return FALSE;
    }
}
```

During initialization, it sets up the error kind using global variable szExceptionType and centers the dialog; it uses *FreeAllResources*, which is shown in Listing 11-4.

Listing 11-4.   FreeAllResources

```
void FreeAllResources() {
    FRAME*   pfrm = Frame_GetPtr(g_app.hwndMain);
    CLIENT*  pcli = Client_GetPtr(pfrm->hwndClient);
    VWWND*   pv   = View_GetPtr(pcli->hwView);
    HISTWND* ph   = Hist_GetPtr(pcli->hwHist);
    HDC      hdc;
//views
//   View
    G3D_GEnv_Destroy(pv->genv);
    if ( hrgnClip )
        DeleteObject(hrgnClip);
//   Hist
    G3D_GEnv_Reset(ph->henv,ID_FONT);
    G3D_GEnv_Reset(ph->henv,ID_BITMAP);
    G3D_GEnv_Destroy(ph->henv);
    hdc            = GetDC(ph->hwnd);
    SelectObject(hdc, ph->hfo);
    ReleaseDC(ph->hwnd,hdc);
    DeleteObject(ph->hf);
//global
    FreeGrayBrushArray();
    FreeRGBBrushArray(pv->mWorld->Colors);
    DeleteObject(pv->mWorld->Scene->hbc);
}
```

This in turn leads us to the floating-point exception classes, the ToolHelp exception classes, and the handling of each. The first step in both cases is installing the handlers. For floating-point errors, this is done by *InstallSignalHandler*, a modeler-specific function. For Toolhelp errors, an interrupt-handler function must be registered using **InterruptRegister**, a Windows and Toolhelp function.

The installation of a floating-point signal handler is shown with the implementation of *InstallSignalHandler* in Listing 11-5. It shows the pre-processor directives to conditionally compile for a DLL or an application.

Listing 11-5.   InstallSignalHandler for Apps and DLLs

```
#ifdef _WINDLL
BOOL FAR PASCAL _export DLLInstallSignalHandler(uSignalType)
#else
BOOL InstallSignalHandler(uSignalType)
#endif
UINT uSignalType;        // which signal handler to install:  ours or
default
{
// Initially, the signal handler is whatever default is provided
// by the C runtime libraries or by Win87Em.  Since this function
// acts as a toggle, the OldFPHandler function pointer must be
// initialized to our signal handler...
    static void (_cdecl *OldFPHandler)(int, int) = FPHandler;

    switch (uSignalType) {
    case SIG_INSTALL:
        #if !defined(EMULATOR) || !defined(_WINDLL)
        if (OldFPHandler != FPHandler)   {
            DebugSay("Attempt to re-install signal handler.");
            break;                           // don't reinstall it
        }
// The following call to signal generates compiler warnings because
// it's prototyped for only 1 parameter, so shut up this compiler
// warning temporarily.
        #pragma warning(disable:4113)
        if ((OldFPHandler=signal(SIGFPE,FPHandler)) == SIG_ERR )
        #pragma warning(default:4113)
        {
            DebugSay("\n\rCouldn't install our signal handler.");
            return FALSE;
        }
        #endif
        fSignalHandlerInstalled = TRUE;
        break;

    case SIG_REMOVE:
        #if !defined(EMULATOR) || !defined(_WINDLL)
        if (OldFPHandler == FPHandler) {
            DebugSay("Attempt to re-remove App signal handler.");
            break;                       // using the default handler
        }
// The following call to signal generates compiler warnings because
// it's prototyped for only 1 parameter, so shut up this compiler
```

```
// warning temporarily.
        #pragma warning(disable:4113)
        if ((OldFPHandler=signal(SIGFPE,OldFPHandler) == SIG_ERR )
        #pragma warning(disable:4113)
        {
            DebugSay("Couldn't restore default signal handler.");
            return FALSE;
        }
        #endif
        fSignalHandlerInstalled = FALSE;
        break;
    }
    return TRUE;
} // end of InstallSignalHandler()
```

The **signal** RTL function is used to install the handler function *FPHandler* shown in Listing 11-6. The reporting function *FPExceptionInfo* hits the user interface with an error message, the control word is monkeyed around with, and the floating-point package is reset using **_fpreset**. The **_control87** function that is used to get and restore the control word around the reset, as well as the reset function **_fpreset**, and the **_fpinit** and **_fpterm** functions are all described in the Windows documentation.

Listing 11-6.   FPHandler

```
void FPHandler(sig, subcode)
int sig;        // in our case this will always be SIGFPE
int subcode;    // indicates which floating point error occurred
{
#if defined(EMULATOR)
    WORD wFCW;      // floating point control word
#endif

    if (sig != SIGFPE)
    {
        DebugSay("Signal error: exception should be SIGFPE.");
        return;
    }
    uNumExceptions++;           //Increase count of exceptions detected

    FPExceptionInfo(subcode);//Report on type of exception occurred

//Reset fp package.Note that this sets the fp
//control word (FCW) back to its initial _CW_DEFAULT value (see
//FLOAT.H); the default masks denormal, underflow, and inexact
//exceptions.If we don't do something about that, then we might no
//longer see exceptions that we wanted to see; consequently, we
//save/restore the FCW around _fpreset().
```

Listing 11-6. (*cont.*)

```
#if defined(EMULATOR)
    wFCW = _control87(0,0);       // Get the current control word
#endif
    _fpreset();                   // Reset the floating point package
#if defined(EMULATOR)
    _control87(wFCW, 0xffff);     // Restore previous control word
#endif
} // end of FPHandler()
```

What is not described in the documentation are the six types of conditions that may be signaled by status flags or traps. Table 11-5 lists these "error classes" for you.

Table 11-5. Floating-Point Error Classes

Exception	Description
Numeric overflow	The exponent of the result is too large to be represented.
Numeric underflow	The exponent of the result is too small to be represented.
Zero divide	This is possible not only for explicit divide errors but for operations that perform division internally.
Precision	Occurs when the result will lose significant digits when stored in the destination format.

Three additional floating-point details round out the discussion — non-normal numbers, formats, and pre-versus-post signaling. Internally, floating-point numbers are stored in a normalized form of exponent and mantissa. This should be straightforward. We're concerned here with the edges of floating-point. The concept of "non-normal" numbers exists to represent numbers that cannot be represented in the standard format. These are denormals to represent underflows, and NaNs or "not-a-number" values that can signify what happened or allow processing to continue. The details of source and destination format are mostly unimportant, but they help you understand that it is most often the operation of transferring the internal result to the destination format that causes underflow and overflow situations. The invalid, zero-divide, and denormal exceptions are signaled before the instruction that would have generated it is executed. The underflow, overflow, and precision exceptions are not signaled until a result is calculated.

With that out of the way, the *FPExceptionInfo* function in Listing 11-7 should make a little more sense now that the categorization is clear.

Listing 11-7. FPExceptionInfo

```
void FPExceptionInfo(uSignalSubcode)
UINT uSignalSubcode;          // signal type passed to handler
{
    char szExceptionType[80];

    switch (uSignalSubcode)// global  set by exception handler
    {
```

```
        case FPE_INVALID:
            lstrcpy(szExceptionType, "INVALID");
            break;
        case FPE_DENORMAL:
            lstrcpy(szExceptionType, "DENORMAL");
            break;
        case FPE_ZERODIVIDE:
            lstrcpy(szExceptionType, "ZERODIVIDE");
            break;
        case FPE_OVERFLOW:
            lstrcpy(szExceptionType, "OVERFLOW");
            break;
        case FPE_UNDERFLOW:
            lstrcpy(szExceptionType, "UNDERFLOW");
            break;
        case FPE_INEXACT:
            lstrcpy(szExceptionType, "INEXACT");
            break;
        case FPE_UNEMULATED:
            lstrcpy(szExceptionType, "UNEMULATED");
            break;
        case FPE_SQRTNEG:
            lstrcpy(szExceptionType, "SQRTNEG");
            break;
        case FPE_STACKOVERFLOW:
            lstrcpy(szExceptionType, "STACKOVERFLOW");
            break;
        case FPE_STACKUNDERFLOW:
            lstrcpy(szExceptionType, "STACKUNDERFLOW");
            break;
        case FPE_EXPLICITGEN:
            lstrcpy(szExceptionType, "EXPLICITGEN");
            break;
        default:
            lstrcpy(szExceptionType, "Other exception type");
            break;
    }
    /* Use the dialog box to determine what to do with the fault */
    lpfnDlg = MakeProcInstance((FARPROC)FaultDialogProc,
                                g_app.hinst);
    nResult = DialogBox(g_app.hinst, MAKEINTRESOURCE(IDD_FAULT),
                        g_app.hwndMain, (DLGPROC)lpfnDlg);
    FreeProcInstance(lpfnDlg);
} // end of FPExceptionInfo()
```

In Listing 11-8, *App_Initialize* is shown calling *InstallSignalHandler* after *FPMaskException* and *CheckCoprocessor*.

Listing 11-8.   App_Initialize and InstallSignalHandler

```
BOOL App_Initialize(APP* papp)
{
    char szBuffer[MAXNAMELEN];

    Splash("Splash");
    if (!App_InitializeHook(papp))
        return FALSE;

    if (!Frame_Initialize(papp))
        return FALSE;

    if (!Client_Initialize(papp))
        return FALSE;

    LoadString(papp->hinst, IDS_APPNAME, szBuffer, MAXNAMELEN);
    papp->hwndMain = Frame_CreateWindow(
            szBuffer,
            CW_USEDEFAULT, CW_USEDEFAULT,
            CW_USEDEFAULT, CW_USEDEFAULT,
            papp->hinst);

    if (papp->hwndMain == NULL)
        return FALSE;

    fHave87 = CheckCoprocessor();

#ifdef EMULATOR       // we're in EMULATOR math...
    FPMaskExceptions(FALSE);//Clear 87 cw to allow exceptions.
#endif

    // set the signal handler to be the application's own;

    InstallSignalHandler(SIG_INSTALL);
    ParseCommandLine(papp->cmdShow,papp->lpszCmdLine);

    Splash(NULL);
    return TRUE;
}
```

Listing 11-9 follows with *App_Terminate* and a call to *InstallSignalHandler* with the remove flag SIG_REMOVE, which invokes the remove block from Listing 11-5.

Listing 11-9.   App_Terminate and InstallSignalHandler

```
void App_Terminate(APP* papp, int codeTerm)
{
    if (codeTerm != TERM_ENDSESSION){
        if (papp->hwndMain) {
            DestroyWindow(papp->hwndMain);
```

```
                papp->hwndMain = NULL;
            }
        }

    Client_Terminate(papp, codeTerm);
    Frame_Terminate(papp, codeTerm);

    InstallSignalHandler(SIG_REMOVE);
    App_TerminateHook(papp);
    GlobalCompact(-1);
}
```

The *CheckCoprocessor* and *FPMaskException* functions are shown in Listing 11-10, and are straightforward implementations. *FPMaskException* uses **_control87** from the RTL. Note that this will operate slightly differently under BC. *CheckCoprocessor* uses the **GetWinFlags** function.

Listing 11-10.   FPMaskException and CheckCoprocessor

```
#ifdef EMULATOR
static WORD wFCW_Masked =   0x133f;      // Floating point control word
static WORD wFCW_Unmasked = 0x1320;      // values to [un]mask exceptions.
#endif

BOOL FPMaskExceptions(fMask)
BOOL fMask;       // TRUE = mask them; FALSE = unmask them
{
#ifdef EMULATOR
    WORD wFCW;

    if (fMask)
        wFCW = wFCW_Masked;
    else
        wFCW = wFCW_Unmasked;

        wFCW = _control87(wFCW, 0xffff);
        break;
    }
#endif
    return fMask;
} // end of FPMaskExceptions()

BOOL CheckCoprocessor(void)
{
    return (BOOL) (GetWinFlags() & WF_80x87);
} // end of CheckCoprocessor()
```

Now floating-point exceptions are at least trapped and the possibility of recovery exists. Combining the signal handler with the TRY/CATCH style allows crude recovery. The offending sequence is "thrown" out of and "caught." This terminates any ongoing calculations, but at least the application does not crash. Without more sophisticated handling to unravel the stack and perform partial restarts, this is the best our floating-point signal handler can do.

That still leaves the integer operations, GP 13 segment overruns, and the normal exceptions that happen without adding floating-point to the mix.

Toolhelp introduced the ability to trap an application's interrupts with the **InterruptRegister** function, and to de-install an interrupt handler with the corresponding **InterruptUnregister** function. The Toolhelp library lets us install handling for the classes of errors shown in Table 11-6. Even though the Toolhelp library supports all of these, we don't need the INT_1 and INT_3 here. Between this and the floating-point errors, plus the TRY/CATCH style and the reporting mechanism, error handling and the modeler's usage of it provide a relatively robust environment.

Table 11-6. Toolhelp Error Classes

Name	Number	Description
INT_DIV0	0	Divide-error exception
INT_1	1	Debugger interrupt
INT_3	3	Breakpoint interrupt
INT_UDINSTR	6	Invalid op code exception
INT_STKFAULT	12	Stack exception
INT_GPFAULT	13	General protection violation
INT_BADPAGEFAULT	14	Page fault not caused by normal virtual memory

Listing 11-11 contains **WinMain** to show how this is set up. The **InterruptRegister** function and the corresponding **InterruptUnregister** function bracket the code. They do not handle floating-point exceptions, but the *InstallSignalHandler* function and its floating-point error handling is installed inside *App_Initialize*. It is deinstalled in *App_Terminate*.

Listing 11-11. WinMain and Toolhelp InterruptRegister Handler Installation

```
int PASCAL WinMain(HINSTANCE hinst, HINSTANCE hinstPrev,
                LPSTR lpszCmdLine, int cmdShow)
{
    // install our Fault handler and our notification handler
    (FARPROC)lpfnFault = MakeProcInstance((FARPROC)FaultHandler,
                                          hinst);

    if (!InterruptRegister(NULL, lpfnFault)) {
        OutputDebugString("Interrupt hook failed!!\r\n");
        return 1;
    }
```

```
        // Initialize the APP structure
        g_app.hinst      = hinst;
        g_app.hinstPrev  = hinstPrev;
        g_app.lpszCmdLine = lpszCmdLine;
        g_app.cmdShow    = cmdShow;
        g_app.hwndMain   = NULL;
        g_app.codeExit   = 1;        // Assume failure
        g_app.fQuit      = FALSE;

        // Initialize, run, and terminate the application
        if (App_Initialize(&g_app))
            App_Run(&g_app);

        App_Terminate(&g_app,
                      (g_app.codeExit == 0 ? TERM_QUIT : TERM_ERROR));

        // Get rid of our handler
        InterruptUnRegister(NULL);
        FreeProcInstance(lpfnFault);
        return g_app.codeExit;
}
```

The details of the Toolhelp handler remain. **InterruptRegister** installs function _FaultHandler_ as the interrupt function. The interrupt function _FaultHandler_ is an assembly function shown in Listing 11-12. It calls C function *THExceptionInfo*. This functions' main purpose is to invoke a dialog to report the error (as previously shown by dialog function *FaultDialogProc*) and to implement the ternary handling logic of terminate the app, continue or restart the instruction, or chain to the next handler. *THExceptionInfo* is contained in Listing 11-13. Notice also the usage of global szExceptionType for error display.

Listing 11-12.   Toolhelp FaultHandler asm Callback

```
cProc   FaultHandler, <FAR,PUBLIC>
cBegin  NOGEN

        push    bp                 ;Make a stack frame
        mov     bp,sp
        pusha                      ;Save all registers
        push    ds
        push    es

        ;** Get instance data segment and prepare for C call
        mov     ds,ax              ;Since this function uses
                                   ;  MakeProcInstance(), AX has the
                                   ;  DS value in it.

        ;** Call the C function:  It returns 0 to nuke the app,
        ;*      1 to restart the instruction, 2 to chain on
  cCall   THExceptionInfo
```

Listing 11-12. *(cont.)*

```
        ;** Decode the return value
        or      ax,ax               ;Check for zero
        jz      MFH_TermApp         ;kill it
        dec     ax                  ;Check for 1
        jz      MFH_Restart         ;Restart instruction

MFH_ChainOn:
        pop     es                  ;Chain on to next fault handler
        pop     ds
        popa
        pop     bp
        retf

MFH_Restart:
        pop     es                  ;Clear stack
        pop     ds
        popa
        pop     bp
        add     sp,10               ;Clear the return stuff
        cCall   Throw,<_pcbEx, 1>   ;Return the exception
        iret                        ;Restart instruction

MFH_TermApp:
        pop     es                  ;Clear stack
        pop     ds
        popa
        pop     bp
        add     sp,10               ;Point to IRET frame
        iret

cEnd    NOGEN

sEnd
```

Listing 11-13.   THExceptionInfo

```
WORD FAR _cdecl THExceptionInfo(
    WORD wES,WORD wDS,WORD wDI, WORD wSI,
    WORD wBP,WORD wSP,WORD wBX,WORD wDX,WORD wCX,
    WORD wOldAX,WORD wOldBP,
    WORD wRetIP,WORD wRetCS,
    WORD wRealAX,WORD wNumber,WORD wHandle,
    WORD wIP,WORD wCS,WORD wFlags)
{
    FARPROC lpfnDlg;
    int     nResult;

// See if we're already here.  If so, tell routine to chain on
    if (wReentry)
        return 2;
    wReentry = 1;
```

```
//If this was a CtlAltSysRq interrupt, just restart the instr.
    if (wNumber == INT_CTLALTSYSRQ){
        wsprintf(szText, "CtlAltSysRq at %04X:%04X\r\n", wCS, wIP);
        OutputDebugString(szText);
        wReentry = 0;
        return 1;
    }
    switch(wNumber) {
        case 1:             // do not handle int 1 and int3
        case 3:
            return 1;
            break;
        case INT_DIV0:
            lstrcpy(szExceptionType,"Integer Zero Divide");
            break;
        case INT_UDINSTR:
            lstrcpy(szExceptionType,"Undefined Instruction");
            break;
        case INT_STKFAULT:
            lstrcpy(szExceptionType,"Stack Fault");
            break;
        case INT_GPFAULT:
            lstrcpy(szExceptionType,"General Protection (Lucky 13)");
            break;
        case INT_BADPAGEFAULT:
            lstrcpy(szExceptionType,"Bad Page Fault");
            break;
        default:
            lstrcpy(szExceptionType,"other Toolhelp exception type");
            break;
    };
// Use the dialog box to determine what to do with the fault
    lpfnDlg = MakeProcInstance((FARPROC)FaultDialogProc,
                                    g_app.hinst);
    nResult = DialogBox(g_app.hinst, MAKEINTRESOURCE(IDD_FAULT),
                        g_app.hwndMain, (FARPROC)lpfnDlg);
    FreeProcInstance(lpfnDlg);
//We're getting out now, so undo reentry flag
    wReentry = 0;
    return (WORD)nResult;
}
```

If you want more detail on Toolhelp and interrupt handling several sources exist. *Undocumented Windows*, by Schulman, Maxey, and Pietrek (Addison-Wesley, 1992), covers it in a section of Chapter 10. The whole of their Chapter 10 is devoted to Toolhelp and all it can do, which is quite a bit. It includes the Coroner program, which has an interrupt handler.

Another source is Ray Duncan's three-part series on Toolhelp in the Power Programming column of *PC Magazine* (August 1992; September 15, 1992; and September 29, 1992). The last one in this series includes an interrupt-handler function as well.

With the underpinnings secure beneath us, it is time once again to tackle control architecture. In Chapter 10, you saw how the linked-list services and the function-pointer group stored in each object allowed a nice, clean, iterative model of operation that amounted to looping across a list and executing a function stored in each element of the list. Pretty simple. The next questions are when to do that, and who is in charge. That is the purpose of the controller.

Control
Modeler Architecture II:

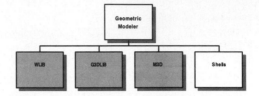

In Chapters 2 and 8, I developed the simple MVC paradigm as both a conceptual and a physical structuring. While most of the discussion of "model" has meant "3D model," in this discussion I use "model" to mean the pure "data model" notion of data structures. Data structures, especially user-defined types, are meant to give user-programmers the ability to model concepts in the problem domain and to define new data types and names that make the conceptual difference between program and problem as small as possible. Two good articles on this aspect of conceptual thinking are "Models of Models" and "Secondary Aspects of Modeling" by Michael Blaha, in *Journal of Object-Oriented Programming* (September 1992 and March–April 1993), which provide discussions of metamodels and metadata. He also discusses additional, less-fundamental but still important issues like versioning and attributes that affect models and our ability to use them to organize thought.

MVC provides a similar conceptual framework, but in an architectural sense. Conceptually, the model or core data structures are transformed and presented in a view with a controller managing the keyboard and mouse interactions that modify the data contained in the model and update the view. The formal MVC provides a good deal more. I use a less formal form of MVC to guide this implementation. Figure 11-3 repeats the figure from Chapter 8, and shows the triangular relationship of the MVC architecture. In the implementation sense, the MVC conceptual model is carried through by a modular structuring and a "contract" between various subsystems, rather than by any formal means.

You've already seen parts of this strategy. The details of the data structures that represent the abstractions the 3D modeler uses were covered in Chapters 8 and 9. The model script and its associated user-defined color table and material table, plus the 3D object list, the light list, and the viewpoint from the scene script, all taken together are the model in the data-modeling sense.

The multiple-view additions from Chapter 2, on top of the MakeApp base application framework from Chapter 1, provide these multiple views of the data in multiple child windows within the main parent window. Figure 11-4 shows a screenshot of the WinMod3D modeler with the multiple views. While the screenshot in Chapter 2 was very similar, it needed labels to clarify which view was what; this one needs no labels. The other screenshot was a blank tablet; this one has much of the picture filled in.

Figure 11-3. **MVC Relationships in Detail**

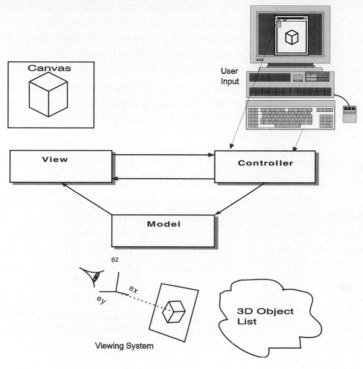

Figure 11-4. **Modeler Screen Shot**

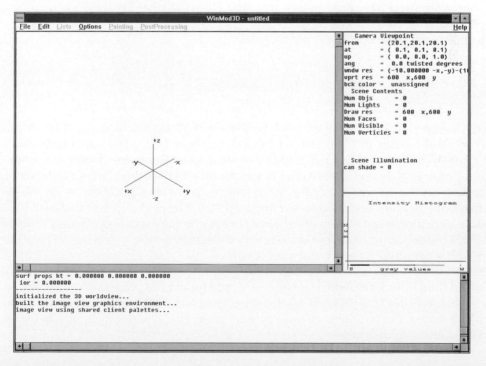

The image view pane with the 3D axis indicates that the modeler is ready. The info pane displays viewpoint, scene, and shading information. The histogram pane contains a crude x-y line plot of the 236-slot histogram that holds the grayscale information. At this point, only the axes and labels are visible because there is no data available to plot.

The final element of the pie is the controller that manipulates the model and manages the presentation of a representation of the model in the view windows. The processes involved in modifying the model, which causes updating of the views, are the same transformation, visibility, and rendering processes from Chapter 10. Hooking up the code from Chapters 8 and 9 populates the model and hooking up the code from Chapter 10 drives the image-view pane.

The Controller

With the MVC model, the controller is the piece of code that sits between the user at the interface and the data contained in the model (as represented in the views). In practice, users often think of the controller as the application. Back in Chapter 8, I introduced the use of a state machine as the basis of the controller. A state machine is more formally known as an FSM or Finite State Machine. The technique of using a state machine as a process controller is a well-founded one. James Rumbaugh's "Modeling and Design" column in *JOOP* includes two articles, "Controlling Code: How To Implement Dynamic Models" (May 1993) and "Objects in the Twilight Zone: How To Find and Use Application Objects," (June 1993) that present the state machine as a natural but underused method of solving the control problem. While these articles naturally include object-oriented material that does not fit C, they also include good information about the larger design and conceptualization issues that lead to using a state machine. He also brings up the implementation point that while many programmers have used parser-generators like yacc that use these techniques, most have never hand-coded a state machine.

His approach to this coding is not complex:

1. Make a state transition diagram.
2. Make the state transition diagram into a table.
3. Write an interpreter to execute the table.

Another good description of the implementation of a state machine is in "State Machines in C" by Paul Fischer in *The C User's Journal* (December 1990). The implementation used here resembles Fischer's, but I've updated it for this environment. A state transition diagram represents state and context, and is a common tool in parsers, where action is highly dependent on the recent past of the input stream. You saw a bit of this with the simple tokenizer of Chapter 8 and its **getc** and **ungetc** policy. The next step is to make a table from the state transition diagram. Finally, the interpreter and the execute cycle need to be implemented. This sequence of actions implements the state machine — a relatively simple creation with a primitive memory and a set of rules.

State transition diagrams are used as a tool to represent program behavior. They are more advanced than flowcharts, which are typically used for overall program flow of control. The state transition diagram (STD) is used with a process to indicate action and context. As Chapter 8 stated, the terminology here includes state, event, and transition. Chapter 8 also used the following definitions:

- *state*: the current activity or process of machine.
- *event*: an input to the machine.
- *transition*: a change of state based on valid input.

An event is legal in a certain state, and defines a transition to the next state as shown in the arc (line) connecting the current state and the next state in Figure 11-5, a repeat from Chapter 8.

Figure 11-5.   State Transition

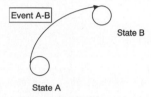

So now our task is to go from the phases of the modeler and the interactions of the manipulation phase to a state transition diagram. The first step is the power-up/power-down action. Machine booting and powering down must be explicitly called out in this type of system. Once the machine is powered-up, it is in a quiescent-but-empty state, because no data has been specified to populate the model. The File/Open menu choice and the standard FileOpen dialog populate the model and move the machine into the ready state. The File/New choice indicates a choice of the NULL model, a release of the existing model occurs, and the machine moves back into the quiescent state. When the machine is in the ready state, many actions are possible. The image can be rendered, saved to a file, copied to the clipboard, or printed. The axis, background, grayscaling, histogram, and print options modify various attributes. The axis, background, and grayscaling options have a direct effect on the image. The options on the Painting menu affect the rendering, forcing a re-imaging in all cases. The keyboard is enabled to modify the camera position, which also forces re-imaging. Finally, the quantization step requires a re-imaging, and this is under machine control as well.

This is the complete set of inputs and actions. The key states are the quiescent "no data" state, the "ready" state (from which most actions can occur), and the transitions that exist in the process of applying options and re-imaging before returning to the ready state. Figure 11-6 illustrates this set of states, events, and actions in a state transition diagram for the state machine used in the 3D modeler's controller.

The next step is to transform the diagram of Figure 11-6 into a table that can be used by an interpreter in an execution phase. Chapter 8 introduced the table fragment shown in Listing 11-14. This is based on the *STATE* structure and the *S_TABLE* state table structure, which are defined in Listing 11-15. The *STATE* structure is used to maintain current information, the primitive memory. The *S_TABLE* structure contains the rules that the interpreter uses.

Figure 11-6. State Diagram for Modeler Controller

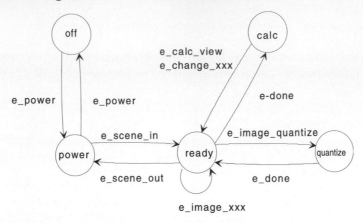

Listing 11-14. State Table Fragment

```
// State      Event        Next_State         F_List
//------------------------------------------------------------
   S_OFF,    E_POWER,     S_POWER,           power_state,0,0,0,
```

Listing 11-15. STATE and S_TABLE Structures

```c
typedef struct tagSTATE
{
   int  cur_state;
   int  cur_cmd;
} STATE;
// state table

typedef struct tagS_TABLE
{
   int  c_state;
   int  t_event;
   int  n_state;
   int  (*flist[4])(STATE * cur);

} S_TABLE;

typedef S_TABLE FAR * LPS_TABLE;
```

The *STATE* structure maintains the current state and the current menu command ID; this is related to the event that triggered the state transition, but they're not the same. The addition of this element makes user-interface manipulation easier for the controller. This provides the simple memory of the state machine. All it needs to know is the current state so the incoming event can be compared to the current state; if it is a legal event in that state, a transition occurs.

The machine uses this simple memory and the rules contained in the instance of the *S_TABLE* structure. The rules are quite simple, and are personified in the first three elements of the structure. These are the c_state, the t_event, and the n_state.

The c_state element is the current state. This element is used in matching the similar element of the *STATE* structure; this is how the state machine decides which rule to test. This matching step requires an external value to test against, and exposes the duality of the table and the external current context — one cannot function without the other. The simple memory of the *STATE* structure and the *S_TABLE* rule table prime the pump of the interpreter, but one without the other is insufficient.

The t_event is the legal event. For any given state, more than one t_event can be legal. Using the c_state current state or rule and the event that triggered this state machine session, the t_event is searched for. Each state in the table may have multiple legal events, so an enumeration across all the legal events is necessary for the matching phase. A while loop across the elements in the table that match the current state is all that's needed to sweep and test for the legality of the event.

If the event is legal, the n_state entry in the table record contains the new state after the transition occurs. The transition between the current state and the next state is accompanied by the execution of the control logic, as indicated by the array of function pointers, which are defined in the *S_TABLE* as the flist. In addition, the *STATE* is passed as a parameter to the control function as it is invoked. This propagates the memory downwards and allows the delegation of responsibility to the control functions. This is central to the correct execution of the state machine. A main driver manipulates the table to determine the functions to call. The main driver itself is independent of table contents. In this respect, this is a general-purpose state machine. You can easily take this code and create a state machine to control a dialog box of buttons that manipulate a device like a sound board, or to control a process like communications, DDE, or whatever. The concept of a state machine is quite powerful.

The states are both the target for a match with the current state and the destination result of the transition due to the event. States are source and destination, and are bridged with the event, as depicted by the arcs in the state transition diagram. Listing 11-16 shows the possible states. This is derived from the state circles in the state transition diagram of Figure 11-6.

Listing 11-16. Possible States

```
// states
#define S_OFF     1
#define S_POWER   2
#define S_READY   3
#define S_CALC    4
#define S_QUANT   5
```

The legal events are shown in Listing 11-17, which repeats Listing 8-3. This is used to generate first the state-event mapping, and then the state-event-nextstate mapping that defines the rules of the state machine. Table 11-7 contains the state-event mapping. From this and the state transition diagram, the generation of the state-event-nextevent mapping as defined by the full table in Listing 11-18 should be clear. Ignore the function-pointer array entries for the moment. The description implies the next state entries in Listing 11-18.

Listing 11-17.   Possible Legal Events

```
//events
#define E_POWER           1
#define E_SCENE_IN        2
#define E_SCENE_OUT       3
#define E_CALC_VIEW       4
#define E_CHANGE_VIEW     5
#define E_CHANGE_RENDER   6
#define E_CHANGE_OPTIONS  7
#define E_IMAGE_QUANT     8
#define E_IMAGE_COPY      9
#define E_IMAGE_SAVE     10
#define E_IMAGE_PRINT    11
#define E_STOP           12
#define E_TIMEOUT        13
#define E_DONE           14
#define E_LAST           15
```

Listing 11-18.   The State Table Definition

```
static S_TABLE s_table[] =
{
//State          Event              Next_State        F_List
//-------------------------------------------------------------
   S_OFF,     E_POWER,           S_POWER,       power_state,0,0,0,
   S_OFF,     E_SCENE_IN,        S_READY,       scenein_state,
                                                ready_state,0,0,
//
   S_POWER,   E_POWER,           S_OFF,         off_state,0,0,0,
   S_POWER,   E_CHANGE_OPTIONS,  S_POWER,       ch_options_state,
                                                calc_state,
                                                power_state,0,
   S_POWER,   E_SCENE_IN,        S_READY,       scenein_state,
                                                ready_state,0,0,
//
   S_READY,   E_POWER,           S_POWER,       power_state, 0,0,0,
   S_READY,   E_SCENE_IN,        S_READY,       scenein_state,
                                                ready_state,0,0,
   S_READY,   E_SCENE_OUT,       S_POWER,       sceneout_state,
                                                power_state,0,0,
   S_READY,   E_CHANGE_VIEW,     S_CALC,        calc_state,0,0,0,
   S_READY,   E_CHANGE_RENDER,   S_CALC,        ch_render_state,
                                                calc_state,0,0,
   S_READY,   E_CHANGE_OPTIONS,  S_CALC,        ch_options_state,
                                                calc_state,0,0,
```

```
    S_READY,    E_CALC_VIEW,        S_CALC,         calc_state,0,0,0,
    S_READY,    E_IMAGE_QUANT,      S_QUANT,        quant_state,0,0,0,
    S_READY,    E_IMAGE_COPY,       S_READY,        copy_state,0,0,0,
    S_READY,    E_IMAGE_SAVE,       S_READY,        save_state,0,0,0,
    S_READY,    E_IMAGE_PRINT,      S_READY,        print_state,0,0,0,
//
    S_CALC,     E_STOP,             S_READY,        stop_state,
                                                    cycledone_state,
                                                    ready_state,0,
    S_CALC,     E_DONE,             S_READY,        cycledone_state,
                                                    ready_state,0,0,
//
    S_QUANT,    E_DONE,             S_READY,        cycledone_state,
                                                    ready_state,0,0,
//
    END,        END,                END,
                                                    0,0,0,0
};
```

The state transition diagram has been created and transformed into tabular form. Next we need the state machine interpreter. This interpreter, which guides the modeler, uses the state table shown in Listing 11-18 as its rules. The process of building the state machine interpreter and the machine boot process are next.

Table 11-7.   State-Event Mapping

State	Event	Description
S_OFF	E_POWER	Transition into power state
	E_SCENE_IN	Transition into ready state
S_POWER	E_POWER	Transition into off state
	E_CHANGE_OPTIONS	Change options that require no model
	E_SCENE_IN	Transition into ready state
S_READY	E_POWER	Transition into off state
	E_SCENE_IN	File/Open circular arc, implied transition to S_CALC and back (reimage)
	E_SCENE_OUT	File/new transition into power state
	E_CHANGE_VIEW	Transition into calc state
S_CALC	E_STOP	Interrupt, very important especially in ray-trace mode, transitions to ready state
	E_DONE	Imaging completion, transition to ready state
S_QUANT	E_DONE	Quantization phase ended, transition to ready state

Control Architecture I: State Table Interpreter and Machine Boot

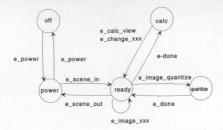

With the state transition diagram and its transformation into the state table done, the machine itself is the next piece of our puzzle. There is an interpreter that manages the comparison of the input event against the table. If the event is legal, the state transition logic is executed and the current state is changed to the indicated next state. The interpreter (or driver) cannot bring itself into existence. It must be booted into a known startup state before it can assume control. Its termination process is, similarly, a two-step process.

The controller is made up of:

- a main driver,
- bootstrap and shutdown procedures, and
- state transition logic.

Loosely, we can consider this to be the control and logic of the state machine. Listing 11-19 shows the function declarations for the *driver*, *init_machine* bootstra, and *term_machine* termination functions. The *driver* function is the place to start.

Listing 11-19.   Internal Control Function Declarations

```
// control
int FAR init_machine(void);
int FAR driver(int ev, STATE * cur);
int FAR term_machine(void);
```

In the end, it all boils down to a single function. Some piece of code must handle the examination of the current context, match the current event against the allowable events in the current state of the current context, and execute the state transition logic if the event is valid. This code is usually referred to as the driver or main driver, and is appropriately named *driver* here. This function is invoked by the code that handles the menu, by the code that handles the image-view pane, and at certain key points in phases where transitions occur. Remember, this is still code and, while there is a certain amount of formality to this approach, some parts of this architecture happen by agreement and nothing more. A certain messiness and embedded procedural knowledge is inevitable.

The *driver* function as declared in Listing 11-14 has four main parts:

1. Find the first entry of the current state.
2. Iterate across all entries of that state and compare the event.
3. If event is valid, change the state.
4. If event is valid, loop and execute all valid function pointers.

The first two steps of this process use the first three elements of the state table as depicted in Listing 11-20. If an error occurs either in finding the current state or validating the event, the function *ProcessError* is used to report the error and the *driver* function is exited.

Listing 11-20.   S_TABLE Elements for the First Part of Driver

```
typedef struct tagS_TABLE
{
    int  c_state;
    int  t_event;
    int  n_state;
...
} S_TABLE;
```

The *STATE* parameter to the *driver* function contains the current context. From there, the function follows the four steps. Listing 11-21 has the implementation of the **driver** function.

Listing 11-21.   The Driver Function

```
int  FAR driver(int ev, STATE * Cntrller)
{
    FRAME* pfrm = Frame_GetPtr(FindWindow("WinMod3D_Frame",NULL));
    int    cur  = Cntrller->cur_state;
    int    i,j;
    char   szBuffer[128];
    int    (*func)(STATE * cur);
//
// get the state
//
    for ( i = 0;
        (cur != s_table[i].c_state || s_table[i].c_state == END);
        i++) {
        ;
    }
    if ( s_table[i].c_state == END)
    {
        ProcessError(pfrm,STABERR_INVALIDSTATE);
        return -1;
    }
//
// find the event for this state
//
    for ( ;
        (s_table[i].t_event != ev && s_table[i].c_state == cur);
        i++)
        ;
    if ( s_table[i].c_state != cur )
    {
```

Listing 11-21. (*cont.*)

```
      ProcessError(pfrm,STABERR_INVALIDEVENT);
      return -2;
   }
//
// set the next state
// execute the func
//
   Cntrller->cur_state = s_table[i].n_state;
   for ( j = 0;
         j < MAX_FUNCS;
         j++)
      if ( (func = *(s_table[i].flist[j])) != 0 ) {
         (*func)(Cntrller);
      }
   return 1;
}
```

The first two steps are matching steps. Using the *STATE* parameter, it finds the first entry in the state table that matches the current state. From that point, using the current event, the set of entries that match the current state are tested against the event. If the event is invalid, an error is reported and the machine stops processing.

If the event is valid, the state is updated to the next state as indicated by the entry in the state table. The third step is a simple assignment to the input parameter's c_state element of the next state. Next the state transition logic in the table is executed in a loop. The last step depends on the function array element in the state table, and uses the temporary function pointer declared on the stack in the *driver* function. Listing 11-22 contains declarations for both of these functions to highlight their importance to the last step.

Listing 11-22. State Table and Function Pointer Array

```
int    (*func)(STATE * cur);

// state table

typedef struct tagS_TABLE
{
...
   int   (*flist[4])(STATE * cur);

} S_TABLE;
```

At that point, both the current context as maintained by the *STATE* parameter and the transition logic indicated by the transition have played their part. This dual manipulation of the crude memory of the state and the execution of state transition logic drives the machine. Listing 11-23 shows you the transition logic function names. The functions themselves are best considered in relation to the states and events.

Listing 11-23.   The State Transition Logic Function Declarations

```
// logic
int  FAR off(STATE * cur);
int  FAR power(STATE * cur);
int  FAR scenein(STATE * cur);
int  FAR sceneout(STATE * cur);
int  FAR ready(STATE * cur);
int  FAR calc(STATE * cur);
int  FAR quant(STATE * cur);
int  FAR stop(STATE * cur);
int  FAR cycledone(STATE * cur);
int  FAR ch_options(STATE * cur);
int  FAR ch_render(STATE * cur);
int  FAR copy(STATE * cur);
int  FAR save(STATE * cur);
int  FAR print(STATE * cur);
int  FAR disp(STATE * cur);
```

The machine bootstrap and termination phases are next.

The bootstrap process initializes the machine to a known state and, from that moment on, driver calls can manipulate the state memory. This is easy to accomplish in application initialization. The key question is where in the process to boot the machine. The main initialization function *App_Initialize* is perhaps too early and, yet, too late to initialize the machine. Once the main window is created, the machine can be initialized. And it should be immediately after this point so that child windows have not done more than update themselves once. In the *Frame_Create* function after the *Client_CreateWindow* call, the basic resources the machine must marshall are available. If any resource creation fails, the function backs out. This means that *init_machine* will not be invoked in the failure case, but will be if the application is going to load correctly. Performing this operation here means that testing for successful creation is left to the MakeApp framework, onto which the state machine controller is carefully grafted. Listing 11-24 shows the *init_machine* call highlighted in gray.

Listing 11-24.   Frame_Create

```
BOOL Frame_OnCreate(FRAME* pfrm, CREATESTRUCT FAR* lpCreateStruct)
{
    pfrm->haccel = LoadAccelerators(lpCreateStruct->hInstance,
            MAKEINTRESOURCE(IDR_MAINACCEL));

    if (!pfrm->haccel)
        return FALSE;

    MakeHelpPathName(pfrm->szHelpFileName);
    lstrcpy(pfrm->szInFileName,"");
    lstrcpy(pfrm->szOutFileName,"");
```

Listing 11-24.   (*cont.*)

```
    pfrm->hwndClient = Client_CreateWindow(pfrm->hwnd,
        0, 0, 0, 0,
        TRUE);

    if (!pfrm->hwndClient)
        return FALSE;

    pfrm->bData  = FALSE;
    pfrm->bDraw  = FALSE;
    pfrm->bDirty = FALSE;

    init_machine();
    fInitMenu(pfrm,pfrm->hwnd);

    return TRUE;
}
```

Listing 11-25 implements *init_machine*. The important first step is initializing the global variable curState, the global *STATE* structure, and its cur_state element. This places the machine's memory into a known state. The invocation of the *driver* function with the E_POWER event invokes the memory-update and state-transition logic to place the machine into the quiescent state. Two entries exist for the S_OFF state: the E_POWER event just discussed and the E_SCENE_IN event to be discussed later. Listing 11-26 shows the function entries again.

Listing 11-25.   The init_machine Function

```
int  FAR init_machine(void)
{
    char szBuffer[128];

    curState.cur_state = S_OFF;
//
// bring the machine up
//
    driver(E_POWER,&curState);

    return 1;
}
```

Listing 11-26.   S_OFF Entries

```
//
S_OFF, E_POWER,    S_POWER,  power_state,0,0,0,
//
S_OFF, E_SCENE_IN,S_READY,  scenein_state,ready_state,0,0,
```

The *term_machine* function brings the machine down. It is called from *Frame_OnDestroy* as one of the last actions of the modeler. Listing 11-27 presents the source to *Frame_OnDestroy* with the *term_machine* call highlighted in gray.

Listing 11-27. Frame_OnDestroy

```
void Frame_OnDestroy(FRAME* pfrm)
{
    term_machine();
    pfrm->haccel      = NULL;
    pfrm->hwndClient  = NULL;
    SaveDimensions(pfrm);
}
```

The usage of *term_machine* is followed by the implementation in Listing 11-28. You can see that this is an extremely simple function. It calls *driver* with the E_POWER event in an almost symmetrically opposite action to *init_machine*.

Listing 11-28. Function term_machine

```
int  FAR term_machine(void)
{
    char szBuffer[128];
//
// bring the machine down
//
    driver(E_POWER,&curState);
    return 1;
}
```

The state transition logic is executed within the driver to handle any modeler-specific shutdown details. Listing 11-29 contains the table entries that show the transitions from the S_POWER state, including the transition back to the S_OFF state that *term_machine* forces.

Listing 11-29. S_POWER Logic, Including the "Off" Entry

```
//
S_POWER,    E_POWER,          S_OFF,     off_state,0,0,0,
//
S_POWER,    E_CHANGE_OPTIONS, S_POWER,   ch_options_state,calc_state,
                                         power_state,0,
//
S_POWER,    E_SCENE_IN,       S_READY,   scenein_state,ready_state,0,0,
```

This brings us to the interface between the application framework and the controller. These are the "hot spots" in the application that must be tweaked to call *driver* and submit to the control of the state machine. It is easiest to consider this from the point of view of the phases of the modeler.

Control Architecture II: The World Generation Phase

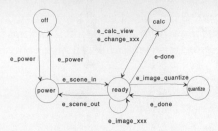

Until the model is populated, there's not much you can do with the application. A modeler without data isn't much use. The world-generation process, as its name suggests, populates the core modeler data structures — the "model" in the architectural MVC sense.

The E_SCENE_IN and E_SCENE_OUT events control the world-generation process. From the S_OFF, S_POWER, or S_READY states, a new world can be specified. Listing 11-30 shows the entries in the state table that control world generation. The end result of this is a transition to the ready state. The process of transitioning includes loading the model and script using *parse_model* and *parse_scene*.

Listing 11-30.   World Generation and the State Table

```
...
//
S_OFF,          E_SCENE_IN,       S_READY,          scenein_state,
                                                    ready_state,0,0,
...
//
S_POWER,        E_SCENE_IN,       S_READY,          scenein_state,
                                                    ready_state,0,0,
//
...
S_READY,        E_SCENE_IN,       S_READY,          scenein_state,
                                                    ready_state,0,0,

S_READY,        E_SCENE_OUT,      S_POWER,          sceneout_state,
                                                    power_state,0,0,
```

You met these functions for the first time in Chapter 8. The *parse_model* function is invoked as a result of the machine receiving one of the event transitions. It is not invoked directly, though. Function *LoadModel*, in Listing 11-31, controls the invocation of *parse_model* and does necessary checks and setup.

Listing 11-31.   LoadModel and the parse_model Invocation

```
LPMODEL WINAPI LoadModel(FRAME * pfrm,VWWND * pv,LPSTR szFileName,
                         FILE FAR * infile)
{
...
//
// load the model
```

```
//
    parse_model (pfrm,pv,theModel,szFileName,infile);
...
}
```

The *parse_model* function in turn calls *LoadScene,* which is shown in Listing 11-32. *LoadScene,* likewise, contains checks and balances before invoking *parse_scene,* in Listing 11-33.

Listing 11-32.   Parse_model and LoadScene Invocation

```
void  WINAPI parse_model(FRAME * pfrm,VWWND * pv,LPMODEL theModel,
                    char FAR  *szFileName FILE FAR  * Infile )

{
...
//
// load the scene
//
   theModel->Scene = LoadScene(pv,theModel,szBuffer);
...
}
```

Listing 11-33.   LoadScene and parse_scene Invocation

```
LPSCENE WINAPI LoadScene(VWWND *pv,LPMODEL mWorld,
                    LPSTR szFileName)
{
...
//
// parse the scene
//
   parse_scene (pfrm,pv,mWorld,lpsFrame,szFileName, infile);

...
}
```

For now, the trail ends here. You can see how the sequence works, and you saw the details of *parse_model* and *parse_scene* in Chapter 8; later, the placement of this sequence in relation to the controller and the application will add the last brush strokes to the front-end picture.

An implied transition exists through the S_CALC state immediately after the model load. Internally, the state machine allows for this and forces it through. The S_CALC state includes both the manipulation and rendering phases.

Control Architecture III: The World Manipulation Phase

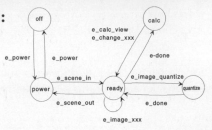

This modeler includes the simple manipulation of the 3D objects, up to but not including the rendering phase. The manipulation also includes the basic camera-motion control that the keyboard interface provides, and this is also under machine control. The S_CALC state actually contains the actions assigned to both manipulation and rendering, as defined here, because to complete an image, you need both processes.

The set of events that cause state transitions within the realm of manipulation includes those that force a re-transformation and re-visibility process:

- E_CHANGE_VIEW,
- E_CHANGE_RENDER,
- E_CHANGE_OPTIONS,
- E_CALC_VIEW.

From the ready state, there are various command-level or menu operations like save and print, as well as an imaging interrupt, that also fall within the manipulation arena. These include:

- E_IMAGE_COPY,
- E_IMAGE_SAVE,
- E_IMAGE_PRINT,
- E_IMAGE_STOP.

Listing 11-34 contains the sub-segment that deals with manipulation, and it overlaps the rendering sub-segment. These interactions focus around the Options and Painting menus.

Listing 11-34.   Manipulation States

```
...
S_READY,      E_CHANGE_VIEW,     S_CALC,   calc_state,0,0,0,
S_READY,      E_CHANGE_RENDER,   S_CALC,   ch_render_state, calc_state,0,0,
S_READY,      E_CHANGE_OPTIONS,  S_CALC,   ch_options_state, calc_state,0,0,
S_READY,      E_CALC_VIEW,       S_CALC,   calc_state,0,0,0,
S_READY,      E_IMAGE_COPY,      S_READY,  copy_state,0,0,0,
S_READY,      E_IMAGE_SAVE,      S_READY,  save_state,0,0,0,
S_READY,      E_IMAGE_PRINT,     S_READY,  print_state,0,0,0,
//
S_CALC,       E_STOP,            S_READY,  stop_state,cycledone_state,
                                           ready_state,0,
S_CALC,       E_DONE,            S_READY,  cycledone_state, ready_state,0,0,

...
```

The screenshots in Figures 11-7 and 11-8 show the Options menu. The Options menu in

Figure 11-7 lets you toggle the axis on or off, pick a background color, set the grayscale method, toggle histograms on or off, and set various printing options consistent with the PRINTOPTIONS structure introduced in Chapter 4.

Figure 11-8 contains the Background submenu of the Options menu. The White and

Figure 11-7.   Options Menu

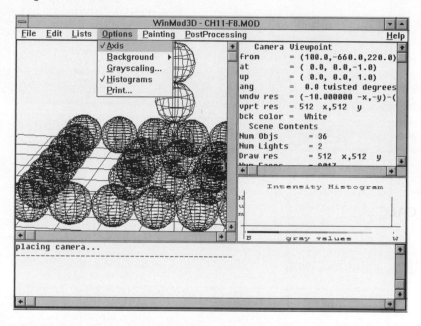

Black choices correspond to the WHITE_CANV and BLACK_CANV styles. The user's choice enables the background color and ambient illumination as the method of calculating background color.

The screenshots in Figures 11-9 and 11-10 show the Painting menu. The Painting menu provides Image and Rendering submenus. I'll cover the Rendering submenu in the next section. Figure 11-10 displays the Image submenu of the Painting menu. The Image submenu controls "double-drawing," and shows two choices — by frame and by primitive. These choices correspond to only updating when the entire frame is done (no double-drawing) and updating each drawing primitive (double-drawing), respectively.

The Lists menu, Figure 11-11, contributes to our simple debugging facility. Besides the *Trans_Printf* calls throughout the modeler that contribute to the running transcript, the Lists menu is also hooked up to the transcript. The color and material tables can be dumped, as can details for each light in the light list. The Objects submenu, shown in Figure 11-12, lets you look at much of the internals of each object.

Figure 11-8.   Background Submenu

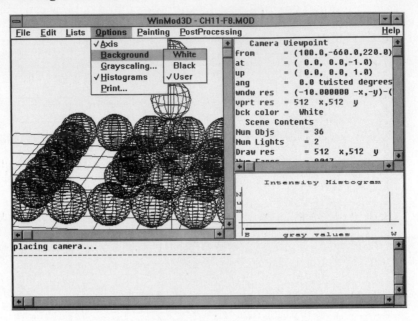

Figure 11-9.   Painting Menu

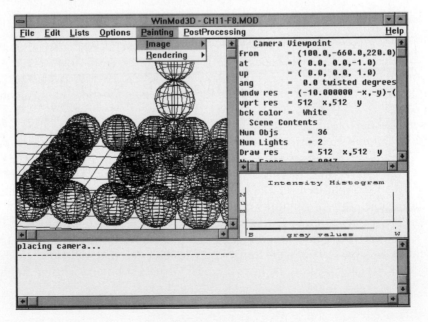

Figure 11-10.   Image Submenu

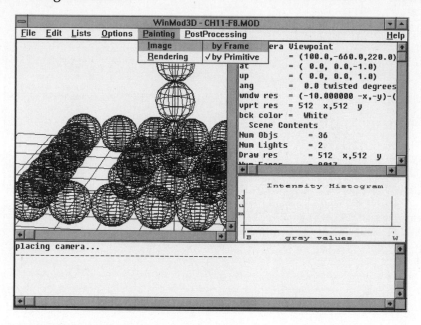

Figure 11-11.   Lists Menu

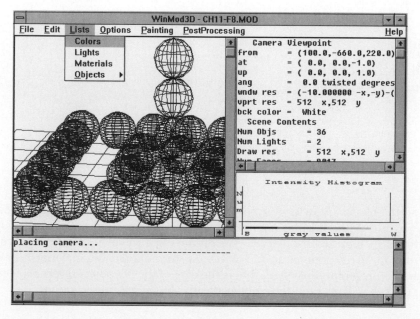

Figure 11-12.   Objects Submenu

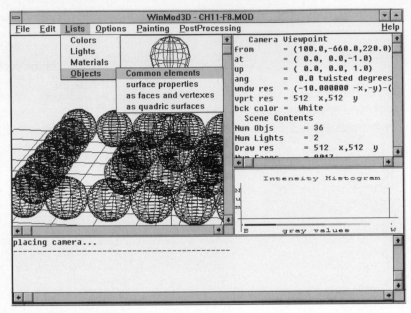

All of the code that provides this must be hooked to the state machine and the events that drive the transitions. After we look at each phase from this high-level view, I'll refine each of them later in this chapter. But first, we must consider rendering and post-processing.

Control Architecture IV: The World Rendering Phase

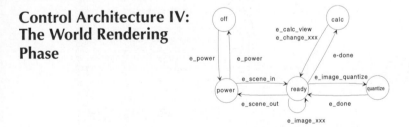

The rendering phase follows manipulation so closely that the distinction is almost artificial here. If we added the editing capability that is so often identified with manipulation, the distinction would be clearer. The rendering phase here takes place when the transformation-matrix generation and object transformation using that matrix have occurred.

The dual representation system that is the core of the 3D object internals means that the modeler (in general) and rendering (specifically) have two major modes:

- polygon mode, for face and vertex, and
- ray-trace mode, for object and intersection.

The visibility step sits as a "bridge" between them. On one hand, there are the faces and vertices being manipulated in polygon mode and the objects, rays, and intersections being manipulated in ray-trace mode; on the other hand is the feeding of the *ShadePoly* and *ShadePoint* functions. So it really doesn't matter whether visibility is classified in manipulation or in rendering.

What matters here is the rendering phase in relation to the state machine controller and its transition logic. With that said, it's time to examine the states that relate to the rendering phase. These make up a subset of the states relevant to manipulation, and include those that force a re-transformation and re-visibility process:

- E_CHANGE_VIEW,
- E_CHANGE_RENDER,
- E_CHANGE_OPTIONS,
- E_CALC_VIEW.

This is reflected in Listing 11-35.

Listing 11-35.   States, Events, and the Rendering Phase

```
...
S_READY,          E_CHANGE_VIEW,     S_CALC,        calc_state,0,0,0,
S_READY,          E_CHANGE_RENDER,   S_CALC,        ch_render_state,
                                                    calc_state,0,0,
S_READY,          E_CHANGE_OPTIONS,  S_CALC,        ch_options_state,
                                                    calc_state,0,0,
S_READY,          E_CALC_VIEW,       S_CALC,        calc_state,0,0,0,
...
```

The Rendering submenu of the Painting menu provides five renderings:

1. wireframe,
2. hidden mono,
3. hidden solid-color,
4. flat-shaded, and
5. ray-traced.

The Rendering submenu is shown in Figure 11-13. I've used a hidden-line view to contrast with the wireframe renditions in the screenshots for the manipulation phase. Note the info pane and the counts of faces, visible faces, and vertex points. This screen capture happens to contain a reasonably sized scene, but is still in monochrome. The solid-color mode does display in color directly, but cannot be reproduced here because of the lack of color plates.

Figure 11-13.   Rendering Submenu

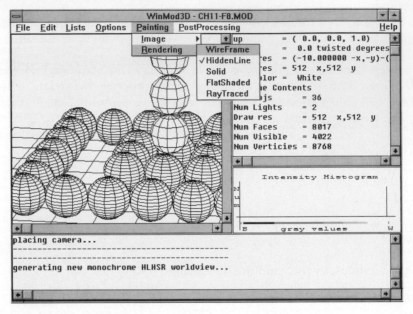

Figure 11-14 shows a grayscaled version of the solid-color rendering. Comparing it to the grayscaled version of the flat-shaded rendering, also in grayscale, you should see two differences. First, the solid-color rendering, even in grayscale, shows the skeletal structure of the underlying polygons because each polygon is outlined in black. The flat-shaded image, on the other hand, removes the edge lines to minimize the intrusion of the underlying structure of the polygons and face-vertex representation. In addition, the flat-shaded image, because of its use of the illumination model, does not use just one color for each object. Each polygon can have a different color, resulting in a gradient of colors or shades. See Figures 11-15 and 11-16.

These figures also show the capabilities of the modeler; according to the info panes for these figures, the scene that is repeated here contains over 8,000 polygons, with over 4,000 of them visible. You also can see the grayscale histogram plot in the hist pane in the flat-shaded and ray-traced renditions. This is produced during the grayscale imaging pass and supports the color post-processing and re-imaging.

Let's make one more thing clear: the solid-color image is in grayscale because this book is published in black and white. The flat-shaded and ray-traced images are in grayscale because they depend on color post-processing to generate color images. They also depend on the grayscaling, the grayscale palette, the grayscale algorithm, the histogram and histogram plot, and the intensity buffer — the players in the next act of our play.

Figure 11-14.   Solid-Color Rendering in Grayscale

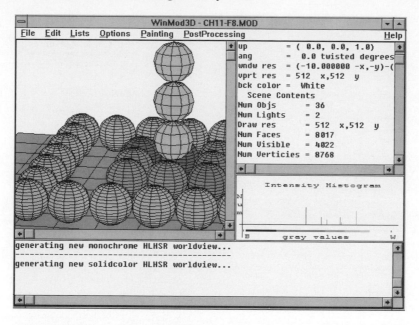

Figure 11-15.   Flat-Shaded Rendering in Grayscale

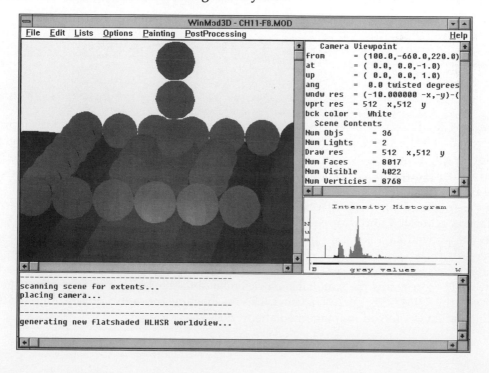

Figure 11-16.   Ray-Traced Rendering in Grayscale

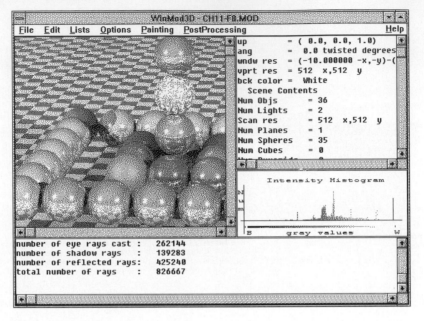

Control Architecture V: The Post-Processing Phase

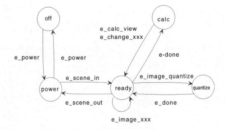

The subtitle of this section is "The Post-Processing Phase," but it might be more appropriate to call it "The Grayscale and Post-Processing Phase" because the grayscaling and the colorizing code are closely related. To review, the shading process for both flat-shaded polygon and ray-traced modes is performed in gray initially. The intensity values calculated by the respective rendering modes are retained for the quantization and colorization steps, then are mapped into the 236 slots of the gray palette for 256-color mode. At the end, a color image is generated and dropped into place. Some implementations do this as a separate process or even as a separate program, which makes it even more of a post-processing operation.

Before exploring the process, we'll cover the relation of this phase to the states and events. Listing 11-36 contains the state table entries related to the post-processing phase. As you can see, the E_IMAGE_QUANT event cycles the machine through a process. Implied in the quantization is a forced re-image step after it does the colorizing.

Listing 11-36.   Quantization States and Events

```
. . .
S_READY,        E_IMAGE_QUANT,    S_QUANT,        quant_state,0,0,0,
//
S_QUANT,        E_DONE,           S_READY,        cycledone_state,ready_state,0,0,
. . .
```

Table 11-2 showed the post-processing phase information by color mode and rendering. The gray process uses the calculated values, the gray palette, and the grayscale method to produce the grayscale image. At the same time, it retains the calculated values, not the truncated gray values, to set up the quantization. The histogram bins are filled during the rendering, allowing the crude x-y histogram plot to give you feedback on the color content of the image. The density of the plot suggests which quantization method to use. Three methods are supported:

1. popularity,
2. median cut, and
3. native or direct.

Figure 11-17 shows a screenshot with the Post-Processing menu exposed.

Figure 11-17.   Post-Processing Menu

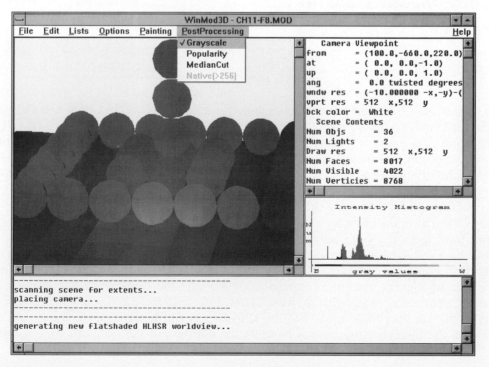

You can see that this was snapped in 32K-color mode because native mode is only available in resolutions greater than 256. Only in modes with 32K or more colors is the native color used directly. In that mode, we use direct color assignment using the retained values, generating 24-bit images. The 15- and 16-bit drivers truncate for us, while the 24-bit drivers use the image as is.

As far as the plot goes, simpler plots indicate fewer color gradations, and also indicate that the popularity algorithm will give acceptable results. More intense plots indicate that the median-cut algorithm is needed to retain any accuracy. The more intense the plot, though, the more unlikely that any quantization algorithm will give acceptable results in 236 colors. The 32K and higher color modes with their direct or native color usage are the ticket then.

That concludes the round-robin look at the controller architecture by phase. The states and events and their relationship to the modeler and the user should be a little clearer. But there are still details left for the implementation sections. The ability for command line, ini-file, and drag-and-drop world generation, for example, as well as the connections to the menu command layer, the keyboard interface, the grayscale methods and dialog, the histogram plot, and the quantization methods all remain.

First, though, it is wise to review your architectural knowledge in relation to the underlying MakeApp framework. There is a superstructure onto which the machine control is grafted. Once that orienting step is completed, we'll start the final round of implementation, including the state-transition logic functions that bind all of this together.

Modeler Architecture III: MakeApp Revisited

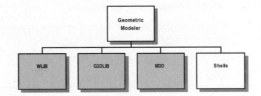

The MakeApp application bequeaths us its architecture, as stated in Chapter 1. This is the standard Windows main, application, and desktop window with a few niceties. First, everything uses message crackers and STRICT in an attempt to be as 16- to 32-portable as possible. Second, the main-application and desktop levels (including WM_COMMAND message handling) are all broken out into clean layers. *App* and *Frame* manage the application and desktop level window, with *Frame_OnCommand* parceling out the WM_COMMAND messages to the menu command handlers named *File_XXX* and *Edit_XXX*. Third, the client area is immediately turned over to the *Client* class, freeing the *Frame* layer from any view management.

In Chapter 2, I developed the additional source components necessary to provide multiple child windows within the *Client* class, or multiple subviews. This added the image view, the histogram view, the information view, and the transcript view panes to the modeler's interface, along with the *View*, *Hist*, *Info*, and *Trans* classes. While it was possible to do this by adding mainly to the *Client* class and ignoring everything above the *Client* in the hierarchy (nothing is perfect), the addition of the state machine controller prevents such a lackadaisical approach.

Before we begin, Figure 11-18 shows the parent-child window class hierarchy that the view hierarchy follows. In addition to the window-view hierarchy, the event-command architecture is another key element of any Windows application (and for most other GUIs as well). The event-command architecture is even more important when we consider the process of grafting the state machine controller.

Figure 11-18.   Window and View Hierarchy

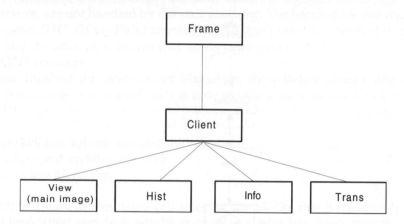

The term *event-command* is used in reference to commands because the notion goes beyond just the WM_COMMAND commands. Three types of event-commands are used as triggers here, and they each have slightly different delivery mechanisms. The three types and delivery mechanisms are shown in Table 11-8.

Table 11-8.   Event Command Types and Delivery

Event Command Type	Delivery Mechanism
Window messages	Delivered to window procedure
Command messages	Menu commands
Alternate sources	Command-line, ini-file, drag-drop

The window procedure handles the window messages, the WM_COMMAND message handler is invoked, and the alternates provide a category for command-line and ini-file "events" that have no message, as well as the WM_DROP handler and the "drop" event. The WM_COMMAND handler is what is usually called the *command handler*, but that can be a limiting notion of commands; the richer definition is valuable here.

A high level of the event-command architecture is shown in Figure 11-19. You can see the three primary categories of event commands handled by the command layer and passed through the controller to manage the views. This is a simplified picture.

Listing 11-38.   App_Initialize and App_Terminate Call Trees

```
BOOL App_Initialize(APP* papp)

    Splash()
    App_InitializeHook()
    Frame_Initialize()        ————frame layer initialize
    Client_Initialize()
    LoadString()
    Frame_CreateWindow()      ————frame layer create
    CheckCoprocessor()
    FPMaskExceptions()
    InstallSignalHandler() —floating-point install
    ParseCommandLine()
    Splash()

void App_Terminate(APP* papp, int codeTerm)


    InstallSignalHandler();—floating-point de-install
    DestroyWindow()
    Client_Terminate()
    Frame_Terminate()  ————————frame layer term
    App_TerminateHook()
```

The *App_Run* function, in Listing 11-39, calls *App_ProcessNextMessage*, which was discussed in Chapter 2 with "good" background processing.

Listing 11-39.   App_Run Source

```
// Process messages until it's time to quit.
//
void App_Run(APP* papp)
{
    while (App_ProcessNextMessage(papp))
        ;
}
```

The *App_Initialize* function cascades into the *Frame* initialization and the state-machine boot. In the handling of the WM_CREATE message by *Frame_OnCreate*, **init_machine** is invoked to boot the controller. The termination code of *Frame_Terminate* likewise takes the machine down. Listing 11-40 shows the call trees for these functions.

Listing 11-40.   Frame Initialization and Termination Call Trees

```
BOOL Frame_OnCreate(FRAME* pfrm, CREATESTRUCT FAR* lpCreateStruct)

    LoadAccelerators()
    MAKEINTRESOURCE()
    MakeHelpPathName()
    lstrcpy()
    lstrcpy()
    Client_CreateWindow()
    init_machine()          ——————————control startup

    fInitMenu()

/////////////////////////

void Frame_OnDestroy(FRAME* pfrm)

    term_machine()          ——————————control shutdown
    SaveDimensions()
```

The *Frame* window procedure sits at the top of the event well. The *Frame* window is the top-level window and, as such, is the direct recipient of desktop messages like WM_DROP.

With the startup of the *App* and *Frame* layers, the exception handlers, and the boot of the state machine, it is time to consider the event-command architecture viewpoint.

Scaffolding II: Event-Command Architecture

The event-command architecture defines three types of event commands:

1. messages,
2. WM_COMMAND command messages, and
3. alternates.

When we say "commands," we usually mean menu commands, although I use a richer definition here because of the perspective it gives in considering command architecture. Every category of input can be placed into these three slots. Again, I'll use pseudo-call trees to present the source, with indentation levels replacing a graphical tree representation.

At the top of the heap stands the *Frame* window procedure, as shown in Figure 11-20. There are two sets of actions taken here. Action one controls events by using the state machine. Action two propagates events by using the normal Windows dispatch mechanism. The separation of events (Windows messages) into "control" and "propagate" classes is straightforward. The events that are chosen for propagation relate, mostly, to handling the desktop user interface. Moving, sizing, icon-drawing, painting (both normal and background), palettes, and menu-initialization messages are all propagated. Creation, destruction, menu function, keyboard control, and drag-drop are all controlled. This separation means the state machine controls the generation of the off-screen canvas, but the details of posting the canvas to the client area, desktop management, and other relatively trivial details are left to the normal processing, as seen in *MakeApp*, and the multiple view extensions of Chapter 2.

By way of the *Frame* window's parentage, it is the first stop for delivery of most messages; for these propagated messages, it performs the second dispatch after the main message pump. Some messages are simply routed to *DefWindowProc*, others are forwarded using the forwarder macros (from windowsx.h discussed in Chapter 1), and many are handled directly. Listing 11-41 contains a definition of *Frame_WndProc* and *Frame_CreateWindow* to link back to the application level.

Listing 11-41. Frame Window Message Handling Split

```
HWND Frame_CreateWindow(
        LPCSTR lpszText,
        int x,
        int y,
        int cx,
        int cy,
        HINSTANCE hinst)

    LoadString()
    CreateWindowEx()

/////////////////////////
LRESULT CALLBACK _export Frame_WndProc(
    Frame_GetPtr()
        LocalAlloc()
        sizeof()
        Frame_SetPtr()
        Frame_DefProc()

    HANDLE_MSG()
    LocalFree()
    Frame_SetPtr()

    HANDLE_WM_MSGFILTER()

// controlled
    HANDLE_MSG(pfrm, WM_CREATE,         Frame_OnCreate);
    HANDLE_MSG(pfrm, WM_DESTROY,        Frame_OnDestroy);

    HANDLE_MSG(pfrm, WM_CLOSE,          Frame_OnClose);
    HANDLE_MSG(pfrm, WM_QUERYENDSESSION,Frame_OnQueryEndSession);
    HANDLE_MSG(pfrm, WM_ENDSESSION,     Frame_OnEndSession);

    HANDLE_MSG(pfrm, WM_COMMAND,        Frame_OnCommand);
    HANDLE_MSG(pfrm, WM_KEYDOWN,        Frame_OnKey);
    HANDLE_MSG(pfrm, WM_DROPFILES,      Frame_OnDropFiles);
```

```
//propagated
    HANDLE_MSG(pfrm, WM_NCCALCSIZE,      Frame_OnNCCalcSize);
    HANDLE_MSG(pfrm, WM_MOVE,            Frame_OnMove);
    HANDLE_MSG(pfrm, WM_SIZE,            Frame_OnSize);
    HANDLE_MSG(pfrm, WM_QUERYDRAGICON,   Frame_OnQueryDragIcon);

    HANDLE_MSG(pfrm, WM_PAINT,           Frame_OnPaint);
    HANDLE_MSG(pfrm, WM_ERASEBKGND,      Frame_OnEraseBkgnd);

    HANDLE_MSG(pfrm, WM_QUERYNEWPALETTE,Frame_OnQueryNewPalette);
    HANDLE_MSG(pfrm, WM_PALETTECHANGED, Frame_OnPaletteChanged);

    HANDLE_MSG(pfrm, WM_INITMENU,        Frame_OnInitMenu);
    HANDLE_MSG(pfrm, WM_INITMENUPOPUP,   Frame_OnInitMenuPopup);
    Frame_DefProc()
```

///////////////////////////

The controlled events include WM_CREATE, WM_DESTROY, WM_CLOSE, WM_QUERYENDSESSION, WM_COMMAND, WM_KEYDOWN, and WM_DROPFILES. In addition, the command-line and ini-file events qualify here. You saw the *Frame_OnCreate* and *Frame_OnDestroy* functions showing the state machine boot and termination signature in Listing 11-40.

Before considering the WM_COMMAND and WM_KEYDOWN, we need to cover the alternate events, including startup and termination events that the controller must know about. In the startup phase, if the user specifies a valid.mod modeling script on the command line, *ParseCommandLine* extracts the filename from the command line and tests for its validity. If it is a valid file, the modeler loads the data by indicating to the state machine that the E_SCENE_IN event occurred; the controller does the rest. The messages WM_CLOSE and WM_QUERYENDSESSION signify application shutdown. This also indicates the state machine needs to be informed, and the E_POWER event does that. Listing 11-42 shows call trees for the alternate blocks. The *driver* function is used in all cases to pass events to the machine.

Listing 11-42.   Frame Alternates

```
void Frame_OnDropFiles(FRAME* pfrm, HDROP hDrop)

    DragQueryFile()
    DragQueryFile()
    sizeof()
    lstrcpy()
    DragFinish()
    driver(E_SCENE_IN,&curState)           - dragdrop
```

///////////////////////////

Listing 11-42.   (cont.)

```
BOOL WINAPI ParseCommandLine(int nShow, LPSTR lpcl)

   Frame_GetPtr()
   GetWindowText()
   lstrcpy()
   RestoreDimensions()
      lstrcpy()
          driver(E_SCENE_IN,&curState)      - command line
          driver(E_SCENE_IN,&curState)      - ini-file
   SetDesktop()

/////////////////////////
void Frame_OnClose(FRAME* pfrm)

   driver(E_POWER,&curState)  ─────────term control
      QueryforClose()
         PostQuitMessage()

/////////////////////////

BOOL Frame_OnQueryEndSession(FRAME* pfrm)

   driver(E_POWER,&curState)  ─────────term control
      QueryforClose()

/////////////////////////
```

That brings us to the main body of the event-command architecture: the WM_COMMAND handling. While this is not the sole source of events in the command architecture used here, it is still a major source. Listing 11-43 shows a call tree of *Frame_OnCommand* and its subsidiary functions. At this point, only the FILE and EDIT menu functions are controlled, but we can change that as simply as modifying the state table, adding new transition logic, and hooking it up to the command layer just as we are showing here. Of particular interest are *File_OnNew*, *File_OnOpen*, *File_OnSave*, *File_OnSaveAs*, *File_OnPrint*, and *Edit_OnCopy*.

Listing 11-43.   Frame_OnCommand and Separation

```
/////////////////////////
void Frame_OnCommand(FRAME* pfrm, int id, HWND hwndCtl, UINT code)

      File_OnNew()         ─────────────control
      File_OnOpen()        ─────────────control
      File_OnSave()        ─────────────control
      File_OnSaveAs()      ─────────────control
      File_OnPrint()       ─────────────control
      File_OnExit()        ─────────────control
      Edit_OnCopy()        ─────────────control
```

```
   Frame_OptGrayscale()    ──────────propagate
   Frame_OptPrint()        ──────────propagate
   Help_OnIndex()          ──────────propagate
   Help_OnKeyboard()       ──────────propagate
   Help_OnCommands()       ──────────propagate
   Help_OnHelp()           ──────────propagate
   AboutDlg_Do()           ──────────propagate
   FORWARD_WM_COMMAND()
```

The user toggles between the data-in and data-out states by opening a modeling script using FILE | OPEN and zeroing the modeler using FILE | NEW. Listing 11-44 contains the call tree that shows the usage of *driver* in these cases.

Listing 11-44.   New and Open

```
void File_OnNew(FRAME* pfrm, int id, HWND hwndCtl, UINT code)

   ClearFile()
   driver(E_SCENE_OUT,&curState);

////////////////////////////////

void File_OnOpen(FRAME* pfrm, int id, HWND hwndCtl, UINT code)

   sizeof()
   AllocAndLockMem()
   InitializeStruct()
   GetOpenFileName()
      Client_GetPtr()
      View_GetPtr()
      lstrcpy()
         LoadFile()
         driver(E_SCENE_IN,&curState);
         SetCursor()
         LoadCursor()
      ProcessError()
      SetCursor()
      LoadCursor()
      ProcessError()
      CommDlgExtendedError()
      SetCursor()
      LoadCursor()
   GlobalFreePtr()
   SetCursor()
   LoadCursor()
```

These two functions use the E_SCENE_OUT event for FILE | NEW and the E_SCENE_IN event for FILE | OPEN.

The two file save functions, *File_OnSave* and *File_OnSaveAs*, are also controlled. They respond to FILE|SAVE and FILE|SAVEAS. Listing 11-45 shows these functions and the use of the E_IMAGE_SAVE event.

Listing 11-45.   Save in Its Two Flavors

```
void File_OnSave(FRAME* pfrm, int id, HWND hwndCtl, UINT code)

    SaveFile()
    driver(E_IMAGE_SAVE,&curState);

/////////////////////////

void File_OnSaveAs(FRAME* pfrm, int id, HWND hwndCtl, UINT code)

  sizeof()
  AllocAndLockMem()
  InitializeStruct()
  GetSaveFileName()
     lstrcpy()
     SaveFile()
     driver(E_IMAGE_SAVE,&curState);
     ProcessError()
     CommDlgExtendedError()
  GlobalFreePtr()

/////////////////////////
```

Likewise, the print and clipboard-copy functions *File_OnPrint* and *Edit_OnCopy*, which respond to FILE | PRINT and EDIT | COPY (there are actually several different types of copy, but more on that later), are controlled. What you are seeing is that any function with a direct effect on or that needs access to the canvas is controlled. Listing 11-46 shows the print and copy function call trees and the events E_IMAGE_PRINT and E_IMAGE_COPY.

Listing 11-46.   Print and Copy

```
void File_OnPrint(FRAME* pfrm, int id, HWND hwndCtl, UINT code)

  sizeof()
  AllocAndLockMem()
  InitializeStruct()
  PrintDlg()
     DeleteDC()
     PrintFile()
     driver(E_IMAGE_PRINT,&curState);
     GlobalFree()
     GlobalFree()
```

```
    ProcessError()
    CommDlgExtendedError()
  GlobalFreePtr()
```

`///////////////////////`

```
void Edit_OnCopy(FRAME* pfrm, int id, HWND hwndCtl, UINT code)

  CopyFile()
  driver(E_IMAGE_COPY,&curState);
```

`///////////////////////`

Now the command architecture has been discussed. The next time you see these events and the state machine it will be to implement the state transition logic and the high-level modeler functions that are directly invoked by the state transition functions. That will finish off the implementation. Before that, though, we need one more look at the scaffolding — this time, the view hierarchy.

Scaffolding III: Window-Class/View Hierarchy

The last piece of the scaffolding in this review of our MakeApp-based modeler is the Window/View hierarchy. This view of the application is still important, because even though the state machine has control over most of the application's core, some events (Windows messages) are propagated (delivered) instead of controlled. Who they get propagated to and why are the key details.

Figure 11-18 showed you the view hierarchy, and we've covered the *Frame* layer extensively. We haven't talked much about the **Client** layer and its descendants other than to name them: image view, hist view, info view, and trans view. Since the discussion centers around the propagated messages, it is perhaps best to show a message-view mapping. Table 11-9 does this for us.

Table 11-9   Message-View Mapping

Message	View	Description
WM_NCCALCSIZE	F	Uses ini-file and SaveDimensions
WM_MOVE	F	Uses ini-file and SaveDimensions
WM_SIZE	F,C	Children sized like parent
WM_QUERYDRAGICON	F	Display icon during dragging
WM_PAINT	F,C,V,H,I,T	Children follow parent
WM_ERASEBKGND	F,C,V,H,I,T	Children follow parent
WM_QUERYNEWPALETTE	F,C,V,H	Image view "owns" palette
WM_ONPALETTECHANGED	F,C,V,H	Image view "owns" palette
WM_INITMENU	F	Perform menu initializations
WM_INITMENUPOPUP	F	Perform menu initializations

Key
F=FRAME, C=CLIENT,
V=IMAGEVIEW, H=HISTVIEW, I=INFOVIEW, T=TRANSVIEW

From this, you can see that the *Frame* layer still leaves its fingerprint on the WM_NCCALCSIZE, WM_MOVE, WM_SIZE, WM_QUERYDRAGICON, WM_INITMENU, and WM_INITMENUPOPUP messages. These are all desktop-level actions that the top level window can or must deal with. The state machine and the underlying views don't need to be aware that any particular desktop is above them, and the MakeApp framework already does an admirable job of that level of management. In this way, we maintain modularity, while, at the same time, the basic application architecture is extended in the critical directions of better control and multiple subviews.

Of these messages, only three are worth exploring in detail with call trees: the painting and palette messages. While parts of the other message handlers might prove interesting, they do not affect the main flow, so discussing them is enough. If that piques your interest, you can examine the code on the disk. The WM_NCCCALCSIZE message is trapped and handled to enable the desktop layer to save the *Frame*'s current size in the ini-file, along with the minimized state. The WM_MOVE message is likewise trapped for current position on the desktop and stored in the ini-file. WM_SIZE messages are propagated to the **Client**. The **Client** knows all children, including positional. It used this same procedural knowledge in *Client_OnCreate*.

Listing 2-31 in Chapter 2 showed the window-creation segment of this function, using size calculations similar to the handling for the WM_SIZE message. The WM_QUERYDRAGICON message lets the application paint the icon during a dragging operation. This is an icon-dragging operation — not the File Manager's drag-and-drop. The two menu messages, WM_INITMENU and WM_INITMENUPOPUP, let the application enable, disable, check, uncheck, or otherwise manipulate the menu bar. This is taken advantage of by utility function *fInitMenu*. It is not worth exploring beyond a brief mention; it does the enabling and checking you would expect, based on the command set seen so far.

That leaves WM_PAINT, WM_QUERYNEWPALETTE, and WM_ONPALETTECHANGED, ignoring the WM_ERASEBKGND message as it was covered with MakeApp in Chapter 2. The interrelationship between palette messages, the canvas, and the paint message is complex.

Remember that, in Chapter 2, Windows palette handling was divided into two components: the data structures and API on the one hand and the application policy and message handling necessary to be good Windows citizens on the other. On top of that, the grayscale and post-processing code was given responsibility for the appearance of the image.

This depended on the library development and the API built in the earlier chapters. Chapter 4 used the data structures and the API to develop the *WL_Pal_* routines. Chapter 5 used these immediately in the *CANVAS* abstraction, building screen and printer palettes into the *CANVAS* and, by extension, into its owning *GENV* graphics environment. The updated RGBCube demo at the end of Chapter 5 demonstrated the basic palette-handling policy for the two palette messages. The handling here continues with that basic treatment.

The only real caveat is palette synchronization. The palette in the final destination client DC and the off-screen DC of the *CANVAS* must be in sync, or garbage will result on the screen from the mismatch. To that end, the palette messages and the paint message are propagated all the way to the image view, which assumes responsibility for palette realization from the desktop level.

In the image view, the WM_PAINT handler uses *G3D_GEnv_Paint* to display the canvas. Listing 11-47 contains *View_OnPaint* and this usage. I show you the source here instead of the call tree because the particulars are of interest in the view discussion, while the command discussion sets up the implementation sections that follow.

Listing 11-47.   WM_PAINT Handler for Image View

```
void View_OnPaint(VWWND* pv) {
    PAINTSTRUCT ps;
    RECT        rDst,rSrc;
    HDC         hdc;
    int         xScroll,yScroll;

    hdc    = BeginPaint(pv->hwnd, &ps);
    xScroll = GetScrollPos  (pv->hwnd, SB_HORZ);
    yScroll = GetScrollPos  (pv->hwnd, SB_VERT);
    rDst.left    = 0;
    rDst.top     = 0;
    rDst.right   = rV.right;
    rDst.bottom  = rV.bottom;
    rSrc.left    = xScroll;
    rSrc.top     = -yScroll;
    rSrc.right   = rV.right;
    rSrc.bottom  = rV.bottom;

    G3D_GEnv_Paint(pv->genv,
                   hdc,
                   rDst, rSrc,
                   g_app.ds.fRectDefined);
    EndPaint(pv->hwnd, &ps);
}
```

That leaves the palette handling. Source code for the two functions *View_OnQueryNewPalette* and *View_OnPaletteChanged* are shown in Listing 11-48. They perform both a *RealizePalette* and a *G3D_GEnv_Use* to sync the palettes. You should take special note of the multiple checks in *View_OnPaletteChanged* to avoid recursive realization.

Listing 11-48.   Palette Handlers

```
BOOL View_OnQueryNewPalette(VWWND* pv)
{
    HPALETTE hOldP;
    HDC      hdc;
    HWND     hwP;
    int      nc = 0;
```

Listing 11-48. *(cont.)*

```
    hdc    = GetDC(pv->hwnd);
    G3D_GEnv_Use(pv->genv,ID_SCREENPALETTE);
    nc     = RealizePalette(hdc);
    if ( nc )
    {
        InvalidateRect(pv->hwnd,NULL,FALSE);
        UpdateWindow(pv->hwnd);
    }

    ReleaseDC(pv->hwnd,hdc);
    return (nc != 0 );
}
void View_OnPaletteChanged(VWWND* pv,HWND hwndPaletteChange)
{
    FRAME*    pfrm  = Frame_GetPtr(g_app.hwndMain);
    CLIENT*   pcli  = Client_GetPtr(pfrm->hwndClient);
    HISTWND*  phist = Hist_GetPtr(pcli->hwHist);
    HPALETTE  hOldP;
    HDC       hdc;
    int       nc;

    if (( hwndPaletteChange != pv->hwnd ) &&
        ( hwndPaletteChange != phist->hwnd ) &&
        ( hwndPaletteChange != g_app.hwndMain ))
    {
        hdc    = GetDC(pv->hwnd);
        G3D_GEnv_Use(pv->genv,ID_SCREENPALETTE);
        nc     = RealizePalette(hdc);
        if ( nc )
        {
            InvalidateRect(pv->hwnd,NULL,FALSE);
            UpdateWindow(pv->hwnd);
        }
        ReleaseDC(pv->hwnd,hdc);
    }
}
```

With that, we complete the common handling for the views. You've seen the controller and how it is inserted into the command stream. A richer definition of command makes this process easier to understand. The view hierarchy, the messages it deals with, and its interdependencies have all been covered briefly. The details of individual drawing logic remain, but that is the purpose of the next section. There, the implementation of the state transition logic that binds high-level modeler guts to the state machine will finish our construction of the modeler.

Implementation I: World Generation

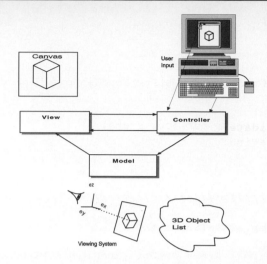

The previous two sections, Control and MakeApp Revisited, covered the state machine controller, event-command architecture, and hooking to state-machine transition logic. Now it is time to implement the state transition logic functions, which loosely correspond to the phases of the modeler. With that as our point of view, the final construction leaves no corner untouched.

World generation occurs in response to E_SCENE_IN events; world shutdown responds to E_SCENE_OUT and E_POWER events.

These events come from either the menu (menu commands), the command line (alternate), or the ini-file (alternate). Listing 11-30 showed the related state table entries and defined the state-transition functions shown in Listing 11-49.

Listing 11-49.   World Generation State Transition Logic

```
int   FAR off_state(STATE * cur);
int   FAR power_state(STATE * cur);

int   FAR scenein_state(STATE * cur);
int   FAR ready_state(STATE * cur);
int   FAR sceneout_state(STATE * cur);
```

The E_POWER event and the S_POWER state are a contrivance to allow a "slot," between machine off and machine ready, to perform actions. This "quiescent" but dataless state of power, S_POWER, responds to the E_POWER event much like S_OFF by kicking the machine to the next level of functionality. It is a two-step machine, like a VCR or drillpress, in that respect. The first step just turns the machine on. The second step is what makes it do something. The same is true in reverse, so the S_READY state responds to the E_POWER event *not* by shutting the machine off, but by terminating the use of the current data in the model. Listing 11-50 shows the *off_state* and *power_state* functions that participate in this.

Listing 11-50. Off and Power Functions

```
int  FAR off_state(STATE * cur)
{
   FRAME*  pfrm = Frame_GetPtr(FindWindow("WinMod3D_Frame",NULL));
//
   if ( pfrm )
      settitle(pfrm,cur->cur_state);
//
   return 1;
}
//
////////////////////////////////////////////////////////////////////////
//
int  FAR power_state(STATE * cur)
{
   FRAME*  pfrm = Frame_GetPtr(FindWindow("WinMod3D_Frame",NULL));
//
   if ( pfrm )
   {
      settitle(pfrm,cur->cur_state);
      pfrm->bDraw    = FALSE;
   }
//
   return 1;
}
```

The ready state is entered by populating the model with data. The *scenein_state* function does this for us. It first uses *LoadView* to load the model for the modeler. Next, it forces a transition through the S_CALC state and generates an image. It uses *driver* and the E_CALC_VIEW event to force a transformation and rendering run. Listing 11-51 has the implementation.

Listing 11-51. Scene Loading Function scenein_state

```
int  FAR scenein_state(STATE * cur)
{
   FRAME*  pfrm = Frame_GetPtr(FindWindow("WinMod3D_Frame",NULL));
   CLIENT* pcli = Client_GetPtr(pfrm->hwndClient);
   VWWND*  pv   = View_GetPtr(pcli->hwView);
//
// perform the operation
//
   SetCursor(LoadCursor(NULL, IDC_WAIT));
   LoadView(pv,pfrm->szInFileName);
   SetCursor(LoadCursor(NULL, IDC_ARROW));
//
// state variables
```

```
//
   bPosts                 = FALSE;
   pfrm->bData            = TRUE;
   pfrm->bDirty           = FALSE;
//
   settitle(pfrm,cur->cur_state);
   fInitMenu(pfrm,pfrm->hwnd);
   pfrm->bDraw            = TRUE;
   driver(E_CALC_VIEW,&curState);
// update info window
   Info_BuildBuffer(pinfo);
   return 1;
}
```

Following *LoadView* leads us to *parse_model* and *parse_scene*, at which point the trail ends for world generation. Once the scene-clearing function is discussed, this section will be over and you will be ready for manipulation and rendering. *LoadView* is shown in Listing 11-52. It has three parts:

- file I/O and model handling,
- scene and camera setup, and
- view setup.

Listing 11-52.   LoadView

```
void WINAPI LoadView(VWWND* pv, LPSTR szFileName)
{
    FRAME*  pfrm = Frame_GetPtr(g_app.hwndMain);
    CLIENT* pcli = Client_GetPtr(pfrm->hwndClient);
    FILE *  infile;

    Trans_Printf(winio_hwnd,
                  (LPSTR)"Loading modeling file %s...\n",szFile);
// first open modeling info file
    infile=fopen(szFileName, "rt"); /* modeling .mod run file */
    if(infile==NULL)      {
       MessageBox(NULL,"modeling file open failure!",
                  "modeler package",MB_OK);
       pfrm->bData        = FALSE;
       return ;
    }
//   out with old in with new
    FreeModel(pv,pv->mWorld);
    pv->mWorld = LoadModel(pfrm,pv,szFileName,infile);
    Trans_Printf(winio_hwnd,"loaded model...%s\n",szFileName);
// then close modeling info file
    fclose(infile);
```

Listing 11-52.   *(cont.)*

```
// setup world globals
    Trans_Printf(winio_hwnd,"scanning scene for extents...\n");
    ScanObjectList( pv,pv->mWorld,pv->mWorld->Scene);
    Trans_Printf(winio_hwnd,"moving camera...\n");
    pv->mWorld->Scene->Eye.view_vd = G3D_V4D_VMag4D(
                            pv->mWorld->Scene->Eye.view_from);
    G3D_View_MoveCamera(pv->genv,tParaProj,
                            pv->mWorld->Scene->Eye.view_from,
                            pv->mWorld->Scene->Eye.view_at,
                            pv->mWorld->Scene->Eye.view_up,
                            pv->mWorld->Scene->Eye.view_horzangle,
                            pv->mWorld->Scene->Eye.view_vd,
                        pv->mWorld->Scene->Eye.view_vs);
    G3D_View_MoveCamera(pv->genv,tPerspProj,
                            pv->mWorld->Scene->Eye.view_from,
                            pv->mWorld->Scene->Eye.view_at,
                            pv->mWorld->Scene->Eye.view_up,
                            pv->mWorld->Scene->Eye.view_horzangle,
                            pv->mWorld->Scene->Eye.view_vd,
                            pv->mWorld->Scene->Eye.view_vs);
    if ( rtype == CMD_SOLID )  {
      HDC hDC;
      G3D_GEnv_SetVal(pv->genv,ID_SCREENPALETTE,(DWORD)hprgb);
      G3D_GEnv_Use(pv->genv,ID_SCREENPALETTE);
      hDC       = GetDC(pv->hwnd);
      pv->hpOld = SelectPalette(hDC,hprgb,0);
      RealizePalette(hDC);
      ReleaseDC(pv->hwnd,hDC);
    }
    View_OnShadeType(pv,rtype,NULL,NULL);
//
    InvalidateRect(pv->hwnd,NULL,TRUE);
    InvalidateRect(pcli->hwInfo,NULL,TRUE);
    return ;
}
```

The file open and close operations are handled by *LoadView* itself, and if an open succeeds, the current model is released by *FreeModel*, and a new one is loaded by *LoadModel*. Then the file is closed and the second part of *LoadView* takes over. Here, *ScanObjectList* and *G3D_View_MoveCamera* set up the CTM matrices for both parallel and perspective projections. Once that is done, various view-related operations occur, mostly involving keeping palettes, canvas, and DC in sync for solid-color rendering mode.

Even though the release function is before the load, let's follow the load path first. *LoadModel* is shown in Listing 11-53. It uses the TRY/CATCH style, while performing memory allocation (using *WL_Mem_Alloc*). Its other major feature is the invocation of *parse_model*.

Listing 11-53.   LoadModel

```
LPMODEL WINAPI LoadModel(FRAME * pfrm,VWWND * pv,
                         LPSTR szFileName,FILE FAR * infile)
{
// order imp for mdi children cannot directly descend from frame
    LPMODEL   theModel;
    char      szBuffer[256];
    BYTE      t, cnt;
    int       n;

    Trans_Printf(winio_hwnd,(LPSTR)"allocating modeling mem...\n");
    TRY
    {
        theModel      = WL_Mem_Alloc(GHND,sizeof(MODEL));
        if ( !theModel )
        {
            Throw((LPCATCHBUF)&_ci.state,GENERR_ALLOCFAILURE);
        }
        else
        {
            Trans_Printf(winio_hwnd,
                        (LPSTR)"Parsing modeling run info...\n");
            theModel->nxVRes    = 0;
            theModel->nyVRes    = 0;
            theModel->Projection = CMD_PERSP;
            theModel->Rendering = CMD_WIRE;
//
// parse the model run file
//
            parse_model (pfrm,pv,theModel,szFileName,infile);
//
            Trans_Printf(winio_hwnd,
                        (LPSTR)"returning modeling run info...\n");
            return theModel;
        }
    }
    CATCH
    {
        switch(_exk)
        {
        case GENERR_ALLOCFAILURE:
        default:
            ProcessError(pfrm,_exk);
            break;
        }
        return NULL;
    }
    END_CATCH
}
```

Following the trail one level further, you see the SCENE block repeated from *parse_model* and the invocation of *LoadScene* in Listing 11-54.

Listing 11-54.   parse_model and LoadScene

```
void  WINAPI parse_model (FRAME *pfrm,VWWND *pv,LPMODEL theModel,
                          char FAR  *filename, FILE FAR * infile)
{
...
   switch ((int) state)
   {
...
        case SCENE:
        {
             char      szName[144];

             theModel->Noise     = InitNoise();

             LoadText(infile,(LPSTR)szName);
             lstrcpy((LPSTR)theModel->szSceneFileName,
                    (LPSTR)szName);
//
// then parse scene
//
             _getcwd (szBuffer, sizeof (szBuffer));
             lstrcat(szBuffer,"\\");
             lstrcat(szBuffer,theModel->szSceneFileName);
//
// single frame modeler
//
             theModel->Scene = LoadScene(pv,theModel,szBuffer);
//
        }
        state = NEUTRAL;
        break;
    }
}
```

LoadScene itself is contained in Listing 11-55, which is a repeat from Chapter 8. With its invocation of *parse_scene*, the trail in this direction ends. This function performs the open/close file I/O operation for *parse_scene* and guards memory allocation with the TRY/CATCH handling. It also invokes *InitVisFace*.

Listing 11-55. LoadScene

```
LPSCENE WINAPI LoadScene(VWWND * pv,LPMODEL mWorld,
                         LPSTR szFileName)
{
    FRAME*         pfrm = Frame_GetPtr(g_app.hwndMain);
    SURFPROPS      surfprops;
    LPSCENE        lpsFrame;
    COLORREF       c;
    FILE *         infile;
    char           szSceneFile[MAXBUFFERLEN];
    int            i,x,y;
// open the scene file
    lstrcpy((LPSTR)szSceneFile,szFileName);
    if ( (infile = fopen(szSceneFile,"rt")) == NULL) {
        ProcessError(pfrm,GENERR_OPENSFILEFAIL);
        return 0;
    }
    TRY
    {
        lpsFrame = WL_Mem_Alloc(GHND,sizeof(SCENE));
        if ( !lpsFrame ) {
            Throw((LPCATCHBUF)&_ci.state,GENERR_ALLOCFAILURE);
        }
        else {
            _fmemset((char far *) lpsFrame,'\0',sizeof(LPSCENE));
// cheat and init visface here,parse the scene,close scene file
// return the frame ( scene ) pointer
            InitViewpoint(lpsFrame);
            InitVisFace(lpsFrame);
            parse_scene(pfrm,pv,mWorld,lpsFrame,szFileName, infile);
            fclose(infile);
            return lpsFrame;
        }
    }
    CATCH
    {
        switch(_exk) {
            case GENERR_LOADSFILEFAIL:
            case GENERR_ALLOCFAILURE:
            default:
                ProcessError(pfrm,_exk);
                break;
        }
        return NULL;
    }
    END_CATCH
}
```

The *InitVisFace* function in Listing 11-56 creates a dummy visible face array. This dummy array makes the handling of *AddVisFace* easier. It gets to assume a valid handle and uses *WL_Mem_Realloc* exclusively. That is not the only place that tests or uses the visible face array, and the dummy allocation avoids any GP faults. Now on to model clearing.

Listing 11-56.   InitVisFace

```
void WINAPI InitVisFace(LPSCENE Scene)
{
   if ( !Scene->VisFaces )
   {
      Scene->VisFaces          = (LPFACELIST)WL_Mem_Alloc(GHND,
            sizeof(FACELIST));

      Scene->VisFaces->fi      = (HPFACE)WL_Mem_Alloc(GHND,
            sizeof(FACE));
      Scene->VisFaces->fiNum   = 0;


   }
}
```

Listing 11-57 contains function *sceneout_state*, which the state machine uses during the E_SCENE_OUT event. It has two purposes: to initialize the views, as seen by the direct tweaking of the histogram and image view panes, and to call *FreeFile*.

Listing 11-57.   Scene Clear Function sceneout_state

```
int  FAR sceneout_state(STATE * cur)
{
   FRAME*  pfrm   = Frame_GetPtr(g_app.hwndMain);
   CLIENT* pcli   = Client_GetPtr(pfrm->hwndClient);
   VWWND*  pv     = View_GetPtr(pcli->hwView);
   HISTWND* phist = Hist_GetPtr(pcli->hwHist);
//
// state variables
//
   bPosts               = FALSE;
   pfrm->bData          = FALSE;
   pfrm->bDirty         = FALSE;
   lstrcpy(pfrm->szInFileName,"");
   lstrcpy(pfrm->szOutFileName,"");
//
// hist window
//
   G3D_Hist_Clear(phist->lph);
   SetupHistCanvas( phist,bckclr,pv->mWorld->Scene);
   Plot_Hist(phist,(HDC)G3D_GEnv_GetVal(phist->henv,ID_DC));
   InvalidateRect(phist->hwnd,NULL,TRUE);
   UpdateWindow(phist->hwnd);
//
```

```
// perform the op on the view window
//
   SetupViewCanvas(pv,bckclr);
   FreeFile(pv);
   Trans_Printf(winio_hwnd,"new session starting...\n" );
//
   settitle(pfrm,cur->cur_state);
   fInitMenu(pfrm,pfrm->hwnd);
//
   return 1;
}
```

Function *FreeFile* in Listing 11-58 undoes the world-generation process. Besides some user-interface work, mostly on the menus, it invokes *FreeModel*.

Listing 11-58.   FreeFile

```
void WINAPI FreeFile(VWWND *pv)
{

// free modeling and scene data
   FreeModel(pv,pv->mWorld);
// init dummy model
   pv->mWorld = InitModel(pv);

   CheckMenuItem(GetMenu(GetParent(GetParent(pv->hwnd))),bckclr,
                 MF_UNCHECKED);
   if ( bckclr = CMD_USER )
   {
      lstrcpy(pv->mWorld->Scene->szBackColor,"unassigned");
      if ( pv->mWorld->Scene->hbc )
      {
         DeleteObject(pv->mWorld->Scene->hbc);
         pv->mWorld->Scene->hbc = NULL;
      }
//    bckclr  = CMD_BLACK;
   }
}
```

FreeModel (Listing 11-59) releases all resources associated with the model. The scene is released first using *FreeScene*. Then, in quick succession, the noise array and the material table are released using *FreeNoise* and *FreeMaterialLookupTable*. The color table and color are a bit trickier. First, if the color palette and brush array that are based on the color lookup table are in use (as signified by solid-color rendering and the CMD_SOLID constant) some palette juggling occurs. This dovetails with the palette-syncing code you saw in the loading process. Then *FreeRGBBrushArray* takes care of the GDI resource, and releases the color table with *FreeColorLookupTable*. Finally, *WL_Mem_Free* releases the memory and

FreeModel invokes **GlobalCompact** with the special value -1. The call to **GlobalCompact** forces the Windows Kernel memory manager to sweep its tables and relink the free list. This is the same action that Heapwalk takes in response to the "GC(-1)..." menu choices. Since the modeler does allocate a lot of memory in many pieces, this is slightly friendlier to yourself and the system. It's friendly to the system since you know that lots of little blocks just got released, and every application's memory management will be smoother after a compact. It's friendlier to you since it will already be taken care of the next time a model is loaded.

Listing 11-59.　FreeModel

```
void    WINAPI FreeModel(VWWND * pv,LPMODEL theModel)
{
   FreeScene(pv,theModel->Scene);

   if ( theModel->Noise)
      FreeNoise(theModel->Noise);
   if ( theModel->Materials)
      FreeMaterialLookupTable(theModel->Materials);
   if (theModel->Colors)
   {
      if ( rtype == CMD_SOLID )
      {
         G3D_GEnv_Reset(pv->genv,ID_SCREENPALETTE);
         if ( pv->hpOld )
         {
            HDC hDC;

            hDC = GetDC(pv->hwnd);
            SelectPalette(hDC,pv->hpOld,0);
            ReleaseDC(pv->hwnd,hDC);
         }
      }
      FreeRGBBrushArray(theModel->Colors);
      FreeColorLookupTable(theModel->Colors);
   }
   WL_Mem_Free(theModel);
   GlobalCompact(-1);
}
```

FreeScene is shown in Listing 11-60. The background brush, another GDI object, is cleared out, the linked lists are de-allocated using *FreeList*, any existing visible face list is cleared using *FreeVisFace*, and the scene memory itself is reclaimed.

Listing 11-60. FreeScene

```
void    WINAPI FreeScene(VWWND * pv,LPSCENE theScene)
{
    int i;

//background
    if ( theScene->hbc )
    {
       DeleteObject(theScene->hbc);
       theScene->hbc = NULL;
    }
//lists
    if ( theScene->LightList )
    {
       FreeList(&theScene->LightList);
    }
    if ( theScene->ObjectList )
    {
       FreeList(&theScene->ObjectList);     /* return memory */
    }

//   cheat and free visfaces here too
    FreeVisFace(theScene);

//finally the scene itself
    WL_Mem_Free(theScene);
}
```

Next, *FreeVisFace* in Listing 11-61 clears the visible face array of structures, a dynamic array. Because scenes can be quite large, this array is potentially huge (you can see the use of the HP prefix to the typecasts to indicate "Huge Pointer"). The face array is another instance of a dynamic or variable-sized array.

Listing 11-61. FreeVisFace

```
void WINAPI FreeVisFace(LPSCENE Scene)
{
   if ( Scene->VisFaces )
   {
      if ( Scene->VisFaces->fi )
         WL_Mem_Free(Scene->VisFaces->fi);
      WL_Mem_Free(Scene->VisFaces);
      Scene->VisFaces = NULL;
   }
}
```

Finally, both *scenein_state* and *sceneout_state* use *settitle* to invoke often-used title combinations. Remember, the title is used as a significant method of feedback, since the modeler has no status bar. Listing 11-62 presents this implementation and shows that, for the

S_POWER, S_READY, and S_QUANT, the initial title for each state is constructed and **SetWindowText** is used to make it visible. The modeling process itself modifies the title to let you know which step of the process is under way in a similar manner.

Listing 11-62.   State Machine Helper Function settitle

```
int  FAR settitle(FRAME * pfrm,int state)
{
  char      szBuffer1[MAXNAMELEN];
  char      szBuffer2[MAXNAMELEN];
  switch(state)
  {
    case S_POWER:
      LoadString(g_app.hinst, IDS_APPNAME,
                 szBuffer1, MAXNAMELEN);
      lstrcat(szBuffer1," - untitled");
      SetWindowText(pfrm->hwnd,(LPSTR)szBuffer1);
      break;
//
    case S_READY:
      SplitPath(pfrm->szInFileName,szDrive,szPath,szFile,
                nFileOffset,szExt,nExtOffset);
      LoadString(g_app.hinst, IDS_APPNAME,
                 szBuffer1, MAXNAMELEN);
      lstrcat(szBuffer1," - %s");
      wsprintf((LPSTR)szBuffer2,szBuffer1,(LPSTR)szFile);
      lstrcat(szBuffer2,".");
      lstrcat(szBuffer2,szExt);
      SetWindowText(pfrm->hwnd,(LPSTR)szBuffer2);
      break;
//
    case S_QUANT:
      LoadString(g_app.hinst, IDS_APPNAME,
                 szBuffer1, MAXNAMELEN);
      lstrcat(szBuffer1," -  image quantizing underway...");
      SetWindowText(pfrm->hwnd,(LPSTR)szBuffer1);
      break;
  }
  return state;
}
```

That wraps up the front end. You have seen the state-transition logic functions *scenein_state* and *sceneout_state* and followed the data structure creation path. Combine that with the parsing of Chapter 8, the instance-creation details of Chapter 9, and the overall architectural scheme, and you now have a populated data model. Additionally, the state machine is ready to control the manipulation and rendering process. The process of reading a model implied an E_CALC_VIEW event, so that is where we'll start.

Implementation II: World Manipulation and Rendering

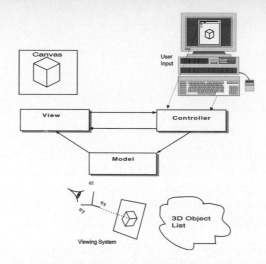

It's appropriate to consider the manipulation and rendering phases together because their relationship is symbiotic in this modeler. The manipulation of the camera forces a re-transformation and re-rendering. The former feeds the latter here, and the two cannot be separated.

Besides the camera and the resultant image data, the canvas itself can and will be manipulated, with the copy, save, and print operations. In addition, we still need to cover alternate actions like the LIST menu and its debugging dump facility for key values. While most of this centers around the S_CALC state, the manipulation and rendering phases are best considered in four parts:

1. imaging actions,
2. view actions,
3. command actions, and
4. user and alternate actions.

Imaging actions include the S_CALC state, its associated logic function *calc_state*, and the various options. View actions cover the info and image panes and modifications to them. Command actions cover the events specifically related to menu actions. Finally, the user and alternate actions cover the Lists menu and keyboard handling.

Imaging Actions

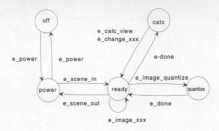

The imaging actions all revolve around the S_CALC state. There are many paths by which you can enter the S_CALC state. Table 11-10 shows, by events, how interactions force the machine through the S_CALC state. These interactions are of two types: direct (explicit) and indirect (implied). This table also shows the state-transition logic functions that are of major concern here.

Table 11-10.   S_Calc Transitions, Implied and Explicit

Event	Explicit/ Implied	Function	Description
E_SCENE_IN	Implied	scenein_state	Auto-gen first image
E_CHANGE_VIEW	Explicit	calc_state	Change in Viewing menu
E_CHANGE_OPTIONS	Explicit	ch_options_state	Change in Options menu
E_CHANGE_RENDER	Explicit	ch_render_state	Change in Rendering menu
E_CALC_VIEW	Explicit	calc_state	Keyboard moves camera
E_IMAGE_QUANT	Implied	quant_state	Reimage after quantization

The *scenein_state* function was shown in the last section, and although I briefly mentioned the *driver* call and its forcing of the S_CALC state, I didn't cover the *calc_state* function. That will be rectified here. At the other end of the table, the quantization event awaits us. Note that the "Image" submenu only changes a Boolean controlling double-drawing, and is treated as a global directive with no state machine impact. The Options and Rendering menus, on the other hand, force transitions, and the functions that provide that state transition logic will be examined. The Rendering menu and associated transitions affect both the 3D-graphics aspect of the modeler and the *Image*, *Hist*, and *Info* view panes. The Options menu and its transitions affect the *CANVAS* and lead us into the View hierarchy as well.

The *calc_state* function, shown in Listing 11-63, uses the TRY/CATCH exception-handling style. This means that any error has a high probability of being trapped. Within this sandwich, it calls the *RenderObjectList* function, shown in Listing 11-64. It, in turn, calls *PolyRenderObjectList* for all polygon modes and *RayRenderObjectList* for ray-trace mode. You've seen these functions already in Chapter 10, albeit in piecemeal fashion.

Listing 11-63. The calc_state Function

```
   int  FAR calc_state(STATE * cur)
{
   FRAME*  pfrm = Frame_GetPtr(g_app.hwndMain);
   CLIENT* pcli = Client_GetPtr(pfrm->hwndClient);
   VWWND*  pv   = View_GetPtr(pcli->hwView);
//
   SetCursor(LoadCursor(NULL, IDC_WAIT));
   TRY
   {
      RenderObjectList( pv,
                        (HDC)G3D_GEnv_GetVal(pv->genv,ID_DC),
                        rtype);
   }
   CATCH
   {
      switch(_exk)
      {
         default:
            G3D_Error_Process(_exk);
            break;
      }
      return 0;
   }
   END_CATCH
   SetCursor(LoadCursor(NULL, IDC_ARROW));
   if ( pfrm->bDraw )
      driver(E_DONE,&curState);
   return 1;
}
```

Listing 11-64. RenderObjectList

```
void WINAPI RenderObjectList( VWWND *pv,
                              HDC    hDC,
                              int    rtype)
{
   switch(rtype)
   {
      case CMD_RAY:
         RayRenderObjectList(pv,hDC,rtype);
         break;
      default:
         PolyRenderObjectList(pv,hDC,rtype);
         break;
   }
}
```

When the rendering process is complete, *calc_state* completes a cycle by invoking **driver** with the E_DONE event. The whole process can also be interrupted with E_STOP. This sets the bDraw flag used by the rendering loops and prematurely terminates the process. In both cases this resets the machine to the ready state. In addition, *cycledone_state* forces an update to refresh the display at the end of every cycle. The *cycledone_state* and *stop_state* functions are shown in Listing 11-65. Once "done" or "stopped," the transition to ready occurs and the ready state has a function, shown in Listing 11-66 (just a stub).

Listing 11-65.   The "done" and "stop" Functions and View Synchronizing

```
int  FAR cycledone_state(STATE * cur)
{
   FRAME*  pfrm = Frame_GetPtr(g_app.hwndMain);
   CLIENT* pcli = Client_GetPtr(pfrm->hwndClient);
   VWWND*  pv   = View_GetPtr(pcli->hwView);
//
   SetCursor(LoadCursor(NULL, IDC_ARROW));
//
// force a render of the view buffers
//
   InvalidateRect (pv->hwnd, NULL, FALSE);
   InvalidateRect(pcli->hwInfo,NULL,TRUE);
   InvalidateRect(pcli->hwHist,NULL,TRUE);
   return 1;
}


int  FAR stop_state(STATE * cur)
{

   Trans_Printf(winio_hwnd,"interrupt of rendering...\n" );
   Trans_Printf(winio_hwnd,"———————————\n");
   return 1;
}
```

Listing 11-66.   The Ready State

```
int  FAR ready_state(STATE * cur)
{
   FRAME*  pfrm = Frame_GetPtr(g_app.hwndMain);
   CLIENT* pcli = Client_GetPtr(pfrm->hwndClient);
   VWWND*  pv   = View_GetPtr(pcli->hwView);
//
   return 1;
}
```

That really is all there is to it. The entire process amounts to calling the driver with the right event, which calls *calc_state*. It then calls *RenderObjectList*. From there, the visibility and shading of Chapter 10 take over. All the hard work of Chapters 8, 9, and 10 (and, of course, all of Part II) makes the modeler's job that simple.

That brings us to the change functions *ch_options_state* and *ch_render_state*. These are shown in Listings 11-67 and 11-68 respectively. Remember from the state transition entries for these functions that the *calc_state* function is also invoked. Each table entry can have up to four functions, and cascading them together is the easiest way to grow the system.

Listing 11-67.   The Change Options Function ch_options_state

```
int  FAR ch_options_state(STATE * cur)
{
    FRAME*  pfrm = Frame_GetPtr(g_app.hwndMain);
    CLIENT* pcli = Client_GetPtr(pfrm->hwndClient);
    VWWND*  pv   = View_GetPtr(pcli->hwView);
//
    switch(cur->cur_cmd)
    {
        case CMD_AXIS:
          break;
        case CMD_WHITE:
        case CMD_BLACK:
          View_OnColor(pv,cur->cur_cmd,NULL,0);
          break;
        case CMD_USER:
          View_OnColor(pv,cur->cur_cmd,NULL,0);
          break;
        case CMD_LOOKAT:
          break;
        case CMD_HISTS:
          break;

    }
    return 1;
}
```

Listing 11-68.   The Change Rendering Function ch_render_state

```
int  FAR ch_render_state(STATE * cur)
{
    FRAME*  pfrm = Frame_GetPtr(g_app.hwndMain);
    CLIENT* pcli = Client_GetPtr(pfrm->hwndClient);
    VWWND*  pv   = View_GetPtr(pcli->hwView);
//
    switch(cur->cur_cmd)
    {
        case CMD_WIRE:
        case CMD_HIDDEN:
        case CMD_SOLID:
          bPosts      = FALSE;
          break;
        case CMD_FLAT:
```

Listing 11-68. (*cont.*)

```
    case CMD_RAY:
      bPosts      = TRUE;
      break;
  }
  fInitMenu(pfrm,pfrm->hwnd);
  View_OnShadeType(pv,cur->cur_cmd,NULL,0);
  return 1;
}
```

For these two change-event sequences, the logic is *ch_options_state*, *calc_state*, *ready_state* or *ch_render_state*, *calc_state*, and *ready_state*. In addition to the re-imaging, most of what both of these functions do is to modify and prepare the CANVAS of the image view using *View_OnColor*, and *View_OnShadeType*. The *ch_render_state* function also meddles with the menu using *fInitMenu*. The *OnColor* function handles the options menu background choice. The *OnShade* function handles the Rendering menu choices. Add that to the *SetupViewCanvas* function shown earlier, and you can begin to see what the image view is all about. Some details of the image view still remain uncovered, though. Since these functions are all image-view related, this is an ideal way to move into the View actions.

View Actions: Info and Image

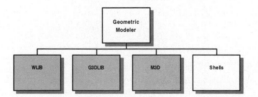

The four subviews — image, info, hist, and trans — are all tightly coupled. The trans view exists solely for session transcripting, and you have seen *Trans_Printf* calls in many places. These add to the running transcript, and the guts of the transcript-exported window class take care of updating and scrolling the *Trans* window. The *Info*, *Image*, and *Hist* views, on the other hand, are specialized views developed for the modeler. The info and image views are covered in more detail here, while the hist view is deferred until the next section, Implementation III.

The Info view is so drab that it does not even use a *CANVAS*. It simply uses **TextOut** and draws, directly on the client area, a text-based display of:

- camera viewpoint information,
- scene content information, and
- scene illumination information.

This enables a user to tell at a glance where they are and how much "stuff" is around them. Quite useful, but it's still not worth the cost of a *CANVAS* for this pane. The only code of real interest is the WM_PAINT handler. Besides that, the only real work appears in the font-creation code that the WM_CREATE handler uses to create a small fixed-pitch font. If you are interested in the font creation code, you'll have to check out the disk.

The WM_PAINT handler is shown in skeletal form in Listing 11-69. There, *Info_OnPaint* does the usual **BeginPaint/EndPaint** sandwich, and uses the created font to set the DC attributes. The info output takes place in three large blocks. These handle the camera, the content, and the illumination information.

Listing 11-69.   Info_OnPaint

```
void Info_OnPaint(INFOWND* pinfownd)
{
    FRAME*   pfrm   = Frame_GetPtr(g_app.hwndMain);
    CLIENT*  pcli   = Client_GetPtr(pfrm->hwndClient);
    VWWND*   pv = View_GetPtr(pcli->hwView);
    PAINTSTRUCT ps;
    TEXTMETRIC  tm;
    HDC         hdc;
    HFONT       hFontF;
    HFONT       hfTmp;
    char        buffer[128];
    LPOBJECT    LightSource;
    LPLIGHTSRC  l ;

    hdc = BeginPaint(pinfownd->hwnd, &ps);
    hFontF = GetStockObject(SYSTEM_FIXED_FONT);
    hfTmp  = SelectObject(hdc,hFontF);
    GetTextMetrics (hdc, &tm);
    LineHeight  = tm.tmHeight + tm.tmExternalLeading;
    ColumnWidth = tm.tmAveCharWidth;
    if ( pv->mWorld->Scene )
    {
// camera viewpoint block
...
// scene contents block
...
//scene illumination block
...
    }
    SelectObject(hdc,hfTmp);
    EndPaint(pinfownd->hwnd, &ps);
}
```

Listing 11-70 contains the camera viewpoint block. It presents a wide range of information. The three main vectors, the from, the lookat, and the up, are displayed. So is the twist angle on the camera. Window and viewport ranges are also included, which tells you the range of floating-point values and the size of the image.

parallel and perspective matrices. The gray palettes, on the other hand, are created at the *Client* level because they are shared between the *Image* and *Hist* views. I'll say more on the gray-palette initialization when we get to the Implementation III section.

Listing 11-75. View_OnCreate

```
BOOL View_OnCreate(VWWND* pv, CREATESTRUCT FAR* lpCreateStruct)
{
    FRECT rW;
    HDC   hdc;
// initial values for from,at
    pv->mWorld = InitModel(pv);
// create the genv, preselect the load bitmap
// set viewport rectangle for initial calcs
    pv->rV.left          = (long)0;
    pv->rV.top           = (long)0;
    pv->rV.right         = (long)width  = pv->mWorld->nxVRes;
    pv->rV.bottom        = (long)height = pv->mWorld->nyVRes;
    pv->rW.left          = -10.0;
    pv->rW.bottom        = -10.0;
    pv->rW.top           = 10.0;
    pv->rW.right         = 10.0;
    pv->genv  = G3D_GEnv_Create(pv->hwnd,
                                HEAVY,INT32,BLACK_CANV,
                                (FRECT)pv->rW,(LRECT)pv->rV);
    if ( ! pv->genv )      {
       Trans_Printf(winio_hwnd,"%s\n",
                   "graphics environment creation failure");
       return -1;
    }
//
    hdc     = GetDC(pv->hwnd);
    SetMapMode(hdc, MM_ANISOTROPIC);
    SetWindowOrg(hdc,  0,           rV.bottom);
    SetWindowExt(hdc,  rV.right,-rV.bottom);
    SetViewportOrg(hdc, 0,                  0);
    SetViewportExt(hdc, rV.right, rV.bottom);
// set the palette
    if ( rtype == CMD_SOLID ) {
       G3D_GEnv_SetVal(pv->genv,ID_SCREENPALETTE,(DWORD)hprgb);
       pv->hpOld = SelectPalette(hdc,hprgb,FALSE);  //foreground
       G3D_GEnv_SetVal(pv->genv,ID_PRINTPALETTE,(DWORD)hpprn);
    }
    else {
       G3D_GEnv_SetVal(pv->genv,ID_SCREENPALETTE,(DWORD)hpprn);
       pv->hpOld = SelectPalette(hdc,hpprn,FALSE);  //foreground
       G3D_GEnv_SetVal(pv->genv,ID_PRINTPALETTE,(DWORD)hpprn);
    }
    G3D_GEnv_Use(pv->genv,ID_SCREENPALETTE);
    RealizePalette(hdc);
//
```

```
    RenderObjectList( pv,
                        (HDC)G3D_GEnv_GetVal(pv->genv,ID_DC),
                        rtype);
//
    ReleaseDC(pv->hwnd,hdc);
    return TRUE;
}
```

Listing 11-76 shows *SetupViewCanvas*. This function does DC and *CANVAS* initialization, depending on the background color or style. For the WHITE background (corresponding to the WHITE_CANV style) or the BLACK background (corresponding to the BLACK_CANV style), this function has a much easier time than for a USER color. In all cases, the text color and background are monkeyed with and the screen and *CANVAS* are wiped clean. In USER-color mode, it needs to do significantly more work to accomplish this modest goal. The background color's ASCII name is used with *LookupColorByName* to get the RGB values, and from there it generates the GDI color.

Listing 11-76.   SetupViewCanvas

```
BOOL WINAPI SetupViewCanvas(VWWND * pv, int bckclr)
{
    HDC      hdc1,hdcmem;
    hdc1   = GetDC(pv->hwnd);
    hdcmem = (HDC)G3D_GEnv_GetVal(pv->genv,ID_DC);
    switch(bckclr)
    {
     case CMD_WHITE:
         SetTextColor(hdc1,RGB(0,0,0));
         SetBkMode(hdc1,OPAQUE);
         SetBkColor(hdc1,RGB(255,255,255));
         SelectObject(hdc1, hBlackPen);
         FillRect(hdc1, &rV, GetStockObject(WHITE_BRUSH));
         G3D_GEnv_SetVal(pv->genv,WHITE_CANV,NULL);
         G3D_GEnv_Clear(pv->genv,
                         GetStockObject(WHITE_BRUSH));
         break;
     case CMD_BLACK:
         SetTextColor(hdc1,RGB(255,255,255));
         SetBkMode(hdc1,OPAQUE);
         SetBkColor(hdc1,RGB(0,0,0));
         SelectObject(hdc1, hWhitePen);
         FillRect(hdc1, &rV, GetStockObject(BLACK_BRUSH));
         G3D_GEnv_SetVal(pv->genv,BLACK_CANV,NULL);
         G3D_GEnv_Clear(pv->genv,
                         GetStockObject(BLACK_BRUSH));
         break;
     case CMD_USER:
```

Listing 11-76. *(cont.)*

```
    if ( pfrm->bData )
    {
        LONG    lsClr;
        SetTextColor(hdc1,RGB(0,0,0));
        SetBkMode(hdc1,OPAQUE);
        lsClr = PALETTERGB(pv->mWorld->Scene->bc.cRed,
                           pv->mWorld->Scene->bc.cGreen,
                           pv->mWorld->Scene->bc.cBlue));
        SetBkColor(hdc1,lsClr);
        SelectObject(hdc1, hBlackPen);
        FillRect(hdc1,&rV, pv->mWorld->Scene->hbc);
        G3D_GEnv_Clear(pv->genv,pv->mWorld->Scene->hbc);
    }
    break;
}
ReleaseDC(pv->hwnd,hdc1);
return TRUE;
}
```

To finish the cycle, we need to consider the *View_OnDestroy*. Listing 11-77 contains this function, and shows its nature as a counterpart to *View_OnCreate*. It releases GDI resources, the model data (using *FreeModel*), the CTM matrices (using *G3D_M4D_MDel4D*), and the *GENV* and the *CANVAS* (using *G3D_GEnv_Destroy*).

Listing 11-77.   View_OnDestroy

```
void View_OnDestroy(VWWND* pv)
{

    G3D_GEnv_Destroy(pv->genv);
    Trans_Printf(winio_hwnd,"%s\n",
                 "freed the graphics environment...");

}
```

Changing our course back to the helper functions brings us to *View_OnColor*. This function is a shell that invokes *SetupViewCanvas*. While *View_OnColor* directly invokes *SetupViewCanvas*, and that's all, *SetupViewCanvas* is more than a menu-command handler. It hides all the details of wiping a *CANVAS* and resetting text details, so many places that need to wipe the screen (like the state machine) take advantage of it. See Listing 11-78 for *View_OnColor*.

Listing 11-78.   View_OnColor

```
void WINAPI View_OnColor(VWWND* pv,int id,HWND hwndCtl,UINT code)
{
   FRAME*  pfrm  = Frame_GetPtr(g_app.hwndMain);
   CLIENT* pcli  = Client_GetPtr(pfrm->hwndClient);
//
// redraw
//
   SetupViewCanvas(pv,id);
}
```

Listing 11-79 contains *View_OnShadeType*. Here you see some of the deeper strategy. This function implements the palette-selection policy. Several different palettes are created globally and used in both the *CANVAS* and the image-view client area DC. These include the gray palette, the solid-color palette (directly based on the color table), and any palette generated by the post-processing quantization phase. Depending on combinations of current rendering type in variable rtype, current post-processing state in bPosts, and the existence of the genned palette, this routine takes the appropriate action. You can also see the use of *SetupViewCanvas*.

Remember the special handling during parsing, in case the CMD_SOLID solid-color rendering was specified? At that point, some palette juggling had to take place, partially to keep palettes in sync and partially because the color table and its associated RGB palette were being destroyed and re-created. That all dovetails with this function, and the palette message-handling policy to present the palette-aware and palette-friendly face our modeler has.

Listing 11-79.   View_OnShadeType

```
void WINAPI View_OnShadeType(VWWND* pv, int rtype, HWND hwndCtl, UINT
code)
{
   FRAME*  pfrm  = Frame_GetPtr(g_app.hwndMain);
   CLIENT* pcli  = Client_GetPtr(pfrm->hwndClient);
   double  xt,yt;
   HANDLE  hbmp;
   HANDLE  hp;
   HDC     hDC,hdcmem;
//
   hDC   = GetDC(pv->hwnd);
   G3D_GEnv_Reset(pv->genv,ID_SCREENPALETTE);
   if ( pv->hpOld )
        SelectPalette(hDC,pv->hpOld,0);
   if ( rtype == CMD_SOLID )
   {
      G3D_GEnv_SetVal(pv->genv,ID_SCREENPALETTE,(DWORD)hprgb);
      pv->hpOld = SelectPalette(hDC,hprgb,0);
   }
```

Listing 11-79. *(cont.)*

```
   else if ( bPosts && hpgen != NULL)
   {
      G3D_GEnv_SetVal(pv->genv,ID_SCREENPALETTE,(DWORD)hpgen);
      pv->hpOld = SelectPalette(hDC,hpgen,0);
   }
   else
   {
      G3D_GEnv_SetVal(pv->genv,ID_SCREENPALETTE,(DWORD)hpprn);
      pv->hpOld = SelectPalette(hDC,hpprn,0);
   }
   G3D_GEnv_Use(pv->genv,ID_SCREENPALETTE);
   RealizePalette(hDC);
   ReleaseDC(pv->hwnd,hDC);
//
// redraw
//
   SetupViewCanvas(pv,bckclr);
}
```

This finishes the view treatment, and our path now leads onward to the Command Actions. Here, we'll explore the static actions on a valid *CANVAS*.

Command Actions

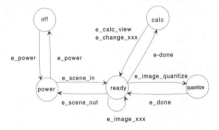

Command actions include EDIT | COPY, FILE | SAVE, FILE | SAVEAS, and FILE | PRINT. While the dialog handling and help could be added to the state machine for monolithic control, that is not done here. Only the actions that affect or use a *CANVAS* are controlled.

These begin with the *copy_state* state-transition logic function, which is invoked by the state machine, as shown previously. The body of this function is in Listing 11-80. It is a shell to call *CopyView*, which manipulates the image-view *CANVAS*. Notice that the "Image" has been dropped from these functions. *CopyView* is also shown in Listing 11-80. It calls *View_OnCopy* where, finally, we use *WL_Clip_RenderImmed* for the CF_DIB, CF_BITMAP, and CF_PALETTE clipboard formats, as shown in Listing 11-81. Note that the palette used is the same one in the DIB that is created for the clipboard action. This ensures that the elements placed in the clipboard agree. If any color mappings perturb the DIB, the palette placed on the clipboard reflects this.

Listing 11-80.   Functions copy_state and CopyView

```
int  FAR copy_state(STATE * cur)
{
   FRAME*  pfrm = Frame_GetPtr(g_app.hwndMain);
   CLIENT* pcli = Client_GetPtr(pfrm->hwndClient);
   VWWND*  pv   = View_GetPtr(pcli->hwView);

   SetCursor(LoadCursor(NULL, IDC_WAIT));
   CopyView(pv,pfrm->szInFileName);
   SetCursor(LoadCursor(NULL, IDC_ARROW));
//
   return 1;
}
//
/////////////////////////////////////////////////////////////////////
void WINAPI CopyView(VWWND* pv, LPSTR szFileName)
{
    FRAME* pfrm  = Frame_GetPtr(g_app.hwndMain);
    HPALETTE hp;
//
// copy genv = copy bitmap and dib and palette
//
    View_OnCopy(pv,curState.cur_cmd,NULL,NULL);
    return ;
}
```

Listing 11-81.   View_OnCopy

```
void View_OnCopy(VWWND* pv, int id, HWND hwndCtl, UINT code)
{
  HPALETTE hpCopy;
  BITMAP   bm;
  HBITMAP  hbm;
  HANDLE   hp,hd;
  RECT rDst,rSrc;

  switch(id)
  {
    case CMD_EDITCOPYGEN:
       if (bPosts && hpgen != NULL)
          hpCopy = hpgen;
       else
          return;
       break;
    case CMD_EDITCOPYSOLID:
       hpCopy = hprgb;
       break;
    default:
```

Listing 11-81. (*cont.*)

```
      case CMD_EDITCOPYGRAY:
         hpCopy = hpprn;
         break;
   }
   if (OpenClipboard(pv->hwnd) )
   {
      HDC    hdc = (HDC)G3D_GEnv_GetVal(pv->genv,ID_DC);
      hbm = WL_Clipbrd_RenderImmed(pv->hwnd,
                      CF_BITMAP,
                      hdc,
                      (HBITMAP)G3D_GEnv_GetVal(pv->genv,ID_BITMAP),
                      hpCopy);
      hd  = WL_Clipbrd_RenderImmed(pv->hwnd,
                          CF_DIB,
                          hdc,
                          hbm,
                          hpCopy);
      hp = WL_Clipbrd_RenderImmed(pv->hwnd,
                          CF_PALETTE,
                          hdc,
                          hd,
                          NULL);

      CloseClipboard ();
   }
}
```

Saving to a file is even simpler. Listing 11-82 contains *save_state* and *SaveView* (in two flavors). The first flavor of *SaveView* correctly uses *G3D_GEnv_Save*. This is how it should be — the API making life easy for us. Just to further illustrate this, the second flavor shows (more or less) what *G3D_GEnv_Save* is doing. After calling through the *CANVAS* and *BMPBUFF* layers, *WL_File_DDBtoDIBFile* is used to save the *CANVAS* as a DIB. The current screen palette is used in this operation as shown in the second flavor.

Listing 11-82.   Functions save_state and SaveView

```
int  FAR save_state(STATE * cur)
{
   FRAME*  pfrm = Frame_GetPtr(g_app.hwndMain);
   CLIENT* pcli = Client_GetPtr(pfrm->hwndClient);
   VWWND*  pv   = View_GetPtr(pcli->hwView);

   SetCursor(LoadCursor(NULL, IDC_WAIT));
   SaveView(pv,pfrm->szOutFileName);
```

```
      pfrm->bDirty = FALSE;
      SetCursor(LoadCursor(NULL, IDC_ARROW));
//
      return 1;
}
//
//version a
void WINAPI SaveView(VWWND* pv, LPSTR szFileName)
{
      FRAME* pfrm  = Frame_GetPtr(g_app.hwndMain);
      HPALETTE hp;
//
// save genv = save bitmap as dib, using screen palette
      if ( G3D_GEnv_Save(pv->hwnd,pv->genv,szFileName)
      {
          pfrm->bDirty          = FALSE;
      }
      return ;
}
//
//version b
void WINAPI SaveView(VWWND* pv, LPSTR szFileName)
{
      FRAME* pfrm  = Frame_GetPtr(g_app.hwndMain);
      HPALETTE hp;
//
// save genv = save bitmap as dib, using screen palette
      if ( WL_File_DDBtoDIBFile(pv->hwnd,
                                pv->genv->lpcanv->bb->hbmMem,
                                pv->genv->lpcanv->bb->hpS,
                                szFileName))
      {
          pfrm->bDirty          = FALSE;
      }
      return ;
}
```

That leaves *print_state* and *PrintView*. These are pretty much what you would expect: the logic function matches the signature of the function-pointer array that invokes the view-related function with a different interface. *PrintView* uses *G3D_GEnv_Print* and produces the required two callbacks for printer job interruption — the abort and abort dialog procs. These are based on the DIBView example as well, although for this basic functionality Petzold's examples would serve just as well. Listing 11-83 has these two functions. That leaves us only the user and alternate actions to cover.

Listing 11-83.   Functions print_state and PrintView

```c
int  FAR print_state(STATE * cur)
{
   FRAME*  pfrm = Frame_GetPtr(g_app.hwndMain);
   CLIENT* pcli = Client_GetPtr(pfrm->hwndClient);
   VWWND*  pv   = View_GetPtr(pcli->hwView);

   SetCursor(LoadCursor(NULL, IDC_WAIT));
   PrintView(pv,pfrm->szInFileName);
   SetCursor(LoadCursor(NULL, IDC_ARROW));
//
   return 1;
}
//
//////////////////////////////////////////////////////////////////////////
void WINAPI PrintView(VWWND* pvwwnd, LPSTR szFileName)
{
    FRAME*      pfrm = Frame_GetPtr(g_app.hwndMain);
    HWND        hwCChild;

    lpAbortProc = MakeProcInstance((FARPROC)PrintAbortProc,
                      g_app.hinst);
    lpAbortDlg  = MakeProcInstance((FARPROC)PrintAbortDlg,
                      g_app.hinst);

    if ( hDlgAbort   = CreateDialog(g_app.hinst, szPrintDlg,
                        pvwwnd->hwnd, (DLGPROC)lpAbortDlg))

    {

// print genv = print bitmap using gray-scaled printer palette

        G3D_GEnv_Print(g_app.hinst,
                    pvwwnd->hwnd, pvwwnd->genv,
                    lpAbortProc,
                    lpAbortDlg,
                    hDlgAbort,
                    (BOOL FAR *)&bAbort,
                    (LPPRINTOPTIONS)&poInfo,
                    szFileName);
        DestroyWindow (hDlgAbort);
    }

    FreeProcInstance(lpAbortProc);
    FreeProcInstance(lpAbortDlg);

    return ;
}
```

User and Alternate Actions

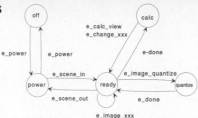

Two more topics exist before we move to the final phase of the modeler: post-processing. These are the keyboard-control code and the Lists menu debugging facility. The keyboard facility lets the user move the camera according to the four arrow keys (x and y dimension control) and the PgUp and PgDn keys (z dimension control). The Lists menu controls the dumping of information into the transcript. Since the transcript is saved into a log file that defaults to transcript.log in the current working directory, this provides a basic debugging capability, as well as information that is too detailed to be contained in the *Info* view display.

Listing 11-84 shows *View_OnKey* in husk form. All of the VK_ key handling has been gutted in this listing to let us look at the forest while ignoring the trees. You can see the increment setup, based on the distance from the origin. This system is, therefore, optimized for scenes clustered at or about the origin. It would be better to remove this code and add an interface to access more of the camera control. Step increment is an obvious parameter that users should be able to change directly by typing it in. In addition, the range approach used here as a default has some value. Again, adding a user interface, even a simple one like a slider with marks like the AVIEditor, which lets you specify range-increment pairs, would be nice.

Listing 11-84.   Husk of View_OnKey, with VK_handling Removed

```
void View_OnKey(VWWND *pv,UINT vk,BOOL fDown,int cRepeat,
                UINT flags) {
   FRAME*  pfrm    = Frame_GetPtr(g_app.hwndMain);
   CLIENT* pcli    = Client_GetPtr(pfrm->hwndClient);
   VECTOR4D sv;
   double   nfx,nfy,nfz,nfa,dist;
   dist = G3D_V4D_VMag4D(pv->mWorld->Scene->Eye.view_from);
   if ( dist > 1000. )
      t_inc = 50.0;
   if ( dist > 75. )
      t_inc = 10.0;
   else if ( dist > 25. )
      t_inc = 5.0;
   else
      t_inc = 1.0;

   switch ( vk )  {
      case VK_...
```

Listing 11-84.   *(cont.)*

```
...
      default:
          return ;
          break;
  }
//
// set the camera
//
  Trans_Printf(winio_hwnd,"generating new worldview...\n" );
  G3D_View_MoveCamera(pv->genv,tParaProj,
                         pv->mWorld->Scene->Eye.view_from,
                         pv->mWorld->Scene->Eye.view_at,
                         pv->mWorld->Scene->Eye.view_up,
                         pv->mWorld->Scene->Eye.view_horzangle,
                         pv->mWorld->Scene->Eye.view_vd,
                         pv->mWorld->Scene->Eye.view_vs);
  G3D_View_MoveCamera(pv->genv,tPerspProj,
                         pv->mWorld->Scene->Eye.view_from,
                         pv->mWorld->Scene->Eye.view_at,
                         pv->mWorld->Scene->Eye.view_up,
                         pv->mWorld->Scene->Eye.view_horzangle,
                         pv->mWorld->Scene->Eye.view_vd,
                         pv->mWorld->Scene->Eye.view_vs);
// invalidate generated color palette
// delete old generated color palette
// rewalk objects
  bPosts       = FALSE;
  if ( hpgen )     {
     WL_Pal_Destroy(hpgen);
     LocalFree(hgen);
     hpgen = NULL;
     hgen  = NULL;
  }
  fInitMenu(pfrm,pfrm->hwnd);
  View_OnShadeType(pv,0,NULL,0);
  driver(E_CALC_VIEW,&curState);   return ;
}
```

The VK keys this handles are:

- VK_LEFT,
- VK_RIGHT,
- VK_UP,
- VK_DOWN,
- VK_PRIOR, VK_NUMPAD9, and
- VK_NEXT, VK_NUMPAD3.

Listing 11-85 shows the VK_UP block as a representative sample. This updates the view_from position, and checks to avoid making the from point identical to the at point (a very bad thing).

Listing 11-85.   VK_UP Code Block

```
case VK_UP:
   nfy = pv->mWorld->Scene->Eye.view_from.y+t_inc;
   if ( nfy >= pv->mWorld->Scene->Eye.view_at.y +
    pv->mWorld->Scene->Eye.view_vd /
    pv->mWorld->Scene->Eye.view_vs )
      pv->mWorld->Scene->Eye.view_from.y += t_inc;
   else if ( nfy <= pv->mWorld->Scene->Eye.view_at.y - 1 *
    pv->mWorld->Scene->Eye.view_vd /
    pv->mWorld->Scene->Eye.view_vs )
      pv->mWorld->Scene->Eye.view_from.y += t_inc;
   else
   {
      dist  = pv->mWorld->Scene->Eye.view_vd /
            pv->mWorld->Scene->Eye.view_vs;
      nfx = pv->mWorld->Scene->Eye.view_from.x;
      nfz = pv->mWorld->Scene->Eye.view_from.z;
      if ( ( dabs(nfx) > dist ) || ( dabs(nfz) > dist ))
         pv->mWorld->Scene->Eye.view_from.y += t_inc;
      else
         pv->mWorld->Scene->Eye.view_from.y =
         pv->mWorld->Scene->Eye.view_at.y +
         pv->mWorld->Scene->Eye.view_vd /
         pv->mWorld->Scene->Eye.view_vs;
   }

   Trans_Printf(winio_hwnd,"Camera move in + y to %lf %lf %lf\n",
                pv->mWorld->Scene->Eye.view_from.x,
                pv->mWorld->Scene->Eye.view_from.y,
                pv->mWorld->Scene->Eye.view_from.z);
break;
```

That brings us to the Lists menu. It includes:

- colors,
- lights,
- materials, and
- objects.

Objects is a submenu of the Lists menu that contains:

- common elements,
- surface properties,

- face and vertex information, and
- quadric surfaces.

These are all handled as menu commands at the image-view level. A simple wrapper function contains a switch statement and case blocks for each menu item. The case blocks are the most important, and Listing 11-86 shows the first one, the one for the Colors item.

Listing 11-86.   Colors Block

```
case CMD_COLORS:
   Trans_Printf(winio_hwnd,"————————\n",szBuffer);
   Trans_Printf(winio_hwnd,"Traversing ColorTable...\n");
   Trans_Printf(winio_hwnd,"————————\n",szBuffer);
   for ( i = 0; i < pv->mWorld->Colors->iEntries; i++ )
   {
      Trans_Printf(winio_hwnd,"Color %24s r:%lf g:%lf b:%lf\n",
         pv->mWorld->Colors->ceColors[i].ce_name,
         pv->mWorld->Colors->ceColors[i].ce_color[0],
         pv->mWorld->Colors->ceColors[i].ce_color[1],
         pv->mWorld->Colors->ceColors[i].ce_color[2]);
   }
   break;
```

Listing 11-87 shows a block that iterates across the light list and prints light-source information using *PrintList.*

Listing 11-87.   Lights Block

```
case CMD_LIGHTS:
   Trans_Printf(winio_hwnd,"————————\n",szBuffer);
   Trans_Printf(winio_hwnd,"Traversing Light List...\n");
   Trans_Printf(winio_hwnd,"————————\n",szBuffer);
   PrintList(pv->mWorld->Scene->LightList,
            winio_hwnd);
   break;
```

A more complex block in Listing 11-88 prints out the contents of the material table. It does this by directly accessing the material table, which, obviously, is not very modular. We'll soon need another print function.

Listing 11-88.   Materials Block

```
case CMD_MATERIALS:
   Trans_Printf(winio_hwnd,"————————\n",szBuffer);
   Trans_Printf(winio_hwnd,"Traversing MaterialTable...\n");
   Trans_Printf(winio_hwnd,"————————\n",szBuffer);
   for ( i = 0; i < pv->mWorld->Materials->iEntries; i++ )
   {
```

```
    Trans_Printf(winio_hwnd,"Material %s has texture %s and\n",
                pv->mWorld->Materials->meMaterials[i].m_name,
                pv->mWorld->Materials->meMaterials[i].m_texture);
    Trans_Printf(winio_hwnd,
              "surf props ka = %lf %lf %lf\n",
  pv->mWorld->Materials->meMaterials[i].m_surfprops.surf_ka.x,
  pv->mWorld->Materials->meMaterials[i].m_surfprops.surf_ka.y,
  pv->mWorld->Materials->meMaterials[i].m_surfprops.surf_ka.z);
    Trans_Printf(winio_hwnd,
              "surf props kd = %lf %lf %lf\n",
  pv->mWorld->Materials->meMaterials[i].m_surfprops.surf_kd.x,
  pv->mWorld->Materials->meMaterials[i].m_surfprops.surf_kd.y,
  pv->mWorld->Materials->meMaterials[i].m_surfprops.surf_kd.z);
         Trans_Printf(winio_hwnd,
      "surf props ks = %lf %lf %lf\n shine = %lf\n",
   pv->mWorld->Materials->meMaterials[i].m_surfprops.surf_ks.x,
   pv->mWorld->Materials->meMaterials[i].m_surfprops.surf_ks.y,
   pv->mWorld->Materials->meMaterials[i].m_surfprops.surf_ks.z,
  pv->mWorld->Materials->meMaterials[i].m_surfprops.surf_shine);
         Trans_Printf(winio_hwnd,
        "surf props kt = %lf %lf %lf\n ior = %lf\n",
  pv->mWorld->Materials->meMaterials[i].m_surfprops.surf_kt.x,
  pv->mWorld->Materials->meMaterials[i].m_surfprops.surf_kt.y,
  pv->mWorld->Materials->meMaterials[i].m_surfprops.surf_kt.z,
  pv->mWorld->Materials->meMaterials[i].m_surfprops.surf_ior);
    Trans_Printf(winio_hwnd,"——————\n",szBuffer);
  }
  break;
```

The next blocks are all related to the 3D objects. Listing 11-89 prints out the common information used to position the objects.

Listing 11-89. Objects Common Elements Block

```
case CMD_OBJECT:
  Trans_Printf(winio_hwnd,"——————\n",szBuffer);
  Trans_Printf(winio_hwnd,
              "Traversing Object List... for common elements\n");
  Trans_Printf(winio_hwnd,"——————\n",szBuffer);
  this = pv->mWorld->Scene->ObjectList;
  i    = i;
  while (this)
  {
      LPEX3DOBJECT lp3DObj;

      lp3DObj = this->o_edata;
      Trans_Printf(winio_hwnd,"object id %d\n",this->o_id);
      Trans_Printf(winio_hwnd,"object local transforms\n");
      Trans_Printf(winio_hwnd,
```

Listing 11-89. (*cont.*)

```
                    "scale       transform x %lf y %lf z %lf\n",
                              lp3DObj->l_transforms.S.x,
                              lp3DObj->l_transforms.S.y,
                              lp3DObj->l_transforms.S.z);
          Trans_Printf(winio_hwnd,
                "rotate      transform x %lf y %lf z %lf\n",
                              lp3DObj->l_transforms.R.x,
                              lp3DObj->l_transforms.R.y,
                              lp3DObj->l_transforms.R.z);
          Trans_Printf(winio_hwnd,
                "translate transform x %lf y %lf z %lf\n",
                              lp3DObj->l_transforms.T.x,
                              lp3DObj->l_transforms.T.y,
                              lp3DObj->l_transforms.T.z);
          Trans_Printf(winio_hwnd,"——————————\n");
//
// next
//
              i++;
              this = this->next;
          }
        break;
```

Listing 11-90 prints out the object surface property information.

Listing 11-90.   Object Surface Properties Block

```
case CMD_OBJECTPROPS:
    Trans_Printf(winio_hwnd,"——————————\n",szBuffer);
    Trans_Printf(winio_hwnd,"Traversing SurfProp List...\n");
    Trans_Printf(winio_hwnd,"——————————\n",szBuffer);
    this = pv->mWorld->Scene->ObjectList;
    i    = i;
    while (this)
    {
        Trans_Printf(winio_hwnd,
"object surface properties for object # %d\n",this->o_id);
        PrintSurfPropInfo(this->o_surfprops,winio_hwnd);
        Trans_Printf(winio_hwnd,"——————————\n");
//
// next
//
        i++;
        this = this->next;
    }
    break;
```

Listing 11-91 prints out the face and vertex information and Listing 11-92 prints out the quadric surface information.

Listing 11-91. Objects as Face and Vertex Information

```
case CMD_POLYOBJECT:
    Trans_Printf(winio_hwnd,"——————\n",szBuffer);
    Trans_Printf(winio_hwnd,
        "Traversing Object List... for polygon rep elements\n");
    Trans_Printf(winio_hwnd,"——————\n",szBuffer);
    this = pv->mWorld->Scene->ObjectList;
    i    = i;
    while (this)
    {
        LPEX3DOBJECT lp3DObj;

        lp3DObj = this->o_edata;
        Trans_Printf(winio_hwnd,"——————\n");
        Trans_Printf(winio_hwnd,
        "object id#%d has %d faces and % d verticies\n"
         defined in data file %Fs\n",
                    this->o_id,
                    lp3DObj->nF,
                    lp3DObj->nVinF,
                    lp3DObj->szDatFile);
//
// next
//
        i++;
        this = this->next;
    }
    break;
```

Listing 11-92. Objects as Quadric Information

```
case CMD_RAYOBJECT:
    Trans_Printf(winio_hwnd,"——————\n",szBuffer);
    Trans_Printf(winio_hwnd,
        "Traversing Object List...for quadric surface elements\n");
    Trans_Printf(winio_hwnd,"——————\n",szBuffer);
    PrintList(pv->mWorld->Scene->ObjectList,
            winio_hwnd);
    break;
```

That wraps up the user actions of the keyboard and alternate actions of the Lists menu. Next is the final phase of the modeler, post-processing to create color images. In addition, I'll go over the details of the supporting grayscale and histogram functions to round out the implementation.

Implementation III:
Grayscale and Color
Post-Processing

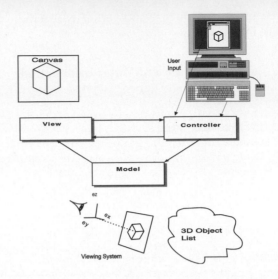

The post-processing code cannot and does not stand alone. It stands on the shoulders of the gray palette and brush array, the grayscale method, the histogram plot, and the retained values of the face and memory buffers. And the interrelationships do not end there. Remember, the gray palette is shared by the *Image* view, and the data represented in the histogram plot of the *Hist* view is the *Image*-view data. This section is, therefore, started with a look at the gray palette and brush array initialization; when we've finished that, we'll look at the grayscale process itself, then examine the *Hist* view and the histogram plot. Finally, I'll cover the quantization code itself, which includes the following methods of palette generation:

- popularity,
- median-cut, and
- direct.

Sharing the gray palette implies that the subviews cannot own its creation or deletion. Listing 11-93 shows the block from *Client_OnCreate* that has this responsibility, as well as the block from *Client_OnDestroy* that cleans up.

Listing 11-93.   Gray Block from Client_OnCreate and Client_OnDestroy

```
BOOL Client_OnCreate(CLIENT* pcli,
                     CREATESTRUCT FAR* lpCreateStruct)
{
...
//
// starts transcripting right away
// builds gray palette and a brush array
```

```
//
    hpprn     = InitGrayPalette();
    InitGrayBrushArray();
    hWhitePen = GetStockObject(WHITE_PEN);
    hBlackPen = GetStockObject(BLACK_PEN);
    hNullPen  = GetStockObject(NULL_PEN);
//
    Trans_Printf(winio_hwnd,
      "%s\n",(LPSTR)"built the gray palette...");
...
}
void Client_OnDestroy(CLIENT* pcli)
{
...
//
// clean up global resources
//
    FreeGrayBrushArray();
    Trans_Printf(winio_hwnd,"%s\n",
                 "(LPSTR)freed the gray palette...");
}
```

Figure 11-21 shows the gray palette that results from this setup. You can see that it is an identity palette, with the system entries at the start and end. Of course, since this is a grayscale figure, the system colors at either end appear in gray instead of in color.

Figure 11-21.   The Gray Palette

Listing 11-94 contains *InitGrayPalette*, which is used in Listing 11-93 to create the gray palette for all drawings. Listing 11-95 contains *InitGrayBrushArray*, also used in Listing 11-93, this one to create the cached brush array resource used particularly in polygon drawing. Listing 11-95 also contains *FreeGrayBrushArray*, which releases the resources on the downside of this process.

Listing 11-94.   InitGrayPalette

```
HPALETTE WINAPI InitGrayPalette(void) {
    HBRUSH      hBrush;
    long        r, g, b, n;
    CRT         crtValue;
    RGB         rgbColor;
    LONG        lsClr;
    char        Col[25];
    HPALETTE    hp;
    int         i;
//
// setup print palette to shadow the rgb colors
//
    pgryPal = WL_Mem_Alloc(GHND,sizeof(LOGPALETTE) +
((NUMGRAYCOL + 2*palpad) * sizeof(PALETTEENTRY)) );
    if ( !pgryPal )
       return 0;
    pgryPal->palNumEntries = NUMGRAYCOL + 2 * palpad;
    pgryPal->palVersion    = PALVERSION;
//
    for ( i = palpad; i <= NUMGRAYCOL + palpad ; i++ )
    {
        /* assign into palette */
        pgryPal->palPalEntry[i].peRed   = min(255,i+palpad);
        pgryPal->palPalEntry[i].peGreen = min(255,i+palpad);
        pgryPal->palPalEntry[i].peBlue  = min(255,i+palpad);
        pgryPal->palPalEntry[i].peFlags = PC_RESERVED;
    }
    WL_Pal_MakeIdentityPal(pgryPal);
    hp = WL_Pal_Create(pgryPal);
    return hp;
}
```

Listing 11-95. InitGrayBrushArray and FreeGrayBrushArray

```
//
// create a gray" palette brush array
//
BOOL WINAPI InitGrayBrushArray(void)
{
    int     n;
    COLORREF c;

    for (n=palpad; n<=NUMGRAYCOL+palpad; n++)
    {
        c = PALETTERGB(pgryPal->palPalEntry[n].peRed,
                       pgryPal->palPalEntry[n].peGreen,
                       pgryPal->palPalEntry[n].peBlue);
        rgbGray[n-palpad] = CreateSolidBrush(c);
    }

    return TRUE;
}
//
// release a gray palette brush array
//
BOOL WINAPI FreeGrayBrushArray(void)
{
    int       n;

    for (n=0; n<=NUMGRAYCOL; n++)
        if ( rgbGray[n] )
            DeleteObject(rgbGray[n]);
    if ( hpprn )
    {
        WL_Pal_Destroy(hpprn);
        WL_Mem_Free(pgryPal);
        hpprn   = NULL;
        pgryPal = NULL;
    }
    return TRUE;
}
```

FreeGrayBrushArray actually releases the palette as well. That prepares the way to do the grayscale. The grayscale is performed according to the gray method, after which gray support exists at the pixel level. The *Hist* window displays a grayscale histogram plot as well, but the *Hist* window class has yet to set up the histogram bins and other details that are covered in the View section.

Grayscale

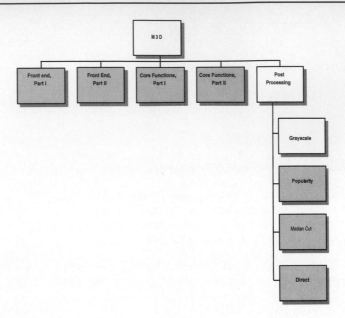

The grayscale process itself is controlled by the grayscale method. Four methods are supported here:

- simple average (1/3 from each component),
- red channel,
- blue channel, and
- green channel.

The simple average is the default. In addition, each color channel (red, green, and blue) can also be specified to give you a quick "peek" at the intensities of the color components.

The *PerformGray* function implements these methods. Figure 11-22 shows the dialog that controls this. It maps directly to the methods, and is not worth examining in detail. The usage of *PerformGray* is shown for polygon mode in Listing 11-96 and then for ray-trace mode in Listing 11-97. This corresponds to the flat-shaded rendering and the ray-traced rendering. You can see how this simply changes the calculation method ahead of the use of the gray intensity.

Listing 11-96.   PerformGray in Polygon Mode

```
...
// apply illumination model and map to gray
   ShadePoly(pv,&pv->mWorld->LoclW,this,vN,P,&Intensity);
   PerformGray(&Intensity,&col,gtype);
   fi->i = Intensity;
// draw flat shaded polygon
   run   = max( 0,col);
```

```
   run    = min( NUMGRAYCOL,col);
   G3D_GEnv_Polygon(pv->genv,(LPPOINT)&pgdi,(long)fi->ni+1,
      (DWORD)hNullPen,(DWORD)rgbGray[max(run,0)]);
// force a render of the hist alternate view draw buffer
   if ( bHists ) {
      G3D_Hist_Set(ph->lph,1 + run);
   }
...
```

Listing 11-97.   PerformGray and DrawGrayPixel in Ray-Trace Mode

```
   MakeRay (pv,Ray.r_origin,rS,rU,rV,ix,iy,&Ray);
   Trace (pv,&pv->mWorld->MaxW,depth,
         &Ray,&Intensity);
   PerformGray(&Intensity,&col,gtype);
   run     = min( NUMGRAYCOL,col);
   DrawGrayPixel(hdcscr,ix,pv->mWorld->Scene->scanY-iy,run);
   DrawGrayPixel(hDC,   ix,pv->mWorld->Scene->scanY-iy,run);
   G3D_GEnv_SetMem(pv->genv,iy,ix,col);
   G3D_Hist_Set(phist->lph,1 + run);
```

Figure 11-22.   Grayscale Method Control

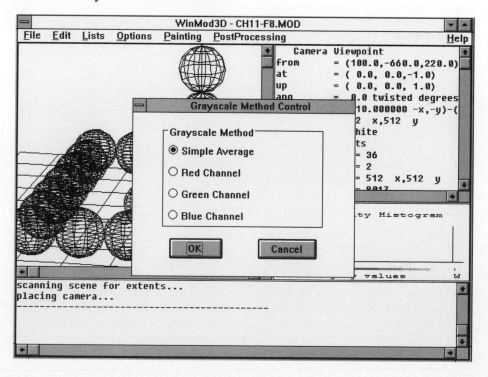

The **PerformGray** function itself is shown in Listing 11-98. It is a straightforward implementation of the four methods described. The first one sums and divides by three (the number of terms) for a simple average. The red, green, and blue methods simply use one of the three values.

Listing 11-98.   PerformGray

```
void WINAPI PerformGray(LPVECTOR4D vI,long far * col, int type)
{
   switch(type)
   {
      default:
      case CTL_SIMPLE:
            vI->x*=255;
            vI->y*=255;
            vI->z*=255;
            *col    = ((vI->x+20+vI->y+20+vI->z+20)/3);
            break;
      case CTL_RED:
            vI->x*=255;
            vI->y*=255;
            vI->z*=255;
            *col    = ((vI->x+20));
            break;
      case CTL_GREEN:
            vI->x*=255;
            vI->y*=255;
            vI->z*=255;
            *col    = ((vI->y+20));
            break;
      case CTL_BLUE:
            vI->x*=255;
            vI->y*=255;
            vI->z*=255;
            *col    = ((vI->z+20));
            break;

   }
}
```

The *DrawGrayPixel* function is an oddball. It is used instead of *G3D_GEnv_Point* because that function requires a brush. By bypassing the API in this one case and using **SetPixel,** life is a little easier. This is made into a separate function rather than using **SetPixel** in-line, because we may need to revisit this decision someday. This way, the main ray-trace loop has high hopes of being insulated from a change in low-level drawing primitive or attribute usage. *DrawGrayPixel* is in Listing 11-99.

Listing 11-99.   DrawGrayPixel

```
void WINAPI DrawGrayPixel(HDC hdc,int xc, int yc, int graycol)
{
  COLORREF  crgray;
  HBRUSH    hbr;

  crgray = PALETTERGB(graycol,graycol,graycol);

  SetPixel(hdc, xc,yc, crgray);

}
```

That wraps up the grayscale coverage. Let's move on to the **Hist** view pane and the details of histograms and plotting histograms. After that, all we'll have left is the quantization code itself.

View Actions: Hist

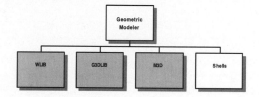

The *Hist* view has one purpose in life: to present a crude histogram plot as visual feedback on the color content of the image in the *Image* view. It uses the histogram bins to feed the drawing process. With this plot, you can get a rough idea of the color content of an image and can use the complexity of the graph to determine which quantization method to use.

Three parts interest us here:

- *Hist* window initialization,
- *Hist CANVAS* helpers, and
- plotting functions.

The histogram bin structure must exist for all of this to work. This means the *Hist* window initialization has at least one interesting feature. Listing 11-100 shows the use of *G3D_Hist_Create* and *G3D_Hist_Destroy*.

Listing 11-100.   Histogram Bin Creation and Destruction

```
...
   if ( ph == NULL )
      if (msg == WM_NCCREATE)
      {
          ph = (HISTWND*)LocalAlloc(LMEM_FIXED | LMEM_ZEROINIT,
                    sizeof(HISTWND));
```

Listing 11-100.   *(cont.)*

```
            if (ph == NULL)
                return 0L;

            ph->hwnd = hwnd;
            ph->lph  = G3D_Hist_Create(2 + NUMGRAYCOL);
            Hist_SetPtr(hwnd, ph);

            G3D_Hist_Clear(ph->lph);
        }
        else
        {
            return Hist_DefProc(hwnd, msg, wParam, lParam);
        }
    }

    if (msg == WM_NCDESTROY)
    {


        G3D_Hist_Destroy(ph->lph);
        LocalFree((HLOCAL)ph);
        ph = NULL;
        Hist_SetPtr(hwnd, NULL);

        //return result;
    }
...
```

These are called in the window procedure during the WM_NCCREATE and WM_NCDESTROY messages (respectively), which guarantees that the histogram bin structure is available for all messages, including the first WM_PAINT.

The next important function is *SetupHistCanvas*. It performs tasks similar to what *SetupViewCanvas* did for the image view. For the WHITE, BLACK, and USER-color backgrounds, it manipulates the text color and background and wipes the client area with the correct brush. See Listing 11-101 for *SetupHistCanvas*.

Listing 11-101.   SetupHistCanvas

```
BOOL WINAPI SetupHistCanvas(HISTWND  * ph, int bckclr,LPSCENE theScene)
{
    HDC hdc    = GetDC(ph->hwnd);
    HDC hdcmem = (HDC)G3D_GEnv_GetVal(ph->henv,ID_DC);
    switch(bckclr)
    {
        case CMD_BLACK:
          G3D_Hist_Clear(ph->lph);
            SetTextColor(hdc,RGB(255,255,255));
            SetBkMode(hdc,OPAQUE);
```

```
                SetBkColor(hdc,RGB(0,0,0));
                SelectObject(hdc, hWhitePen);
                FillRect(hdc, &rVh, GetStockObject(BLACK_BRUSH));
                G3D_GEnv_SetVal(ph->henv,
                               BLACK_CANV,NULL);
                G3D_GEnv_Clear(ph->henv,GetStockObject(BLACK_BRUSH));
                break;
            case CMD_WHITE:
                G3D_Hist_Clear(ph->lph);
                SetTextColor(hdc,RGB(0,0,0));
                SetBkMode(hdc,OPAQUE);
                SetBkColor(hdc,RGB(255,255,255));
                SelectObject(hdc, hBlackPen);
                FillRect(hdc, &rVh, GetStockObject(WHITE_BRUSH));
                G3D_GEnv_SetVal(ph->henv,
                               WHITE_CANV,NULL);
                G3D_GEnv_Clear(ph->henv,GetStockObject(WHITE_BRUSH));
                break;
            case CMD_USER:
                G3D_Hist_Clear(ph->lph);
                SetTextColor(hdc,RGB(0,0,0));
                SetTextColor(hdcmem,RGB(0,0,0));
                SetBkMode(hdc,OPAQUE);
                SetBkMode(hdcmem,OPAQUE);

                SetBkColor(hdc,RGB(255,255,255));
                SetBkColor(hdcmem,RGB(255,255,255));
                SelectObject(hdc, hBlackPen);
                SelectObject(hdcmem, hBlackPen);
                FillRect(hdc, &rVh, GetStockObject(WHITE_BRUSH));
                G3D_GEnv_Clear(ph->henv,GetStockObject(WHITE_BRUSH));
                break;
        }
        ReleaseDC(ph->hwnd,hdc);
        return TRUE;
}
```

This brings us to the details of plotting the actual histogram. Figure 11-23 shows the crude x-y plot of the data contained in the histogram bin structure. Let's examine the "zoomed" version of this figure in Figure 11-24.

Figure 11-23.   Histogram Plot, Actual Size

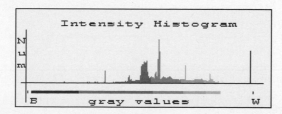

Figure 11-24.   Zoomed Area of Histogram Plot

From these two images you should be able to see a couple of important details. First, from the small figure you can see that there are two areas of the image. The axes and labels are the "outside"; the plot itself is the "inside." Second, from the large figure you should be able to see that the inside consists of individual lines, one of each color in the grayscale palette and histogram bin structure.

That leaves the outside. It has an x-y axis, a title, a dependent (or y-axis) label, and a special label for the independent (or x-axis) label. This also reflects the best way to break down the source code.

Listing 11-102 contains *Plot_Hist*. This function plots a main title, a y-axis title, x-y axes themselves, and an x-axis title. In addition, the x-axis is further labeled (just underneath the axis) with the colors that the plot represents. Finally, *Draw_Hist* is used to plot the "inside."

Listing 11-102.   Plot_Hist

```
id WINAPI Plot_Hist(HISTWND* ph,HDC hdc)
{
    FRAME    *pfrm  = Frame_GetPtr(GetParent(GetParent(ph->hwnd)));
    HFONT    hfTmp;
    RECT     rect;
    LOGPEN   lgp;
    POINT    pt;
    HPEN     hpen, hpenold;
    char     buffer[128];
    int      i, gap, binpix,binstart;
```

```
        ilg    = 5;
        irg    = 5;
        gap    = 5;
        ibg    = 17;
        itg    = 15;
//
        MaxHeight    = 140;
        MaxWidth     = ((ph->rWh.right-2)-(ph->rWh.left+5));
        MaxHistBins = NUMGRAYCOL+1;
//
        if ( bckclr == CMD_BLACK )
            hpenold         = SelectObject(hdc, hWhitePen);
        else if ( bckclr == CMD_WHITE )
            hpenold         = SelectObject(hdc, hBlackPen);
        else
            hpenold         = SelectObject(hdc, hBlackPen);
//
// main title
//
        draw_graph_title(ph,hdc);
//
// axes and labels
//
        draw_graph_ytitle(ph,hdc);
        draw_graph_axes(ph,hdc);
//
// drw black on left
// scale hist pixel line
//
        binpix           = min(1,MaxWidth/MaxHistBins);
        binstart         = 0;
        pt.x = (ph->rWh.left + 8) + gap;
        pt.y =  ph->rWh.bottom + iLineHeight+4;
        draw_line(hdc,
                   pt.x-1,pt.y,
                   pt.x-1,
                   pt.y - 3);
        SelectObject(hdc,hpenold);
//
//
//
        draw_graph_xcolor(ph,hdc,gap,binpix,binstart);
//
// drw white on right
// scale hist pixel line
//
        binpix             = min(1,MaxWidth/MaxHistBins);
        binstart           = (NUMGRAYCOL + 1) * binpix;
        pt.x = (ph->rWh.left + 10) + gap + binstart;
        pt.y =  ph->rWh.bottom + iLineHeight+4;
// draw hist pixel line
```

Listing 11-102. **(cont.)**

```
if ( bckclr == CMD_BLACK )
    hpenold           = SelectObject(hdc, hWhitePen);
else if ( bckclr == CMD_WHITE )
    hpenold           = SelectObject(hdc, hBlackPen);
else
    hpenold           = SelectObject(hdc, hBlackPen);
draw_line(hdc,
            pt.x+1,pt.y,
            pt.x+1,
            pt.y - 3);
//
    draw_graph_xtitle(ph,hdc);
    SelectObject(hdc,hpenold);
//
// actual hist
//
    if ( pfrm->bData )
        Draw_Hist(ph,hdc,ph->lph);
//
}
```

Simple plot routines *draw_line* and *draw_label* act underneath *draw_graph_title*, *draw_graph_ytitle*, *draw_graph_axes*, and *draw_graph_xtitle*. The two simple routines are shown in Listing 11-103, and all the others are shown in Listing 11-104.

Listing 11-103. **Simple Helpers**

```
void WINAPI draw_line(HDC hdc,int x1, int y1, int x2, int y2)
{
    MoveTo(hdc,x1,y1);
    LineTo(hdc,x2,y2);
}
void WINAPI draw_label(HDC   hdc,int   x1, int y1,LPSTR buffer)
{
    TextOut(hdc,
            x1,y1,
            buffer,lstrlen(buffer));
}
```

Listing 11-104. **Additional Helpers**

```
void WINAPI draw_graph_title(HISTWND * ph,HDC hdc)
{
    char        buffer[128];
    lstrcpy(buffer,"Intensity Histogram");
    draw_label(hdc,
            (ph->rWh.right - ph->rWh.left)/2 - (lstrlen(buffer)/2)
```

```
                *iColumnWidth,
            MaxHeight + iLineHeight + 5,buffer);
}
//
void WINAPI draw_graph_ytitle(HISTWND * ph,HDC hdc)
{
    char          buffer[128];
    lstrcpy(buffer,"N");
    draw_label(hdc,
            1,ph->rWh.bottom + iLineHeight * 9, buffer);
    lstrcpy(buffer,"u");
    draw_label(hdc,
            1,ph->rWh.bottom + iLineHeight * 8,buffer);
    lstrcpy(buffer,"m");
    draw_label(hdc,
            1,ph->rWh.bottom + iLineHeight * 7,buffer);
}
//
void WINAPI draw_graph_axes(HISTWND * ph,HDC hdc)
{
    char          buffer[128];
    draw_line(hdc,
            ph->rWh.left+10, ph->rWh.bottom+5,
            ph->rWh.left+10, MaxHeight+5);
    draw_line(hdc,
            ph->rWh.left+5,  ph->rWh.bottom+iLineHeight*2,
            ph->rWh.right-10,ph->rWh.bottom+iLineHeight*2);
}
void WINAPI draw_graph_xtitle(HISTWND * ph,HDC hdc)
{
    char          buffer[128];
    lstrcpy(buffer,"gray values");
    draw_label(hdc, (ph->rWh.right - ph->rWh.left)/2 -
        (lstrlen(buffer)/2)*iColumnWidth-10,
                ph->rWh.bottom + iLineHeight,buffer);
    lstrcpy(buffer,"W");
    draw_label(hdc,
            pt.x,
            ph->rWh.bottom + iLineHeight, buffer);
    pt.x = (ph->rWh.left + 10) + gap - 1;
    lstrcpy(buffer,"B");
    draw_label(hdc,
            pt.x,
            ph->rWh.bottom + iLineHeight, buffer);
}
```

Now we have to plot the axis colors. Function *draw_graph_xcolors* does this valuable deed, as shown in Listing 11-105. It loops across the slots of the gray palette and histogram bin structure and draws a 3-pixel-high line. During the loop, it adjusts for the black pen if the *CANVAS* background is black as well. Note this loop well, because *Draw_Hist* also uses a variation of it.

Listing 11-105.   Color Label Function draw_graph_xcolors

```
void WINAPI draw_graph_xcolors(HISTWND * ph,HDC hdc,
                               int gap, int binpix, int binstart)
{
    HPEN         hpen, hpenold;
    LOGPEN       lgp;
    POINT        pt;
    int          i;
//
// x labels = color patches
// setup  hist line color for display context
//
    for (i = 1;  i <= NUMGRAYCOL; i++) {
        lgp.lopnStyle    = PS_SOLID;
        lgp.lopnWidth.x = 1;
        lgp.lopnWidth.y = 1;
        lgp.lopnColor    = MapColorRangetoCRef(i, NUMGRAYCOL+1);
// hack for black canvas
        if ( lgp.lopnColor == CLR_BLACK )
        {
          switch(bckclr)
          {
            case CMD_BLACK:
                lgp.lopnColor  = CLR_WHITE;
                break;
            case CMD_WHITE:
                lgp.lopnColor  = CLR_BLACK;
                break;

          }
        }
// create colored pen
// calc hist patch start loc
// draw hist patch
        hpen             = CreatePenIndirect(&lgp);
        hpenold          = SelectObject(hdc, hpen);
        binpix           = min(1,MaxWidth/MaxHistBins);
        binstart         = i*binpix;
        pt.x = (ph->rWh.left + 10) + gap + binstart;
        pt.y =   ph->rWh.bottom + iLineHeight+4;
        draw_line(hdc,
                  pt.x,pt.y,
                  pt.x,
                  pt.y - 3);
// remove colored pen
        SelectObject(hdc,hpenold);
        DeleteObject(hpen);
    }
}
```

The *Draw_Hist* function is shown next, in Listing 11-106, and it's a little long. It basically repeats *draw_graph_xcolors*, but includes the details of scaling the size of the graph (using *G3D_Hist_FindMostPopular*) and the related sizing of each plot line. In addition, it still does the special-case checks.

Listing 11-106.   Draw_Hist

```
BOOL WINAPI Draw_Hist(HISTWND* ph,HDC hdc,LPHIST lph)
{
    HPEN          hpen, hpenold;
    POINT         pt;
    LOGPEN        lgp;
    RECT          rect,fr;
    int           i, gap;
    long          scale;
    int           binpix,binstart;
    double        dval;
    WORD          val;
//
// first establish max
//
    scale =  G3D_Hist_FindMostPopular(lph);
    scale =  max(1,scale);
//
    gap = 5;
    GetClientRect(ph->hwnd,&rect);
    fr.left   = ph->rWh.left + 10;
    fr.top    = ph->rWh.top   - iLineHeight*2;
    fr.right  = ph->rWh.right  - 2;
    fr.bottom = ph->rWh.bottom +iLineHeight*2+1;
    switch(bckclr)
    {
       case CMD_BLACK:
          FillRect(hdc, &fr, GetStockObject(BLACK_BRUSH));
          break;
       case CMD_WHITE:
          FillRect(hdc, &fr, GetStockObject(WHITE_BRUSH));
          break;
    }
// drw black on left
// scale hist pixel line
    binpix          = min(1,MaxWidth/MaxHistBins);
    binstart        = 0;
// draw hist pixel line
    dval =   ((double)lph->Hist[0] *
             (double)(MaxHeight-20)/(double)scale);
    val  =   (WORD)min((DWORD)dval,(DWORD)MaxHeight-20);
    if ( bckclr == CMD_BLACK )
       hpenold            = SelectObject(hdc, hWhitePen);
```

Listing 11-116.   (cont.)

```
    gcColors.hpCEntry  = (HPPPCOLORENTRY)WL_Mem_Alloc(GHND,
                           1*sizeof(PPCOLORENTRY));
    if ( !gcColors.hpCEntry ){
        Trans_Printf(winio_hwnd,
"failed to allocate quantization array...free some memory!\n" );
        return;
    }
//build analysis structures, analyze, pass back gcColors
    switch(rtype){
        default:
          generateMedianFromFace(pv,(LPGENNEDCOLORS)&gcColors);
          break;
        case CMD_RAY:
          generateMedianFromMemBuff(pv,(LPGENNEDCOLORS)&gcColors);
          break;
    }
//
// make a palette using gcColors
//
    hpgen = MakeGenPalette(gcColors);
//
// release working memory
//
    WL_Mem_Free(gcColors.hpCEntry);
    gcColors.hpCEntry = NULL;
    DeAllocCubeandBoxes();
    if ( !hpgen )
        return;

    break;

  case CMD_NATIVE:
...
    break;
  }
...
```

Next is the generate function pair *generateMedianFromFace* and *generateMedianFromMemBuff*. The code used here owes a lot to Craig Lindley's implementation in *Practical Ray Tracing in C* (Wiley, 1992). It has been heavily modified for this environment in terms of function interfaces and memory management, but at its core, the debt is still clear. Like the popular pair, they differ in the source of intensity values; after that, the main body is identical. Listings 11-117 and 11-118 contain these functions.

Listing 11-117. GenerateMedianFromFace

```
BOOL WINAPI generateMedianFromFace(VWWND* pv,LPGENNEDCOLORS lpMC)
{
    int i,indx;

    for ( i = 0; i < pv->mWorld->Scene->VisFaces->fiNum;i++) {
        HPFACE          pfi;
        char _huge *    p;
        long            offset;
        BYTE            R,G,B;
//
        p         = (char _huge *)pv->mWorld->Scene->VisFaces->fi;
        offset    = (DWORD)((DWORD)i * (DWORD)sizeof(FACE));
        p         +=offset;
        pfi       = (HPFACE)p;
// pass 1 get cached intensity and build RGBCube
        R = (pfi->i.x);
        G = (pfi->i.y);
        B = (pfi->i.z);
        R = R >> 3;
        G = G >> 3;
        B = B >> 3;
        (RGBCube[R][(B*COLLEVELS)+G])++;
//    allow some other tasking
        if (PeekMessage(&g_app.msg, NULL, 0, 0, PM_REMOVE)) {
            TranslateMessage(&g_app.msg);
            DispatchMessage(&g_app.msg);
        }
    }
    gcColors.NumColors = 0;
    for (c=0; c < COLLEVELS; c++)
      for (k=0; k < COLLEVELS*COLLEVELS; k++)
        if (RGBCube[c][k])
          gcColors.NumColors++;
    if ( gcColors.NumColors > 0 ) {
// pass 2  build "boxes" around colors - 236 only
        BuildColorBoxes(pv);
// pass 3 - sort boxes
        SortColorBoxes();
    }
// map scolvals to gcColors
    ScaleColVals();
    gcColors.hpCEntry = (HPPPCOLORENTRY)WL_Mem_Realloc(
      gcColors.hpCEntry,(2 + gcColors.NumColors) *
      sizeof(PPCOLORENTRY),GHND);
    for (k=0; k < gcColors.NumColors; k++) {
        G3D_V4D_VSet4D(&(gcColors.hpCEntry+(k))->val,
          255*((double)SColVals[k].cRed  /(double)COLLEVELS),
          255*((double)SColVals[k].cGreen/(double)COLLEVELS),
          255*((double)SColVals[k].cBlue /(double)COLLEVELS),ONE4D);
    }
    return TRUE;
}
```

Listing 11-118. GenerateMedianFromMemBuff

```
BOOL WINAPI generateMedianFromMemBuff(VWWND* pv,
                    LPGENNEDCOLORS lpMC)
{
    int        ix, iy, sy, indx;
//   sweep the image array for colors
    for ( iy = 0 ; iy <= pv->mWorld->Scene->scanY-1 ; iy++) {
        for ( ix = 0; ix <= pv->mWorld->Scene->scanX-1 ; ix++) {
            PPCOLORENTRY  pCE;
            HPDWORD       hpl;
            BYTE          R,G,B;

            hpl    = G3D_MemBuff_GetMem(pv->genv->lpcanv->mb,ix,iy);
//
// pass 1 get cached intensity and build RGBCube
//
            R = GetRValue(*hpl) >> 3;
            G = GetGValue(*hpl) >> 3;
            B = GetBValue(*hpl) >> 3;
            (RGBCube[R][(B*COLLEVELS)+G])++;
//
        }
    }
//    allow some other tasking
        if (PeekMessage(&g_app.msg, NULL, 0, 0, PM_REMOVE)) {
            TranslateMessage(&g_app.msg);
            DispatchMessage(&g_app.msg);
        }
    }
    gcColors.NumColors = 0;
    for (c=0; c < COLLEVELS; c++)
      for (k=0; k < COLLEVELS*COLLEVELS; k++)
        if (RGBCube[c][k])
          gcColors.NumColors++;
    if ( gcColors.NumColors > 0 ) {
// pass 2  build "boxes" around colors - 236 only
        BuildColorBoxes(pv);
// pass 3 - sort boxes
        SortColorBoxes();
    }
// map scolvals to gcColors
    ScaleColVals();
    gcColors.hpCEntry = (HPPPCOLORENTRY)WL_Mem_Realloc(
        gcColors.hpCEntry,(2 + gcColors.NumColors) *
        sizeof(PPCOLORENTRY),GHND);
    for (k=0; k < gcColors.NumColors; k++) {
        G3D_V4D_VSet4D(&(gcColors.hpCEntry+(k))->val,
         255*((double)SColVals[k].cRed  /(double)COLLEVELS),
         255*((double)SColVals[k].cGreen/(double)COLLEVELS),
         255*((double)SColVals[k].cBlue /(double)COLLEVELS),ONE4D);
    }
    return TRUE;
}
```

In each case, a three-dimensional histogram is first generated from the source intensities in variable RGBCube. It might not be clear from Figure 11-25 and the discussion of 24-bit color, but, in theory, this color cube would be 256x256x256x4 bytes in size — a 16.7MB three-dimensional array. This is impractical in most cases, and in practice the least-significant color bits are shifted away to make the array size more convenient. Here, since 32K colors is our implicit target, shifting by 3 leaves 5 bits of color for each of red, green, and blue — 2^{15} entries, which is 32K total colors that can be represented.

The net result (besides the memory savings) is additional color truncation; ignoring the lowest 3 bits means that the nearest 8 shades of color are "lumped" together. Each histogram entry thus represents 8x8x8 (512) colors in the image.

Notice the form of the cube. It is convenient to organize the cube in the 3D RGB triplet manner for the median-cut. This means it can be addressed using the R,G,B values to access or retrieve the counts. As each intensity is decoded, the corresponding triplet is updated.

Once this process is complete, two more passes at the cube are made. In the next pass, the boxes are constructed by *BuildColorBoxes*. Then they are sorted and averaged by *SortColorBoxes*. Next, the color values are scaled in an attempt to compensate for the shifting process in *ScaleColVals*. These functions do the hard work and, along with their helpers, are borrowed from the Lindley versions. Finally, the box averages are moved into the *GENNEDCOLORS* structure in preparation for *MakeGenPalette*.

These three major functions, the minor functions, and the memory helpers are next. Listing 11-119 contains *AllocCubeandBoxes* and *DeAllocCubeandBoxes*. These allocate the working storage for the color cube and the averaged values (scaled and unscaled).

Listing 11-119.   Alloc and DeAlloc Functions

```
unsigned WINAPI AllocCubeandBoxes( void )
{
   unsigned Index;

   for (Index=0; Index < COLLEVELS; Index++)
      RGBCube[Index] = NULL;
   for (Index=0; Index < COLLEVELS; Index++)  {
      RGBCube[Index] = (unsigned long far *) WL_Mem_Alloc(GHND,
         ((unsigned long)COLLEVELS*(unsigned long)COLLEVELS)
         *sizeof(unsigned long));
      if (RGBCube[Index] == NULL) {
         return(FALSE);
      }
      else {
      /* clear it to all zeros */
         _fmemset((char far *) RGBCube[Index],'\0',
                  COLLEVELS*COLLEVELS*sizeof(unsigned long));
      }
   }
```

Listing 11-119. (*cont.*)

```
   Boxes   = (HPMEDIANBOXES)WL_Mem_Alloc(GHND,
                (1+MAXNUMCOLREGS)*sizeof(MEDIANBOXES));
   SBoxes  = (HPMEDIANBOXES)WL_Mem_Alloc(GHND,
                (1+MAXNUMCOLREGS)*sizeof(MEDIANBOXES));

   ColVals  = (CRT far *)WL_Mem_Alloc(GHND,
                  (1+MAXNUMCOLREGS)*sizeof(CRT));
   SColVals = (CRT far *)WL_Mem_Alloc(GHND,
                  (1+MAXNUMCOLREGS)*sizeof(CRT));
   return(TRUE);
}
//
void WINAPI DeAllocCubeandBoxes( void )
{
   unsigned Index;

   for (Index=0; Index < COLLEVELS; Index++)
      if (RGBCube[Index] != NULL)
        WL_Mem_Free((char far *) RGBCube[Index]);

   WL_Mem_Free(Boxes);
   WL_Mem_Free(SBoxes);

   WL_Mem_Free(ColVals);
   WL_Mem_Free(SColVals);
}
```

Listing 11-120 contains helper *OtherAxes*; Listing 11-121 contains helper *Shrink*. These two functions provide *BuildColorBoxes* with axis manipulation, box construction support, and zero-plane removal support. Zero planes are elements in each box with a zero count.

Listing 11-120. OtherAxes

```
//
//This function sets the indices to the numbers of the other axis
//after a main axis has been selected.
//
void OtherAxes(unsigned MainAxis, unsigned *Other1, unsigned *Other2)
{
   switch (MainAxis)  {
   case 0:
     *Other1 = 1;
     *Other2 = 2;
     break;
```

```
    case 1:
      *Other1 = 0;
      *Other2 = 2;
      break;
    case 2:
      *Other1 = 0;
      *Other2 = 1;
  }
}
```

Listing 11-121.   Shrink

```
void Shrink(unsigned BoxIndex) {
  unsigned axis,aax1,aax2;
  unsigned ind[3], flag;

  /* Along each axis: */
  for (axis=0; axis < NUMAXIS; axis++)  {
    OtherAxes(axis,&aax1,&aax2);
  /* Scan off zero planes on from the low end of the axis */
    flag = 0;
    for(ind[axis]=Boxes[BoxIndex].RGBLo[axis];
        ind[axis] <= Boxes[BoxIndex].RGBHi[axis];
        ind[axis]++) {
      for (ind[aax1]=Boxes[BoxIndex].RGBLo[aax1];
           ind[aax1] <= Boxes[BoxIndex].RGBHi[aax1];
           ind[aax1]++)  {
        for (ind[aax2]=Boxes[BoxIndex].RGBLo[aax2];
             ind[aax2] <= Boxes[BoxIndex].RGBHi[aax2];
             ind[aax2]++)
          if (RGBCube[ind[0]][ind[1]*COLLEVELS+ind[2]])  {
            flag=1;
            break;
          }
        if (flag) break;
      }
      if (flag) break;
    }
    Boxes[BoxIndex].RGBLo[axis] = ind[axis];
  /* Scan off zero planes from the high end of the axis */
    flag = 0;
    for (ind[axis]=Boxes[BoxIndex].RGBHi[axis];
         ind[axis]+1 >= Boxes[BoxIndex].RGBLo[axis]+1;
         ind[axis]-)  {
      for (ind[aax1]=Boxes[BoxIndex].RGBHi[aax1];
           ind[aax1]+1 >= Boxes[BoxIndex].RGBLo[aax1]+1;
           ind[aax1]-)  {
        for (ind[aax2]=Boxes[BoxIndex].RGBHi[aax2];
             ind[aax2]+1>=Boxes[BoxIndex].RGBLo[aax2]+1;
             ind[aax2]--)
```

Listing 11-121.   (*cont.*)

```
            if (RGBCube[ind[0]][ind[1]*COLLEVELS+ind[2]])  {
                flag = 1;
                break;
            }
          if (flag) break;
        }
        if (flag) break;
    }
    Boxes[BoxIndex].RGBHi[axis] = ind[axis];
  }
}
```

BuildColorBoxes is in Listing 11-122. First, it initializes the cube to be one box and removes unused zero planes using *Shrink*. Then the loop iterates for each target entry. The box with the most elements that are not of a single color-value is chosen as the box to split further. Degenerate entries are re-used, and the longest axis of the box is chosen to split along. The code sums the planes of the box from the low end until the sum exceeds half of the total. That is the new box. More code to avoid degenerate cases is followed by touching up the entries in the new box; then *Shrink* is called twice to remove zero planes again. At that point, the new box is constructed and the total count of boxes updated before the top of the loop is reached. This is repeated until it reaches either the number of colors or 236, whichever is smaller.

Listing 11-122.   BuildColorBoxes

```
void WINAPI BuildColorBoxes(VWWND * pv){
   register unsigned SelectedBox, c;
   unsigned ind[3], Max, axis, TargetBox, k;
   unsigned aax1,aax2;
   unsigned long LongMax, PlaneSum, ElementSum;

  for (c=0; c < NUMAXIS; c++)  {
     Boxes[0].RGBLo[c] = 0;
     Boxes[0].RGBHi[c] = COLLEVELS-1;
  }
  switch(rtype)
  {
     case CMD_RAY:
        Boxes[0].NumElements = ((long)pv->mWorld->Scene->scanX *
                                (long)pv->mWorld->Scene->scanY);
        break;
     default:
        Boxes[0].NumElements =
             pv->mWorld->Scene->VisFaces->fiNum;
        break;
  }
```

```
NumBoxes = 1;

Shrink(0);

while(NumBoxes < MAXNUMCOLREGS &&
      NumBoxes <= gcColors.NumColors)  {

  LongMax = 0;
  SelectedBox = 1000;
  for (c=0; c < NumBoxes; c++)  {
    if ((Boxes[c].NumElements > LongMax) &&
        ((Boxes[c].RGBLo[0] != Boxes[c].RGBHi[0]) ||
         (Boxes[c].RGBLo[1] != Boxes[c].RGBHi[1]) ||
         (Boxes[c].RGBLo[2] != Boxes[c].RGBHi[2])))  {
      LongMax = Boxes[c].NumElements;
      SelectedBox = c;
    }
  }
  if (SelectedBox == 1000)
    break;
  axis = 0;
  Max = Boxes[SelectedBox].RGBHi[axis] -
        Boxes[SelectedBox].RGBLo[axis];
  for (k=1; k < NUMAXIS; k++)  {
    if (Max < (c=(Boxes[SelectedBox].RGBHi[k]-
                  Boxes[SelectedBox].RGBLo[k])))  {
      Max = c;
      axis = k;
    }
  }
  TargetBox = NumBoxes;
  for (c=0; c < NumBoxes; c++)  {
    if (Boxes[c].NumElements == 0)  {
      TargetBox = c;
      break;
    }
  }
  OtherAxes(axis,&aax1,&aax2);
  if( Boxes[SelectedBox].RGBHi[axis] !=
      Boxes[SelectedBox].RGBLo[axis] )  {
    ElementSum = 0;
    for (ind[axis]=Boxes[SelectedBox].RGBLo[axis];
         ind[axis] <= Boxes[SelectedBox].RGBHi[axis];
         ind[axis]++)  {
      PlaneSum = 0;
      for (ind[aax1]=Boxes[SelectedBox].RGBLo[aax1];
           ind[aax1] <= Boxes[SelectedBox].RGBHi[aax1];
           ind[aax1]++)
        for (ind[aax2]=Boxes[SelectedBox].RGBLo[aax2];
             ind[aax2] <= Boxes[SelectedBox].RGBHi[aax2];
             ind[aax2]++)
```

Listing 11-122.   *(cont.)*

```
                    PlaneSum+=RGBCube[ind[0]][ind[1]*COLLEVELS+ind[2]];
                    ElementSum += PlaneSum;
                    if (ElementSum > Boxes[SelectedBox].NumElements/2)
                        break;
                }
            if (ind[axis] == Boxes[SelectedBox].RGBHi[axis])  {
                ind[axis]—;
                ElementSum -= PlaneSum;
            }
            for (c=0; c < NUMAXIS; c++)  {
             Boxes[TargetBox].RGBLo[c] = Boxes[SelectedBox].RGBLo[c];
             Boxes[TargetBox].RGBHi[c] = Boxes[SelectedBox].RGBHi[c];
            }
            Boxes[TargetBox].RGBLo[axis] = ind[axis]+1;
            Boxes[TargetBox].NumElements =
            Boxes[SelectedBox].NumElements - ElementSum;

            Boxes[SelectedBox].RGBHi[axis] = ind[axis];
            Boxes[SelectedBox].NumElements = ElementSum;

            Shrink(SelectedBox);
            Shrink(TargetBox);

            if (TargetBox == NumBoxes)
                NumBoxes++;
        }
    }
}
```

Following the creation of the boxes by *BuildColorBoxes, SortColorBoxes* arranges the boxes and does the averages for us. Listing 11-123 provides the source to this function. Besides the averaging, it bubble sorts the boxes by brightness.

Listing 11-123.   SortColorBoxes

```
void WINAPI SortColorBoxes(void) {
    unsigned Index,c,flag,temp,r,b,g,indices[MAXNUMCOLREGS];
    unsigned long weightedcolor[MAXNUMCOLREGS],rsum,bsum,gsum,tmp;

    for (Index=0; Index < NumBoxes; Index++)  {
        rsum = bsum = gsum = 0;
        for (r=Boxes[Index].RGBLo[0];
             r<=Boxes[Index].RGBHi[0]; r++)
            for (b=Boxes[Index].RGBLo[1];
                 b<=Boxes[Index].RGBHi[1]; b++)
                for (g=Boxes[Index].RGBLo[2];
                     g<=Boxes[Index].RGBHi[2]; g++)  {
                    tmp = RGBCube[r][b*COLLEVELS+g];
                    rsum += r*tmp;
```

```
                bsum += b*tmp;
                gsum += g*tmp;
            }
        ColVals[Index].cRed   = rsum/Boxes[Index].NumElements;
        ColVals[Index].cBlue  = bsum/Boxes[Index].NumElements;
        ColVals[Index].cGreen = gsum/Boxes[Index].NumElements;
    }
    for (Index=0; Index < NumBoxes; Index++)  {
        indices[Index] = Index;
        weightedcolor[Index] = ColVals[Index].cRed  *30 +
                               ColVals[Index].cBlue *11 +
                               ColVals[Index].cGreen*59;
    }
    flag = 1;
    while (flag)  {
        flag = 0;
        for (Index=0; Index < NumBoxes-1; Index++)
           if( weightedcolor[indices[Index]] >
               weightedcolor[indices[Index+1]])  {
               temp = indices[Index];
               indices[Index] = indices[Index+1];
               indices[Index+1] = temp;
               flag = 1;
           }
    }
    for (Index=0; Index < NumBoxes; Index++)  {
     SColVals[Index].cRed   = ColVals[indices[Index]].cRed;
     SColVals[Index].cBlue  = ColVals[indices[Index]].cBlue;
     SColVals[Index].cGreen = ColVals[indices[Index]].cGreen;
     SBoxes[Index].NumElements = Boxes[indices[Index]].NumElements;
       for (c=0; c < NUMAXIS; c++) {
           SBoxes[Index].RGBHi[c] = Boxes[indices[Index]].RGBHi[c];
           SBoxes[Index].RGBLo[c] = Boxes[indices[Index]].RGBLo[c];
       }
    }
}
```

SortColorBoxes also remaps the color values in preparation for *ScaleColVals*, which is shown in Listing 11-124. *ScaleColVals* attempts to compensate for the earlier truncation. That leaves the direct method and the re-imaging pass.

Listing 11-124.   ScaleColVals

```
void ScaleColVals(void)
{

    register unsigned Index;
    register unsigned Temp;
```

Listing 11-124.   (*cont.*)

```
/* Find the maximum value of any RGB component value */
MaxValue = -1;
for (Index = 0; Index < MAXNUMCOLREGS; Index++)  {
   if (SColVals[Index].cRed > MaxValue)
     MaxValue = SColVals[Index].cRed;
   if (SColVals[Index].cGreen > MaxValue)
     MaxValue = SColVals[Index].cGreen;
   if (SColVals[Index].cBlue > MaxValue)
     MaxValue = SColVals[Index].cBlue;
}
/* Scale all color register components accordingly */
for (Index = 0; Index < MAXNUMCOLREGS; Index++)  {

   /* temp used to prevent overflow of BYTE value */
   Temp = SColVals[Index].cRed * (unsigned) MAXCOLREGVAL;
   Temp /= MaxValue;

   SColVals[Index].cRed = Temp;

   Temp = SColVals[Index].cGreen * (unsigned) MAXCOLREGVAL;
   Temp /= MaxValue;

   SColVals[Index].cGreen = Temp;

   Temp = SColVals[Index].cBlue * (unsigned) MAXCOLREGVAL;
   Temp /= MaxValue;
   SColVals[Index].cBlue = Temp;
}
}
```

Direct Method and Re-Imaging

The direct method operates exactly as its name implies — it directly assigns colors in the final image. This, in turn, implies that the direct block in *View_OnQuantize* needs to do no work. This is confirmed in Listing 11-125.

That leaves the re-imaging code. As you see in Listing 11-125, the pair of functions *DrawFromFace* and *DrawFromMemBuff* are used to do the re-imaging.

Listing 11-125.   **Direct and Re-Imaging Block**

```
switch (id)
{
  case CMD_POPULAR:
...
            return;
    break;

  case CMD_MEDIAN:
...
    break;
```

```
                sp
                ls
                sp

                ls
                Se
        }
     Relea
     lstrc
     lstrca
     lstrca
     SetWir
     returr
}


Listing 11-1

void WINAF

{
   HDC
   HBRUSH
   POINT
   int
   long
   COLORRE
   LPEX3DO
   VECTOR4

   for ( i
        v
        G

        G

        p
        p
   }
   cr

   hbr
   lp3DObj
   switch(t
      defau
      case
      case
      case
      case
      case
```

```
        case CMD_NATIVE:
//
// no-op here
//

                break;
          break;
        }
//
// rewalk objects
//
        View_OnShadeType(pv,qmethod,NULL,NULL);
        switch(rtype)
        {
           case CMD_RAY:
               DrawFromMemBuff(pv);
               break;
           default:
               DrawFromFace(pv);
               break;
        }
```

These functions borrow heavily from the core of the render functions *PolyRenderObjectList* and *RayRenderObjectList*. *DrawFromFace* is shown in Listing 11-126, and it uses the standard rendering code for polygons. However, it calls *DrawFaceGennedFace* instead of the function pointer for face drawing. This function is shown in Listing 11-127. These two functions are straightforward modifications of the previous rendering code, and are used mainly to enforce the use of the colors in *DrawFaceGennedFace*.

Listing 11-126. DrawFromFace

```
BOOL DrawFromFace(VWWND * pv)
{
    FRAME*    pfrm  = Frame_GetPtr(GetParent(GetParent(pv->hwnd)));
    HBRUSH    hbr,hOldBrush;
    HPEN      hpo;
    COLORREF  cr;
    HDC       hDC,hdcmem;
    int       i,j;
    char szBuffer1[MAXBUFFERLEN],szBuffer2[MAXBUFFERLEN];
    char szBuffer3[MAXBUFFERLEN];
// re-gen bitmap with new palette
    LoadString(g_app.hinst, IDS_APPNAME, szBuffer3, MAXNAMELEN);
    hDC     = GetDC(pv->hwnd);
    hdcmem = (HDC)G3D_GEnv_GetVal(pv->genv,ID_DC);
```

Listing 11-127. *(cont.)*

```
// close the poly, no need to transform 1st point again
        pgdi[4].x = pgdi[0].x;
        pgdi[4].y = pgdi[0].y;
        break;
    case T_PYR:
// if last face do rectangle
        if ( i == lp3DObj->nF-1 ) {
            pgdi[4].x = pgdi[0].x;
            pgdi[4].y = pgdi[0].y;
        }
        else {
            pgdi[3].x = pgdi[0].x;
            pgdi[3].y = pgdi[0].y;
        }
        break;
    }
    G3D_GEnv_Polygon(pv->genv,(LPPOINT)&pgdi,
                    (long)fi->ni+1,(DWORD)hNullPen,(DWORD)hbr);

    if ( bDbl ) {
        HBRUSH hcOld;
        hdc = GetDC(pv->hwnd);
        SelectObject(hdc, hNullPen);
        hOldBrush = SelectObject(hdc, hbr);
        Polygon(hdc,(LPPOINT)&pgdi,(long)fi->ni+1);
        SelectObject(hdc ,hOldBrush );
        ReleaseDC(pv->hwnd,hdc);
    }
    DeleteObject(hbr);

    if (PeekMessage(&g_app.msg, NULL, 0, 0, PM_REMOVE))
    {
            TranslateMessage(&g_app.msg);
            DispatchMessage(&g_app.msg);
    }
}
```

DrawFromMemBuff in Listing 11-128 extends the ray-traced rendering in a very similar manner. The core code is duplicated from ray-traced rendering, and within that the drawing uses the new color (calculated or direct) instead of the grayscale color.

Listing 11-128. DrawFromMemBuff

```
BOOL DrawFromMemBuff(VWWND * pv)
{
    FRAME*  pfrm    = Frame_GetPtr(GetParent(GetParent(pv->hwnd)));
    HDC     hdcscr,hdccan;
    int     ix, iy, sy, run;
    char    szBuffer1[MAXBUFFERLEN],szBuffer2[MAXBUFFERLEN];
    char    szBuffer3[MAXBUFFERLEN];
```

```
            LoadString(g_app.hinst, IDS_APPNAME, szBuffer3, MAXNAMELEN);
//    sweep the image array for colors
            hdccan = (HDC)G3D_GEnv_GetVal(pv->genv,ID_DC);
            hdcscr = GetDC(pv->hwnd);
            for ( iy = 0 ; iy <= pv->mWorld->Scene->scanY-1 ; iy++)
            {
                for ( ix = 0; ix <= pv->mWorld->Scene->scanX-1 ; ix++)
                {
                    HPDWORD        hpl;
                    BYTE           R,G,B;

                    hpl    = G3D_MemBuff_GetMem(pv->genv->lpcanv->mb,ix,iy);

                    SetPixel(hdccan, ix,pv->mWorld->Scene->scanY-iy, *hpl);
                    SetPixel(hdcscr, ix,pv->mWorld->Scene->scanY-iy, *hpl);
                }
//    allow some other tasking
            if (PeekMessage(&g_app.msg, NULL, 0, 0, PM_REMOVE))
            {
                TranslateMessage(&g_app.msg);
                DispatchMessage(&g_app.msg);
            }
//
//    update title bar
//
                lstrcpy(szBuffer1,szBuffer3);
                lstrcat(szBuffer1," - ");
                sprintf((LPSTR)szBuffer2," line %d  of %d ...",iy+1,
                        pv->mWorld->Scene->scanY);
                lstrcat(szBuffer1,szBuffer2);
                SetWindowText(pfrm->hwnd,(LPSTR)szBuffer1);
            }
//
        lstrcpy(szBuffer1,szBuffer3);
        lstrcat(szBuffer1," - ");
        lstrcat(szBuffer1,pfrm->szInFileName);
        SetWindowText(pfrm->hwnd,(LPSTR)szBuffer1);
        return TRUE;
}
```

They both accomplish the coloring similarly, too. They depend on the palette already being in place, or no palette in 32K-color mode. Then they use the calculated intensity. If Windows is in a palette mode, then its own nearest-neighbor algorithm color matches for us. If Windows is in a 32K-color or higher mode, the color is used directly. The driver itself needs to truncate these 24-bit colors to 15-bit colors, but in most images this will not be noticed.

That wraps it up. You've now seen the final step in generating images. With only grayscale in this book, it is impossible to show you the output of the colorizing process — but you only have to render a scene and post-process it to see it for yourself. Once you have these images, they can be shared using the clipboard, saved to a file, or printed. The image is saved to a file as a DIB that contains the palette. This means the saved file is a standard Windows DIB and can be used for wallpaper, for instance.

Using the Modeler

This modeler is a Windows program; using it is as simple as using other Windows programs, but there are some details you still need to know. These include setup, conceptual steps to using the modeler, and some debugging tips.

The visible parts of execution include clicking on the icon to launch, "mousing" the menu, and scrolling, but there is more to do than just that. Certain key files must exist where the modeler can find them. Beyond that is the question of the data that the modeler needs. Remember that way back in Part I I mentioned that the search for geometry was a major task? You should now see that this is your largest problem. The last issue is the process of scene debugging, or fixing a scene that appears a little wrong. First, though, we'll cover the setup process.

Setup

Once you've built the source included on the disk (see Appendix B for more details on the build process), you need to make sure all the necessary components exist. These include DLLs, .mod modeling scripts, .scn scene geometry scripts, .dat modeling information files, and .dat object geometry files.

Lets take these in reverse order. You should have the following object .dat files:

- cone.dat, which was programmatically generated in Chapter 9,
- box.dat, which you hand-generated in Chapter 9,
- cylinder. dat, which was programmatically generated in Chapter 9,
- plane.dat, which was programmatically generated in Chapter 9,
- pyramid.dat, which you hand-generated in Chapter 9,
- sphere.dat, which was programmatically generated in Chapter 9.

The data in these files defines the explicit representations. These files are critical to the operation of the modeler. If any modeling and scene description scripts exist and try reference any non-existing .dat files, bad things will probably happen. The modeler only implements a minimum of checking, so it's easy to cause a fatal error. I repeat Groucho Marx's advice — "Don't do that." To avoid this, the support files must exist in the current working directory, which will be the directory you launch the modeler from.

In addition, the modeling script lets users define lookup tables for colors and materials. A default set is provided and includes the following:

- colors.dat   X/11 color palette values,
- material. dat   default surface material properties table.

These files must exist, although nothing is sacred about their contents. If they do not exist in the directory the modeler is launched from, the modeler will crash when it reads a modeling script.

Part II implemented two DLLs: the WL library and the G3D library. These DLLs must exist either in the path or in the current working directory. Windows checks this and will prevent the program from loading if it does not find these DLLs in the fight place.

That leaves modeling and scene scripts. Modeling and scene script files must exist for the modeler to do anything interesting. These are the .mod and .scn files, and are usually in the current directory as well (although they are not shipped that way on the disk), because the .dat files they reference contain no path information. I've included some scenes on the source disk, but these are mostly of the debugging variety because of space limitations. However, I have included a few more-interesting scenes that include a large test (more than 100 spheres, which is in excess of 24,000 polygons), a table on the infinite plane, and a set of spheres in a mirrored comer. Object hierarchies are not implemented even though they would make composite objects like the table much easier to manipulate. It is still possible for simple objects like a table to do without.

Conceptual Steps

Once you've successfully installed the source, built the system, and mastered the mechanics of usage presented here, you become the scene compositor; your mental point of view shifts to something between artist-painter and director-cinematographer. You must compose your scenes and the general rules of scene composition from art — like foreground and background — begin to be important.

The details of scene composition are beyond the scope of this section. Briefly, though, you should keep in mind that placement, relative sizes, point of view, and the other common details an artist manipulates affect the visual appearance of the scene and its effect on the viewer.

Some scenes work and others do not. The basic process of scene building boils down to:

1. Build the model and scene scripts.
2. Generate test runs and fine-tune the results in an iterative phase.
3. Do the final imaging.
4. Post-process the final image to get color.

The easiest way to build new scripts is to cannibalize old ones with the DOS copy command and your favorite text editor. Building new "entities" in scenes like the table are a little harder. They take some patience, and after doing a few of them you'll want to add hierarchical objects. The problem is that the table is not really a table. It is four legs and a top. The legs know nothing about each other or the top, and the top is just as ignorant. What you really need is the ability to call those five objects a "table" and apply a local transformation to the table, for example, to move it to [50,50,0], instead of having to figure out by hand where all the pieces have to go. For basic composite objects like a table, the current scheme is not too bad, but it quickly becomes unacceptable.

One final set of changes you can contemplate, short of writing code, is adding new entries to the existing color and material tables, or even defining a new color lookup table or material specification table. These extend the range of appearances the existing objects can take. They don't change what can be in a scene, just how the objects look.

There are a few general rules about scenes that I can pass on to you. First, worry about foreground and background. Something should occupy the viewer's attention in each region of the image or it will appear unbalanced.

Think about the scale of the elements in a scene in relation to each other and the final image size. Take a 512x512 canvas, and objects that extend between –50 and + 50 in x, y, and z. The window range is then 100, and each pixel will represent about .20 units in the scene (100 / 512 = .1953125). That means that before dividing from perspective (and ignoring aspect ratio correction), the window-viewport mapping says that an object 5 units long in window space (which corresponds to object-world-eye space) occupies 25 pixels in viewport space (which corresponds to screen and canvas space). The final number depends on your camera position (so your mileage may vary), but you should begin to get the idea.

Next, in practice, it works best to place objects around or near the origin, since the only way to manipulate the at point is by changing the script file. Adding the ability to adjust the at point interactively greatly enhances the system's capabilities.

Finally, it would be nice to be able to tweak the vd and vs using direct manipulation.

Those caveats aside, the process becomes an iterative one of tweaking positions, lights, and materials until you get the effect you want. With practice, you will start to see how changes in the parameters are transformed into changes in the image, and, indeed, that is exactly how art students learn — they draw using many different materials and techniques. Only by rendering and spending time with a system like this will you get a feel for how to put a scene together, what elements interact and affect each other, and which views are interesting. At that point, you will be ready to change the code to remove the limitations inherent in this system.

Debugging

The "black art" of debugging is no better in the realm of 3D; in fact, it's even harder. Still, it boils down to the same principles — gather information and make incremental changes.

The Lists menu, the transcript window, and the transcript log file (transcript.log) all provide ongoing commentary about the activities in the modeler. In many of the code blocks throughout this book, the transcripting was removed or abridged. Using it, you can generally see what the internals think happened. If, for instance, a crash occurs on a scene, you can compare that log to one that did not crash to ascertain the cause. Likewise, the Lists menu gives you specific access to various tables and lists. The Lists menu contains the following entries:

- Colors   Dump the colors table.
- Lights   Dump the light source list.
- Materials   Dump the materials list.
- Objects   View the 3D object list as:

    -common elements of both representations,
    -surface properties of objects,
    -laces and vertexes for polygon data,
    -quadric surfaces for analytic data.

This, plus the ongoing log entries, allows a pretty thorough dump of the internals.

Hopefully, you're tracking down appearance problems and not fatal exits. While this code has been tested, it is not guaranteed. Appendix B discusses how I hope to handle bugs; it basically boils down to "If you report them, I'll try to fix them and post a new version." I give you more detail on this (and my CompuServe ID) in Appendix B.

For scene details like object geometry, surface appearance, and lighting, the visual appearance is at least as important as the textual representation of the internals. One of the best things about debugging graphics is that you can see the scene. Much of your debugging amounts to looking at the picture and determining whether or not it appears correct. Determining appearances is best handled with test pictures. I've provided some basic scenes for this on the source disk. These include a variety of test scenes that take three flavors:

1. single objects,
2. multiple objects of a single type,
3. lighting.

The single object tests validate the definition of each object. Once that is established, testing translation, scaling, and rotation for the object are next. Simply by placing an object out each axis, you can test the translation and scaling with almost no mental effort in scene generation. The result of this is a set of scenes of an object type arranged about the origin on the axes. These validate the basic object geometry. By viewing these test scenes from multiple angles, but at least from above and below, you can verify both the geometry of the object and the renderer.

Lighting tests are a little harder. These amount to assessing whether "a believable reflection occurs" first and then quickly checking "Is that reflection too bright or too light," or "is the size of the highlight too large or too small," or "Does that color or material look correct." These can only be tested by a lot of rendering runs.

Remember one thing, in the lighting model distance is not accounted for. In pure physics terms, the light diminishes or is attenuated by dividing by the light distance squared; in practice, this goes too far the other way and we use the term (Ld * b), where b is in the range $0 <= b <= Ld$ (which means the divisor is not quite the square). This has implications for shadows and multiple objects of similar material separated by some appreciable distance.

In any case, the lighting is adequate and the best approach is a gradual one even if you fix the lighting model. Use one or two lights to get a feel for the scene, and if you want additional overall brightness or highlights, add additional lights once all other details are correct. Remember the LdotN test and the fact that the angle counts in diffuse calculations; the calculation of R, the reflected vector for ray-traced mode, is affected as well.

The key in test scenes is to come up with one or two test cases that show a lot of different variables, then use these as "known good scenes." When extending the modeler you can also use these to verify that your old code base is not broken and that your new one is correct, by comparing the old versions of the known good scenes with new runs. If you have problems, use only small changes. Make objects slightly larger or smaller. Move them about one axis at a time to make sure movement is as you expect. If objects intersect when you don't think they should, move their positions slightly. This is usually an effect of not using the centroid combined with large polygon sizes working together to defeat the hider.

When testing appearances, jitter the lights and the camera slightly to see if this makes a difference. Sometimes a small change gets you past a threshold that may be due to angles you are not visualizing, or they could be due to bugs — either way, this may help. Even though this code has been tested a lot, it is hard to test everything. That is the benefit of shipping the source — you can fix problems instead of sitting there, helpless. That leads to examples of what is possible as is and the issue of what to change or add to make the modeler more powerful.

Examples

You need some examples. Figure 11-26 shows an image that contains "one of each." It has one of each object, and uses one of each texture type. This is contained in scene file ag2.scn (all on a grid, version 2). The objects are a sphere, a plane, a box, a pyramid, a cone, and a cylinder. The sphere is a smooth mirror. The plane is a checkerboard. The box is wood. The pyramid is basic marble. The cone is grit. The cylinder is Italian marble. This is a good basic test scene for textures.

Figure 11-26.   One of Each

Figure 11-27 provides a good quick-and-dirty reflection test. It contains three mirrored spheres of differing sizes around a much smaller Italian marble sphere. This shows how a small scene can give a good test.

Figure 11-27.   Three Mirrored Spheres

Expanding on this in Figures 11-28 and 11-29 is a "vale" of spheres. Here are two rows of spheres with an empty area between them providing for an interesting interplay of reflection. Figure 11-28 shows the scene from a distance, and 11-29 shows the scene with the d/s ratio changed for a closeup. Add a couple of spheres that are textured instead of mirrored and, once again, relatively simple geometry provides an interesting image.

An even more interesting variation is shown in Figure 11-30. This scene simply takes the clump of spheres that makes up the "vale" and duplicates it, in an upside-down fashion, making a scene of one hundred spheres.

Finally, to show a more interesting set of geometry, Figures 11-31 and 11-32 show a temple and a kitchen, respectively. Having seen these examples, you should now be able to conceptualize scenes on your own.

Figure 11-28.   The Vale of Spheres

Figure 11-29.   A Closer Look at the Vale of Spheres

Figure 11-30. One Hundred Spheres in massive.scn

Figure 11-31.   A Temple

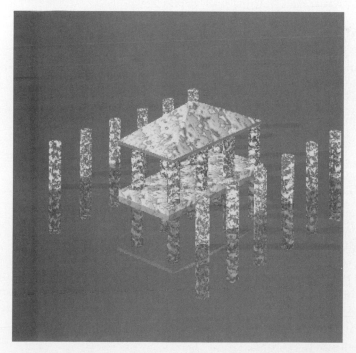

Figure 11-32. A Kitchen

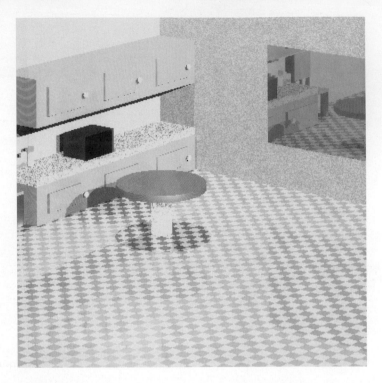

Possible Extensions

The possible changes to this modeler are legion, but the ones that make the most sense boil down to nine categories:

1. representation,
2. objects,
3. control,
4. hidden-line,
5. rendering,
6. memory,
7. underlying 3D support,
8. underlying raster/Windows support,
9. representation.

The current representation of the polygon mode is extremely naive and could be greatly enhanced. Two forms of this would be a version that adds adjacency information and a spline-based patch mesh approach. In addition, the whole notion of hierarchies needs to addressed soon.

That leads to objects. Besides the oft-discussed addition of hierarchical object definitions (as in PHIGS), new object types, "named" objects, and the object database and support files could all use some work. New object types can be added by duplicating any object module (cone, cube, cylinder, plane, pyramid, sphere) and implementing the functions. Shell module quadric.c provides a husk example. No implementation is provided, but the substructure is there. From that starting point, you should be able to see your way to adding the necessary code to the front end. Once the lists in memory are created, as long as you follow the interface for the individual object functions, the function pointer invocations in the processing loops will work. You will probably find it easier to get polygon mode up first, and then deal with ray-traced mode.

Besides the notion of a composite or hierarchical object definition, you will run into cases where a new primitive (like a table) is available and you have no idea how it is constructed. You can instantiate instances of it, but you are going to want "named" objects as well. This lets you make specific instances of the underlying primitive "table" available in some predetermined size, orientation and surface appearance, and save redefinition time. This also gives you "endtable," "coffetable," and "dinnertable" relatively easily from "table."

Once you have names, proliferation is next. Object non-proliferation treaties are defeatist. They do tend to make directory maintenance simpler, but at the cost of limiting the possibilities. Taking the object .dat files and the default color and material table and placing them in some master file is the answer. OLE 2.0 and its structured storage offer some opportunities here. While there are other features to add (quartic surfaces and the toroid come to mind), this is a good starting set of object enhancements.

Control right now is limited to extremely basic camera positioning. You need multiple cameras and better specification over camera parameters. In this light, the manipulation of the lookat point is needed as well. Light source control is also non-existent outside of the script file. It would be nice to clean this up. All of this can be solved by a "monitor" dialog and some tricky use of the indirect calls at run time to respond to the current environment. Specifying multiple cameras and switching between them is another subject, though. Currently, the sole camera is used as the basis of all space. Defining another camera and transformation matrix solves this. I leave you to mull over the intricacies of changing the user interface to indicate existence of multiple cameras and signal their location, switching, etc.

In the visibility and rendering areas, the hidden algorithm should use the centroid instead of its current choice of one corner on which to base the surface normal. Alternatively, you could toss this implementation in favor of something like a z-buffer. That dovetails with the desire to add to polygon rendering incremental rendering techniques like Phong shading that use interpolated values. These additions also require the representation to carry adjacency information because the values being interpolated are averages over the current face and the adjacent faces. They also need a polygon-scan converter, because Phong shading places a unique color at each pixel. The method currently used is to call the Windows GDI routine Polygon and fill with one color based on a solid brush. Adjacency, scan-line converting, and the z-buffer all go together.

The attenuation by distance should also be added to lighting calculations at that point. Adding refraction, the other part of transmission, greatly extends the modeler. Right now, the reflection half of transmission is implemented; adding refraction lets you do glass and other transparency effects.

Again, this is not the only, or even the best, way to build applications or modelers. It simply provided a structuring mechanism that gave a lot of bang for the buck. It also made a reasonable-sized code base intelligible. Between the two DLLs, the support library, and the modeler itself, the code base is about 30,000 lines of code. The run-time size of the modeler plus the DLLs is close to 460K total (320K for the modeler and 140K for the DLLs). And the DLLs provide services to any other client application, as well.

This is not large, but isn't exactly small either. This is a medium-sized project, and the architectural and design decisions were made with that in mind. If the target goal had been a system of 300,000 lines or 3,000,000 lines (do not laugh, AutoCAD is over 1,000,000 lines of code, so these numbers are not that unrealistic as a range for a commercial application), we would surely have had to use a different approach. The point is, you know what, why, how, and when for the entire system presented here, and you have the full source code. You can make the call on scaling it up, or using it as is and simply extending it within this scale. Hopefully, you'll at least find this material useful enough to justify the time you've spent reading it.

Appendices

Appendix A
Glossary

Terms defined in the glossary are in italics in the text. Definitions are solely in the context of computer graphics; many terms have alternate definitions outside of this context.

aliasing
When a signal is undersampled, high frequencies can take the appearance of lower ones. This is referred to as taking on an "alias" and producing artifacts.

anti-aliasing
Taking precautions to limit or eliminate *aliasing* artifacts.

ambient light
An imaginary non-directional light striking everywhere in a scene, defined in an *illumination model*.

back-face culling
A form of culling in which faces that lie on the back side of an object (relative to the *viewpoint* or camera) and cannot be seen are removed early in the *viewing pipeline*.

bounding volume
A simpler surface surrounding a more complex one, making it possible to test the simpler surface first, saving time during certain processes in the *viewing pipeline*. If the first test fails, time has been saved because only if the first test succeeds does the more expensive operation need to take place. False hits are thus very costly.

boundary representation
B-rep, or boundary representation is the representation scheme used here. The surface of an object is approximated by using *polygons*.

camera, camera model
Viewing system based on photographic principles. At a minimum, it allows specification of from point, lookat point, up direction of camera, and perhaps some control over the field of view. Camera model refers to this method; camera refers to the current *viewpoint* in a system supporting a camera model.

coordinates
Typically, an [x y z] triple in some space used to represent a coordinate or a point. Here, used as a 4D homogenous [x y z w] 4-valued set to make points and *vectors* equivalent and thus eliminate conversions.

coordinate space
A mathematical world with a defined range of valid values.

cross (product)
Vector math operation, used to generate parts of the viewing transformation and surface *normal*.

CSG
Constructive Solid Geometry, an alternate representation technique.

diffuse reflection
A uniform radiation of light from a surface that makes it appear uniformly smooth.

dot (product)
Vector math operation, used in visible surface testing (dot surface *normal* with eye).

explicit surfaces
Surfaces represented by an explicit collection of points.

eye point, eye ray
The eye point is the *viewpoint* and the eye ray is the *ray* from the eye to the screen, or the root ray for some pixel.

frequency
Speed of an oscillation in cycles per second.

Gouraud
Early *shading* technique, interpolates color values across surface.

highlight	The portion of radiated light due to *specular* effects.
HLHSR	Hidden-line, hidden-surface removal.
illumination model	The particular equation used when *shading*, synonymous with the shading model. A "local" illumination model only describes light sources and surface orientation. A "global" illumination model deals with interaction of objects to simulate *reflection*, *shadows*, and *refraction*.
intersection	In ray tracing, this refers to the point that is on both a ray and a surface, and the process of finding that point.
mathematical surfaces	Surfaces represented by an implicit set of points that can be generated by evaluating equations. Also called "analytic" here.
nanometer	10^{-6} meter in length. A millimeter is 10^{-3} and a micrometer is 10^{-6}. Angstroms are 10^{-10} of a meter.
normal	A *vector* perpendicular to a plane.
Nyquist limit	Sampling theorem that states that the sampling rate must be greater than twice the frequency of the information.
object	A geometrically defined entity for use in a graphics system.
object instance	(Or just "instance") Refers to a specific object, not the prototypical example on which it is based.
object database	Collection of prototypical objects available for instantiation.
O-Notation	"Big-oh" notation describes the "order of magnitude" of run time for algorithmic analysis, also sometimes called "asymptotic notation."
optics	Branch of physics that studies light.
Painters algorithm	Drawing technique that uses the *z-sorted* face list to draw faces in a "painter's" order, back to front, which "hides" non-visible surfaces (with some major limitations on objects within a scene).
parametric equations	Mathematical technique that definines equations in one variable, typically *t* or time. Equations of two or three variables can be transformed into a parametric representation with some algebra; most notably by solving a system of simultaneous equations using the "method of substitution" or back-substitution. Parametrics are natural for an iterative process.
pinhole camera	Simple imaginary *camera model*, used as basis of *viewing system*.
Phong	*Shading* technique that interpolates *normals* across surface.
polygon	Any region of a plane bounded by a set of linear edges, here limited to triangles and rectangles.
polyhedron	3D object constructed of *polygons*.
point-sampling	A family of rendering techniques to which *ray tracing* belongs
quadric surfaces	Algebraic surfaces of order 2 (quadratic), including sphere, plane, cone (special-case pyramid), cylinder (special-case cube), paraboloid, and hyperboloid.
quartic surfaces	Algebraic surfaces of order 4. The torus is the most common example.
quicksort	Sorting algorithm that has NlogN behavior, as opposed to bubblesort which is N-squared (the dreaded quadratic).
ray	Infinite line bounded at one end, described with an origin and a direction. A ray can be described mathematically as a *parametric* line.
ray-object intersection	The process of finding any or all points that lie both on a ray and on an object.
ray tracing, tracing	Process using *parametric* lines and *mathematical surfaces* to find points belonging in the set generated by intersecting lines with *mathematical*

	surfaces. These points represent the parts of each surface visible in a scene and are then colored using an *illumination model* and a *shading* process.
reflection	The process that describes light that strikes a surface at a point and bounces off the material, leaving from the same side. The angle of reflection is equal to the angle of incidence. During *shading,* the color of this point is determined by combining the values from the surface intersection with the values from any additional intersections after the bounce "redirects" the ray.
refraction	The process that describes light that strikes a surface and passes through a transparent material to leave from the opposite side. The angle of refraction is based on Snell's Law of *optics.* During *shading,* the color of this point is determined by combining the values from being transmitted through the material and the values from after being transmitted through and continuing on in the scene.
scan-converting	Raster technique used in polygon drawing for pixel-level shading (i.e., *Gouraud, Phong*).
shading	Here, this is a process that is the application of a *illumination model* across the points of surfaces in an image (also can mean a shading technique, like *Phong* shading). "Shading model" and "illumination model" are synonymous. Shading is also used to describe the process of applying the equations.
shadow	Part of a scene visible to the *viewpoint* but not visible to at least one light source.
spectrum	The forms of radiant energy arranged by size of wavelength or *frequency.* The visible part is known as "light" and is wavelengths of 380-730 *nanometers.*
specular reflection	Reflection of light producing a "highlight" and the process in computer graphics that produces such highlights.
rendering	The process of going from the object database to a final image on screen.
surface normal, normal	*Vector* perpendicular to plane of polygonal surface.
texturing, texture mapping	Process and technique for modifying the color value of a surface. The most prevalent type of texture mapping involves a bitmap as the source of color values. Here, a mathematical function is used instead. In either case this can be seen as accessing in some form an "array" of color intensity information to be used in calculating the final color of a surface point.
vector	Implemented here as a 4D homogeneous value of [x,y,z.w]. Can be synonymous with "point" in space.
vertex normal	Used in more advanced polygon-shading processes, similar to what is used here, except that a normal is generated at each vertex instead of once per surface.
viewpoint	*Pinhole camera* operates on a scene using a viewpoint or from point focused on a lookat point.
z-sort	Process of sorting faces after the visibility test and before drawing.

Appendix B
Source-Code Details

If you want to play with the code, this section will probably interest you. It contains a discussion of what you need to compile and run the programs presented in this book. Then I describe the contents of the source disk so that you know what you have. Next I'll cover the installation process so that you know how to get at this source. Finally I'll discuss the process of building the source so that you'll know how to use it.

What You Need

To compile and run the programs presented in this book you will need the following software:

- Microsoft Windows 3.1,
- Microsoft Windows Software Development Kit 3.1,
- Microsoft C (command-line compiler for MSVC 1.0 and later works just fine, and it should even work with MSC 7.0); including the linker, librarian, make, and other tools,
- a programmer's editor.

To run Windows, the SDK, and the programs developed here, you need the following hardware:

- A Windows Enhanced-Mode-compatible machine that is at least a 386 with 8 MB of RAM, a fast, large, hard-disk, and a mouse is best. A math co-processor, while not assumed, will make the programs run faster.
- A Super-VGA monitor and graphics adapter is required.

The graphics presented here assume a minimum of 256 colors. With a card capable of at least 32K colors, or with 15-bit or greater color resolution, the routines used here take advantage of higher resolution; but 256 colors will be our least-common-denominator. Don't worry—we can make some pretty nice pictures with 256 colors, and 32,768 colors is really nice. Anything better is golden.

The code used in the book was cross-compiled for Windows NT at various stages in both the book's and NT's life. The principal delivery system is Windows/DOS. The Windows/DOS versions of the code was tested on NT's 16-bit Windows subsystem.

What You Have

Your source disk includes the libraries, sample applications, generators, the modeler and support services, scenes, and the MakeApp-derived shells that provide an app-generation tool. For our purposes, let's refer to this source as the 3DGPW project. A readme file named "readme.1st" and a packing list file named "packing.lst" are provided as part of the installation process. Look for them in your target installation directory. The components in the 3DGPW are broken down in Table B-1.

Table B-1.   Components of Source Disk

Delivered Components	Description
Libraries	
WLib	Helper functions for Windows at the primitive level.
G3DLib	Higher level services, provide new "types."
M3D	Modeler support services, built as part of modeler.
Samples	
Chapter 4 RGBCube	Basic RGB color cube using color routines.
Chapter 4 RGBCube Part II	Repeat using palette routines from WLib.
Chapter 5 RGBCube Fixed	Repeat using fixed canvas style.
Chapter 5 RGBCube Variable	Repeat using variable canvas style
Chapter 6 RGBCube Prim	Repeat using canvas output primitives.
Chapter 6 Primtest	Test all canvas output primitives.
Chapter 7 3DCube	Spinning 3D cube using 4-parameter viewing system.
Chapter 7 Surf3D	3D surface plots using 4-parameter viewing system.
Chapter 7 Camera	Spinning 3D cube using pinhole camera viewing system.
Applications	
Generators Part I	Object database generator apps. DOS command-line apps.
Generators Part II	Procedural scene generator. DOS command-line app.
WinMod3d	The geometric modeler and scene renderer application.
Model and Scene Files	
Scenes	Variety of scenes; both for testing and fun
Tools	
Shells	MakeApp-derived shells for SDI, MDI, static demos, Dynamic demos, and a DLLS.

The first two important components are the WLib and G3DLib DLLs. They provide a wide range of services and are the foundation of the graphics application development of Chapters 7–11. These services are used in the Sample Applications from Chapters 4–7 as a validation process. Conceptually, there is a third library — the M3D modeler support services — but they are built as part of the modeler. We implement generators for the object database of points and a sample procedural scene generator as DOS command-line apps. These come from Chapters 9 and 10. Then the modeler proper, WinMod3D, and some sample scenes provide the main feature of the source disk. The M3D support services are conceptual only and are included as part of the modeler build. While Chapter 11 implements the modeler; the M3D modeler support services are developed as part of Chapters 8-11. The M3D services require some function interface work to truly be a stand-alone library. Finally, the MakeApp-derived application generators are included as basic construction tools.

How You Get It

Batch file install.bat. is on your source disk. It provides a "usage" output if you execute it with no parameters. This output looks like:

```
usage: install "%1" "%2" where:
      "%1"                    = source drive with : but no terminating \
      "%2"                    = target drive and root directory with no terminating \
      "%2\install.log"        = derived path for logfile of install
for example:
      install a: c:\3DGPW
```

To install, you must put the disk into a drive, then use this batch file as shown above. As you execute, the batch file both writes a log file (saved as install.log in the target directory) and echoes progress to "stdout." In addition, a batch file to set the environment variables needed to compile the source is also written to the target directory. This batch file is named"setvars.bat." Once installed, the files take approximately 8 MB of disk space.

How You Use It

Each build component has a makefile, optional linker response file, and build batch file to make regeneration easy. Simply make sure the compiler is installed correctly and that the 3DGPW project environment variables are set up to point to the proper directories (as per previous instructions) and invoke the batch file. This will cause the make process to execute the inference rules to force a rebuild of that component. Table B-2 lists the build component support in terms of batch files and makefiles.

Table B-2.   Build Details

Build Element	Build Support
Libraries	
WLib	makefile and mw.bat
G3DLib	makefile and mg.bat
M3D	n/a; built with WinMod3D
Samples	
Chapter 4 RGBCube	makefile and brgb.bat
Chapter 4 RGBCube Part II	makefile and brgb.bat
Chapter 5 RGBCube Fixed	makefile and brgb.bat
Chapter 5 RGBCube Variable	makefile and brgb.bat
Chapter 6 RGBCube Prim	makefile and brgb.bat
Chapter 6 Primtest	makefile and btest.bat
Chapter 7 3DCube	makefile and mc.bat
Chapter 7 Surf3D	makefile and ms.bat
Chapter 7 Camera	makefile and mc.bat
Applications	
Generators Part I	
fvl - face and vertex support	makefvl.mak, bfv.bat
cone	makecone.mak, makecone.lnk, and bcone.bat
cylinder	makecyl.mak, makecyl.lnk, and bcyl.bat
plane	makepl.mak, makepl.lnk, and bpl.bat
sphere	makesph.mak, makesph.lnk, and bsph.bat
Generators Part II	
sphereflake	makesflk.mak, makesflk.lnk, and bsf.bat
Modeler	
WinMod3d	makefile and mc.bat
Model and Scene Files	
Scenes	variety of scenes, both for testing and enjoyment
Tools	
Shells	
SDI	makefile and ms.bat
MDI	makefile and mm.bat
Static	makefile and mpgd.bat
Dynamic	makefile and migd.bat
DLL	makefile and mdll.bat

A "master" batch file that builds the libraries, the samples, the generators, the modeler, and the MakeApp-derived application construction tools (named buildall.bat) is generated as part of the installation process. This batch file assumes that all environment variables are correctly set, both for the compiler execution (PATH) and for source compilation and linking (INCLUDE, INC, and LIB). You will see it in the main target directory, and its execution begins the build process.

Each subdirectory contains at least one executable. In the case of the object database generators, there are multiple executables in the /GENERATE/OBJECTS subdirectory. Table B-3 lists the executables that can be launched once the build process has completed successfully. The generators are DOS command-line tools, while all of the others are Windows executables with the exception of the DLLs and the DLL shell.

Table B-3.   Execution Details

Delivered Components	Launching
Libraries	
WLib	DLL, publish to Windows directory
G3DLib	DLL, publish to Windows directory
M3D	N/A; built with WinMod3D
Samples	
Chapter 4 RGBCube	RGBRGB.EXE from Windows
Chapter 4 RGBCube Part II	RGBPAL.EXE from Windows
Chapter 5 RGBCube Fixed	RGBCFWV.EXE from Windows
Chapter 5 RGBCube Variable	RGBCVWV.EXE from Windows
Chapter 6 RGBCube Prim	RGBCPWV.EXE from Windows
Chapter 6 Primtest	PRIMTEST.EXE from Windows
Chapter 7 3DCube	CUBE3D from Windows
Chapter 7 Surf3D	SURF3D from Windows
Chapter 7 Camera	CAM3D.EXE from Windows
Applications	
Generators Part I	
fvl - face and vertex support	makefvl.mak, bfv.bat
cone	MAKECONE from DOS command line
cylinder	MAKECYL from DOS command line
plane	MAKEPL from DOS command line
sphere	MAKESPH from DOS command line
Generators Part II	
sphereflake	MAKESFLK.EXE from DOS command line
Modeler	
WinMod3d	WINMOD3D.EXE
Model and Scene Files	
Scenes	Variety of scenes, both for testing and enjoyment
Tools	
Shells	
SDI	MSDIAPP.EXE from Windows
MDI	MMDIAPP.EXE from Windows
Static	MPGDAPP.EXE from Windows
Dynamic	MIGDAPP.EXE from Windows
DLL	DLL, not executable

That wraps up the details of the source disk. If all else fails, the files are compressed using COMPRESS.exe, which comes with the Windows SDK. EXPAND.exe is provided on the source disk and with the SDK and can be used to expand files on a file-by-file basis from the compressed format on the source disk. Launching the Windows executables are the same as for any other Windows executables.

Philip H. Taylor
CIS:75130,1714

Appendix C
Bibliography

Books (alphabetical by category)

Math, Physics, and Engineering

Beckenbach, Edwin F. et al. *Modern College Algebra and Trigonometry, 5th Edition*. Wadsworth Publishing Company, 1986.

Bueche, Frederick J. *Physics for Scientists and Engineers, 2nd Edition*. MacGraw-Hill, 1975.

Debeer, Ferdinand P. and Johnstone, E. Russel, Jr. *Mechanics: Statics and Dynamics, 3rd Edition*. MacGraw-Hill, 1977.

Press, William H. (et. al). *Numerical Recipes in C*. Cambridge University Press, 1988.

Morgan, Don. *Numerical Methods*. M & T Books, 1992

Purcell, Edwin J. *Calculus and Analytic Geometry*. Prentice-Hall, 1972.

Programming and Software Engineering

Bentley, Jon. *Programming Pearls*. Addison-Wesley, 1986.

——. *More Programming Pearls*. Addison-Wesley, 1988.

Brooks, Frederick P. *The Mythical Man-Month*. Addison-Wesley, 1982.

Knuth Donald E. *The Art of Computer Programming*, Volume 1, 2nd edition, "Fundamental Algorithms." Addison-Wesley, 1973.

——. *The Art of Computer Programming*, Volume 2, 2nd edition, "Seminumerical Algrorithms." Addison-Wesley, 1981.

——. *The Art of Computer Programming*, Volume 3, "Sorting and Searching." Addison-Wesley, 1973.

McClure, Carma. *CASE Is Software Automation*. Prentice-Hall, 1989.

Plauger. P.J. *Standard C Library*. Prentice-Hall, 1992.

Yourdon, Edward Nash, ed. *Classics in Software Engineering*. Yourdon Press, 1979.

Graphics

Ammeraal, Leendert. *Programming Principles in Computer Graphics*. Wiley, 1986.

Angel, Ian O. and Griffin, Gareth. *High Resolution Computer Graphics Using FORTRAN 77*. Wiley, 1987.

Arvo James, ed. *Graphics Gems II*. Academic Press, 1991.

Bartels, Richard H. et al. *An Introduction to Splines for use in Computer Graphics & Geometric Modeling*. Morgan Kaufman, 1987.

Barzal, Ronen. *Physically-Based Modeling in Computer Graphics*. Academic Press, 1992.

Blake, John W. *PHIGS and PHIGS+*. Academic Press, 1993.

Bower, Adrian. and Woodwark, John. *A Programmer's Geometry*. Butterworths, 1983.

Burger, Peter, and Gillies, Duncan. *Interactive Computer Graphics*. Addison-Wesley, 1989.

Cohen, Michael F. and Wallace, John R. *Radiosity and Realistic Image Synthesis*. Academic Press, 1993.

Durrett, H. John, ed. *Color and the Computer*. Academic Press, 1987.

Enderle, G. et al. *Computer Graphics Programming GKS—The Graphics Standard*. Springer-Verlag, 1984.

Farin, Gerald. *Curves and Surfaces for Computer Aided Geometric Design, 2nd Edition*. Academic Press, 1990.

Foley, James D. and Van Dam, Andries. *Fundamentals of Interactive Computer Graphics*. Addison-Wesley, 1984.

——,et al. *Computer Graphics Principle and Practice, 2nd Edition*. Addison-Wesley, 1990.

Glassner,Andrew S., ed. *An Introduction to Ray Tracing*. Academic Press, 1989.

——,ed. *Graphics Gems*. Academic Press, 1990.

Harrington, Steven. *Computer Graphics: A Programming Approach, 2nd Edition*. MacGraw-Hill, 1987.

Heiny, Loren. *Advanced Graphics Programming Using C/C++*. Wiley, 1993.

Hill, F. S., Jr. *Computer Graphics*. Macmillan, 1990.

Kirk, David. *Graphics Gems III*. Academic Press, 1992.

Lindley, Craig A. *Practical Ray Tracing in C*. Wiley, 1992.

Mandelbrot, Benoit B. *The Fractal Geometry of Nature*. W. H. Freeman and Company, 1983.

Mantyla, Martti. *Introduction to Solid Modeling*. Computer Science Press, 1988.

Newman, Willam M. and Sproull, Robert F. *Principles of Interactive ComputerGraphics*. McGraw-Hill, 1979.

Peitgen, Heinz-Otto and Richter, P. H. *The Beauty of Fractals*. Springer-Verlag, 1986.

——. and Saupe Dietmar, ed. *The Science of Fractal Images*. Springer-Verlag, 1988.

Rankin, John R. *Computer Graphics Software Construction*. Prentice-Hall, 1989.

Rimmer, Steve. *Bit-mapped Graphics*. Windcrest, 1990.

Rogers, David F. and Adams, J. Alan. *Mathematical Elements for Computer Graphics, 2nd Edition*. MacGraw-Hill, 1990.

Snyder, John M. *Generative Modeling for Computer Graphics and CAD*. Academic Press, 1992.

Stevens, Roger T. *Fractal Programming and Ray Tracing in C and C++*. M & T Books, 1990.

——. and Watkins, Christopher D. *Advanced Graphics Programming in C and C++*. M & T Books, 1991.

Taylor, Walter F. *The Geometry of Computer Graphics*. Wadsworth, 1992.

Upstill, Steve. *The Renderman Companion*. Addison-Wesley, 1990.

Watkins, Christoper D. and Sharp, Larry. *Programming in 3 Dimensions*. M & T Books, 1992.

——.et al. *Photorealism and Ray Tracing in C*. M & T Books, 1992.

Watt, Alan. *Fundamentals of Three-Dimensional Computer Graphics*. Addison-Wesley, 1989.

——. and Watt, Mark. *Advanced Animation and Rendering Techniques*. Addison-Wesley, 1992.

Weiskamp, Keith et al. *Power Graphics using Turbo C*. Wiley, 1989.

Windows programming

Durant, David et al, *Programmers Guide to Windows*. Sybex, 1987.

Heiny, Loren. *Windows Graphics Programming with Borland C++*. Wiley, 1992.

Heller, Martin. *Advanced Windows Programming*. Wiley, 1992.

Microsoft. *Microsoft Windows 3.1 SDK Guide to Programming*. Microsoft Press, 1992.

Microsoft. *Microsoft Windows 3.1 SDK Programmers Reference Volume 1: Overview*. Microsoft Press, 1992.

Myers, Brian and Donner, Chris. *Graphics Programming under Windows*. Sybex, 1988.

Norton, Peter and Yao, Paul. *Peter Norton's Windows 3.0 Power Programming Techniques*. Bantam, 1990.

Petzold, Charles. *Programming Windows*. Microsoft Press, 1988.

——. *Programming Windows, 2nd Edition*. Microsoft Press, 1990.

Pietrek, Matt. *Windows Internals*. Addison-Wesley, 1993.

Richter, Jeffrey M. *Windows 3 : A Developers Guide*. M & T Books, 1991.

Rimmer, Steve. *Windows Bitmapped Graphics*. Windcrest/MacGraw-Hill, 1993.

Schulman, Andrew et al. *Undocumented Windows*. Addison-Wesley, 1992.

Journal Articles (by date, by publication)

Computing Surveys

Computing Surveys, March 1974. *A Characterization of Ten Hidden-Surface Algorithms.* Sutherland, Ivan E. et al.

Computer Graphics

Computer Graphics, Vol 11, No 2, Summer 1977. *Shadow Algorithms for Computer Graphics,* Crow, Franklin C.

Computer Systems

Computer Systems, Vol 1., No 1., Winter 1988. *Dynamics for Computer Graphics: A Tutorial.* Wilhelms, Jane.

Communications of the ACM

CACM, June 1975. *Illumination for Computer Generated Pictures.* Phong, Bui Tuong.

CACM, Oct 1976. *Texture and Reflection in Computer Generated Images.* Blinn, J. F. and Newell, M. E.

CACM, June 1980. *An Improved Illumination Model for Shaded Display.* Whitted, Turner.

CACM, June 1982. *Computer Rendering of Stochastic Models.* Fournier, A. et al.

ACM Transactions on Graphics

ACM TOG, Jan 1986. *Stochastic Sampling in Computer Graphics.* Cook, Robert L.

ACM TOG, Apr 1987. *An Experimental Comparison of RGB, YIQ, LAB, HSV and Opponent Color Model.* Schwartz, Michael W. et al.

ACM TOG, Apr 1988. *On the Power of the Frame Buffer.* Fournier, Alan and Fussel, Daniel.

ACM TOG, Oct 1988. *Color Gamut Mapping and the Printing of Digital Color Images.* Stone, Maureen C. et al.

ACM TOG, Apr 1990. *Letters to the Editor: Comments on "Stochastic Sampling in Computer Graphics."* Comment 1 by Pavlidis, Theo. Comment 2 by Wold, Erling and Pepard, Kim.

ACM TOG, Oct 1990. *A Simple Method for Improved Color Printing of Monitor Images.* Lamming, Michael G. and Rhodes, Warren L.

IEEE Computer Graphics and Applications

IEEE CG & A, Aug 1985. *Advances in Computer-Generated Imagery for Flight Simulation.* Yan, Johnson K.

IEEE CG & A, Feb 1986. *An Implementer's View of PHIGS.* Abi-Ezzi, Salim S. and Bunshaft, Albert J.

IEEE CG & A, April 1986. *A Raster Display Graphics Package for Education.* Rogers, David F. and Rogers, Stephen D.

IEEE CG & A, July 1986. *Are PHIGS and GKS Necessarily Incompatible?* Schoenhut, Jurgen.

IEEE CG & A, Aug 1986. *GKS-3D: A Three-Dimensional Extension to the Graphical Kernel System.* Puk, Richard F. and McConnel John I..

Conference Tutorial Notes (by conference and tutorial)

SIGGRAPH 1986

SIGGRAPH 1986 Course 2 Notes: Introduction to Color Raster Graphics
SIGGRAPH 1986 Course 8 Notes: Introduction to Solid Modeling
SIGGRAPH 1986 Course 9 Notes: Advanced Topics in Solid Modeling
SIGGRAPH 1986 Course 10 Notes: Geometry for Computer Graphics and CAD
SIGGRAPH 1986 Course 11 Notes: Fractals : Basic Concepts, Computation and Selected Topics
SIGGRAPH 1986 Course 12 Notes: Developments in Ray Tracing, especially
Simple Ray Tracing
SIGGRAPH 1986 Course 15 Notes: State of the Art in Image Synthesis, especially
Ray Tracing and Radiosity
SIGGRAPH 1986 Course 16 Notes: Image Rendering Tricks, especially
The Hackers Guide To Making Pretty Pictures
System Aspects of Computer Image Synthesis and Computer Animation
104 SIGGRAPH 1986 Course 25 Notes: Understanding CGI
105 SIGGRAPH 1986 Course 26 Notes: An Introduction to PHIGS

SIGGRAPH 1990

SIGGRAPH 1990 Course 2: Notes: Color and Computer Graphics
SIGGRAPH 1990 Course 9 Notes: PHIGS PLUS
SIGGRAPH 1990 Course 12 Notes: Solid Modeling: Architectures, Mathematics, and Algorithms
SIGGRAPH 1990 Course 15 Notes: Fractals: Analysis and Modeling
SIGGRAPH 1990 Course 18 Notes: The Renderman Interface and Shading Language
SIGGRAPH 1990 Course 19 Notes: X3D-PEX
SIGGRAPH 1990 Course 24: Radiosity, especially
An Annotated Bibliography
SIGGRAPH 1990 Course 24: Advanced Topics in Ray Tracing, especially
Implementation Notes for Ray Tracers
The Ray Tracing Kernel
Ray Tracing Bibliography
Locus Classicus

MSDN CD(alphabetical)

GDI

Coordinate Mapping. Gery, Ron.
DIBS and Their Uses. Gery, Ron.
GDI Objects. Gery, Ron.
Palette Awareness. Gery, Ron.
Palette Manager: How and Why. Gery, Ron.
Using DIBs with Palettes. Gery, Ron.
Using True Color Devices. Gery, Ron

Animation in Windows. Rodent, Herman.
Flicker-Free Displays Using An Off-Screen DC. Rodent, Herman.

Kernel

Floating Point in Windows. Long, David.

Popular press (by date, by publication)

General Programming, Finite State Machines, Math, Exception Handling, and Debugging

Programmer's Journal

> May/June 1991. *Numeric Exception Handling*. Barrenechea, Mark J.

C Users Journal

> Feb 1989. *How To Do It ...In C: An Introduction to Finite State Machines*. Ward, Robert.
> Feb 1989. *Scaffolding for C and C++*. Burk, Ron and Custer, Helen.
> June 1990. *Generating Source for <float.h>*. Prince, Dr. Timothy.
> Aug 1990. *Evaluating Your Floating Point Library*. Sheppard, Gene.
> Dec 1990. *State Machines in C*. Fischer, Paul.
> Mar 1991. *Implementing a Trap Command*. Don Libes.
> Aug 1991. *Exception Handling in ANSI C*. Colvin, Gregory.
> Oct 1991. *Debugging in C - An Overview*. Baldwin. Wahhab.
> Jan 1993. *Designing an Extensible API in C*. Mirho, Charles.
> Jan 1993. *Using Wrappers To Improve Portability of Commercial Libraries*. Van Camp, Kenneth E.

> Windows/DOS Developer's Journal

> May 1992, Q&A. *Trapping FP Exceptions under Windows*. Bonneau, Paul.
> July 1992. *A Windows assert(0 with Symbolic Stack Trace*. Pietrek, Matt.

Windows Tech Journal

> April 1992. *Catch and Throw*. Plamondon, James.

Graphics Programming

Dr Dobb's Journal

> Nov 1988. *Photorealism in Computer Graphics*. Upstill, Steve.
> Sept 1990. *Ray Tracing*. Lyke, Daniel.
> Oct 1991–Feb 1993. *Graphics Programming Column, X-Sharp*. Abrash, Michael.

C Users Journal

Aug 1988. *A Simple Model for Hiding Surfaces*. Anderson. Jay Martin.
Aug 1989. *Masked 3-D Plotting*. Brannigan, Michael.
Aug 1989. *Clipping Techniques*. Stevens, Dr. Roger T.
Aug 1989. *Shading 3-D Reconstructions*. Vannier, Michael and Geist, Danny.
Dec 1991. *3-D Solid Modeling*. Mooallem, Saul.
Nov 1992. *A Versatile Plotting Routine*. Smith, Lowell.

Byte

Dec 1986. *Graphing Quadric Surfaces*. Haroney, George.
Dec 1987. *Three-Dimensional Perspective Plotting*. Daulton, Tyrone.

Windows Programming

Microsoft Systems Journal

MSJ July 1988. *Color Mixing Principles and How Color Works in the Raster Video Model*. Welch, Kevin P.
MSJ, Mar 1989. *MDI, An Emerging Standard for Manipulating Document Windows*. Welch, Kevin P.
MSJ, July 1990. *A New Multiple Document Interface API Simplifies MDI Application Development*. Petzold, Charles.
MSJ, Nov 1990. *Learning Windows Part IV: Control Windows and MDI Support*. Adler, Mark.
MSJ, March 1991. *Learning Windows Part V: Exploring the Graphics Device Interface*. Adler, Mark.
MSJ, May 1991. *Learning Windows Part VI: Bitmaps, Fonts, and Printing*. Adler, Mark.
MSJ, Sep 1992. *GDI Comes of Age: Exploring the 32-Bit Graphics of Windows NT*. Petzold, Charles.

PC Magazine

Petzold, Volume 10 Number 10–Volume 10 Number 15, Petzold" *Environment* columns on DIBs.
Schulman, Andrew, Volume 11, No 2–3, *Undocumented Windows* articles.

Byte

Aug 1991. *The Hungarian Revolution*. Heller, Martin and Simonyi, Charles.

Misc

Microsoft internal. Jan 1988. *Naming Conventions (Hungarian)*. Klunder, Doug.

Index